2
8

D1711950

# A HISTORY OF PSYCHOLOGY

# IN AUTOBIOGRAPHY

## Volume V

# THE CENTURY PSYCHOLOGY SERIES

Richard M. Elliott, Gardner Lindzey, and
Kenneth MacCorquodale

*Editors*

# A HISTORY OF PSYCHOLOGY
## in
# AUTOBIOGRAPHY

## Volume V

*Edited by*

Edwin G. Boring
HARVARD UNIVERSITY

Gardner Lindzey
UNIVERSITY OF TEXAS

New York
APPLETON-CENTURY-CROFTS
*Division of Meredith Publishing Company*

# Preface

Autobiography improves with age as it ripens into history. When the first volume of *A History of Psychology in Autobiography* appeared in 1930 psychologists found it interesting. Its readers for the most part were familiar with the writings of the men and women who spoke through its pages; often they knew the biographers personally or had at least listened to them, and they profited from seeing how the owner of an important name regarded his own work and what importance he assigned to events that appeared to have shaped his life. When first written, these stories lay, nevertheless, almost in the present, for—except in the speculation about how childhood forms a man—an intellectual autobiography that covers forty years does not consider that it is speaking of the past until much later. Now, however, thirty years have gone by since those first three volumes of 1930–1936 were published, and the lives described in them are now history—recent history, to be sure, but long enough ago for psychologists to send their students to sense in these accounts the attitudes of an earlier generation and the atmosphere in which it thrived, the spirit of a time when psychology was smaller, less complex and more intimate.

How the value of present effort increases with time becomes evident when one examines the table at the end of this preface. There you see the ages of the contributors to this series and the dates of their deaths. Of the fifty-eight psychologists who contributed to the first four volumes, only five are still living. Of the forty-three who wrote for the first three volumes only one is left—Sir Frederic Bartlett. It is necessary to get these personal records before mortality intervenes, yet not before the lives described are approaching completion. The present committee has lost Heinz Werner, who died after accepting our invitation to contribute, but we are fortunate in being able to include Kurt Goldstein, who completed his biography before he died. Three other psychologists (Heymans, Höffding, de Sanctis) died before the volume containing their contributions could be published, and three others (Calkins, Zwaardemaker, Hull) died in the year of publication.

Yet all in all the great men and women of psychology have been a hardy lot. Of the fifty-four contributors who have passed on at the date of this writing only one, Woodworth, reached the 90's. The youngest to die was Klemm at 54, and the next youngest was Franz at 59. The median age of these autobiographers at death is at present between 77 and 79, in between Drever and Terman. Two were in their 50's, eleven in their 60's, fifteen in their 70's, twenty-five in their 80's, and one in his 90's.

At the end of the 1920's, when the new historians of the still new psychology were complaining that insufficient information was available about the lives, and thus the motivations, of the eponyms whom it was their task to describe, the present series was begun by Carl Murchison and the Clark University Press. At the time, the committee asked that the contributors tell of the motivations that guided them in their professional careers, not fully realizing in the then unformed state of motivational psychology how little a man knows correctly of his own motivations. When, after a lapse caused first by the exhaustion of the pool of sufficiently mature prominent psychologists and then by the distraction of World War II, the project was revived twenty years later, the invitation was changed to stress conscious motivation less and the events of the life more. Here follows an excerpt from the Preface of Volume IV, published in 1952:

The reader of this volume will see how much our autobiographers differ from one another in the nature of their efforts. Perhaps they differ most in the degree with which they find unity in their lives. Presumably every one of them would like to see his intellectual history as the evolution of a single purpose, for integrity is good and simplicity is elegant. No one, of course, fully succeeds in this undertaking, for the story of every life is constrained by the exigencies of its owner's environment.

Some of these accounts are more intellectualistic than others, and it may be that they show the greater unity, either because some irrelevancies are omitted from the life history or because irrelevancies are actually, at least to a certain degree, omitted from the actual living. Other accounts are more environmentalistic, because social and institutional events and accidents have figured so largely in them. The environmentalistic autobiographer may have had a chief long-term goal, have pursued it, have achieved it with some fair degree of success, yet he may feel that the unforeseeable accidents of living have determined much of his life and have perhaps even altered his goal. The intellectualist, if such we may call him, may, on the other hand, have suffered disruption of plans less than his colleague, but it is probable that he has also been less interested in the effect of external forces upon himself.

No one, not even the members of this group of distinguished psychologists, can hope to deal adequately with the springs of his motivation. What he tells about himself and what he shows about his values can, however, go far toward instructing the reader as to how human motive moves to make science progress. The accidents of living do not always seem irrelevant to progress when they operate in the manner shown in the pages of this book. Psychology in autobiography cannot be complete, but it can make a contribution to the history of psychology which is unique.

Here follows an excerpt from the invitation to contributors to the present volume. It is an extension and modification of the instruction for 1952.

The important decisions in regard to the contents of your autobiography are yours. We hope, however, that the document will devote some attention to the historical details of your life. In connection with the *facts of life,* we hope you will identify yourself with regard to such matters as place and date of birth, significant educational and professional experiences, and family. We are, of course, particularly interested in the *intellectual and professional* aspects of your life as they have influenced and been influenced by events, ideas, and persons in and out of the field of psychology. Your perception of major developments and issues within psychology during your lifetime and your relation to these events will be of special importance. We should appreciate any discussion of your *feelings, motives, and aspirations* or of significant events that would increase the reader's understanding of you and your contributions to psychology. In brief, we are interested in your intellectual life history, but at the same time we feel that it should be illuminated by as much information about your personal background and inner motives as you are ready and able to divulge.

Considerable pressure has been put upon the committee to include a complete bibliography of the contributors. Complete bibliographies for such men as these would run from 100 to more than 500 citations apiece. Psychologists look wistfully at Murchison's *Psychological Register* of 1932 and hope for its updating, but neither that nor the inclusion of bibliographies here is practicable. The committee has space for only fifteen biographies of 12,000 words each, and it would have to decrease this number to add the bibliographies. Also, there would be duplication, for complete bibliographies are often published elsewhere for distinguished psychologists. The memoirs of academies sometimes include them. There are, moreover, already available some fairly complete bibliographies of psychologists whose publications have been listed in the *Psychological Index* and in *Psychological Abstracts* from 1894 to 1958; they are in the *Author Index* to those two serials published in four volumes in 1960 by G. K. Hall and Company of Boston.

Why are only Americans included as contributors in the present volume? The early volumes were divided approximately in the proportion of eight Americans to seven Europeans. Of course psychology was then and is even more now predominantly American; the language of this book is English and its character American. Nevertheless the present committee began with the expectation that its American character would be assured by our choosing those foreigners who had made an impression upon American thought in psychology, the Europeans or others who appeared as most important in the United States even if not in their own countries. We did indeed correspond with some Europeans and quite early met with two declinations, but the crucial desideratum that fixed our decision was the great scarcity of psychologists in Europe and elsewhere who had notably influenced the thinking of

American psychologists, who had not already contributed to a previous volume, and who were over 60 years old. Let the critic who suspects us of xenophobia try naming a few psychologists, foreign to America, who meet these three specifications.

On the other hand, this committee, whose authority ceases with the publication of this volume, looks forward hopefully to a Volume VI that will again be truly international. With the multiplication of psychologists on six continents it becomes more difficult to choose the outstanding names than it was when psychology seemed limited to Western Europe, Great Britain, and America, but the discrimination should not be impossible.

In the first four volumes sixty-one psychologists were invited to contribute and only three declined (Cattell, Lashley, and Köhler). For the present volume eventually we asked twenty-two psychologists. Werner died. Three would have liked to participate but had too many commitments for even our deferred deadline. They thought that if they could be asked early for a Volume VI, they could accept. Three others declined for personal reasons.

The present committee was formed by accretion. The idea of reviving the series began with Lindzey, who secured the agreement of Appleton-Century-Crofts to undertake the publication. Boring, who has been on all five of the committees and had conducted the negotiation with President Jefferson of Clark University for the transfer of the rights from Clark University to Appleton-Century-Crofts, agreed to act as chairman if Lindzey would be Executive Officer. The Committee is grateful to President Jefferson and Clark University for relinquishing these rights in the interests of this historical and scientific enterprise. MacCorquodale was included because of his long association with Lindzey and Appleton-Century-Crofts in the editing of the Century Psychology Series. Wapner was a natural continuation of the Clark ancestry for the series. Werner at Clark had been a member of the previous committee. Newbrough and Sharp had on their own initiative been conducting a poll of psychologists to assess the desirability of reviving the series. Clearly it was best to fuse the two enterprises. The American Psychological Association was asked to sponsor the undertaking, as it had Volume IV, appointing a new committee if it deemed wise, but it declined, believing that the present committee did not need its help. Nevertheless we felt that our committee could profit from more intelligence, so we added Beach and Hobbs to our membership. This committee has prepared the present volume, but it is not self-perpetuating. We believe, however, that Lindzey will be an adequate care-taker for the interests of the series between volumes. Especially must we mention the indispensable assistance of Miss Leslie Segner in the final preparation of the manuscript for publication.

We thank the contributors. They will receive no royalties but we hope they find satisfaction in this bit of immortality that it is possible for us to give them. They have now gained posterity for an audience, and long years after they are gone they can still be speaking to the strange new psychologists who will be their intellectual descendants. The small royalties that accrue from the sales of this volume quite properly go to the American Psychological Foundation.

Frank A. Beach
*University of California*
Edwin G. Boring, *Chairman*
*Harvard University*
Nicholas Hobbs
*George Peabody College for Teachers*
Gardner Lindzey, *Executive Officer*
*University of Texas*

Kenneth MacCorquodale
*University of Minnesota*
J. R. Newbrough
*National Institute of Mental Health*
Joseph C. Sharp
*Walter Reed Army Institute of Research*
Seymour Wapner
*Clark University*

January, 1967

# Contributors to Volumes I–V

## VOLUME I

### 1930

J. M. Baldwin (1861–1934)
M. W. Calkins (1863–1930)
E. Claparède (1873–1940)
R. Dodge (1871–1942)
P. Janet (1859–1947)
J. Jastrow (1863–1944)
F. Kiesow (1858–1940)
W. McDougall (1871–1938)
C. E. Seashore (1866–1949)
C. Spearman (1863–1945)
W. Stern (1871–1938)
C. Stumpf (1848–1936)
H. C. Warren (1867–1934)
T. Ziehen (1862–1950)
H. Zwaardemaker (1857–1930)

## VOLUME II

### 1932

B. Bourdon (1860–1943)
J. Drever (1873–1950)
K. Dunlap (1875–1949)
G. C. Ferrari (1869–1932)
S. I. Franz (1874–1933)
K. Groos (1861–1946)
G. Heymans (1857–1930)
H. Höffding (1843–1931)
C. H. Judd (1873–1946)
C. L. Morgan (1852–1936)
W. B. Pillsbury (1872–1960)
L. M. Terman (1877–1956)
M. F. Washburn (1871–1939)
R. S. Woodworth (1869–1962)
R. M. Yerkes (1876–1956)

## VOLUME III

### 1936

J. R. Angell (1869–1949)
F. C. Bartlett (1886–    )
M. Bentley (1870–1955)
H. A. Carr (1873–1954)
S. De Sanctis (1862–1935)
J. Fröbes (1866–1947)
O. Klemm (1884–1939)
K. Marbe (1869–1953)
C. S. Myers (1873–1946)
E. W. Scripture (1864–1945)
E. L. Thorndike (1874–1949)
J. B. Watson (1878–1958)
W. Wirth (1876–1952)

## VOLUME IV

### 1952

W. V. D. Bingham (1880–1952)
E. G. Boring (1886–    )
C. L. Burt (1883–    )
R. M. Elliott (1887–    )
A. Gemelli (1878–1959)
A. Gesell (1880–1961)
C. L. Hull (1884–1952)
W. S. Hunter (1889–1954)
D. Katz (1884–1953)
A. Michotte (1881–1965)
J. Piaget (1896–    )
H. Piéron (1881–1964)
C. Thomson (1881–1955)
L. L. Thurstone (1887–1955)
E. C. Tolman (1886–1959)

VOLUME V

1966

G. W. Allport (1897–    )
L. Carmichael (1898–    )
K. M. Dallenbach (1887–    )
J. F. Dashiell (1888–    )
J. J. Gibson (1904–    )

K. Goldstein (1878–1965)
J. P. Guilford (1897–    )
H. Helson (1898–    )
W. R. Miles (1885–    )
G. Murphy (1895–    )
H. A. Murray (1893–    )
S. L. Pressey (1888–    )
C. R. Rogers (1902–    )
B. F. Skinner (1904–    )
M. S. Viteles (1898–    )

# Contents

Gordon W. Allport

1

# Gordon W. Allport

Bergson held that every philosophic life pivots on a single "personal idea," even though the attempt to express this idea never fully succeeds. This dictum, savoring as it does of idealism and romanticism, is alien to the Lockean image of man that dominates Anglo-American psychology. And yet I confess I am attracted to this proposition. It seems to state in a broad way a testable hypothesis.

One might say that my own personal idea is to discover whether such broad hypotheses concerning the nature of man are empirically viable—at least as viable as the associationistic and reactive hypotheses that today govern the American psychological outlook. Although I suspect that Bergson exaggerates the potential unity of human personality, I also think that he, as well as other Leibnitzian, neo-Kantian, and existential writers, sets a challenge to empirical psychology; and that something should be done to test these views. The philosophy of man and the psychology of man should be brought to confront one another.

Let me suggest some relevant empirical questions. How shall a psychological life history be written? What processes and what structures must a full-bodied account of personality include? How can one detect unifying threads in a life, if they exist? The greater part of my own professional work can be viewed as an attempt to answer such questions through piecemeal and stepwise research and writing. If my theoretical writings exceed in bulk my output of research, it is because of my conviction that significant, not trivial, questions must be posed before we lose ourselves in a frenzy of investigation.

In 1940 I assigned my Harvard seminar the problem "How shall a psychological life history be written?" The seminar included the following members: Jerome Bruner, Dorwin Cartwright, Norman Polansky, John R. P. French, Alfred Baldwin, John Harding, Dwight Fiske, Donald McGranahan, Henry Riecken, Robert White, and Freed Bales. I mention their names because it seems to me that while these scholars have pursued diversified and distinguished careers, much of their subsequent creative work has been broadly relevant to the topic of the seminar.

We did not succeed in our self-imposed task. It is true that we designed a set of rules and composed cases to fit the rules, but at the end we were

3

distressed by the hollowness of the product. Our abortive rules were never published, yet from the seminar issued several important published researches, some of them summarized in my monograph *The Use of Personal Documents in Psychological Science* (1942).

I still do not know how a psychological life history should be written. And here I am, faced ironically enough with the assignment of writing my own psychological vita. Lacking a method I shall have to bumble along as best I can, hoping that psychologists of the future will learn how such an assignment should be carried through.

## 1897–1915

Every autobiographer finds his own genealogy of captivating interest and knows that his family relationships are of highest explanatory importance. But the reader is likely to find the same material dull—something to be tolerated because it *ought* to be relevant. The writer has great difficulty showing the reader just *what* is relevant, and *where* and *why*. He himself does not know how to separate primary formative influences in his heredity and early environment from those that are of minor or negligible significance. My own account will be as brief as possible.

Father was a country doctor who learned his profession after a career in business and after having a family of three sons. I, the fourth and last of the family, was born November 11, 1897, in Montezuma, Indiana, where my father had set up his first medical practice. My mother and I were, I believe, his first patients. Soon afterward he moved his practice to Streetsboro and to Hudson in Ohio. Before I started school he moved again to Glenville (Cleveland), where I had the advantage of twelve years of sound and uninterrupted schooling.

Since my brothers were considerably older (Harold, nine years; Floyd, seven years; Fayette, five years) I fashioned my own circle of activities. It was a select circle, for I never fitted the general boy assembly. I was quick with words, poor at games. When I was ten a schoolmate said of me, "Aw, that guy swallowed a dictionary." But even as an "isolate" I contrived to be the "star" for a small cluster of friends.

Our family for several generations had lived in rural New York State. My paternal grandfather was a farmer, my maternal grandfather a cabinetmaker and Civil War veteran. My father, John Edwards Allport (born 1863), was of pure English descent; my mother, Nellie Edith Wise (born 1862), was of German and Scottish descent.

Our home life was marked by plain Protestant piety and hard work. My mother had been a school teacher and brought to her sons an eager sense of philosophical questing and the importance of searching for ultimate religious answers. Since my father lacked adequate hospital facilities for his patients, our household for several years included both patients and nurses. Tending office, washing bottles, and dealing with patients were important aspects of my early training. Along with his general practice my father engaged in many enterprises: founding a cooperative drug company, building and renting apartments, and finally developing a new specialty of building and supervising hospitals. I mention his versatility simply to underscore the fact that his four sons were trained in the practical urgencies of life as well as in a broad humanitarian outlook. Dad was no believer in vacations. He followed rather his own rule of life, which he expressed as follows: "If every person worked as hard as he could and took only the minimum financial return required by his family's needs, then there would be just enough wealth to go around." Thus it was hard work tempered by trust and affection that marked the home environment.

Except for this generally wholesome foundation, I cannot identify any formative influence of special importance until after my graduation from Glenville High School in 1915, at which time I stood second highest in a class of 100. Apparently I was a good routine student, but definitely uninspired and uncurious about anything beyond the usual adolescent concerns.

Graduation suddenly brought up the problem of further schooling. Wisely my father insisted that I take a summer to learn typing at a business college—a skill I have endlessly prized. During this period my brother Floyd who had graduated from Harvard in 1913 suggested that I apply there. It was late to do so, but I was finally admitted after squeezing through the entrance tests given in Cambridge in early September. Then came an experience of intellectual dawn.

### 1915–1924

Did ever a Midwestern lad receive a greater impact from "going East to college"? I doubt it. Almost overnight my world was remade. My basic moral values, to be sure, had been fashioned at home. What was new was the horizon of intellect and culture I was now invited to explore. The undergraduate years (1915–1919) brought a welter of new influences.

First and most important was the pervading sense of high standards. Harvard simply assumed, or so it seemed to me, that excellence should prevail. At the first hour examinations I received an array of D's and C's. Profoundly shattered, I stiffened my efforts and ended the year with A's. As a prize I was awarded a *detur* (what might that be?) in the form of a *de luxe* edition of *Marius, the Epicurean* (who was he?). In the course of fifty years' association with Harvard I have never ceased to admire the unspoken expectation of excellence. One should perform at the highest level of which one is capable, and one is given full freedom to do so. Although all my courses were valuable to me, my focus was soon directed toward psychology and social ethics. Taken together these two disciplines framed my later career.

Münsterberg, looking like Wotan, was my first teacher in psychology. My brother Floyd, a graduate student, was his assistant. From Münsterberg's guttural lectures and from his textbook *Psychology: General and Applied* (1914), I learned little except that "causal" psychology was not the same as "purposive" psychology. The blank page dividing the two corresponding sections of the textbook intrigued me. Could they not be reconciled and fused? I wondered. Harry Murray had also started to study with Münsterberg. In "What Should Psychologists Do About Psychoanalysis?" (1940), he reports that he was so revolted by the chill of Münsterberg's approach that he fled to the nearest exit, thereby retarding by several years the choice of his later profession. Meat for me was poison for Murray. The question arises then: What is a "good" teacher? I drew nourishment from Münsterberg's dualistic dilemma as well as from his pioneer work in applied psychology.

Soon I found myself taking courses with Edwin B. Holt, Leonard Troland, Walter Dearborn, and Ernest Southard. Experimental psychology I took with Herbert Langfeld and my brother. Between times and out of hours I gained much from my brother's more mature reflections on the problems and methods of psychology. He invited me to serve as a subject in his own researches on social influence. Münsterberg had persuaded him to follow the Moede tradition and discover the differences resulting from the performance of tasks in groups and alone.

World War I dislocated my program only slightly. As an inductee in the Students' Army Training Corps I was allowed to continue my courses (with sanitary engineering and map-making added). Even at our training camp I prepared, with Langfeld's encouragement, reports on psychological aspects of rifle practice. Although my contribution was sophomoric, the assignment was beneficial. The Armistice was signed on my twenty-first birthday, November 11, 1918. Demobilization and a return to my chosen program followed rapidly. At commencement, 1919, I received my A.B. degree, and Floyd received his Ph.D.

A final line of undergraduate influence came through my studies in the Department of Social Ethics, chiefly with James Ford, and especially from the accompanying field training and volunteer social service which heavily engaged my interest. All through college I conducted a boys' club in the West End of Boston. At various times I did volunteer visiting for the Family Society and served as volunteer probation officer. During one summer I held a paid job with the Humane Society of Cleveland; during another I worked for Professor Ford as field agent for the registration of homes for war workers in crowded industrial cities of the East. At the Phillips Brooks House I held a paid job as executive of the committee to assist foreign students and as secretary of the Cosmopolitan Club. All this social service was deeply satisfying, partly because it gave me a feeling of competence (to offset a generalized inferiority feeling) and partly because I found I liked to help people with their problems.

This social service interval reflected my search for personal identity. It blended also with my attempt to achieve a mature religious position. Like many undergraduates I was in the process of replacing childhood conceptions of doctrine with some sort of humanitarian religion. A few years later, however, I reacted against this essentially Unitarian position because it seemed to me that to exalt one's own intellect and affirm only a precarious man-made set of values cheapened the whole quest. Humility and some mysticism, I felt, were indispensable for me; otherwise I would be victimized by my own arrogance. Arrogance in psychological theorizing has always antagonized me; I believe it is better to be tentative, eclectic, and humble.

My two lines of study gradually merged into an important conviction. If one were to do effective social service, one needed a sound conception of human personality. Sound theory must underlie application. This conviction was clearly expressed later in my Ph.D. thesis, which was titled "An Experimental Study of the Traits of Personality: With Special Reference to the Problem of Social Diagnosis." This, of course, was an early formulation of the riddle: How shall a psychological life history be written?

After graduation I had no clear idea what I should do. Vaguely I felt that social service administration might be a better line for me than teaching. But an opportunity came to give teaching a trial. For one year I taught English and sociology at Robert College in Constantinople during the last gasp of the Sultan's reign (1919–1920). I greatly enjoyed the year—its freedom and novelty and sense of achievement. When by cable I was offered a fellowship for graduate study at Harvard I knew that teaching was not such a bad career for me, and I accepted the opportunity. Two life-long friendships were formed at Robert College—one with the family of Dean Bradlee Watson, who later became professor of dramatic literature at Dartmouth and our son's godfather; the other with Edwin Powers, later Deputy Commissioner of Correction for the Commonwealth of Massachusetts.

En route from Constantinople to Cambridge, an event of pungent significance occurred, namely, my one and only encounter with Sigmund Freud. I have told the story many times but it must be repeated, for it had the character of a traumatic developmental episode. My brother Fayette was at that time in the United States trade commission in Vienna. It was during the period of Hoover relief activities. My brother invited me to stop for a visit.

With a callow forwardness characteristic of age twenty-two, I wrote to Freud announcing that I was in Vienna and implied that no doubt he would be glad to make my acquaintance. I received a kind reply in his own handwriting inviting me to come to his office at a certain time. Soon after I had entered the famous red burlap room with pictures of dreams on the wall, he summoned me to his inner office. He did not speak to me but sat in expectant silence, for me to state my mission. I was not prepared for silence and had to think fast to find a suitable conversational gambit. I told him of an episode on the tram car on my way to his office. A small boy about four years of age had displayed a conspicuous dirt phobia. He kept saying to his mother, "I don't want to sit there . . . don't let that dirty man sit beside me." To him everything was *schmutzig*. His mother was a well-starched *Hausfrau,* so dominant and purposive looking that I thought the cause and effect apparent.

When I finished my story Freud fixed his kindly therapeutic eyes upon me and said, "And was that little boy you?" Flabbergasted and feeling a bit guilty, I contrived to change the subject. While Freud's misunderstanding of my motivation was amusing, it also started a deep train of thought. I realized that he was accustomed to neurotic defenses and that my manifest motivation (a sort of rude curiosity and youthful ambition) escaped him. For therapeutic progress he would have to cut through my defenses, but it so happened that therapeutic progress was not here an issue.

This experience taught me that depth psychology, for all its merits, may plunge too deep, and that psychologists would do well to give full recognition to manifest motives before probing the unconscious. Although I never regarded myself as anti-Freudian, I have been critical of psychoanalytic excesses. A later paper entitled "The Trend in Motivational Theory" (1953) is a direct reflection of this episode and has been reprinted, I believe, more frequently than any other of my articles. Let me add that the better balanced view of motivation expressed in later neo-Freudian, ego psychology is more to my taste.

Back at Harvard I found that the requirements for the Ph.D. degree were not stiff (not nearly stiff enough); and so with only two years' additional course work, a few examinations, and the thesis, I qualified for this degree in 1922 at the age of twenty-four. McDougall had joined the staff and was one of the readers of my thesis, along with Langfeld and James Ford. During this period Floyd, an instructor, was editing Morton Prince's *Journal of Abnormal and Social Psychology.* I helped him with the work, thus making an early acquaintance with the journal I myself was later to edit (1937–1948).

During this period I suffered from vocational misgivings. Unlike most of my student colleagues I had no giftedness in natural science, mathematics, mechanics (laboratory manipulations), nor in biological or medical specialties. Most of the psychologists I admired had competence in some adjuvant field. I confessed my misgivings about my fitness to Professor Langfeld. In his laconic way he remarked, "But you know there are many branches of psychology." I think this casual remark saved me. In effect he was encouraging me to find my own way in the humanistic pastures of psychology.

But did I have enough courage and ability to develop my deviant interests? No other psychologist, at least at Harvard, seemed to be interested in social values as an academic problem nor in developing a lifelike psychology of personality. Indeed the available relevant work included not much more than a few early studies by June Downey (Wyoming), Walter Fernald (Concord Reformatory), and R. S. Woodworth (Columbia), who during the war had devised his "Personal Data Sheet," an early pencil-and-paper personality test. I believe that my own thesis was perhaps the first American dissertation written explicitly on the question of component traits of personality. It led to my maiden publication (with my brother) entitled "Personality Traits: Their Classification and Measurement" (1921). In this connection I may add that I suspect my own course given at Harvard in 1924 and 1925, titled "Personality: Its Psychological and Social Aspects," was probably the first course on the subject offered in an American college.

Standing at a frontier was a somewhat alarming business. The climax of my conflict came in connection with my single encounter with Titchener. I had been invited to attend the select gathering of his group of experimentalists, which met at Clark University in May, 1922, just as I was finishing my thesis. After two days of discussing problems in sensory psychology Titchener allotted three minutes to each visiting graduate to describe his own investigations. I reported on traits of personality and was punished by the rebuke of total silence from the group, punctuated by a glare of disapproval from Titchener. Later Titchener demanded of Langfeld, "Why did you let him work on that problem?" Back in Cambridge Langfeld again consoled me with the laconic remark, "You don't care what Titchener thinks." And I found that I did not.

The whole experience was a turning point. Never since that time have I been troubled by rebukes or professional slights directed at my maverick interests. Later, of course, the field of personality became not only acceptable but highly fashionable. But, although the field itself became legitimate, my own theoretical position was not always approved.

I have implied that my graduate years at Harvard were not particularly productive intellectually. They did, however, lead to two benefits over and beyond the degree. Within the congenial circle of graduate students I found my future wife, Ada Lufkin Gould, a Boston girl, who, after taking her master's degree, worked in the field of clinical psychology. Our interests were closely parallel. I was also awarded by Harvard a Sheldon Traveling Fellowship, which gave me two years in Europe. For me these years were a second intellectual dawn.

The German tradition in psychology was still strong in America, although Germany itself had been flattened by World War I and inflation. It was only natural for me to head for Germany. William James and E. B. Titchener had immortalized in their textbooks the Teutonic foundations of our science, and my own teachers had studied there. From Harvard philosophers R. B. Perry and R. F. A. Hoernle, I had gained further respect for German thought.

I was not prepared, however, for the powerful impact of my German teachers who included the aged Stumpf and Dessoir, the younger Max Wertheimer, Wolfgang Köhler, and Eduard Spranger in Berlin, and in Hamburg, William Stern and Heinz Werner. A fellow student was Heinrich Klüver, who helped me with my halting German, and who has remained a cherished friend ever since even though our paths of psychological interest have diverged.

At that time Gestalt was a new concept. I had not heard of it before leaving Cambridge. It took me some weeks to discover why my teachers usually started their two-hour lectures with a castigation of David Hume. Soon I learned he was the natural whipping boy for the German structural schools of thought. *Ganzheit* and *Gestalt, Struktur* and *Lebenformen,* and *die unteilbare Person* were new music to my ears. Here was the kind of psychology I had been longing for but did not know existed.

Of course I realized that romanticism in psychology could poison its scientific soil. (I myself had been brought up in the Humean tradition.) At the same time it seemed to me that the high quality of experimental studies by the Gestalt school, the original empirical investigations at Stern's Institute, and the brilliance of the Lewinian approach (which I came to know at second hand) gave safe anchorage to the kinds of concepts that I found congenial.

Thus Germany gave me support for the structural view of personality that I had pieced together for myself. For the *American Journal of Psychology* I wrote a brief *Bericht,* "The Leipzig Congress of Psychology" (1923), outlining the various German movements that reflected the *Strukturbegriff: Gestalt,* Stern's *Personalistik,* Krueger's complex qualities, and the school of *Verstehen.* From Stern in particular I learned that a chasm exists between the common variety of differential psychology (which he himself had largely invented along with the concept of the IQ) and a truly personalistic psychology that focuses upon the organization, not the mere profiling, of an individual's traits.

I became acquainted also with German doctrines of types. Among them were the elaborate speculations and investigations of E. R. Jaensch on eidetic imagery. I ventured to replicate some of his work a year later while in Cambridge, England. Three papers resulted: "Eidetic Imagery" (1924), "The Eidetic Image and the After-image" (1928), and "Change and Decay in the Visual Memory Image" (1930). Later I was horrified by Jaensch's prostitution of his scientific work to provide psychological underpinning for Nazi doctrine. His paranoid efforts explained to me some of the weaker portions of his earlier eidetic theory.

The year in England was spent largely in absorbing my German experiences. Professor Frederic Bartlett was courteous in providing me with facilities for work. Ivor A. Richards invited me to contribute a paper on "The Standpoint of Gestalt Psychology" to *Psyche* (1924); but I confess I chiefly ruminated on my German year and enjoyed myself by studying Faust with Professor Breuel.

Thus did my years of formal training come to an end. A cable from Professor Ford offered me an instructorship in social ethics at Harvard to begin in the fall of 1924. Besides taking over his course on social problems and social policy, I was invited to offer a new course in the psychology of personality—a pioneer enterprise.


## 1924–1930

Temperamentally I am a bit of a worrier, and for this reason I prepared my courses with conscientious thoroughness. When my chairman, Dr. Richard Cabot, implied that my platform manner "lacked fire" I tried to add animation to substance in my teaching. Ada and I were married in 1925, and for forty years she has had to tolerate the strain that marks all my preparations.

Our son Robert Bradlee was born in 1927 after we had moved to Dartmouth College. He later became a pediatrician, and it pleased me to find myself sandwiched between two generations of physicians.

Profoundly important professional friendships resulted from my first two years of teaching at Harvard. The first was with Dr. Richard Cabot, who held a double professorship at Harvard in cardiology and in social ethics. He proved to be a man of remarkably forthright social conscience. At the top of his field in medicine, he somehow found time to establish medical social service, to write many lucid volumes in medicine and in ethics, and to stir undergraduates profoundly with his uncompromising teaching of his own Puritan brand of ethics. Himself a wealthy Boston Brahmin, Cabot followed a theory and practice of philanthropy that appealed directly to my own sense of values. He believed as strongly as I in the integrity of each individual human life and would give financial and spiritual assistance when he felt he could aid in another's growth at some critical and crescent moment. (In 1936 he gave me support so that I could take a semester of free time to complete my book *Personality: A Psychological Interpretation,* 1937.) Gradually I became involved in his projects, inheriting after his death the general supervision of the Cambridge-Somerville Youth Study (Powers and Witmer, 1951). Likewise he asked me to be a trustee of the Ella Lyman Cabot Trust which has continued year by year to carry through his own philanthropic conception of "backing persons with projects." In connection with this Trust I have been associated with Dr. Cabot's famous successor, Dr. Paul Dudley White, and with other friends in a unique and highly congenial philanthropic activity.

My second friendship was formed with Edwin G. Boring who had come to Harvard while I was studying abroad. Fearing that my appointment in social ethics might remove me from psychology proper, I asked Boring if I could assist him in his introductory course, the famous Psychology 1. He agreed to the arrangement, and so I gained some experience teaching sections in experimental psychology (but not in arranging demonstrations, at which I should certainly be a failure). With Boring's encouragement I wrote further on imagery (1928). Acquaintance with a man of such amazing strenuosity and profound personal integrity, such deep historical erudition, and meticulous standards was, and is, a great influence and a major gratification in my career.

Less intimate, but likewise influential, was my contact with William McDougall. I assisted him as well as Boring in his elementary course. Needless to say, the two courses were in marked contrast. Although I admired McDougall for his vigor and independence, I harbored all the prevailing anti-McDougall prejudices. I deplored his doctrines of instinct, interactionism, and the group mind (all of which I, like most other Americans, only half understood). Although Germany had converted me from my undergraduate semifaith in behaviorism, I felt that McDougall's antagonism to the prevailing American psychological creed went too far. His solution to the causal-purposive problem seemed as dualistic as Münsterberg's, and no more satisfactory. At the same time I was fully exposed to his point of view and found it became more persuasive in later years. McDougall always had a bad press in America. In spite of his forensic gifts, his British style of polemic diminished his effectiveness. After about seven years at Harvard he moved to Duke University where he continued his monumental heresies until his death in 1938. To Duke he brought my other teacher and friend, William Stern, a Hitler fugitive who outlived McDougall by two years. He also provided a haven for Rhine and his parapsychological research, once again exhibiting his independence of the prevailing psychological ethos.

My brother had left Harvard for the University of North Carolina before my instructorship began. Besides our joint article we published "A Test for Ascendance–Submission" in 1928. This was a scale to measure dominant and submissive tendencies (one of the earliest pencil-and-paper personality tests). Apart from these two papers we never collaborated, even though we have occasionally helped each other with criticism. The truth, of course, is that our psychological views diverged. His *Social Psychology* (1924) was too behavioristic and too psychoanalytic for my taste. While our later works on political and social attitudes and on prejudice were similar in orientation, his theories became more positivistic, more monistic, and in a sense more interdisciplinary than my own. Floyd was a stricter logician and more systematic in his use of method than I. It should also be said that he had artistic, musical, and manual giftedness that I lacked. Over the years we pursued our own ways, but because of our common and unusual surname and divergence of points of view we managed to confuse students and the public. Were there one or two Allports?

It is clear to me now that the common quality in Stern, McDougall, Boring, Cabot, and my brother is a fierce personal and professional integrity. Unconsciously no doubt I have drawn much encouragement from them in pursuing my own personal idea in the face of contrary fashion.

To this list of senior intellectual mentors and friends I must add the name of Pitirim A. Sorokin, whom I met when he came to Harvard in 1930 to head the Department of Sociology (to replace Social Ethics). Later I dedicated my book *Becoming* (1955) to this colleague of powerful erudition and blazing conviction. How he maintained his own moral and intellectual integrity during the Russian Communist Revolution he himself tells in his autobiography, *A Long Journey* (1964). In comparing my life with his I realize how sheltered my own career has been.

Another influential figure has been my amiable and supportive colleague Harry A. Murray. Our fields of interest lie so close together that by unspoken agreement we allow a "narcissism of slight differences" to keep us in a state of friendly separation. I derive from Murray a great deal of stimulation and encouragement.

Somewhat later, in the 1940's, I met Peter A. Bertocci, now Bowne Professor of Philosophy at Boston University, devoted to the personalist school of thought and well read in psychological theory. Over the years we have had frequent amiable arguments in and out of print. While he approves the general trend of my thought, he would like me to subscribe to an agent-self and to a larger measure of voluntarism. On these issues I demur, but I deeply prize his philosophical monitoring and his friendship.

An offer from Charles Stone at Dartmouth now broke my connection with Harvard for a period of four years. In Hanover I found myself in a pleasant and more relaxed atmosphere, free to pursue my own inclinations. I helped with the general introductory course and taught both social psychology and personality. During summer sessions I generally returned to teach at Harvard. The Baker Library during the long winter days at Hanover provided me with German journals so that I could keep abreast of thinking in typology, Gestalt, and *Verstehen*. Ever since the days of my thesis I had been haunted with the idea that I should write a general book on personality. Hanover gave me an opportunity to read and to think about this project. As one product, I might mention my first professional paper offered at the Ninth International Congress, held at Yale in 1929. It was titled "What Is a Trait of Personality?" (1931). The problem of the structure of personality was already much on my mind. (I resumed the theme thirty-six years later in a lecture to the APA in 1965, acknowledging my Distinguished Scientific Contribution Award. I titled it "Traits Revisited.")

Among my Dartmouth undergraduate students were Hadley Cantril, Henry Odbert, Leonard Doob, all of whom followed me to Harvard for their Ph.D. degrees. When McDougall left Harvard there was a gap in the area of social psychology. During 1928 Boring invited me to return as assistant professor, but it was September 1930 before I entered upon this final academic assignment. It is obvious to the reader that I had from 1915 a deep attachment to Harvard—an infatuation that has continued to this day.


## 1930–1946

Back in Cambridge the frenzy began. In Hanover I had started an editorial connection with the *Psychological Bulletin,* being responsible for survey articles in the field of social psychology, and I had formed the habit of reading the *Psychological Abstracts* from cover to cover (a habit soon extinguished by competing stimuli). All in all I felt fairly familiar with the then current field of general psychology and so enjoyed colloquia and luncheon discussions with my colleagues: Boring, Pratt, Beebe-Center, Chapman, Murray, White, and others. Graduate students in social psychology formed a band we called "The Group Mind." For some years we met to discuss one another's research programs in the fields of attitudes, expressive behavior, propaganda, and radio. Philip Vernon came from England for a time and brought a tornado of initiative. With him I was able to work out two investigations of lasting significance: *Studies in Expressive Movement* (1933) and *A Study of Values* (1931). Both of these projects rested upon my own German background but were sparked by Vernon's energy. *A Study of Values* was an attempt to establish empirically the six primary dimensions of personal values defined by Eduard Spranger, my Berlin teacher: the theoretical, economic, aesthetic, social, political, and religious. The resulting test, although unconventional in many ways, has shown astonishing vitality over the years. Gardner Lindzey assisted with a revision in 1951 and again in 1960. It is my contention that a measuring instrument in the field of personality is far better if based on good a priori analysis than if based on factorial or other adventitiously achieved dimensions.

My mention of Vernon and Lindzey leads me to a warm and grateful acknowledgment of the happy collaboration I have enjoyed with many of my students. My joint publications (listed in the bibliography published as an appendix to *Personality and Social Encounter,* 1964) include as co-authors, besides Vernon and Lindzey, the names of Hadley Cantril, Henry Odbert, Leo Postman, Jerome Bruner, Bernard Kramer, James Gillespie, Thomas Pettigrew, and a dozen others. I can only hope they have shared my satisfaction in our joint labors.

Psychology was a rapidly growing subject in the 1930's. The social emphasis was suddenly enhanced by the impact of world events: the depression, the rise of Hitler, the threat of war, and other fractures in the social edifice. There were relatively few social psychologists. Thus a host of responsibilities came my way. The Social Science Research Council and National Research Council wanted me for committees. The *Journal of Abnormal and Social Psychology* wanted me as editor. After Boring had successfully piloted a final break between philosophy and psychology at Harvard, he wanted me to assume chairmanship of the now finally independent Department of Psychology. Lashley joined the department, and I was promoted to the third permanency on the staff (1937). Astonishing to me was my election as president of the American Psychological Association for the year 1939.

But for me the event of chief significance in this decade was the publication by Holt of *Personality: A Psychological Interpretation* (1937). This book, as I have said, had been "cooking" in my head since my graduate days. My ambition was to give a psychological definition of the field of personality as I saw it. My vision, of course, was influenced by my encounters with social ethics, Anglo-American empiricism and German structural and personalistic theories. I wanted to fashion an experimental science, so far as appropriate, but chiefly I wanted an "image of man" that would allow us to test in full whatever democratic and humane potentialities that he might possess. I did not think of man as innately "good," but I was convinced that by and large American psychology gave man less than his due by depicting him as a bundle of unrelated reaction tendencies. I did not write the book for any particular audience. I wrote it simply because I felt I had to define the new field of the psychology of personality as I saw it. Although there were books in the related areas of mental hygiene and abnormal psychology, I regarded my own approach as being in the tradition of academic psychology, and I felt that my emphasis should be on normality rather than on pathology. I also had a desire to avoid jargon and to try to express my thoughts in proper and felicitous English. The result was that some readers regarded the book as difficult and pretentious, others labelled it as "classic," and for twenty-five years it stood as more or less standard reading in the field. Perhaps its major importance was that it defined (for the first time) the topics which well-bred texts in the field of personality should cover.

To establish my main point (that a full-bodied psychology of the human person is possible) I had to devise and adapt a number of rather novel supporting propositions. Chief among them was the concept of *functional autonomy*. No theory of motivation, I maintained, could be adequate if based on the exclusive primacy of drives and on the reactive aspects of human nature. I hesitated to adopt McDougall's concept of purpose because it was anchored to dubious instinct theory. I felt that in the course of life, motives can, and usually do, undergo radical transformation and that the propelling force lay in the present on-moving structure of personality, not in some anachronistic conditioning of past motives. The book also emphasized the neglected topics of expressive behavior and faced up to the problem of the normative criteria for maturity. It dealt with the epistemological problem of our knowledge of other personalities and throughout reiterated the challenge that any adequate psychology of personality must deal with the essential uniqueness of every personal structure. The latter insistence, of course, scandalized readers who felt that a man's individuality was sufficiently dealt with by regarding him as a point of intersecting common dimensions. I never implied that differential psychology was irrelevant to the psychology of personality, but I did insist that our science was at fault for neglecting the problem of patterning. When at long last I undertook a complete rewriting of this text in order to update the material and simplify the exposition, I selected the title *Pattern and Growth in Personality* (1961).

While my chief intellectual love has always been personality theory, perhaps half of my research and writing has dealt with more general topics in social psychology. Even while working on *Personality* I took time off to dig as deeply as I could into the concept of "attitude," which resulted in my topical chapter, under this title, in C. C. Murchison's *Handbook of Social Psychology* (1935). A number of papers on social attitudes and newspaper psychology and a book on *The Psychology of Radio* (with Cantril, 1935) attest the same interest.

World War II placed a still heavier demand on social psychologists. Although I served with the Emergency Committee in Psychology under the APA, I avoided offers of employment in government agencies. My abilities, I felt, were not equal to the urgent and often vague demands placed upon the new agencies proliferating overnight in Washington. I felt that if I had any contribution to make, it would be best made by remaining at Harvard. Telephone lines were hot with the inquiry, "What do we know about civilian morale?" Speaking for myself, I knew nothing. But, in collaboration with Harry Murray, I decided some useful things might be discovered if we offered a seminar in "morale research." Until Murray himself was called to Washington to head an important project for the Office of Strategic Services, we directed a number of student projects, ranging in type from an analysis of Hitler's character to studies of wartime rumor and riots. A bound (but not published) volume resulted entitled *Worksheets in Morale*.

The seminar had a long-range consequence. It continued year after year, with a gradual focusing on what seemed to be the most urgent problem of national unity, namely, group conflict and prejudice. The products of this seminar over a twenty-five-year period have been numerous. I shall speak of them later.

Meanwhile there were other wartime demands. Ever since the advent of Hitler in 1933, a flood of refugee psychologists was pouring into the United States, many of them the finest type of scholar: Koffka, Stern, Köhler, Lewin, Werner, Egon and Else Brunswik, and many others. To find jobs for such stars was not difficult, but the second string of unknown refugees created a serious problem. Together with Barbara Burks, Gardner Murphy, and others, I did what I could to make contacts for them. The refugee problem had great interest for sociologists as well as for psychologists. J. S. Bruner and E. M. Jandorf collaborated with me in publishing an analysis of ninety personal documents written by Hitler fugitives under the title "Personality under Social Catastrophe" (1941).

Some of my time was given to making speeches, semipopular writing on morale, and rumor analysis, leading to a daily syndicated feature in the *Boston Traveler* entitled "Rumor Clinic" in which we endeavored to scotch harmful wartime rumors. We classified them as of three types: "bogies," "pipe dreams," and "wedge-drivers." The third type, based on prejudice and group antagonism, was the most serious. For much of this work I leaned upon the investigations of my student Robert H. Knapp. Soon Leo Postman joined forces with me in giving a course on race relations to Boston police officers and in publishing a book *The Psychology of Rumor* (1947).

As the close of the war approached, many psychologists became concerned with the conditions required for writing a lasting and effective peace. I pointed up a statement signed by 2038 psychologists entitled "Human Nature and the Peace" and published it in the *Psychological Bulletin* (1945). In retrospect our formula for peace may seem somewhat quixotic, but it still stands as a tribute to the social ideals of our profession.

The profound public concern of most American social psychologists, not only in wartime but throughout these troubled decades, is a fact worthy of comment. In 1936 the Society for the Psychological Study of Social Issues (SPSSI) was born. Early leaders included Gardner Murphy, Goodwin Watson, George Hartmann, Kurt Lewin, Edward Tolman, and Theodore Newcomb. I served as president of the Society in 1944. My membership in this group is one that I find congenial, for at heart I am both a political liberal and a social reformer.

From my early Dartmouth days I had found close intellectual and personal companionship with my student Hadley Cantril. We both wanted to fashion a social psychology that would be accurate and applicable to significant problems. Between us we called it "L-P" (*Lebenspsychologie*). Our book about the psychology of radio (1935) was one product of our collaboration. He was director of the "Tensions Project" at UNESCO in Paris and invited me to attend a memorable conference there in 1948, resulting in the book he edited, *Tensions that Cause Wars* (1950). For it I wrote a chapter entitled "The Role of Expectancy."

As the war drew to a close, most of my colleagues and students, it seemed, were in Washington or in the armed services. For us stay-at-homes it became necessary to plan on a huge postwar influx of veterans into our universities. In particular at Harvard we faced a local situation of some urgency. Although I was continuing as chairman of the Department of Psychology it seems that some far-reaching type of change was needed. Our department, like that of sociology, was small. The interests of our own staff were clearly divided, with the "biotropes" (Boring, Stevens, Lashley, Beebe-

Center) on one side and the "sociotropes" (the terms are Boring's) on the other (Murray, White, Allport). A corresponding division of interest was evident in the Department of Anthropology, with Kluckhohn, representing cultural anthropology, finding much in common with sociologists and sociotropes. Together a group consisting of Parsons, Murray, Kluckhohn, Mowrer, and myself held many meetings devising a new department. To change any basic organization within a university (especially within an older institution) is a task as cumbersome as moving a cemetery. However, plans were laid, and in January 1946 the Faculty of Arts and Sciences voted that the new department should be created.

Before leaving this era I wish to report a stroke of personal good fortune. During the last three years of my chairmanship of the Department of Psychology, Mrs. Eleanor D. Sprague served as my secretary. She continued with me in the new department, where my administrative job was chairmanship of the Committee of Higher Degrees. She was my right hand until her retirement in 1964. Thanks to her competent assistance I covered more ground than would otherwise have been possible.


1946–1966

Six P.M. was the sacred hour of adjournment for faculty meetings. At a meeting in January 1946 the faculty authorized the formation of the new department but at 5:50 P.M. had not yet christened it. The name Human Relations was suggested, but that would never do because Yale already had an institute by that name. It would be too suffocating to call it the Department of Sociology, Social Psychology, Clinical Psychology, and Social Anthropology, although that is what it was. At about 5:59 P.M. someone proposed "Social Relations," and owing to the lateness of the hour the name was adopted without debate. The new organization, involving as it did a splitting of the previous Departments of Anthropology and Psychology, was a drastic move for Harvard and startled that portion of the academic world which watches changes in Harvard's educational policies. But the war was over, the need urgent, and veterans were flocking back with a keen interest in the basic social sciences, which, they vaguely felt, must hold some solution to the troubled world's problems.

With the enthusiastic cooperation of the Provost, Paul Buck, the new department rapidly enlarged its staff with returning Harvard people (George Homans, Jerome Bruner, Brewster Smith, Donald McGranahan, and others) and with brilliant new members including Samuel Stouffer, Frederick Mosteller, and Richard Solomon. A new curriculum was offered commencing in July 1946. I myself (with George Homans) gave the introductory course for a few years. Within a year or so it became the largest elective course in college with nearly 900 Harvard and Radcliffe students registered in it. In fact soon after its beginning the department had large enrollments, a concentration of about 400 undergraduates and close to 200 candidates for the Ph.D. degree. Advanced degrees were not offered in Social Relations but rather in each of the four constituent disciplines. The problem of the department has always been to balance the needs of specialization with a measure of desired cross-disciplinary training. Our policies have followed a wavering course between specialism and integrationism, with no satisfactory proportion yet discovered.

This bold academic experiment could not have succeeded, I think, were it not for the fact that in the course of their wartime service most of our staff members had lost their strict academic identities. A man could be a good social scientist whether or not his main training had been in psychology, sociology, anthropology, statistics, or some other discipline. The war thus prepared our minds for such integration as was achieved. Intellectual leadership toward the formation of a "common language" in our field came from Talcott Parsons, joined for a time by Edward Shils and Edward Tolman. Whether the effort was premature or whether Harvard's tradition was one of individualism and dissent, it did not turn out to be possible to establish a common basic language for the department. But dyads, triads, and small clusters of colleagues did manage to work together on projects of common interest, and a general atmosphere of convergence prevailed. Much credit for such unification as was achieved goes to Parsons. For ten years he was our enthusiastic chairman and from the beginning the true leader of the enterprise.

As one of the department's founding fathers I was eager to see the experiment succeed. My specific duty was to chair the Committee on Higher Degrees (with Mrs. Sprague's able assistance) and, wherever I could, to uphold the arms of other administrative officers. (Talcott Parsons, Robert White, and David McClelland served successively as chairmen, and Samuel Stouffer and Freed Bales as laboratory directors.)

My own teaching continued much as it always had. I finally dropped the large elementary course into the able hands of Bob White and gave over formal course instruction in social psychology to younger colleagues—Jerry Bruner, Roger Brown, Gardner Lindzey, and more recently Herb Kelman, Elliot Aronson, Stanley Milgram, Kenneth Gergen, and the oncoming procession of younger talent. I gave a middle-level course in theories of personality and conducted two graduate seminars—one for second-year graduate candidates in clinical and social psychology and one a continuation of the morale seminar, which had become entirely devoted to problems of group conflict and prejudice.

It was in connection with the latter course that I directed several relevant Ph.D. theses and began a series of publications of my own, climaxed by The Nature of Prejudice (1954). To my mind the significance of this book, which still circulates widely in a paperback edition, lies in its table of contents. As was the case with the field of personality, I spent several years deciding what subject matter was truly central to a new, ill-defined psychological territory and what the proper order of topics should be in any comprehensive text.

While many able students collaborated in this work, one grew to the stature of a torch-bearer. I was greatly impressed by the research abilities and expository skills of Thomas F. Pettigrew, a Virginian. I invited him to accompany me to South Africa as special scholar at the Institute for Social Research at the University of Natal, where we spent six fruitful months in 1956. It was, of course, fascinating to compare the ethnic frictions of South Africa with those of the United States and thus in a way to test the cross-cultural validity of my recently published book. My conclusion was that all the personal forces making for prejudice were present in both lands, but that my own psychological bias had perhaps led me to underestimate the forces of history and of traditional social structure more strikingly evident in South Africa.

Pettigrew and I made some cross-cultural perceptual investigations in South Africa. One of them, entitled "Cultural Influences on the Perception of Movement" (1957), seemed to us to show that social factors in perception are prominent only when there is inherent ambiguity in the stimulus situation.

After a year at North Carolina, Pettigrew returned to Harvard and gradually assumed a large portion of my own teaching and administrative duties, adding them to his own heavy program of work in the field of race relations. Under his direction the long-standing seminar continues to make its contributions to the study of morale.

Returning to the field of personality theory (always central in my interests), I found myself burdened with requests for named lectures in assorted universities, sometimes single lectures, sometimes a series. Likewise there were presidential and other honorific papers to prepare, as well as chapters for symposia and handbooks. In fact most of my writing for the past twenty-five years seems to have been dictated by such obligations. Each obligation I tried to employ as an occasion to say something relevant to personality theory. Thus, to the Eastern Psychological Association I offered "The Ego in Contemporary Psychology" (1943). Sometimes this paper is cited as reintroducing the concept of self into academic psychology—a bit of an overstatement, I think. Again, the Merrick Lectures at Ohio Wesleyan and the Lowell Lectures in Boston gave me incentive to prepare *The Individual and His Religion* (1950). The assignment of the Terry Lectures at Yale resulted in *Becoming: Basic Considerations for a Psychology of Personality* (1955). A large number of additional occasional papers were gathered together in *Personality and Social Encounter* (1960). It seemed appropriate in this latter volume to list in an appendix my complete bibliography, revised in the paperback edition (1964).

To my mind there is a distinct unity in these writings, including those on prejudice. Personality, as I see it, is composed chiefly of generic attitudes, values, and sentiments. (See, for example, "Mental Health: A Generic Attitude," 1964.) Therefore the prejudice-complex, the religious sentiment, the phenomenological ego, and one's philosophy of life are important subterritories to explore in individual lives.

While giving much of my attention to these generic formations that are found in many, if not all, lives, I still place higher in my scale of scientific values the search for the pattern that binds sentiments, values, and traits within each unique individual life. I chose this theme for an address in 1961 to the *Berufsverband deutscher Psychologen* in Hamburg. The lecture was titled "Das Allgemeine und das Eigenartige in der Psychologischen Praxis" (1962). This assignment I accepted partly as an excuse for a sentimental journey. I was happy to repay the profound stimulation that German structural concepts had given me and especially to return to the scene of my studies with Stern almost forty years previously. But I felt too that German psychologists might understand my plea for morphogenic (idiographic) methods, geared to the structure of individual lives, somewhat better than did most of my American colleagues. This line of thought, of course, relates to my perennial question, "How shall a life history be written?"

For many years I had used in my teaching a remarkable series of 300 intimate letters written by a woman from the age of fifty-eight until her death twelve years later. The letters deal with a mother-son tangle and are written in a fiercely dramatic, personal style. Here surely is a unique life, calling for psychological analysis and interpretation. Having had considerable experience in teaching with the aid of these letters, I decided to present them as a challenge to others and to sketch the available modes of psychological analysis applicable to this single case; thus I produced the book *Letters from Jenny* (1965).

Among the occasional assignments that took much time and effort I should mention the chapter for Lindzey's *Handbook of Social Psychology* (1954) entitled "The Historical Background of Modern Social Psychology." I had for several years offered a course in this subject and so welcomed the opportunity to give a compendious statement of the roots of modern social psychology as I saw them to be. Although a revision of the *Handbook* is now called for, I find little to change in the chapter. Someone, however, should write a much fuller and more detailed history of the subject.

I knew, of course, that a revision of the 1937 edition of *Personality* was needed. It should be brought up to date; the account of functional autonomy required restatement, and the new movements in the fields of cognition, role studies, and existential theory should be included. *Pattern and Growth in Personality* (1961) represented this updating and likewise a simplification of exposition. Being older (and feeling personally more secure) now I can dispense with my earlier inflated vocabulary.

Meanwhile the Department of Social Relations had grown and grown. With a staff of nearly 100 instructors, further evolution and change were bound to occur. It was time to turn the controls over to younger colleagues. The department had existed for eighteen years in seven separate buildings and was largely cut off from the biotropic Department of Psychology. When the Fund for Harvard College announced as one of its goals the building of a large and inclusive Center for the Behavioral Sciences it seemed that at last a geographical union of these disparate units might be achieved. We moved into the new fifteen-story William James Hall in January 1965, just as I was entering a period of semiretirement. By arrangement with President Pusey I had agreed to teach in the fall semesters for a few years but to keep the spring terms free for writing and travel. I found it a wrench to leave Emerson Hall, which as student and teacher I had inhabited continuously for fifty years (less seven years for my work abroad and the interval at Dartmouth).

One final chapter in my formal relations with Harvard should be recorded. In March 1966 the Corporation appointed me the first Richard Clarke Cabot Professor of Social Ethics. In announcing the establishment of this new chair President Pusey took occasion to "welcome the formal reappearance of Social Ethics in a community which owes much to the dedication and example of Richard Clarke Cabot and, before him, Francis Greenwood Peabody." Pusey added that "In a time of widespread confusion about moral issues, there is also in our day a resurgence of concern for human and ethical values, especially for character and moral sensibility." Since Dr. Cabot was my first "boss" at Harvard, having much influence upon my career first and last, the appointment seemed to me to complete fittingly an intellectual cycle as well as a cycle of sentiment.


A POLEMIC-ECLECTIC

Much of my writing is critical of prevailing psychological idols. At times I have crossed swords with learning theory, dimensionalism in personality research, and with what seems to me to be an overemphasis on unconscious processes, projective tests, and simplified drive theories of motivation. I have felt that these fashionable explanatory principles are able to deal only with the peripheral or "opportunistic" layers of personality, or else that they make too much of some improbable formulations of depth psychology. (Yes, my single encounter with Freud was traumatic.)

In place of (or, more accurately, as a supplement to) these popular formulae, I have advocated what seemed to me necessary principles. These are principles dealing with "propriate" functions (anchored to the self-image), insightful capacities for learning, complex integrative generic attitudes and ways of perceiving one's world, expressive (not merely projective) behavior, the formations that mark maturity in personality, and values and orientations toward the future—in short, with the course of growth and becoming. It is within this web of concepts that one would find my personal idea.

Bergson, of course, was right in saying that no philosophic mind ever succeeds in fully realizing his idea. It is my experience also that such a mind may all the while be half-distrustful of the idea's validity. Although much of my writing is polemic in tone, I know in my bones that my opponents are partly right.

When asked to give an occasional paper at the XVII International Congress of Psychology in Washington, I titled it "The Fruits of Eclecticism: Bitter or Sweet?" (1964). In it I tried to trace eclectic trends in the psychology of the past and to argue that a systematic eclecticism is not impossible in the future. But here I insisted that no enthusiastic particularism, however fashionable, will ever be adequate. I implied that only a view of the "Open System in Personality Theory" (1960) will really serve the purpose. Any investigator, of course, has the right to restrict his variables and neglect, momentarily, irrelevant aspects of behavior, *but he has no right to forget what he has decided to neglect.*

As I have said elsewhere, some of my colleagues treat personality as a quasi-closed system. I respect their work and know that eventually their contributions will fit into the larger frame. I feel no personal animosity toward the associates with whom I have ventured to disagree. But what I dislike in our profession is the strong aura of arrogance found in presently fashionable dogmas. To my mind humility is a virtue appropriate for social and psychological scientists to cultivate. I am not fond of the label "behavioral sciences" now in vogue. From a certain point of view it is harmless enough, but to me it somehow implies that if we were all to embrace the creeds of positivism and behaviorism, all our problems would be solved. I cannot agree. Our methods would be restricted, our theories one-sided, and our students would be intimidated by a tyrannical and temporary scientism. Humility requires a more tentative position. William James was right—our knowledge is a drop, our ignorance a sea. James himself, to my mind, sets a worthy model for psychologists to follow in his open-mindedness, his respect for multiple avenues to truth, and his personal humility.

The irrelevance of much present-day psychology to human life comes from its emphasis on mechanical aspects of reactivity to the neglect of man's wider experiences, his aspirations, and his incessant endeavor to master and to mould his environment. Of course not all psychologists have this blind spot. Carl Rogers, Abraham Maslow, Gardner Murphy, Harry Murray, and many others have clearer vision.

What then is my personal idea? I suppose it has to do with the search for a theoretical system—for one that will allow for truth wherever found, one that will encompass the totality of human experience and do full justice to the nature of man. I myself have never had a strictly defined program of research, nor have I tried to establish a "school" of psychological thought. Students who have worked with me have been encouraged to tackle any significant problem, so long as it dealt with persons, with parts of persons, or with groups of persons.

Dedicated as I am to a program so broad and loose, I find it surprising that many specific honors have come my way. I shall report only one—the one that has pleased me most deeply, for it succeeds in summing up my personal idea better than I can do. In connection with the XVII International Congress of Psychology, which met in Washington in 1963, fifty-five of my former Ph.D. students presented me with two handsomely bound volumes of their own writings with the following dedicatory inscription: "From his students—in appreciation of his respect for their individuality." This is an intimate honor, and one I prize above all others.

## REFERENCES

*Selected Publications by Gordon W. Allport*

(with F. H. Allport) Personality traits: their classification and measurement. *J. abnorm. soc. Psychol.*, 1921, *16*, 6–40.
An experimental study of the traits of personality: with special reference to the problem of social diagnosis. Unpublished doctoral dissertation, Harvard College Library, 1922.
The Leipzig congress of psychology. *Amer. J. Psychol.*, 1923, *34*, 612–615.
The standpoint of Gestalt psychology. *Psyche*, 1924, *4*, 354–361.
Eidetic imagery. *Brit. J. Psychol.*, 1924, *15*, 99–120.
The eidetic image and the after-image. *Amer. J. Psychol.*, 1928, *40*, 418–425.
(with F. H. Allport) A test for ascendance-submission. *J. abnorm. soc. Psychol.*, 1928, *23*, 118–136.
Change and decay in the visual memory image. *Brit. J. Psychol.*, 1930, *21*, 133–148.
What is a trait of personality? *J. abnorm. soc. Psychol.*, 1931, *25*, 368–372.
(with P. E. Vernon) *A study of values.* Boston: Houghton Mifflin, 1931; revised eds. (and G. Lindzey) 1951, 1960.
(with P. E. Vernon) *Studies in expressive movement.* New York: Macmillan, 1933.
(with H. Cantril) *The psychology of radio.* New York: Harper & Row, 1935.
Attitudes. In C. Murchison (Ed.), *A handbook of social psychology.* Worcester, Mass.: Clark Univer. Press, 1935, ch. 17.
*Personality: a psychological interpretation.* New York: Holt, Rinehart and Winston, 1937.
(with J. S. Bruner & E. M. Jandorf) Personality under social catastrophe: ninety life-histories of the Nazi revolution. *Charact. & Pers.*, 1941, *10*, 1–22.
*The use of personal documents in psychological science.* New York: Social Science Research Council, 1942, Bull. 49.
The ego in contemporary psychology. *Psychol. Rev.*, 1943, *50*, 451–478.

Human nature and the peace. *Psychol. Bull.* 1945, 42, 376–378.

(with L. Postman) *The psychology of rumor.* New York: Holt, Rinehart and Winston, 1947.

*The individual and his religion.* New York: Macmillan, 1950.

The trend in motivational theory. *Amer. J. Orthopsychiat.*, 1953, 25, 107–119.

The historical background of modern social psychology. In G. Lindzey (Ed.), *Handbook of social psychology*, Vol. 1. Reading, Mass.: Addison-Wesley, 1954, ch. 1.

*The nature of prejudice.* Reading, Mass.: Addison-Wesley, 1954; abridged ed. Garden City, N.Y.: Doubleday Anchor, 1958.

*Becoming: basic considerations for a psychology of personality.* New Haven, Conn.: Yale, 1955.

(with T. F. Pettigrew) Cultural influences on the perception of movement: the trapezoidal illusion among Zulus. *J. abnorm. soc. Psychol.*, 1957, 55, 104–113.

The open system in personality theory. *J. abnorm. soc. Psychol.*, 1960, 61, 301–310.

*Personality and social encounter: selected essays.* Boston: Beacon Press, 1960; revised ed., 1964.

*Pattern and growth in personality.* New York: Holt, Rinehart and Winston, 1961.

Das Allgemeine und das Eigenartige in der psychologischen Praxis. *Psychol. Beiträge*, 1962, 6, 630–650.

The fruits of eclecticism: bitter or sweet? Proceedings of the XVII International Congress of Psychology, Amsterdam, 1964; also published in *Psychologia*, 1964, 7, 1–14; and in *Acta Psychol.*, 1964, 23, 27–44.

Mental health: a generic attitude. *J. Relig. Hlth*, 1964, 4, 7–21.

*Letters from Jenny.* New York: Harcourt, Brace & World, 1965.

## Other Publications Cited

Allport, F. H. *Social psychology.* Boston: Houghton Mifflin, 1924.

Cantril, H. (Ed.) *Tensions that cause wars.* Urbana: Univer. of Illinois Press, 1950.

Münsterberg, H. *Psychology: general and applied.* New York: Appleton-Century-Crofts, 1914.

Murray, H. A. What should psychologists do about psychoanalysis? *J. abnorm. soc. Psychol.*, 1940, 35, 150–175.

Powers, E. & Witmer, Helen. *An experiment in the prevention of delinquency.* New York: Columbia, 1951.

Sorokin, P. A. *A long journey.* New Haven: College & University Press, 1964.

Leonard Carmichael

The Smithsonian Institution

# Leonard Carmichael

I was born on November 9, 1898, in the Germantown section of Philadelphia, Pennsylvania. I am an only child. I come from a predominantly
professional family. My father was a successful physician with a special interest in neuroanatomy and neurology. If his IQ had been measured, it would
have been very high. He was a traveled and broadly informed man. My
mother, Emily Henrietta Leonard, did her major work in logic and psychology
at Wellesley College where she established lifelong friendships with M. W.
Calkins, the "self-psychologist," and E. A. McC. Gamble, an authority on the
psychology of taste and smell. Before her marriage my mother taught at Miss
Porter's School (Farmington) and went on to be vice president, to use the
present title, of the State Teachers College at Fitchburg, Massachusetts. As
a young matron in Philadelphia she early became active in the work of volunteer charitable boards. Her interests, I now see, were centered in agencies
concerned with helping children and the indigent ill. She also organized a
successful movement to save a fine eighteenth-century house in Germantown.
At the time of her death she had been for eight years chief of the Bureau
of Recreation of the City of Philadelphia. This appointive post was, I believe, the highest position held up to that time by any woman in the city
government of Philadelphia.

My father's family on the Carmichael side came from the North of Ireland (county, Londonderry). Some of them had been clergymen in the
Anglican Church of Ireland. My maternal grandmother came to Philadelphia
from the British West Indies. Her family were plantation owners and clergymen.

My mother's father, Charles Hall Leonard, D.D., LL.D., was professor
of homiletics and for many years dean of the Crane Theological School of
Tufts University. I suspect he was a master of his subject because the famous
Phillips Brooks journeyed out from Boston for a full term to take his lectures.
He lived to be ninety-six years old and even published a book after he was
ninety. His father had been a small manufacturer and represented Haverhill
in the General Court (the state legislature of Massachusetts). My maternal
grandmother, Phebe Bassett, was a teacher of mathematics before her marriage. She had studied Greek and Latin at Brook Farm, the famous New Eng-

land transcendentalist utopian community. Her lifelong interest was in the branch of mathematics called celestial mechanics. She found her recreation in astronomical computations such as those required in establishing the orbits of comets. Through this grandmother's line I am descended from a colonial American of some distinction, Wyseman Clagett. *The Dictionary of American Biography* says of this ancestor that he was the last chief legal officer of the Crown in the colony of New Hampshire and the first such officer in the new state of New Hampshire. He largely wrote its constitution. A fine portrait of his wife, now in the Brooklyn Museum, was painted by Blackburn, who had as sitters many of the notable families of the 1750's in New England. I own a good oil copy of this portrait.

It was my good fortune to attend what was at the time, and probably still is, one of the best and largest private secondary day schools in America, the Germantown Friends School, though my parents were not Quakers but Episcopalians. In school I was, I think, only a high average student and occasionally on the honor roll. Each year the faculty of the school devised a printed examination, an "Information Test," that was given to the entire upper school without previous warning. Its detailed questions ranged over science, history, biography, and current events. Perhaps in this respect I achieved distinction outside of regular courses by scoring highest in the whole school several times.

Several of my teachers have had a profound influence on me throughout my entire life. Among them was H. A. Domincovich, a teacher of Latin and English and an outstandingly brilliant man. Another was an excellent art teacher, who was herself an artist of real ability. She taught me the pleasure of going to art galleries and to periodic gallery shows and introduced me to a number of well known artists. From this teacher, Miss E. H. Schick, I learned the elements of drawing, a skill that later helped me very distinctly in my college study of zoology. A few of my anatomical drawings are still included in various textbooks of zoology and psychology. This early and continuing interest in art proved to be a very real help to me when later in life I found myself, as secretary of the Smithsonian, concerned with the management of four great galleries of art that are bureaus of the Smithsonian Institution.

I certainly was not an outstanding athlete, but participating in sports meant much to me. I won school letters for playing on the first team in basketball, football, and soccer. I was also editor of the school paper and president of my class. I was given a cane, an old tradition, by my class, as its most popular member. Many of my lifelong friendships were formed in this school.

Germantown, for more than a century technically a part of Philadelphia, retained in my boyhood its independent character as an old community. Certainly it seemed to me then and now to be an ideal place in which to grow up. Germantown had all the advantages of being part of what some have called America's most historic and also most artistic and culturally sophisticated city, but the Germantown part of Philadelphia also provided many of the advantages of country living. The house I was born in was large and distinctive enough to be included in a definitive book on historical houses of Philadelephia. Part of it dated back to a time before the hard-fought Revolutionary Battle of Germantown in which General Washington was defeated. The history of Germantown, its old Georgian mansions, its beautiful old mahogany furniture, and the hand tools of its artisans had an abiding fascination for me. My senior essay at school was written on the pietistic German university men who established in the seventeenth century an astronomical observatory in Germantown.

My friends and I early gained an interest in natural history from our teachers and from our books. I made a fair collection of the butterflies and moths of this region and mounted them with care.

The house in which I was born had its own stables, outbuildings, and large flower and vegetable gardens. From our gardener I learned something of the old-world nurture of plants. Gardening has been one of my continuing interests. A chauffeur of my father's taught me the proper use and care of basic woodworking and metalworking hand tools, and even the elements of blacksmithing. Later, in laboratory shops and at home, the use of tools has been a pleasant part of my life.

As a child I read constantly, going through the plays of Shakespeare, many of the works of Thackeray, and my favorite, Anthony Trollope, whom I now consider the greatest psychologist among novelists.

History has always interested me. College courses in history made this subject a minor interest of mine through life. Before going to college I had read such books as Bergson's *Creative Evolution,* Royce's *The Spirit of Modern Philosophy,* and the two volumes of my mother's first edition of James' *Principles of Psychology* with her good notes in the margin. She had studied this book under the direction of Yale's distinguished psychologist George Trumbull Ladd. It is indeed fortunate for one to have parents with scientific interests and a well-stocked library! Our conversation at home was about books, letters, and science. Sermons were employed to teach me the principles of formal logic. It was a rare dinner when someone did not rush for the encyclopedia to prove a point.

As I have noted, my grandfather was a dean at Tufts, and my uncles had gone to this college. I entered Tufts in 1917 and was graduated four years later with the B.S. degree, *summa cum laude,* and academically second in my class. I was elected to Phi Beta Kappa as a junior. After America entered the war, I volunteered; but as soon as I put on my uniform as a private, I was assigned to help in a course in military sanitation and hygiene.

As an undergraduate I was an active member of the Theta Delta Chi Fraternity of which my uncles had also been members. Fraternity life, often criticized today, was for me both pleasant and worthwhile. I was almost too involved in extracurricular affairs. I was editor-in-chief of the undergraduate college paper, president of the college dramatic society, and had other duties and offices. Each day I wrote news about the academic, social, and athletic events at Tufts for the then famous *Boston Transcript*.

After receiving my freshman marks I applied for a scholarship and found that since my father's income was at a satisfactory level I was not eligible. This so-called "financial means test" for the award of scholarships and academic honors, commonly practiced by colleges, annoyed me then and has continued to annoy me. I at once applied for an assistantship in biology, which I received, for which there was no "means test." This meant that besides my own studies and extracurricular activities, afternoons during my college years were spent as a laboratory assistant in zoology. This science became my major interest. I believe that I have worked hard all my life, but never harder than when I was a college undergraduate. Morning after morning I set my alarm for 4 A.M. or even earlier in order to get essential studying done.

Laboratory teaching was interesting and I profited by it. In a limited way this teaching made me something of a comparative anatomist and histologist. In my senior year H. V. Neal, my major professor of zoology, allowed me to do a small research problem on the embryology of the eye muscles in one of the sharks. This started my great interest in the significance and the evolutionary history of sense organs as directors of animal behavior. It also showed me how basic is the science of descriptive and experimental embryology. As a college senior I thus decided that I wanted to spend the rest of my life learning all I could about the sense organs and especially about the role of the receptors in determining the discriminations that organisms make in their adaptive responses to varied environmental energies. At this time I was almost equally attracted to the study of anatomy, physiology, embryology, and especially the study of animal behavior as seen in the quantifiable tropistic reactions that were then being most actively investigated.

The two men whose books influenced me most as an undergraduate were the biological ultramechanist Jacques Loeb and the proponent of emergent evolution C. Lloyd Morgan. I finally decided, especially after reading Howard C. Warren's *Human Psychology*, that psychology rather than anatomy or physiology was the best place for me to anchor a study of the sense organs when considered in a general functional and biological setting.

The question then arose as to the place for graduate work. My father had generously agreed to support me as long as I wished to study. E. B. Twitmyer, the able and objectively-minded psychologist at the University of Pennsylvania, offered me a very generous Harrison Fellowship, but I decided to go to Harvard for my graduate work.

A teacher at Tufts, Edwin A. Shaw had taken his Ph.D. at Harvard in educational psychology under Walter F. Dearborn. He suggested that I go to Cambridge and talk to Dearborn about studying psychology at Harvard.

Dearborn offered me a much smaller fellowship than the one at Pennsylvania. I accepted, although I told him I was not primarily interested in education with a capital "E." Dearborn told me that in his opinion all psychology and especially educational psychology was most likely to be advanced by people who understood and maintained a basic biological approach to the science. He therefore most cordially urged me to accept the fellowship on my terms, and he assured me that I could take any pattern of graduate courses at Harvard that I wished in preparation for the Ph.D. degree. During my three years at Harvard as a graduate student I therefore took a number of courses in zoology as well as psychology. Indeed, the first piece of graduate laboratory research I undertook was a quantitative study of the light reactions of the meal worm (*Tenebrio molitor*). It will never be possible for me to overemphasize the importance of the privilege of studying so closely during these years with the man who directed this research, G. H. Parker, then a professor of zoology at Harvard. His graduate lectures on the nervous system and the sense organs were models of clarity and scholarship. I tried to emulate his lectures in all my later teaching.

Among the experiences at Harvard for which I am most grateful was the opportunity to take the courses or to audit the lectures of such distinguished teachers as the great E. G. Boring, L. T. Troland, and William McDougall.

Throughout my graduate years, my association with Dearborn was especially close and satisfactory. He assigned me, for my own exclusive use, a fine large office and an adjoining research room on the third floor of Emerson Hall. These were rooms once used by Hugo Münsterberg. Dearborn gave me the privilege of rebuilding in the Harvard shop an improved model of the famous Dodge-Dearborn eye movement recording camera. In the laboratory shop I worked at a bench with Troland and thus came to know him quite well. Troland introduced me to a quantitative and truly functional or operational point of view in psychology.

At Harvard I did experimental work in the zoological laboratory and in Emerson Hall. Much of my time was spent in apparatus construction and in learning new biological techniques basic to later behavior study. Dearborn introduced me to W. R. Miles, then at the Carnegie Institution of Washington's Nutrition Laboratory adjacent to the Harvard Medical School. In Miles' laboratory I had the privilege of watching the use of string galvanometers and other advanced pieces of physiological and psychological apparatus. This laboratory allowed me to formulate an idea of what a really well-equipped psychological laboratory could be. It also started me on a lifetime of admiration of this really distinguished man.

When it came time for me to select a topic for my Ph.D. thesis I talked at length with Dearborn about my basic interest in the sensory control or release of inborn patterns of behavior. This led both student and teacher to much discussion of the psychology and biology of so-called "human and animal instincts." Finally Dearborn convinced me that it would be most advantageous for me at this time in my career to do my dissertation on a theoretical and historical subject. The result of this decision was that I prepared a 445-page analysis of the history of technical thought about human and animal instincts as my Ph.D. thesis. A summary of some of the conclusions of this paper was later published under the title "Heredity and Environment: Are They Antithetical?" (1925). This title was not mine but was selected in an oral conference with Morton Prince, then the editor of the *Journal of Abnormal and Social Psychology*. He had talked to me about my thesis and asked me to write the paper for him. In his charming manner he pounded his desk and said, "Give it a title people will sit up and notice!" Prince is another psychologist whom I consider myself fortunate to have known well. He was an original thinker in addition to being a wealthy, dashing, sport-loving gentleman.

In reviewing the literature for my thesis I became especially interested in the German publications of William Preyer. Later this scientist's book, *Specielle Physiologie des Embryo, Untersuchungen über die Lebenserscheinungen vor der Geburt,* opened my eyes to the specific area of research in my chosen field of the sensory and neural control of behavior on which I was to spend many years. The accidental finding of this book, which I had never heard of before, in the Harvard library was a turning point in my life. Here at last I saw a way to investigate the topic of major interest to me—the morphological growth of the receptors and nervous system in relation to changes in behavior as responses are released at various stages during the early ontogenetic development in each mammal before learning begins or at least before it becomes important.

During my Harvard student years I also did the research that was basic to my part of a monograph, *Special Disabilities in Learning to Read and Write,* which was published with Dearborn and E. E. Lord (1925). My portion of this monograph dealt with data that I collected on spontaneous mirror-writing. Then and now this topic seems to me to be an interesting example of the complexities of the development of perception, cognition, and human receptor-directed motor skills in relation to probably inborn human lateral dominance.

One of the influences of my graduate years was the opportunity to learn about the new Gestalt psychology from Dearborn's able friend, R. M. Ogden of Cornell. One day Dearborn handed me K. Koffka's *The Growth of the Mind* (1924) in its first German edition, saying, "Read this and tell me what it is about." Contrary to Dearborn's expressed doubts this book seemed to me to be interesting and significant. Later it was my privilege to know Koffka quite well and to enjoy at first hand his truly original mind.

The year before my Ph.D. was conferred I was offered an assistant professorship of educational psychology at Cornell at, as I remember it, for the time a very fine salary. I refused as I wanted to get my Ph.D. degree before accepting a university appointment.

Two other graduate students and I took a seminar on animal behavior given by a visiting lecturer at Harvard, Wallace Craig. His ethological point of view ever since has been important in my thinking. He antedated in many ways the present-day systematic position of men such as N. Tinbergen and K. Lorenz, as they now fully acknowledge. The lack of recognition that Harvard gave to Craig astonished me at that time and does so even more now. He was far ahead of his time.

I think I received A grades, except for one A-minus, in all my graduate courses at Harvard. As a result Dearborn proposed me for the coveted prize of a Sheldon Fellowship. Sheldon Fellowships provide a stipend large enough to allow each recipient to travel and study in a very free way for a year after receiving the doctorate.

My father was pleased to learn that I had been awarded this fellowship allowing me to travel and study for a year in Germany, and he again reminded me that he would be delighted to underwrite any additional needed years in Germany to get an M.D.

All these plans were suddenly changed! H. S. Langfeld called me to his office in Emerson Hall one day in the spring of 1924 and told me that he was planning to accept an appointment at Princeton to be director of its psychological laboratory. I can still remember Langfeld's charming, smiling face as he asked me to come to Princeton with him. He told me that each undergraduate senior psychology major at Princeton had to dissect a human brain, that he had found it a little hard to think of a graduate student in psychology who was qualified to undertake the task of teaching physiological psychology in this way, and he knew from his friends Dearborn and E. B. Holt that I could do it. After a difficult debate with myself I relinquished the idea of long study in Germany and instead accepted the Princeton offer.

Slowly I walked to the office of Dean Briggs who was in charge of Sheldons to tell him my decision. He kindly suggested that I keep the fellowship, go off to Germany at once, come back at the latest possible time, and then, but not before, resign my fellowship. This generous administrative action by one of America's greatest educators won my lifelong gratitude.

During my graduate student years a fellow student J. G. Beebe-Center came to be one of my good friends, and in later years he was, I think, my closest academic acquaintance. He was that *rara avis* in professional psychology, a truly literate man. We not only studied neurology and optics together, but we also read and talked about the writings of such men as Descartes, Hobbes, and Pascal.

During this period the psychological system of William McDougall interested me as did his deep knowledge (which today is too often forgotten) of the facts of behavior. His vitalism or near vitalism was always most unattractive to me. At my oral doctoral examination were both G. H. Parker, a most clear-minded and radical biological mechanist, and McDougall. I can still remember Dearborn's helpful words to me as he led me into the examination room: "Say exactly what seems correct to you. We will agree with you and not with McDougall."

My "The Report of a Sheldon Fellow" was published in the *Harvard Alumni Bulletin* in 1925. I had elected first to go to the University of Berlin where academic doors were pleasantly opened for me as a recent Harvard Ph.D. by the head of the American Institute of the University of Berlin. This Institute had been founded largely through the efforts of Harvard's great Münsterberg. Through the courtesy of Professor Wolfgang Köhler I was privileged to attend lectures in psychology and also to observe research in progress. I heard some of Köhler's lectures to his large and enthusiastic classes. These lectures were models of organization and interest. Ever since that time I have been a deep admirer of the greatness of Köhler's mind.

At Berlin I saw the elaborate apparatus developed by C. Stumpf for his famous auditory studies. I was especially interested in the views of German psychologists about the then novel Gestalt psychology. I went to meetings of a small, admiring group who sat almost worshipfully around Max Wertheimer, a man who then and now seemed to me to have great originality and insight.

Among the other psychologists that I met and talked to during this time in Germany were H. Rupp, O. Bobertag, O. Klemm, F. Krueger, A. Kirschman, T. Ziehen, G. E. Müller, N. Ach, and E. R. Jaensch. In England I met Karl Pearson's associate, Miss Elderton, and had the pleasure of meeting for the first time F. C. Bartlett of Cambridge, certainly one of the most gifted trailblazers among the scientific psychologists of this generation.

On my return from my Sheldon Fellowship period I went at once to Princeton where I began my life as a teacher and investigator. Princeton was academically satisfying and delightful. My courses were physiological psychology (including the dissection by each student of a real human brain) and the history and systems of psychology. I assisted in graduate instruction and in the supervision of some of the required senior theses of undergraduate major students. Some of these experimental studies were later published. Probably the most interesting part of my teaching was the conduct of small preceptorial conferences. I had preceptorial sections of students from Langfeld's courses and from the course in social psychology given by H. C. McComas. It should be noted that Langfeld in turn had preceptorial conferences of students from my lecture courses. The exchange of ideas thus engendered made this plan, fostered at Princeton by Woodrow Wilson, outstanding as a method of instruction in higher education. I was honored while at Princeton to receive mention in the annual student poll as one of the university's best preceptors.

In 1924 the Princeton Department of Psychology occupied the entire upper floor of historic Nassau Hall. But when I arrived Eno Hall, the fine new laboratory of psychology, was nearly complete. As the youngest member of the staff it was my obligation to supervise the movement of equipment and apparatus from Nassau Hall to the new building. H. C. Warren had generously contributed to the funds that made this building possible. Warren was a rare man. He was an original, distinguished, and scholarly psychologist and also the possessor of an inherited fortune that made it possible for him to help psychology at Princeton in many ways. The word "gentleman" and the word "Warren" are synonymous for me. Eno Hall was dedicated with a fine address by E. B. Titchener, resplendent in his customary academic gown.

I came to Princeton with a planned research program. I intended to do experimental work on the development and especially the embryology of animal behavior in general and the growth of receptor-controlled behavior in particular. I also planned to keep myself busy writing papers based on library research on the history of physiological psychology and on topics related to the theory of receptor action and the role of primary sensory experience in mental life. Somewhere the great art critic Bernard Berenson says that he counted each day lost in which he did not write something for publication. I must admit that from my Princeton days on, I have had this feeling, but I must quickly add there have been many lost days.

I postponed the use of fetal mammals in experimentation and began work on the behavior of larval amblystoma and frog tadpoles. Several papers on the results secured by raising experimental groups of these animals under an anesthetic were published. The anesthetic used allowed structural growth but no movement. The drugged group was then compared with other groups of similar organisms that had been allowed to move normally as they grew. These studies supported a hereditary rather than an environmentalistic theory of the determination of the growth of organized behavior. At the time, the results of these experiments surprised and almost shocked me. They did not support my then strongly held belief in the determining influence of the environment at every stage in the growth of behavior.

On the theoretical side my first paper was a long study of current attitudes toward the definition and psychological meaning of the word "sensation." The problem analyzed in this paper grew out of thoughts started by the treatment of this topic by Boring in his truly great two-year course at Harvard dealing with sensation, feeling, imagery, thought, and related topics. A few days after this paper appeared I was amazed and delighted to receive a long letter from Titchener about it. He complimented me on the paper. He commended me for having read everything that he (Titchener) had written. He stated that it was a good thing for a young psychologist to become completely familiar with the works of one older psychologist. As he had chosen Wundt, he said he was glad that I had chosen him.

At that time studies for a projected book on the history of research on reflex action were begun. Two papers preliminary to the proposed volume were published, one on Sir Charles Bell and one on Robert Whytt. The book was never written. F. S. Fearing's volume, *Reflex Action*, appeared in 1930, and I did not feel that two books on the subject were needed. However, some interesting, close, and continuing academic friendships, such as those with the neurologists C. J. Herrick and J. F. Fulton, developed from these papers.

My frequent reference to the many contributions to psychology of Sir Charles Bell amused my graduate students. Even now at the annual meeting of the American Psychological Association, my former graduate students and colleagues dine together calling themselves, much to the confusion of the uninitiated, "The Sir Charles Bell Society."

An important event of my Princeton years was the invitation of Warren to collaborate with him on a complete rewriting of his textbook on psychology. Some of this work was done at Woods Hole, the great summer center of American biology. Here I met and came to know many of the leaders of the time in physiology, experimental embryology, and genetics.

Our book, *Elements of Human Psychology* (1930), when published by Houghton Mifflin Company, proved to be an immediate success. It was used as an introductory book for years in many major universities and smaller colleges.

Warren and I both enjoyed the formulation of crisp definitions for the glossary of our textbook. This interest led me to help Warren with work on his important *Dictionary of Psychology* (1934). After Warren's sudden death I was able to assist in the preparation of the book for its publishers, also Houghton Mifflin Company. I was by that time editorial advisor in psychology for this firm. This publishing connection has continued throughout my whole academic life and has given me great satisfaction. More than forty books published by this distinguished company have been under my editorship. Most have had interpretative introductions by me.

My associations have been most rewarding with the following authors and indeed with many others: L. F. Shaffer, F. D. Brooks, N. L. Munn, C. R. Rogers, N. R. F. Maier, M. A. Merrill, V. M. Axline, N. Cameron, J. J. Gibson, W. C. Trow, Sir G. H. Thompson, A. Magaret, J. E. Horrocks, G. G. Thompson, M. D. Glock, T. Gordon, J. M. Seidman, E. H. Porter, D. Rogers, F. McKinney, R. S. Daniel, T. A. Ringness, H. J. Klausmeier, A. J. Singer, Jr., E. J. Shoben, Jr., D. J. Levenson, E. B. Gallagher. I should like especially to speak of my very close and friendly association through the years with one of the authors listed above, Norman Munn. His great textbooks, the outstanding *Handbook of Psychological Research on the Rat,* the various editions of *The Evolution and Growth of Human Behavior,* and his other books have in my view been real contributions to scientific psychology and far more than what one sometimes hears called mere textbooks.

Association with my academic colleagues at Princeton was delightful. I learned about psychological aesthetics from Langfeld. This subject has continued to interest me. I have been chairman of the Division on Aesthetics of the American Psychological Association. I am also a member of the American Society for Aesthetics. In art I like inventiveness and ingenuity in an aesthetic world of strict rules. Pope is my favorite poet because of his psychological insight and his cleverness with words. J. S. Bach, his contemporary, is my favorite composer. The baroque not only pleases my ears but my eyes, and I especially like this style in painting, sculpture, architecture, and in the work of ceramists and silversmiths. Lawlessness and romantic anarchy in the arts leaves me cold. Most tested aesthetic rules are in a way absolutes and have, it seems to me, a psychological and even a physiological base, as the wise Bernard Berenson well observed.

In this connection I should perhaps note that I have always had a deep bystander's interest in academic philosophy. Santayana has been a guiding star in the establishment of my *Weltanschauung*. I also learned much at Princeton by observing the truly urbane Langfeld as to how to live a wise, reasonable, hardworking, intellectually rewarding, and at the same time pleasant academic life.

My knowledge of intelligence testing and other forms of objective examining was increased by my associations with C. C. Brigham who was then a Princeton professor but devoting much of his time to the development of the Scholastic Aptitude Tests for the College Entrance Examination Board. Later, as a result of my work in this area I was asked to take over the general direction of this work for the College Entrance Examination Board on a full-time basis, but this interesting offer was refused.

Undergraduate and graduate students at Princeton were then, as now, highly selected and able. In my first year as a teacher I had a small senior class of some five students. In this class were a number of men who later became well known psychologists. These men who had notable later careers included C. W. Bray, J. J. Gibson, the late Harold Schlosberg, and G. S. Horton. It was later my privilege to assist each of them except Horton with Ph.D. work.

For a number of years I taught educational psychology with great pleasure at the Harvard summer school. These large classes were a delight. They contained many visiting students from abroad. During one summer at Harvard I also worked in physiology (with an emphasis on the techniques of neurophysiology) at the Harvard Medical School.

During the summers that I taught at Harvard, I learned to row a single scull on the Charles River. All-in-all, these summers were most satisfactory. I enjoyed my teaching, and yet there was time to get into shape for publication the research of the previous winter. Incidentally, before this time for seven summers I served as the chief counsellor at a summer camp for boys. I came to know the state of Maine and especially its wilderness rivers very well during this time. Here I acquired my continuing love of sport fishing.

At Princeton it was my privilege to live in the superb gothic Graduate

College. I learned there to know well the patrician Andrew Fleming West, dean of the graduate school. West's philosophy of graduate education was sound. He emphasized limiting such training to highly selected full-time students with high marks in a broadly chosen basic undergraduate program. During term time a few young faculty members and almost all the full-time graduate students in all academic fields dined together in academic gowns in the Great Hall of the Graduate College. Conversation here was good and always stimulating.

While still an instructor at Princeton I was offered and I refused a full professorship at Smith College by its famous president, William Allen Neilson. Possibly as a result of this offer I was made an assistant professor at Princeton. Other institutions, including the Graduate School of Education at Harvard, asked about my interest in moving from Princeton, but I always replied in the negative.

In 1927 came an offer that I did accept from the able biologist A. D. Mead, who was the vice president and active administrative head of Brown University. He offered me a full professorship and the directorship of the laboratory at Brown. He promised me a satisfactory laboratory budget and large funds for fellowships for my graduate students. When I was trying to make up my mind, President Hibben of Princeton offered me "permanent tenure" if I would stay. When the decision to go was reached, I asked Mead not to announce that I was a full professor in my first year. This was done because of my age and possible faculty feeling at Brown. It was agreed that the full professorial title should come to me in my second year. Even with this delay I was a full professor in one of the old "Ivy League" universities while I was still in my twenties. It has been said that I was the youngest or one of the youngest full professors in the long history of Brown.

Brown was my academic home for nine of the most pleasant and productive years of my life. Providence is a city of historic charm, with a happy mingling of "town and gown." At Brown I at once plunged into the organization of a modern laboratory and the equipping of it for research and training in experimental and animal psychology. I have always had a real interest in apparatus and have published a number of papers in this field. From the first, E. B. Delabarre, who had been at Brown since 1891, gave me full cooperation in all aspects of my work. Delabarre's original scientific work should give him an important place in the history of American psychology.

Soon after I came to Brown, the great depression overwhelmed America and the world. The University budget and all faculty salaries were necessarily cut, but Brown never reduced the stipends or the number of graduate fellowships promised me when I came to the University. These fellowships became widely known. Many very able university graduates all over the country applied for them. Thus, Brown's small group of graduate students in psychology soon became quite outstanding. The department took virtually no part-time graduate students.

During my entire time at Brown I personally gave all the lectures in the undergraduate elementary course. Soon those electing this course filled the largest teaching auditorium, and in a few years it was necessary for me to repeat the same lecture three times. The auditorium was filled from 9:00–10:00, 10:00–11:00, and 11:00–12:00. I also taught a number of advanced undergraduate courses, conducted graduate seminars, and directed undergraduate and graduate research. In spite of this heavy load of interesting teaching (at one time twenty-one hours a week) I found enough time for my own research. I cannot resist noting that in my days at Princeton, Brown, and Rochester, I alone or my wife and I together, and most of the teaching staff went to the laboratories morning, afternoon, and evening, including weekends except an occasional Saturday evening. In this way the graduate students and staff became a hardworking family. The research of each member was of interest to all.

At Brown for the first time I was able to begin in a serious way the program of study of the prenatal development of behavior in mammals that I had so long planned. The first research of this sort was a study of the fetal cat. J. D. Coronios wrote his dissertation on this work. Following this investigation, other fetal mammals were studied. Some of these were done by me alone, others in cooperation with colleagues and graduate students. For more than two years I worked on the experiments basic to my long monograph on stimulus-released behavior of the fetal guinea pig. In this study, 87 fetal litters of known insemination age were prepared for study. Sixty of these litters were in all respects adequate for research reports, and thus, the stimulus-released behavior of a total of 178 fetuses was investigated in detail. Records of the responses given by the organisms were made by a specially constructed and electrically activated motion picture camera. As the organisms were stimulated, I often wore a head-supported dissecting microscope. One hundred and four points were established as important stimulus zones and all of these points were stimulated in each organism and used at each fetal stage studied. The stimuli were calibrated hair esthesiometers, needles, single break electric shocks, and warm and cool drops of liquid. In relatively mature fetuses, rotation and righting reactions were elicited by moving the total organism in various planes. Protocols were dictated recording the responses of each fetus to each stimulus. The novel results of this study appeared when these protocols were later assembled in connection not with each fetus but with each stimulus zone. Thus previously unrecognized and amazingly uniform behavioral sequences came to light. Specific patterns of behavior were typical of each zone stimulated. This behavior was remarkably constant from fetal stage to fetal stage. To use a modern term, here was displayed for the first time a whole repertory of "species-specific responses" of a fetal mammal. These and related studies led me to formulate what I have sometimes recently heard called "Carmichael's Law." This is the generalization that most specific receptor neuromuscular response mechanisms may be activated by experimental means *before* the time in the normal development of the organism at which the response in question must play its biologically essential role in the adaptive behavior of the organism. Examples of such responses are rhythmic fetal locomotor movements elicited by paw stimulation while the organism is still in the amniotic fluid and chest movements basic to later air breathing that can be called out by stimulation while the fetus is also still immersed in liquid.

These experiments did demonstrate that speed of reaction increases and what may be called "precision of behavior" became greater as fetal age increased. But in general, in an analogy, one may say that the same pushbutton elicits the same response to an amazing degree throughout much of active fetal and early neonatal life.

I have discussed in several places the significance of these studies of the fetal growth of mammalian responses for a general understanding of behavior. Here my old interest, which began as an undergraduate, in the receptor control of behavior of a forced or tropistic sort took on a new dimension. In later fetuses, specific behavior acts were also seen in so-called spontaneous reactions that resulted from changes in the very important internal environment of the organism or from metabolic or other activities of the central nervous system itself.

While these experiments were in progress I wrote a chapter for the 1933 edition of C. Murchison's *A Handbook of Child Psychology* entitled "Origin and Prenatal Growth of Behavior." This chapter, which has since been twice revised, is longer than many separate books. It puts in historic and scientific focus known facts about the growth of response before birth in all organisms of which I could find satisfactory published reports. Only a relatively small number of copies of this so-called "Murchison Handbook" were printed. This led me to undertake the editing of my own *Manual of Child Psychology*. The first edition of this new large volume appeared in 1946 and a second appeared in 1954. This manual contained contributions by many distinguished psychologists who have ever since been my friends and also contained revisions of my own long article on the early development of behavior. The preparation of my two editions of this manual required thousands of hours of work, but I believe that the labor was justified. My good and generous friend, the late Professor Henri Piéron of the Sorbonne, saw fit to arrange to have the book translated into French and published in 1952 in three volumes by the Presses Universitaires de France. Piéron also made me an honorary member of the French Psychological Society, and I think I can only say "had me elected" as his successor as president of the Section of Experimental Psychology and Animal Behavior of the International Union of Biological Sciences. As this autobiography is written I still hold this office. The manual has also been translated and published in full in Spanish.

At the invitation of E. G. Boring, H. S. Langfeld, and H. P. Weld, I also wrote at this time "The Response Mechanism," which appears as chapter two in their *Psychology, A Factual Textbook* published in 1935. I rewrote this chapter for subsequent editions of this book. Later I wrote a chapter, "Ontogenetic Development," in S. S. Stevens' *Handbook of Experimental Psychology*.

During my Brown and Rochester years I had other research interests, such as the postnatal growth of reflex capacity of kittens to right themselves in the air when falling. Newborn kittens fall without giving any indication of turning. By six weeks the well known air-righting reflex of the adult cat (*i.e.* the falling cat always lands on all four legs) has practically come to a mature state. The development of this capacity has, in my opinion, many general implications for understanding the growth without learning of many other adaptive responses in the ontogeny of mammals including man.

At my invitation H. H. Jasper was called to the Brown faculty. He had taken his Ph.D. degree in psychology at Iowa and just before coming to Brown had received the Sc.D. degree in physiology in Paris. In a conversation one day he remarked that a German scientist, Hans Berger of Jena, had discovered that electrical potentials correlated with human brain activity could be recorded by placing electrodes on the scalp and amplifying and recording them. Some anatomical and physiological doubts occurred to me, but I did borrow the German journals in which Berger had published his findings. The results reported in these papers surprised me. Soon Jasper and I, working at Brown University's affiliated Bradley Hospital, assembled a new type of high-gain amplifier and a Westinghouse mirror oscillograph system. I can still remember our delight and amazement when, after appropriately applying electrodes to the scalp (the subject was Carl Pfaffmann, now a distinguished physiological psychologist), we secured an excellent and most typical record of alpha waves. The results of this study were published in *Science* on January 11, 1935. This joint article with Jasper is, I believe, the first report of human electroencephalographic work on this continent. Following this initial study Jasper and I and a number of other associates carried on a wide range of psychological experiments in which electroencephalographic recording was used. These included studies of the senses and of learning or conditioning.

Neuroembryology, neuroanatomy, and neurophysiology have been central in my scientific interest from my student days to the present. Many of my closest research friendships have been with workers in these fields, such as G. E. Coghill, A. Forbes, H. Klüver, H. S. Gasser, and above all that amazingly original thinker and experimentalist, K. S. Lashley. It was Gasser who suggested that I join the American Physiological Society, which has provided me through the years with much information and many valuable professional associations.

During my period at Brown and later at Rochester a number of studies on brain mechanisms and behavior were carried out in which I participated. Among those who worked in this field were K. U. Smith (now professor at Wisconsin), J. L. Kennedy (now chairman of the Department of Psychology at Princeton), W. E. Kappauf (now professor at Illinois), C. S. Bridgman (now professor at Wisconsin), and L. C. Mead (now acting president of Tufts). The central theme of these investigations was the role of the visual cortex and of subcortical visual centers in various aspects of optically controlled behavior in the cat.

Among my other students who took doctorates in this period were L. F. Beck (now with the E. C. Brown Trust), R. Cruikshank (now Mrs. Bussy and an authority on genetic development of animals), the late P. M. Fitts (until his sad recent death, professor at Michigan), A. C. Hoffman (scientific editor), G. F. J. Lehner (director of the Psychological Clinic, U.C.L.A.), C. T. Morgan (outstanding author and editor of psychological publications and recently lecturer at the University of California, Santa Barbara), L. A. Pennington (Division of Childhood and Youth, state of Wisconsin), E. T. Raney (professor at Wayne University), J. Warkentin (a psychiatrist who holds both the Ph.D. and M.D. degrees), and N. Y. Wessel (the former president of Tufts University). C. Pfaffmann, now vice president of the Rockefeller University, was an undergraduate student in psychology at Brown and did two years of graduate work in my department before becoming a Rhodes scholar and taking his Ph.D. with E. D. Adrian at Cambridge. All of these students without exception have made distinguished contributions in teaching, research, or administration. It is interesting to note that most of these students worked in quantitative animal psychology, which seems to have turned out to be an especially good preparation for later eminence in human factors work, engineering psychology, and also in administration. Space keeps me from listing all of my students who took some graduate work in my department during these years and then went on to further study under other auspices, but I cannot resist mentioning in this connection S. Bojar, J. D. Coronios, A. I. Goldfarb, T. S. Krawiec, C. H. Pearce, S. O. Roberts, M. F. Smith, G. Riley, and D. Rugg.

At Brown some of my students and I worked on a number of studies of learning including delayed response in the cat and what I consider to be a new phenomenon in learning in which initial maze learning of a special type modifies the subsequent capacity for such learning in the rat.

In 1930 I was invited to become a member of the psychology faculty at Harvard. After carefully considering this flattering offer I decided to stay at Providence. The position that was vacant at that time was then ably filled by Gordon Allport who later asked me why I had the bad judgment to turn down Harvard! Later I was queried about the possibility that I might be offered the Chair of Psychology at Oxford, but I felt that I did not wish to move to England.

In 1935 Professor E. G. Boring was on leave. At his invitation I became a visiting professor at Harvard and taught the introductory courses in psychology at Harvard and Radcliffe. During this period I commuted by automobile from Providence to Cambridge, often carrying with me lecture demonstration material to be used in class, both in the large lecture room in Emerson Hall and at Radcliffe. Thus, during the same single semester I taught all the elementary psychology at Brown, Pembroke, Harvard, and Radcliffe. Since my Brown lectures were each repeated three times, there were days when I really felt familiar with the subject matter of elementary psychology! A small but pleasing reward was being chosen several times by Brown University students as their "favorite professor."

In 1931 and 1932 I drove to Worcester once a week as a visiting professor in experimental psychology at Clark University, carrying at the same time my full program at Brown.

During the Brown years a number of other offers of positions came to me. These included a full professorship at the University of Iowa, graciously tendered me by the distinguished Dean C. E. Seashore, and one at Ohio State University. Tempted as I sometimes was by these and other offers, it seemed wise not to accept them.

The most important event of my Providence years was my marriage on June 30, 1932, to Pearl L. Kidston of Hudson, Massachusetts. After finishing college she had worked for a number of years at Harvard in the Graduate School of Education. Beside her gay outlook on life, it may be mentioned that she has an excellent applied mathematical mind. Her knowledge of statistics and accounting enabled her through the years to do the family bookkeeping—a great boon to me. She was the joint author of what seems to me to be one of the best vocabulary tests ever constructed. In my early experimental work she got up with me at any hour of the night or early morning to go to the laboratory to take down in shorthand the long protocols that were later basic in the studies of the early development of behavior. Later she has had to share with me the transition from college teacher to college president and then to the headship of one of our nation's greatest research institutions, the Smithsonian. She says sometimes that our lives have at least not been quiet or dull!

We have only one child, a daughter, Martha, born during my last year at Brown; but this one child has brought us great satisfaction. She is now Mrs. S. Parker Oliphant and has named our first grandchild Leonard Carmichael Oliphant. She majored in zoology with a minor in psychology at Wellesley and before her marriage became a quite proficient brain physiologist, histologist, and an expert on the behavior of the squirrel monkey. Under the fine guidance of her distinguished laboratory director at the National Institute of Health, Dr. Paul D. MacLean, she acquired special knowledge of the limbic system.

In 1936 with great reluctance I left Brown to go to the University of Rochester to become dean of the Faculty of Arts and Sciences and professor of psychology. The very able young president of Rochester, Alan Valentine, offered to allow me to develop there in a new large building a fully adequate experimental psychological laboratory for the type of physiological and behavioral experiments in which I was most interested. He also provided even more adequate funds for graduate fellowships than I had had at Brown. Before the days of federal funds for fellowships, this was most important. Through the generous benefaction of George Eastman, founder of Eastman Kodak Company, Rochester had, I believe, more endowment per student than any other university in the United States.

My two years at Rochester, like the years at Providence and Princeton, were very pleasant. Before coming to Rochester I had arranged with the Brown authorities to transfer most of my graduate students from Providence to Rochester. W. S. Hunter who came on my strongest recommendation to assume my position at Providence, similarly brought his graduate students from Clark to Brown.

The debt of gratitude that I owe to K. U. Smith for all that he did in setting up the psychological laboratories at Brown and at the University of Rochester should be attested here. I also wish to express deep gratitude to Bertram Wellman, an able inventor and electronics engineer who, at Rochester and later at Tufts, assisted me in invaluable ways in the invention, construction, and use of the involved electronic apparatus which made possible many of my experiments. At Rochester, even though I was a dean as well as a professor, I continued to teach all the elementary courses in psychology at both the women's college and the men's college on their two separate campuses. I also taught graduate courses and advised Ph.D. candidates on thesis research.

One of the able graduate students at Rochester was A. C. Hoffman, II. Contrary to the tradition of the laboratory, he insisted on doing a Ph.D. dissertation in human, not mammalian psychology. Following a lead given us by the distinguished Rochester physiologist W. O. Fenn, my electronics associate and I had developed in our laboratory a device for the electrical recording of the eye movements of animals. It occurred to me that it might be interesting to compare quantitatively the use of this new electrical technique of recording human eye movements with the old optical techniques that I had used in my student years in the study of reading. These electrical techniques were proved to be reliable, and they have the advantage that they can be used with subjects sitting comfortably in a chair and without the head clamps required in photographic studies.

During this Rochester period A. F. Rawdon-Smith, Wellman, and I collaborated on the study of the electrical cochlear response of the fetal guinea pig. This study clearly showed the relationship between the development of electrophysiological response of the auditory receptor organ and my previously determined time for the onset of behavior which could be released by airborne auditory stimuli in this typical fetal mammal. Similarly, a number of studies on compulsory optokinetic nystagmus in a number of different mammals and in human babies demonstrated the usefulness of the electrical eye movement recording technique in the study of many and quite various visual phenomena. In this connection it may be pointed out that much of my experimental work has involved the measurement of differences in the release of inborn rather than learned patterns of behavior by altering the physical stimuli acting on the organism.

In 1937 John A. Cousens, president of Tufts College, who had only a few days before given me my first honorary D.Sc. degree, died. The presidency was offered to me but it took many weeks before I could bring myself to decide to leave the field of research and teaching and enter that of administering my alma mater. This was in 1938. The fact that the Tufts trustees agreed that I be allowed to continue my personal scientific work helped me decide, and I went to Medford. At Tufts I established a laboratory of sensory physiology and psychology, of which I served as the director as long as I was at the college.

Before going to Tufts I was offered a professorship and the chairmanship of the Department of Psychology at the University of Chicago. President R. M. Hutchins promised to see that a proper new psychology laboratory was built at Chicago if I would come, but I decided against the move.

During much of my academic life I have been active in psychological and other scientific and academic organizations. I was treasurer of the American Psychological Association from 1932 to 1936. I was president of the American Psychological Association in 1940. My presidential address was entitled "The Experimental Embryology of Mind" (1941). In this address I presented the view that the experimental embryology of behavior provides a basis for the understanding of some aspects of adult human behavior in a way that is comparable with the explanatory role of a knowledge of embryology in the study of adult anatomy. This address was a public retraction of what I had come to see as the incorrect conclusions of some of my early publications in which I had interpreted experimental findings from too strongly an environmentalist point of view.

In the years since this presidential address it has become even more clear to me on the basis of my study of fetal and newborn animals, that genetically determined maturation is of the utmost importance in understanding much behavior at the adult level as well as in the early stages of human and animal development. This conclusion seems to me to apply even in some ways to a validation of properly stated nativistic theories of perception and some phases of cognition. I cannot help feeling that the next half century will profitably give more attention than has the preceding half century to a better understanding of what older workers called "the original nature of man." The word "instinct" as applied to any aspect of human behavior may continue to be suspect, but under some such name as "species-specific behavior" there can be no doubt, it seems to me, that an increasing number of alterations in the reactions of human individuals, during what may be called the full trajectory of life, will be found on careful analysis to result from genetic coding. Such coding must be considered in relation to the development of many individual differences in function and capacity as well as in the behavior that is characteristic of each species. To put this in a single phrase, it seems to me that my studies suggest that much more human and mammalian behavior change, even in adult life, is a result of genetic determination than has been thought to be true in recent decades by some students of learning and especially by some psychoanalytic theorists. In all my work involving the description of behavior, whether external stimulus-released or so-called "spontaneous" in nature, I have tried to say what the movements are that the organism makes rather than calling behavior by such names as "epimeletic," "agonistic," "comfort-seeking," or other names for the ends secured by behavior as given by modern zoologists such as J. P. Scott. The objective description of behavior that I have always attempted to present is much more easily related to underlying neural and physiological mechanisms than is behavior named in terms of the ends that the observer thinks the behavior he is observing will secure for the animal.

During all of my fourteen years at Tufts, in spite of complicated administrative tasks, I succeeded in maintaining at least some free time for work in my laboratory and for psychological writing and editing. Under a Carnegie grant, Dearborn of Harvard and I, with the cooperation of A. C. Hoffman and L. C. Mead, the present Mrs. Jane Hildreth, Mrs. John L. Kennedy, and others carried on an elaborate research of reading and visual fatigue using the electrical recording method previously noted. This study demonstrated that college and secondary school subjects could read continuously for six hours either directly from books or from microfilm without any measurable fatigue. The results of this study are reported in a full-length book, *Reading and Visual Fatigue* (1947). This book also reviews the history of the scientific study of eye movements.

During an early year of my work at Tufts I was able to accept from a cherished friend, E. R. Guthrie, a visiting professorship at the University of Washington for the summer term. I gave a series of lectures on the psychology of learning.

In 1939 and 1940 the nation was clearly preparing for what turned out to be inevitable war. At the suggestion of my lifelong patron and friend, the great and inventive psychologist Robert M. Yerkes, I was asked to come to Washington to direct the mobilization of scientists and engineers for the war effort. This I agreed to do but not on a full-time basis. The title of my position was Director of the National Roster of Scientific and Specialized Personnel. Before the war was over, my office grew to have a staff of over 400 persons and did, I think, invaluable work in the recruitment and assignment of scientists for the atomic energy project, the radar project, and many others. From 1939 to 1945 I commuted between Tufts in Massachusetts and Washington once or twice weekly, spending more than a year of nights on a sleeping car between Boston and Washington. The human brain can stand a good deal of shaking!

During the war years I also served as chairman of the Division of Anthropology and Psychology of the National Research Council. This position gave me an opportunity to work in many ways for the advancement of psychology as a science and as a profession. For example, in the period just before the war the United States had no psychological warfare program of importance. I was asked to advise Army Intelligence on the setting up of work in this field. I elicited the assistance of W. S. Hunter, and soon we were able to bring E. R. Guthrie from the University of Washington to establish this work. He and his associates did an outstanding job.

My position at the National Research Council also allowed me to help in the administration of the Emergency Committee, which did much for the nation and for the psychological profession during the war. The National Research Council had provided outstanding war service during the First World War, but Vannevar Bush, James B. Conant, and others quite rightly decided that a new agency was needed for scientific work in the Second World War. This led to the establishment of the National Defense Research Committee and later the Office of Scientific Research and Development. These new agencies were closely related to the National Research Council and the National Academy. The history of this work, *Scientists Against Time* by J. P. Baxter, summarizes the contributions of psychology. I played a minor role in having psychology included in this organization and in nominating W. S. Hunter to head this work. I served under Hunter's direction on war-related research. The work that I was primarily concerned with was the validation of synthetic training devices and the development of selection procedures.

During the war and immediately thereafter I was also a member of the Science Committee of the National Resources Planning Board, the Committee on Research Personnel of the War Manpower Commission, and the Committee on Human Resources of the Research and Development Board. From 1947 to 1952 I was a member of the Naval Research Advisory Committee. I have had a similar post on the Army Scientific Advisory Panel. For a number of years I lectured on human engineering before each new class at the Naval War College in Newport. I have also given a number of special lectures in various universities including the Arthur Dehon Little Lecture at the Massachusetts Institute of Technology and a series of lectures at the Rice Institute in Texas. These latter lectures were published in 1956 as a book, *The Making of Modern Mind.*

Through the years it has been my pleasure to have many honorary associations with educational and related institutions. From 1947 to 1948 I was chairman of the American Council on Education. I served for a number of years as vice chairman of the Harvard Foundation for Advanced Study and Research. I have also had the honor of serving as chairman or as a member of visiting committees at Harvard, Princeton, Johns Hopkins, Tulane, and other institutions. I have been for more than a quarter of a century a member, and for much of that time chairman, of the Board of Scientific Directors of the Yerkes Laboratories of Primate Biology. I am now also on a similar board of the Delta Regional Primate Research Center at Tulane. For years I have been on the Board of Scientific Overseers of the Jackson Memorial Laboratories at Bar Harbor where outstanding work on genetics in relation to mammalian behavior is conducted. My interest in the psychology of primates has been active since my early graduate years, and I am proud at the present time to be serving as president of the newly-formed International Primatological Society.

From 1950 to 1954 I was chairman of a New England committee for a comprehensive economic survey of the region. This project had the support of the federal government and resulted in important publications by the Yale University Press.

I now serve as trustee of the Brookings Institution, as a director of the Research Corporation of New York, and from 1954 until a few months ago I was president of the Board of Trustees of Science Service. From 1952 to its termination (when it became the National Aeronautics and Space Administration) I was a member of the board of the National Advisory Committee for Aeronautics, and from 1956 to 1958 I was vice chairman of this truly great research organization that did so much for the development of America's leadership in aviation and also began, in such an effective way, America's participation in the scientific conquest of space. Under an appointment of President Eisenhower, I had the title of Ambassador Extraordinary and was chairman of a delegation at an international conference at The Hague to represent our country and ultimately to sign, in the presence of the Queen of the Netherlands, a treaty for the protection of cultural property in time of war.

In 1952 I was offered the secretaryship of the Smithsonian Institution in Washington. I was very happy at Tufts where my efforts to improve the university plant, especially at the medical and dental schools, had met with success. I also had secured trustee agreement in increasing faculty salaries each year and in giving more financial support for research. Some fourteen million dollars of special gifts came to Tufts during my presidency. Thus, after saying "no" for a number of weeks I was finally prevailed upon to accept the challenge of becoming the chief executive of the Smithsonian. I still continue as a Tufts trustee, and I have thus watched with pleasure the progress of the institution under the presidency of my former student and good psychologist, N. Y. Wessell. I am grateful that Tufts has named its largest new dormitory Carmichael Hall. A dynamic undergraduate social service society also honored me by its name, the Leonard Carmichael Society.

I left Tufts and took up my new responsibilities in Washington on January 1, 1953. This move was in no sense a departure from the academic world. The Smithsonian is a very great research institution, especially in astrophysics, anthropology, archeology, ethnology, zoology, botany, geology, paleontology, oceanography, and in general, social history. The research staff of the Smithsonian, in its areas of specialization, is as distinguished as the faculty of any university in the world.

The Smithsonian has eleven bureaus most of which are primarily concerned with research, but it also emphasizes museum work. In 1953 when I came, there were some 37,000,000 catalogued objects in the Smithsonian museums. When I retired in 1964 there were over 57,000,000 such objects. The annual number of visitors during this period rose from 3,500,000 to over 10,000,000.

One of the great privileges of serving as the principal administrative officer of the Smithsonian was the opportunity of working closely and intimately with its Board of Regents, which included during my time official Washington Chief Justices Fred M. Vinson and Earl Warren, Vice Presidents Richard M. Nixon and Lyndon B. Johnson, Senators Clinton P. Anderson, Leverett Saltonstall, H. Alexander Smith, J. William Fulbright, and Robert A. Taft, and members of the House of Representatives Clarence Cannon, Frank T. Bow, M. J. Kirwan, J. M. Vorys, Overton Brooks, and Leroy Johnson. "Citizen Regents" in this period included John Nicholas Brown, William A. M. Burden, Robert V. Fleming, Crawford H. Greenwalt, Caryl P. Haskins, Jerome C. Hunsaker, Arthur H. Compton, Vannevar Bush, Owen J. Roberts, and Everette L. DeGolyer. I feel deep friendship and admiration for all of these men. I feel an especially personal debt of gratitude to Clarence Cannon, parliamentarian, historian, and chairman of the House Committee on Appropriations; Chief Justice Warren, chancellor of the Smithsonian during almost my whole tenure of office; and Robert V. Fleming, chairman of the Institution's Executive Committee, who has one of the wisest financial minds and is one of the greatest administrators I have ever known.

During the eleven years of my secretaryship, funds for buildings and the planning of buildings appropriated by the congress amounted to over sixty-one million dollars. The annual appropriations for the central units of the Smithsonian rose from two and a half million to over thirteen million. In this same dozen years over thirty-two million dollars came to the Institution from foundations and other sources in addition to direct federal appropriations.

My years in Washington have been most interesting. I have come to know quite well each of the presidents and many ambassadors who served here during this period. I have been, for some years, a vestryman of St. John's Episcopal Church (the church of the presidents). I am also a member of the Chapter (*i.e.,* trustee) of the Washington National Cathedral. I am now a trustee of the National Trust for Historic Preservation. It has been my great privilege to come to know, besides government officials, many of the academic, artistic, and literary leaders of this generation who have visited or worked in Washington. I met nearly every major crowned head and many chiefs of state who came to Washington during my Smithsonian years.

One of my most pleasant memories concerns the work I was allowed to do personally in association with President and Mrs. John F. Kennedy for the better preparation of the White House for visitors.

In 1964 at age sixty-five I insisted on retiring from the Smithsonian, although I was repeatedly urged by the Board of Regents to continue my tenure as secretary at least to age seventy. One of my last official acts at the Smithsonian was to preside over the dedication of the great new thirty-six-million-dollar Museum of History and Technology, which was conceived, planned, and built during my administration as head of the Smithsonian. President Johnson and Chief Justice Warren spoke at these exercises. This is, I believe, the largest and most adequate building ever built in the world for a general museum.

To my surprise, on the announcement of my retirement I was offered by the National Geographic Society's distinguished president and editor, Dr. M. B. Grosvenor, my present position as vice president for Research and Exploration of this great nonprofit society which has as its function "the increase and diffusion of geographic knowledge" and which has done much through the years for research in anthropology, archeology, human prehistory, animal behavior, as well as in more specific geological and geographic fields. I had been a trustee of the National Geographic for a number of years and also for some time, chairman of its Committee for Research and Exploration. My present position involves serving as chairman of the Society's able research committee and the administration of grants for research to university and other workers now totaling each year approximately one million dollars.

I have spoken of my long-time personal interest in primate research. Recently I was privileged to observe troops of wild temperate-zone monkeys in Japan, and I have also had the great opportunity of watching for some days over thirty wild chimpanzees deep in the forests of East Africa.

I still continue my work as editor of books in psychology for the Houghton Mifflin Company. In 1957 at the request of Random House I wrote *Basic Psychology,* which gives my general point of view about psychology and was written not as a textbook but as a volume for the educated general reader. This book has surprised me by its wide and continuing sale each year since its publication. During this period I have also written a number of articles and chapters for books dealing with psychological topics. A 1964 publication was a chapter, "The Early Growth of Language Capacity in the Individual," in a book edited by E. H. Lenneberg, *New Directions in the Study of Language.*

If I were asked what thread seems to me to have run most consistently through my career, I could answer the question in one word: *research.* As I have noted, I began a little investigation as an undergraduate at Tufts, and ever since that time my own research, or the administration and funding of the research of others, has been my central day-in and day-out interest.

During the last decade I have observed as many births and as many newborn animals of different species as possible at the National Zoological Park, which as a bureau of the Smithsonian Institution was under my general administration. Also, with the help of a full-time research associate, Dr. Mozelle B. Kraus, I have attempted during recent years to bring together, from all the journals of the world, summaries of papers that deal with animal infancy. I have undertaken this comprehensive study of early postnatal mammalian life as a complement to my earlier studies of prenatal life. This recent work has added to my conviction that many psychologists in the last half century have given far too little weight to the role of inheritance in evaluating the changes in behavior that take place as an individual develops. The recent growth of knowledge concerning the role of DNA and RNA in the determination and coding of genetic information provides a new basis for understanding the role of inheritance in behavior change. I can now say that my lifetime of study of receptor-initiated behavior, which I began as an undergraduate, has given me each year a better and better understanding of the mechanisms of adaptive response and of mental life.

It was suggested by the editors of this autobiography that as it is intended, at least in part, for psychologists, it might be well to present some reference to the individual writer's "feelings, personal motives, and aspirations." I do not know how to do this, so the following description will have to suffice. A Rorschach test was given to me some years ago and scored by one of the great authorities in this field. The results of this test showed that I did especially well in my ability to organize relations not commonly seen and in grasping connections between elements. On the Z factor my total was 145.5, which is among the highest scores that had been recorded. The range at that time for the healthy superior was said to be 50–85. I am not quite sure how to interpret this, but it is as close to a formal psychological analysis of my personality as anything that I know of.

My life has not been all hard work. I have enjoyed the company of friends in large and small groups. Club membership has meant much to me. Among the clubs to which I have belonged with pleasure are the Art Club (Providence), the St. Botolph and Country Clubs (Boston), the Cosmos, Metropolitan, and Chevy Chase Clubs (Washington), and the Century Association (New York). I have also enjoyed membership in discussion clubs such as the Pundits (Rochester, N. Y.), the Examiner (Boston), and the Literary Society (Washington).

A number of honors have come to me during my career. I was elected to the American Academy of Arts and Sciences in 1932 and to the American Philosophical Society in 1942. I served as vice president of this society from 1962 to 1965. I was elected to the National Academy of Sciences in 1943, and I have been chairman of its section on psychology.

I have noted that I am a trustee of Tufts. I am also on the Board of Trustees of George Washington University. I have recently been elected a

Fellow of Brown University (that is, a member of its "upper house" of trustees). Brown has also honored me by giving my name to the large auditorium in the W. S. Hunter Psychological Laboratory there.

I may note also that I have received a number of special honors, including a Presidential Citation given by President Truman for my war work and one from President Eisenhower for my contribution to "the advancement of man's knowledge of the science of flight and to the practical solution of many attendant problems." On August 22, 1964, Mrs. J. F. Kennedy wrote me: "President Kennedy was going to give you the Citation of Merit this last Fourth of July in his beloved Rose Garden for all that you did for the Smithsonian in your glowing years there." As a reminder of this she honored me by sending a beautiful gold box engraved in script as follows:

The
Seal of the President
of the United States

Leonard Carmichael
with deep appreciation for
January 20, 1961–November 22, 1963
Jacqueline Kennedy

I have also received the following foreign decorations: Commander of the Order of Danneborg (kingdom of Denmark), Commander of the Order of Merit of the Republic of Italy, Knight Commander's Cross with Star of the Order of Merit of the Federal Republic of Germany, and Knight Commander of the Order of Alfonso the Wise of Spain.

During my life in Washington and in connection with my many governmental consulting positions I have always tried to explain what modern psychology is to fellow physical scientists in places such as the Pentagon and to many members of Congress at the almost endless hearings at which I have testified. I cannot help believing that cumulatively I may have helped a little in this way in developing a better understanding of the scientific field of psychology in these great power centers of our national life.

I have received, in all, twenty-three honorary doctor's degrees including an LL.D. from Harvard, which in its Latin citation uses these words: *"psychologiae studiosum qui non minus excellit in scientia sua quam in rerum academicarum sagaci administratione."* This in English translation reads, "A psychologist who combines distinction in his science with success in administration." This phrase is surely too generous, but it does summarize the two aspects of my life at which I have worked hard in the past and at which I am now continuing to work as actively as is my habit. For me, administration and psychology (and, a little paradoxically it may be, especially quantitative comparative animal psychology) are not separate fields. Administration in many, many instances is real psychology applied in the real world. Certainly for me, from my college days on, the scientific study of the behavior of animals and men as an expression of the physiology of the living organism has been a satisfying philosophers' stone which has given meaning and coherence to all my thought and action.

# REFERENCES

*Selected Publications by Leonard Carmichael*

An evaluation of current sensationism. *Psychol. Rev.,* 1925, *32,* 192–215.
(with E. E. Lord and W. F. Dearborn) Special disabilities in learning to read and write. *Harvard Monogr. Educ.,* 1925, *I,* II(1), 1–76
Heredity and environment: are they antithetical? *J. abnorm. soc. Psychol.,* 1925, *20,* 245–260.
The report of a Sheldon fellow (German psychological laboratories). *Harvard Alumni Bull.,* 1925, *27,* 1087–1089.
The development of behavior in vertebrates experimentally removed from the influence of external stimulation. *Psychol. Rev.,* 1926, *33,* 51–58.
Sir Charles Bell: a contribution to the history of physiological psychology, *Psychol. Rev.,* 1926, *33,* 188–217.
A further study of the development of behavior in vertebrates experimentally removed from the influence of external stimulation. *Psychol. Rev.,* 1927, *34,* 34–47.
The history of mirror drawing as a laboratory method. *Pedag. Sem. J. genet. Psychol.,* 1927, *34,* 90–91.
Robert Whytt: a contribution to the history of physiological psychology. *Psychol. Rev.,* 1927, *34,* 287–304.
A further experimental study of the development of behavior. *Psychol. Rev.,* 1928, *35,* 253–260.
(with H. C. Warren) *Elements of human psychology.* Boston: Houghton Mifflin, 1930.
(with H. P. Hogan and A. A. Walter) An experimental study of the effect of language on the reproduction of visually perceived form. *J. exp. Psychol.,* 1932, *15,* 73–86.
Origin and prenatal growth of behavior. In C. Murchison (Ed.), *A handbook of child psychology.* Worcester, Mass.: Clark Univer. Press, 1933.
The genetic development of the kitten's capacity to right itself in the air when falling. *Pedag. Sem. J. genet. Psychol.,* 1934, *44,* 453–458.
(with E. T. Raney) Localizing responses to tactual stimuli in the fetal rat in relation to the psychological problem of space perception. *Pedag. Sem. J. genet. Psychol.,* 1934, *45,* 3–21.
An experimental study in the prenatal guinea pig of the origin and development of reflexes and patterns of behavior in relation to the stimulation of specific receptor areas during the period of active fetal life. *Genet. Psychol. Monogr.,* 1934, *16,* 337–491.
The response mechanism. In E. G. Boring, H. S. Langfeld, and H. P. Weld (Eds.), *Psychology, a factual textbook.* New York: Wiley, 1935.

(with H. H. Jasper) Electrical potentials from the intact human brain. *Science,* 1935, *89,* 51–53.

A re-evaluation of the concepts of maturation and learning as applied to the early development of behavior. *Psychol. Rev.,* 1936, *43,* 450–470.

(with G. F. J. Lehner) The development of temperature sensitivity. *J. genet. Psychol.,* 1937, *50,* 217–227.

(with H. H. Jasper and C. S. Bridgman) An ontogenetic study of cerebral electrical potentials in the guinea pig. *J. exp. Psychol.,* 1937, *21,* 63–71.

(with Z. Y. Kuo) A technique for the motion-picture recording of the development of behavior in the chick embryo. *J. Psychol.,* 1937, *4,* 343–348.

Learning which modifies an animal's subsequent capacity for learning. *J. genet. Psychol.,* 1938, *52,* 159–163.

(with A. F. Rawdon-Smith and B. Wellman) Electrical responses from the cochlea of the fetal guinea pig. *J. exp. Psychol.,* 1938, *23,* 531–535.

(with A. C. Hoffman and B. Wellman) A quantitative comparison of the electrical and photographic techniques of eye movement recording. *J. exp. Psychol.,* 1939, *24,* 40–53.

(with J. Warkentin) A study of the development of the air-righting reflex in cats and rabbits. *J. genet. Psychol.,* 1939, *55,* 67–80.

The national roster of scientific and specialized personnel. *Science,* 1940, *92,* 135–137.

The experimental embryology of mind. *Psychol. Bull.,* 1941, *38,* 1–28.

(with J. G. Beebe-Center and L. C. Mead) Daylight training of pilots for night flying. *Aeronaut. Engng. Rev.,* 1944, *3,* 1–10.

(Ed.) *Manual of child psychology.* New York: Wiley, 1946.

(with W. F. Dearborn) *Reading and visual fatigue.* Boston: Houghton Mifflin, 1947.

Ontogenetic development. In S. S. Stevens (Ed.), *Handbook of experimental psychology.* New York: Wiley, 1951.

The phylogenetic development of behavior patterns. *Genetics and the inheritance of integrated neurological and psychiatric patterns* (Proceedings of the Association for Research in Nervous and Mental Disease). Baltimore: Williams and Wilkins, 1954, 87–97.

*The making of modern mind* (The Rockwell Lectures presented at Rice Institute, March, 1955). Houston, Texas: Elsevier, 1956.

*Basic psychology.* New York: Random House, 1957.

Evidence from the prenatal and early postnatal behavior of organisms concerning the concept of local sign. *Acta Psychol.,* 1961, *19,* 166–170.

The early growth of language capacity in the individual. In E. H. Lenneberg (Ed.), *New directions in the study of language.* Cambridge: M.I.T., 1964.

### Other Publications Cited

Baxter, J. P. *Scientists against time.* Boston: Little, Brown, 1946.

Koffka, K. *The growth of the mind.* New York: Harcourt, Brace & World, 1924.

Preyer. *Specielle Physiologie des Embryo. Untersuchungen über die Lebenserscheinungen vor der Geburt.* Leipsig: Grieben, 1885.

Warren, H. C. *Dictionary of psychology.* Boston: Houghton Mifflin, 1934.

Karl M. Dallenbach

# Karl M. Dallenbach

I am a descendant of a German-Swiss family. My surname, which is alternative with "Tällenbach," which means "valley brook," is almost as frequently seen and heard in Canton Berne as "Smith" in America. The name has been traced back to the thirteenth century, to the national hero of Switzerland, Wilhelm Tell (Täll, Taellen), who, according to family legend, was the founder of the family. Since the interchange of "T" and "D," which comes from flatting, is one of the commonest of Grimm's etymological laws, the story is not incredible, as it speaks of the "Tells" who lived by the "brook." It is a nice legend, whether true or not.

The first member of the family to migrate to America was Jorg Martin Dällenbach. He was one of the "poor" Palatines brought by the English Queen Anne to the Hudson Valley in 1710 to manufacture naval stores for the British Navy. After serving in the Colonial Army (1711) in the war against the French in Canada and working out his indebtedness to the Crown for his passage to and subsistence while in the Hudson Valley, he received a patent of land near Stone Arabia in the Mohawk Valley of New York, where he remained the balance of his life. Many of his descendants still reside there but under several variants of his surname which range from Dellenback, Dellenbeck, Dallenbaugh, Tillapach, to Tillapaugh (Dillenback & Dallenbach, 1935, p. xv).

The second migration of Dällenbachs to America occurred in 1824 when two brothers, Christian and Jacob, both of middle age, heads of families, and men of moderate means, left Nidenberg and Safneran, neighboring villages near Lake Bienna, for the New World. Christian, the elder, a cheese maker, settled on dairyland near North Georgetown, Ohio; Jacob, the founder of my twig of the family, a vintner, settled on land more suited for vineyards, a farm on the north bank of the Allegheny River, now in the center of Pittsburgh, North Side, but then on the outskirts of Allegheny City.

The two families prospered in America. Christian's family, which settled in a predominately English-speaking community, soon adopted the Anglicized spelling and pronunciation of their surname as "Dellenbaugh." Jacob and his family, who lived in the German community in Allegheny City, were more resistant. The most that any of them yielded in the spelling of their surname was to change it to "Dellenbach." Jacob and his son John, my grandfather, persisted in using the Swiss spelling, Dällenbach, throughout their lives.

My grandfather worked for his father until he married Rosanna Angler, a recent immigrant from Arlenbach, Switzerland, in March, 1848. He then struck out to seek his own fortune, settling first at Ripley, Ohio, which had the promise of developing into a metropolis. He opened a market and general store and remained there for eight years, during which his first four children were born; among them was my father, John Jacob, the third child and first son, who was born on June 7, 1853 (Dillenback & Dallenbach, 1935, p. 360). Ripley was, however, by-passed for Cincinnati in the competition for river traffic. Its promise to become an important river port was not fulfilled. That, connected with the death of their fourth child, decided my grandparents to go farther west. My grandfather wished to go to the gold fields of California, but my grandmother, as small a woman as he was a large man—he was over 6 feet in height and 250 pounds in weight—would not hear of it. As she ruled the family, they compromised by taking a covered wagon to a homestead in Champaign County, Illinois. The land was all that it was claimed to be; it grew crops, but was so far from a market that there was little that could be done with them after they were harvested, particularly when corn was 9 cents a bushel and other produce correspondingly low.

While still solvent, my grandfather gave up the profitless struggle on the soil and moved to a little settlement that sprang up several miles to the west of Urbana, Illinois, with the laying of the tracks of the Illinois Central Railroad. He established a market there and engaged in the profitable business of shipping livestock on the new railroad to the Chicago market. The little village, first called West Urbana and then officially Champaign, flourished and with it John's fortune and family. Six children—five sons and one daughter—were born here, making ten children in all, but two died before reaching maturity. When John retired in 1877, he turned his market and wholesale livestock business over to his two older sons, my father, John Jacob, and my uncle, William Christian, who conducted it successfully until they retired after forty years, in 1917, without anyone in the family to succeed them.

My maternal grandparents, Christian Franz Philipp and Johanna (Schnieber) Mittendorf, and their three daughters immigrated to America from Wolfenbüttel, Braunschweig, Germany, in the spring of 1853. They first settled in Leiden, Cook County, Illinois, where my mother, Anna Caroline Mittendorf, was born on July 6, 1854. After one year in Leiden, the family moved to a farm outside the village of Champaign. My father, John Jacob, and mother, Anna Caroline Mittendorf, were married in Champaign, November 17, 1880.

## CHILDHOOD

I, the second of three sons of this union, was born October 20, 1887. Since the first-born was a boy, it was hoped I would be a girl. That I was not made little difference in my early rearing. My hair, naturally wavy, was allowed to grow until long, blond curls hung far down my shoulders and back, and I was dressed in skirts until I was nearly four years old. Then I was put in knee-pants and allowed to go barefooted in clement weather, as all boys were in those days. I retained my long hair, however, and was subjected to a fate worse than dresses; namely, a "Little Lord Fauntleroy" suit, a dark velvet sailor-jacket and knee-pants, worn with a fluffy white shirt with a large collar and cuffs and a large white bow tie, patent leather shoes, and knee stockings. This was the garb of the "hero" of Frances Hodgson Burnett's book (*Little Lord Fauntleroy*), who, both in clothes and character, represented a boy many proud mothers throughout the English-speaking world wished their sons to be. I wore this suit to Sunday School and on every occasion when my mother wished to exhibit me, which was much too frequent for me.

As long as I wore dresses, my play was restricted to girls. The boys did not welcome me. When I was put into knee-pants, however, I ventured afield and enlarged my circle of acquaintances. I found the boys, of whom there were many in the immediate neighborhood, different kinds of playmates. They played rougher games and would not give in to my wishes and suggestions and would use force to have their own way. I was at a great disadvantage with long hair and was at the bottom of the pecking line. Nearly every time I ventured to play with the boys, I came running home, crying and bedraggled, for the sympathy that I would get from my mother. One day, Dad chanced to be home when I returned. I got no sympathy from him. He told me if I ever started a fight he would give me a licking when I returned home, as he did not wish a "bully" for a son; and further, if I got licked in a fight I did not start that he would give me another licking when I got home, as he did not wish a "sissy" for a son. As I knew that he would keep his promises and also, from experience, what his lickings were, I had to keep the peace and avoid disputes; I had in short to be a "sissy."

I decided, however, that my hair, my handicap in fighting, must go. I begged to have it cut, but to no avail; Mother would not hear of it. My hair was her pride and joy. I persisted in my requests, but it was not until I announced that I would not go to school with long hair that my mother finally acquiesced. The visit to the barbershop was, however, delayed until the day before the opening of school, and then, when I left with Dad to have it done, Mother began to cry. To my everlasting satisfaction, I ran back, embraced her and said that I would not have my hair cut if she did not wish it. At her "No, go ahead, but bring your curls back," I turned and ran after Dad before she could change her mind. Soon I was an emancipated and happy boy. Fifty years later, when Mother died, the box marked "Karl's curls" was found among her treasures.

Freed from the handicap of long hair, I soon changed my position in the pecking order of the neighborhood. With only a few fights I advanced myself from the bottom to the top. My first fight was with a boy a year older but smaller than I, as I was large for my age. It arose over the distribution of the insects that he and I were jointly collecting. He wished, as I thought, to take the best specimens for his own. I objected, he insisted and, as he had been accustomed to pushing me around, he attempted to make me accept his division by force. He did not realize what a difference my lack of curls would make and got himself thoroughly licked. He never challenged me again and neither did any of the boys who stood below him in the pecking order.

My next fight, or rather series of fights, was with a playmate who stood at or near the top of the pecking order. He also was a year older, and smaller, than I. He taught me to play marbles, at which he defeated me badly at first. Chagrined by my lack of skill, I practiced at home until I became more proficient than he was, and by the time my curls were cut, I was defeating him regularly. Since he had consistently won before, he could not understand the change and sought to make me play over my good shots by accusing me of "shoving," which was not allowed. As I was not shoving, I refused to replay the shots and the game ended in a fight in which he found himself, to his surprise, soundly thrashed. As childhood quarrels are short-lived, we were soon back on the old basis playing marbles again. He consistently lost as I continued my practice and increased my skill. The games almost inevitably ended in fights, because he never gave up. I could not understand his persistency and wished he would stop, for I counted him a friend and disliked to hurt him. Our fights continued, however, until he moved away with his family to another city. Some fifty years later, when we were in Champaign on a visit, he told me why he persisted in fighting me. He knew that he was a year older than I, that he had once been able—when I had long hair—to lick me, and he thought he would be able to do it again if he tried often enough. He showed admirable courage and persistency, but a woeful lack of judgment and the realization that conditions sometimes irrevocably change.

When I was about four years old, and my younger brother was about two years old, our home, a cottage which was too small for the growing family, was moved to the outskirts of town where we lived while a new home, a large two-story, twelve-room house possessing all the modern conveniences of that day and generation, was being built on the old lot. Besides a large cellar with furnace, coal, laundry, and tool rooms, it had a large attic that was finished for our play. It was equipped with blackboards and, in due time, with a wrestling mat on which my older brother taught me the art of wrestling, popular around the turn of the century. Though six years older than I, and by then an athlete in high school, he brought me to the level of achievement at which he could not pin my shoulders to the mat.

After we moved into the new home, particularly after my curls were cut, the center of play of the boys in the neighborhood shifted to our yard and house, not only because of the large playroom in the attic that our friends enjoyed with us in inclement weather, but also because of the many playthings we had at our house.

When our play took my younger brother and me away from home, Mother called us by ringing a farm-bell, but Dad, if he were at home, whistled for us. He used a shrill whistle that came down through the family from Switzerland. It is made with a crooked little finger and can be heard across a section, *i.e.* over a mile, as I determined in an experiment that I induced Dad to make with me. A peculiarity about that whistle is that only one member of a generation of the family learned it, and that it descended down my line. My grandfather acquired it from his father, Dad from his, and I from mine. None of my uncles nor either of my brothers learned it; of my family, only one, John Wallace, my older son, learned it.

### Early Memories

*Meeting of Brothers.* My earliest and most vivid memory during childhood occurred on September 13, 1889, when I was twenty-two months and twenty-three days old. It was my introduction to my newly arrived baby brother.

I had spent the previous afternoon and night at the home of two cousins who were about my age and was taken by my aunt to see my brother the next day. All the aunts from both sides of my house were assembled in our living room to observe my reactions. I was led to *my* crib. I do not know what I expected to see, but what I saw, a little red face occupying *my* place, enraged me. Since my little arms would not reach him, and I could not pull him out, I went to the coal scuttle standing beside the baseburner which heated the room and got the poker to drive him out. It was taken away from me before I could wield it. Then I got the coal shovel, of which I was also relieved, and then the broom and mop from the kitchen pantry, which were also in turn taken away from me. Then, giving up the attempt to drive away the usurper, as everyone seemed against me, I ran out to the back porch and threw myself down on the back steps and bawled. My crib and my place in my mother's affections—since I did not see her in the room—were lost! My aunt, who brought me there, came out and comforted me and took me home with her, where I spent the next two days. Though I was fond of her, she was not Mother, hence when asked if I wished to return home for a visit, I gladly assented. When I got home and found that I had not lost Mother's affections and that I had a new trundle-bed in place of the crib, that I was a big boy and not a baby, I readily agreed, when Mother invited me, to stay home.

In the psychological sense of "an event that is placed, dated, and re-called with the feeling of familiarity," this is a memory. But is it? This event, "the meeting of brothers," was related so often during my childhood and youth that what I now recall may be nothing more than a composite of the stories told me. Had it never been mentioned after its occurrence, it would not, I believe, be "remembered" now.

*Frozen Tongue.* One cold winter day, while playing in the snow (I was still wearing skirts, hence it must have been some time early in my fourth year), I sought to slake my thirst by licking an icicle. At contact, my tongue stuck (froze) fast, and I reflexly pulled it free, losing the skin from its center.

I had a very sore tongue for some time, and when it healed I discovered that I could not taste candy at the center, only around the edges and far back, as my experiments with stick candy revealed. I thought my inability to taste at that area was due to the loss of the skin from there. It was not until many years later, when I studied psychology, that I learned the real reason: that the center was insensitive to taste. This "early memory" may be like "the meeting of brothers," since everyone in my family knew and talked about it for many years and warned the children in the neighborhood against duplicating my experience. It may well be, therefore, that what I "remember" now are the stories told of it and not the original experience.

*Running Away from Home.* The third "early memory" occurred during the spring of my fourth year, while I was still wearing dresses.

After being punished by my mother for not minding her, I announced in anger that I was going to run away. I thought she would beg me to stay, but she wisely did not. I regretted the threat almost as soon as it was made, but having delivered it, I had to go through with it. I dallied around as long as I could to give her opportunity to plead with me to stay home, getting first a wrap and then going to the cooky jar for food to take with me on the trip, and then I walked resolutely out of the front door and down the street. The problems that I faced on that trip were tremendous. I did not know where to "run," but habit settled that, and I turned down the familiar street that led to Grandfather Mittendorf's, a mile out of town. I trudged along slowly; deeply regretting that I had got myself into such a situation and fully aware that it was of my own making.

When I reached the edge of town and the long country road stretched out before me, I sat down on the bank to rest and to consider my problems— and to eat the cookies I had brought with me. Where was I to sleep that night and the nights thereafter? What and where would I eat? It was a dark and dismal world that faced me. Suddenly, the happy thought occurred to me that I *had* run away; that having been accomplished, I was now free to return. I happily retraced my steps homeward and when I got there I rushed through the door with the happy cry, "I'm back!" Mother said, "Good, just in time for supper." Not another word was ever said about the incident. It was evidently to be a secret between Mother and me. She never mentioned it; she did not even ask me where I had gone. I was grateful that it was to be ignored, and I hoped it would be forgotten, but I myself never was able to achieve that.

Here is an "early memory" that was not discussed, but was recalled and revived frequently by me to keep me from ever again thinking about running away from home; a thought which G. Stanley Hall claims is very frequent in youth.

## EDUCATION

*Grammar School.* During the summer before I entered school, the eight-grade schoolhouse, which I was to have attended, burned to the ground. The makeshift necessitated by this fire placed the first grade in the Baptist Church across the alley back of my home. As I could count, recite the alphabet, and read a few simple words, I found the first grade, except for the play with children of my own age, tedious and boring.

Grammar schools at that time were organized into grades of about forty pupils each, every grade being divided into an A- and B-class upon the basis of the teacher's opinion of the pupils' competency. Except for the prestige of being in the A-class, it made little difference into which class one was placed, as both used the same books and studied the same subjects. The teacher taught the A-class while the B-class was studying and then the B-class while the A-class was studying. There was no surcease from labor for the teacher; she alternated between the classes throughout the day except during the fifteen-minute recess held every morning and afternoon, and the periods devoted to singing and drawing, when the classes were combined. Of the eight grades through which I passed, two, the second and seventh, stand out in memory.

The second grade was in the new brick schoolhouse built on the site of the one that had burned. I remember it in particular because the teacher made arithmetic "fun," it became a contest in which I determined to and did excel; and also because she read to the combined classes in the last period of every week if we had been "good children" during the preceding days. She read the most fascinating stories that I had ever heard: those of "The Gods and Heroes of Greece and Rome." We were entranced and every pupil was not only a monitor of his own behavior but of every other child's; it was the best-behaved class I ever attended.

When she finished this book, we insisted upon her rereading it rather than turning to another, hence we heard those tales over and over, the teacher finally permitting us to call for the ones we desired. Twice-told tales do not bore children; indeed, they wish to hear stories that they know so well that they can correct the narrator when he deviates from them. I called for the "labors of Hercules" and for the stories of Prometheus and Epimetheus. What I know about the gods and heroes of Greece and Rome, which is, I think, considerably more than the average person, was learned in this grade. It was while listening to these tales that I gained insight into my character. I wished very much that I could identify myself with Hercules or Prometheus (whose name, as we were told, meant "forethought"), but truth and honesty forced me to the realization that I was an Epimetheus, an "afterthought." I tried very hard to change my character to that of a "forethought," but without success.

I was mischievous, a "Peck's bad boy," in the grades following the second. There were no rewards for being good, such as those offered to the children in the second grade, hence I behaved naturally. My reputation for misbehaving, which had been building up ever since I left the second grade and had reached its climax in the sixth grade, preceded me to the seventh, the teacher of which was prepared to "break that frisky colt."

The first day in class I met a new boy whose family had just moved into the city. He was put in the B-class in a seat next to me. We soon became fast friends and fellow connivers in mischief: the teacher now had two "colts" to break. She set about it with a will; she paddled the palms of our hands with a ruler and whipped us with switches. Our code of manhood would not permit us to cry, and we did not, though we both realized that the punishment would be less severe if we did. Lickings followed lickings with no apparent effect, hence she tried a different attack; she expelled us from school for a week, requiring us to take our books with us. She did not inform our parents, and since we hid our books and left and returned home every day at the usual time, they never learned of it. Except for the constant fear that they would, we had a pleasant vacation. We were, however, glad when the time passed and we could again return to school.

I went back to my old seat but my accomplice was placed two seats in front of me. Undaunted by the separation, I stuck a pin through the tip of my shoe, extended my leg, and stuck him in the hip while the teacher was busy with the A-class. He screamed. Without asking for an explanation, the teacher told us to stay after school. This on the first day after we had returned from our expulsion! When we reported to her after school, she told us to take seats in front of her desk and went about her other duties, permitting us to stew in the juices of our imagination. Finally she turned to us and said, "Boys, I do not know what to do with you; punishment and expulsion have accomplished little. I believe that you are bad because you do not have enough to do. I am therefore giving you more to do. Tomorrow morning I shall promote you to the A-class. If you do not keep up with the work there, back to the B-class you will go." Carrying my books across the room to the A-class the next morning was the proudest moment of my life. To avoid the disgrace of being demoted, which hung heavily over me, I resolved to be an exemplary pupil, and my companion in "crime" felt the same as I. In this we were aided by the teacher, who removed temptation by placing us in seats widely separated. The entire course of my life was, I believe, changed. From an indifferent pupil, satisfied merely with a passing grade, I strove thereafter to be at or near the head of my class.

## CULTURAL TRAINING

Mother was determined that her boys should be cultured as well as educated. She insisted that we receive religious and musical training and permitted us to be exposed to the theater.

*Religious.* Mother was an ardent member of the Congregational Church, and I was sent to the primary class in its Sunday School at an early age. I do not remember attending in girls' dresses but do recall being there in the "Lord Fauntleroy" suit, hence I must have entered sometime around my fourth birthday. I enjoyed Sunday School and attended it regularly until I was old enough to accompany Mother to church, where I served as an usher until I left home for graduate study.

*Musical.* Sometime during my eighth year, my brothers and I were subjected to piano lessons. I demurred, but to no avail. Perhaps because of my mechanical ability, I rapidly learned to read and to play music, and soon I was playing in my teacher's recitals. Though I preferred popular music, I was forced to play classical, specializing in Liszt and Chopin. At the recitals, I pounded out the pieces my teacher selected for me, while Mother sat entranced, planning, as I discovered later, to make a concert pianist out of me.

Mother played the guitar. Her instrument stood in the corner of the music room and once in a while she would play it for us and sing the old-time songs. Once, in an unguarded moment, I expressed the wish that I could play it and found that she had engaged a teacher for me. I quickly learned the chords of the various keys and to read and play music written for the guitar, but I could not play any compositions, on piano or guitar, without the music before me, unless I had practiced the piece and had learned to play it "by heart." I simply lacked an ear for music. My piano teacher recognized this and told Mother that I had progressed with her as far as I possibly could. Thus, after six long years, my musical training was ended. I have ever since, however, been grateful to Mother for her persistence for I did acquire an appreciation for and a knowledge of music that I otherwise would have lacked.

*Theatrical.* Shortly before the conclusion of my musical training I was offered a position as an usher at the local opera house. As it was the only theater in the community and was well attended by the people of the two towns, Champaign and Urbana, and by the students of the University, the best of the Chicago plays and operas came to it. The position carried no salary, only the privilege of seeing the productions. It was with trepidation that I asked Mother whether I could accept. To my delight, she gave her consent because she agreed it would be a cultural experience—a point I had emphasized in making my request. I saw several hundred productions— good, bad, and indifferent—during my years of service. I never, however, became stage struck; at no time did I become attracted to a career in the theater.

## GOALS

While Mother was planning a musical career for me, I was planning careers of my own. Indeed, throughout my life, as far back as I can recall, I had a goal in mind.

*Fireman.* My first ambition was to be a fireman. We lived close to the fire-station. Whenever the fire-bell rang, signaling the district of the fire, my playmates and I ran or rode our bicycles to it. What an exciting life the fireman had. Dad, moreover, had served as a volunteer fireman when young. What he had been, I also wished to be.

*Policeman.* I did not go to many fires before I noticed there was always a man in a blue coat, a roundish helmet, with a club in his belt, who ordered everybody around, keeping the best place from which to view the fire for himself. When I learned that he was a policeman and that he could arrest and put people in jail, I decided not to settle for less; I would become a policeman.

*Lawyer.* One day I overheard my father address a man as "squire." As that title was new to me, I asked, "What's a squire?" To his reply, "a lawyer," I again asked "What's a lawyer?" To end my questions, he said, "A man who gets a dollar every time he opens his mouth to speak a word." Upon hearing that, I immediately decided to be a lawyer, and from that moment until I was well along in graduate school, my goal was the law.

## EARLY MANHOOD

### HIGH SCHOOL

I could do nothing in grammar school toward shaping my career for law and only a little in high school, but what could be done was done. I registered in high school for the academic course.

*Academic.* During the first semester of my freshman year, after dropping my musical training, I found free time on my hands and my Epimetheusian characteristics were again coming to the front. To submerge them, I elected an additional course every semester and was graduated with enough additional units to secure fifteen credit-hours at the University of Illinois—a dividend that I had not anticipated.

I enjoyed and did well in mathematics (algebra and all the geometries—

plane, solid, spherical, and analytical), in science (chemistry, physics, and physiology), geography, history (American, English, Greek and Roman, Medieval, and modern), drawing (freehand and mechanical), and manual training—the meaty subjects, those in which one could set his teeth; and relatively poorly in English, German, Latin, poetry, public speaking, composition, and rhetoric—the less factual literary subjects, but the very ones in which a lawyer should excel. To supplement these courses, I joined the debating and literary societies and competed in every oratorical and declamatory contest for which I was eligible. I was determined to overcome my inherent shyness and stage fright.

During the spring of my senior year, I was chosen for the lead in the class play and elected as one of the commencement orators; more than should have been given to any one boy. The play passed pleasantly; it was fun and I learned why some people choose a theatrical career, but I was wedded to the law! During the excitement of the commencement exercises the following evening, I forgot to bring a copy of the oration I had written and I did not think of it until it was too late to return home for it. I was consequently without a prompter in the wings, and I could not recall a single word of my speech, only the lines of the play of the previous evening. I sat in agony until my turn to speak came and I was introduced. Not knowing what else to do, I went forward. When I placed my hand on the podium in the nonchalant manner in which I had been coached, the first and succeeding words came to mind, and I sailed through my speech without an error or hesitation; the best delivery I had ever made. It was not until years later, after I had studied psychology, that I found an explanation for this "miracle."

*Athletics.* Champaign High School, when I entered it, fielded teams in three sports: football, baseball, and track-and-field. Basketball was introduced in my senior year. I competed for and won positions on all of them; I played tackle and fullback in football; catcher in baseball; threw the hammer and put the shot in track-and-field; and played guard in basketball. Football was my favorite sport despite the fact that my right collarbone was broken in my sophomore year, and I received a brain concussion in my senior year. Since I wrote with my right hand, I thought that I was doubly unfortunate in this injury because I had, in order to keep up with my classes and avoid the academic loss of the semester, to learn to write with my left hand. I practiced assiduously and soon was handing in my assignments on time and going to the blackboard in my turn. I did not stop with writing; I learned to do all the unimanual activities with my left hand, and by the time I had regained the use of my right arm and hand, I was ambidextrous. Before the accident, however, I was definitely of the RRL type, the mixed type, of handedness (Downey, 1927, p. 319; Titchener, 1899, pp. 474 ff.) in which the bimanual activities (batting, chopping, shoveling, sweeping) are done lefthandedly. That I was of the mixed type may be the reason I became ambidextrous so easily. I am still able, after more than fifty years, to write with either hand. My writing with the right hand, a degenerated Spencerian, is much more rapid but less legible than with my left hand—a rounded vertical.

Both injuries were received during practice; I was never injured during a game, nor after high school.

Every summer, during my childhood and young manhood, after returning from a vacation spent visiting distant relatives or at a northern lake, I hunted up the hardest job I could find so that I would be in good physical shape for football. One summer I worked with a ditching gang extending sewers into the new additions being laid out at the edge of town; the next two I worked on a cement gang laying sidewalks; and then with a dredging gang. The work on all of these jobs was done by hand. Ditch-digging machines and cement mixers were not even dreamed of in those days. The working hours in all of them were from 7 to 12 A.M., and 1 to 6 P.M., and the pay was 25 cents per hour. By the time school opened and football practice got under way, I was in excellent physical shape.

*Checkers, Chess, and "Go."* My father's chief diversion during my childhood was checkers, which he played every Sunday evening with a friend. Because Dad played checkers, I wished to play and was given permission to watch the game when played at our house, if I sat quietly by and did not disturb them. I complied, but after a session of silent and attentive observation, I asked to be taught the game. To my delight, they agreed.

They were good teachers, and I was soon defeating them. Instead of being resentful at losing to a lad, they were proud of the player they had developed and matched me with the best players in town, in the county, and, when I reached high school, with the former champion of Central Illinois, an elderly man who had given up tournament play. In the twenty-game match with him, we drew seventeen, he won one, and I won two. He was the best player I had ever met.

During my sophomore year at the University, I participated in the organization of The University Chess and Checker Club, which annually sponsored tournaments in those games. I entered the checker tournament in my sophomore and junior years and won the championship both times. In my senior year, I took up chess, that is, I learned how the different pieces were moved, and I also learned the Japanese game of "Go." I was introduced to "Go" by my cousin, a librarian at the Chicago Public Library, who had himself learned of it by reading a German book on the game which had been received by the library. We had previously played checkers, but when I reached the point in my play when I defeated him regularly, he shifted to "Go," a game with which I was unfamiliar. He gave me a "Go"-board, and a set of the "stones" and taught me the rules and a bit of the strategy of play. After my introduction to chess and "Go," I gave up checkers. There simply was not enough time to play all of them—indeed, there was not enough time to play any of them—but nevertheless, I made time. They all are fine games, but, in my opinion, "Go" stands to chess as chess does to checkers—and as

checkers stands to "mill," a game my grandmother taught me during childhood.

*Golf.* I began playing golf during middle childhood at about nine years
of age, when the boys of the neighborhood were urged to serve as caddies
at the nine-hole course that had just been opened in the city. As caddies were
permitted to play golf on the course when not otherwise engaged, several of
the larger boys and I did more playing than caddying. By the time I was
sixteen years old, I was playing near-par golf and was disappointed when I
did not break forty; once I made thirty-three. This group practically lived on
the links, going out early in the morning and staying until late afternoon. I
discovered, as other claims on my time arose, that I had to play daily or
become a "dub." Since I could not play daily and my self-imposed standards
would not permit me to be a "dub," I abruptly quit the game, intending to
return to it when time permitted, which it has not as yet done.

## University of Illinois

Before I registered at the University, my father made it quite clear to me
that I was not to play football or to join a fraternity until I had demonstrated that I could do university work. Though I wished to do both, there
was too much at stake, hence I agreed.

*Academic.* I registered as long planned for the law course in the College
of Arts and Sciences. The fifteen advanced credits I had received from high
school freed me from the necessity of taking mathematics and science—the
courses I liked most and in which I did best. My work was therefore concentrated in fields in which I was less interested and did not do as well. Since
they were required in the pre-law course, I had to take them.

Near the end of the first semester, to aid me in my courses, I joined
the Adelphic Literary Society, an organization that was founded at the opening of the University. There were, at the time of my joining, six literary
societies: three for men and three for women. All held weekly meetings and
the programs of all of them were much the same. The Adelphic's meetings
were opened by music, vocal or instrumental, and followed by orations,
essays, declamations, book reviews, and a debate of a popular subject that
was decided by the vote of the audience. The meetings were closed by a
"critic," usually a faculty member of the society, who reviewed the evening's
events and criticized them kindly. The societies were thus extra-curricular
laboratories for the Departments of Rhetoric, English, and Public Speaking.
The members learned to express themselves on their feet. In addition to the
weekly programs, the society, in conjunction with one or another of the
women's societies, produced a play every year. To overcome my natural shyness, I attended the meetings regularly and accepted any and every assignment. I consequently participated in many programs, every annual play,
the Intra- and Inter-Society declamation contests, and competed every year

for the University Debating Teams. I never, however, succeeded in making a University Debating Team. My failure was due chiefly to my inability to shift loyalties. After I had studied a question and had evaluated the arguments pro and con and had come to a conclusion that I thought was right, I could not, with conviction, argue for the other side. A debater, as I learned, must be able to do that; indeed, he frequently does not know which side he is to represent until shortly before he is to speak. Debating is not a search for truth, like science, but is a game, like chess or checkers, in which the more skillful manipulators of the arguments win. I simply was not cut out to be a debater—nor, perhaps, to be a lawyer. Could I, with conviction, defend a client I knew to be guilty?

After I had passed the first semester's work, I was permitted to join a fraternity, Delta Upsilon. During the second semester, one of the upper classmen of that fraternity advised me regarding the selection of courses for my sophomore year. He strongly recommended elementary psychology, which I had avoided because I identified it with phrenology. As he was a pre-law student, I accepted his recommendation and registered for the course with John Wallace Baird. The class was large. To avoid the time-consuming task of calling the roll, he seated the class alphabetically and thereafter marked the absentees, which were few, by noting the numbers on the vacant seats. He stood during his lecture, spoke extemporaneously, richly demonstrated his lectures, and invited questions, which I, sitting in the front row, frequently asked. When he came to color blindness, he sought to demonstrate the Holmgren test. He called for a volunteer; none offered and without making a second appeal he called upon me to take it. He demonstrated the method with me and, to his delight, found that I was color-blind. I then knew why I wished white instead of red flags on the golf course; why I could not see cherries on a tree from a distance; and I also learned later why I could not taste at the center of my tongue—it was not because I had pulled the skin from it during childhood, but because there were no end organs there. Baird used Tichener's *An Outline of Psychology* (1899) as his textbook, which was so simply, clearly, and interestingly written that it invited its own study. The course was the most interesting I had ever taken; it was Science.

Lacking the prerequisites to take Baird's courses during the second semester, I elected Frederick Kuhlmann's course in abnormal psychology. Though Kuhlmann used a heavily written book as a text, M. W. Barr's *Mental Defectives* (1910), and sat at his desk and lectured from notes, as did most of my teachers, I found the course very interesting. He took the class to institutions for the feebleminded and insane where inmates, illustrating the various types he had discussed in class, were brought before us. The course opened up aspects of human life of which I previously knew nothing.

As I had discovered in high school, I did best in my academic subjects when I submerged my Epimetheusian characteristics by extra work. I therefore, after my freshman year, elected an extra course every semester which fell outside the pre-law curriculum. Among those elected were mechanical and freehand drawing, clay modeling and sculpture, and astronomy.

During my sophomore year, I conceived the idea of taking notes in class in shorthand and transcribing them with a typewriter and of handing in typewritten reports. Thus, instead of hunting for the hardest work I could find the following summer to prepare myself for football, which I was contemplating playing again in the fall, I attended Champaign Business College and learned shorthand and typing. I thought that notes in shorthand would be better than those in longhand and that their transcription would be all that would be required in the way of studying, and also that typewritten reports would receive higher grades than those in longhand. I was wrong about the first two assumptions—my notes in shorthand were not better than my handwritten ones, and their transcription did not relieve me from further study. My third assumption was, however, correct; typewritten reports, rarely submitted by students in those days, did receive higher grades than longhand.

In my junior year, I elected Baird's two-semester course in experimental laboratory. Titchener's *Student's Manual of Qualitative Experiments* (1902) was used as a text and worked through during the course of the year. Baird lectured upon the experiments as we took them up, and he circulated among the class, assisting the laboratory-pairs in their work. The courses were the most interesting I had ever taken, even more interesting than elementary psychology. Every experiment was an adventure into a new world of experience. They were not work; they were fun. I did, however, work upon my reports. Because of my training in the art department, I was able to illustrate my reports richly with drawings of the apparatus, and my results by charts, diagrams, and graphs. My grade on the first semester reports, which were typewritten after I received a typewriter at Christmas, was "99," with the notation "Except for misspellings, your grade would have been a possible." To correct my spelling, my weakest subject in grammar school, I looked up every word about which I had any doubt and handed in reports during the second semester without misspellings. At the end of the semester, Baird gave me a "possible." He asked me for my reports, had them bound, and deposited them in the laboratory as an example for later students to emulate.

In addition to Baird's experimental course, I took social psychology and child psychology under S. S. Colvin, the head of the department; comparative psychology under Kuhlmann; the seminary conducted by the departmental staff; and the courses in philosophy that were germane to psychology (ancient and medieval philosophy) under D. H. Bode. Colvin, like Kuhlmann, remained seated during his lectures and was tied to his notes. I did not enjoy his courses as much as I did the others, since they were more theoretical, speculative, and less factual. Bode, like Baird, stood while he lectured and spoke extemporaneously. His courses were interesting, easy to follow and understand.

In March of my junior year (1909), Titchener visited the University and gave his *Lectures on the Experimental Psychology of the Thought-Processes* (1909)—his answer to the work on "imageless thought" done by Külpe and his students at the University of Würzburg. Though I did not know who Külpe was, nor had I heard of the Würzburg school against which Titchener inveighed, I attended every one of his lectures and was entranced by them. Baird, a former student of Titchener, took him through the laboratory, introduced him to the students assembled there to meet him, and showed him my laboratory reports as a sample of the work done in it. After looking through my reports, Titchener complimented me upon them and suggested that I come to Cornell for a doctorate in psychology. His mention of a "doctorate in psychology at Cornell" was a wedge between my long-sustained desire for the law and my recently acquired interest in psychology.

The courses in experimental psychology were popular and the capacity of the laboratory was taxed. Baird taught the courses alone until the end of my junior year, when he was granted a student assistant, effective the following term. He offered the position to me, and I gladly accepted. The appointment greatly increased my indecision about my life's work. Until then I had been studying psychology for the aid it would give me in law, but now I was considering turning to psychology and studying it for its own sake. The decision was not urgent as I had another year in which to consider it.

Because of the advanced credits I received from high school and the extra courses I had carried every semester following my freshman year, I needed only six credits for graduation at the end of my junior year. I could have taken them during the following summer school and have received my degree in August. I did not choose to do that, however, for several compelling reasons: I did not wish to be graduated before my class; I did not wish to miss the trip that my parents were planning to the West Coast and the visit with my older brother, who was practicing medicine in Seattle where the Alaska, Yukon, Pacific Exposition was being held that summer; and I did not wish to make myself ineligible for athletics during the coming year, which a degree would do.

One evening during the winter of my junior year, while sitting in the lounge in front of the grate in my fraternity, I heard one of the members tell of his trip to Europe the previous summer on a "cattleboat." His tale was so interesting and the trip was so inexpensive, I decided to take a similar one during the summer following my graduation. I immediately told my father about it and asked his permission to take it. He refused, but all the friends with whom I discussed it were interested and enthusiastic and many more agreed to go than I thought could be accommodated. I did not, however, refuse or discourage anyone, thinking future events would cause my father to change his mind. I continued to discuss the trip with my father and with others in his presence. Since the trip was so far in the future, over a year, I thought he would be reconciled to it by the time I planned to go. Sure enough, he was. When I overheard him telling a visitor that I was going to work my way to Europe the following summer on a cattleboat, I knew the trip was assured.

In my senior year, in addition to the assistantship under Baird and the required courses in pre-law, I elected the seminary in psychology, a course with Kuhlmann in mental and physical tests, one with Bode on Kant, and clay modeling (sculpture) in the Department of Fine Arts. My work as an assistant was pleasant and agreeable. It consisted chiefly in removing apparatus from the shelves before the students arrived, in replacing it after they had left, and in supervising their work while in the laboratory.

During the first semester, I sought Baird's advice about making psychology my vocation. He opened the conference by saying that he never gave advice, that he did not wish to bear the responsibility of another person's decision, but that he would gladly discuss my problem with me. He said further that I had done well thus far, that I might become a good psychologist, but that "psychology was a long and rocky road and that the only person who should enter it was one who could be happy in traveling no other." I was not discouraged in my talk with him; indeed, I admired him more than ever for his point of view and adopted it as my own. I have never since given advice. I gladly talk over the pros and cons of a problem that a person brings to me, but the decision must be his own. The differences among people in regard to giving advice are great. Some, like Baird, after discussing the advisee's problem with him, cast it back into his lap in the hope and expectation that he will be able to resolve the problem himself. Many others, like my instructor in clay modeling, a course I greatly enjoyed and in which I did well, give advice freely. Upon the basis of my work in a single course, he advised and urged me to become a sculptor. He said I had talent and predicted a future for me in that art. I was not moved in the slightest by him, as I was at that time deeply engaged in the struggle between psychology and law, with psychology a bit in the ascendancy. I have often pondered, however, what I would have become and where I would now be, had I followed his advice; the mystery of "what might have been."

In January, 1910, at the end of the first semester of my senior year, Baird left Illinois for the chair in experimental psychology at Clark University, vacated by Edmund C. Sanford's elevation to the presidency of Clark College. Baird was replaced at Illinois by Arthur Sutherland, who had obtained his doctorate the previous spring (June, 1909) at the University of Chicago. He was not an experimentalist, but he wisely did not alter the routine of the experimental course. He gave the weekly lectures but placed me in charge of the laboratory, as he was not familiar with the experiments that were scheduled.

Though I had more than enough credits for my degree at the end of the first semester, I avoided January graduation because I still wished to retain my eligibility for spring athletics. I entered the graduate school and started research on an M.A. thesis under Kuhlmann on "The Relation of Memory Error to Time Interval" (Dallenbach, 1913), an aspect of the *Aussage* problem, the subject considered in the seminary the previous semester. To complete my schedule that semester, I elected the departmental seminary and another course in philosophy under Bode. I was graduated in June with 150 credit hours.

After Baird left, my desire for psychology was dimmed. A decision—law or psychology—had to be made that spring, and law was again in the ascendancy. Shortly before the end of that semester, I saw a circular upon the departmental bulletin board announcing a fellowship in psychology for the following year at the University of Pittsburgh. Here was a way out of my dilemma. I applied for it and asked Baird to write in my behalf. If I received it, I would go forward to an M.A. degree in psychology and postpone the decision between law and psychology for another year; if I did not, I would go to Harvard the following fall for a degree in law. I would let events, for the time being at least, decide my problem for me. This decision, if it may be regarded as one, was a great relief.

*Athletics.* In keeping with the letter of the promise that my father extracted from me when I entered the University, I did not play football that first fall. Nothing, however, was said about coaching, hence I assisted the coach of the Champaign High School team. I did this because new rules regarding the forward pass had just been adopted, and I thought, if I were ever to play football again, I should keep abreast of the new developments. After the football season was over, I went out for the freshman swimming and the track-and-field teams. I made the freshman water polo team, but found little pleasure in the game, which was very different from the one played now. It was chiefly a wrestling match in water; fighting for the possession of a half-inflated rubber ball and attempting to carry it forward and to touch the goal at the ends of the pool. I had, in consequence of playing it, a head cold all winter. I stuck to the game for the season, but never again went out for it, although urged by the coach and players to do so. It was not "fun." I made the freshman track-and-field team in the hammer and shot and was elected its student manager, an "errand-boy" for the coach.

In my sophomore and succeeding years, I ventured, in addition to track-and-field, to go out secretly for football. I played guard with the sophomore team that won the interclass championship and with the varsity teams in my junior and senior years. From my freshman to senior years, after the close of the football season, I wrestled, boxed, and lifted weights until the opening of the outdoor season for track. I did not improve much in track; I was mediocre throughout the years, but still good enough to make the squad and now and then to win a third place. I was good enough in wrestling, however, to represent my class at the interclass matches. Wrestling was not at that time an intercollegiate sport, but intra- and interclass championships, at the different weights, were annually held. In my senior year, I again won the right to represent my class in the heavyweight division and finally won the University championship.

It was with regret and a tinge of sadness that I played the last game of football in my senior year. I thought my football days were over. I was greatly pleased and highly complimented, therefore, when the director of athletics and the head and line coaches individually summoned me to their offices after the season and informed me that I had another year of eligibility and asked and urged me to delay my graduation a year, since a degree would make me ineligible. My teammates and many of my friends and acquaintances urged me to do it, but I finally decided in the negative because I could not permit my class to be graduated without me.

## European Trip on the Cattleboat

As the time for the trip to Europe on the cattleship neared, my classmates, who once were enthusiastic for the trip and had promised to go, dropped out one by one until only one was left. Having talked so much about the trip and knowing nothing about its hardships, I would have taken it even if it meant going alone. Fortunately, that was saved me. My companion and I left the afternoon of commencement for Montreal to take ship to London. My father accompanied us to the railroad station, and before the train pulled out he gave me an envelope containing a liberal amount of money. I had not asked him for half, as I had said from the first mention of the trip that I would pay for it out of my own savings. Though I had not as yet heard from Pittsburgh regarding my application for the fellowship in psychology, I left all worry behind.

As soon as we arrived in Montreal, we hunted at the docks for the employment agency whose business it was to supply laborers for ships leaving for Europe. To our surprise and great pleasure, we found two of our classmates there, the survivors of a group who had separately planned a cattleboat trip to Europe. We joined forces, took ship that afternoon, and steamed away early the next morning for London.

The work was hard, and it had to be done whether one was seasick or not (which I was most of the trip), and our food was as bad as we were warned it would be. Both were tolerable with companions in misery, but I would not choose to make the trip alone. We docked at London, where we stayed a week during which we visited Hampton Court to see its famous maze, facsimiles of which Kuhlmann used in one of his courses in psychology. Then, starting in Holland, we spent the remainder of the summer on the continent, arriving back at Amsterdam the afternoon before our ship was to leave for home.

## University of Pittsburgh

When I arrived home, I learned that I had been awarded the fellowship in psychology. My hope for another year of grace before coming to a decision regarding my life's work had been vouchsafed me.

*Academic.* My fellowship was one of six that had been granted in as many different departments to mark the establishment of the graduate school at Pittsburgh. Though late in receiving the notification of my appointment, I was at Pittsburgh in time to attend a conference of the fellows, called by the dean of the graduate school, at which we met each other and were welcomed to the University. With two of the fellows, Karl S. Lashley, in biology, and Roy H. Uhlinger, in chemistry, I formed close and lasting friendships.

Uhlinger, reporting early, had found for himself a rooming house within a short walking distance from the University. As there was still a vacancy there, he took me, after the dean's brief meeting, to see it. I signed up for it immediately and then returned to the University for a conference with J. H. White, professor and sole member of the Department of Psychology. White had recently taken his doctorate at Clark University under G. Stanley Hall. Though not himself an experimental psychologist, he had acquired Hall's interest in and respect for the laboratory and had, during the previous spring, announced and ordered apparatus for the new course.

At the conference with White, my duties were defined and my course of study was planned. My principal duty was to organize and teach the laboratory. The apparatus, Stoelting Company's duplication of that used in Titchener's manual, was still packed in the boxes in the room reserved for the laboratory. I was familiar with that apparatus and soon had the boxes unpacked and the various pieces arranged upon the shelves provided for them. I followed Baird's organization of the course and his method of teaching; I knew no other.

My course of study was a perplexing problem. As I had taken every course offered in psychology at Illinois, there was none at Pittsburgh I had not taken. Since the die committing me to a career in psychology now seemed to have been cast, I thought I should learn more about the human organism and therefore proposed courses in biology and physiology. White highly approved, but suggested, since those courses in the College of Arts and Sciences were chiefly concerned with animals and only incidentally with man, that I take them in the Medical College. His point was well taken, and so it was decided.

We then turned to the discussion of a topic for my M.A. thesis. He asked me for suggestions. I told him of the *Aussage* problem I had started during the past semester at Illinois under Kuhlmann's direction and suggested, since only half the work planned had been completed, that it be continued (1913). After explaining the specific problem undertaken and describing the results obtained and the work still to be done, I readily gained his assent. Work on my thesis was therefore well underway.

The courses I wished to take in the medical school—neurology, physiology, and embryology—were given in the sophomore year of medicine. For a student to elect sophomore courses before completing the prerequisites in the freshman year was unprecedented; my registration was refused. I reported this to White, he to the dean of the graduate school, and he to the president of the University and the dean of the medical school. Because I was not a medical student, but a fellow in the graduate school, the problem was resolved in my favor, and I was permitted to take such courses as I desired.

All of the fellows, as I learned later, had courses or laboratories to teach. Lashley taught the laboratory in biology that I would have taken with him had I not been granted the privilege of registering in the medical school. He wished to take the laboratory in psychology with me. As elementary psychology was a prerequisite, and he did not have time to satisfy it, he requested that it be waived. My experience in registering in the medical school had bearing upon his request, and White immediately granted it. Lashley's first course in psychology was therefore a qualitative laboratory. He skillfully performed the experiments and was one of the best introspectors in the class. In addition to this association, we played chess as frequently as time permitted, though neither of us knew little more about the game than how the different pieces were moved.

My work went well throughout the year, which passed quickly and busily. I completed the experimental work on my thesis by the end of the first semester and presented the manuscript to White early in May. It was lengthy and richly illustrated with charts, figures, tables, and diagrams, which my undergraduate courses in drawing made possible. White was pleased with it, and I received my M.A. degree that June (1911).

During the year, I became fascinated by the courses in the medical school. They were scientific. Except for Baird's courses in psychology, I had studied nothing so interesting since chemistry, physics, and physiology in high school—subjects I had avoided in college because of my dedication to a career in law. Medicine, during the course of the year at Pittsburgh, had replaced law; now my mental struggle was between medicine and psychology. After weeks of worry and mental conflict, I again decided to permit events to decide.

Recalling the invitation that Titchener had given me at Illinois, I applied to Cornell and only to Cornell, putting all my eggs in one basket, for the Sage Fellowship in Psychology. If I received it, I would go forward to a doctorate in psychology; if I did not, I would enter the medical school at Pittsburgh. I asked Baird and White to write Titchener in my behalf and settled back, resolved to be content with whatever came to pass.

I might have applied to Clark for a fellowship with more hope of success and have worked under Baird, who was my inspiration and ideal, but I did not. Five of his students at Illinois followed him to Clark for their doctorates; that I, the student he had chosen for his assistant, did not was not due to my lack of admiration of or respect for him. Quite to the contrary, my application was to Cornell and Cornell alone, because of my admiration for him. He had studied and had taken his doctorate under Titchener. I wished to do as he had done; nothing less would satisfy me. My feeling for Baird is best shown by the fact that my first son, John Wallace, was named after him—a name to which my wife readily agreed because they were also the first names of my father and of hers.

Titchener, when acknowledging receipt of my application, invited me to Cornell for an interview during the coming Easter vacation. I made the trip and was received graciously in his home. The interview extended over an afternoon. He asked about my work at Pittsburgh and approved highly of my studies in the medical school, which encouraged me. But when he said, "Oh, a study in applied psychology" after I had described my master's thesis— the disparaging tone more than the words, discouraged me. I did not know that I had been working in applied psychology; indeed, I did not know at that time the difference between applied and other kinds of psychology.

I broke the lull which followed that remark by asking him in which theory of vision he believed. He replied: "Believe? Believe! Why, I don't believe in any." Then followed a discourse upon theory and its place in experiment which ended with the admonition to "carry your theories lightly" (Dallenbach, 1953). That was strange advice to me, since throughout my training thus far theory had played an important role. We had, even in Baird's and Bode's courses, discussed and ardently defended the theories of our choice. As the fellowship for which I was applying was not mentioned during the interview, I returned to Pittsburgh that evening with small hope that my application would be seriously considered. My thesis was in applied psychology; I had displayed my ignorance regarding the place of theory in science. Soon after I returned to Pittsburgh, however, I was notified that I had been awarded the Sage Fellowship. The die had again been cast in favor of psychology.

*Athletics.* For many years, fall meant football to me. The Pittsburgh papers were full of news of the University's team. Though practice was open to the public, I did not go out to see it because I was too busy getting registered, my laboratory in order, and my room arranged. Finally, a few days before the first game, I went to the practice field. I was struck by the size and maturity of the players. While watching practice, the urge for the game returned in full force, and I introduced myself to the coach, told him of my football experience, and offered my services for free as an assistant coach. Instead of accepting my offer at once, as I hoped he would, he questioned me, and then astonished me by asking me whether I would be interested in playing on the team. It seemed that my degree, which made me ineligible for further play at Illinois, made me a free agent and eligible at Pittsburgh. I was interested and played right guard on the team which played nine games, won them all, scoring 282 points to our opponents' 0; under present methods of scoring, about 360–0. During the following spring, I threw the hammer on the track-and-field team.

As soon as I "made" the football team, the fraternities, both social and medical, rushed me. Since I was a member of a social fraternity, I could not join another, but as a member of the sophomore class in the medical school, I could and did join a medical fraternity, Nu Sigma Nu.

While I was playing football, Uhlinger, my roommate, enlisted in the student company of the Pennsylvania National Guard. Its drill hall bordered the University and its officers were members of the Pittsburgh faculty. Nothing would satisfy him until I too enlisted, which I did when I learned that rifles and ammunition were furnished to those who wished to improve their marksmanship. By practicing assiduously, I rapidly passed through the grades of marksman, sharpshooter, to expert rifleman.

## CORNELL UNIVERSITY (1911–1912)

To get a good start upon my work at Cornell, I arrived in Ithaca a week early. After locating a rooming house and a boarding club close to the campus, I reported to Professor Titchener. He gave me an appointment for the next afternoon. With time on my hands, I visited the Cornell chapter of my fraternity, where I met the captain of the Cornell football team. Our conversation quite naturally turned to football and he hoped, and raised in me the hope, that I might be allowed to play for Cornell.

At my conference with Professor Titchener the next afternoon, I asked him about my playing football. To my surprise and delight, he approved. He had been an athlete in his student days, being on the tennis and fencing teams at Oxford, and coaching the fencing team at Cornell for several years after joining that faculty. He had, therefore, an athlete's point of view. After sanctioning my play of football, which the registrar, a stickler for rules, later vetoed, Titchener explained briefly the Cornell system of graduate study and then turned to the research that he wished me to undertake for my doctoral dissertation.

*System of Graduate Study.* The Cornell system of graduate study, a transplant from Germany, was unlike any educational system I had ever encountered. From the first grade through my graduate year at Pittsburgh, I was assigned work and there was a teacher standing over me to see that I did it and to grade my performance. This was not the case at Cornell; no graduate courses were offered, none of the undergraduate courses were required. The graduate student was allowed perfect freedom to prepare himself for his final oral examination in any way he wished; by studying in the library, by experimenting in the laboratory, or by attending undergraduate courses of his choice. Many students were unable to survive this degree of freedom; they required the compulsion of a teacher. Those who did survive, who learned to depend upon their own initiative, were the productive scholars of the future.

In addition to the major subject, every doctoral student was required to elect two minors. As some of the professors directing "minors" tried to get "major" work from their minors, many students "shopped around" among the different departments and elected minors entailing the least work. Some curious combinations of major and minors resulted from this procedure. Though Titchener advised me to "shop around," I did not. I knew precisely the minors I wished to elect. My first, under Professor Benjamin F. Kingsbury, was in histology and embryology in the medical school (the first two years of which were then given in Ithaca); it was work that would later count toward an M.D. degree, my urge for which still lingered. My second, under Professor G. M. Whipple, an engaging man and teacher, was in educational psychology, a popular and rapidly growing field. I would have been wiser had I followed Titchener's advice, or at least have had their course requirements stipulated in writing, because, finding a willing worker, both of these men added research to their already heavy requirements. I was eventually carrying what amounted to three majors.

As I did not then know enough to direct my study in the library and laboratory, I elected undergraduate courses in which the instructors organized the work. Since a graduate student was merely a "visitor" in an undergraduate course, he was not required to take the examinations given in it; I did, however, to mark my progress. The doctorate depended solely upon the candidate's dissertation and his performance in his final oral examination.

Among the outstanding undergraduate courses I attended was Professor Madison Bentley's in systematic psychology. Bentley's course made me aware, for the first time, of the division of psychology into schools. I was distressed to learn that psychology was a Hydra-headed subject, but glad to discover that Titchener was the leader of the school with which I had unknowingly affiliated myself during my work with Baird. I also learned in this course the significance of the lectures on "imageless thought" that I had heard Titchener give at Illinois. In psychophysics I was, as I recall, the only student; and Boring and I worked through the experiments in Titchener's *Student's Quantitative Manual* (1905, Part I) and read the *Instructor's Manual* (1905, Part II) in conjunction with them. Working together in this course, we established a life-long friendship.

*Dissertation.* After Titchener's appointment in 1909 to a professorship in the graduate school, he did not go to the University except on Monday evenings of the second semester when he met his seminary. He conducted his work from his study at home. Students wishing to see him—he directed the work of all the doctoral students—had to make appointments long in advance. Because he was particularly interested in the dissertation he had assigned me, "The Measurement of Attention," he saw me promptly whenever I requested a conference. His interest in my work derived from his postulation that clearness (vividness, attensity) was an intensive attribute of sensation and, as such, was the elementary basis of attention (Titchener, 1910, p. 53; 1913, pp. 191–317), the doctrine he developed in his *Lectures on the Elementary Psychology of Feeling and Attention* (1908).

In his review of the literature on attention, Titchener found that the writers on the topic described the processes attended to as being clearer and more vivid, outstanding, insistent, impressive, and *eindringlich,* than those attended from. He had therefore many terms from which to choose, and he unfortunately chose "clearness." Unfortunately, because his use of that term, even when qualified by "sensory" or "attributive," was confused with "cognitive" clearness, *i.e.* clearness to the understanding. If he had used "vividness" at the outset, much confusion would have been avoided, since "vividness" is an experiental, not a cognitive, term. During the course of my study at Cornell, I had the temerity to ask him why he had selected "clearness." He readily admitted that his choice had been unwise and told me that it had been made purely on the basis of empathy (*Einfühling*) (Titchener, 1909, p. 21); that the word "clearness" was round and forward-flowing, whereas "vividness" was angular and prickly. He dropped "clearness" for "vividness" in his *A Beginner's Psychology* (1915, p. 66) and later coined the term "attensity" for this dimension of experience (Titchener, 1924).

Upon the assumption that the phenomenon measured is like in kind to the units measuring it (*e.g.* if measurable in feet or meters, it is like those units a spatial phenomenon; if in seconds, a temporal phenomenon), Titchener assigned L. R. Geissler the problem of measuring attention in terms of attributive clearness (Geissler, 1909). Working in the field of vision, Geissler demonstrated that attention could be measured in terms of attributive clearness. Since, however, his experiments were limited to the field of vision, which itself possesses an anatomical focus and margin and is subject to sensory as well as attentional adaptation, Geissler obtained no conclusive results. His method of measuring attention had to be tested by experiments in audition, touch, and imagery—fields that lack physiological foci and margins. The measurement of attention in the field of audition, which lacks sensory adaptation in addition to a focus and a margin, was assigned to me. My study corroborated Geissler's results. I, too, found that attention could be measured introspectively in terms of attributive clearness. The need to carry the work into the fields of touch and imagery was not, therefore, as great, but the work was planned for touch and completed later with corroborative results (Dallenbach, 1916).

*Chess.* During the fall of my first semester at Cornell, my landlord, a devoted chess player, taught me the game. Due probably to the identical elements in checkers and chess—planning and foreseeing moves—I improved my game rapidly. I was, under his instructions, making moves with a plan in mind, not merely, as in the games with Lashley, because it was my move. Very soon I was defeating my landlord consistently; he was not a strong player. He brought up the subject of blindfold play and we marveled together over that "strange ability." He told me that he had once attempted it and proudly said that he had carried it twenty moves before breaking. He badgered me into playing a game blindfolded, though I thought it ridiculous for me to attempt it and utterly impossible for me to do. All I hoped for was to carry the play farther than he had done. To my great surprise and his chagrin, I carried the game sixty-three moves through a pawn-ending and mated him. I found that blindfold play was not difficult; indeed, I believe that anybody playing a moderately fair game can play it. The difficulty in blindfold play is in overcoming the mental block—something like that involved in the running of the first four-minute mile.

Several months later, at a conference with Titchener, I casually mentioned that I had played a game of chess blindfolded. He was greatly interested and asked many questions about the mental processes involved. I had requested the conference to discuss my dissertation, but it was chiefly devoted that evening to blindfold chess. He urged me to continue the play and to undertake its study. If I would, he would place me on the program of the experimental psychologists the coming spring at Clark University (Dallenbach, 1916, pp. 41 f.). I was puzzled by his interest and request, but was not rash enough to ask the reason. I gladly agreed, and played two blindfolded games simultaneously, then three, intending to increase the number until I broke. Since the mental processes involved in multiple play were very different from those involved in a single game, he told me to devote the present study to the single game and to take up multiple play later. The mental processes involved in my play consisted of visual images, kinesthetic images, sensations, verbal motor and verbal auditory images, concomitant attitudes, and feelings.

I discovered at the spring meetings at which I read my paper the reason for Professor Titchener's interest. He and Thorndike led a symposium on "imageless thought." My analysis of the processes involved in blindfold chess gave no support to the Würzburg School. Awaiting the resumption of my study of multiple play, which I have never found time to do, the paper I read at Clark was withheld from publication until I was invited to contribute it to the *Festschrift* published in Titchener's honor in 1917 (Dallenbach, 1917).

*Meals.* Before the end of the first semester at Cornell, I found myself so involved in work that I had to stay up later and later to accomplish it. Since breakfast was not served at my boarding house after 8:00 A.M., I missed more and more breakfasts. I seemed to get along without them, so I finally decided to omit that meal and to sleep as long as I desired. I have ever since then eaten but two meals a day. After I was married and could breakfast at home at my convenience, I omitted the noon meal, thus saving the noon hour for work, a custom that I have since followed. My weight, which jumped to 210 pounds after I had given up athletics, remained there until I reached old age. By omitting the noon meal, I have gained, over the years, thousands of hours, with no ill effects as far as I am aware.

*Seminary.* Titchener's seminary was held on Monday evenings during the second semester every year. Though held in the graduate laboratory, it was not listed in the University catalogue. It was private, attendance being restricted to those he invited. He gave the paper at the first meeting on the topic to be studied by the seminary that year; dividing it into various sub-topics which he assigned the members. After a discussion of his paper and setting the dates at which the members' papers would be read, he served refreshments, thereafter provided in rotation by the members. The social hour usually ended about midnight.

Titchener demanded a high level of achievement in the papers pre-sented in his seminary. If they did not meet his standard, his criticism was purposely severe so that the quality of the papers following would be raised. The topic of my first seminary at Cornell was "Applied Psychology," and I was assigned a paper on the "Binet Mental Tests." I had but a week in which to prepare it; I did the best I could in that time, but it was not good enough; it drew his severe criticism. As he had anticipated, however, his criticism "bore fruit." Every one of the papers following mine was excellent; many were worthy of publication, and some were published. In my second seminary, which was on "Functional Psychology," I was assigned the task of discovering the source of the systematic use of "function" in psychology. My search car-ried me back to "phrenology," the pseudo-science that delayed my study of psychology. My paper was scheduled for a date near the end of the semester, hence I had several months to work on it. This time it was well received, and Titchener encouraged me to publish it (Dallenbach, 1915).

*Smoking.* During the course of my first seminary at Cornell, Titchener, a chain smoker of cigars, pressed one of his big, black cigars upon me with the facetious remark that "a man could not hope to become a psychologist until after he had learned to smoke." I accepted his dare; it was "my first cigar." I smoked it slowly during the seminary, and it seemingly had no effect upon me. It was, however, a delayed bomb; it began to take effect as I walked to my room after the seminary, and by the time I reached it I was suffering from nicotine poisoning. It was worse than seasickness, and I could not escape it by sleeping. It was seemingly an antidote to sleepiness from which I suffered every evening about midnight, frequently falling asleep at my desk when I should have been studying. Smoking might, as I thought, be the solution of that problem. If I smoked just a little—plainly, a cigar was too much—I might escape the resulting illness and enjoy the induced wakeful-ness. I therefore bought a pipe and a small can of tobacco and tested my theory. It worked; one pipeful sufficed, it induced wakefulness but not ill-ness. Thereafter, whenever I became sleepy, a few puffs on my pipe enabled me to work as late as I wished. One small can of tobacco lasted me for weeks. With the passage of time, I smoked more and more for the pleasure of it, until now, as I fear, I am a chain pipe-smoker. What I need now, in the fall of life, is an antidote to wakefulness.

*Modeling.* During my first year at Cornell, particularly during the fall when the time previously devoted to football was vouchsafed me, I played around with the things I had learned in clay modeling at Illinois. I introduced into experimental psychology plaster of Paris armrests as replacements for the wooden and felt rests then in use. The plaster rests cast especially for every observer were not only more comfortable, but they insured that the tissue would be brought to the same relative position at successive experimental periods. The superiority of the plaster rests was immediately recognized; they were thereafter used at Cornell from whence their usage spread to other laboratories. In addition, I modeled a bas-relief plaque of Titchener, made plaster casts of it for the members of the department, and later, as time permitted, I made life masks of the members of the department, and mounted the heads in a frieze which Titchener hung in his office. Titchener did not wish to be left out and asked me to make a life mask of him, but I did not dare attempt it because of his full beard and bristly moustache. I did, however, make casts of his right hand—one with fingers spread and one with closed fist.

## University of Bonn

The graduate group of students then at Cornell was small, friendly, cooperative, and intensely competitive; what one did, the others wished to do and to do better. When I told them of my cattleboat trip to Europe, their interest was aroused, and they proposed to take a similar trip during the coming summer (1912) and asked me to accompany them. I readily agreed, and we made plans to go to Leipzig to see Wundt and to attend his lectures. As the time for our departure neared, the same thing happened as at Illinois two years before; the number making the trip dwindled until only W. S. Foster, A. S. Edwards, and I were left. Three were sufficient, hence the trip was not abandoned. Agreeing to meet me on a specific date at a designated hotel in Montreal, Foster and Edwards left for their homes. Before I left to keep the date, Titchener gave me a number of his cards with introductions written upon them so that I would be received by Wundt and other psychologists I chanced to meet in Europe.

On my way to Montreal, I stopped at Oswego, Edwards' home town, and learned that he could not take the trip because of severe illness in his family. I therefore went on alone to keep the date with Foster. I registered at the hotel at which I was to meet him and then engaged passage for the two of us on a cattleboat that was leaving the next afternoon. As Foster had not appeared by the next morning, I cancelled the passage and waited for him to show. After waiting another day, I booked passage on a White-Star liner to Liverpool, England. Knowing the hardships involved in working one's passage on a cattleboat, I simply did not have the courage to face them alone.

The passage to Liverpool was enjoyable, as was the trip across England, during which I stopped at Stratford-on-Avon to see the Shakespeare country and at Oxford to see the various colleges, lingering the longest at Brasenose, Titchener's college. There I met the porter of the college, who became very friendly when I gave him one of Titchener's cards and told him that I was one of Titchener's students. He remembered Titchener well and took me to see the room Titchener occupied while in the college. He also told me of some of Titchener's escapades while there. In his youth, Titchener was far from being the sedate, dignified man that he became as an adult in America.

From Oxford I went to London, saw some of the places I had missed during my first visit, and then on to Cologne to call upon the American Consul, Hirum Dunlap, a close and old friend of my parents. When Mr. Dunlap learned the purpose of my trip, to meet Wundt and to attend his lectures, he telephoned Leipzig and learned that Wundt was at his summer home in Heidelberg and would not receive callers. What to do was now a perplexing question. Mr. Dunlap suggested that I spend the summer at the University of Bonn, which was a short distance from Cologne. If I did, Mrs. Dunlap added, I should plan to have dinner with them every Sunday. I still hesitated because I knew nothing of that University, not even the professor of psychology there. When Mr. Dunlap, obtaining a catalogue, said, "A man by the name of Külpe," my hesitation immediately vanished, as Külpe, next to Wundt, was the man in Europe under whom I most desired to study.

Mr. Dunlap accompanied me to Bonn the next morning and assisted me in registering in the University, which I doubt I could have accomplished without the aid of the United States Consul. Then I went to see Külpe. He was not in his office, hence I went to his home. I introduced myself and gave him one of Titchener's cards. He received me most kindly, and extended me the privileges of a visiting colleague, a kind and generous act as it relieved me of the necessity of paying tuition. The next day I attended his lectures in elementary psychology and his seminary, which was held weekly in the evening.

Külpe's lectures in elementary psychology were given daily at 11:00 A.M. in a large room holding nearly 400 auditors. Promptly on the hour, he walked to the rostrum from a door directly behind it and began his lecture. At the same time, the doors of the lecture room were locked from the inside. The disturbance caused by late arrivals, as I learned to my surprise when I was a minute late one day, was not permitted. As soon as Külpe appeared, the students stamped their feet, and they stamped throughout the hour whenever he made a humorous observation or demonstrated an interesting experiment. It was their method of applauding. His lectures were richly illustrated, hence they were frequently interrupted by this, to me, strange applause. He closed promptly on the hour, and his audience again stamped but did not move until he had left the rostrum.

Külpe's seminary was conducted much like Titchener's. He introduced me to the members as a "colleague from Cornell." Among those present were Karl Bühler, then a *Privatdocent* who had followed Külpe to Bonn from

Würzburg, and Robert S. Woodworth and Lillian J. Martin, from America, who were spending sabbatical leaves there. Bühler, who proposed that "image-less thought" be accepted as a new element in psychology (Bühler, 1907; 1908) was gracious and invited me to attend his lectures on "The Psychology of Thought." I gladly accepted, but he spoke so rapidly that I could not follow him and got little out of the course. He was very friendly, however, and did everything he could to assist me. So also did my fellow compatriots. Woodworth helped me to find a furnished room and took me to the *Stammtisch* at which the more advanced of Külpe's students, those I had met in the seminary, came together every noon. At his, or Külpe's, or on the initiative of the members of the *Stammtisch* itself, I was invited to join it. I was pleased to be included. Because of his many kindnesses, I felt toward Woodworth as toward an older brother—and this feeling still persists.

The members of the *Stammtisch* met immediately after Külpe's elementary lecture, which they all attended. Throughout the meal and long after it, they sat around the table talking psychology. The discussions usually started from the topic treated by Külpe in the morning's lecture and went from there wherever they listed. I had never before seen anything like it. The German students lived, ate, slept, and dreamed psychology. None of them played chess or checkers or games of any kind, and none indulged in sports. They were dedicated to psychology. How, I thought, could the students of psychology in America, who went their own ways after class, who discussed sports, politics, and the news of the day when they did by chance come together, hope to compete with their German confreres? I was greatly discouraged about the status of study in America.

Shortly before the close of the term, I asked Külpe for his photograph and he gave me one. Forty years later I ran it in *The American Journal of Psychology* as the frontispiece to R. M. Ogden's *Nachruf* of Külpe (Ogden, 1951). The members of the *Stammtisch* were astonished and envious when I showed them the photograph. None of them would have dared be so bold as to request one. I was unaware that I had done anything indecorous or untoward. Külpe had been very kind to me during my stay in Bonn. He once had me to his home for dinner, and he also invited me to the formal celebration of his fiftieth birthday. I was pleased but a bit embarrassed because I did not have formal clothes with me—who would think of taking dress clothes on a cattleboat? When I told him of my lack, he said, "come as you are." I did and was the only one there in informal dress. I wished his photograph. As none was on sale in the bookstores in Bonn, the only way I knew how to get one was to ask him for it. If that was being forward, let him who thinks so do without a photograph!

On the way to Hamburg to board the ship for home, I made an *Ausflug* to Wolfenbüttel to see my maternal grandfather's youngest sister. I had no address for her and knew of her only as "Witwe Hartman." With the aid of the officials at the *Rathaus,* who rendered every assistance, I found my great-aunt. After introducing myself and telling her of her American relatives, I was taken by her son-in-law to my grandfather's former home, which had not been changed since he had left it fifty-nine years earlier.

## Cornell University (1912–1913)

While in Germany, I grew a beard, an imperial, which I kept short and neatly trimmed, to surprise my professors and fellow students at Cornell. They were surprised but no more so than I, as two of my fellow students, W. S. Foster and C. A. Ruckmich, also returned with beards that they had grown over the summer for reasons similar to mine. Except for the fact that our beards were neatly trimmed (and also that the word had not been coined), we were the "beatniks" of that day and generation. After we had exhibited our beards, it became a matter of pride to see which of us would weaken and be the first to cut his off. I would gladly have been second, but if the other two wished to be stubborn, so could I. They were; hence we wore beards and received our doctorates the following spring still wearing them. I have worn mine ever since.

Upon my return to Cornell, I learned why Foster had failed to meet me in Montreal. His parents would not permit him to work his passage to Europe on a cattleboat. He did not telegraph because he thought that Edwards and I would realize that if he was not there on the appointed date, he was not coming, and we would go on without him!

To remove myself from the temptation of playing chess, I left my old rooming house and moved into Cascadilla Hall, a University dormitory chiefly occupied by graduate students. Shortly after moving there, I joined the Acacia Fraternity, an organization that was then restricted to students belonging to the Masonic Lodge, which I had joined as an undergraduate when I turned twenty-one years old. Its members were graduate students and its chapter house, where I could get my meals, was only a short distance away. I greatly enjoyed my associations that year. It was very different from a boarding club.

During the summer when I was away, Bentley accepted a call from Illinois and Titchener resumed charge of the undergraduate department and again taught, during the fall semester, a section of the elementary course from which he had been relieved when elevated to his graduate professorship (Boring, 1927, p. 500; Dallenbach, 1956, p. 173). Though attendance at his lectures was restricted to sophomores, I attended them with his knowledge but without his sanction. If I ever were to hear his lectures, it had to be then, since I was coming up for my degree the following spring. He lectured twice a week, on Tuesdays and Thursdays at 11 o'clock. He delivered his lectures in an academic gown and precisely as the chimes sounded the opening hour he appeared on the rostrum behind a desk heavily laden with demonstrational apparatus. He spoke extemporaneously without notes and closed his summary just as the class bell sounded. I could see from whence Baird had derived his form and style of lecturing.

With three researches to complete and write up, the undergraduate courses I was attending, the observational hours I had to spend on others' experiments, and the study that I was doing in preparation for my doctoral examination, I found that Külpe's students, whose dedication I had so greatly admired, had nothing on me. Between pipe-smoking, which I had begun the previous spring to keep me awake, and the elimination of breakfast, I was able to carry on, bring my work to a close, and come up for my doctoral examination in early June of 1913.

Titchener advised me against spending the morning of the examination in frantic study; he told me to get out of my room and spend the hours in strolling leisurely through the gorges running through the Cornell campus. This seemed to be excellent advice, for nothing could be accomplished during that morning's study that could have any bearing upon the outcome. If a candidate does not know enough to pass the examination without that study, he will not be able to pass with it. I did, therefore, as he advised. As I walked through the gorges, I kept asking myself questions that I could not answer, and I had no means of looking up the answers. I believe that I would have spent a less fretful and anxious morning in my room with my books, hence I am not sure about the excellence of the advice.

My examination, conducted by the chairmen of my major and minors, was opened by Titchener. To remove my tension, he began by asking questions about my early training—a procedure I have ever since followed in conducting doctoral examinations so that the candidate would be put at ease —turned to more and more searching questions, and then to my dissertation. He had me explain its historical background, its object, procedure, results, and their significance. He exhibited me, showing what he had accomplished with me to the other members of the committee. He set the style of the examination. Kingsbury, chairman of my first minor, followed Titchener's example. After general and specific questions about histology and embryology, he turned to the research that I had conducted under his direction, namely, the embryological age at which Nisel granules appeared in nerve cells. He had me explain the methods and techniques used and the results obtained. I found Nisel granules in the nerve cells of mice embryos at all the stages I was able to examine. I was unable to solve that problem, hence the study was not published. Whipple, chairman of the second minor, questioned me upon the *Manual of Mental and Physical Tests* (1914) he had recently published and the undergraduate courses that I had taken with him and then turned to the study I had done under his direction (Dallenbach, 1910; 1919).

Titchener began the examination promptly at 2 P.M.; Whipple closed it as the chimes struck 6 P.M. It was the longest doctoral examination in the history of the Cornell Department. When Whipple closed his questioning, I was excused, but due to the lateness of the hour I was not held in suspense for long. I was called back and Titchener formally announced that the committee was recommending me for the Doctor of Philosophy degree. As I look back upon that afternoon, it seems to me that the members of the committee were more concerned in demonstrating what they had accomplished with me than in examining me.

Titchener felt the obligation, as few directors of doctoral candidates do now, of obtaining positions for his students. He secured the option of three for me, among them being an instructorship at the University of Oregon, where a man was needed to supervise the construction and equipping of a new laboratory, something on the order of what I had done at Pittsburgh. I was grateful for his efforts in my behalf, but not enthusiastic, as I was then flirting with the idea of returning to Pittsburgh for an M.D. degree, fervor for which was kept alive by my minor with Kingsbury. I thought Titchener would approve of that idea, but he did not. I had to go to Oregon, as he did not intend to have his training and work with me wasted. I went to Oregon, remaining, however, at Cornell the summer following the receipt of my degree to prepare a paper for publication, which I had read at Titchener's seminary that spring (Dallenbach, 1915). When I left Cornell my formal training was over, but my career as a teacher and an experimental scientist, which had its roots in 1909 as Baird's assistant, was begun. What I did with this training, or, more truthfully, what it did to me, is told in Boring's biography and shown by Mrs. McGrade's bibliography, contributed to the *Festschrift* published in 1958 by colleagues in Europe and America to mark my seventieth birthday and formal retirement (Boring, 1958; McGrade, 1958). Boring touched lightly on my childhood and young manhood, and concentrated on my career in psychology. Since space will not permit me to treat of both periods, I have chosen to write fully of the formative years of my life and to omit the later.

Boring's biography ends with my retirement. What has come to pass since then may briefly be brought up to date. I have served and am still serving the University of Texas on "modified service," the most enlightened system of retirement that I know. It permits me to carry on: to teach, direct graduate research, publish such articles and notes as I wish, edit *The American Journal of Psychology*, and, in addition, to enjoy the academic life and environment. I am well and still vigorous and know of no better way of passing my declining years.

## REFERENCES

*Selected Publications by Karl M. Dallenbach*

The effect of practice upon visual apprehension in school children. *J. educ. Psychol.,* 1910, 5, 321–334, 387–404.
The measurement of attention. *Amer. J. Psychol.,* 1913, 24, 465–507.

The relation of memory error to time interval. *Psychol. Rev.*, 1913, *20*, 323–337.
The history and derivation of the word "function" as a systematic term in psychology. *Amer. J. Psychol.*, 1915, *26*, 473–484.
The measurement of attention in the field of cutaneous sensation. *Amer. J. Psychol.*, 1916, *27*, 445–460.
Blindfold chess: the single game. In *Studies in psychology: Titchener commemorative volume*. Worcester, Mass.: Louis N. Wilson, 1917.
The effect of practice upon visual apprehension in the feebleminded. *J. educ. Psychol.*, 1919, *10*, 61–82.
The place of theory in science. *Psychol. Rev.*, 1953, *60*, 33–39.
Madison Bentley: 1870–1955. *Amer. J. Psychol.*, 1956, *69*, 169–186.
Across the years with Boring. *Contemp. Psychol.*, 1961, *6*, 332–337.
(with A. L. Dillenback) *The Dallenbachs in America: 1710–1935*, St. Johnsville, N.Y.: Enterprise and News, 1935.

## Other Publications Cited

Barr, M. W. *Mental defectives, their history, treatment and training*. Philadelphia: Blakiston, 1910.
Boring, E. G. Edward Bradford Titchener: 1867–1927. *Amer. J. Psychol.*, 1927, *38*, 488–500.
———. The Society of Experimental Psychologists. *Amer. J. Psychol.*, 1938, *51*, 410–421.
———. Karl M. Dallenbach. *Amer. J. Psychol.*, 1958, *71*, 1–40.
Bühler, Karl. Tatsacken und Problem zu einer Psychologie der Denkvorgange: I. Ueber Gedenken, *Arch. ges. Psychol.*, 1905, *9*, 297–365; II. Ueber Gedenkenzusammenhange, *Arch. ges. Psychol.*, 1908, *12*, 1–23; III. Ueber Gedenkenerinnerungen, *Arch. ges. Psychol.*, 1908, 24–92.
Downey, J. E. Types of dextrality and their implications. *Amer. J. Psychol.*, 1927, *38*, 317–367.
Geissler, L. R. The measurement of attention. *Amer. J. Psychol.*, 1909, *20*, 473–529.
McGrade, M. C. A bibliography of the writings of Karl M. Dallenbach. *Amer. J. Psychol.*, 1958, *71*, 41–49.
Ogden, R. M. Oswald Külpe and the Würzburg School. *Amer. J. Psychol.*, 1951, *64*, 4–19.
Rife, J. M. Types of dextrality. *Psychol. Rev.*, 1922, *29*, 474–480.
Titchener, E. B. The postulates of a structural psychology. *Psychol. Rev.*, 1898, *2*, 449–465.
———. *An outline of psychology*. (3rd ed.) New York: Macmillan, 1899.
———. *Experimental psychology: a manual of laboratory practice*. I, i. *Quantitative experiments, student's manual*. New York: Macmillan, 1902.
———. *Experimental psychology: a manual of laboratory practice*, II, i. *Quantitative experiments, student's manual*. New York: Macmillan, 1905.
———. *Experimental psychology: a manual of laboratory practice*. II, ii. *Quantitative experiments, instructor's manual*. New York: Macmillan, 1905.
———. *Lectures on the elementary psychology of feeling and attention*. New York: Macmillan, 1908.

———. *Lectures on the experimental psychology of the thought-processes.* New York: Macmillan, 1909.

———. *A text-book of psychology.* New York: Macmillan, 1910.

———. *A beginner's psychology.* New York: Macmillan, 1915.

———. The term "attensity." *Amer. J. Psychol.,* 1924, 35, 56.

Whipple, G. M. *Manual of mental and physical tests.* Baltimore: Warwick & York, 1914.

Fabian Bachrach

# John Frederick Dashiell

## BACKGROUND AND CHILDHOOD

The surname *Dashiell* is a Scottish misspelling of a French name—which assertion is less a quip than an epitome of genealogy. Forbearers of the family name *de Chiel* have been traced back at least to the year 1025 in the Department of Leon. After the revocation of the Edict of Nantes, a Protestant generation fled to Scotland; and later one scion emigrated to Maryland's Eastern Shore, bringing with him his spelling of the name. (Descendants of his three sons spread westward through the states.) Two other lines of ancestry of the present writer were the Scotch-Irish Montgomerys (including the general of that name in the French and Indian and Revolutionary Wars) and the Myerses who had been among the Dutch patroons in New York State. Vocationally the more immediate progenitors numbered fairly successful farmers, merchants, artisans, a shipbuilder, and ministers.

Born in Indianapolis in 1888 to John W. Dashiell, D.D., and Fannie S. Myers Dashiell, I was the ninth of twelve children, among whom were to be found the diversities of physique and of temperament to be expected of siblings, with no extreme deviants. One child died following accidents. All but one of the other eleven attended college; which fact implies that my father and my mother were both idealistic and realistic. Father was a minister in the Methodist Church, at one period serving as district superintendent and for many years as treasurer of the Indiana Conference; and Mother was an active officer in the Foreign and the Home Missionary Societies of that church. Both parents were strong in their faith, but not literalists nor evangelical nor pietistic. I found interesting reading—historical, archeological, humanistic—in my father's library. My mother's reading chair was reserved for her always, and, though she deplored excessive "novel reading," she kept up with many sacred and secular works of fiction. In our family a book was a suitable gift for any occasion.

Both Father and Mother were physically strong and vigorous. This obviously determined the fact that my brothers and I were athletes, serving as captains on varsity teams of basketball, baseball, and football. My daughter and granddaughters are excellent swimmers, as well as high-grade students and quite comely. Mother had been rather gifted musically, and we children had our occasional "sings" about her piano; two of the sisters also played piano and violin. As for myself I enjoyed membership in the glee club and in a touring male quartet. One striking incident was revealing, I think, of personality make-up. In my middle forties and with no real reading knowledge of music, I made so bold as to take up study of the cello. After exactly eight months' intensive practice on that noble instrument I was startled one evening to find myself the only cellist at rehearsal of the university orchestra—and we were to work on Schubert's Eighth ("Unfinished") Symphony, a composition both movements of which assign the lead for substantial passages to the cello. It was like looking over a precipice. But fate was kind. Somehow I did get through that rehearsal without the grossest of blunders. What had I done! Was it possible? Could I really play it (or even play *at* it), the music that had enthralled me as a listener for so many years? Then upon stepping out-of-doors I broke down and in a moment of exaltation found myself weeping. Another incident of the same evening serves to exhibit that characteristic duality of interests. Following the orchestra rehearsal I was to attend a program of the Society of the Sigma Xi. I had been looking forward to this with high interest. Some years earlier when elected to membership in that scientific research society I felt that I had reached a significant milestone; I was a scientist! My gratification was high a few years later when I was elected vice president and chairman of Section I of the American Association for the Advancement of Science (AAAS) (1939). Yet, now, the particular evening of which I was speaking found me for that one time almost indifferent to all this. My prideful wooing of scientific facts had weakened for the time before the allure of Euterpe.

This duality of interests in the sciences and the arts has continued, and alongside my shelves of technical and academic psychology stands a library of 199 recordings extending back to some of Caruso, the Flonzaleys, Toscanini, Melba, and others of such age and vintage. All of which serves to soften an apparent opposition in ideals and programs that is obsessing educational America as of this date of writing. (Why the opposition: is it that man's propensity to categorize then freeze the categories has invaded here too?)

Whatever the clinical psychologst may or may not be inclined to make of this, it is a fact that side by side with a lively interest in music, in my own case there has been a lifelong impairment of hearing. An attack of scarlet fever in infancy left an aftermath of total deafness in one ear and partial deafness in the other. The impairment has always proved a handicap, of course, with embarrassing episodes. But I will confess that occasionally I found it convenient to exploit the weakness, as when I let inattentiveness to teacher's instructions be passed off as due to my poor hearing. I will not deny employing another "alibi" throughout the adult years: that of being an absentminded professor. One or the other explanation often served as an ever-present help in time of trouble. And, more seriously, I find it wise and socially convenient to wear a hearing aid, and not too inconspicuously.

Also in regard to my psychological character, I realized that I was a clear case of Binet's *visile* rather than *audile,* though such classification, we know now, is not usually clean-cut. This point was impressed upon me when Dr. McKeen Cattell asked if I could visualize the whole word "Constantinople"; and upon my claiming that I could, he challenged me to call out the letters in backward order. That demonstrated to me the truth of one of Francis Galton's cautious findings regarding imagery. Another but positive one was to be found in my constant references to imaginal number forms. There is one master form that has served me through the years for arranging many sorts of serial materials—months of the year, children's ages, ancient and modern centuries, and times of the clock. And for more complexly disposed materials, what can be more absorbing than a map—any map!

I seem never to have been much intrigued by the supernatural or the magical. At the age of ten or twelve years I did have a flare-up of curiosity about fortune-telling which ran, I think, the usual course. Astrology! Think of it! To be able to read a person's fateful future by the positions of the stars did seem to be an exciting quest. It is a matter of note, however, that I soon found the signs of the zodiac, the individual stars and planets themselves, eclipses and seasons and zones, and all the purely factual material so absorbing on their own account that I soon forsook the original interest in horoscopes to bury my nose during school hours in my sister's college astronomy, carefully screened behind my large geography. Is not this shift of interest from the useful to the factual similar to that brought out in the simple demonstration of growing children's changing definitions of words? A horse to the youngest is "to ride on," and only later "an animal," "a quadruped," and eventually perhaps an *Equus equidae.* And on a more heroic scale is not the history of a civilization to be marked as advancing from a preoccupation with the practically useful to inquiries into the factually true?

This is as good a place as any at which to say clearly that I have never felt any appeal in the disinterring of dead issues once assigned by scientists to the limbo of disproven, rejected notions about nature or human nature— telepathy, alchemy, astrology, clairvoyance, and the like—by these or by other new names. Surely there is some limit beyond which open-mindedness becomes credulity impelled by a Will to Believe. "ESP" and "PK" have, I fear, been resorted to too often as if they were universal solvents for almost any psychological problem. No, these notions have always left me quite cold, in spite of thirty years of friendship with their exponents. Had I not in childhood been disillusioned with magical numbers, formulae, and abracadabra, I wonder if I would have been made credulous by the odd circumstance that my dissertation for the doctorate consisted of thirteen chapters, was submitted on the thirteenth of the month, and led to my receiving the degree in the year 1913.

Twelve children of one family whose lives overlapped sufficiently to have afforded such memorable memories as of all twelve lining up after the Christmas morning prayers in reversed age sequence before bursting into the parlor to discover what Santa had left—those twelve would seem to promise interesting material for group analysis. As it happens, however, the individual differences, from Myers the eldest to Mary the youngest, an age span of but twenty-one years, were not such as to arouse comment. "In-groups," "peck-right hierarchy," "isolates," "deviates," and most of the concepts found useful by the sociometrist or the group dynamics analyst would not have proved especially useful in characterizing this family complex. Which is not to say that the Dashiells found or made life humdrum; indeed one of us should have been a story writer, for there was material! What is probably of more present interpretative value is the nature of the parent-child relationships. If a midpoint be struck between the extremes of authoritarianism and permissiveness, it is pretty certain that each parent in his handling of each of the children varied but little from that midpoint. To be sure, there was a gradual reduction in whatever austerity was shown the earlier-born children as the later-born came into the family; but all twelve had reason to be grateful that precept, praise, or punishment from either parent was, though definite, moderated in degree. Always there was maternal and paternal affection, and it was returned.

I had experiences relevant to psychology outside the family too. In one city in which we lived an interesting parallelism could be seen between the "territoriality" behavior so observable in many animal forms and an unwritten law regulating gang and intergang behavior in humans. A boy in ward X might visit a boy in ward Y; but he would do well to be circumspect and not dilatory, for upon departing he might find an aggressive pack of Y warders at his heels with full and obvious intents. Yet once he had reached the middle of the boundary street between the two wards he could saunter as he pleased with no bully from Y to dare molest him.

## EDUCATION

Indiana has always ranked high among the states of the Union in the standards maintained in her public schools. I was fortunate, then, and doubly so since both my parents regarded attending college as a matter of course, even for children of a man in the poorly paid ministry. The college we attended was not widely known—Moores Hill College, later to be moved to and rechristened Evansville. Unquestionably the atmosphere I found was more sectarian and a bit more monastic than it was contemporary-world oriented; but I was fortunate in having at least two teachers who, though not Ph.D.s, equipped me for pursuit of learning. The one, biologist A. J. Bigney, secretary of the Indiana Academy of Science, lectured and directed his laboratories with an infectious enthusiasm, the solid results of which I realized in later years when I was to teach a year of zoology, and again when I offered courses in physiological psychology and comparative psychology, the latter being a favorite to this day. Also at college I had Charles E. Torbet who was almost the opposite of Bigney in temperament; yet his careful and balanced induction of students into literature and history was crucial in shaping my permanent interests. The reading of the Victorian poets, especially Wordsworth, awakened new emotional insights and sympathetic perceptions in this seventeen-year-old, thus dispelling a vocational choice of the law in favor of philosophy and its not-yet-divorced partner, psychology. The other of Torbet's fields, history, was absorbing too; and especially since I was privileged to teach an ancient history class in the academy, or prep school of the college.

I obtained two bachelor degrees in successive years; one in science, the other in literature. A bit unusual, indeed; but had not my father done this years before at this same college? There was of course much overlapping of these curricula. In the last spring I was lucky enough to win scholarships at Columbia and at Harvard. (I understood that graduate schools were at that time inclined to encourage more applicants from the smaller colleges.) The choice presented me was of course an impossible one to resolve; thus I let certain extrinsic factors decide for me, and I enrolled at Columbia.

My professors at Columbia University that first year (what a group of Four Horsemen!) were Cattell, Woodworth, Thorndike, and Dewey. I, newly come from a freshwater small college with no experience in seminars or even in large lecture-halls, found myself at sea for a while; but as the eminence of each man was matched by his reassuringly informed matter-of-factness, loyalty replaced awe. And the meaning of "psychology," which I had known within the generous limits of William James' rich *Briefer Course* (1892) studied at college, became now further expanded.

Cattell, with his quiet but pointed and purposeful ways of thinking, his utter objectivity and preciseness and literalness in technical matters as well as in personal relationships, was pushing the question of "how people do *differ,* and on what these differences depend." Much influenced in general by British thinking, Cattell was a strong Galtonian. I was one of the fortunate graduate students whom he employed at quite adequate pay to help in editing the third edition of his directory of *American Men of Science;* and I was profoundly moved to find myself, in a later edition, rated with a star by colleagues in my field. Cattell's interest in human differences, coupled with a gift for dealing with practical affairs such as publishing, made him a prophet well ahead of his times. He recognized that psychology need not be limited to an academic-scientific area, but by making laboratory experiments convertible into individual measures or tests, psychology could be applied to practical affairs. Today of course it is difficult to believe that in 1910 the director of Harvard's laboratories, Dr. Hugo Münsterberg, could be bewailing to a very young fellow like myself the public hostility aroused by the tentative beginning in applied psychology put forth in his book *On The*

*Witness Stand* (1909). One of the permanent fruits of Cattell's leadership in the opening up of applied psychology is seen today in the Psychological Corporation. This organization has been one of the potent forces acting to further but also to control the burgeoning profession of testing. Now, applied psychology could have flourished in two quite opposite directions. The one was quick popularization and rapid promotion of job opportunities in dealing with the square-peg-square-hole manpower needs of industry, business, individual-advisement, advertising, and so forth. The other direction was the cautious, checked and rechecked research entries into such fields. I will not forget a query heard in 1928: "Can you help me find an applied psychologist who is also a sound scientific man?" Imagine having such a request nowadays; the historical progress of applied psychology has been unquestionably in the direction of the measured, the sound, and the sane. The spirit of Cattell found kindred spirits in those of W. V. Bingham, D. G. Paterson, and others, and in the alertness of the APA Committee on Scientific and Professional Ethics (on which I enjoyed serving for two different periods), as well as the appropriate committees of state psychological associations, so effective because so firmly on the ground.

Another teacher of mine, Dr. R. S. Woodworth, who seemed so young, was a most important director of the graduate student's work. His modest, almost hesitatingly delivered, lectures in physiological and experimental psychology furnished solid ballast for the advanced students' programs. The lectures in the former subject were the basis for what soon was to be known as the "Ladd and Woodworth" (1911). A full forty years later when I offered a lecture course in physiological psychology at the University of California at Los Angeles—with students second to none in motivation and in competence—I found my Columbia course was a surprisingly solid pier from which to throw a bridge to span that great time interval. In the experimental laboratory, too, Dr. Woodworth's effectiveness was evidenced by the ovation that greeted the announcement at a Columbia luncheon that "The Bible has come out!" This is shown again by the fact that I, like others, learned to save up problems of research until I could consult the (always youthful) Old Man. E. B. Titchener's four-volume classic was not displaced (will it ever be?); but a far broader recognition of experimental problems and methods was now available in Woodworth's and later in Woodworth and Schlosberg's great book.

The lectures of Dr. E. L. Thorndike in "educational psychology" puzzled this callow new graduate student. His monumental three-volume text by that name had not yet appeared, and the thin single volume available seemed to run to columns of figures, always figures. Where was the meat and juice of human nature? But soon one came to recognize his working principle: "Everything that exists or happens, exists or happens in some amount"; and to see the compacted wisdom in "Correlation, not compensation, is the general rule in human nature." The many easy generalizations about psychology, teaching, learning, and other topics, I now came to realize and recognize for what they were. It was fascinating for me to observe how, as soon as you quantify a statement, you pull yourself up, you stop to look at things more critically, and more precisely. What did it matter that Thorndike's talks were not tailored to a neat course organization: what he had to say was invariably pithy, arresting, and suggestive. Then when we read and discussed G. Stanley Hall's *Adolescence* (1922)—a work surely at the opposite pole from Thorndike's in subject matter and style—we appreciated our teacher's catholicity and his utter fairness. Most grateful and delighted we were whenever he set a question-and-answer hour, for then we found ourselves tapping unlimited resources.

Ethics to an undergraduate at a church-supported college had tended to have connotations and implications of superhuman authoritativeness, of universal sanctions and imperatives; and the language abounded in "oughts," "shalls," and "musts." But in the lectures of John Dewey the hearer found himself a natural human being in a natural world. A key sentence quoted by him (from Hobhouse or Westermarck) ran: "Social approval and disapproval is the primary ethical fact." Many students were a bit baffled by Professor Dewey's apparent casualness and even occasional absentmindedness. Some were seen to be taking but few notes in meeting after meeting, then suddenly to catch an inspiration and to write furiously for the rest of the hour. Similarly, I observed that in a logic seminar with Dewey, we thirty ardent participants might debate for most of the two-hour period, then in the last quarter hour hear suggestions from Dewey that led many of us to mutter on leaving, "Wish I'd thought of it that way!" Dr. and Mrs. Dewey—she, a person of considerable personality—held Sunday afternoon teas at which you could count on meeting fascinating people of gown and town and diplomatic renown.

Psychology in America in those days was largely in the German tradition that derived from the work of those physicists and physiologists who had become interested in applying their methods to human beings—J. Müller, Fechner, Helmholtz, and others. Thus, universities in America were rated in psychology on the basis of their laboratories; and many of us graduate students thought of the abnormal psychology of France and Germany (multiple personality, Mesmerism, insanity, feeblemindedness, and so on)—if we thought of it at all—as outré. One of our circle of graduate students now famous for work in applied psychology warned the others of us that to dabble in that stuff might make *us* just a bit "touched." When Wisconsin's Joseph Jastrow came as a visiting professor to Columbia for a semester this indifference toward human odds and ends as objects of serious study was punctured. His fluent lecturing presented such material graphically enough to enlist our curious interest. Even so, our research problems and seminars continued largely in the experimental tradition.

Another whose writings did much to shape my intellectual development was William James. Certainly, as Cattell had said, his two-volume *Principles of Psychology* (1890) is the greatest single publication in psychology, and of all time, I would add. Candidates facing a Ph.D. oral examination were advised to read the great classic. As philosopher-psychologist Mary W. Calkins once declared, James' *Principles* is like the Bible, quotable on just about any (psychological) topic. And through the years since hearing that remark in 1911 I have time and again keenly realized its appositeness. The $4.44 those two volumes cost me in 1909 is the best investment I ever made, that's a surety! "The perceptive state of mind is not a compound" (p. 313). What better corrective for all the atomism and reductionism that has insinuated itself into modern psychology, including the experimental! And the James-Lange theory of emotion I have always held to be one of the most illuminating insights in modern man's study of man, normal or abnormal. Ah yes, you can find it inadequate; you can add here and take away there, correct this detail and rewrite that phrase; but for setting the reader's thinking in the right directions, it is inspired writ. Give me these two Jamesian ideas and I could expand them into almost a complete psychology.

It is my lifelong regret that I never had an opportunity to meet Professor James. I did have occasion to call at a home next door to his at the time the APA was holding its 1909 convention in Cambridge, but James was too ill to attend the sessions. I missed seeing the great man by that one doorknob.

One other of the Olympians whom I was never to have the privilege of knowing was E. B. Titchener, whose interest in meetings was displaced from the APA to his own selected group, the Experimental Psychologists. (The contemporary organization of that name continues the same scientific research ideals but with far wider recognition of what subject matter truly *is* "psychology.")

One more source of inspiration I hasten to acknowledge. For one of my three years as a graduate assistant I was privileged to work with Frederick J. E. Woodbridge, editor of the *Journal of Philosophy, Psychology, and Scientific Method* and lecturer in the history of philosophy. This class included some of Columbia College's most brilliant students. Woodbridge lectured three times a week; as his assistant I held small-group discussion sessions devoted to the philosophical or psychological classics named by the professor to parallel his lectures. I lost no opportunity to attend those lectures, as did some other graduate students, for Woodbridge's presentations were themselves classics. He would sketch in the origins and historic backgrounds; then by presenting each man or system sympathetically, he taught us to seek understanding from the inside out. When lecturing on Plato he was a thorough Platonist, when on Descartes, a thorough Cartesian. I think the ardent young student is all too eager to plunge into advocacies and polemics; and I hold that to be derisive of another's field of study, be it philosophy, esthetics, mathematics, advertising, or choreography, is a clear mark of immaturity. That year's work confirmed my predilection for the historical approach, and consistently I have preferred the history of psychology as my favorite teaching subject.

An effective teaching device I early hit upon in such a course was the constructing of a ceiling-to-floor chart by each student, with parallel vertical columns for the proper dating of men and their books and researches as they fall into the German, French, British, or miscellaneous traditions, and with different colors of ink for notations of experimental, clinical, physiological, theoretical, or other subject matter. One artistically gifted student embellished his chart with truly excellent portraits. It is sometimes surprising how much devices of this sort can lend reinforcement to the student's interest in the essential subject matter itself and facilitate long-time retention. Query: Why does not every college of liberal arts set up as one required course the history of philosophy to be taught by wise, enlightened humanists who are scientists and by scientists who are humanists with historical perspective?

My second choice as a teaching subject has pretty consistently been comparative or animal psychology. My aforementioned work with college courses in zoology, as student and as teacher, had made laboratory contacts with animal phyla familiar and fascinating enough; and moreover the realization dawned on me that many of the problems of behavior at the human level could be dealt with in infrahuman forms and so much more simply, suggestively, and revealingly. (And this is not as trite as it sounds.)

Though of questionable relevance at this point, I am impelled on two counts to mention a family pet, a gentle Chihuahua. She had been obtained in the desperate hope that friends' tales might have truth in them: that an asthmatic patient is often benefited by keeping a purebred Chihuahua in close physical proximity. Whether it be a matter of counterallergy or of psychosomatics, my wife Thelma's long-time asthma has during these ten years been strikingly relieved—and we are content to be pragmatic as to the explanation. This pet appears legitimately in one photograph in the *American Psychologist* for 1959.

A second psychological observation prompted by this pet is a noticeable gentling in my own handling of laboratory animals. I have never performed any slightest surgery without anesthesia, of course, and I have done my share of letting off-duty albino rats sniff and snuggle at my shoulder and neck; yet I detect recently a more restrained handling of them—a generalization from my handlings of the family pet. Indeed, I confess to qualms about the present-day exploiting of "stress" problems in animal research by run-o'-mine students. After all, I submit, intense fear, like intense pain, is evil; and I shall never be able to forget that experiment reported at an APA session some years ago in which a tame rat had been actually frightened to its death by a vicious gray rat introduced into the same cage "to provide a stress situation"!

My third choice of courses for teaching has been developmental or child psychology. But only if the course be pretty strictly contained, that is, biologically oriented and in the spirit of a natural science undistracted by too many emotional, educational, and mental-hygienic considerations. To study the human child dispassionately and objectively as a member of *Homo sapiens* is surely the first approach to sound knowledge of the developing individual, the beginning of wisdom. This is the truly scientific approach.

Let me add that there are certain other considerations that lead me to be less actively and personally interested in the more useful and practical courses in childhood to be found listed in college curricula. At times I have found it disappointing to see what strikes me as an overplaying of a very few favorite "explanations." So many and so interlaced are the contributing factors that determine a human being's actions, feelings, and thoughts at a given juncture, that—as a cynic would put it—in any particular case you can *always* find an Oedipal situation, some traumatic circumstance of weaning, a castration anxiety, an order-of-birth family pattern, or a too authoritarian or too permissive handling in childhood. Which *one* of these or other equally simplified formulas is applied to the case may represent the consultant's own individual bias. Also, in many cases a freedom of interpretation is provided by those ever-present helps in time of trouble: the mechanisms of projection, identification, regression, and especially compensation. But to be fair, it must be recognized that the clinician has many more variables to control than has the experimentalist in his neat laboratory. All these and many others are of course valuable weapons in the armament of the clinician.

## TEACHING APPOINTMENTS
## AND ADMINISTRATION

My first academic appointments provided me with variety. In 1913–14 I had the ponderous title of Professor of Education and Biology at Waynesburg College. The next year I served as an instructor in philosophy at Princeton University and the next two years as instructor in philosophy and then in psychology at the University of Minnesota. In the two academic years 1917 to 1919 I enjoyed teaching "pure" psychology at Oberlin College where that discipline had already been separated from philosophy.

After receiving appointment at the University of North Carolina in 1919, I was permitted a year later to pull together the psychology courses being taught in the Departments of Philosophy and Education to form an autonomous Department of Psychology. Year by year additions to course offerings and to staff were made under two guiding principles: that psychology is basically a biological science and that accordingly there should be an emphasis upon laboratory or other concrete work. In the very first two-term introductory course I worked out appropriate experiments for the students working in pairs, the experiments closely paralleling the lectures. The other natural science departments, who were always conscientious about their own offerings, welcomed psychology to their group. Indeed, our courses "1" and

"2" were made available as electives for discharging the college's natural science requirement for the A.B. or B.S. degree. So far as I have been able to learn, I can probably claim priority in the setting up of psychology as a natural science with a full laboratory. The testimony of competent students supported this approach to the field of psychology, and after a year's trial the faculty accepted it. The plan continued, and has been established at a number of other institutions. Incidentally, assignment of selected graduate majors to handle these laboratory sections offers invaluable teaching experience and by the same token offers a useful basis for appraising the assistants as candidates for professional appointments elsewhere.

Many years later, after statutory retirement at North Carolina, I was given opportunity at Wake Forest College again to organize an independent undergraduate Department of Psychology. There I had the friendly cooperation of Dr. H. C. Reid, chairman of the philosophy department, who, having once been a student of Titchener's, was handling the psychology work. He was, however, now glad to be relieved of the psychology to devote full time to his philosophical work and colleagues. It was a source of real gratification that in the new Life Sciences building, the psychology department was invited by the biologists to share generous space. I was glad to submit a list of specifications of rooms and utilities. I was also further heartened by the students' naming their psychology club for me.

But to return to earlier years and the University of North Carolina. Our working quarters there were inadequate, and the need was recognized as so imperative that in 1928 we were allotted a three-story building, New West. This historic structure had been serving as home for an historic debating society and a men's dormitory. Loyalty feelings on the part of "old grads" of the society were not to be offended by razing the structure for replacement, but a compromise was accepted. The society's assembly room was moved to the top floor; the building was gutted leaving the four brick walls; and we of the department were given *carte blanche* to have the architects and builders pour inside that shell a new concrete building according to our specifications (1930b). Thus were satisfied both sentiment and science. Having spent a summer during my college years at blueprint work with Westinghouse in Pittsburgh, I found this opportunity to design rooms, fixtures, and even special furniture for New West one of the exciting occupations of my life. Because provision was made for animal research, the genial University Business Manager dubbed the building a "mouse-o-leum," with no ghoulish implications. (As this is being written in 1964 the active department is acquiring also the former botany-zoology building. But that is for others to tell.)

I should amend my account on earlier pages in which the natural science orientation of the Department of Psychology was stressed. My emphasis was due to the unusual nature of that characterization in the American academic world. In fairness I want to point out that psychology was rated as a natural *or* as a social science at the University of North Carolina. Indeed, I am proud of the fact that for two decades many members of the social science faculties had audited or had enrolled in courses in the psychology department, most commonly the one in animal behavior or the one in neuroses and psychoses.

During my years as chairman the North Carolina department awarded thirty-six M.A. degrees in psychology and twenty-five Ph.D.s. Of the advanced students at North Carolina I was frequently made proud by their attitudes toward psychology. This was revealed well by their lively participation in seminars, with or without course credit. I can think of but three or four out of the many institutions in which I have held appointments where equal initiative and earnestness was manifested. Just for contrast I recall one state university where my graduate class in learning voted to continue as a lecture course rather than change to a seminar with optional reporting of journal articles and books. Yes, those evening psychology seminars at Carolina will always be vivid in recall!

In the early 1920's I was fortunate in the psychologists who accepted appointments as colleagues: Dr. Harry W. Crane from Ohio State with a strong medical background, Dr. English Bagby from the Yale department, and Dr. Floyd H. Allport from the Harvard department. Bagby was soon to publish his *Psychology of Personality* (1928), and Allport his trailblazing *Social Psychology* (1924). In the 1930's renewed emphasis upon experimental and statistical psychology was made possible by the appointments of Dr. A. G. Bayroff of New York University and North Carolina, Dr. W. J. Daniel of North Carolina, and Dr. R. J. Wherry from Ohio State. In the next decade, after Wherry left to go to the Pentagon, Dr. Dorothy C. Adkins of Ohio State took charge of the teaching of statistics and group testing and published her book *Construction and Analysis of Achievement Tests* (1947), then quite lately her *Statistics: An Introduction for Students in the Behavioral Sciences* (1964). Upon resigning the chairmanship in 1949 I followed the unanimous counsel of the members of the department, and nominated her to the chancellor for the chairmanship. One of my last acts as chairman was the nomination of Drs. Harold G. McCurdy, Irwin S. Wolf, and James W. Layman to round out the personnel for training in personality and clinical psychology. Dr. Layman formally organized a curriculum that was later approved by the APA. Excellent relations were soon cemented.

The "rolling stone" adage is peculiarly applicable here. One device to prevent a teacher's becoming a "mossback" is to have faculty appointments in different institutions. In that regard I consider my life as having been blessed. After appointments at Princeton, Minnesota, and Oberlin, I became a fixture at the University of North Carolina from 1919 on; but on leave I have used opportunities to work summers or semesters at a number of institutions to be mentioned later. The more interesting contrasts and comparisons, however, are not those to be drawn between different sections of the country, but between the universities themselves.

In 1948 personal tragedy struck, when an unsuspected malignancy took away my wife Sylvia. A sympathetic chancellor, R. B. House, recognized my need of change of scene without disengagement from mental occupation, and he permitted an arrangement which was, I would guess, unique in university practice. Without any change in my faculty status or salary at North Carolina nor any compromise of retirement expectations there, I was permitted to serve as a visiting professor for one semester at the University of California at Los Angeles and for another semester at the University of Florida. My earnings at those institutions were directly transmitted to the treasurer at North Carolina, and a thoroughly competent substitute for me was thus provided in the person of Dr. Eugene R. Long, Jr., from the University of Virginia. The changes of scene afforded me intensive working opportunities, not play vacations, under morale-bolstering conditions, and neither university was handicapped. I will add that though this was a more extreme departure from the usual static employment conditions, it did strengthen my belief in the salutary effects on teachers and students of exchange professorships. Why not have more of them across the land?

A few words I must say about Sylvia herself. After graduating from the same Indiana college two years after me, she had waited for me a third year, teaching, while I worked at my Columbia graduate studies. Then when my doctorate was clearly in sight, we married and lived for a year in the Big Town, with its opera, Metropolitan and other museums, Broadway, its art auctions (one sale including a Rembrandt), and other world-size fascinations as well as the social life of a university. I recall that after my oral examination I signalled Sylvia by entering our apartment sounding the Triumphal March from *Aida*. And I want to add that Sylvia understood and supported my professional hopes and ambitions. Besides being a willing sharer in the trials and privations of the earlier years of my getting established professionally, she continued warmly to back my aspirations; and I recall her disappointment once when I declined being considered for the secretaryship of the APA. She took an active part in the home entertaining of my classes and of the graduate psychology group, especially when visiting psychologists were in Chapel Hill. Many will remember her alert sprightliness.

## EDITORIAL DUTIES

Any inquiring reader knows the tremendous convenience of having access to a file of reference volumes furnishing correct and complete topical listing year by year or month by month of all psychological books and journal articles. This service has been provided by the Publications Board of the APA in the Psychological Index since 1894. A further boon to the reader was furnished in 1927 in the form of authoritative condensations of the pith and substance of each publication—the reader's first resort and ever-present help in time of need—the *Psychological Abstracts*. Under the editorial guidance of Walter S. Hunter and R. R. Willoughby this service was extended to cover all the material appearing anywhere in the world. Voluntary assistance was enlisted from members of the Association, to each of whom was then assigned books or the file of certain journals for immediate abstracting and reporting back to the editors.

Now abstracting has always seemed to me a most rewarding exercise for the abstractor himself—a challenge to get so much said or implied in so little space and with objective fidelity. It was my privilege and real pleasure to serve as one of the many cooperating abstractors for many years in the first two decades of the *Abstracts*. I recall but one journal article too resistant to my efforts: a doctoral dissertation that attempted to reduce maze learning to changing patterns of flexor and extensor reflex thrusts—surely about the nadir in reductionist theory!

Other much heavier editorial opportunities were to come my way soon. In 1931 I was invited to become the consulting editor of the McGraw-Hill Publications in Psychology.

The success of that series owed much to the already established prestige of such authors as Kurt Lewin, N. R. F. Maier, J. P. Guilford, T. C. Schneirla, Cliffort T. Morgan, Carl E. Seashore, S. Howard Bartley, Elizabeth B. Hurlock, and many others. Recognizing that this business of critically reading the manuscripts of fellow psychologists who might as appropriately be sitting in judgment on *my* books was a reflection calculated to keep me on the qui vive. After nearly twenty years (1950) the pressure of old and some new professional involvements persuaded me to resign this post. But I left it with a feeling of indebtedness toward so many cooperative authors and with memories of extremely happy associations I had been having with everyone I had known in the publishers' offices. It had been easy for me to identify with the company and to feel a bit of personal pride in that imposing office building they erected on Forty-second Street.

A second editorial responsibility I assumed in the 1930's was that of editing the *Psychological Monographs,* one of the official journals of the APA. My tenure extended from 1935 until 1947. This post afforded me the advantage of getting to know some of the liveliest research going—a matter of gratification to one who was helping direct projects in his own laboratory and trying to cover essentials of the field of psychology for presentation in college textbook form. In one respect this post was a relatively easy one: the vast majority of the manuscripts were doctoral dissertations that had passed the critical reading and oral examinations of graduate departments and could on their face be presumed to be acceptable. But there were exceptions. In a few cases it appeared that a student's dissertation had been passed on the strength of its literary presentation rather than as a contribution to human knowledge on the subject. And in one case I remember with chagrin letting my editorial scruples *con* be outweighed by the emphatically expressed judgments *pro* of two full professors in a well known university.

Still a different kind of editorial work, as it too is called, involves not judging of others' writings as such, but reworking and gathering into a single form what others have written. I was asked to contribute eighteen articles on psychology to the *Encyclopedia Americana* (1960 edition). This was an opportunity like no other, for its execution would require the kind of treatment of subject matter combining a textbook's systematic order, a semihistorical perspective, an abstractor's getting at the heart of the matter—all rolled into one. That my enthusiasm paid off is suggested by the words of a reviewer: "Dashiell writes with rare insight and illuminating clarity. His [encyclopedia] articles . . . form the most important contribution . . . to the coverage of psychology" (Metcalf, 1959). I slept well after reading that.

Summary surveys of lesser scope I was given opportunities to make in later years, such as chapters in books edited by others—chapters on general principles of behavior, general principles of learning, and the like.

A conscientious bit of field survey by library research I concluded for a chapter in *A Handbook of Social Psychology* (1935a). I tried to make this live up to its title, "Experimental Studies of the Influence of Social Situations on the Behavior of Individual Human Adults." I had been asked to do this by the book's editor, Carl Murchison, since I had published an experiment in 1930 in which I carried further Floyd H. Allport's method of making measured comparisons of what the individual can or will perform when alone versus when he is in different sorts of social surroundings. My own specific finding had been the modest one that when a working person is aware that his start-stop signals are simultaneous with and under the same physical control system as are the other workers', even though they be in other rooms or other buildings, his scores differ from those he makes when he is quite alone. To have a true social situation then, the physical presence and proximity of fellow men is not a *sine qua non*. The handbook chapter turned out as intended, since I have had testimony from recent workers in relevant social psychology that they have used it as a point of departure.

In a recent year I was asked to do another encyclopedia job, that of providing an article or series of articles on the history of psychology. Nothing would have given me a greater lift! What a keen disappointment then, that an early publishers' deadline plus commitments I had made to fill certain teaching engagements made that impossible. It still has a place in my fantasies.

## RESEARCH PUBLICATIONS

As mentioned earlier, in the first two decades of the twentieth century the line of difference between philosophy and psychology was not heavily drawn, either in the literature or in university departments and courses. (A survival, albeit a vigorous one, is found today in the Southern Society for Philosophy and Psychology.) For my master's degree I majored in psychology and minored in philosophy, then for my doctorate switched the two. The

1913 master's thesis was an attempt to bring out inconsistencies and inadequacies in the conception of a "social consciousness" of Schaeffle, Lilienfeld,
and others—a critical job done definitively later by Floyd H. Allport.

As a philosophy major I had come under the influence of both Dewey
and the New Realists; and my doctoral dissertation, "The Philosophical Status
of Values," was an examination of contemporary systems of value theory,
coming up with a presentation in nonsubjective instrumental terms.

After eight quite minor papers in philosophy, I published my first psychological venture, a comparison of preferences among color-combinations
and among tone-combinations on the part of kindergarten children and college sophomores (1917). This was a study in what in those days was called
judgment. Although the trends of the collected data were in line with statements of other investigators the study now can be seen to be poorly controlled
statistically. Historically viewed, the problem and procedure were illustrative
of methods to be used in experimental esthetics.

During my first year at Columbia I had had some opportunity to handle
white rats in a simple maze, in after-hours following work on Cattell's *American Men of Science*. Later, my teaching at Oberlin brought me into close
association with Dr. R. H. Stetson, whose acuteness I was soon to recognize
and whose generosity to appreciate. He had devised a multiple-unit system of
constructing mazes that permitted the taking down and reassembling of the
wall sections in changing patterns. Together we adapted the idea to animal
mazes of different wall heights and runway lengths, and similarly, to child
mazes on a much larger scale. The very plasticity and adaptability of this
apparatus suggested a number of research problems with animal subjects
(1919). I was enabled (1) to exhibit higher and lower level (space) habit
hierarchies, (2) to compare the problem-value of different kinds of culs-de-
sac at side, straight ahead, and so forth, (3) to bring out prevalence of forward over backward oriented running (with A. G. Bayroff, 1931b), (4) to
identify spatial habit elements readily transferable from maze to maze
(1920a), (5) to prove animals' abilities to reroute themselves after having
been blocked, and (6) to observe variability in routing when no blocking has
been encountered.

One very minor study furnished an amusing lesson for my students.
Employing fairly simple mazes identical in pattern but of different sizes
accommodated to the experimental subjects, I found that the mean number
of trials taken by albino rats to learn it was 13 ± 5, while the score for
kindergarten children was 12 ± 4.

Incidentally, at that early stage (about 1915) of child psychology, many
a young Ph.D. was counselled: "pick out a few likely-looking tests from
G. M. Whipple's *Manual of Mental and Physical Tests* (1914), and apply
them to various groupings of children by age, sex, grade, nationality, or what
have you." Was this shotgun research? Trailblazing, rather!

If the old saw is true that politics makes strange bedfellows, it is equally true that a lively spirit of inquiry ofttimes raises strangely different queries and questions. The scientist or other investigator whose problems and inspirations grow out as so many sprigs from one single parent trunk is not very far from mono-ideism. And though we customarily emphasize the devotion of an inquiring scholar or scientist to his one area of intensive attention, it is my belief that a psychologist biographer would find not only that variability and imagination are essential in creativity (a big word at the time of this writing), but also that many-sidedness characterizes the interests and personal involvements of most productive thinkers. Be that as it may, I find in the sequences of research interests of myself and my students a rather puzzling degree of noncontinuity, after due allowance is given the half-dozen maze problems mentioned above growing out of exploiting a new technique. Some of the various research problems to which we addressed ourselves were as follows:

1. a comparison of complete *vs.* alternate methods of practicing two habits (1920b)
2. the effects of practice upon two mental tests
3. psychological principles that bear upon (Wilsonian) internationalism
4. temporal *vs.* spatial sequences in learning multiple stimuli
5. an examination and restatement of the history of educational theory through the centuries
6. some "racial differences" measured by the Will-Temperament Test
7. a physiological-behavioristic description of thinking and, later, the physiological location of the seat of thinking (1926) (these have gotten into textbooks as comparisons of the central *vs.* peripheral view of thinking)
8. a re-examination of urban *vs.* rural children with Binet and then Pintner-Paterson tests (with W. D. Glenn, 1925b)
9. a quantitative demonstration of animal drive (this found its way into elementary and some advanced texts, 1925c)
10. learning of inclined planes by rats (directly stimulated research elsewhere)
11. changes in psychomotor efficiency in a diabetic (1930a)
12. apparatus for measuring serial reactions (1930c)
13. the objective nature of "intent" in legal usage
14. affective value-distances as a determinant of time taken to choose (with Sybille K. Berwanger, 1937)
15. the role of vision in spatial orientation by the white rat (1959a)
16. monocular polyopia induced by fatigue (1959b).

To such a listing of more and less related topics I should hasten to add that my interest lay not in their disparateness; frequently I went on to urge their relatedness. As described by a friendly editorial commentator, "The most definite effect he [Dashiell] has had upon his students and upon other members of his profession has been a tolerance for conflicting viewpoints and an open inquiring attitude. . . . His writings have frequently emphasized the synthesis and coordinations between different lines of psychological research." If there be any truth in the quotation, an example is furnished in the paper

I read before Section I of the AAAS in 1935, "A Survey and Synthesis of Learning Theories" (1935). At that time the manifold theories of learning were tending to be grouped into three general types: the trial-and-error, the conditioned response, and the Gestalt types. Debates between the advocates of these three were at times spirited; and, as is so often seen, vigorous advocacy led to mental myopia and astigmatism, and to the either-or error. In my analysis I set forth some eleven of the major emphases made by this or that one of the three schools; then I canvassed the outstanding experimental reports of all three to see whether such emphasized points might not actually be found in the procedure and data of all three. To make a long story short: they were!

Here is a convenient place to urge a very general historical consideration, especially on the part of young readers. In the panorama of intellectual history, suppose that a new insight or a new construction emerges. Then later a newer insight or newer construction breaks through. Is the previous one then discredited and dismissed? In most cases, no! It is eventually absorbed into the body of doctrines, and that in turn enriches it. For example, the Gestalt movement of the early twentieth century may not be explicitly at the center of attention with most psychologists of the sixties, but that is precisely because the spirit of that movement has become absorbed into the whole field of psychology. This is true also of the schools of structuralism, functionalism, behaviorism, and psychoanalysis. And further, within any large area of competing doctrines, such as the many psychoanalytic theories, it is wisdom to expect to find interpenetration and cross-fertilization. The history of psychology is not so much a story of acceptances-rejections as one of adaptations, absorptions, and assimilations.

A writing effort that gives some substance to the statement that I was more interested in tracing essential similarities than in exploiting differences was my vice presidential address to this same Section I in 1939 entitled "A Neglected Fourth Dimension to Psychological Research" (1940). Besides present stimulus, habit, and genetic factors, it was pointed out that the human being's responses are determined by his "set." More impressive polysyllabic names were to be found for this in many time-honored experimental reports— as on attention, reaction time, psychophysics, work curves, imageless thought, inspiration, and many more—but it had not previously been isolated for full recognition. A few months after my address some direct studies on "set" did appear in the journals and with that word in the titles.

But a more sweeping sort of reconciling of oppositions and differences had urged itself on me for my presidential address before the American Psychological Association in 1938. The time was ripe for some such effort. In fact, one of the more colorful oldsters of the Association was having much to say about "the threatened dismemberment of psychology." At the time of that convention, then, centrifugal forces were much in evidence. The researches being reported were, of course, more and more about less and less:

specializations magnifying differences. A clear symptom of this divisive *Zeitgeist* had been displayed in the organizing of an American Association of Applied Psychology, its membership drawn almost completely from that of the APA. (This splinter-grouping ended when the APA was reorganized less than ten years later.)

There were other disjunctive forces at work also. "There goes Doctor X: what's he?" Such a query was to be overheard from almost any group of students. It was an indoor sport to sort and classify psychologists. There can be no question that this was a consequence of preoccupation with the great schools of psychology: structuralism, functionalism, behaviorism, Gestalt, and psychoanalysis. Predictably enough, partisanship developed.

And so it seemed fitting at that moment of psychological history in America that for one evening attention be directed to harmonizing trends, trends toward more mutual understanding and more cooperative effort. A number were pointed out in this presidential address (1939). The following are some relationships to the mother, philosophy:

1. The two-thousand-year-old divorcement of mind from body was still preoccupying some Wundtian psychologists; and it was high time that such a dualistic split be recognized for the irrelevance that it was.
2. Modern psychology's ardent espousal of scientific method had recently o'ershot the mark in disavowing any relation to philosophical disciplines; but method is logic, is philosophical.
3. More specifically, operationism, enunciated first by physicists, had been recently adopted as a principle of rigor by a number of experimenting psychologists.
4. Another new methodological emphasis was Hull's upon postulates and deductions therefrom.
5. Then there had appeared Lewin's topological envisagement of psychological relationships; and meanwhile a reemphasis upon the individual as individual.
6. Psychology in the 1930's was also developing more rapport with biology as shown by Tolman's redescription of animal and human behavior in purposive and molar instead of mechanical and molecular terms.
7. Several of the older concepts of biology were being dusted off and given new piquancy and relevance to psychology. The heredity-environment dichotomy was being dedichotomized, *e.g.,* when do environmental factors first come into play?
8. The Spencerian concept of adjustment had for some years been adopted and made basic in mental hygiene and abnormal psychology.
9. But now this concept was projected on a still greater canvas, that of homeostasis or organismic regulation. Indeed, certain of our elementary textbooks are still presenting it as a basic concept to tie together all the various aspects of psychology.
10. The biological concept of emergence also has been of great value to psychology, for it serves to show that sudden inspirations, insights, and creativity are natural events in a natural world.

On the other hand I was finding myself in those years caught up in certain more major problems of research, especially the last two listed on a preceding page as (15) and (16), both on vision.

At the International Congress of Psychology meeting at New Haven in 1929 I presented reports on three of the studies just mentioned. One, which seemed to be quite favorably received there, may be worth a further word, not only for whatever intrinsic interest it may furnish the reader but also because it serves to illustrate a general point about research activity in general: namely, that a fruitful subject of inquiry has often popped up quite incidentally to the investigators' primary concern. I happened to be interested in the question of whether an animal when facing many alternative paths all leading eventually to the reward (positive reinforcement) would tend to follow walls, or take more bee-line or crow-fly directions, or take some intermediate course. A rat maze with an open-alley multiple-choice design was constructed which would permit travel from entrance to exit via as many as twenty criss-crossing and equal-length alternative routes. There was much theoretical importance to the outcome. At that date there had been considerable use of the ultrasimple S-R description of learning as involving the sensory stimulations which the organism receives while it traverses a pathway becoming associated with the motor responses it then makes; and the habit as a whole being conceived as a learned sequence of S-R's. Nothing of the sort occurred in our laboratory! In a sequence of runs from entrance to exit, the animal was commonly observed to vary its routing, sometimes running unhesitatingly down certain sections of pathways it had never entered previously (*i.e.,* with nonidentical stimuli in operation). The report of these findings (1930d) we may fairly consider to have been one of the crucial experimental refutations of the doctrine that behavior reduces ultimately to patterns of S-R's or of reflex arcs, a beautifully simple conception while it lasted! (This report attained the dignity of a monograph.)

I should mention one more bit of research, and this one too because it combines a question that is interesting on its own account with another question of vastly greater import (1959b). From the age of eight or ten years and throughout my life I have observed a phenomenon that is nowhere reported in the journals and that, to my dismay and disgust, is challenged by some authorities in a relevant field. It is as follows: after any prolonged bout of reading or other intensive eye work I see more than the one image; I see the object as partly duplicated. Importantly, this is true of each eye and is not the everyday experience of seeing double that anyone with binocular vision can report. To my astonishment I find both practicing and teaching oculists and ophthalmologists who have never run across this phenomenon following eye work; and a dean of ophthalmology in a western state university has challenged the reported experience, that is, of accessory images resulting from eye fatigue. They are unable to explain it in terms of what they know concerning the eye's refractive mechanisms. This skepticism is not shared by all these "eye men," however, and I have the positive supporting testimony of certain psychologists, including physiological psychologists and sensory-introspective psychologists, who are of recognized authority, including S. Howard Bartley, S. Smith Stevens, and F. Nowell Jones. What an interesting scientific dilemma is posed! Has our skeptical reaction against conscious experience as a source of scientific knowledge carried us so far overboard that we are to repudiate any subjective evidence of a process, event, or change, until we can demonstrate a parallel physical process, event, or change?

## TEXTBOOKS

It is a practice in many university psychology departments for every member of the staff to have charge of at least one elementary psychology class in every two years, for example. I suppose there is a double reason in this. For one: perhaps there is no academic subject which for its very first presentation demands breadth of background and mastery and authoritativeness in the same degree as does psychology. It is not the intrinsic difficulty of the subject, for one can think of other academic disciplines calling for as close application and as frequent reviewing; rather it is because of the variety of directions of approach and especially the many different points of contact with everyday life at which the student can readily go astray. Then again, for the professor's own sake it is to be recommended that he frequently come down from his ivory tower and keep his narrowed research visions oriented and articulated with trends in knowledge as a whole. For whichever reason, many professors have never lost their interest in the introductory courses. And I want to be counted with that company.

As a young teacher my attention went to the textbooks themselves. James' *Briefer Course* (1892), on which I had cut my milk teeth, I readopted along with others in some of the early years of teaching the introductory course. J. R. Angell's text—even when taught by a professor named Lord (a standard Columbia undergraduates' pun, not mine)—was solidly established in the predominantly functionalist institutions of America. Clear and masterly (the author was later president of Yale), it was a pleasure to teach, that is, to lecture alongside it. Nor was it completely supplanted by the Woodworth introductory text appearing in 1921.

It was in the year 1912 that two new understandings of human hows and whys, the behaviorist and the Gestaltist, were brought to psychology. The behaviorist insight arose in the work being done in laboratories at Petrograd (Pavlov) and Moscow (Bekhterev), and was then presented forcefully in this country by Watson; Gestaltism originated in work at Frankfurt and Berlin (Wertheimer, Köhler, and Koffka). The impact of Gestaltism was to hit American psychologists a little later. But Watson's virile presentation of behaviorism had its prompt appeal to the younger men of American psychology; and I was swept along. In truth I had been "softened up" when majoring in philosophy at Columbia by the prevailing antisubjective New Realism there. It came to be an ambition of mine to bring out an introductory textbook in this behaviorist direction, even following it out further. As an "objective" psychology (Bekhterev's term) it could properly include the nonsubjective physiological material of psychology that was not properly "behavior." At the other extreme it could deal further with the intellectual processes, especially by adapting and exploiting the Harvey Carr–Walter Hunter "symbolic processes" brought into the light in their delayed reaction experiments and the fresh and simple treatment of "perception" in Stevenson Smith and Edwin R. Guthrie's *General Psychology in Terms of Behavior* (1921). Accordingly I named my textbook, published in 1928, *Fundamentals of Objective Psychology*.

Consistent with the atomistic and reductionist ways of thinking prevailing in those first decades of the century (and before?), the organization of my textbook proceeded by first describing reflex behavior and sensorimotor arcs, though not to the extreme of some of the then current psychology and neurology texts which furnished page-long lists of the reflexes of man out of which his living and moving as a person was to be compounded. The long accepted S-R formula was adopted; but one chapter was given to making explicit "modifications and amplifications" of that formula, and another to the integration of such action units (*à la* Sherrington). With such a machine-like framework the problem of what makes it operate so as to move and act like a living being became a real problem. There was little to go on in the textbooks or other systematic writings, little that could be described in completely objective terms. Some promise appeared in the "drives" of the animal psychologists; but too often these seemed verbal and not taken far enough back to their physical origins in identifiable "matter." I was insistent upon going all the way back and identifying tissue conditions within the organism which gave rise to intra-organic stimulations which excited the organism to overt activity. My persistent demand was for bodily—identifiable bodily— tissues. Hunger served as a simple model. Instead of attributing the activity of a person who seeks food to his "instinct of hunger" we could see the start of the business in the physically recordable contractions of his stomach when empty, as by balloon and by x-ray. Similarly it did not require extreme ingenuity to find experimental physiological demonstrations of the needs of other bodily tissues as initiating other types of "motivated" activity. One more link in this story: when the organism in its activity came upon a situation (as food) in which the tissue demand ceased, then the said activity ceased. All of this, to be sure, was in the making in the mid-1920's, but I am supported by others who agree that it had not been as completely and clearly formulated, not so well based upon demonstrated tissue-needs as in my *Fundamentals of Objective Psychology*.

The book was well received by teachers of psychology. I was satisfied by the degree to which it extended the application of objectivism; and apparently it was teachable. After this has been said, however, I must add a comment. When teaching this or any other behaviorist text I found it sensible and fair to address my students thusly: "Now, we know that after all our interest in psychology is an interest lots of times in how we and other people feel or have enthusiasms or how our thoughts come and go. That is human nature, too!" Then I gave them more traditional material. And I frequently found it clarifying for them to hear the snatch facetiously quoting a Christian Scientist:

> Said credulous mistress O'Neil:
> "Though I know that pain isn't real,
> When I sit on a pin that punctures my skin
> I dislike what I *fancy* I feel."

Nine years later a second textbook was issued by me with a change of title to *Fundamentals of General Psychology* to permit change of contents to include subjective or phenomenological approaches to many topics.

Naturally there were other changes of emphasis reflecting the changing times. "Growth" of the individual had become "development," as the organismic, even the homeostatic, concepts came into greater use. Not unrelated to that shift of emphasis was the consolidation of the gestalt (now spelled with a small "g" as befits coin of the realm) correctives of atomism and reductionism. The motivated organism was now interpreted by principles of life as much as by principles of machinery and indeed by principles that are also biosocial. Further, it is true that our psychology must continue to be basically and in its methods a natural science; but also it should be addressed toward questions that are intrinsically human and humane. In my efforts to represent the current thinking of psychologists, I was indeed grateful for almost daily consultations with Dr. A. G. Bayroff. That this general textbook as well as my other work was in line with American psychology of the times, I took to be indicated by my election to the presidency of the APA in 1938.

Twelve years later I attempted a textbook resurvey of psychology without change of title for the new crops of college sophomores. There had been no revolution in basic theory, viewpoints, nor systematic terminology. But the experiences of war years had widened psychologists' ken in applied directions, most emphatically in clinical study of individual deviates.

From the first it has been one of my credos that to study human nature, just as in studying any other nature, the student should study *it,* not merely words about it. If he be given textbooks about man and his behavior, let him also have guidance in observing that behavior and in experimenting with it. In this faith we teachers of the introductory classes at North Carolina drew up mimeographed directions for each week's laboratory session, organized about the conventionally accepted sections: problem, materials and/or subjects, procedure, results, discussion, and references. Then, after some years of revisions and rewritings, the whole collection of sixty instructions was brought out in book form in 1931 as *An Experimental Manual in Psychology* issued by the same publishers as brought out my texts then and later, the Houghton Mifflin Company, whose conservative handling of all matters assures correctness in procedures and in details. We have not attempted revisions of this manual; it is almost a universal preference of laboratory men that they work out their own mimeographed sheets of instructions.

## OTHER PHASES OF LIFE

Of academic experiences with "pure" psychology I seem to have had my full share. Though continuously a member of one (North Carolina) faculty since 1919, I have enjoyed earlier and interim appointments of a term or more at twenty-two different universities and colleges. To mention a half of them, east to west, will suffice for the picture: Clark, Rochester, Princeton, Oberlin, Duke, Florida, Minnesota, Texas, Wyoming, Oregon, Southern California, and California at Los Angeles. It would be fun to hazard specific comparisons, of course, but so gratuitous! In certain departments emphasis is more on experimental, in some it is theoretical, others emphasize clinical; some are better equipped for advanced courses; at one institution all the students seemed lacking in any sense of humor as reported by other visiting professors as well as me; at another they were (all) excessive workers; and I could go on. Differences of psychology faculties, too, are easily recognizable along various dimensions. A most tempting field for surveying, yes; but not for genetic nor historical purposes.

For all that, my peregrinations have not been extensive geographically. My only trips "abroad" numbered two in eastern Canada at the times of psychology conventions, two in western Canada, a four-day visit in the Hawaiian Islands, a two-day tour of pre-Castro Cuba, and a ten-day sight-seeing tour of Mexico. All were fascinating. Two of these trips were especially valuable for their object lessons in social psychology. A sojourn in Honolulu and Hilo afforded opportunity to observe an absence of race barriers. A gracious and gifted teacher I met there turned out to be part Hawaiian, part Chinese, and part Irish. In those islands the term "native" is as likely to connote aristocracy as any lower status. In Mexico, again, the stereotypes "lazy," "dirty," and "mean looking" that one picks up from "greaser-baiters" near the border simply were totally inapplicable. I could relate incidents quite in line with a Canadian psychologist's and a Florida psychologist's warm praises after extended residence in Mexico by each. A particular instance that speaks volumes was related to me by the latter, who often spent a whole summer in this or that Mexican village, just living among the people there. Discovering that in one of his villages there was no law-enforcing official, he was moved to inquire what in the world they do with a fellow who might attempt to steal a burro or a wife or a purse of pesos. He received this answer, "Oh, we lead him down to the village square; and then we all stand around him and laugh at him!"

The story of psychology in America is, of course, for the major share of it an academic story, though the last two decades have witnessed an impressive flowering in the many clinical directions and areas of application. What is more, for me psychology has been limited to the nonapplied or "pure." My defects of hearing aforementioned barred active participation in either world war; though I served as a member of a sedentary Washington committee imposingly named Expert Consultants to the Secretary of War. My closest indirect experience with the physical fighting in World War II was through my son, Frederick Knowles ("Dick") Dashiell, who though in his middle thirties and with a family, was a volunteer "combat-correspondent" front line sergeant with the Marines throughout the Iwo Jima campaign. Later (through marriage to Mrs. Thelma Hill Smith) I retroactively got other vivid secondhand contacts with combat through her two sons. One, Donald M. Smith, Jr., of the Coast Guard, had survived an explosion, sinking, and a day of being "lost" after the Omaha Beach landing; and the other son, Adrian W. ("Duke") Smith of the Navy, narrowly survived a Japanese kamikaze divebombing. Now for a note of lighter vein. After the war Adrian was married to my daughter Dorothy Ann; then some months later I was married to his mother, thus making him both my stepson and my son-in-law, also making my daughter my stepdaughter-in-law. Other changes in stating this factual matter are readily apparent, and they make it a fertile conversation piece. This daughter incidentally had once consented to serve as the subject in a picture in the third (1949) edition of my textbook representing (in a strained posture) the use of a serial exposure apparatus.

And now, in no spirit of levity, let me say that these later years of life with Thelma have known an unhurried, unworried, gay, well-oriented serenity—even through illnesses—such as I would wish to be the lot of other senior citizens. One factor in this was a girlhood spent happily as a general's daughter in the heart of Wilsonian Washington and also as a nurse in training, while another is an undemonstrative devotion to her Church. There has been a contrast between our *Lebensanschauungen,* mine being of course the scientific and academic, hers the business, military, and political: we do not debate questions of religion nor of politics. I am often reminded of the familiar Browning passage beginning, "Grow old along with me . . ."; for it has acquired enrichment of meaning.

My son Dick is now assistant director of press and radio for the National Educational Association. His elder son is teaching mathematics at the University of California at Berkeley. My son-in-law "Duke" is on the board of directors of Hickey-Freeman. It seems a pity that comments on the academic, artistic, personality, social, and athletic achievements of most of my grandchildren and step-grandchildren would be out of place in a scientific and professional autobiography!

Was it the inheritance of an energetic constitution from my father and my mother or the result of stimulating opportunities? Whatever the interpretation, the remarks of some students and associates were to the point; and in the 1920's and 1930's I was a "glutton for activity." These activities included: organizing a new department; working out all details, lecture and laboratory, for the two-term introductory course; trying out courses I had neither studied nor taught before (abnormal, legal, industrial); sketching out all pre-blueprint details for a new psychology building, including animal laboratories; conducting or directing my own and advanced students' researches, including three of mine leading to papers for the International Congress; serving as chairman of local chapters of Sigma Xi and of the American Association of University Professors; twice serving on the advisory committee to the University president; taking up study of the cello; serving on a church committee; purchasing and remodeling a twelve-room home; holding on-leave appointments at universities from East to West Coasts; serving twice on the APA council, and twice as chairman of APA's committee on ethics. It has been a full life, and I am grateful.

Any professional man has memberships in "learned societies"—national, regional, and state. They do, of course, furnish some of the sources of his motivation, and they constitute some of the media and environment in which he works. I will take space for naming only those in which I happen to have held office. In chronological order they are:

Southern Society for Philosophy and Psychology, president, 1925
American Psychological Association, president, 1938
Society of Experimental Psychologists, chairman, 1938
American Association for the Advancement of Science, vice president and chairman, Section I, 1938
North Carolina Psychological Association, president, 1959
North Carolina Academy of Science, president, 1960
Southeastern Psychological Association, president, 1961.

Of the APA annual conventions, I can recall attending thirty-three, and finding inspiration at thirty-three.

Even in a matter-of-fact survey of his professional life one finds it impossible not to recognize that in some measure his morale and dedication has been partly maintained by feedback tokens he had received from students and from colleagues. I am reminded of them daily as my eye or mind's eye falls upon so many things: a pair of all-silk-and-lacquer vases brought over from Foochow, a Kreisler album with heartening inscription, a gasoline-propelled miniature airplane-on-leash, a framed parchment from a student's psychology club given my name, a sterling carving set, a combination gold-lettered leather briefcase and handbag, a complete desk set of blotter and

many pieces in brass and gold-stamped leather, a scalloped sterling serving
tray bearing thirty-three facsimile signatures, a tooled-leather billfold from
Egypt, and (in my study) a full-sized heavy photograph of a bronze wall
plaque that is mounted in the psychology building at Carolina, fashioned by
Dr. H. G. McCurdy's son John who had been commissioned by eighty-three
friends—the sculpture faithfully portraying my pleasure in handling a speci-
men of *Mus norvegicus albinus.*

Finally, I was presented the Gold Medal Award for 1960 from the American Psychological Foundation annually struck "in recognition of . . . long
devotion to Psychology as a science and as a profession"; and on the parchment accompanying the medal, testimony to the generosity of spirit of my
professional colleagues, for there it is inscribed: "inspiring teacher, lucid
writer, ingenious investigator, able administrator, and genial friend." To
quote a favorite author, Oliver Wendell Holmes:

> Call him not old, whose visionary brain
> holds o'er the past its undivided reign.

# REFERENCES

*Selected Publications by John Frederick Dashiell*

Children's sense of harmonies in colors and tones. *J. exp. Psychol.,* 1917, 2, 466–
475.

(with R. H. Stetson) A multiple unit system of maze construction. *Psychol. Bull.,*
1919, *16,* 223–230.

Some transfer factors in maze learning by the white rat. *Psychobiol.,* 1920, 2,
329–350. (a)

A comparison of complete versus alternate methods of learning two habits. *Psychol. Rev.,* 1920, 27, 112–135. (b)

A physiological-behavioristic description of thinking. *Psychol. Rev.,* 1925, 32, 54–
74. (a)

(with W. D. Glenn) A re-examination of a socially composite group with Binet
and with performance tests. *J. educ. Psychol.,* 1925, *16,* 335–340. (b)

A quantitative demonstration of animal drive. *J. comp. Psychol.,* 1925, *5,* 205–
208. (c)

Is the cerebrum the seat of thinking? *Psychol. Rev.,* 1926, 33, 13–29.

*Fundamentals of objective psychology.* Boston: Houghton Mifflin, 1928.

Variations in psychomotor efficiency in a diabetic with changes in blood-sugar
level. *J. comp. Psychol.,* 1930, *10,* 189–198. (a)

The new psychological laboratory at North Carolina. *J. exp. Psychol.,* 1930, *13,*
217–219. (b)

Some simple apparatus for serial reactions. *J. exp. Psychol.,* 1930, *13,* 352–357. (c)

Direction orientation in maze running by the white rat. *Comp. Psychol. Monogr.,*
1930, 7, No. 32. (d)

*An experimental manual in psychology.* Boston: Houghton Mifflin, 1931. (a)

*Fundamentals of general psychology.* Boston: Houghton Mifflin, 1937; revised, 1949.

(with A. G. Bayroff) A forward-going tendency in maze-running. *J. comp. Psychol.*, 1931, *12*, 77–94. (b)

Experimental studies of the influence of social situations on the behavior of individual human adults. In C. Murchison (Ed.), *A handbook of social psychology*. Worcester, Mass.: Clark Univer. Press, 1935. 1097–1158. (a)

A survey and synthesis of learning theories. *Psychol. Bull.*, 1935, 32, 261–275. (b)

(with Sybille K. Berwanger) Affective value-distances as a determinant of esthetic judgment-times. *Amer. J. Psychol.*, 1937, *50*, 57–67.

Some rapprochements in contemporary psychology. *Psychol. Bull.*, 1939, 36, 1–24.

A neglected fourth dimension to psychological research. *Psychol. Rev.*, 1940, 47, 289–305.

The role of vision in spatial orientation by the white rat. *J. comp. physiol. Psychol.*, 1959, 52, 522–526. (a)

Monocular polyopia induced by fatigue. *Amer. J. Psychol.*, 1959, 72, 375–383. (b)

### Other Publications Cited

Adkins, Dorothy C. *Construction and analysis of achievement tests.* Washington: GPO, 1947.

———. *Statistics: an introduction for students in the behavioral sciences.* Columbus, Ohio: Merrill, 1964.

Allport, F. *Social psychology.* Boston: Houghton Mifflin, 1924.

Angell, J. R. *An introduction to psychology.* New York: Holt, Rinehart and Winston, 1918.

Bagby, E. *Psychology of personality.* New York: Holt, Rinehart and Winston, 1928.

Hall, G. *Adolescence.* New York: Appleton-Century-Crofts, 1922.

———. *Psychology: briefer course.* New York: Holt, Rinehart and Winston, 1890.

James, W. *Psychology: briefer course.* New York: Holt, Rinehart and Winston, 1892.

Ladd, G. T. & Woodworth, R. S. *Elements of physiological psychology.* (Rev. ed.) New York: Scribner, 1911.

Metcalf, J. T. Psychology in the encyclopedias. *Contemp. Psychol.*, 1959, *4*, 97–105.

Münsterberg, H. *On the witness stand.* New York: Doubleday, 1909.

Smith, S. & Guthrie, E. R. *General psychology in terms of behavior.* New York: Appleton-Century-Crofts, 1921.

Whipple, G. M. *Manual of mental and physical tests.* Baltimore: Warwick and York, 1914.

Woodworth, R. S. *Psychology, a study of mental life.* New York: Holt, Rinehart and Winston, 1921.

Woodworth, R. S. & Schlosberg, H. *Experimental psychology.* (Rev. ed.) New York: Holt, Rinehart and Winston, 1954.

# James J. Gibson

I was born in 1904 in a little river town in southeastern Ohio. The Muskingum Valley had been settled very early by New Englanders. The Indians had long since disappeared, but arrowheads still turned up in the spring ploughing, and my father had a large collection. A river town, with a dam and a water-powered mill smelling of grain, is a memorable place for a small boy.

My mother taught all the grades in a country school until she married my father. He had learned to be a surveyor for railroads after a couple of years in college. Soon after I began school, his job took him into raw new country in the West. His family went along; only after some years in the Dakotas and Wisconsin did we settle down in a suburb of Chicago. By that time, at the age of eight, I knew what the world looked like from a railroad train and how it seemed to flow inward when seen from the rear platform and expand outward when seen from the locomotive. The son of a railroad man had a better opportunity than others in those days to *see* things: saw-mills, mines, ore-boats, mountains, canyons, deserts, rivers, viaducts, tunnels, and the geometrical wonder of steel rails tracing an even path over a wrinkled earth.

By the time I was fully settled in school I had two younger brothers. We lived within walking distance of Lake Michigan. But I never learned to be a swimmer; I had rather climb trees, and I conquered a whole grove in the backyard with my brothers. But they were four and eight years younger; I was something of a solitary youth and I had few outside friends until nearly through high school. There, at the age of sixteen, my entry into social life was provided by a teacher who cast me in a play. I was a wicked courtier.

I delighted in acting. For the next twenty years I sought every opportunity to try out for parts in the "little" theater. Amateur players are a special fraternity, I think, with peculiar ego-needs, and my proudest moments have been obtained on the stage. The achieving of a dramatic role, the expressing of a character, has given me deeper satisfaction than the playing of any of the other roles that an academic career affords—or the military, scientific, professional, or administrative roles. Wherever I have lived, the North Shore, Northwestern University, Princeton, Smith College, and Cor-

127

nell, the amateur theater has made a bridge between college and community and across disciplines, and those who are addicted to it, as I was before I became deaf, are persons to my taste.

The only thing I remember learning in high school was Euclidean geometry. The beauty of geometrical insight and geometrical proof made a lasting imprint on my thinking; I recall asking the teacher whether every theorem that *was* true could be *proved* true. After secondary school I went to Northwestern for lack of any other planning of where I might go to college. It was just down the lake shore, and I could commute from home.

In 1922 I transferred from Northwestern to Princeton (which strangely would accept a Midwestern sophomore without much Latin, but not a freshman) and found myself out of place again except among the little theater enthusiasts. My friends in college were the eccentrics instead of the club members. I had no idea what I wanted to do or be, choosing to major in philosophy and spending the summers as an inadequate bank clerk, a bewildered oilfield laborer, and a miserable salesman. It was the Princeton celebrated by F. Scott Fitzgerald. I was an emancipated youth but, alas, not a gilded one. I was deeply impressed by that environment, like the unhappy novelist himself, but I dimly realized that I did not like it. However, in my last year we put on a production of a blood-and-thunder play of the twelfth century from the manuscript of which Shakespeare had stolen the plot of Hamlet. The characters were the same even if their speeches were bombast. It was a great success, especially the duelling, which I had coached, and we took it to New York for two nights. I fell in love with our Ophelia who had been borrowed from the cast of the Garrick Gaieties. This last was the first "intimate revue" produced in New York, and I became a familiar backstage visitor. Philosophy was neglected. I scraped through the comprehensive exams in May, however, and she came to my commencement in 1925. To be sure, she jilted me during the following year, when I was a graduate student, but I had become a sophisticate. I could stroll casually through a stage door.

At the beginning of my senior year I had taken a course in experimental psychology run in permissive fashion by H. S. Langfeld, newly arrived from Harvard. The eight students were a mixed group but an *esprit de corps* developed. Some catalyst was present that precipitated four psychologists from them: Bray, Gahagan, Gibson, and Schlosberg. Langfeld was delighted with us; he had a touch of the German professor, but he winked at the horseplay with which we enriched the laboratory exercises. Toward the end of the year he was able to offer three of us assistantships. This stroke of luck gave me an identity; I was an academic; not a philosopher, but even better, a psychologist.

My lack of aptitude for business had been clearly demonstrated, and my father was willing to take the burden of two sons in college at the same time. Graduate study in psychology suited me. I brought to it a taste for pragmatism in philosophy and I soon became excited by the behaviorist revolution. Howard Crosby Warren, the founder of Princeton psychology after James Mark Baldwin, was a friend and champion of Watson, who spoke to the colloquium. I thought him brash. The next year Langfeld brought E. B. Holt to the department from Harvard, and we took to his ideas with enthusiasm. Holt was a slow writer but a great teacher. He had a contempt for humbug and a clarity of thought that has never been matched. He had shown how cognition might itself be a form of response, and he was engaged in extending conditioned-reflex theory to social behavior, amending the gaps in the published textbook that his student Floyd Allport had recently written. He shocked his students by violent predictions in the mildest possible manner of speaking.

Holt's motor theory of consciousness provided a way of encompassing the facts of Titchener without either trying to refute them or simply to forget about them. It was a more elegant theory than that of any other behaviorist. For thirty years I was reluctant to abandon it, and it is still very much alive today, but the experimental evidence is now clearly against it. Awareness seems to me now an activity but not a motor activity, a form of adjustment that enhances the pickup of information but not a kind of behavior that alters the world. Instead of the contrast between consciousness and behavior that used to preoccupy us, I think we should look for the difference between observational activity and performatory activity. But this is getting ahead of the story.

Graduate instruction at Princeton was not split up into different fields. It was centered around a weekly colloquium at which we made frequent reports in the form of papers written out and read. The faculty then criticized. There was a group of young instructors, including Leonard Carmichael who lectured on the evolution of the nervous system. We also learned from each other and from graduate students in other disciplines. The Graduate College, where we lived, had a life of its own apart from the University. It stood on a hill a mile from the campus. Its dean had won the only academic battle ever lost by Woodrow Wilson in placing it there. We had dinner in gowns in a great hall. The trappings were a mere imitation of Oxford, no doubt, but this did not bother us, for the intellectual air was bracing and the conversations were wide-ranging. The wine cellar included in the plans for the building was empty, but New Jersey applejack was to be had, and a stomach for it could be learned, if not a taste.

I did my thesis on the drawing of visual forms from memory to refute the just-published results of Wulf at Berlin, a student of Koffka's, purporting to show that memories changed spontaneously toward better *Gestalten*. The drawings of *my* subjects differed from the originals only in accordance with laws of perceptual habit, not laws of dynamic self-distribution, I concluded with great confidence. Form perception was learned. Otherwise one fell into the arms of Immanuel Kant. I was a radical empiricist, like Holt, who suspected that the very structure of the nervous system itself was learned by neurobiotaxis in accordance with the laws of conditioning. Little did I know that within six months I would be facing Koffka himself weekly across a seminar table.

I reported my research one spring under the wing of Langfeld at a meeting of Titchener's invited group of experimentalists. The great man sat at the head of a table, like Jehovah in black broadcloth, with an enormous cigar emerging from a great white beard. I received a few words of advice, very penetrating, as I recall. He inspired genuine awe, for he quite simply knew more psychology than anyone else. But my generation had no need for his theory or his method. His influence was on the wane and he died soon after. I was later deeply influenced by Boring's modification of the Titchenerian theory, a modification that permitted psychophysics to go about its business, but not by analytical introspection. The assumption that all consciousness, or even all cognitive consciousness, can be reduced to sensory elements is surely untenable.

So it was that in 1928 I was considered qualified to teach psychology. I went to Smith College (at $1800 a year). Harold Schlosberg went to Brown; Chuck Bray stayed at Princeton. At Smith I was to remain for many years. And within my first week I met that extraordinary man Kurt Koffka, a kind of person entirely new to my experience.

Koffka had been brought to Northampton by William Allan Neilson, who installed him in an old house off the campus, permitted him to import assistants from Russia, Poland, Germany, and elsewhere, and let him experiment to his heart's content. Neilson had not consulted his department of psychology in making this research appointment, and the teaching staff did not quite know whether to be honored or offended. But Koffka promptly set up a weekly seminar to which we were cordially invited.

Koffka did most of the talking, and I listened regularly from 1928 to 1941. I sometimes reported my own work and I occasionally ventured to argue with him, for my bent was skeptical and pragmatic. Koffka hated positivism. The emerging doctrines of Gestalt theory seemed to me tender-minded, but I learned a great deal, for the seminar was centered on evidence and the analysis of evidence. In 1933, after the original research funds had been exhausted, Koffka became a member of the department, teaching one course. He then began to put together the *Principles of Gestalt Psychology* (1935), requiring his undergraduates to summarize sections of his manuscript in class as he went along. This strange method of teaching, you might suppose, would soon bring his course enrollment to zero (the worst of all fates at a college), but, on the contrary, the girls were dazzled. He chose the brightest. It was a serious book, dedicated to difficult problems, and there was no compromise with difficulty.

Of course it is also true that Koffka loved Smith College and that women melted in his presence. It was once explained to me that such worship of an odd-looking man with a high-pitched voice came from the fact that he gave absolute attention to any girl he met. But I do not pretend to understand why they worshipped him. He wrote one of the great books of this century, as I came to realize later. It took a long time for the *Principles* to sink in, and I had to reject the notion of organization and reinterpret the notion of structure before I could assimilate it, but Koffka, along with Holt, was a main influence on my psychological thinking.

I had my own teaching, of course, during all this time. There were never less than nine class hours a week. I had a regular course in social psychology that ran throughout the year. After fifteen years of it I knew the field pretty well, but I never tried to publish in it. I also did my stint of teaching the introductory course and the beginning experimental course. But my specialty was advanced experimental psychology, which met six hours a week for thirty-two weeks a year. There were always eight to a dozen seniors in it, and we ran experiments on every possible problem. They were generally new experiments, with little or no published evidence as to what the results might be. Bright students, especially girls, will work like demons when the outcome will be a contribution to knowledge. At the high point of this course the students would choose a problem from my offerings, run the subjects, analyze the data, and write up a report at the rate of one a month. I still have copies of the best of these papers, and every so often I find a published experiment that was first performed essentially by one of my students in the thirties. A good many *were* publishable. The apparatus was makeshift (but it was used only once), the statistics were elementary (but one gets a feeling for reliability), and a satisfying number of the questions we put to test gave clear answers. There must have been 500 or more such projects in my years at Smith, and I am sure that they constitute my main backlog of psychological knowledge. And there is still another backlog in the files of unanswered questions that I had to dream up in order to keep ahead of those lovely creatures who had a zeal for discovering how the mind works.

One year, 1930 to 1931, there were eight or nine girls in the course who were all smart (and all pretty). The mysterious catalyzer of an intellectual group developed. We made astonishing discoveries—that a conditioned withdrawal-reflex would transfer to the unconditioned hand, for example (with E. G. Jack & G. Raffel, 1932). We had a lovely time and ended the year with a splendid picnic. Five of the group went on to become psychologists. Two of them, Eleanor Jack and Sylvia MacColl, with another from a previous year, Hulda Rees, became graduate assistants at Smith. That year, 1931 to 1932, was an illustrious one for me. As a prosperous bachelor with a salary of $2500 in the deep depression, I could take around all three girls at once, and they were charming as well as being my professional colleagues. We had weekends in New York and mountain climbing expeditions to New Hampshire. By summer I was in love with the prettiest of all and pursued her to Illinois where she was persuaded to marry me in September.

This is the place, perhaps, to jump ahead and speak of my wife's part in the psychological history here being attempted. I will say nothing about our personal life save that we have had a fine time, have raised two handsome offspring who seem to be intellectuals like ourselves, and have had our share of adventures. We have never been a "research team," as many married scientists have, for we collaborate only indifferently. She went to Yale for a year and got a degree with Clark Hull in a burst of mutual admiration. She was and is a very tough-minded investigator, for all of being a nice girl. Down deep she is a Hullian, as I am a Holtian; a rat-behaviorist, as I am a philosophical behaviorist. The influence of Koffka was weaker on her than on me. She is bored by the epistemological problem, whereas I am fascinated by it. Nevertheless, we converge in the developing belief that the weakness of the stimulus-response formula in American psychology lies on the side of the stimulus, not on that of the response. The experiments on learning that convince her of this are not the same as the experiments on perception that convince me of it, but we agree on where to look for the trouble, and we both think that modern psychology is in deep trouble.

We have no patience with the attempts to patch up the S-R formula with hypotheses of mediation. In behavior theory as well as psychophysics you either find causal relations or you do not. After much travail we managed to write a paper together ten years ago on perceptual learning (with E. J. Gibson, 1955). Perception, as we said, is a matter of differentiating what is outside in the available stimulation, not a matter of enriching the bare sensations of classical stimulation. We barely touched upon the many questions that arise, however, and agreed upon scarcely more than a few slogans. Leo Postman saw this paper as a threat to the whole theory of association (Postman, 1955), and it was, but he rightly argued that an alternative theory of perceptual learning had not been spelled out. References to "the Gibsons' theory of perception," therefore, have given us a bit of a turn, for we were neither wholly in agreement at the time nor was that paper a theory.

In the last few years, however, we have been working semi-independently on different levels of the input side of the S-R formula. We now have a theory. At this moment I have finished a book entitled *The Senses Considered as Perceptual Systems* (1966) and my wife has nearly finished one on perceptual learning and development. The one is consistent with the other. I have formulated a theory of stimulus information and redescribed the sense organs as mechanisms for picking it up. She has examined the ways in which growth and experience enhance the pickup of the invariants that carry information. As a whole it is new, and the theory has radical implications for all parts of psychology. But once more I have gotten ahead of the story.

Returning to 1932, I did an experiment that summer before getting married. I had previously been using a pair of spectacle frames with optometrist's trial-prisms in them to verify the old result that one soon learned to reach for things in the right direction despite their apparent displacement. I had also observed the curvature adaptation that resulted from wearing the prisms and assumed that this too was a correcting of visual experience by tactual, in accordance with Bishop Berkeley's theory of visual perception. But there was disturbing evidence against this presumably self-evident explanation (even in Stratton's original experiment of this type), and I thought of a control experiment that would surely put the doctrine of sensory empiricism back on its feet. I would look at a field of *actually* curved lines equivalent to the prismatic distortion for as long as I could stand to do so and show that no change in apparent curvature would then occur. But to my astonishment it did occur. Apparent curvature still decreased and straight lines thereafter looked curved in the opposite direction.

This result was shocking to an empiricist. How could sensory experience be validated except against other sensory experience? It might, of course, be validated against behavior, which came to the same thing, but there had *been* no behavior in my experiment. I could only conclude that the perception of a line must be like the sensation of a color or temperature in being susceptible to the negative afterimage caused by some process of physiological normalization. This was equally puzzling, however, for it called in question the very notion that perceptions were based on physiological sensations. This crucial experiment (see 1933), subsequently elaborated in many ways, has motivated my thinking for thirty years.

I never pursued the more strenuous experiment of wearing distorting spectacles for weeks or months, as Ivo Kohler did at Innsbruck in the mid-thirties, and I failed to discover the full range of phenomenal adaptation to visual distortion that he did (Kohler, 1951). His results are even more destructive of classical theories than mine. Distortion of the visual feedback from movements of the observer, it now appears, is even more important than a distortion of visual *form* with a stationary observer. If I had followed up this lead I might have come sooner to my present conviction that optical transformations in time are the main carriers of information, not optical forms frozen in time.

I continued to work on various problems in the decade before the war. A great deal of encouragement for research came from the annual opportunity to report it at the meetings of the Psychological Round Table, a somewhat raffish group of young psychologists in the East, founded on the inflexible principle that members became emeritus at the age of forty. Promotion of assistant professors was not rapid in those days and elevation to membership in the Society of Experimental Psychologists, which was full up with venerable holdovers from Titchener's day, was not to be expected. At its first meeting the group voted tolerantly *not* to call itself the Society of Experimenting Psychologists. It was concerned *not* to issue invitations on the basis of weighty deliberation. On Saturday night a scientific address was delivered on sexual or scatological questions. Despite the lightheartedness of these meetings, discussions and new ideas were fruitful, and criticism was sharp.

In 1937 one of my friends, an engineer, was a bug on automobiles, and it was the time of the first driver clinics. The tests being given, I felt, were nonsense, for the skill of driving a car (on which I prided myself) had never been analysed. So we analysed it (with L. E. Crooks, 1938). Lewin had begun to formulate his theory of behavior as locomotion, with fields, valences, and vectors, but it was static and did not apply very well to visually-guided real locomotion, so other concepts had to be worked out—the clearance-lines of obstacles, the margin of safety considered as a ratio, and the temporal flow of the necessary information for accelerating, decelerating, and steering. Our paper was not spectacular, but the problems encountered came up again in my wartime work on aircraft landing (see 1947, 1955) and my later attempt at a general theory of locomotion (1958). No fact of behavior, it seems to me, betrays the weakness of the old concept of visual stimuli so much as the achieving of contact without collision—for example, the fact that a bee can land on a flower without blundering into it. The reason can only be that centrifugal flow of the structure of the bee's optic array specifies locomotion and controls the flow of locomotor responses.

As the reader may gather, I prefer radical solutions to scientific problems whenever possible. General explanations are always preferable to piecemeal explanations ("models" as they are nowadays called), and this is all that is meant by a radical theory. As the depression deepened in the thirties, I became convinced that a radical solution of politico-socio-economic problems was possible. Social psychology looked a great deal easier then than it does now. Marxian socialism provided the only general theory for social action, and it was internally consistent as compared to the intellectual muddles of liberalism, and rational as compared to the stupidities of fascism. I was converted from skepticism and pragmatism to radicalism almost overnight in a strange way: by reading *The Education of Henry Adams*. In this effete and indecisive American I seemed to recognize myself. The old American radicals, men like Thorstein Veblen (with whose nephew I had taken a course in non-Euclidean geometry at Princeton), were men who had rightly been soured by the rationalizations of satisfied citizens, but they could accomplish nothing because they had no political backing. The mass support for social reform could only come, of course, from Labor. So I became a left-winger and joined the Labor movement.

A group of us on the Smith faculty took out a charter as Local 230 of the American Federation of Teachers. It was, I think, the first such college union. We bored from within the American Association of University Professors. We sent a delegate to the Northampton trade union council. The lack of any feeling for socialism among the local unionists puzzled me, and I must have puzzled them. President Neilson, who often was invited to AAUP dinners, was hurt by our minority, for he considered himself a radical. So he was, of course, but with a difference. We never did persuade any public or secondary school teachers to join our local. My wife and I once went up to organize the Dartmouth faculty, who in truth were exploited worse than we were, but we got so distracted by a round of parties on the Carnival weekend that the necessary papers went unsigned.

The truth is, I suppose, that the intellectual radicals of the depression years, and even the Communist Party, never got to the really hungry people. Marx could not foresee this. Social behavior was less predictable than we thought it was. I have reluctantly given up theorizing about politico-economic problems. The Society for the Psychological Study of Social Issues, which I helped to found and the motivation of which I understood, has become a group that I no longer understand. No one has a theory any more, only a conscience. And this is too bad, for, as Lewin said, there is nothing as practical as a good theory.

The failures of international politics in that era were heartbreaking to one of my generation. Things might have been different and Hitler might have been prevented if statesmen and parties had been wiser, that is, if they had understood what was going on. But to understand, to be able to explain and predict, entails the knowing of laws. It is our own fault if we do not know the laws. Because no radical solution to the problems of politics has been found does not mean that it does not exist. Psychologists are simply, on an absolute scale, dullards.

When the war came in 1941, I felt little idealism about it. Nevertheless, it was as good a war as could be expected if there had to be one, and there were opportunities for a psychologist to make a practical contribution. I left in the middle of the year and spent some months in Washington where the program of psychological research units in the Army Air Force was being organized. I then spent eighteen months in Fort Worth, Texas, at the headquarters of the Flying Training Command and another two and one-half years at Santa Ana Army Air Base in California.

Psychological research units were mainly needed for personnel selection. At one time, something like the equivalent to the entire college population of the country was being trained for flying duty of one sort or another, and selection for aptitude was essential. There was some research on training, of which I will speak, but testing was our main responsibility. Most of the psychologists recruited for this job were experimentalists like myself, not test psychologists. There was to be an entirely new approach to aptitude testing.

One of the new ideas was to use motion picture screening for the presentation of test items. And another, more obvious, was the development of tests for the visual perception of space. The Army Air Corps had to be at home in the "wild blue yonder." The motion picture unit became my responsibility and the ancient problem of space perception was my burden. It was worrisome, for, as I gradually came to realize, nothing of any practical value was known by psychologists about the perception of motion, or of locomotion in space, or of space itself. The classical cues for depth referred to paintings or parlor stereoscopes, whereas the practical problems of military aviation had to do with takeoff and landing, with navigation and the recognition of landmarks, with pursuit or evasion, and with the aiming of bullets or bombs at targets. What was thought to be known about the retinal image and the physiology of retinal sensations simply had no application to these performances. Birds and bees could do them, and a high proportion of young males could learn to do them, but nobody understood *how* they could.

The Aviation Psychology Program included four or five research units besides the motion picture unit. We made tests for aircrew aptitudes, hundreds upon hundreds of them; and we tested the tests in the Anglo-American tradition of statistical prediction. We validated against the criteria of pass-fail in the flying schools, and the navigator, bombardier, and gunnery schools, and thus lifted ourselves by our own bootstraps. We analysed the factors in the correlations between tests and struggled to interpret them. But I, at least, have never achieved a promising hypothesis by means of factor-analysis. The so-called "spatial" abilities extracted from existing tests still seem to me unintelligible. The fact is, I now think, that the spatial performances of men and animals are based on stimulus-information of a mathematical order that we did not even dream of in the 1940's. There are invariants of structure or pattern under transformation. Moreover, the information is so redundant in natural situations, with so many covariant equivalent variables and so many ways of getting information that substitute for one another, that the isolation of cues for testing these perceptual skills is a problem we will not soon solve. Perceiving is flexible, opportunistic, and full of multiple guarantees for detecting facts. It is no wonder that the hope of fairly sampling perception with paper-and-pencil tests, pictorial tests, or even motion picture tests has not been realized. And the building of apparatus to simulate the stimulus-information in life situations is difficult when one does not know what the information is.

The test-construction work of my own unit has been described elsewhere (1944, 1947) and need not be repeated. Adapting the motion picture for group testing was a fascinating problem. Our test films were partly shot and were always processed and printed in a militarized motion picture studio staffed with industry personnel who had simply put on uniforms. Air Force training films were also produced in this studio where the Hal Roach comedies had been made. We also had the facilities of Hollywood available. I became as sophisticated about film studios as I had been about the stage. I learned a great deal about the technology of film-making and something about the psychology of the sort of perception that the film can mediate. A true understanding of this sort of vicarious experience would be a triumph for both psychology and the cinema if it could be achieved. But there is a vast gulf between what the film expert knows and what the perception psychologist knows. The cinematographer knows how to convey astonishing versions of reality on a sheaf of light-rays but cares nothing for the eye. The psychologist thinks he knows about the eye but has never paid any attention to the subtleties in the sheaf of rays. The two do not communicate.

Toward the end of the war my research unit was finally asked to work on a problem that had long interested us, the question of how a training film taught, or conveyed information, and what kinds of subject matter the cinema was uniquely adapted to teach. The previous experimental literature on educational films in schools and colleges and the controversies over "visual education" were almost useless. The Air Force had been using training films on an unprecedented scale for all sorts of purposes and literally hundreds of them were available: for orientation, for morale, for propaganda against picking up girls not approved by the USO, and for instruction in all the classes of all kinds of training schools down to technical films on how to rivet aluminum. The AAF Production Unit in Culver City would make a training film on any subject whatever. But nobody had any clear idea as to whether or not they did any good. We had been analysing some of the shooting scripts of instructional films in advance of production to see if we could develop a theory of what a motion picture shot could do that nothing else could. And this led to an experiment.

R. M. Gagné, who had once been my student in peacetime and who was the only other pure experimental psychologist ever assigned to us as an officer, worked on it with me. Essentially what we did was to take an instructional film that we considered excellent and compare it with the best possible illustrated manual and the best possible illustrated lecture on the same material. The auditory instruction with the motion sequences ran only fifteen minutes; the written and oral instruction with the static pictures was fuller and ran thirty minutes. Despite the time difference, aviation cadets learned significantly more from the teaching with sequential displays than they did from the teaching with the graphic displays. The reasons were fairly clear. What had to be learned was a system of how to aim at a moving target (fighter plane) from a moving platform (bomber). As the situation changed, the action changed. The film *showed* how one thing varied with another; the book and the talk could graph it, represent stages of it, and describe it in several ways, but could not display the continuous covariation in time. Moreover, and this impressed me, the film could make use of the "subjective camera," taking the point of view of the learner and displaying how the situation would look *to him*, not merely what things looked *like*. The experiment is more fully described in my book (1947, ch. 10).

Gagné and I also worked on aircraft recognition, the discrimination and identification of small dark silhouettes against the sky with only slight differences in form. It was a life-and-death matter in certain theaters of the war. Weeks of training were spent on it in all branches of the service. Perhaps no other such peculiar perceptual skill has ever been so widely learned and taught. A large number of instructors was required, and it once seemed to me that half the English professors of America must be serving their country by teaching the subject. But how to do it? The psychologist Renshaw, at Ohio State, had early convinced the military that the secret of recognition was promptness and the way to get quick perceptual reactions was to give quick stimuli, that is, to show photographic slides of airplanes with a tachistoscope. The English professors were endlessly flashing pictures on a screen so as to speed up their students' perceptions. The only thing that could be said for such training was that it was less boring than most military courses. The trouble was that when the boys got overseas they could not recognize aircraft.

By the end of 1943 there began to be disillusion with the Renshaw flash system, and a few aviation psychologists were allowed to take a crack at the problem. An airplane has to be recognized in any of its possible orientations. We advocated the use of solid models, the changing shadows of solid models on a translucent screen, motion picture shots, and instead of pictures, caricatures or cartoon drawings of the different airplanes that exaggerated their distinctive features. Gagné and I did a lot of nice research on the kind of learning involved in this perceptual skill (Gibson, 1947, ch. 7). We learned more about the perception of objects, I think, than we would ever have done by running standard laboratory experiments on form-perception. For one thing, I got a nagging suspicion that nobody ever really sees a flat form in life, that is, a picture of a thing. One sees a continuous family of perspective transformations, an infinity of forms, that somehow specifies the solid shape of the object. This puzzle remained with me for twelve years until I was able, in collaboration with my wife, to conclude that the invariants in a family of transformations are effective stimuli for perception (with E. J. Gibson, 1957).

The suggestion that it is the distinctive features in the transformations of objects, not the forms as such, that enable us to recognize them is a very fruitful if radical hypothesis. What a caricaturist does is to freeze the differences between one human face and all others in a drawing, emphasizing the differences and omitting the similarities. A caricature therefore is not usefully understood as a distortion of a face or a misrepresentation, for it specifies the person and conveys information about him. This is information in the recently discovered meaning of the term which implies that a stimulus is definable as what it is *not* instead of as what it *is*.

I was lucky in the war, for unlike most I got to work finally at what I could best do. I did not care much for military life (the few psychologists who revelled in it were not ones I respected), but I made a lot of friends, and putting my education to a practical test was a new education. I discovered that what I had known before did not work. I learned that when a science does not usefully apply to practical problems there is something wrong with the theory of the science. So, after writing up my contribution to the shelf of volumes on aviation psychology, I got out, returned to my teaching at Smith, and began at once to write a book on visual perception that took off from new assumptions. This was *The Perception of the Visual World* (1950).

Koffka had died, and my wife and I felt that the spark had gone out in the old Smith College department, so we were glad to go to Cornell in 1949. Unhappily, she could no longer teach as she had done since 1932 (with time out) under Neilson's canny policy of hiring husbands and wives in the same department and getting two for the price of one-and-a-half. Smith has experienced no difficulty with the supposed evils of nepotism, and it is a pity that universities will not try the experiment of tolerating spouses. I doubt that they put their heads together any more than other academic pairs.

The book came out during the first year at Cornell. The crux of it came in the third chapter where the experience of the *visual world* was contrasted with the experience of the *visual field*. The former was the awareness of one's surroundings; the latter was an awareness of one's visual sensations when the eyes were fixated. I was out to give an explanation of the former, not of the latter. Depth and distance and objects of constant size and shape were *seen*, I suggested, not judged or inferred, and the question was how this could be explained. The perceptual impression was primary and the sensory impressions were secondary, being obtained only with an introspective attitude. The "cues for depth" were what depth and distance looked like when they were not simply seen as depth and distance. The real stimuli for perception (I should have said stimulus-*information* for perception) were gradients of the retinal image (I should have said *invariants* of the *optic array*).

The main new idea I introduced was that of optical texture, which enabled me to define and illustrate gradients of the *density* of optical texture. Such a gradient was asserted to be in psychophysical correspondence with the recession or slant of a phenomenal surface. This assertion has been checked by a good many experimenters in the last fifteen years and it seems to hold up. At least it does if optical "texture" is treated generally as the overall structure of the optic array. It subdivides into many other hypotheses that cannot be detailed here.

The idea that such a gradient might be a stimulus opened up a quite new possibility of explaining how perception might be veridical, for the gradient of density was a consequence of the perspective projection of light from the real surfaces of the environment. The correspondence of phenomenal surfaces to physical ones might be thus accounted for without any appeal to innate intuition, or the correction of sensations by past experience, or a spontaneous organization of the sensory data in the brain—in short, with no appeal to any theory of perception whatever. Here was a new basis for a realist solution to the epistemological problem.

My sixteen years at Cornell have been largely devoted to the developing, testing, and sometimes the altering of the ideas set forth in the *Visual*

*World*. They keep generating fresh ideas and opening up new explanations. A great number of exploratory experiments and some twenty or more published ones have come out pretty much as expected. Most of these involve surface-perception in one way or another: extending to the edges of surfaces; the layout of surfaces; the motions of surfaces, both rigid and non-rigid; the perception of human faces as elastic surfaces; the tactual perception of surface-layout; and recently the perception of impending collision with a surface (Schiff, 1965).

These experiments are not concerned any more with the perception of space but with the perception of the features of the world, the furniture of the environment, and what they afford. The old puzzle of depth-perception, I think, can be dismissed. Space, so-called, is not separable from meaning. An example is provided by the experiments done by my wife and Richard Walk on detection of a "visual cliff" (Gibson & Walk, 1960). Animals and babies are very sensitive to the optical information that specifies depth downward at an edge. This specifies (or "means," if I may use the term) a falling-off place. For a terrestrial animal it affords falling and hence injury. It might be expected therefore that this unique discontinuity in a transforming optic array would be readily picked up by terrestrial animals. Their behavior shows that it is. But this result does not in the least imply that animals and babies possess innate depth-perception in the sense intended by Immanuel Kant. It implies that their visual systems first detect those gross features of the layout of the world that are important for animals and babies. The information for a cliff is in the ambient light. The notion that they are born with depthless visual sensations to which the third dimension is added by *any* operation, learned or unlearned, now seems to me quite ridiculous.

There was a period in the 1950's when we explored the possibilities and the limitations of the kind of visual perception that is mediated by still pictures, drawings, photographs, and the like. I learned from it a great respect for painters and the art of painting. I was bewildered by the continuing controversy of art considered as representation versus art in the styles loosely called nonrepresentative. I have come to think that the futile debates about nonrepresentative art stem from our ignorance about the information in light. Psychologists and artists have misled one another; we have borrowed the so-called cues for depth from the painters, and they in turn have accepted the theory of perception we deduced from their techniques.

Eventually I came to realize how unlike the pictorial mode of perception is from the natural one. The former is perception at second hand; the latter is perception at first hand. The framed optic array coming from a picture to an eye is quite unlike the natural optic array coming from the world to an eye. The latter is only a sector, a sample, of the total ambient array. Eyes evolved so as to see the world, not a picture. Since this became clear to me I have tried to give up any use whatever of the term "retinal image." The assumption that there is a picture on the retina has led to all sorts of unnecessary and insoluble problems, problems for psychology, art, and optics. I have ventured to assume that classical instrumental optics comprises a set of convenient fictions for a rather dull branch of applied physics and that a new ecological optics can be worked out (1961).

I now assume that perception does not depend on sensory impressions at all, but instead only on the pickup of stimulus information. Sense-data are incidental symptoms of experience, not its foundation, and the effort of Titchener and his predecessors to make an inventory of them was almost wholly wasted.

The theory of perception as the registering of information and of perceptual learning as the education of attention to information in the available stimulation applies as well to touching, listening, smelling, and tasting as it does to looking. It illuminates the evolution of perceptual systems in animals. It explains the development of the subtle perceptual skills of man. The theory will be open to examination with the publication of my new book (1966) and the forthcoming one written by my wife on perceptual learning. I have had to contradict the most venerable doctrines of sensory physiology, and she has had to throw away the laws of association, seemingly the only foundation for empiricism since Locke. It is too soon to say whether the alternative ideas will catch on in physiology, psychology, and education. We shall see.

In conclusion, a kind of self-examination may be revealing. What I have most wanted to do all my life is to make a contribution to knowledge. If you feel you are doing this it is much more fun than running things, or being a military commander, a departmental chairman, a participant in the brotherhood of workers, a mountain climber, or even an actor. And it seems to me that one can contribute to knowledge without being very bright (which I am not) but merely by being stubborn about it. Such a contribution, of course, has to be expounded and clarified, and this is where teaching comes in. It is a two-way process, and no one does it for himself. One must listen as well as talk; read as well as write. Knowledge is not knowledge until it is preserved in dusty libraries for the future. But despite all that, the big satisfaction comes from the thinking that first went into it, the satisfaction of seeing old facts and new data fall into place.

I have been a lucky member of a rich society that has made it materially easy for someone who wants to contribute to knowledge to do so. At least it has been easy since the Great Depression. I have been given all the breaks. I have had time for thinking and writing at most of the havens provided for the leisure of the theory class, as someone put it. I have been to Oxford University (1955–56), the Institute for Advanced Study at Princeton (1958–59), and the Center for Advanced Study in the Behavioral Sciences (1963–64). They are wonderful places. My career has been made possible by the fact of endowments, and my research has been generously supported by the federal taxpayer. I am a creature of a prosperous age.

I seem to be, to my surprise, a member of a large profession. There are some 20,000 psychologists in this country alone, nearly all of whom have become so in my adult lifetime. They are all prosperous. Most of them seem to be busily applying psychology to problems of life and personality. They seem to feel, many of them, that all we need to do is consolidate our scientific gains. Their self-confidence astonishes me. For these gains seem to me puny, and scientific psychology seems to me ill-founded. At any time the whole psychological applecart might be upset. Let them beware!

I have, in my time, experienced the gratification of having people unburden themselves about their emotional problems and the fascination of getting inside the complex personality of another. I have felt the urge to help others. I even think I might have been a successful clinician. But nothing that I know as a scientist would have helped me to be one.

As to my personal peculiarities, the principal one is my deafness. I have had to wear a hearing aid for the last twenty years, and the loss seems to be progressive. The earliest of the surgical remedies for otosclerosis failed in my case and the later ones would probably not do me much good. The standard wisecrack that it must be a great advantage to be able to turn off the noises of the world at will gives me a hollow laugh. Deafness is isolating. For some reason I could never learn to pick up the visual information for lip-reading, although I have occasionally tried. On the other hand, I think I am fairly acute at understanding facial and gestural expressions. This is a contradiction I cannot resolve. I have tended to compensate for deafness by advertising it instead of trying to hide the necessary apparatus. Most people, in face-to-face conversation, react appropriately to this signal, and to them one is grateful. A few are disconcerted and, worst of all, a few shout. Conversation is nevertheless fairly satisfactory. The main frustration is in group discussion and in the failure of auditory localization. It is very hard for someone to realize that when he calls to me I do not know which way to look for him.

It is interesting that my vision has held up well even past the age when presbyopia limits the unaided acuity of most persons. I use my eyes for all sorts of purposes; I have educated them, and I sometimes wonder if that has anything to do with it.

I think I have a new solution to the ancient puzzle of how animals and men perceive. It is pieced together, of course, from selected bits of all the old solutions, but it has one new piece that makes everything fit—the concept of available stimulus-information and the relegation of stimulus-energy to its own level. There are other psychologists who have thought about perception almost as I do, but not quite. The one with whom in recent years I have been in strikingly near agreement is Albert Michotte, of Louvain—in everything but the notion of external information and external meaning. (His death, since this was first written, is a great loss to psychology.) It is a notable lesson in the convergence of experimental science that such a man as he and such a one as I, from totally different backgrounds, should have found ourselves agreeing so thoroughly and so delightedly—he, a student of Cardinal Mercier and I of the materialist Holt; he, a believer and phenomenologist and I a skeptic and behaviorist; he, a member of the conservative Belgian nobility, a prince of the Catholic Church, and I a Midwestern Sunday-school radical with an underlying suspicion of popery. We got the same results. This is what counts. It makes one believe in the possibility of getting at the truth.

## REFERENCES

### Selected Publications by James J. Gibson

(with E. G. Jack & G. Raffel) Bilateral transfer of the conditioned response in the human subject. *J. exp. Psychol.*, 1932, *15*, 416–421.

Adaptation, aftereffect, and contrast in the perception of curved lines. *J. exp. Psychol.*, 1933, *16*, 1–31.

(with L. E. Crooks) A theoretical field-analysis of automobile driving. *Amer. J. Psychol.*, 1938, *51*, 453–471.

History, organization, and research activities of the Psychological Test Film Unit, Army Air Forces. *Psychol. Bull.*, 1944, *41*, 457–468.

(Ed.) Motion picture testing and research. *Aviat. Psychol. Res. Rep.*, No. 7 (Washington: U. S. Government Printing Office), 1947.

*The perception of the visual world.* Boston: Houghton Mifflin, 1950.

(with E. J. Gibson) Perceptual learning: differentiation or enrichment? *Psychol. Rev.*, 1955, *62*, 33–41.

(with P. Olum & F. Rosenblatt) Parallax and perspective during aircraft landings. *Amer. J. Psychol.*, 1955, *68*, 372–385.

(with E. J. Gibson) Continuous perspective transformations and the perception of rigid motion. *J. exp. Psychol.*, 1957, *54*, 129–138.

Visually controlled locomotion and visual orientation in animals. *Brit. J. Psychol.*, 1958, *49*, 183–194.

Ecological optics. *Vision Res.*, 1961, *1*, 253–262.

*The senses considered as perceptual systems.* Boston: Houghton Mifflin, 1966.

### Other Publications Cited

Gibson, E. J. & Walk, R. The "visual cliff." *Scientific American,* 1960, *202* (No. 4), 64–71.

Koffka, K. *Principles of Gestalt psychology.* New York: Harcourt, Brace & World, 1935.

Kohler, I. *Über Aufbau und Wandlungen der Wahrnehmungswelt.* Vienna: R. M. Rohrer, 1951.

Postman, L. Association theory and perceptual learning. *Psychol. Rev.,* 1955, *62,* 438–446.

Schiff, W. Perception of impending collision. *Psychol. Monog.,* 1965, *79* (No. 604), 1–26.

# Kurt Goldstein

(Edited by Dr. Walther Riese)

I was born in Kattowitz, a small town in Upper Silesia, Germany, now a part of Poland. I went to a so-called classical *Gymnasium* in which my interest in learning was directed mainly toward the humanities. We were taught the Latin and Greek languages and their literature for many hours a week. Modern languages were somewhat neglected and we read their literature in German translation. We also were taught mathematics, physics, botany, zoology, and geography.

When I had received my bachelor degree (*Abiturium*), I went to the University of Breslau and from there for one term to Heidelberg, returning for the rest of my education to Breslau, where I received my medical degree and my license to practice.

I was undecided in the beginning whether to major in philosophy or natural science, particularly after I went to Heidelberg, where I became very much interested in philosophy and literature. I chose natural science as a profession and became a physician.

Due to the organization of German universities I had ample opportunity, as all students had, to explore many other fields. During the first two years no examination had to be passed and one could elect his studies according to his own time and preference, thereby acquiring knowledge in many areas simultaneously. Medicine appeared to me best suited to satisfy my deep inclination to deal with human beings and to be able to help them. The vague knowledge I had of medicine concerned mainly diseases of the nervous system, which seemed to me to be particularly in need of attention. At that time these diseases were generally considered to be caused by abnormal bodily conditions. Thus, the study of anatomy and physiology was taken for granted, and so they became first the chosen area of my studies and very soon of my research.

Dr. Goldstein died September 19, 1965. Dr. Riese was Dr. Goldstein's associate and is presently emeritus associate professor of neurology, psychiatry, and the history of medicine at the Medical College of Virginia. Formerly he was consulting neuropathologist to the Department of Mental Hygiene and Hospitals of the Commonwealth of Virginia, chargé de recherches du Centre Nationale de la Recherche Scientifique (Paris), and Privatdozent of neurology at the University of Frankfurt a/M.

Even as a senior medical student I became most interested in the theoretical problems which could be worked out in the laboratory. I was therefore attracted to the work of researchers who were especially active in the field of my endeavors. The anatomist Professor Schaper, whose specialty was the embryonic development of the nervous system of man, was an example for me. Another was the famous psychiatrist, Professor Karl Wernicke, who investigated the symptomatology of psychosis in connection with the post-mortem findings in the brain, and I became interested in his use of psychology to understand psychic phenomena. In that era there was more interest in psychosis than in neurosis and, indeed, each was usually treated separately. Neurology as an independent field gained interest much later. There was, for a long time, dispute as to whether neurological cases should be treated in a medical department or in a psychiatric institute. Only when men like Nonne, Erb, Ottfried, Förster, Edinger, Kussmaul, and others began to work exclusively in neurology did it become an independent specialty of study and teaching.

I am very grateful and devoted to those teachers of mine, not only because I had the opportunity to acquire so much knowledge from them, but because each of them developed in me certain characteristic procedures of scientific investigation, which I learned only later to appreciate at full value. Schaper taught me to appraise and give painstaking attention to the most minute details and impressed me by his precise and detailed observations and descriptions of data often mistakenly considered unimportant, as well as by his complete personal dedication to his work. I learned from him how to observe developmental processes and come to an understanding of living nature without falling prey to mechanical interpretations. With Wernicke I became aware of the interrelation of matter and function, which led to a psychological interpretation of the symptoms of nervous diseases. His recognition of the significance of psychology for psychiatry was far beyond that of other psychiatrists of his time.

In Edinger I found an excellent interpreter of the great variations in the relationship of the structure of the nervous system to the behavior of animals; thus, he created a new field of science: "the comparative anatomy of the nervous system." Although my basic concepts later diverged from his, he had a lifelong effect upon my thinking. His was an all-embracing attitude toward living beings; he turned particularly to the study of the central nervous system of man. It led him to strive for a treatment center as the goal of his work, a wish that unfortunately was never to be fulfilled. The strength of his intention was shown in the fact that he not only gave me, his *Oberarzt* (first assistant) in his institute, whom he needed very badly, permission to organize my special institute for brain-injured soldiers, but he even dismissed me from his laboratory with the words, "Your work with human beings is of much greater importance than my theoretical work in the laboratories." How deep this concern of his was, could be seen in the seriousness with which this famous man treated the patients in the small outpatient department of his institute. I remember vividly his kindness to patients and co-workers alike. He used to say, when a young researcher wrote a paper about a topic that he himself wanted to study, "How good! Now I won't have to do it," and at once wrote those words in a kind letter to the author.

When he died in 1919, I became, as he had been, *o.ö. Ordinarius* (professor in ordinary) of neurology at the University of Frankfurt a/M. As such I had to teach neurology at the University. He left me with the difficult task of becoming the director of the neurological institute and of the institute for brain-injured soldiers, which I had founded under military authority during the First World War and which was under my care from 1916 until 1933, when I left Germany. It demanded much theoretical and practical work. In addition I had at the same time to treat a considerable number of war-neurotics; this, from both theoretical and practical points of view, was very fortunate. Management of this great caseload was possible only because I found a considerable number of young co-workers.

My major activity was directed toward rehabilitation of the brain-injured in all physical and psychic aspects. The institute staff included medical doctors, one of whom was Professor Walther Riese; psychologists, including Professor Egon Weigel; schoolteachers; and a number of craftsmen who taught patients trades according to the latters' remaining abilities. This therapeutic vocational program was organized after careful observation and study of each patient by our professional staff. Psychological examination and training of aphasic patients was my special interest for many years and thus became an outstanding subject of study in the institute. I had engaged for this special purpose a number of competent psychologists to assist me. I want to mention the invaluable help I received from my late friend and co-worker, the psychologist Adhemar Gelb. The details of our work during the first years are recorded at length in the book *Die Behandlung, Fürsorge und Begutachtung hirnverletzter Soldaten* (*Treatment, Social Care and Evaluation of Brain-Injured Soldiers*) published in 1919.

Thousands of brain-injured soldiers passed through our hospital where we had developed my method for the application of psychology to the investigation of disordered brain functions. I had dedicated myself for many years previously to psychology and psychotherapy, and as far back as 1927 I had taken part in the organization of the International Society for Psychotherapy. When a new department of neurology was contemplated at the Moabit Hospital of the City of Berlin I accepted the offer to become its director. This neurological department of the general hospital was built according to my plans and provided the facilities I needed for the treatment of patients and the development of my theoretical work. In this way the vision of Ludwig Edinger became a reality.

I left my *o.ö.* professorship at the University of Frankfurt a/M., one of the few chairs of neurology in Germany, with great regret. Unfortunately,

I could not enjoy this very interesting and, I think, promising work for longer than a few years because I was one of the first professors at the University to be arrested by the Nazis, and I had to leave Germany.

I then accepted an invitation to be the guest of the University of Amsterdam. That year was a particularly fruitful one for the development of my ideas, as it gave me time to write my book *Der Aufbau des Organismus,* first appearing in Holland in 1934 in the German language edition and in 1938 in English in the United States under the title *The Organism.* In this book I presented my views on the organization and functions of the central nervous system from the "holistic approach." I tried to explain not only my procedure in the treatment of patients but also my convictions about research in biology. The latter resulted in a definite interpretation of the nature of man that I consider to be the basis of my treatment.

In 1935 I left Amsterdam and arrived in New York where I obtained a license to practice medicine. I was given the opportunity to work at the New York State Psychiatric Institute and became clinical professor of psychiatry at Columbia University. At the Montefiore Hospital the director organized a laboratory of neurophysiology for me. During 1938–39 I was appointed by the president and fellows of Harvard College to read the William James Lecture on Philosophy and Psychology. This lecture was published under the title *Human Nature in the Light of Psychopathology* (1940). From 1940 to 1945 I was clinical professor of neurology at Tufts Medical School in Boston under a grant from the Rockefeller Foundation. From then on I was engaged in the private practice of neuropsychiatry and psychotherapy, as visiting professor of psychopathology at the College of the City of New York, as visiting professor at the New School for Social Research in New York, and later as professor at Brandeis University on the same subject.

In trying to present a review of my research and the theoretical foundation of my activities I feel somewhat embarrassed at the sheer volume of my publications, which may be simply the effect of my long life. The widely diversified topics, belonging to different problems, even to different fields of science, may look as if they had little interrelationship and were simply the result of a scattering of interests. That is not so. Some papers were inspired accidentally by the presence of patients who presented specific problems calling for special investigations and, as a matter of fact, issued from practical problems with which I was confronted.

Increasing knowledge taught me that one can understand each single phenomenon correctly only when one considers it in relation to others, all the normal patterns and abnormal symptoms a patient presents (see *The Organism,* p. 78). It is of the utmost importance that one evaluate any aspect of the human organism in relation to the condition of the organism in its totality. On this understanding is based what I have called self-realization. The trend toward self-realization is not merely a stimulus but a driving force that puts the organism into action. What one usually calls the influence of the environment is the coming to terms between the organism and the world in "adequacy."

As stated in an early paper, the cause of poor results in the therapy of organically damaged patients was the neglect of the aforementioned problematic character of the symptom. Even experts, masters in their field, started their investigation from a "primary symptom" that was often selected by theoretical consideration. One can say that a basic reason for their failure was the *associationist psychology*, which had at that time a prevailing influence on the thinking of physicians in general. My practical procedure, though not determined by any theory, induced me to formulate some methodological postulates which, I thought, had to be taken into consideration in all investigations and which I still consider the most important before we attempt any interpretation.

The first postulate is *to consider initially all the phenomena* presented by the organism, giving no preference in the description to any special one. At this stage, no symptom is to be considered of greater or lesser importance for the diagnosis. It must be left to future investigation to determine to what extent one symptom rather than another is essential for understanding the underlying defect of a function.

The second methodological postulate concerns *the correct description of the observable phenomena*. It was a frequent mistake to write down what amounted to the mere description of the simple positive or negative results obtained from an investigation that issued from a theory. A correct result may be ambiguous in respect to its underlying function. Therefore only a thorough analysis and presentation of the way in which the effect, whether success or failure, was achieved can provide clarification of the performance. Equally ambiguous can be the wrong answer or the missing one or saying, "I do not know." Though only positive phenomena can be used for gaining knowledge, the negative ones can be very important indirectly. They are an indication that something is going wrong. The patient may not be able to answer, but if one is able to eliminate the secondary phenomenon that hindered him, then one may gain knowledge of what he *is* able to do, and that alone is of importance. Often one will find that it is not the negative result itself which indicates the incapacity of the individual. A feeling of insufficiency, which may or may not produce a number of other disturbances, may in turn produce different effects. What happens in this respect depends on the evaluation of the insufficiency by the *patient himself* and on the effect of the relationship between the physician and the patient, on what we call the *transference*. What is going on in the patient is not simply the failure to answer; his reaction can be interpreted only in relation to an often very complicated network of events.

The older psychopathological protocols usually confined themselves to a consideration of whether or not the patient answered a question correctly.

This plus-or-minus method is inadequate, no matter whether the answer is correct or false. If we regard a reaction only from the standpoint of the actual solution of a task, a correct answer can be presented in spite of a wrong procedure. That may lead us to overlook a deviation from normality since the individual may fulfill the task by a detour which may not be evident in the answer.

The third methodological postulate is *a careful description of the present condition of the organism in which the answer appears*. Many errors would have been avoided in psychopathology if these postulates, quite definitely stated by Hughlings Jackson in a similar way decades ago, had not been so frequently neglected.

There are two objections to our methodological postulates. The first is that one can never really determine at what point an examination can be regarded as completed. When, within the frame of reference of our postulations, we seek to analyze as many individual performances of a patient as possible, this technique will certainly obviate the grossest errors even though it may not lead to absolutely incontestable results. The investigation should be carried far enough to insure at least that a theory can be developed which will render understandable all observed phenomena and point out the ones not yet observed, leaving these latter open for further investigation.

A second objection to our postulates may be that our procedure necessarily limits the number of cases investigated. As a matter of fact, we have on occasion based our results on a few or even a single case, the results of which advanced our knowledge. Conversely, the study of a great number of patients is often misleading because, as the literature bears witness, one cannot investigate them all in the same careful manner. It seems to me that the only alternative is to carry out the examination of each patient to the extent we have indicated before. Investigations of other patients may induce us to modify our first assumptions, but if the analysis of the first one was sufficiently thorough, additional investigations will not destroy the concept, only round it out. I would like to illustrate our procedure by an example of one patient with a speech disturbance, showing how "step-by-step" investigation can gain results that bring us nearer to the truth. I used this method of investigation in my first paper on the subject, amnesic aphasia (1905). I had not yet come to the interpretation that I later considered the right one, but even this unfinished presentation was important as a stepping-stone for the development of my theoretical point of view insofar as I already realized that we have to consider two different forms of man's relationship to the world, a realization that proved important for deeper understanding of the symptoms (see *The Organism*, ch. VII).

The clinically outstanding symptom of this patient with brain damage was his inability to name an object in spite of recognizing it and being able to speak the word for it in the next sentence—a symptom-complex frequently observed in brain damage. For example, a woman patient was unable to say the word "umbrella" when asked "What is this? What do you call it?" but immediately afterward said, "I have three umbrellas at home." This seeming contradiction was explained by further examination which showed that the patient was impaired in a special mental capacity which we later called "abstract attitude." This defect was overlooked at first. Was the failure related to the defect of the abstract attitude? Subsequent experimental studies on normal people confirmed the assumption. We understand now that the missing capacity was not at all a defect of a special function of finding words or a defect of an association between the "image" of objects and particular words, as we had assumed. That made understandable why therapy based on this assumption was so unsuccessful.

Other symptoms that the patient presented and that had previously been considered the effect of another damage of the brain could then likewise be explained simply as the impairment of abstraction. We came more and more to the conclusion that the whole clinical picture might well be understood by the application of the holistic approach, which began to play an increasingly important role in my attempt to understand the behavior of human beings, normal and pathological. But another very important question arose which could not be answered yet.

I was aware from the beginning that the orientation that tries to evaluate each single phenomenon in relation to the knowledge of the whole organism confronts us with an epistemological problem of the first order (see The Organism, p. 399 ff.). Certainly such knowledge cannot be derived from the results of natural science methodology. So this became my main problem: How can we move from the quantitative experiences of natural science to the qualitative ones of biology? In The Organism I stated that we should not hesitate to assume a creative power of the living being as the basis of such an endeavor. This we find in the practice of medicine, as witnessed by a great number of my own experiences with patients. Medicine is based on scientific experiences, not on theoretical ideas from which its practice can simply be deduced; it is a kind of artistic enterprise and so mirrors the nature of man, which requires risk-taking and courage (see The Organism, p. 306). As I have said, "Courage in its final analysis is nothing but an affirmative answer to the shocks of existence which must be borne for the actualization of one's own nature."

I presented the investigation of this patient in order to show how an apparently inconspicuous symptom, such as the loss of ability to find a word under special conditions, could be masked in other situations by the patient. Thus, I came to devote my efforts to solving the most complicated and essential epistemological problem of biology and medicine, a problem that accompanied my endeavors to understand patients and their treatment all my life and for which I found a solution much later. It applied to many conditions we confront in clinical neurology and psychiatry, particularly aphasia, agnosia, and apraxia. Therapy was not in all respects satisfactory. Because the psychological analysis was not sufficient, our task was mainly custodial, bringing the patient relief from stress by medication and other means.

My greatest problem grew out of my awareness at this period that I could not achieve my goal with the method of natural science. Certainly, the objects of natural science are a part of our life and the results of this method are of great significance, but they are of a different nature from the objects of our present studies, the objects of biology. The dissimilarity of the "facts" that we study does not mean that they derive from two different worlds; the differentiation is the product of man's ability to look at things from a variety of viewpoints which correspond to different goals. It is always the one living world which we are confronted with, but we make use of the experiences therein for other purposes than those of natural science. The purpose of the world of natural science is to gain security; of the other, to live in its full nature. Man's most dangerous conflict is that he overestimates his trend toward security to such a degree that he even comes to believe that he can experience the living world with the same method. This mistake has created the catastrophe which we feel now and which we fear if we once begin to be aware that it may be the earmark of any culture and particularly of our own. This general consideration was the basis of my urge to find a better method for understanding the behavior of living beings and of sick people in the attempt to help them.

The result of my experiences was that natural science presupposes the living world but the living world is not the world of natural science. Knowledge of the latter, however important it may be, represents only one aspect of the living world. Indeed, to be scientific we always have to begin our work with the quantitative method of natural science since it alone gives our knowledge the order we need. This order can be gained only by the experience of beginning with the isolated stimuli which issue from ourselves and from the world. We call this process "perception," in which phenomena have to be taken much more holistically than is usually done. With this experience we build a definite concept of the nature of the scientific natural world and so also of the living organism. But one should never forget that, by this procedure, "thinking" enters into natural science only when it can be used for guaranteeing order. The world of natural science is an abstraction, a creation of man in which directly experienced objects do not exist, or better, exist only in the abstraction of natural science statements; such a construction of the world is not suitable for the understanding of life. It is not even able to bring together man and world—the basis of all knowledge. The relation between man and world from both perspectives is based on adequacy, adequacy of the happenings between man and world. In respect to this point there is no difference between natural science and the living world; however, the kind of adequacy in each is not the same.

The world in which we live is a much more encompassing sphere than the world of natural science; what concerns natural science is quantitative results, whereas our living world is based upon qualitative experiences. Security needs the material world, that is, a product of the application of natural science by which the spiritual side of man is intentionally by-passed. Existence in the living world presupposes qualitative experience, not simple "order." To understand how we can move from the quantitative results of natural science to the qualitative activity of life is a problem that has always caught the imagination of man. I cannot go into the details here, but I want to emphasize that adequacy is achieved by man's creative power; it is, so to say, a secret activity of life by which our self-realization becomes possible. That procedure demands that we take the risk of insecurity; only when confronted by some insecurity are we able to realize ourselves, which means to exist.

There are two ways by which we enter into the sphere of adequacy. One of them is language. As equivocal as language may be in relation to the world, an example of which we have seen in our discussion of the patient with difficulty in naming, it will nevertheless give us some key to attaining adequacy. The other way is the "preferred behavior," which I have dealt with in detail in *The Organism*. It has been my observation that the correct performances, the ones that fulfill a particular task, are those that are performed in a preferred way. We are by no means always conscious of how we perform, but we are not unconscious of it. We are, so to say, in a sphere which promotes correct behavior. Many experiences have taught me that when we perform a special task correctly, the whole organism is in a "preferred condition" and we are on the way to being adequate. Neither preferred condition nor adequacy is in itself a goal of the organism; they are but the basis for self-realization. Adequacy represents a secret procedure of life, and life demands it for existence. It does not occur consciously; we become aware of it in modifying our behavior when our sense of moving in the direction of adequacy is disturbed. We should never forget that our activities toward self-realization are always hampered by the difficulties of life, especially by the influence of the world of natural science. We have to bear these imperfections in our activities, as they belong to human nature.

The usefulness of the step-by-step procedure induced us to apply the same method again and again with the same patient and with other patients with similar symptoms that we had not fully understood before. This method was especially elucidating because during World War I, I had an opportunity to see the same brain-injured patients for many months and some for even longer. After my departure from Germany, there was no contact until I went there in 1958 to see and examine many of these patients again. In the meantime my findings on the same problems, for instance of speech disturbances, were frequently published: in 1905, 1909, 1910, 1914, 1915, 1924, 1933, 1936, 1938, and 1948, until 1950, when I published a book in which I used all the results concerning the phenomena of pathological speech, of therapy, and of normal language.

I want to mention some problems which I treated in the same manner: the problem of localization in the brain cortex, the restitution and regulation of defects, the problem of brain injuries (which occupied me from 1916 to 1933), and, later on, the problems of anxiety, psychophysical relationship, abstract and concrete behavior, consciousness and the so-called "unconscious," catastrophic condition, and therapy. I also deal with these problems and their implications in my books.

When I review my scientific work I feel that I can divide it into three periods. In the first period I was influenced, as were most physicians at that time, by the atomistic approach of natural science. The chief problem I had in mind in the first period of my research was that of better understanding the symptom complexes of patients from the physiological and psychological points of view, as well as the localization of the damage of the brain corresponding to the disturbed performance.

Concerning localization, I presented the result of my research of the enormous literature available and of my own great experience in a paper of 242 pages, in which I discussed this problem from the anatomical, psychological, and clinical standpoints. I came to the conclusion that there are no facts to justify the assumption of the localization of performance in definite regions of the brain cortex. The central nervous system represents a network which is related to different peripheries in which the performances appear to us. Wherever the damage of the brain is located, the basic function of the brain, which we call the figure-ground function, is disturbed. This is followed by varying symptomatology because the different functions underlying the performances are disturbed in differing degrees of severity by this damage. To this corresponds a modification of a performance, better said, of behavior, which we call, according to Hughlings Jackson's concept, "dedifferentiation." The defect of a performance related to the lesion of a definite region is determined by the influence that the disturbance of the particular structure of the network at this place exerts on the total process of the nervous system. Inevitably, we have to deal in all lesions with the modification of the nervous substance. This disturbance always has the same structure in principle, no matter which part of the nervous system is involved, be it the cortex, subcortex, spinal cord, or the peripheral nerve. This modification is the effect of isolation which takes place in all damage. Pathology consists of isolation of the part of the nervous system which is damaged. When we want to understand the defect of a performance we have to consider the effect that isolation produces in general on the functioning of the nervous system and especially on the particular part which is damaged. As the observation and analysis of a great number of symptoms have taught us, the effect of isolation differs as to extent and intensity. The symptoms that we observe are, however, not simply the effect of the damage alone but also of the reaction of the organism to this defect in its attempt, despite this defect, to come to a new order which guarantees its existence. The remaining defect does not prevent the organism from seeking adequacy again, albeit in a different world. This should never be forgotten in any attempt to put performance in relation to a specific damage in the brain.

A considerable part of my research was directed toward the very complicated problem of helping patients to find a new organization for their lives. Although opposed to the theory of localization, I certainly do not deny the significance of the brain for performance. But we cannot say that because we find a definite defect in our performances in a definite region of the brain, that it is in this region that the function is normally performed. Monakow, who carried out very careful research, has protested correctly against this. Strangely enough, one finds even in modern textbooks these brain maps in which different functions are attributed to definite regions, even functions that are only psychologically understandable, but not spatially demonstrable.

Our main goal was and must be to better understand individual symptoms as an expression of dedifferentiation before we consider them at all in relation to a definite brain function. I have tried to contribute some knowledge of this in my book *The Organism.*

It would create the greatest difficulty if I were to assume that the problem of psychophysical unity should be thought of as being directly related to brain function. Our observations of normal and pathological behavior have taught us that the activities of the organism cannot be understood as effects of fixed patterns of reaction to stimuli coming from the outside or inside, as was generally assumed in mechanical concepts, such as reflexes, drives, instincts, or will.

The assumption of these agencies is untenable. The activities of the normal and pathological organism can be understood only if looked upon as determined by the basic trend of the organism, the trend to realize itself in the world as completely as possible under the given conditions. This situation we call "existence." This is the driving force of the organism, each of whose activities represents a definite condition of the excitation of the nervous system or, one could better say, of the whole organism. If it sometimes appears that the organism is under the influence of reflexes, then the relation of the organism to the world is not in a normal condition.

The reflex and similar theories cannot be based on experimental results because we are confronted, as in pathology, with the results of phenomena going on in isolation. It seems to me pertinent here to make some remarks about the origin of the holistic approach which made such a great number of symptoms understandable. It gave me a new impetus to study the nature of man; some results of this study were presented in my William James Lecture at Harvard in 1938.

The holistic approach did not originate from any idea. It was forced upon me by concrete experience. The holistic approach was not unknown in Germany; it had been proclaimed by such famous internists as Kraus,

Krehl, Christian, and others. It was particularly Ludwig Binswanger who dared to express similar ideas and to put the person into the center of his concept of sickness and therapy, so giving meaning to psychological and physiological phenomena. One might think that Freud's concept was not far from this, but the introduction of reflexes, drives, and instincts made Freud's use of it more than doubtful. The work of the famous English neurologist, Hughlings Jackson, could have been very important, but was very little known, particularly in Germany, until after the First World War when his pupil, Henry Head, published his work about aphasia in which he followed Jackson's concepts. Those few who accepted Jackson's concepts in principle were not yet ready to consider the concept of the organism as a whole, not even so far as he went concerning the functions of the brain. For a considerable time I was nearly alone among the neurologists in my consistently holistic approach. In 1932 about twenty physicians, famous in their special fields, arranged a meeting in Austria at which they developed in principle similar holistic ideas in connection with material pertaining to their respective specialties. For the first time at this meeting I presented my concept and became more convinced that I should continue examining and treating patients in my own way.

I was still more encouraged when I learned that my basic concept was much in accordance with the theoretical interpretation of the French physiologist Claude Bernard, as published in his *An Introduction to the Study of Experimental Medicine* (1866). Claude Bernard, as famous as he was in Germany for his medical discoveries, was to me and most other physicians there completely unknown for his theoretical interpretation, which he had developed from his practical work. Some of his comments may illustrate his point:

In the organism of the living being we have to consider an ensemble, a harmony of phenomena, an individual. One should always return to this ensemble before one draws definite conclusions . . . One should see without doubt that the parts which constitute the organism are inseparable in the physiological sense . . . The physiologist and the physician should always consider at the same time the organism and its ensemble and other details . . . Living is a contact between the organism and the outer world, if one suppresses the one or the other of the two conditions, life ceases . . . All theories grew out directly from the practical experience.

It was particularly interesting for me that Claude Bernard was inclined to philosophical deliberations in practical work as much as he was strictly against confusing philosophical concepts. He wrote, "If new discoveries will help us to understand life better, that would not modify our attitude towards what philosophy means in the biological sciences, namely an intrinsic factor of knowledge." When I read that, I felt at home.

It was of particular significance for the further development of my research to find that brain damage could produce a change of behavior in its totality in a characteristic way. This observation induced us to distinguish two forms of behavior in man, which we called "abstract attitude" and "concrete behavior." Briefly, we can say that the abstract attitude is necessary for taking a mental set voluntarily, for shifting voluntarily from one aspect of an object to another, for making a choice, grasping the essential part of a given presentation, planning ahead, assuming an attitude to the merely possible, and finally detaching the ego from the outer world. When we find a failure in any performance belonging to one of these groups, we are able to assume that the patient will fail in all performance fields where this attitude is needed. In concrete behavior our reactions and thinking are directed by the immediate claims or a particular aspect of an object or a situation. The patient with impairment of the abstract attitude may behave correctly in all performances that can be executed with concrete behavior. It is understandable that many symptoms may be wrongly interpreted if one neglects this possible origin of the defect. This origin of a defect can be easily evaluated because the tests we have developed can demonstrate directly that the abstract attitude is impaired and so facilitate investigation. Many phenomena that were previously interpreted as a special defect, for instance defect of memory and attention, should be regarded with doubt; they may instead be the effect of failure in abstract attitude.

The symptoms that we find in a defect of the concrete behavior appear, for instance, as a failure of the motor-sensory performances and to these belong simple motor aphasia and similar symptom complexes. I do not consider it necessary to say here anything more about concrete behavior. It is more important to look carefully at patients who show abnormally strong concreteness. This can have two different causes. One is the lack of mental development in infancy. The abstract attitude normally develops before the end of the first year. In some children it does not develop in a normal way and in others only very belatedly. It is understandable that these infants are struck by catastrophe when the world around them imposes tasks with which they cannot cope. Then they withdraw into concrete behavior, the sole way in which they can protect themselves against catastrophe. If the infant maintains concreteness as a habit, which can occur under different circumstances (which I cannot discuss here), he will readily show abnormal concreteness later on, particularly when he is confronted with a task he has difficulty in carrying out. This is the abnormal concreteness which, for instance, the schizophrenic shows. The schizophrenic does not lack the abstract attitude, but his concreteness is the only way to avoid such activities as would endanger him. In a similar way, the patient with brain damage sticks to concrete behavior which shows in perseverance and rigidity.

There are mental conditions in infancy that have been interpreted as a psychosis resulting from an abnormal relationship between mother and infant due to "libidinous disturbances" and that have been treated with

psychoanalysis. I demonstrated that these children have an abnormal concreteness due to mental underdevelopment, to a defect or a retardation of
the development of abstraction. In spite of that, in a number of publications
the condition has still been considered a psychiatric anomaly. I have no doubt
that my interpretation is correct. Careful scrutiny of the entire question by
B. Rimland (1964), based on the study of all relevant material and personal
observations, has proved my assumption. Consequently, the treatment of
these children must be changed. The explanation of the defect by our method
of investigation based not on a probable theory but on observable facts, was
successful both theoretically and practically.

Further studies have taught me that the two behavioral attitudes—
abstract and concrete behavior—belong together and that they represent a
unit in which each part plays a particular role. The abstract attitude has,
so to say, to prepare the condition in which an individual can perform a
demanded task. If for any reason an individual is *forced* to perform in a
situation that requires abstract attitude, he sticks to the concrete behavior.
Indeed, from what we have just said, it is clear that a task can never be
performed with concrete behavior alone.

I was able to use my results for the interpretation of the concrete behavior of so-called primitive societies. It had been assumed that primitive
people have inferior minds—a misconception still widely held. I thought that
their overt concreteness must have a special reason because on some occasions
they were perfectly able to use abstract attitude. The explanation came from
an observation by an anthropologist, Paul Radin, that in all primitive tribes
one can distinguish between two types: the thinkers and the nonthinkers.
The nonthinkers are competent to behave abstractly, but they frequently do
not use this attitude because their living is so organized by the thinkers that
their concrete behavior is sufficient to fulfill their tasks. As Radin says further,
they are essentially not different from the people of civilized societies. With
that, the comparison of the behavior of primitive people with that of mentally defective human beings, which has caused great misunderstanding of
the latter, can be rejected. Something similar takes place in our society; for
instance, if the worker in a large industrial plant, who always performs the
same concrete action, were to think about what he does, he would disrupt
the whole routine. He can fulfill his task concretely because the machines
are so constructed by the experts that the worker does not have to think
about what he is doing. He has the ability to behave abstractly but does not
use it. So we can say in general that if we see people behave very concretely,
we should not consider them abnormal; the difference between their kind
of concreteness and that of the mental patient should be distinguished.

In the third period of my research I never stopped testing the usefulness
of the holistic approach on different material. A number of papers concerning a variety of neurological and psychiatric problems were the result. I continued my studies on normal and mentally ill infants. In my lectures I have

talked about Freud, but I have never written comprehensively about psycho-analysis. I dislike discussions of theories if one is not able to know in detail the material on which they are based; in psychoanalysis this is impossible. Even if we have to deal basically with the same problems (as I have explained in my paper "The Relationship of Psychoanalysis to Biology," 1929), my observation of phenomena differs markedly from that of the analysts. My different approach and my procedure, which is to consider the phenomena insofar as possible without preconceived theoretical interpretation, brought very different material to the fore. In an attempt to clarify some special problems of universal concern I have reported on anxiety, aggression, conscious-ness, and so-called infantile sexuality (1929, 1939), which are important for both disciplines, the holistic one and psychoanalysis.

My main interest now is directed toward the problem of the relation between biology and philosophy. I have already explained in the concluding chapter of *The Organism* (p. 507) that my work ultimately led me into realms far removed from the usual biological considerations. I expressed the hope that the reader might realize this and see that transition into philo-sophical problems is not determined by the casual personal inclination of the author but that the material itself imposes the obligation upon us if we desire to find our way through. This became apparent first in the presenta-tion of language in my book *Language and Language Disturbances* (1948) and gave me additional impetus to study the problem of the relation between man and world and, in turn, of the relationship among the parts of the organism. Here it was particularly the problem of the tendency of the parts to come together in units. How do these units originate? This intriguing question has vexed me in all my attempts to understand organismic behavior, such as my study of the development of the corpus callosum in the brain. It occupied me from my study of the much discussed problem of stimulus-response to the attempt to understand the highest mental phenomenon, the building of concepts; it occupied me especially in my consideration of the problem of the categorical attitude, which is of such importance in acquiring knowledge in general and also in biology.

I can refer here only briefly to the problem of categories. The men-tioned behavior forms have usually been considered as the effect of the use of the mental capacity of a subject. I came to the conclusion that they are not determined by consciousness and that it would be meaningless to call them unconscious. They represent living events and are not the result of intellectual activities. I could no longer accept the assumption that experience is the product of mind or brain functions alone, especially after it became my conviction that the external world is always connected with it.

Pathology has shown how important the world is for the understanding of anything at all. Man cannot live without world and world does not exist without man. The study of the world of the brain-injured proved to be no less important to our knowledge than the study of the disturbance of the performance. Indeed, though the patient's behavior is certainly determined by the brain defect, it can only be understood as a phenomenon going on in the totality of his modified personality in relation to the world.

The holistic approach induced me to bring psychophysical relationship into the foreground. It became obvious that it was directed by the tendency to come to terms with the world in which the individual feels he lives. There are two different behavior forms in his being in the "man-world" entity. We start an activity with the abstract attitude if the concrete way is not forced upon us (see what I have said before concerning the behavior form of primitive people, p. 160). When in a given condition the abstract attitude does not occur, e.g., in brain defect or in anxiety, then the concrete behavior comes to the fore. The patient sticks to that which brings him into a feeling of adequacy. What we call categories are living events that are effective. The patient experiences either success or failure; we describe this behavior in our terms. In either case, the adequacy between him and the world can come to pass. When he is not able to achieve adequacy in one form or the other, then something occurs which we call catastrophe. This is a condition in which there is no adequacy possible, the situation which is characteristic of anxiety, as I have shown in various papers. As we have said, the patient does not experience catastrophe when we have arranged his world in such a way that he can behave concretely or, as sometimes may happen, when he has learned from indications to recognize how to come to terms in this concrete way. He is generally not able to learn from indications because due to his impairment he cannot make a choice. For him there does not exist the possibility of trial and error. If he has found the right way, he is simply living in what is for him an adequate condition. He is always, except in catastrophe, living in adequacy. What is going on in his behavior is so complex that only by the most careful analysis has one a chance of explaining it.

When I learned about the approach which the philosopher Edmund Husserl, who has gained increasing acceptance in recent years, had taken toward knowledge, I felt vaguely that my interpretation of the behavior of patients may prove to be similar to the results of "phenomenological analysis." My presentiment was confirmed when I read the essays of some of Husserl's adherents, who not only showed great interest in our material and interpretation concerning abstract and concrete behavior but found it important for their own philosophical inquiries. I would like to mention particularly Professor Aaron Gurwitsch, the late Professor Alfred Schutz, and the late French philosopher Merleau-Ponty. Gurwitsch (1964) writes: "Husserl had naturally to engage himself in a thoroughgoing analysis and discussion of the theories of abstraction and refuted the empiristic theory of abstraction," a theory which I, too, was unable to accept from my view of behavior. Husserl's results, continues Gurwitsch, have been confirmed by Goldstein and Gelb's studies of brain-injured people. "This appears the more significant and conclusive because their findings were investigated with a mere neurological and psychopathological setting and in complete independence of a phenomenological point of view" (Gurwitsch, 1964). Without going into detail, I want to mention some of Husserl's results that seemed to be in particular agreement with results I arrived at by my analysis of human beings. For instance, he states that:

. . . the *Lebenswelt* (living world) is of a common occurrence, it is present and pregiven, it is the natural everyday life, it includes nature, this nature is given in direct experience not in idealized nature like in Natural Science. Within the *Lebenswelt* we encounter our fellowmen and take it for granted that we do not only exist in the same world but are concretely confronted with the same things as the others. All theoretical truth, logic, mathematics, science . . . finds its validity and justification in evidence concretely occurring in the *Lebenswelt*.

To that correspond the insights I gained in my attempt to understand biology. The great importance that Husserl gives to the problem of the relationship between events interested me greatly. This problem, which played an enormous part in philosophy and came to the fore in a new way in phenomenology, became the focus of the phenomenologists' interest in my work on abstract and concrete behavior and of my interest in Husserl's inquiries.

I shall close this presentation with some remarks on sickness and therapy. I started this biography with the confession that my basic inclination was to help people in their distress, especially patients. In my endeavor I came to see that man is not perfect and that he has to arrange his life with awareness of the difficulties which arise from his nature. Try as he will and should to be perfect, he has to bear imperfection. That concerns also the physician's attitude toward sickness and his procedure in therapy, because the sick individual and the physician are in a similar situation. The latter must, if he wants to eliminate the remaining effect of the sickness, help the patient to understand the human situation and let him feel that therapy is an enterprise between the two. Sickness cannot be understood correctly if one assumes that it is something that befalls the individual from the outside. Our task is not simply to eliminate the disturbance or fight the effect of the sickness. Sickness seen from a higher aspect has to be considered as a disturbance of the relation between man and world, a disorder involving both. The patient primarily experiences his overt distress, but what is more important is that he is so much incapacitated to come to terms with the world in an adequate way that he becomes unable to realize himself. He feels, so to speak, that he is not able "to be," and that shows in anxiety. He will feel recovered and healthy when disorder and anxiety have disappeared. But this can be achieved in some sicknesses only when he is able to bear some distress. In such cases it will depend on how much distress and anxiety the individual is able to bear in order to reach a situation where life is still worth living.

It is then the essential task of the physician to help the patient to find the necessary new orientation toward life that acknowledges restriction. This will be possible only when the physician has gained deep insight into the structure of the personality of the patient, bodily and psychologically. This feeling of a common enterprise develops a kind of communion between patient and physician, it develops in a sphere of immediacy which I have written about elsewhere. In this sphere grows that which I have called transference (which differs from Freud's concept of transference). My concept of it originated in my organismic approach to the study of behavior in general; it arose from my experience in treating brain-injured patients with whom I could achieve success in this way. I wrote a comprehensive paper on the way in which this transference has to be executed in different diseases. According to my conviction, we should always be aware of imperfection, our action will always exceed our knowledge. It is for this reason that the problem of free decision enters into the activity of the physician. The situation becomes more difficult because the decision of the patient himself cannot be disregarded. This often occurs, not only when, for instance, an operation becomes necessary and a decision is demanded of the patient; there are other times, too, when he has to choose between restriction of his freedom and greater suffering. It is clear that we are not to take this as an external alternative—rather it touches, as one might say, on an existential question that can never be avoided by the physician. How will a physician be able to advise and direct? In any case, he will be able to do so only if he is convinced that it concerns the coming to terms of two persons in their attempt to help each other. In this extraordinary event, which happens much more often than one is aware of, the contrast between the factors in the medical situation and the objective procedures of natural science becomes strikingly apparent.

## REFERENCES[1]

### Selected Publications by Kurt Goldstein

Studies on the development of the human brain II: first development of the great brain commissures and the growing together of thalamus and striatum. Beiträge zur Entwicklungsgeschichte des menschlichen Gehirns II: die erste Entwicklung der grossen Hirncommissuren und die Verwachsung von Thalamus und Striatum.) Arch. Anatom. Physiol., Anatom. Abteil., 1903, 29–60.
The problem of amnesic aphasia. (Zur Frage der amnestischen Aphasie.) Arch. Psychiat., 1905, 41.
Theory of hallucinations. (Zur Theorie der Halluzinationen.) Arch. Psychiat. Nervenkrankh., 1908, 44, 584–655; 1036–1100.

[1] A complete bibliography of Dr. Goldstein's publications has been compiled by Joseph Meiers, M.D., 601 West 115th Street, New York City, and is available on request to Dr. Meiers.

On disturbances in the grammar of cases with cerebral injuries. (Über Störungen der Grammatik bei Hirnkranken.) *Mschr. Psychiat. Neurol.*, 1913.

*The brain-injured soldiers: therapy, social care and experts evaluation. (Die Behandlung, Fürsorge und Begutachtung des hirnverletzten Soldaten.)* Leipzig: F. C. W. Vogel, 1919.

(with A. Gelb) On the influence of the impairment of visual image on tactile recognition. (Über den Einfluss des Verlustes des optischen Vorstellungsvermögens auf das taktile Erkennen.) *Z. Psychol.*, 1919, 83, 1–94.

Dependence of motility upon visual processes. (Über die Abhängigkeit der Bewegungen von optischen Vorgängen.) *Mschr. Psychol. Neurol.*, 1923, *LIV*.

The homologous functional cause of symptoms in organic and mental diseases, especially about the functional mechanism of compulsion. (Über gleichartige funktionelle Bedingtheit der Symptome bei organischen und psychischen Krankheiten; im besonderen über den funktionellen Mechanismus der Zwangsvorgänge.) *Mschr. Psychiat. Neurol.*, 1924, *LVII* (4), 191–209.

(with A. Gelb) On aphasia of color names. (Über Farbennamenaphasie.) *Psychol. Forsch.*, 1924, 6, 127–186.

The cerebellum. (Das Kleinhirn.) In Bethe (Ed.), *Handbuch der normalen und pathologischen Physiologie*, 1926, X.

On aphasia. (Über Aphasie.) *Schweizer Arch. Neurol. Psychiat.*, 1927.

Localization in the cerebrum. (Lokalization und Grosshirn.) In *Handbuch der normalen und pathologischen Physiologie*. Berlin: Springer, 1927.

The tendency to preferred behavior. (Über die Tendenz zum ausgezeichneten Verhalten.) *Dtsch. Z. Nervenheilk.*, 1929, *109* (1), 1–61.

The relationship of psychoanalysis to biology. (Die Beziehungen der Psychoanalyse zur Biologie.) Bericht auf dem II allgemeinen Medizinischen Treffen für Psychotherapie in Nauheim, April 1927. *Allg. ärztliche Z. Psychiat.*, Leipzig: Hirzel, 1929.

The holistic approach to medicine. (Die Ganzheitliche Betrachtung in der Medicin.) In *Einheitsbestrebungen in der Medicin*, 1930.

Pointing and grasping. (Über Zeigen und Greifen.) *Nervenarzt*, 1931, 4, 453–466.

The mind-body problem and its significance for medical action. (Das psychophysische Problem in seiner Bedeutung für ärztliches Handeln.) *Ther. Gegenw.*, 1931, 72, 1–11.

*The organism: A holistic approach to biology derived from pathological data in man. (Der Aufbau des Organismus: Eine Einleitung in die Biologie auf Grund der Erfahrungen beim kranken Menschen.)* Holland: Nijhoff, 1934. (English translation) *The organism.* New York: American Book, 1938; introduction by K. Lashley. (French translation) *La structure de l'organisme.* Texte augmenté de fragments inédits et traduits de l'allemand par le Dr. E. Burckhard et Jean Kuntz, Paris: Gallimard, 1951. (paperback in English) Boston: Beacon Press, 1963.

The problem of the meaning of words based upon observation of aphasic patients. *J. Psychol.*, 1936, 2, 301–315.

*Human nature in the light of psychopathology.* Cambridge, Mass.: Harvard, 1940. (paperback ed.) New York: Schocken Books, 1963. Published also in Japanese.

(with E. Rothmann) Physiognomic phenomena in rorschach responses. *Rorschach Res.*, 1945, IX, No. 1.

(with M. Scheerer and E. Rothmann) A case of "idiot savant": an experimental study of personality organization. *Psychol. Monogr.*, 1945, 58, No. 4.

*Language and language disturbances.* New York: Grune & Stratton, 1948. (Spanish translation) *Trastornos del lenguaje: Las afasias su importancia para la medicina y la teoria del lenguaje.* Barcelona, Madrid: Editorial Cientifico Medica, 1950.

Remarques sur le problème epistémologique de la biologie. Translated by Simone et Georges Canguilhem. (Read in absentia at the Conference on Epistemology, Fall, 1949.) In *Actes du congrès international de philosophie des sciences,* Paris, 1949; Vol. I, *Epistémologie,* Paris, 1951, 141–143.

On emotions: considerations from the organismic point of view. *J. of Psychol.,* 1951, *31,* 37–49.

The concept of transference in treatment of organic and functional nervous diseases. *Acta Psychotherapeut.,* 1954, 2, Fasc. 3/4.

The smiling of the infant and the problem of understanding the "other". *J. of Psychol.,* 1957, *44,* 175–191.

New ideas on mental health (Cooper Union Lecture). In J. Fairchild (Ed.), *Personal problems and psychological frontiers.* New York: Sheridan Press, 1957, 96 ff.

Concerning "primitivity": the problem of the lower mentality of primitive people. In *Essays in honor of Paul Radin: culture in history.* New York: Columbia, 1960.

## Other Publications Cited

Bernard, Claude. *An introduction to the study of experimental medicine,* 1866. (Paperback ed.) Dover, 1957.

Binswanger, Ludwig. *Grundformen des menschlichen Daseins.* Zurich: Niehaus Verlag, 1942.

Gurwitsch, Aaron. *Fields of consciousness.* Pittsburgh: Duquesne, 1964.

Head, Henry. *Aphasia and kindred disorders of speech.* New York: Hafner, 1926. 2 vols.

Husserl, Edmund. *Die Krise der europaeischen Wissenschaften.*

Jackson, Hughlings. Affection of speech from disease of the brain. *Brain,* 1878, *I,* 304.

————. Croanian lectures on the evolution and dissolution of the nervous system. London: *Lancet,* 1884.

Merleau-Ponty. *Phenomenology of perception.* New York: Humanities, 1962.

Radin, Paul. *Essays in honor of Paul Radin: culture in history.* New York: Columbia, 1960.

Rimland, B. *Infantile autism.* New York: Appleton-Century-Crofts, 1964.

Schuetz, Alfred. *Collected papers.* Holland: Nijhoff, 1962.

# Joy Paul Guilford

What is a life—a sequence of personal events, of birth, school, marriage and parenthood, work, retirement, and death? I recall one time hearing Charlotte Bühler defend the thesis that, in effect, a life is like a symphony; it has a central theme, with variations on that theme. There is a strong feature of unity about it.

Looking backward, it is sometimes possible to see the threads that seem to follow through, although often in winding fashion. If our genes do provide a kind of life program, certainly it is a program subject to many revisions, as environmental opportunities, or lack thereof, have their say.

If a life is a kind of symphony, an autobiography is written about an unfinished symphony, and it gives only one rendering or interpretation. In what follows, I shall start along chronological lines, but when it comes to matters of career, I shall attempt to follow some of the threads of psychological interest and to inject as much unity into the picture as seems justified. The reader may be able to judge whether there is a central theme.

## BIRTH AND FAMILY

The record is that I began breathing on March 7, 1897. I have often wondered whether I had an unconscious memory of being born, for during childhood, a number of times I had a terrifying dream of being trapped in a tight-fitting, curved, underground passage from which it was difficult to escape. Consciously, I have always had more than a touch of claustrophobia. I could not bring myself to crawl through tunnels or under buildings as other children did.

The locale of my first contact with the external environment was on a farm, about five miles from the village of Marquette, in Hamilton County, Nebraska. My sure knowledge of ancestry does not go back beyond my grandparents, only one of whom I knew personally. My father, Edwin Augustus Guilford, and my mother, Arvilla Monroe, came from farmer parentage. Recent generations had been on the move from Michigan, where both parents and grandparents had been born, to Iowa then to Nebraska, where my

169

father, two of his brothers, and their father took neighboring homesteads in the 1880's. Another brother became a railroad engineer. Both my parents had been limited to a grade-school education. I recall a bit of shock on learning indirectly that my father and mother were first cousins (as were their brother and sister, respectively), both having the same Monroe ancestry, presumably going back to the Monroe clan of Scotland. The Guilford ancestry was undoubtedly English. The Corey blood on my mother's side was probably Irish.

Of quite a number of first cousins of my generation, few went to high school. Three of the female gender taught school temporarily. One of the male gender attended engineering college until an accidental death. There was one of my father's cousins who achieved the status of a bishop in a minor church denomination. Another cousin ended his years as a paranoid patient. He was the most colorful relative I knew.

Although my father rented his farm (he had lost ownership in the drought of 1894), I am sure that he was above the average farmer in intelligence and in managerial ability. He was a leader in his church and community, having taken an active part in organizing and maintaining a farmers' cooperative. There were few skills needed on the farm that he would not undertake to acquire. For example, he did creditably in planning new buildings, laying foundations, carpentry and even amateur veterinary practice including surgery on farm animals. He was very uncommunicative and stern and the one who punished, which set the pattern for my reactions to all those in authority over me.

By community standards, our family would have been regarded as neither poor nor well-to-do. It was one of the first in the community to own a family automobile, a 1912 Studebaker. My parents set quite a religious atmosphere in the home and saw to it that the family attended the rural United Brethren church regularly. My mother was discontented with farm living and frequently let it be known. After retiring from the farm at the age of sixty, my father served several years as deputy county sheriff.

A brother more than five years older than I and a sister almost two years younger completed the family. The most significant relationship to my brother was that he was assigned as my protector, and the relationship to my sister was one of sibling rivalry. My brother was low on academic ability and did not finish grade school, but he was high on drawing skill and in mechanical ability. With his sense of humor and some creative talent, I am sure that he had potential for the art of cartooning. He took a course in auto mechanics and that was his chief type of employment. After finishing grade school, my sister took business-college training and spent a few years before marriage as a bank clerk. It may have been some of the obvious differences in various abilities in my own family that later helped to turn my attention to problems of differential psychology during my professional career.

## CHILDHOOD AND YOUTH

On the farm I had the usual tasks that fall to the growing boy. With the example set by my parents, I learned not to be afraid of hard work and long hours. Compared with other children, I seem to have been unusually observant of natural phenomena of every kind, and I spent an unusual proportion of my time reading. I also did some short-story writing and several times won prizes in the form of books from an Omaha newspaper. I started lessons on the piano at seven, continuing irregularly for a number of years, but never became a good piano player. One or two efforts at composing and at writing poetry were dismal failures never attempted again. I was thus prepared for the recent finding that creative potential depends upon the area in which one would be creative.

My other musical activities included singing in church choirs and in a college chorus and playing the saxophone badly during college days. My love of music (which favors subclassical types) is an aspect of a general aesthetic interest. On the Kuder Preference Record my highest score is on the artistic scale, and on the Strong Vocational Interest Blank my score is highest for architect as well as for psychologist. Architecture or landscape gardening would have been a most appealing occuption for me, but I lack some of the important pertinent abilities, such as drawing ability. My chief hobbies for years have been gardening and color photography.

As a boy, I enjoyed fishing, swimming, and skating, but not hunting and not competitive sports, in which I had little basis for success. Our home possessed an excellent tool shop and I devoted some time to constructing things but never was skilled or much interested in mechanical activities. My disinterest in mechanics increased with the years and is probably a major reason for preferring statistical studies over laboratory studies that involve equipment.

According to family policy, I started to school at the age of seven; on my seventh birthday, in fact, although less than two months remained in the school year. During the first full year of school, I advanced through the "third reader," and it was not long until I was helping my older brother with his arithmetic problems. Of the elementary subjects, I liked arithmetic and physiology best. At the age of eleven, I attempted most of the county eighth-grade examinations and passed them. The following year I passed all of them. Because of my age and the distance to high school, however, I returned to the rural school for "postgraduate" study.

My first semester of high school was spent at the village school in Marquette, living at home. I then transferred to the high school in the county seat, Aurora, living with relatives and family friends at various times.

I graduated in 1914 as class valedictorian in a class of forty-five, having earned an average grade higher than ninety-six percent. Such a level of achievement was not maintained later in college, partly because I placed less emphasis upon getting grades and asserted some degree of independence in some courses, a trend that was to grow through graduate work. I very easily made election to Phi Beta Kappa, however.

In high school the science curriculum was rich, with courses in physical geography, botany, physics, and chemistry, all of which I took. The teaching was excellent. I do not think that I really disliked any subject unless it was second-year Latin. During my junior year, I undertook the program of commercial courses in addition to the academic program. During my senior year, I took the additional subject of "normal training," with the prospect of becoming a teacher.

It was in the normal training that I first became acquainted with psychology as a subject. The teacher had recently studied psychology at the state university and taught us some of it with great enthusiasm. I obtained books by William James from the town library and read much from them. I then realized that some observations that I had made in earlier years were actually psychological observations. For example, I had noticed some phenomena of binocular vision and other visual-perceptual phenomena. The behavior of farm animals and of wildlife had also provided sources of observation. I had also obtained published material on hypnotism and had found it exciting. Perhaps this was part of a pattern of interest in things bordering on the magical. I found fairy tales, stories of Greek mythology, and the Arabian Nights' tales fascinating, and to this day I am not in sympathy with those who would keep such imaginative literature away from children. The rural school that I had attended, curiously, had a good selection of such reading material, as well as the Lambs' tales from Shakespeare.

Upon graduation from high school, because of my relative youth, I did not secure a teaching position during the first year, nor were funds available for entrance into college. The next year I taught in a rural school near Phillips, Nebraska. The following year, I taught in grades five through eight in the Phillips village school.


## UNIVERSITY OF NEBRASKA

In the fall of 1917, I entered the University of Nebraska. It was a keen disappointment not to be permitted to take psychology in the freshman year. For my science requirement, I registered for a course in chemistry known as qualitative analysis. The teacher was one of the most uninteresting that I ever knew. And yet, his way of thinking and his way of quizzing were thought-provoking. The laboratory work was well planned and appealed to me so much that I decided to become a chemist.

A course during the freshman year that left a lasting impression on me was in world history, called "The Growth of a World Society," taught by Fred Morrow Fling. For some years, this foresighted historian had been pointing out the inevitability of a world organization. For the first time, I saw the function of the study of history—to make human life more intelligible, to give the student deeper roots, and to provide him with a time perspective. The part of the course that influenced me most, however, was the "laboratory" work, in which we went through the process of writing the history of a day during the French revolution. We learned how to find source material, how to evaluate it, how to know when a historical fact may be regarded as established, and how to write and document an organized report. I detested the dictatorial manner and methods of the teacher and the laboratory assistant and would have dropped the course in the middle of the year but for the intervention of a dean. I was glad that I had to stay with the course, for I have since realized that one of the most useful things students can be taught is method.

During my freshman year, I joined a local social fraternity, which a few years later became a chapter of Pi Kappa Alpha. This experience made an important contribution to my social development, but it could not make up for all previous retardation in this respect.

The summer of 1918 was spent on my father's farm. Facing the prospect of military draft, I volunteered and entered a training detachment that was being trained for service in the Signal Corps at the Kansas State Agricultural College. For three months we studied radio and the physics basic thereto. I was under orders to proceed with officer training at Yale University when the Armistice came about.

I did not return to the University to complete the academic year 1918–19. Instead, I took a temporary teaching position in grades seven and eight at Hooper, Nebraska, where an Army buddy was teaching. That summer the county superintendent of schools in my native county asked me to serve as acting superintendent while he took the summer off. I returned to the University in the fall of 1919.

During my sophomore year, my educational objective was in the direction of public-school teaching as a career. I took some courses in education, and to supplement my income I did some teaching for pay in the University demonstration high school. I taught general science during the first semester and physics during the second. This supervised teaching was beneficial.

I had not given up the idea of a chemistry major, and thus enrolled in a course in organic chemistry. Although the teaching in both lecture and laboratory was excellent, my interests in chemistry were waning. The details of complex molecular structures were not particularly appealing. I did not complete the full year in organic chemistry; instead, during the second semester I enrolled in a course in introductory zoology, which contributed to background for psychology later.

Being a sophomore, I was permitted to enter the course in beginning psychology, which was a year course with laboratory. To my deep regret, the great teacher Harry Kirk Wolfe, who had taken his doctorate with Wundt, had died. The course did not impress me very favorably during the first semester. The emphasis was on neural anatomy and physiology. The laboratory work was devoted to dissection of sheep's brains. This was not the psychology that I had anticipated. The second semester's work was more interesting, to which Carl Seashore's laboratory manual contributed a great deal.

Toward the end of the school year, I happened to be talking with the teacher in the course, Winifred F. Hyde. I was remarking that I should probably have to take the next year off to teach in order to be able to finance further study at the University. Dr. Hyde asked me whether I would be able to continue next year if given an assistantship in psychology. This came as a surprise, particularly since assistantships were given only to graduate students. I eagerly accepted, and during the two remaining undergraduate years I taught laboratory and quiz sections in general psychology. Undoubtedly, this experience determined my choice of a major and a career. Without the continued aid and encouragement of Winifred F. Hyde, I should probably not have seen my chosen training through. Incidentally, fellow assistants during my tenure in this status included Frederick H. Lund and Arthur T. Jersild, who later became recognized psychologists, and Samuel Brownell, who later became distinguished in the field of education.

I have often thought it unfortunate for my further academic development that, since psychology at the University of Nebraska was regarded as an adjunct to philosophy, I was guided into philosophy courses when I should have been taking courses in mathematics. I did have the opportunity to extend my scientific background by taking a course in optics (after a year of college physics) and a course in genetics. My mathematical experience as an undergraduate was limited to algebra and trigonometry, neither of which was very exciting, in contrast to my three years of mathematics in high school.

I sought to round out my psychology program by taking a course in social psychology in the sociology department under a professor who was said to have more than a local reputation. This was one of the easiest courses that I ever took. The teacher spent the entire semester discussing a few chapters from the textbook in a very elementary way, much to my disgust.

I chose a course in argumentation, chiefly because of the reputation of the teacher, M. M. Fogg (not an apt name for one who coached debating teams), and was greatly rewarded. I learned how to marshal and organize arguments in support of propositions. The orderly thinking of the teacher and the logical nature of the subject appealed to me very much. My term paper was a defense for using academic-aptitude tests for university students. From this course, and from other experiences, I have concluded that the choice of teacher is frequently more important for the student's development than the choice of course.

At the end of my senior year, an opportunity came for me to teach in the 1922 summer session at the Peru (Nebraska) State Normal School. It happened that I was the only assistant in the laboratory and the only one who could be reached on the Saturday morning that the president of the school came looking for a last-minute replacement. I taught three sections of beginning psychology, with laboratory—and sheep's brains. My assistant was Erland N. P. Nelson, who later joined the ranks of psychologists.

The next academic year I returned as a graduate assistant but with added duties. It happened that one of the psychology teachers, C. O. Weber, obtained a leave of absence to take postdoctoral work at Harvard University, leaving the psychology clinic unprovided for. I was asked whether I would take charge of the clinic, which I did; an arrangement that extended into a second year.

My preparation for the role of clinical psychologist was severely limited. I had had one course on intelligence testing and some limited instruction on remedial procedures in connection with a course in educational psychology. Fortunately, my predecessor had left records and literature in such excellent shape that I could see what his operations had been. I read the pertinent sources, which in those days were not very extensive, and by self-instruction learned to administer all the necessary tests. The chief source of "clients" was the State Home for Dependent Children, which wanted advice on the disposition of children coming under its supervision. Other sources were the local juvenile court, seeking information on cases informally, and occasionally the school psychologist in the Lincoln public schools, who asked for assistance on certain cases. Altogether, I handled over a hundred cases during the two years.

This clinical experience provided excellent laboratory instruction for a graduate student. Observation of the children's behavior in response to psychological tests, particularly the performance tests, impressed me with the rich possibilities that were being missed by summarizing all the information in terms of mental age and IQ. The results from 110 cases were systematically recorded and statistically summarized as a basis for my master's thesis entitled "Some Problems Encountered in the Clinical Examination of Children." This thesis emphasized the limitations of information provided by the IQ and urged a much more analytical assessment of individuals.

Only a few university students came to the clinic, some out of curiosity and some with questions about vocational fitness and personality traits. In this connection, I did some preliminary experimenting with the Downey Will Temperament Test, which was new at the time. I also spent some time in drawing up a list of abilities and other traits that might be evaluated in order to achieve a comprehensive assessment of an individual, with an effort to keep the traits as nearly independent of one another as possible. When writing my book *Personality* (1959a) years later, I regretted that I had not saved the list for comparative purposes.

Other experiences during my four years as assistant (during the fourth year I held the rank of assistant instructor) had their influences on the direction of my professional interests. The period shortly after the wartime success with the Army Alpha Examination saw a growing experimental use of academic-aptitude tests. I assisted the head of psychology in administering and scoring the Army Alpha and the E. L. Thorndike battery of aptitude tests to entering freshmen classes and in dealing with the data from those sources.

During one year, the head of the chemistry department asked us to develop a battery of tests that would assist in the classification of students in two beginning chemistry courses. Most of this task fell to me. It provided my first occasion for test construction and research. In this connection it was necessary for me to learn something about statistical methods. I had taken one graduate course in educational measurement, which was on statistics, but it was unbelievably elementary and I learned very little from it. Most of the statistics that I have learned, then and since, has been self-taught. A report on the classification of chemistry students by means of tests constituted my first publication, produced jointly with Winifred F. Hyde (1925).

In my clinical experience, the conviction grew that there is a multiplicity of abilities, not just one—intelligence. As an assistant in the laboratory, I obtained permission to introduce as one exercise a battery of ten word-association tests (the Woodworth and Wells series) along with a simple-reaction-time test for the purpose of obtaining intercorrelations. I had certain a priori hypotheses as to the involvement of three abilities: a reaction-time component and two association-ability components, one having to do with stimuli that converge on one or a limited repertoire of responses (as in giving class names) and the other pertaining to tasks in which the stimulus has a relatively large number of possible responses (as in giving class members). The distinction may have been the seed from which my later distinction between convergent and divergent production came. At any rate, the intercorrelations differed systematically and somewhat as expected. I had heard of Spearman's g at that time but not about his method of factor analysis. I was to do my first factor analysis some ten years later.

In my second year of graduate work, on the basis of my one year of experience in the clinic, I was asked to introduce a new course on abnormal psychology. In preparation for this course I read all the available books on Freudian psychology and on psychiatry. This course broadened considerably my range of interests and was reflected in some later research. I later taught such a course at the University of Kansas and the University of Southern California, but not in recent years.

Between the first and second years of graduate work, I obtained, through a teachers' agency, a teaching position in the West Virginia Wesleyan summer session. In addition to beginning psychology, this position involved teaching three courses in education, preparation for which kept me more than busy, between diversions in the form of boating, fishing, and picnics with some of West Virginia's wonderfully hospitable people. I returned for a second engagement in the summer of 1925.

## CORNELL UNIVERSITY

Through the advice and efforts of Winifred Hyde and others, I was offered an assistantship at Cornell University to continue graduate work under Edward Bradford Titchener. The offer was made more attractive financially by inclusion of permission to make my living quarters in the psychology laboratory, which was then a custom of some of the graduate assistants, an entirely unofficial arrangement.

As assistant in the Department of Psychology at Cornell, it was my duty to set up the demonstrations for the lectures of Titchener to sophomores in beginning psychology and to teach quiz sections. The story of Titchener's very dramatic lectures has been related by Boring (1927). All the psychology staff members and the graduate students were expected to be present. Following the lecture, the staff members gathered with Titchener in a smoke-filled office behind the lecture room (Titchener was noted for being liberal with large, Filipino cigars of great potency) where for an hour discussions were held on almost any subject, scientific or otherwise.

The atmosphere in psychology at Cornell was very different from the philosophical and clinical milieu from which I had come. At Cornell was a close-knit group, devoted to the development and promotion of the point of view of a master who was both revered and feared. Previously, points of view had meant little to me. There had been only revulsions of the philosophers at Nebraska against Watson's behaviorism. Our major textbook there had been written by Walter B. Pillsbury, who did not let any point of view show.

My attention to points of view at Cornell was further heightened by two circumstances. A new instructor, Harry Helson, had just completed a very scholarly dissertation at Harvard on the then new Gestalt psychology. My associations with Helson were close, and he had much influence on my thinking on theoretical issues. A rewarding friendship was formed that has lasted through the years. He was to influence my career in a number of ways, as will be related. We both served as "observers" for Deane B. Judd (now a leading authority on color problems), who was working on visual afterimages for his doctorate in physics. In the psychological laboratory, Helson and Judd were attempting to supply uniform stimulation for adaptation of an entire retina, a study that later led to Helson's derivation of his famous adaptation-level concept and theory.

Another circumstance during the first year at Cornell was the presence of a visiting professor in education, not in psychology; a leader in Gestalt psychology, Kurt Koffka, in whose seminar I enrolled for two semesters. Koffka also gave a series of special lectures, and Wolfgang Köhler paid a brief visit for lectures on the campus. These invasions from a divergent point of view helped to make things interesting. Anticipations of open clashes of views grew, when, during the second semester, Koffka attended Titchener's seminar, as well as the entire psychology staff and Dean R. M. Ogden who had brought Koffka to Cornell. Somehow, Titchener managed to keep open discussions of points of view below the overt level until the very last meeting of the seminar, when a lively session lasted into the wee hours of the morning.

One experience at Cornell that affected me most was a course in psychophysics under Karl M. Dallenbach. This course impressed me with the system and precision with which psychological data could be obtained and treated and with the fact that numerical values and mathematical functions could be employed. I have always been fascinated with numbers and I still enjoy operating a calculating machine. Partly because of this course and partly because of Helson's advice, I changed from a physiology minor to a mathematics minor. The other minor remained education. The mathematics minor included a year course on theory of probability, which was most enlightening as a background for statistics.

The presence in the Department of Psychology of the office of the *American Journal of Psychology,* of which Dallenbach was owner and Titchener was editor, and a general atmosphere of research for publication predisposed the graduate students to seek publication. Dallenbach, particularly, set for his students an example of high devotion to scientific rigor and industry. In one of his lectures on memory, Dallenbach suggested that a memory span could be conceived as a limen and could be measured by utilization of the method of constant stimuli. I soon arranged to do the experimental collection of data and found that the results fully supported his expectation. The result of this study was a joint publication in 1925.

A bit of history was entailed in the publication of this short article. Dallenbach had reason to believe that another psychologist who specialized in psychophysics might soon come into print with the same idea. He therefore urged Titchener to give some priority to publication of this article. In reaction to this pressure, Titchener resigned as editor of the journal. Being free from this editorial obligation, he was slated to be the first editor of the new *Journal of General Psychology,* but death stepped in to change that plan.

For a dissertation topic, Titchener gave me a choice between a problem on the skin senses and a problem on fluctuation of attention. I quickly chose the latter. His suggestion of any problem on attention surprised me, for his seminar had been devoted to the literature on attention to see how it was faring as a systematic concept, with the general consensus, according to my impression, that there was no good place for the concept in any existing system. This outcome, too, had been a surprise, since Titchener had been proud of his treatment of attention as a matter of sensory clearness.

My reading on the problem of fluctuations of attention led me to the hypothesis that a fluctuating sensation under constant environmental stimulation is a phenomenon of the stimulus limen. The significant feature is that the fluctuating sensation is essentially a running picture of changing sensitivity. I obtained good evidence for this proposition with respect to visual stimuli. Subsequently, others have found the same results with respect to auditory and tactual stimuli. Following some leads given by Dallenbach and Koffka, I also demonstrated some of the multiple determiners of the changing sensitivity from both peripheral and central sources.

In the late summer of 1926, Helson, who had been a staff member at the University of Illinois during the preceding academic year, had an offer from the University of Kansas and was told that he would be released to accept the offer if he could find a replacement. I was nominated and invited to fill the vacancy (it would hardly be correct to say that I was a replacement), which I accepted, although I had not written my dissertation. Teaching a full load of quiz sections, laboratory sections, and during the second semester a course on attention, I also attended graduate courses in psychology and mathematics and wrote the dissertation, returning to Cornell at midyear for the final oral. During the same year, I also did two experimental studies, one on learning and one on the autokinetic phenomenon. As a kind of delayed reaction to my Cornell "indoctrination," I wrote several chapters for a general psychology textbook that was to be entirely systematic and from the Titchenerian point of view. Realizing that it could not be a complete psychology, I gave up the project.

## FURTHER TEACHING YEARS

In the spring of 1927, I accepted for the following summer and for the next year an appointment as assistant professor at the University of Kansas. I was to take the place of a professor who had covered instruction in abnormal and social psychology. In connection with the latter course, I used F. H. Allport's *Social Psychology* (1924) as a text. As a class demonstration of perception of emotional expression, a subject given considerable emphasis in the text, I introduced a class experiment on learning to read facial expressions. A full set of more than a hundred lantern slides of the H. Rudolf photographs happened to be available in the department to serve as material. A report of this study was published in 1929, followed by development, with others, of a facial model for synthesizing expressions (with M. Wilke, 1930). Many years later, expressions were to become focal again in a study of social-cognition abilities (with M. O'Sullivan & R. de Mille, 1965).

At the University of Kansas I was asked to give a course to graduate students on psychophysics and statistics. Along with Helson's continued encouragement, this course kept my interest alive in quantitative psychology. The teaching of the course also revealed my weakness in statistics.

Just prior to taking up my duties at the University of Kansas, I was married to Ruth S. Burke, whom I had met during summer sessions at Cornell. She had completed a master's degree in psychology at Northwestern University and most of the work for the doctorate. She has been an important factor contributing to my progress professionally, not only in relieving me of domestic and fiscal responsibilities but also helping me in research in the early days, from which we have a number of joint publications. One child was born a year after our marriage, a daughter, Joan Sheridan. Joan later earned her master's degree in psychology at the University of Southern California, was married, and has three children. More recently she earned the doctoral degree in industrial psychology, then served as program director for the Los Angeles branch of the American Institutes for Research, and is now a research scientist at Douglas Aircraft Corporation.

By the end of the academic year 1927–28, Dr. Winifred Hyde had submitted her resignation from the University of Nebraska in order to be married. I was invited to take her place at the rank of associate professor. I welcomed the opportunity, recognizing the need to build up a department of psychology that would become independent of philosophy and that should become more equivalent in strength to those in neighboring state universities. Within a relatively conservative setting and during depression years, this goal was approached slowly, but within ten years the staff was tripled in size. During an interlude of the fall semester of 1935–36, I was granted a leave to serve as visiting professor at Northwestern University and returned there for the following summer session.

During the semester, I took advantage of the opportunity to visit L. L. Thurstone's evening seminar because of my strong admiration of his stimulating, trailblazing work. There were more visitors than registered students in the seminar, among them being Marion Richardson, Harold Gulliksen, and N. Rashevsky. Charles Spearman was visiting at the University of Chicago at that time, and I had some delightful discussions of factor analysis with him. This was at the time when I was writing the chapter on factor analysis for the first edition of *Psychometric Methods* (1936). Thurstone also made available to me facilities of his laboratory, in which Ledyard R. Tucker was his assistant.

In 1938 I was asked to serve half time as director of the newly established Bureau of Instructional Research at the University of Nebraska. This agency had responsibilities for the testing of all new students, testing in the state-wide scholarship contests, preparation of information for student advisers, and conducting statistical studies. In connection with the scholarship testing function, I took advantage of the opportunity to develop and try out new types of tests. Among these were a test based upon the Gottschaldt figures and a punched-holes test for measurement of visualization, both of which have become relatively permanent fixtures in one form or another in the list of tests now used in research.

In 1940 I resigned from the University of Nebraska to accept an appointment as professor of psychology at the University of Southern California. This change had been preceded by my teaching in the latter institution during the summers of 1938 and 1939, under pleasurable circumstances. The opportunity to be free of administrative duties and consequent additional time for research appealed to me, for I have never welcomed administrative assignments, whereas research has always given me greatest satisfaction.

## RESEARCH TRENDS

I have already indicated the background of some of my research activities. It is time to take a less incidental view. During the 1930's and since, my research interests and attention have been shaped by several determinants. There was the residual interest in individual differences, aroused by the earlier clinical experiences. In 1927 there appeared the monumental book by Charles Spearman, *The Abilities of Man,* which presented for the first time in book form his methods of factor analysis, many results, and much psychological theory. Here seemed to be the promise of an answer to the problems of abilities and other traits that had been bothering me. His emphasis on his g factor, however, left me skeptical, for it ran counter to my own observations. The later development by Thurstone of his generalized, multiple-factor theory and methods seemed to be more promising.

As rapidly as Thurstone developed his methods, I applied them to the analysis of basic traits in the area of C. G. Jung's concept of introversion-extraversion. The reasons for making this application were incidental. One day at Cornell, Samuel Feldman, an instructor, having been reading McDougall's new *Outline of Abnormal Psychology* (1926), jokingly remarked that McDougall had solved the problem of introversion-extraversion and had developed a good test for that trait. Later, at the University of Illinois, Elmer Culler, as his contribution to the psychology seminar, discussed Jung's new book on the subject.

In the early days on the faculty at Nebraska, I instigated some student research on McDougall's theory and his test, which was based upon fluctuating ambiguous figures, and other theories and tests. These studies led to the conviction that several disparate phenomena were then erroneously regarded as belonging under the single concept. Common American conceptions were in general agreement that Jung's types should be regarded as opposite poles of a continuous dimension. It seemed obvious that factor analysis was the way in which to determine whether there was a single dimension of introversion-extraversion or whether more than one dimension is involved.

My first approach, a novel one at the time, was to begin the analysis with intercorrelations of responses to single questions as the experimental variables. Each question was designed to elicit symptomatic indication of some particular behavioral aspect of the area of personality under investigation. The resulting conception of a multidimensional description of introversion-extraversion seemed to be well borne out, as well as the identification of some other dimensions of personality not so pertinent to that concept.

From my associations with G. L. Freeman at Northwestern University, in which we had discussions of individual differences in traits related to physiological variables, there grew an experimental inventory emphasizing psychodynamic aspects of behavior. Items from this inventory were factor analyzed, yielding a factor of "general drive" and also a factor of "nervousness." The former may be the same factor that Raymond B. Cattell has more recently identified as the "id" factor; the latter is probably in much the same direction as the variable called "manifest anxiety."

Later, items from the paranoid scale of the Humm-Wadsworth Temperament Analysis were factor analyzed, with the help of Donald W. Dysinger, to test some hypotheses of Roswell H. Johnson, a marriage counselor, to the effect that three dimensions are involved. The results bore out the hypotheses but have not been published. The Guilford-Martin Personnel Inventory grew out of the findings.

Other such analyses have followed, but the later ones have used combinations of items to provide experimental variables for factor analyses rather than single items. Analyses have been done of both temperament (with W. S. Zimmerman, 1956) and motivational (with P. R. Christensen, N. A. Bond, & M. A. Sutton, 1954) variables, including interests in various kinds of thinking (with P. R. Christensen, J. W. Frick, & P. R. Merrifield, 1961a) yielding a number of what I have called "hormetic" factors (1959a).

In 1927 there appeared the classical article by L. L. Thurstone on psychophysical theory, in which he laid the rational basis for quantifying data obtained from comparative judgments. This opened up a considerable range of possibilities in psychological measurement. One of my reactions was to do a number of studies exploiting the methods of scaling from pair-comparison data. Another was in the form of attention to psychophysical laws. Noting, as R. S. Woodworth had done, that most empirical data involving measured observed increments in stimulus in relation to stimulus quantities came out with mathematical relationships somewhere between Weber's simple proportionality and James McKeen Cattell's square root function, I proposed to gain flexibility and generality by applying the power function $\triangle S = KS^n$, which was first mentioned in 1932.

In the second edition of *Psychometric Methods* (1954), I ventured to integrate this function, in the Fechnerian manner, coming out with the function $R = JS^{(1-n)} + B$, in other words, a power law relating the quantity of a psychological event to its instigating stimulus event. Unfortunately, I failed to specify the restriction under which the integration would be justified. One way of stating this restriction would be in terms of Thurstone's case V (equal discriminal dispersions and equal intercorrelations of deviations). In a 1954 study with Harvey F. Dingman, I proposed that scaled psychological values obtained from ratio judgments are proportional to stimulus values raised to a power that could vary according to the experimental conditions. Such a function was shown to fit data published by R. S. Harper and S. S. Stevens (1948) as well as our own. Later, Stevens and others have shown very extensive generality for the applicability of the power law.

Another line of quantitative research, which had no particular antecedent other than my general aesthetic interest and my urge to quantify, was on color preferences. I felt that the work that had been done on this subject was very deficient in many ways, but chiefly because no investigator had taken the trouble to specify the colors he used, either in terms of stimulus properties or observed visual properties. Two of my major investigations were aimed at determining functional relationships between the affective value (degree of liking or disliking) of a color and its perceived properties—hue, brightness, and chroma. Very systematic relationships were found, with periodic functional relationships of affective value to hue and with generally monotonic relations between affective value and either brightness or chroma (1934, 1940b, 1949). Isohedon charts indicating all such relationships were published with Patricia C. Smith (1959). Two minor studies dealt with the prediction of affective value of pairs of colors from information of color properties (1931) and of affective values of the two color members (with E. C. Allen, 1936). A study of the latter type was also done with odors and odor combinations (with W. Spence, 1933). A theoretical outcome was the proposal of an aspect of psychology to be known as "psychodynamics" (1939b), i.e. having to do with quantitative relationships among observed psychological variables, in my presidential address to the Psychometric Society.

During the 1930's, a few of my students did minor studies with me on conditions of attention and measurement of attention (with R. B. Hackman, 1936; with E. Ewart, 1940). I have often regretted the disappearance of work on attention problems in general, but it is heartening to see that such investigations are coming back under the more manageable rubrics of vigilance, activation level, and filtering.

My experiences during World War II turned my attention again in the direction of abilities, although it cannot be said that those interests were ever dead or even dormant, for the topic of my presidential address to the Midwestern Psychological Association was "Human Abilities" (1940a). In March, 1942, I became director of Psychological Research Unit #3 at the Santa Ana Army Air Base, with the rank of major. The area of research assigned to this unit, which was one of several under the general direction of John C. Flanagan, was that of intellectual abilities, information, and judgment. Early in 1941, Walter V. Bingham had tried to interest me in coming into the Adjutant General Office, with the prospect of heading the psychological test program. But the country was not then at war, and I had barely settled for what I hoped would be a long residence in a home in California, so I declined. Flanagan's call came after Pearl Harbor, and there was no question about what I should do.

The general objective of PRU #3 was the development of tests for the selection and classification of aircrew trainees—aircraft pilots, navigators, bombardiers, and eventually flight engineers and flexible gunners, as well as a distinction between fighter and bomber pilots. Fortunately, assigned to my staff were Merrill Roff and Lloyd G. Humphreys, both of whom were partial to a factor-analytic approach to test problems and both with some experience with factor analysis. This was the first time that factor analysis had been put to use in a vast test-development program.

Several systematic studies were made in the domains of memory, reasoning, judgment, foresight and planning, and mechanical abilities. The feasibility and fruitfulness of a rational approach of this type were amply demonstrated (1948a). The ramifications of some of our studies also extended into the areas of perceptual and psychomotor tests and their factors. The findings were published in a 900-page document entitled *Printed Classification Tests,* which I edited with John I. Lacey (1947). Reflections on the Air Force experiences served as the content of my presidential address to the Western Psychological Association in 1947 (1948b).

Later during the war, I was assigned as chief of the Field Research Unit (Headquarters, Air Force Training Command, in Fort Worth, Texas), with Paul Horst, Robert L. Thorndike, and Launor F. Carter among the members of the unit. In the neighboring office were Laurance F. Shaffer, Edwin E. Ghiselli, and B. von Haller Gilmer, who were supervising the Air Force's testing operations. Frank A. Geldard was the chief psychologist of the headquarters group.

After a brief transfer back to PRU #3 at my own request, at the discontinuation of that unit in the fall of 1944, I was transferred to PRU #2 at the Aviation Cadet Center, San Antonio (now Lackland Air Force Base), at which all test-development research was consolidated. The unit later became the Department of Records and Analysis under the AAF School of Aviation Medicine of Randolph Field. I was separated from military service in January 1946, with the rank of colonel and with the award of the Legion of Merit following shortly. I had returned to teaching during the previous November.

Many unsolved problems left at the conclusion of the wartime research program, particularly problems in the intellectual area, have since kept my attention. Research contracts provided by the Personnel and Training Branch of the Office of Naval Research and the U.S. Office of Education of the Department of Health, Education, and Welfare and grants from the National Science Foundation since 1949 have made possible a continuous and integrated program of research in space provided by the Department of Psychology at the University of Southern California. A number of highly qualified and dedicated graduate students have also made their lasting contributions to the series of studies in the Aptitudes Research Project. Concentrated efforts were directed at domains initially recognized as reasoning, creative thinking, planning, and evaluation. The findings have been published in a series known as *Reports from the Psychological Laboratory*.

The subject of creative abilities had intrigued me since graduate-student days, when I realized that intelligence tests had little in them that would be likely to assess creative talent. On the other hand, I had noted that G. M. Whipple's book, *Manual of Mental and Physical Tests* (1915), had a chapter on tests of creative imagination, which suggested some possibilities along that line. After holding some seminars on the subject of creative disposition in the late 1940's, I selected the topic "Creativity" for my presidential address to the American Psychological Association in 1950. In this address I set forth hypotheses concerning some of the basic traits that should be expected to be important for recognized creative people and that should be represented in tests that call for creative performance. I was most agreeably surprised at the response to this effort and realized that I had for another time experienced the luck of good timing. For it appeared, as subsequent events have shown, that, as E. G. Boring would say, creativity was coming to the fore in our *Zeitgeist*. Since 1950 the quantity of literature on creativity has virtually exploded. Conferences and institutes have been held and continue to grow in number and in attendance. At least one department of creative education has been established, at the State University of New York at Buffalo, and a foundation for creative education has come into existence. It cannot be foreseen at this time where all this will lead. The recent frantic efforts to improve education have clearly been influenced by the "creativity movement."

But research in the Aptitudes Research Project has by no means been confined to creative potential. Significant outcomes will be discussed in the next section under theory. But it can be said that, beginning with the situation as of 1946, when about twenty-five intellectual abilities had been demonstrated by factor analysis, twenty years later about eighty such dimensions of ability have been demonstrated.


## PSYCHOLOGICAL THEORY

I recall Titchener saying more than once that as psychologists grow older, they tend to go in one of two directions; they go either in the direction of applied psychology or in the direction of general theory construction. I have never had ambitions to attempt to build a system of psychology, perhaps because I noted from my Cornell experience how restricting it can be. I had my "fling" at psychotechnology, as Titchener would call it, during wartime years. But recent developments have directed steps towards basic psychological theory.

A precipitating experience was an invitation to attend a symposium on factor analysis conducted by the Centre Nationale de la Recherche Scientifique held in Paris in July of 1955. In preparing for this event I wrote a paper entitled "Les Dimensions de l'Intellect" (1956), in which I attempted to put some degree of logical order into the nearly forty intellectual-ability factors then recognized. I had already noted quite a number of parallels among the factors and the fact that three distinct kinds of information seemed to be involved in different classes of tests for the factors.

The distinction between verbal and nonverbal, or verbal versus performance, or verbal and quantitative, which had become somewhat orthodox, was not sufficient. A further distinction had to be recognized between two classes of abilities for dealing with nonverbal information, for some factors are features of tests composed of visual figures (tests of spatial orientation, visualization, figure analogies, and so on), while others are features of tests composed of numbers or letters. The former group of tests (and their factors) were therefore labeled as "figural" and the latter as "structural" or "symbolic." The verbal category of tests and their factors was later given the label of "semantic" rather than "verbal," in recognition of the fact that tests of symbolic abilities are also composed of words (hence could be called "verbal"), yet only the spelling characteristics are of significance in assessing individual differences, not the meanings attached to those words (symbols).

In the same paper, distinctions were recognized between factors of memory abilities, "discovery" abilities (later to be labeled as cognition abilities), two kinds of abilities pertaining to production of information (both heavily dependent upon memory storage), and evaluation abilities (pertaining to decisions about goodness of information). The two-way distinction between divergent-production abilities and convergent-production abilities was on the basis of the operational difference that divergent-production tests require multiple answers to given information, whereas convergent-production tests call for single, determined, or restricted answers. Distinctions among categories later recognized as products of information were then in a very crude state, but there were a few such distinctions.

Further extensions and clarifications of the theory were published in 1956 and 1957. It was not until there was an invitation to make a presentation at the Seventh Annual Western Regional Conference on Testing Problems, conducted by the Educational Testing Service, that the structure-of-intellect model was fully conceived in its present form. The model was the basis for my Walter Van Dyke Bingham lecture at Stanford University a year later (1959b). Besides combining the three ways of classification into a single system in the form of a three-dimensional matrix, an entire category of abilities was hypothesized and added for abilities that should take into account what some had called "social intelligence" and others had called "social cognition" or "empathy." The type of information involved was labeled "behavioral." It might have been called "psychological" information, as Spearman had forecast in his *The Abilities of Man* (1927). The label of "social" was rejected in order to avoid unwanted, broader connotations.

The structure-of-intellect model became the heuristic source of hypotheses of still undiscovered intellectual abilities. Consequent to its service in that respect, we were led to find about twenty additional factors, and as of 1966 the search proceeds along the same lines. The model is undoubtedly incomplete, for already four abilities having to do with auditory information have been reported. The model can be readily extended. It can be noted that I have also used the matrix type of model in logical classification of factors found in the areas of psychomotor abilities, temperament traits, and dimensions of psychopathology (1959a).

Incidentally, I have been somewhat amused by some general reactions of dismay regarding the large number of factors and some attempts to whisk them away. In general, I feel sure that psychologists have overdone the application of the principle of parsimony. In fact, there is all too apparent the perennial wish to find that a single principle will answer all questions. Let us be reminded that Frank Barron (1953) and others find that the more creative individuals prefer complexity to simplicity. Facetiously, I sometimes wonder, are psychologists an uncreative lot?

But I am sure that the greatest significance of the structure-of-intellect theory is not to be found in the numbers of abilities that it envisages. I have pointed out in a number of places (1960, 1961, 1962, 1964) that factor analysis, properly applied in an experimental-psychology setting, is a powerful method for enabling an investigator to turn up concepts that have general psychological meaningfulness. Concepts in connection with the structure of intellect can be readily utilized in connection with the understanding of thinking, problem solving, and creative thinking, as well as learning and even motivation (1965). The concepts readily lend themselves to empirical research because they are themselves empirically based in terms of kinds of tasks that can be manipulated experimentally. It is, indeed, through experimental manipulation and systematic variation of tasks that we have been able to differentiate the abilities or functions of human behavior.

## MAJOR PUBLICATIONS

Most of my books have been written for students, with the objective of making available to them things that I thought they needed and things that I wanted to say to them. I have never to my knowledge written with the objective of impressing my fellow psychologists but rather with the objective of being understood. I have not attempted to cater to popular views or movements but to say things that I wanted to say. A consequence has been that most of my books have not been widely popular, in this country at least; there have been gratifying uses, with and without translation, in other countries.

*Psychometric Methods* was written to fill a need for an expanding course that I gave in the early 1930's. Starting that course with psychophysics and basic statistics, time added scaling methods, test theory and methods, and factor analysis. My converging of interests brought about some attempt to give in this book a unified treatment of methods of measurement in psychology. The response at the first appearance of this book took me by surprise. But the time was ripe for it. There was a strong undercurrent of interest in psychological measurement, as indicated by the founding of the Psychometric Society and the launching of the journal *Psychometrika* at about the same time. Substantial developments in the field after 1936 called for the second edition in 1954. Earlier, the publisher had persuaded me to write a short introduction to statistical methods, which came off the presses in 1942 as *Fundamental Statistics in Psychology and Education*. The fourth edition of the latter appeared in 1965.

My book *Personality* was a natural outgrowth of my teaching experiences and the growing knowledge of aptitudes and other personality traits as revealed by factor analysis. At the University of Southern California I was asked to teach a course on personality. I found that textbooks then available were likely to be emasculated versions of general psychology under new titles; a more distinctive type of presentation was desired. My only sabbatical leave, during the spring of 1956, made possible the achieving of this writing objective. In the book I tried to give to the subject of personality a rigorous theory and treatment, as an experimentalist of quantitative bent viewed it. From the sales reports, it must have been too rigorous for American consumption. The German translation is said to be popular, and the book has been selected for translation into Asian and African languages; Persian first.

Over the years, I have produced a number of tests and personality inventories for publication, usually in collaboration with students. Being firmly convinced of the ultimate value of assessing traits that have been derived through a combined rational and empirical approach rather than traits derived "by fiat," as Irving Lorge (1935) expressed it; and having developed devices for measurement along these lines, I felt some urge to share them with others, to make them available through publication. My first efforts, the Nebraska Personality Inventory and a revision of the Army Alpha Examination, were rejected by a well known test publisher and distributor. The solution was for my wife, who desired to keep a hand in some kind of psychological service, to publish and distribute my tests, which she has continued to do.

My postwar publications have emphasized aptitude tests, including a battery of seven factor tests known as the Guilford-Zimmerman Aptitude Survey (with Wayne S. Zimmerman, 1947) and a growing series of factor tests arising out of the Aptitude Research Project findings, with various joint authors. Efforts to demonstrate the value of factor tests in improving predictions of behavior have been limited, but a recent study shows what may be expected (Guilford, Hoepfner, & Peterson, 1965). The outstanding success of the U.S. Air Force classification test battery can be cited as a very substantial testimonial, since that instrument has covered a number of aptitude factors and a number of its tests have approached factorial univocality.

My current efforts in research continue along the same direction of testing hypotheses regarding undiscovered intellectual abilities, hypotheses generated from the structure-of-intellect model. My efforts in writing have the objective of putting in book form the significant findings of the Aptitudes Research Project during the past seventeen years and also the construction of a general-theoretical foundation for intelligence testing (1967), something that has heretofore been almost entirely lacking in this country.

# REFERENCES [1]

*Selected Publications by Joy Paul Guilford*

(with K. M. Dallenbach) The determination of memory span by the method of constant stimuli. *Amer. J. Psychol.*, 1925, *35*, 621–628.

(with W. F. Hyde) A test for classification of students in chemistry. *J. appl. Psychol.*, 1925, *9*, 196–202.

"Fluctuations of attention" with weak visual stimuli. *Amer. J. Psychol.*, 1927, *38*, 534–583.

An experiment in learning to read facial expressions. *J. Abnorm. soc. Psychol.*, 1929, *24*, 191–202.

(with M. Wilke) A new model for the demonstration of facial expressions. *Amer. J. Psychol.*, 1930, *42*, 436–439.

The prediction of affective values. *Amer. J. Psychol.*, 1931, *43*, 469–478.

A generalized psychophysical law. *Psychol. Rev.*, 1932. *39*, 73–85.

(with W. Spence) The affective values of combinations of odors. *Amer. J. Psychol.*, 1933, *45*, 443–452.

The affective value of colors as a function of hue, tint, and chroma. *J. exp. Psychol.*, 1934, *17*, 342–370.

*Psychometric methods.* New York: McGraw-Hill, 1936; 1954.

(with E. C. Allen) Factors determining the affective values of color combinations. *Amer. J. Psychol.* 1936, *48*, 643–648.

[1] For a more extensive bibliography see Michael, Comrey, & Fruchter (1963) and Lindsley *et al.* (1964).

(with R. B. Hackman) Varieties and levels of clearness correlated with eyemovements. *Amer. J. Psychol.*, 1936, 48, 371–388.

(with R. B. Hackman) A study of the "visual fixation" method of measuring attention value. *J. appl. Psychol.*, 1936, 20, 44–59.

*General psychology.* Princeton, N.J.: Van Nostrand, 1939 (a); 1952.

A study in psychodynamics. *Psychometrika*, 1939, 4, 1–23. (b)

Human abilities. *Psychol. Rev.*, 1940, 47, 367–394. (a)

There is system in color preferences. *J. opt. Soc. Amer.*, 1940, 30, 455–459. (b)

(with E. Ewart) Reaction time during distraction as an indicator of attention value. *Amer. J. Psychol.*, 1940, 53, 554–563.

*Fundamental statistics in psychology and education.* New York: McGraw-Hill, 1942; 1950; 1956; 1965.

(with J. I. Lacey) *Printed classification tests.* Army Air Forces Aviation Psychology Research Program Report No. 5. Washington, D.C.: GPO, 1947.

(with W. S. Zimmerman) *The Guilford-Zimmerman aptitude survey.* Parts I-VII. *Manual of instructions and interpretations.* Beverly Hills, Calif.: Sheridan Supply Co., 1947.

Factor analysis in a test-development program. *Psychol. Rev.*, 1948, 55, 79–94. (a)

Some lessons from aviation psychology. *Amer. Psychologist*, 1948, 3, 3–11. (b)

System in color preferences. *J. Soc. motion pic. tv Engr.*, 1949, 52, 197–210.

Creativity. *Amer. Psychologist*, 1950, 5, 444–454.

(with P. R. Christensen, N. A. Bond, & M. A. Sutton) A factor analysis study of human interests. *Psychol. Monogr.*, 1954, 68, No. 4 (Whole No. 375).

(with H. F. Dingman) A validation study of ratio-judgment methods. *Amer. J. Psychol.*, 1954, 67, 395–410.

Les dimensions de l'intellect. In H. Laugier (Ed.), *L'analyse factorielle et ses applications.* Paris: Centre Nationale de la Recherche Scientifique, 1956, 321–335. (a)

The structure of intellect. *Psychol. Bull.*, 1956, 53, 267–293. (b)

(with W. S. Zimmerman) Fourteen dimensions of temperament. *Psychol. Monogr.*, 1956, 70, No. 10 (Whole No. 417).

Revised structure of intellect. *Rep. psychol. Lab.*, No. 19. Los Angeles: Univ. Southern Calif., 1957.

New frontiers of testing in the discovery and development of human talent. In *Seventh annual western regional conference on testing problems.* Los Angeles: Educational Testing Service, 1958, 20–32.

*Personality.* New York: McGraw-Hill, 1959. (a)

Three faces of intellect. *Amer. Psychologist*, 1959, 14, 469–479. (b)

(with P. C. Smith) A system of color preferences. *Amer. J. Psychol.*, 1959, 72, 487–502.

Basic conceptual problems in the psychology of thinking. *Ann. N.Y. Acad. Sci.*, 1960, 91, 6–21.

Factorial angles to psychology. *Psychol. Rev.*, 1961, 68, 1–20.

(with P. R. Christensen, J. W. Frick, & P. R. Merrifield) Factors of interest in thinking. *J. gen. Psychol.*, 1961, 65, 39–56. (a)

(with P. R. Merrifield, P. R. Christensen, & J. W. Frick) Interrelationships between certain abilities and certain traits of motivation and temperament. *J. gen. Psychol.*, 1961, 65, 57–74. (b) (with P. R. Merrifield, P. R. Christensen, & J. W. Frick) Some new symbolic factors of cognition and convergent production. *Educ. psychol. Measmt,* 1961, *21,* 515–541. (c)

An informational view of mind. *J. psychol. Res.,* 1962, *6,* 1–10.

Intelligence, creativity, and learning. In R. W. Russell (Ed.), *Frontiers in psychology.* Chicago: Scott, Foresman, 1964, 125–147.

(with M. O'Sullivan & R. de Mille) The measurement of social intelligence. *Rep. psychol. Lab.,* No. 34. Los Angeles: Univ. Southern Calif. Press, 1965.

(with R. Hoepfner & H. Peterson) Predicting achievement in ninth-grade mathematics from measures of intellectual-aptitude factors. *Educ. psychol. Measmt,* 1965, *25,* 659–682.

Motivation in an informational psychology. In D. Levine (Ed.), *Nebraska symposium on motivation.* Lincoln: Univ. Nebr. Press, 1965.

*The nature of human intelligence.* New York: McGraw-Hill, 1967.

## Other Publications Cited

Allport, F. H. *Social psychology.* Boston: Houghton Mifflin, 1924.

Barron, F. Complexity-simplicity as a personality dimension. *J. abnorm. soc. Psychol.,* 1953, *48,* 163–172.

Boring, E. G. Edward Bradford Titchener, 1867–1927. *Amer. J. Psychol.,* 1927, *38,* 489–506.

Hackman, R. B. A study of the "visual fixation" method of measuring attention value. *J. appl. Psychol.,* 1936, *20,* 44–59.

Harper, R. S. & Stevens, S. S. A psychological scale of weight and a formula for its derivation. *Amer. J. Psychol.,* 1948, *61,* 343–351.

Lindsley, D. B., *et al.* American psychological association distinguished scientific contribution awards. *Amer. Psychologist,* 1964, *19,* 941–954.

Lorge, I. Personality traits by fiat. *J. educ. Psychol.,* 1935, *26,* 273–278.

McDougall, W. *Outline of abnormal psychology.* New York: Scribner, 1926.

Michael, W. B., Comrey, A. L., & Fruchter, B. J. P. Guilford: psychologist and teacher. *Psychol. Bull.,* 1963, *60,* 1–34.

Spearman, C. *The abilities of man.* New York: Macmillan, 1927.

Stevens, S. S. On the psychophysical law. *Psychol. Rev.,* 1957, *54,* 153–181.

Thurstone, L. L. Psychophysical analysis. *Amer. J. Psychol.,* 1927, *38,* 368–389.

Whipple, G. M. *Manual of mental and physical tests.* Part II. *Complex processes.* Baltimore: Warwick and York: 1915.

Harry Helson

# Harry Helson

As one sets himself to the task of writing his autobiography, questions immediately arise: What should he include? What should he omit? What will be of interest to his contemporaries, what to posterity, if indeed anyone is interested in the background details of a life behind the public printed record? Who knows what will be important or interesting in another day and age? Can one write of his work, his encounters with others, his disappointments and satisfactions objectively? Is it desirable to be coldly objective if the purpose of these autobiographies is to make the man known as a human being, not merely as a reflection of the scientist as he appears in his published works? These and other questions spring to mind in preparing to delineate the ideas, events, and people in a life that is largely past. The objective facts are available elsewhere. What is not so easy to determine and is known only to the writer—such as, the choice points in his career, the way his teachers and colleagues have affected him, and his aspirations and goals— are matters of personal evaluation and its attendant biasses. But it is in such personal matters that the individual is revealed.

My parents came to this country, following my maternal grandfather, in the 1880's or early 1890's from Cherkassy in the Ukraine. They were married after reaching this country, and I was born November 9, 1898, in Chelsea, Massachusetts. My father abandoned my mother when I was about four or five years of age, taking my older sister with him. I stayed with my mother until I was ten years old when, on account of her serious illness, I was sent to my father who had remarried and settled in Old Town, Maine.

Without normal family relationships until the age of eleven, my childhood was not a happy one, to say the least. During the first few months with my father, I frequently contemplated suicide and even went to the banks of the Penobscot river to end it all. Fortunately, I came upon a group of youngsters swimming and cavorting on the bank and sat down to watch them. Not only was I diverted from my purpose, but it occurred to me that if there were youngsters my age, perhaps no better off than I, who could enjoy life, there was hope for me. I resolved to go back to the "cold" home where I was wanted by neither my father nor my stepmother and to make the best of it. At the end of the summer, my father moved from Old Town

195

to Bangor, and the whole family was so engrossed in the new business that I was completely on my own from early morning till late at night. Finally the fear of entering a dark abode at night and the settling noises of the house as I lay in bed unable to sleep until the others arrived at a very late hour, drove me to seek a home elsewhere. Some friends of my mother, whom she had met some years before, offered to take me in, and I moved my few belongings to their house. It was during the following spring, almost a year after I left my mother in New Bedford, Massachusetts, that I was fortunate to be taken into the home of Frederick and Theodosia Dyer who thereafter became my foster parents. They wished to adopt me, but my mother would not agree; however, they regarded me as their son, and their home was mine as long as they lived.

My father never made the slightest effort to find out where I had gone or to contact me after I left his house! I relate these facts because there is now a widespread tendency to place all the blame for juvenile delinquency and even later troubles on broken homes and bad early environments. No doubt these play a part, but if a child is early imbued with a vision of the good life, subjected to discipline, and given high goals to strive for, the bad effects of a poor early environment may be counteracted to a great extent. My mother did these things for me, and I owe it to her that I did not succumb to the vicissitudes of my early life. In defense of my father, I should point out that after the death of his second wife when I was in my senior year at Bowdoin College, we met by chance, and he became interested and friendly. He helped pay my way through graduate school and made up to a considerable extent for his early neglect.

The Dyers were members of the First Universalist Church in Bangor but were also ardent spiritualists. They seldom, if ever, attended church services; instead they devoted themselves to bringing spiritualist speakers and mediums to Bangor for public meetings and seances in our home. As a result, I early became acquainted at firsthand with mediums, spiritualistic philosophy, and the main manifestations of spiritualism—"spirit controls," messages, telepathy, clairvoyance, and physical manifestations. Several physical phenomena that occurred spontaneously in our own house left an indelible impression of unexplained events that merit further investigation. They impressed me because I am positive they were not the result of trickery or mechanical manipulation by any person in the household. I am convinced of this, not only because of my faith in the integrity of members of the family, but even more because there was nobody *smart enough* in the house to produce them by mechanical or other means. With the reader's indulgence, I will describe two of these phenomena. The first happened during a dark seance in which only members of the household were present. We were seated in a semicircle in the living room with blinds drawn and the room almost totally dark. Suddenly a small patch of light about the size of a quarter appeared on the rug at the feet of the person on the right end of the "circle" and proceeded to move slowly and continuously along the rug a few inches in front of each person. When it came to me, I put my foot on it and it disappeared. I then got down on my hands and knees and covered the spot with cupped hands and saw the light *under my hands*. It was, therefore, not light reflected or transmitted from a source above the floor. After these tests, the light moved to the last person in the circle and there disappeared. During the whole episode, no one moved except myself when I made the tests. I will not use space here to discuss possible sources of this phenomenon, such as an afterimage explanation, because none that I have been able to conjecture then or since seem plausible.

The second phenomenon that has puzzled me for many years occurred as follows. While standing in broad daylight beside the kitchen stove, a hod full of coal was violently shaken, although there was no movement of the floor or anything near it. I fled from the kitchen to the second floor of the house, where I told Mrs. Dyer and her sister what had happened. They told me it was only my imagination and to go back to the kitchen to finish what I was doing. When I returned to the same spot, the hod of coal went through the same performance! Again I fled, and the ladies came downstairs and examined the hod and the stove, and we found nothing. These and other poltergeist phenomena have simply remained in my memory as unexplained physical events without convincing me that there is personal survival after death or even "mental" control of physical objects beyond the confines of one's own body. But they have left me with an open mind toward paranormal phenomena.

My adventures in psychic research were resumed during my third year of graduate work when I became assistant to Gardner Murphy who was Hodgson Psychic Research Fellow at Harvard, while, at the same time, he was teaching at Columbia. It was during that year that we investigated the famous "Margery" mediumship. Margery was the wife of a Boston surgeon who had started in a small way with table tipping and other physicalistic phenomena in seances held in her home for a few friends. Soon she was in competition for a prize of $5000 offered by a magazine if she could prove to the satisfaction of a committee appointed by it that the phenomena were genuine. William McDougall and Murphy were members of the committee, and I was invited to several of the seances. From the first, I was unimpressed by Margery's performances—they were "old stuff" to one who had witnessed table tipping, table rapping, and movement of objects in the dark at seances in spiritualistic camp meetings in Maine and New York. When I discovered the *modus operandi* of one of her tricks, moving a piano stool from its place at the piano to a wall six or seven feet away, and presented McDougall with pieces of the string used to pull the stool by a confederate in the basement, and this evidence was presented to Dr. and Mrs. Crandon, my attendance at the seances was no longer desired. In a book published some time after-wards, Dr. Crandon maintained that my evidence had been withdrawn by McDougall, but this, I understand, was not true.

A year or two later Margery went to Europe, and when she returned, she had a new set of phenomena, among them the production of so-called ectoplasm and spirit photography. By that time I had left the Boston area and knew of her exploits only by hearsay. Suffice it to say, she was not awarded the $5000 prize, although one member of the committee, not a scientist, professed to believe her phenomena were genuine.

The spiritualistic background of my early boyhood inclined me toward an interest in philosophy and psychology, not so much to explicate spiritual-istic phenomena, as to learn what was known about the universe at large and man's place in it. However, the "efficient cause" of my turning to these subjects was my attendance, when I was about fourteen, at the weekly meet-ings of a small group of adults at which Andrew D. White's *History of the Warfare of Science with Theology in Christendom* (1896) was read aloud and discussed. One of the members of the group, a lawyer who held the position of clerk in the municipal court, steered me to the works of the great religious iconoclast Robert G. Ingersoll, Spencer's *First Principles* (1900), and William James' *Psychology* (1892). At that time, I was over-whelmed by what seemed to be the depth and extent of these writers' knowl-edge. I wondered how they were able to learn so much in a single lifetime. My adulation for them was global and undiscriminating. It was many years later before I found out how superficial Spencer actually was, what a mar-velous style Ingersoll had, and how pithy and true was James in his writings. About the same time, I was loaned Locke's two-volume *An Essay Concern-ing Human Understanding*, but most of it was far above my comprehension. The net result of all this reading and a few glimmerings was a resolve to devote myself to philosophy and psychology as soon as I entered college.

In contrast with my later concentration on work to the exclusion of practically all outside interests, in high school I studied violin and played in both the Young People's Symphony and the high school orchestra, was a member of the debating team, editor of the monthly journal, *The Oracle*, during my senior year, and won the boys' senior essay medal, which all members of the graduating class were required to compete for. During my college years, I had less time for outside activities, having to earn money by playing the violin for dances, church functions, and on other occasions. Ex-cept for being on the debating team and contributing slightly to a maga-zine that two of my classmates and I wrote, printed, and distributed, my attention was wholly taken up with my studies. My concentration on, and dedication to, a scholarly life really began in college and continued there-after. As time went on, I spent less and less time on music and, except for indulgence in a concert, play, or movie, I have had no hobbies or extra-curricular interests to speak of. Any diversion that required regular participation, such as a weekly bridge club, bored me and was soon dropped. On the other hand, I count myself a more-than-average social individual, enjoying the society of others on a free give-and-take basis. I have never cared to be a member of any type of organization and have joined only scholarly and scientific organizations. I did join a college fraternity at Bowdoin but never experienced the benefits supposed to inhere in such organizations. Most of my friends were either in other fraternities or were not members of any fraternity. I learned early that organizational affiliations do not necessarily connote men of character and worth, and so have refused to identify myself formally with any particular political, religious, or social groups.

I went to Bowdoin College with the intention of majoring in philosophy and psychology. In those days there were no counselors, no professors to advise with regard to choice of courses, major subject, or distribution. One read the catalogue stating the requirements for the B.S. or B.A. degree and decided for himself what he would take. I do not remember having a consultation with a professor during my whole undergraduate career, either to get advice on preparation for a career or about work in college. As a result, I found myself deficient in mathematics and physics after obtaining the Ph.D. degree. These lacks were partly made up in the years following graduate work. I took courses in mathematics at Cornell, both during regular session and summer school, and at the University of Kansas two years later. During another summer spent at Cornell, I audited courses in general and physical chemistry and worked in the photometry laboratory. Finally, in the thirties, when vacuum tube techniques began to be used for almost everything in the laboratory, I arranged a private course with a young physicist at Bryn Mawr College, whom I paid out of my own pocket, for lectures and laboratory work in electronics. When a group of graduate students in the psychology department at Byrn Mawr asked for a course in neurology, and a member of the biology department agreed to give it, I took the course with them, dissecting dogfish and pig embryos among other laboratory assignments. I mention these efforts at self-improvement because I felt I had much to learn after obtaining the Ph.D. degree. Besides taking courses with formal instruction, I also had to start from scratch on my own with statistics, as there was no course or requirement in this area during my graduate days in the Department of Psychology at Harvard. Now there are grants, career awards, and other means for deepening and broadening one's knowledge in the postdoctoral days if one so desires. Much as I gained from all this work following the doctorate, it would have been much more valuable had I absorbed it much earlier, preferably during my undergraduate days.

I started graduate work at Harvard with the intention of working toward a Ph.D. degree in philosophy, but the arrival of E. G. Boring from Clark University at the beginning of my second year was responsible for my change to psychology. With Boring, whose courses I audited because I was ostensibly a philosophy major, a new, fresh wind seemed to blow across the psychological horizon. After the second or third lecture, I remember looking across the room at Beebe-Center who, when he caught my glance, gave a solemn nod of approval as if to say, "This is what we have been looking for." And indeed it was. Problems of sensation and perception were discussed in the light of all the available experimental, quantitative literature. There was no armchair psychologizing here. And then like a bombshell came Boring's presentation of Wertheimer's and Korte's work on apparent movement, introducing us to Gestalt psychology. There was nothing written in English about Gestaltism except for Koffka's 1922 article in *Bulletin*, which, because of the new way of looking at things, presented more difficulties than enlightenment concerning the Gestalt movement. Now this article seems to me a model exposition of the Gestalt way of looking at psychological problems. So, at the beginning of my third year at Harvard, when it was necessary to decide on a thesis subject, I could not find a philosophical problem that interested me. I had made an appointment one weekend to confer with Ralph Barton Perry on the following Monday to decide on a philosophical subject for a thesis, but over the weekend it suddenly occurred to me, "Why not do an exposition and criticism of the Gestalt psychology?" I was so fired over this possibility, I forgot to cancel my appointment with Perry and, instead, presented the project to Boring.

The idea of a nonexperimental thesis in psychology was alien to Boring and took him somewhat by surprise, but he promised to consult with other members of the department, which then included philosophy and social ethics as well as psychology. In a few days, I received a positive reply and Boring's consent to act as my adviser. (I do not remember that we had formal committees on theses or candidates in those days, but, in addition to Boring, I find acknowledgments to McDougall and Langfeld in my thesis, so these three must have served as my committee.) Then began the most intensive reading and studying I have ever done. Over ninety percent of the 240 references were German, most of them long, difficult, experimental articles, some of them written in the ponderous German style of the Austrians in Graz and Vienna. In the thesis, the concept of Gestalt was traced back to the Greek and modern philosophers and the work of Meinong, von Ehrenfels, Schumann, Benussi, Bühler, Gelb, Rubin, and others. The thesis ran to 484 typed pages and was published as four articles in the *American Journal of Psychology* in 1925 and 1926. These were later reproduced in a bound volume with preface, bibliography, and indexes at the suggestion and with the help of K. M. Dallenbach. The first of the four articles was submitted to Titchener in his last year as editor of the *American Journal of Psychology*. However, the article actually submitted to Titchener was not published for, as he told me, "If this is published you will gain a reputation for scholarship, but nobody will read you." In a few minutes Titchener delineated the kind of exposition that would be of interest, and his judgment proved to be correct as shown by the fact that all the bound volumes were quickly bought, and, even after 200 more were procured, I was unable to fill many requests, including one for sixty copies for Koffka's class in Berkeley where he taught one summer.

Before leaving the Harvard period, I would like to say a few words about McDougall. I audited one or two of McDougall's courses, and, as assistant to Murphy who was Hodgson Fellow in psychic research, I also reported to McDougall on the work we were doing in that area and thus came to know him as a person as well as professor. McDougall was undoubtedly one of the most kindly, finest gentlemen I have ever met in the teaching profession. After each of his lectures, there would always be a long line of students outside his office desiring to confer with him. I am sure these conferences were not merely concerned with problems of classwork. Since my purpose in seeing him was to talk about our last seance with Margery or about some medium I had investigated or about the phenomena at our last table-tipping session in the laboratory, I usually stood last in line in order to allow him as much time as he wished to give our conference without forcing others to wait. In these conferences, McDougall would puff at his pipe, blowing huge smoke rings that floated a foot or so away from his face and then returned to encircle his face like a vertical halo. These smoke rings never lost their fascination for me. During one of our conferences, McDougall announced that one of his grandfathers was Jewish—a fact that few, if any, in this country know. I mention it here for what it is worth as counterevidence for the charge that McDougall was a racist or held objectionable racist theories. He had lost a brother in the First World War and, thereafter, he told me, could never bring himself to read the German literature again. The idea of a *Herrenvolk* was, I am sure, as obnoxious to McDougall as to almost everyone else both then and later.

At the time I obtained my degree in June, 1924, there were no jobs available in psychology, at least for me. Owing to my association with McDougall and Gardner Murphy on the Margery case, I was offered the chance to be Walter Prince's assistant in the Boston branch of the American Society for Psychic Research, with the prospect of succeeding him as research officer and editor of their journal on his retirement. But the idea of spending a lifetime on psychic research with little likelihood of any positive contributions to knowledge did not appeal to me, much as I needed a job and attractive as was the salary offered. Fortunately for me, Boring wrote Titchener asking if he could find a place for me at Cornell as instructor, and Titchener replied he would see what he could do. I went home to Maine to await definite word, which did not come until late August or early September— an instructorship at $1200. Compared with present-day beginning salaries, this amount was pitifully small, but I was single, wanted a university position in *psychology,* and a place to work and learn. Cornell was ideal and I accepted gratefully.

My first meeting with Titchener was somewhat of a disappointment.

He was supervising the cutting down of a tree in his yard and had on an old pair of baggy trousers, a sweater, and shirt open at the neck. In those days people did little yardwork and almost no "do-it-yourself" chores. I made one or two comments, hoping to start him talking about psychology, but his interest was in the way the limbs were coming off the tree. I do remember that he spoke of "the delight in the use of tools" and remarked that "a gentleman never mentioned money matters." Yet, before the afternoon was over, he spoke of how nice it would be if some rich man would offer him his yacht for an extended cruise!

My teaching assignment first semester at Cornell came as a surprise. Titchener informed me I was to demonstrate to the graduate students the main pieces of apparatus in the Cornell laboratory, giving their history as well as their *modus operandi*. "But," I remonstrated, "I don't know anything about apparatus. My dissertation was all library work." "I know," replied Titchener, "that's why I've given you this course. In this way you'll learn." And so I did. Deane B. Judd, with whom I had become acquainted, was a graduate student in physics, and I enlisted his aid. Judd lectured on light-measuring instruments, and I parceled out a report or two to students on other types of equipment. I was also asked to check the inventory of laboratory equipment at Cornell, a task Bentley assigned me the following year at the University of Illinois, and from these assignments I became acquainted with laboratory equipment and its uses.

The year 1924–25 at Cornell was notable both for what I learned and the friends made there. In addition to Judd, J. P. Guilford was also a graduate student. Dallenbach was on the faculty and was the most active researcher in the department. My friendship with these men has continued ever since, buttressed by professional as well as personal affinities. Due to an accidental incision in the left ventral surface of the first phalange of Dallenbach's index finger, it was rendered completely devoid of sensation. Dallenbach gave me the opportunity to be the experimenter to trace the return of sensitivity in a replication of the work of Henry Head and E. G. Boring who deliberately severed nerves in their arms for the purpose of studying this problem. Not knowing how fast various types of sensation might return, we worked every day for several weeks, then once a week, later once a month, and gradually extended the periods between observations to a year or more. Data have accumulated over forty years, but no publication has resulted except for brief reports by Dallenbach or myself at psychological meetings. Such a huge mass of data has accumulated, it is now doubtful that it will ever see the light of day in print.

To me, the most interesting finding in this study is that sensitivity returns simultaneously on all sides of the numb area, a result that is not compatible with the notion of regeneration restricted to the nerves originally severed. It looks as if normal nerve endings on all sides of the affected area, as well as the cut nerves, send branches into the numb region; else why does sensitivity spread from normal tissue on all sides surrounding the anesthetic area?

The work with Dallenbach gave me excellent training in apparatus and methods for investigating skin and underlying sensitivity. It was as good as writing a Ph.D. dissertation in experimental psychology under Dallenbach's direction. I can thus claim two "masters": Boring at Harvard and Dallenbach at Cornell. In addition, that year Judd and I constructed perhaps the first Ganzfeld: a sphere lined on the inside with orange-red Hering paper provided equal and constant chromatic stimulation to all parts of the retina, while the eyes were allowed to move freely. My interest in problems of adaptation thus began at the very start of my career and has continued ever since.

Having studied the Gestalt literature for my thesis, I was fired with enthusiasm for this approach, even though I was not able to agree with their position 100 percent. Compared with the only alternative approach (*i.e.,* analytical introspection) that was available in the mid-twenties for the study of sensory processes, *Gestalttheorie* was far preferable. At Cornell my command of *Gestalttheorie* was largely wasted. There was no chance of offering a course in it or of bringing it explicitly into my teaching because my main job as instructor was handling discussion sections in the introductory course where a Titchenerian point of view prevailed. In those days young instructors with Ph.D.s did largely what graduate assistants now are called upon to do. I did enliven my sections with accounts of Gestalt experiments in perception and Köhler's work with the apes, but there were no questions in the examinations on this material. When Bentley invited me to join his department at the University of Illinois at a considerably higher salary than I was getting at Cornell, I accepted.

During the 1924–25 academic year, Koffka came to Cornell as visiting professor, but not under the auspices of the psychology department. Ogden, dean of arts and sciences and also head of the education department, was responsible for Koffka's appointment, and so he was technically a member of the education department rather than the psychology department. Koffka gave a small seminar attended by Ogden, Dallenbach, Guilford, myself, and two or three others. He also gave the Schiff lectures for the University at large. As stated in the preface to my collected papers on Gestalt, I was indebted to Koffka's seminar and the Schiff lectures for much in several sections of the third article. In addition, Guilford and I were invited to Koffka's home to read German one evening a week, and these informal meetings were most delightful and informative. Koffka told us about the positions of the three young men, Wertheimer, Köhler, and himself, in relation to their older teachers and stalwarts, Stumpf and Schumann, and we learned how deep and radical was the break between *Gestalttheorie* and prevailing approaches to perception. When I once referred to the Graz group, among whom Meinong and Benussi were the leaders, as the left or radical wing of the Gestalt revolution, with their emphasis on *Produktionsvorgang* to produce Gestalten, Koffka retorted, "No—we are the radical group, they are the conservatives." On second thought, it was plain to me that Koffka was quite right, for the resort to higher psychological processes to account for perception of configurations was in the tradition of dualistic accounts of perception; *i.e.,* one type of process for sensory data and another type for perception of patterns or wholes. Postulation of a single, unitary psychophysiological basis for all perceptions, temporal as well as spatial, was indeed a radical break with the past in 1912, the year that Wertheimer published the paper that launched Gestalt psychology on its way.

The seminar given by Koffka was during the first semester and the one given by Titchener was second semester. Since attendance at Titchener's seminar was wholly by invitation, and since only the staff and a few of the best graduate students were invited, we were all agog as to whether or not Koffka would be invited and, if so, whether there would be any fireworks in view of the widely disparate views held by the two men regarding fundamentals in psychology. Titchener had easily disposed of *Gestalttheorie* in personal discussions with some of us by claiming that it did not represent the scientific approach to psychology—dealing as it did with complexes, forms, and meanings, it was an applied psychology and hence really did not concern his position at all. Koffka and Ogden were both invited to participate in Titchener's seminar and never was there anything approaching a confrontation of their opposing views. The subject of the seminar would be, Titchener announced, the meanings of "attention" in the literature. The various journals were parceled out to the members of the seminar, who were required to report on all the ways in which this term was used. Dallenbach and I were assigned the *Zeitschrift für Psychologie,* which at that time comprised about eighty-five volumes! Each of us read about half this number, although I must say after careful reading of five or six volumes, I began skimming, stopping to read only where such words as Aufmerksamkeit, Klarheit, Deutlichkeit, and other words having some relation to attention appeared. Koffka, so far as I can remember, did not report and was not even asked to present the Gestalt criticisms of the concept of attention and all that they entailed; nor did he get a chance to discuss the positive contributions of *Gestalttheorie* to the problem of attention.

At Illinois I began under extremely trying circumstances. Early in the fall, I developed an infection in my left thigh that required hospitalization. I was the first patient in the new University student infirmary. When the infection had proceeded to the point where I could not move my entire leg, my condition was very grave, as evidenced by the fact that a screen was placed around my bed presumably to hide a dying patient. My doctor operated, making two deep incisions. The infection had literally dug a channel deep in the tissue about four inches long. The operation, allowing drainage and medication, saved my life, for there were no antibiotics or sulfa drugs at that time.

I recovered quite rapidly from this illness and resumed my teaching and research. Again most of my work was teaching sections of introductory psychology with Bentley giving the lectures. Again, as pointed out above, I had to make an inventory of the apparatus in the laboratory, finding many of the old standard pieces at Illinois that I had encountered at Cornell. Among the oddities were the plaster brain models that were said to belong to Spurzheim, the phrenologist, that had somehow found their way to the Illinois Department of Psychology. Besides preparing the third and fourth articles in my series on Gestalt for the *American Journal of Psychology,* the only research I was able to do did not pan out, but there was one result that was further investigated thirty-five years later. A graduate student, Joseph Steger, at Kansas State University, learning of it in my seminar, asked to study it out of pure curiosity. I had tried to condition a sensory process, first by pairing light with tone or tone with light and then omitting the second stimulus. The cases where subjects reported a conditioned tone following light or a conditioned light following tone were too few to warrant publication. To conceal the purpose of the experiment, subjects were required to press a key on the appearance of the *first* stimulus, as if it were a reaction time study. I found that the reaction times to the *first* stimulus were longer when the *second* stimulus followed the first than when the second stimulus was omitted. This finding was later amply confirmed with two light stimuli (Helson and Steger, 1962). A number of subsequent studies, in which heteromodal stimuli were employed, have shown that there is facilitation (quickening) of response up to about 25 milliseconds after which there is increasing inhibition up to 100 milliseconds with the effect of the second stimulus on the first diminishing thereafter (Helson, 1964).

Although I was set to remain at Illinois, I received an invitation from R. H. Wheeler to join him at the University of Kansas as assistant professor at a considerable raise in salary. Having started at Cornell as instructor at $1200 and having gone to Illinois at $2000, the offer of $2600 seemed munificent, especially since I planned to be married and money became important. I had become engaged to Lida Anderson, a graduate student in French at Illinois, and we planned to work for a year, she to teach at Alma College in Michigan, while I went to Kansas, in order to save enough to get married on. I returned to Cornell in the summer of 1926 to resume work on Dallenbach's finger and left for Kansas late in August. I met my fiancée in Chicago to drive to Urbana where we planned to visit her sister and brother-in-law, Ahna and David Fiske. We decided then and there to give up the idea of being apart for a year and were married in Chicago. Needless to say, both the Fiskes in Urbana and, a few days later, the Wheelers in Lawrence were quite surprised when a married couple appeared. The

Wheelers helped us find a house, kept us until we could buy some furniture, and otherwise aided in making life comfortable and pleasant during those beginning days.

Kansas was a busy hive of research activity. W. S. Hunter had preceded Wheeler as chairman, so there was a good animal laboratory and even a *Diener* who took care of the animals. With such good animal facilities, I naturally did a rat study, in which the problem was to determine if rats would transpose a brightness discrimination relatively, as Köhler's apes had done. The rats behaved in accordance with expectations from *Gestalttheorie,* and I published my one and only animal study. This study, I think, was the first to invoke "the law of least action" as an explanation in the field of learning and performance (1927). It was also at Kansas that I did experimental work on vision in the blind spot and the study with Guilford showing that perception of phi phenomenon and eye movements did not correlate. Other studies I completed at Kansas were a study of the tau effect with S. M. King, which resulted in two publications, and a description of the Kansas kinohapt with S. H. Bartley. These studies did not appear in print until after I had left Kansas. I cite them to bear cut what I stated in the opening sentence, that is, that Kansas was a beehive of experimental activity during these two years and later, as there were also many studies in progress by other members of the department. I should mention that the work on the phi phenomenon was done with an eye-movement camera that Guilford and I "built." We also constructed the kinohapt with which the tau effect was studied. Then, and until the advent of electronic equipment from commercial sources, research apparatus was usually built or at least assembled by each worker or with the aid of an instrument-maker. There was little money in those days to purchase more than essential parts of apparatus.

During my first year at Kansas, Wheeler strongly opposed my espousal of *Gestalttheorie.* He was then an ardent introspectionist, believing in "complete" analytical introspection that went far beyond Titchenerian-type protocols. Wheeler also advocated a motor theory of consciousness, maintaining, as Dewey and Münsterberg had before him, that the motor side of the reflex arc must be completed before there was any consciousness. By the middle of my second and last year at Kansas, Wheeler had completely embraced *Gestalttheorie* and one day outlined to me a series of books he planned to write within a relatively short time utilizing holistic and allied concepts. It seemed like an impossible task in the time limit he had set himself, but, as the sequel showed, he accomplished it as planned. Into all his activities— intellectual, personal, social—Wheeler put all of his energies. When he turned to his studies of the effects of climate on human behavior, he took an even more radical position than Buckle or Huntington: climatic cycles were responsible for all human activities, including types of government, movements in literature, mathematics, and even the sciences. According to this theory, warm cycles breed individualism, romanticism, atomism, and democracy; cold cycles breed monarchy, dictatorship, classicism, and holism. There never was a more ardent department head or friend than Wheeler; he worked hard to make members of his department happy and furthered their work in every way; no one could have been more appreciative of those under him. It was with genuine regret that I left Kansas.

The reasons for my early frequent moves, from Cornell to Illinois to Kansas to Bryn Mawr, where at last I settled for twenty years, were not wholly as clear to me then as they appear to be in retrospect. Until the Second World War, university faculties were not as dynamic and changing as they are now. Departments were relatively small and static. Promotions were slow and waited on the death or retirement of senior professors. At Cornell, Illinois, and Kansas, I saw myself waiting in line, as it were, for a better salary and promotion. There was no certain prospect, even with good work, of reasonably rapid advancement. When the invitation came to go to Bryn Mawr as director of the laboratory and associate professor, with promotion to full professor assured when the incumbent Professer (James Leuba) retired in five years, the open path I desired materialized. In urging me to remain at Kansas, both Wheeler and Chancellor Lindley held out the prospect of succeeding to professorship and chairmanship of the department when Wheeler left. Neither Lindley nor Wheeler dreamed that it would be nearly twenty years before the latter would leave Kansas. In addition, Bryn Mawr appealed to me because there I could build a laboratory and, to a lesser extent, a new department, as contrasted with the set patterns I had found at Cornell, Illinois, and Kansas. Cornell was strongly Titchenerian in fact and in spirit; Illinois was amorphous both in and outside the department, and I had felt lost; Kansas was dominated by Wheeler, and, much as I liked and admired him, I wanted to have my own show. So to Bryn Mawr I went in September of 1928.

I came to Bryn Mawr College a year after the Ferrees had left for Wilmer Institute at The Johns Hopkins University. Most of their apparatus was still in the psychology laboratory at Bryn Mawr, and they asked to purchase as much of it as I was willing to part with. Since it was apparatus that had been developed for their own special purposes, I was glad to sell most of it for about $20,000 which furnished me with a nest egg for equipping an experimental laboratory such as I desired for teaching and research purposes. When I went to Bryn Mawr, there was little or no equipment in the laboratory for general experimental psychology. The appropriation for all needs in psychology was $500 a year and stood at that figure from 1928 until I left in 1949, partly because I never completely spent all the money received for the Ferree apparatus. (I have always hoarded money received for teaching and research, whether from an institution, a military agency, or private foundation. As of this writing, I have not yet spent all of a grant of about $9000 received about ten years ago, although several publications have appeared as a result of this grant.) At Bryn Mawr, I had the benefit of an excellent instrument-maker, Mr. Norman Powell, whom I shared with the departments of physics, chemistry, biology, and geology! However, most of his time went to psychology, for we spent many hours a week designing, testing, and modifying various pieces of equipment.

These days almost everything in the psychology laboratory is electrical or electronic in nature and bought on the open market at fantastic figures compared with what we expended. The present stands in sharp contrast to my early days when apparatus was either built with one's own hands or in close contact with the college or department instrument-maker. Not possessing the necessary skills myself to work with lathe, drill press, planer, and other equipment, I had to communicate my ideas to the instrument-maker by means of rough sketches with the dimensions of what I had in mind. Powell was strictly a metalworker and refused to do even the simplest jobs in wood—for that I had to go to the boss carpenter who was as able producing what I wanted from my rough descriptions and drawings as Powell was. I was thus able to obtain the equipment needed for both teaching and research in experimental psychology. During my twenty years at Bryn Mawr, among the numerous pieces of research equipment we constructed were an eye-movement camera for photographing and timing a light beam reflected from the cornea; a kinohapt that enabled us to stimulate spots on the skin in any desired order and with controlled time intervals; a mechanical timer for controlling the time of and between three stimuli that had the remarkable accuracy of something like one hundred-thousandth of a second and with greater stability than any electronic timers I have since seen; aesthesiometers ranging from one to fifty millimeters, which were quickly interchangeable; stimulators for error of localization on the skin; a trichromatic colorimeter; a variable gearshift for increasing or decreasing the luminance of the Nagel adaptometer at controlled rates; and a stereoscope permitting variations in interocular distance as well as in depth and in the vertical direction. We also constructed many things for undergraduate teaching needed in quantity that we could not afford to buy in the open market. Since I only had to pay for the materials, our apparatus, counting the amount received from Ferree and the small yearly appropriation, cost us about $30,000 during my twenty years at Bryn Mawr. I cite these facts for the benefit of those who may not be able to obtain large contracts or grants and to contrast what we did with comparatively little money as compared with what is spent nowadays for ready-made equipment.

In the case of most individuals, the early pattern of work and intellectual development is set by the area of the doctoral thesis and/or the interests of a teacher or the director of the dissertation. My first research was therefore concerned with problems having their origin in *Gestalttheorie* as shown in the account of work done at the University of Kansas and some studies during the first years at Bryn Mawr College. Most of my work was published in the *American Journal of Psychology,* and, as Dallenbach received an article for the *Journal* in a new area, he urged me to settle down and work in a single field. But I had to find something that was both interesting and capable of continued exploration. One cannot, it seems to me, *decide* to do programmatic research in a predetermined area; one must find new problems springing from his previous work or work in progress. Nor does one necessarily start with a theory from which problems flow, as many logicians would have us believe scientific exploration proceeds.

The greatest bar to creative work is, I have come to believe, acceptance of scientific shibboleths and doing experiments according to prevailing stereotypes in various fields of investigation. Most of my researches have been inspired by skepticism regarding the validity of generalizations and doubts as to the fruitfulness of various approaches. Thus Judd and I began investigating vision with total as opposed to spot stimulation of the retina. Our studies in strongly chromatic illumination were begun because I did not believe the CIE (International Commission on Illumination) method of color specification was adequate, based as it was on gauging the spectrum with small foveal stimuli against a dark background. In the investigation of sensitivity of the blind spot, I reversed the usual method of demonstrating its insensitivity, which consisted of using a black stimulus on a white surround, by employing instead a bright stimulus against a dark surround. When I found the classical method of constant stimuli to be extremely tedious and time consuming in determinations of the two-point threshold owing to the rule that stimulus-separation had to be changed for each judgment, I did a study with Shaad showing that there was no significant difference between random presentation and repeated presentations of the same stimulus if subjects were warned against making the stimulus error in their judgments. Unsatisfied with the usual descriptive studies of the von Bezold "mixture" effect, I decided to use line stimuli that could be varied in width and separation in place of the artistic designs employed by von Bezold and others. A series of quantitative studies eventuated with Rohles, Joy, and Steger, which showed that color assimilation is subject to lawful, ordered variations in the stimuli, leading from assimilation to contrast with a neutral zone in which there is neither contrast nor assimilation. Finally, contrary to the usual approaches in social psychology, we introduced the method of variation in strength of social stimulation in a study by Edgar Schein during the time that I was Thomas Welton Standord Fellow and acting professor at Stanford in 1948–49, and also in the Texas studies with R. R. Blake and others.

In addition, two specific questions were destined to guide much of my research: Is a neutral gray the end state of chromatic adaptation under *all* conditions, *e.g.,* with moving eyes and constant light flux on the whole retina? What is seen in strongly chromatic illumination if the end result of adaptation is not Hering's midgray? The answer to the second question was embodied in the principle of color conversion: in every viewing situation there is established an adaptation level, such that luminances above AL are tinged with the hue of the illuminant, those below are tinged with the after-image complement to the illuminant hue, and luminances at or near AL are either achromatic or weakly saturated hues of uncertain or changing chromaticness. The work in chromatic illuminants was begun in 1928, and the first publication was not until ten years later. As I have pointed out elsewhere, no rhyme or reason appeared in hundreds of observations until we substituted nonselective for selective stimuli. So long as we used chromatic stimuli, we could not shake ourselves loose from their daylight appearance. We were baffled in our attempts to relate the daylight colors to the chromatically illuminated colors: a daylight green on white background might be seen as reddish or blue-green or neutral in red light, but all greens—light, medium, and dark—were seen as reddish on black background in red light, the former a more saturated red than the latter. After the principle of color conversion was formulated, everything appeared clear and simple. Use of nonselective stimuli freed us from the incubus of their daylight color because their hues in chromatic illumination would have to arise from the prevailing conditions of vision, not from memory or any carry-over effect from previous experience.

The principle of color conversion was responsible for many studies by my colleagues and myself. It was tested by Higbee who used what amounted to self-luminous stimuli in fields illuminated by chromatic sources; by Michels and myself in reverse, so to speak, by requiring observers to synthesize light, medium, and dark grays in the exit pupil of a colorimeter while the surrounding area was illuminated with strongly chromatic light; and by Judd, my daughter (Martha Warren Wilson), Josephine Grove, and myself in a number of studies of color rendition in passing from daylight to incandescent and fluorescent sources of illumination.

That the work in visual adaptation would lead to the theory of adaptation level was certainly not intended or foreseen. The natural history of the theory, which may be of interest, was as follows: first, there was the stark fact that some stimuli in monochromatic light were achromatic, and the reflectance of the achromatic stimuli depended on the background. This led to recognition of the operation of adaptation levels in vision. Then there was recognition that PSE (point of subjective equality) in psychophysics was also a manifestation of the working of adaptation levels in judgments of sensory magnitudes.

Recognition of the role of the neutral point as the determining factor in the qualitative structure of visual fields immediately suggested the possibility of an analytic, quantitative approach to Gestalt phenomena. What the Gestalt psychologists had to assume as a primitive, given datum or postulate, it was now clear, could be accounted for in more general, basic terms. Not only qualities like red and blue-green, warm and cold, pleasant and unpleasant, but sensory magnitudes were also seen to depend upon prevailing adaptation levels. The same sound may be loud or soft, the same light bright or dim, depending on its relation to prevailing levels of stimulation. Adaptation-level theory thus extends *Gestalttheorie* and furnishes a principle according to which qualities and magnitudes can be ordered, thus accounting for the organization of perceptual fields. Outside perception, when stimuli and responses can be ordered on bipolar continua, the concept of adaptation level can also be applied quite naturally. For example, in attitude studies, if statements denoting degrees of agreement and disagreement toward an issue are employed, those that elicit a neutral or indifferent response are indicative of the adaptation level for that universe of discourse. Similar considerations apply in the study of affectivity, learning, cognition, and personality because practically all concepts, involving opposites as they do, can be ordered on bipolar continua in which there are neutral or indifferent zones corresponding to prevailing adjustment levels. Since neutral responses depend upon all the stimuli impinging on the organism, the conditions under which they act (such as their frequency, size, recency, and intensity), and upon residuals from previous stimulation, adaptation levels vary from moment to moment and from person to person. Beginning with the study of sensory processes and psychophysical judgment, my colleagues and I extended our investigations into almost every basic area of psychology. These, as well as studies by others bearing directly on the theory, and a number of unpublished studies of our own were brought together in my book (Helson, 1964b). I was able to start this book while holding appointment as Hogg Foundation Research Scholar at the University of Texas (1956–57) largely because of the support and interest of the associate director of the Hogg Foundation, Dr. Wayne Holtzman. The book grew as I worked on it, and its progress was materially aided by a research leave from the University of Texas in 1958–59 and by a light teaching load at Kansas State University where it was finally completed in 1963.

A comment is in order regarding some demands made on the theory of adaptation level. After the first publication appeared, I received many letters asking what the weighting constants should be for series, background, and residual stimuli under conditions we had not investigated. I have not been able to see why this theory should give answers that no other theory has been asked to give in advance of experimentation. Constants in equations must be determined empirically. Weighting coefficients determined under one set of conditions do not necessarily hold for different conditions. A merit of adaptation-level theory is that it can be applied to many problems, but it must not be oversimplified or used without regard to the sense of concrete situations.

The outbreak of the Second World War was, for many academic as well as other people, a turning point in their lives. Shortly after the attack on Pearl Harbor, I wrote to the Department of the Army offering my services in any capacity whatsoever. I doubt if there was a reply, and I was not one of the psychologists over forty years of age tapped for military service. In the spring of 1942, Drs. Thornton Fry and Samuel Fernberger, representing the National Defense Research Committee (NDRC), came to me and asked if (1) I believed fruitful work could be done in the study of handwheel controls of anti-aircraft guns and allied equipment such as tracking and director devices; and (2) would I be willing to head a project concerned with such study in the neighborhood of Philadelphia? I replied affirmatively to both questions and was invited to participate in a conference held at the Foxboro Company, in Foxboro, Massachusetts. Having gone that far and wishing to participate in some measure in the war effort, I could not refuse to go to Foxboro, even though I had understood originally that it would not be necessary to move my family and household effects in agreeing to head a project. We sold our house in June, 1942, for exactly what we had paid for it, not realizing that the coming inflation would hit housing harder than any other single item in our economy. We moved first to Sharon, Massachusetts, and then to Foxboro. These were the first of half a dozen moves during the war period, with more to come later.

The Foxboro project was actually a joint engineering-psychology affair, with the head of Foxboro's Research and Development Division, Mr. William Howe, and myself as codirectors. The resources of the Foxboro Company engineering staff were at our disposal and intensive work on the design of our research equipment began in June and continued until early fall when we were ready to begin our research. Trained psychologists were not immediately available, but we began with one person besides myself in a small room of one of the buildings and added more personnel and space as we needed them. In less than a year from the time we started, we had produced several reports to the services, and NDRC offered to build more adequate quarters for the project. We persuaded President Atwood of Clark University to grant Dr. Robert Brown leave of absence to join us, and later Dr. Sidney Newhall also came to us. Our nonprofessional staff also grew because hundreds of records had to be analyzed every week, data had to be statistically treated, and apparatus had to be built, rebuilt, and constantly recalibrated.

Since only a small part of the work done at Foxboro was published in public form (Helson, 1949), some idea of the variety and extent of work accomplished in the years 1942 through 1944 may be of interest here. Following is a partial list of subjects covered in reports to NDRC, the services, and various organizations:

Handwheel speed and accuracy of tracking,
Relative accuracy of handwheel tracking with one and both hands,
Inertia, friction, and diameter in handwheel tracking,
Accuracy of tracking by means of handwheel controls,
Simultaneous hand and foot operation of tracking and ranging controls,
Direct tracking and simultaneous stadiametric ranging,
Tracking with illuminated and nonilluminated oscilloscopes,
Influence of visual magnification on accuracy of tracking,

Improvement in direct, aided, and velocity tracking through magnification of data presentation,

Effects of target speeds and rates of turning on accuracy of direct handwheel tracking,

Factors responsible for visual fatigue in the presentation of data with oscilloscopes and suggestions for their alleviation,

Latency in the formation of the retinal image and tracking,

Studies of aided and velocity tracking.

From the many Foxboro studies, I was able to make a number of generalizations having applicability beyond the particular types of equipment and conditions of operation employed in those investigations. The first generalization was the $U$-hypothesis, according to which human performance tends to be optimal over a fairly broad band of stimulus values, such as handwheel gear ratios and inertia, but above and below this band, performance becomes noticeably poorer. We can also subsume sensitivity curves for pitch, loudness, brightness, and other sensory dimensions to the $U$-hypothesis, in that they have the same shape as the error curves found in tracking performance. The $U$-hypothesis now seems to be quite generally accepted by workers in human engineering and human factors. A second generalization, although not as broadly applicable as the $U$-hypothesis, may nevertheless serve as an heuristic principle in the design of equipment. This is the principle of "generality or transferability of the optimal condition." It refers to the fact that a condition or variable that is good in one complex of conditions tends to be good in other constellations of conditions. The third generalization was the principle of offset or compromise, and it states that, if it is not possible to incorporate the optimal value of a parameter in designing equipment, other parameters may be adjusted to offset the deleterious value to a greater or lesser extent. Thus if it is not possible to use gear ratios for fast turning to track distant slow targets because of the much faster rates required for near targets, the radius of the handwheel may be increased, thereby increasing the amount of arm movements which enter into the advantage found in fast handwheel speeds. The fourth generalization concerned the role of internal norms in performance. Internal norms determine the "par" performance of an individual and are set by characteristics of equipment as well as by organismic factors, such as keenness of vision and hearing, muscular development, and the degree of motivation and frustration tolerance.

These generalizations are mentioned because work dealing with design of equipment and human factors has been criticized on the basis that this field is "full of information that is apparently very correct but which represents only one point on what should have been a curve showing how one variable is functionally related to another" (Wood, quoted in Helson, 1964b). As stated above, the approach at Foxboro was to determine the curves relating performance over a wide range of variables, and it was because of this approach that we were able to extract information of a general nature, not only the four principles just discussed, but also others. The moral of all this is, of course, that budding psychologists should be trained to design experiments that will yield general principles. The Foxboro studies showed that it is possible to obtain valid generalizations even from research having a strong practical bias. The rank empiricism that pervades psychology today can be traced to several sources, chief of which is the way students are taught, the types of research which are easiest to get published, and the safety of sticking to particular facts which are valid in themselves, but have few implications beyond their own frames of reference.

By the time all of the Foxboro studies were declassified, my interests had shifted to problems connected with adaptation-level theory, and I laid the Foxboro results aside. Some of the studies became available from the Publication Board, Office of Technical Services, U.S. Department of Commerce, but I myself never saw them in that form and never checked to see how many of the Foxboro studies were available there. I can repeat here the late Franklin V. Taylor's judgment concerning the Foxboro work that "It was the pioneer work in human factors in this country" because I consider it a tribute, not only to myself, but also to Drs. Samuel Fernberger and Thornton Fry, who had the vision of fitting equipment to men in contrast to the traditional approach of fitting men to jobs and machines through selection and training. Of course both approaches, optimal design of machines for human operation and selection and training, are necessary for best performance. The former philosophy was made most explicit in the Foxboro approach, as well as the idea of investigating the whole range of variables like handwheel speed and inertia in order to determine optimal regions and breaking points in the use of manipulanda. The studies concerned with design of equipment since the end of the war may have been due to the Zeitgeist, but I like to think that the Foxboro project had something to do with getting it started, if it is proper to speak of activating a Geist!

While I was at Stanford on sabbatical leave from Bryn Mawr, I was invited to Brooklyn College as chairman and professor, and I decided to accept. I little realized that being chairman of a large department would be so different from being chairman at Bryn Mawr. The paper work seemed never to end—as soon as material for one catalogue was sent in, another had to be done, and the matter of staffing was a constant source of worry. In my second year at Brooklyn, Dallenbach asked me to go to Texas, and I was most happy to relinquish the duties of chairman and resolved never again to accept an appointnment involving administrative work. When I went to Texas, I was in my fifty-third year and did not expect to make another move before retiring, but fate would have it otherwise. One of the best things about life is that it contains unforeseen, pleasant surprises. My move to Kansas State University had its origins in a meeting with Dr. William Bevan at the New Orleans conference of the Southern Society for Philosophy and Psychology in the middle 1950's. My friendship and collaboration with Bevan had its beginnings at that time. We corresponded about mutual psychological problems from then on, and during a research leave from Texas that I spent in Berkeley, he invited me to be visiting professor at Kansas State University during the second semester of the 1960–61 academic year. The semester spent there was so stimulating and fruitful that I accepted the invitation to fill the first named chair at Kansas State.

I have mentioned a number of topics and areas in which I have worked, but some others may come as a surprise to those who are not familiar with them. Though I have not been regarded as a physiological psychologist, several of my publications are either directly concerned with or have a bearing on physiological mechanisms. Among these studies, I would first single out the investigation of vision in the blind spot which forced me to the conclusion there is a primitive type of light sensitivity there that is not explained by light scattering or excitation of receptors contiguous to this area. I believe my view of the sensitivity of the macula coeca will be vindicated in time. Two other studies in the physiological area were undertaken at the suggestion of practicing neurologists. The first was to determine if the paralgesias and formications reported by patients following total or subtotal section of the trigeminal nerve for relief of tic douloureux are "imaginary" or the result of some residual sensitivity in the area deprived of fifth nerve supply. Careful tests, some using psychophysical methods, showed there was indeed some residual sensitivity to deep pressure, in localization of a single point, and in response to extremely hot stimulation. Complete loss of sensitivity to extreme heat occurred when, in addition to section of the sensory root, a thoracic sympathectomy had been performed. In a foreword to this study, published in *Brain* (1932), Dr. Charles H. Frazier asked if these facts did not point to afferent as well as efferent functions of the sympathetic system. The other study, with Lucena Quantius, undertaken at the suggestion of another neurologist, Dr. Theodore Weisenberg, was to determine whether emotional states could influence surface body temperature. The results showed that they could and did under experimentally controlled conditions, thus confirming the clinical observations made by Dr. Weisenberg (with Quantius, 1934).

Three other studies also belong in the physiological category. The first of these was by Guilford and myself (1933), showing that absolute visual thresholds are lower in dark-eyed than in light-eyed individuals, the largest difference being between Negroes and light-eyed whites. However, the differences between eye groups decreased from fovea to periphery, where they ceased to be statistically significant. This study points to a more direct participation of the retinal or choroidal pigment in vision than is usually supposed when it is credited only with reduction in light scattering inside the eye. The interested student will find other types of evidence cited in this article in favor of the importance of the retinal pigment in vision.

Finally, two studies showing the importance of accommodation and surroundings on perception of size should be mentioned here. In the first I found that objects fixated through a pinhole with maximal accommodation and excluding all other objects were perceived to be much smaller than when viewed in free vision. A critical test of the role of accommodation and the influence of surround on apparent size was next made by projecting after-images in tubular vision. Afterimages were projected at various distances through a black tube just large enough to accommodate the images. Although *measured* size increased with distance of projection, *apparent* size did not. Emmert's law does not hold, therefore, in reduced vision. It thus appears that accommodation, perspective, and surround influence perceived size. The breakdown of Emmert's law, so far as perceived size is concerned, must be because there is no relaxation of accommodation and because perspective relations are ruled out in tubular vision.

Although I appreciate attempts to link behavioral and physiological processes, I have tried to avoid the use of extrabehavioral models and inter-pretations to bolster experimental findings. Well established correlations be-tween stimulus conditions and observable behavior can lead to control and prediction of responses and also to fruitful, verifiable theories. I have seen many fads in types of interpretation come and go. By this I refer to the habit of some psychologists to offer explanations of their data in the language of the latest concepts in physics, chemistry, physiology, or engineering in an endeavor to supply a more scientific substrate for their findings. In this con-nection William James said,

> The aspiration to be "scientific" is such an idol of the tribe to the present generation, is so sucked in with his mother's milk by every one of us, that we feel it hard to conceive of a creature who should not feel it . . . (1890, p. 640).

The greatest accomplishments in psychology have seemed to me to con-sist of concepts, generalizations, and theories that stay close to data or have direct reference to observable behavior, such as the Purkinje and Bezold-Brücke phenomena, the laws of association, the principles of conditioning, the concept and "laws" of Gestalt, and the laws of mass action and equipoten-tiality. These concepts do not go outside the universe of discourse of the data they generalize, and I believe they are far more "scientific" and useful than most explanations in terms of hypothetical constructs, which attempt, for example, to equate brain function with computers and sensory-motor be-havior with servomechanisms. Organisms do decode and encode, take advan-tage of feedback, and adjust to rates and accelerations of inputs, but they also do much more and hence should not be completely identified with the latest man-made devices, clever and efficient as they may be. Behavior offers a much richer variety of phenomena than does any machine, and we are far from having exhausted the potentialities for theory immanent in perception, judg-ment, learning, cognition, imagination, and the feelings and emotions.

In closing I would like to make a few personal observations regarding such matters as differences in recall between youth and middle age, the kind of person I think I am professionally, my methods of work, my immediate family, and the kind of world young people now entering psychology seem to me to face.

Differences in recall between youth and middle age were brought home quite forcibly when I was asked to do a critical survey of the "New Look" approach to perception and personality in 1951. While working on this project, the contrast between my ability to recall at twenty-five and at fifty-three years of age was greater than I had supposed before undertaking this job. When reading and writing up the Gestalt literature for my doctoral dissertation, I had an almost photographic memory. I could recall the titles of the articles, the periodical, year, volume, and pages of each publication, and I was able to give the exact page on which a given point was made. Perhaps the concentration required to read the material in German helped fix it so minutely and securely for later recall. But twenty-seven years later, completeness and certainty in recall were far less. Although I could recall various points, I was not always sure who had made them; the exact journal or book would often escape me. Every detail had to be checked against notes on the reading. The same thing occurred in the writing of my book begun five years later, but there were good reasons for this in the case of the book: the number of items read was far greater, and the interval between original impression (reading) and recall was much longer, since it took seven years to complete the manuscript of *Adaptation-Level Theory*. The one bright lining in all this is that I find little or no difference between 1951 and 1965 in my ability to recall what I have read.

Because faculties are so much keener, enthusiasm so much greater, and storage and retrieval of information so much better in youth than in middle and later life, it is a pity that better use is not made of the early years by more people, outside as well as inside academia. There are, of course, compensating factors in later life. One does not need to spend time working in various areas before settling down to a major interest, and one is less likely to be concerned with side issues or unimportant minutiae of problems that more creative minds have explored. I have frequently been struck by the good work older psychologists often produce in what is for them totally new areas, and it must be because they see basic issues better than do many inexperienced younger men.

Self-assessment is difficult and, according to the depth psychologists, can only be made by probing into the subconscious. However, I believe that conscious as well as subconscious motivations play a part in human behavior. So far as I am able to judge, I have not been motivated by a spirit of competition to equal or outdo anyone else. I have set my own standards of accomplishment, and these have been intrinsic to the problems that have engaged me. I have seldom, if ever, been able to meet my own criteria of good work. What McDougall called the "self-regarding sentiment" must be very strong in me, since I feel I have not met my own standards of accomplishment. It was a self-image I have tried to live up to, not position in a group or the accomplishment of other psychologists. Nor have I ever been conscious of being in competition with others in professional matters.

My manner of working and writing can best be characterized as slow, deliberate, and replicative. By this I refer to the fact that in almost every case there was a preliminary or pilot study, followed by the experiment itself, and often a second and third replication. In this way I satisfied myself that results were not due to biassed sampling of subjects or the idiosyncrasies of experimenters. After I considered an experiment completed, I usually laid the results away for several months or years before writing for publication. I write and rewrite at least half a dozen times before sending manuscripts to be published. Writing has been a slow, painful process, not only to achieve a tolerable style but also, and perhaps more important, to communicate my ideas clearly and forcefully. In a science that must largely use language rather than mathematical symbols to convey ideas, the way in which material is presented is of prime importance. I was especially impressed by the importance of good writing during the six years that I was editor of the *Psychological Bulletin*. By this I do not mean that a slick or purely literary form of presentation can make up for a paucity of ideas or superficial thinking. The mature worker in any field can tell how hard and how deeply one has probed by the way one's publications read. The greatest compliment I ever received came from Titchener when he said of the two articles he edited for *American Journal of Psychology*, "I can see that you have sweat blood over these." I have always had a backlog of twenty to thirty unpublished studies and do not expect to have everything in print by the end of my career.

No account of a life is complete without mention of one's immediate family. In many ways the kind of person one is, his goals, aspirations, and pattern of life may be reflected in his immediate family, for they are influenced by the minor as well as major nuances of the paterfamilias. To say that I was most fortunate in choice of a wife may sound hackneyed, but it is true. My wife, Lida, took all the burden of the household, rearing of children, and the social amenities, leaving me free to concentrate on my work. As a result, the little time I had for home life in the days when our children were young was relaxed and pleasant—I did only such chores as I chose, and they took very little time from my work. Moreover, she has given me constant moral support and has put up with my idiosyncrasies, as few in her place would have done. To say the least, I owe her much for whatever success I have had professionally as well as for many other things in our life together.

My son, Henry, early showed a predilection for mathematics and physics, and I helped and encouraged him along these lines as much as I was able. It was not long before he was beyond me in mathematics, and, by the time he entered college, he was ready for advanced work in this subject. He is now a mathematician teaching at Berkeley. My daughter, Martha, was originally bent on a medical career and took the courses in college necessary for entrance to medical school, but she has ended up as a physiological psychologist. In addition, my son's wife, Ravenna Mathews Helson, and my daughter's husband, William A. Wilson, Jr., are also psychologists, and, with my wife's interest in remedial reading, we have become an almost 100 percent family of psychologists!

As one comes to the close of an account of one's personal life in these precarious days, one cannot but be concerned with the problem of mankind's survival. I did not expect to live through two world wars, the second on a greater scale and more savage toward civilian populations than the first, and to face the imminent possibility of total destruction in a third world war. The main problem, it seems to me, from now on is to prevent an atomic war that will obliterate western civilization or set it back for centuries by making the land uninhabitable and by poisoning the water supplies. I do not believe young men now beginning their careers can withdraw as completely from national and world issues as many of my generation have done. Science plays such a large part in government, the military, industry, and wherever we turn, and the issues are so fraught with danger, that the younger generation must find a way of making the most of its scientific capabilities while at the same time doing its share to ameliorate internal as well as external tensions and educate mankind to settle outstanding issues peaceably. Psychology has an important part to play in all this as a scientific discipline, but individual psychologists, along with other scientists and intellectuals, must be prepared for direct personal involvement if we are to avoid catastrophe from within or without. It looks as if life will be more hazardous, will offer more challenges, and will demand much more from the coming generations than it did from ours.

## REFERENCES

*Selected Publications by Harry Helson*

The psychology of Gestalt. *Amer. J. Psychol.*, 1925, 36, 342–370, 494–526; 1926, 37, 25–62, 189–223.
Insight in the white rat. *J. exp. Psychol.*, 1927, 10, 278–296.
The part played by the sympathetic system as an afferent mechanism in the region of the trigeminus. *Brain*, 1932, 55, 114–121.
(with Guilford, J. P.) The relation of visual sensitivity to the amount of retinal pigmentation. *J. gen. Psychol.*, 1933, 9, 58–76.
(with Lucena Quantius) Changes in skin temperature following intense stimulation. *J. exp. Psychol.*, 1934, 17, 20–35.
Design of equipment and optimal human operation. *Amer. J. Psychol.*, 1949, 62, 473–497.
Perception and personality—a critique of recent experimental literature. *USAF*

*School of Aviation Medicine,* Report No. 1 (Project No. 21–0202–0007), 1953, 1–53.

(with J. A. Steger) On the inhibitory effects of a second stimulus following the primary stimulus to react. *J. exp. Psychol.,* 1962, *64,* 201–205.

Current trends and issues in adaptation-level theory. *Amer. Psychologist,* 1964, *19,* 26–38. (a)

*Adaptation-level theory: An experimental and systematic approach to behavior.* New York: Harper & Row, 1964. (b)

## Other Publications Cited

James, William. *Principles of psychology.* Vol. II. New York: Holt, Rinehart and Winston, 1890.

Geraldine Elzin

# Walter R. Miles

I was born on March 29, 1885 in Dakota Territory, where my parents and grandparents had taken up homestead land on the great prairie. They had emigrated from Indiana following the depression of the late 1870's. My grandfather Richard White, a prosperous farmer, lost his good farm and all other property in Indiana through the generous but unfortunate gesture of signing as guarantor for his neighbors. This sad event was sometimes referred to in my childhood but like many other things I then heard I did not understand. There were various verbal confusions in those early days; one was about Indians and Indiana. Our family had come from Indiana but it was here in Dakota that we thought about Indians and their possible incursions.

My earliest recollections are of the great endless prairie. Its clear air afforded me a vast special view of our world. No hills, no trees obstructed the seemingly endless expanse of flat land. Far away the prairie met the sky. As a small boy I tended our flock of sheep, keeping them out of the wheat fields. We, the sheep and I, were visible to the parents at home. There were gophers that ran down holes when I came near; there were skylarks that would fly up and sing. There were wild rose bushes with sweet-smelling blossoms. I seem to have talked to myself about these features of the landscape as my father talked to me when we viewed them together.

Now I can see myself as a small boy sitting on my father's lap as with his oxen he ploughed one long furrow after another. Perhaps more than once a wild duck's nest was ploughed up and we stopped to catch the little ducks. The buffalo had gone from the land but there were white bones sometimes in the buffalo wallows. I found most interesting my father's explaining the buffalo skulls, especially the holes where once had been the eyes and the ears. My father took me with him when he drove to the grain elevator to buy wheat. The great tall elevator gave me my first experience of echo and I loved to repeat it. The elevator ran by horsepower and my job was to keep the horse going. In Dakota most of my play was alone, but after my brother was born when I was five, I was often given care of him. I liked to be with him and there was satisfaction in this responsibility.

Eventually my father sold the homestead and bought a country store.

223

We lived over the store and were all busy together upstairs and down. Across from our store was a blacksmith shop in which I spent free time watching the smith as he formed the iron shoes and fitted them to the horses' hooves.

I remember the one-room school where as the smallest child I sat in the front row. Every morning the big boys brought their revolvers and guns to place on a table by the teacher and near me. I liked to imagine that those were my guns. I suppose I was an attentive child at school; I know I tried to remember what the teacher told us.

When I was eight years old a great change occurred. Our family, the grandparents, and an uncle and his family all moved from North Dakota to the village of Scott's Mills in northwest Oregon about twenty-five miles east of Salem, the capital. To me this change in environment was truly astonishing. Here in this new land we were surrounded by steep hills, and beyond them the high mountains reached to the Cascade Range. Hills and mountains were covered with wonderful wild trees. In our valley were rows of fruit trees bearing cherries, apples, pears, and plums. And nearby was a river of clear water! This gave power for an old sawmill and for an active flour mill. Here in our village was a new two-story schoolhouse and a new Friends' Church with a church bell.

My father bought the large two-story general store building and goods. Grandfather helped him in this store. We lived near. My uncle rented the sawmill and operated it. Soon I was employed after school and during vacations helping him in various ways, with shingles, lath and stacking boards, "big knots, little knots, and clear." By the time I was fourteen I worked at a saw-table cutting parts for fruit boxes and trays for drying fruit. Finally, I was in charge of assembling both boxes and fruit trays, earning good wages. Of course I continued to help in the store when I was needed.

I can never forget the great calamity that befell us when I was twelve. The store caught fire from another burning building one night and burned to the ground. The insurance was days overdue! We were literally wiped out. But everyone was kind. We bought an empty building and went into business again.

The school in Scott's Mills was good for a village of its size in Oregon at that time. We were not all in one little close room. Among the teachers we had I think of two who were outstanding. Mabel H. Douglas, a graduate of Penn College, was a sister of Woods Hutchinson, a popular scientific writer of that period. She was a skillful, understanding, and likable teacher. In the upper grades we were taught by the principal, who knew how to teach us so that we liked to be in his classes. He often acted out the things he was teaching. I graduated from this school in 1900 and was about ready to enter the Preparatory Department of Pacific College in Newberg. The financial problem was solved for the time being by my living at home for one year more and working full time for my uncle. One of my teachers tutored me in Latin and Algebra.

In 1901 I went to the Academy in Newberg some thirty-five miles from Scott's Mills. I was fortunate in being selected as helper or chore boy in return for my room and board in the president's house. My class group numbered twenty-five. This in itself was stimulating. I enjoyed my classes, kept up my work, and was able to play on the football squad. I graduated in June 1902. When autumn came I entered Pacific College. Now in return for my tuition and maintenance, my jobs were stoker of the wood-burning furnace in the main college building and houseman in the men's dormitory. These jobs I held most of the time I was at Pacific College, adding what outside chores I could find. In the summers I returned home and worked for my uncle in the box factory and the prune dryer.

One of my employers in Newberg, Dr. Minthorn, formerly principal of Pacific Academy, told me of his nephew and my cousin Herbert Hoover who after graduating in the first class at Stanford University had become a successful mining engineer. It was about this time that I began to think about further college work and about teaching as a profession. My favorite teacher at Scott's Mills, Mrs. Douglas, was now my history teacher in the college.

In my senior year I found what I had unknowingly been looking for. This was my best course so far, psychology, taught by our President, Edwin McGrew. The textbook for the course was James' *Psychology, Briefer Course*. I found other psychology books and read them. I reread James. My studies, especially those in science, interested me greatly. I also enjoyed instruction in public speaking. I was chosen valedictorian of my class.

During the summer of 1906 I had a fine outdoor job as a forest-fire warden in the mountains of southern Oregon. There were deer, bears, and other wild creatures in this area. On returning home at the end of this delightful experience I gave my rifle to my father to sell. I hoped that I would never have occasion to shoot another wild creature.

Several circumstances now favored Earlham College for my further education. My interest in psychology and public speaking may have helped in Earlham's offering me a scholarship. A widowed aunt of my mother invited me to become her helper and general chore man. She lived comfortably, within walking distance of the college, and I was assured that the conditions she offered would be agreeable. And so it proved. There were some of my advisors at Newberg who regarded Earlham as too liberal in its religious attitude at this time. But for me the opportunity seemed the right one and I never regretted my acceptance.

Professor J. Hershel Coffin while completing his thesis for the Ph.D. in psychology at Cornell had been appointed to succeed Professor Edwin D. Starbuck who, coming from James at Harvard, had set up a small experimental psychological laboratory at Earlham. In a brochure I had seen a picture of it and this had increased my interest in coming to Earlham.

Professor Coffin invited me to become his assistant in the elementary course. He explained that no money was available for this assistantship, but I was glad to accept the opportunity on these terms. My two courses with Professor Coffin came first in my program of endeavor. In the experimental laboratory with an older student as my teammate we worked through one of Titchener's manuals. I still have that notebook. I enrolled also for courses with Professor Elbert Russell in Bible study; Professor Dennis in biology; Edwin Trueblood, public speaking; and William N. Trueblood, English literature. These were all able teachers; several of them had done graduate work at great universities. All of them were devoted in their work and inspiring to me.

Professor William N. Trueblood who was my neighbor also became my friend as I helped him fill his silo and in other farm activities. He adopted me as a sort of nephew. In trips that we made about the country he introduced me to his hobby of fossil collecting. Neither in Dakota nor in Oregon had there been anything like this. I began to read Darwin.

I became an active member of the English Club and in my senior year was its president. I graduated from Earlham in 1908. I was grateful to the College and to Aunt Mary who had helped to make this experience possible. I returned to Oregon with an offer of a pastorate in a Midwestern city, which I appreciated but could not bring myself to accept.

Shortly after my return home I received an offer from Penn College to fill a temporary vacancy in psychology and education. The salary was $600 if single, $700 if married. I accepted the $700. I worked in my father's greenhouses; my parents had sold all their property in Scott's Mills and moved to a place north of Newberg. I assisted my future father-in-law in building a new barn. Elizabeth Mae Kirk, my Pacific College sweetheart, and I were married September 1, 1908, and left Oregon the next day for Oskaloosa, Iowa.

The year of teaching at Penn College was busy and challenging. My psychology students were eager, some recognizably able. Years later one of my students, Alexander C. Purdy, became a leader in the Hartford Seminary and eventually its dean. Another, Clarence Pickett, taught for many years at Earlham and was later general secretary of the American Friends Service Committee.

One morning at Penn College there came quite unexpectedly a stranger to my classroom. He was Professor Carl E. Seashore of the State University of Iowa. A dean of graduate studies, he was engaged in recruiting graduate students to the University. He met other faculty members, lectured to my students, we talked, and I agreed to visit the University at Iowa City. Our discussions and the visit resulted in my acceptance as a graduate student in Iowa University.

During the summer of 1909 my wife and I made a home visit to Oregon. Since our marriage and departure there had been two deaths we both felt deeply, that of her father and of my young brother. The visit helped and refreshed us. With warm sustaining wishes from home we arrived back in Iowa and I began my studies at the University. A graduate scholarship, selling life insurance, and student coaching helped me financially. Lectures, seminars, study, and the writing of a master's thesis filled the time. The thesis, "A Comparison of Elementary and High School Grades" (1910), led to unexpected commendation and a present of books from Professor E. L. Thorndike.

In the spring our son, Thomas Kirk Miles, was born and my wife's mother came to join us and help. My need to be practical and, as it now appears to me, my lack of information regarding the opportunities in psychology, had led me to secure the master's degree in education. But the year's experience, especially the laboratory course with Dean Seashore's able associate, Dr. Mabel C. Williams, and our close association and friendship with Dr. and Mrs. Seashore were influences pulling me toward psychology.

An unexpected offer of a pastorate in the Friends Church of West Branch, Iowa, two hours by train from the University helped my decision. Accepting this gave us comfortable assured living. I could read and study on the train. The pastorate was accepted and the move made. I became a graduate student in psychology, attending lectures and seminars and reading in all my spare time in the library of psychology and philosophy.

I found the work in Dr. Seashore's musicology laboratory fascinating; his ingenious inventions beguiled me. Seashore's tonoscope seemed to me an ideal instrument for research in one of several areas. I chose study of the accuracy of the voice in simple pitch singing. I had seventeen mature men as subjects. Most of them had training in music, all sang solo, quartet, or in glee clubs. How does accuracy of control vary with the range of the voice? How does the intensity of the standard tone affect the pitch of reproduction? There were many phases to work out. The three years of research and seminars were not easy years, travelling back and forth, but they were happy and they were interesting.

Work with the tonoscope and with musical subjects was interesting, sometimes delightful. My course work was completed in 1912 and the thesis a year later. Our daughter, Caretta Elizabeth, was born in West Branch in November 1911. The social life of our family centered around the Friends Church. My interest outside the requirements of preaching and personal parish contacts was in developing overall community events such as lectures and musicales. A lively Chautauqua program took shape and even such socializing as a great barbecue in which all the town and surrounding countryside joined.

At the University I had become, while an education major, a member of the education fraternity, Phi Delta Kappa. This contributed later, as will be seen, to an unexpected eventuality. In the Iowa psychology department I was honored by election to Sigma Xi shortly before Professor E. B. Titchener came to Iowa as Sigma Xi visiting lecturer. During this visit Dr. Seashore asked me to act as aide to our noted guest. This was indeed a prize privilege, especially as it led to later contacts.

In the spring of 1913 I was asked to accept the Iowa Phi Delta Kappa nomination as national secretary. This required visits to chapters in Eastern colleges and attendance at the National Council Meeting in Philadelphia. On this trip East I especially appreciated the opportunity to renew my acquaintance with Professor Titchener at his home in Ithaca. It was during this Phi Delta Kappa meeting in Philadelphia that I received, to my surprise, a telegram from Professor Raymond Dodge asking if I might be interested in filling in for him for a year (1913–14) at Wesleyan. Indeed, I was interested. After a meeting in New York with Professor Dodge and the Wesleyan president the matter was concluded. I knew my wife would concur.

Dean Seashore was pleased, as he said, "to have an Iowan product go East." My final examinations were not all I could have wished but the thesis I felt was satisfactory. It was published as a *Psychological Review Monograph*. That year, 1913, the psychology department presented two of the four Ph.D. candidates at the Iowa Commencement. The other two Ph.D.'s given were one in chemistry and mathematics and one in political science and English. My associate was Thomas Vance, long-time professor at Iowa State College and through the years my friend.

We were sorry to leave our good friends in Iowa, but the new offer seemed ideal. So the Miles family of four plus Grandmother Kirk left for historical New England.

My Wesleyan appointment was announced in the college catalogue as Associate Professor of Psychology with responsibility for four courses, all in psychology. For me this had superb significance. Home life was happy and relaxing. A second little girl, Marjorie Helen, was born in August. We were comfortable in the quiet congenial surroundings of Middletown.

All my working hours were devoted to becoming acquainted with the apparatus in Dodge's laboratory and with experimental methods represented there, learning to know my students, and attempting to arouse in them interest in the new and growing science of psychology. I thought about Wundt's laboratory, Titchener's achievements, and Dodge's work with Erdmann in Halle. I set up and demonstrated the nature and use of many pieces of laboratory equipment. I worked through all of Dodge's publications that I could find and reprints of other articles that were on the shelves in his laboratory office, including such topics as reaction time of the eye, visual fixations in reading, the velocity of horizontal and vertical eye movements, and

other very interesting topics and data. I studied. New graphic ways of measuring human behavior were of much interest to me and I enjoyed introducing them to my classes. In the elementary class we used Pillsbury's text
(1911) as was mentioned in the University catalogue.

Residence in Middletown, Connecticut, opened also a new geographical
area to the westerner. New York, Boston, and New Haven were within
practical reach. My first attendance at the American Psychological Association was in December 1913 when it met nearby at Yale. Professor Warren
of Princeton gave the presidential address on "The Mental and the Physical."
My mentor, Dodge, introduced me to many psychologists hitherto only
names for me. I well remember Münsterberg, Yerkes, Margaret Washburn,
Warren, and Angier who was head of the Yale psychology department. The
friendly secretary, W. V. Bingham, also took me in hand. I was happy to
be elected a member of APA in 1914.

While I was in New Haven, Dodge told me of his work with Dr. F. G.
Benedict at the Carnegie Nutrition Laboratory and invited me to visit him
in Boston. This I was able to do in February and was then much impressed
by the experimental program he was engaged in completing.

My commitment at Wesleyan was for a single year, so now a new position had to be found. Correspondence was initiated. Then came a call from
Dr. Benedict asking me to consider continuing the type of investigation
Dodge had started at the Nutrition Laboratory. The position was full-time
research supported by the Carnegie Institution of Washington at a location
in Boston close to the Harvard Medical School; this was indeed attractive
and I accepted. In the early summer of 1914 the Miles family moved to
Boston. I knew I would miss the teaching and the students, and the friendly
intercourse with the distinguished Wesleyan faculty.

At the Carnegie Nutrition Laboratory the first weeks were fruitfully
and pleasantly spent with Dodge in orientation and in reading the manuscript for the monograph he was engaged in writing. Then I was on my
own. My first assignment at Dodge's suggestion was a rerun of Dodge's Subject VI with vigorous checks. This man was available and his services were
secured. A detailed examination of previous planning was followed by thirty
hours of new testing: six hours per day for five consecutive days in one
week. The worked-up results for this new testing gave satisfactory agreement with the earlier findings, indicating not failure to cooperate on the
subject's part but rather a deviant constitution in his case.

This was my first experience in applying a repeated program of physio-
logical-psychological measurements of a human subject on consecutive days.
It was the type of experimental approach I would use in most of my work
at the Carnegie Laboratory. This first set of data concerned the measurable
influence supposedly produced by a small amount of properly diluted ethyl
alcohol taken at a certain time on alternate days of testing. A report of this

work was prepared in a brief paper introduced by Dr. F. G. Benedict. I had the honor of reading this paper at a meeting at the National Academy of Sciences in Washington, D.C., November 4, 1916.

The Laboratory had publicly announced a program of alcohol-nutritional research. A part of this responsibility now rested upon me and I did my best to discharge this duty in an objective, scientific manner. I devoted much time to self-grounding in nutritional studies while carrying on instrumental planning, devising, and development and published descriptions of some of my developments. Incidentally, we had a good instrument shop in the basement of our laboratory and this was stimulating.

A second and more extensive series of measurements of alcohol effects (1918a) conducted as before under rigid test conditions led to conclusions now generally accepted. Their practical value is familiar to educators and utilized in modern traffic safety programs.

World War I brought new demands. Professor Dodge came to Boston with an interesting problem that involved testing gas masks for both safety and comfort. He came to use some of our equipment and kindly utilized my assistance also. The work resulted in recommendations influencing later mask models.

I was glad to serve on a National Research Council Committee with Leonard Troland and Harold Burtt who was chairman. We studied air pilot aptitude, or tried to, on M.I.T. Flying School personnel. My laboratory sessions with these men, one at a time, were in the evening.

Then came an offer of a captaincy for me in the Army Air Force, but Dr. Benedict persuaded me to stay on in the Laboratory. He was convinced there were war ration problems of first importance that trained researchers were really obligated to attack. At first I was undecided but finally made up my mind to stay and work in this new field. The special project Dr. Benedict had in mind included a number of physiological and psychological factors that we might measure during a rather long period of under-nutrition. Our subjects would be young men of draft age. From Europe had come reports minimizing the effects of reduced civilian rations. What was the truth in this matter? The senior members of our staff worked together in the planning and conduct of this experiment and in addition we had the excellent assistance of Dr. Paul Roth of Battle Creek Sanitarium.

In September 1917 we proceeded, with two "equated groups" of healthy young men from the Springfield Y.M.C.A. College, to test the effects of a regime in which diet was reduced to two-thirds or less of the supposed caloric requirement. In the Carnegie Laboratory a staff of ten workers carried on periodic tests covering a wide range of body systems and functions. Both physiological and psychological findings were clear-cut and the personal integrity and veracity of the subjects was demonstrated. Basal metabolism measurements were made daily with equipment that was kept in the subjects' quarters. Squad A at first restricted their diets until each man had lost twelve percent in weight. Caloric intake was then increased to preserve the lower weight level. The normal demand had been 3200 to 3600 calories per day for these men. To maintain the reduced weight level about 2300 calories were required. The heat output was lowered eighteen percent by the end of this experiment. Pulse rate and blood pressure were markedly lower. I recorded electrocardiograms and found a condition quite comparable to bradycardia resulting from their reduced diet routine. Skin temperature was lowered and the men felt cold weather excessively. The nitrogen output was about nine grams whereas for the control group it was about twice that amount. The men looked emaciated.

Quite a variety of psychological tests were selected as suitable for repetition and were employed in this research. Some examples will illustrate the body burden resulting from the reduced diet. In clerical tasks improvement was slowed; finger movement speed was slowed. Eye movements measured from photographic records were progressively slower. Strength of grip was decreased. Several tests of accuracy showed that the number of errors increased as the duration of the low-intake period lengthened.

Personal interviews after the low-diet experience had terminated revealed that all Squad A members noticed a marked reduction in sex interest and expression during the low-intake period (1919a). However, after the conclusion of the prolonged experimental routine these men soon recovered their feelings of well-being and energy. They had managed to keep up their college work during the low diet months and individually were rather proud of their contribution to the science of nutrition (1918b, 1919a, with F. G. Benedict, 1919b).

Stimulating for me in these Carnegie years was the contact with our near neighbors, the Harvard Medical School men. We met at lectures, seminars, and in the cafeteria. Sometimes their visitors were brought over to see us and our work. Among these medical colleagues and friends were Walter Cannon, Cecil Drinker, Otto Folin, Alexander Forbes, Reid Hunt, and Wallace Fenn.

Occasionally I attended Staff Meetings at the Boston Psychopathic Hospital where Dr. E. E. Southard was chief psychiatrist. He and his research associate Myrtelle M. Canavan, M.D. were at that time bringing out a series of human brain studies of great relevance to psychophysiology. At the Harvard Department of Psychology at Emerson Hall in Cambridge I was a rather frequent visitor attracted there to see and discuss topics of mutual interest with Sidney Langfeld, E. B. Holt, Leonard Troland and Harold Burtt. It was always a pleasure to visit that active laboratory, to see their approach to problems, and to meet and talk with their graduate students. I like to recall loaning Edward C. Tolman a memory drum for use in his Ph.D. work. An annual meeting of the psychologists of the Boston area was always worth attending.

At the Carnegie Laboratory Dr. Eliot P. Joslin and Dr. Howard Root were interested in studies on the metabolism of diabetic patients. Dr. Root and I collaborated in psychological and also physio-anatomical studies of some older diabetics and published our results jointly (with H. F. Root, 1922c, 1926). Dr. Root very kindly aided me by taking, as needed, blood samples of my alcohol research subjects (1922b). My collaboration with Dr. Joslin was of a different type. I aided him in reading the manuscripts and galley proofs of his books. The association with these two men is for me among the most valued in this period. In the spring of 1920 I was scheduled to visit laboratories in England and on the Continent as a representative of our laboratory. We now had a visitor with us for two or three weeks, Dr. E. C. Van Leersum from Amsterdam. He was engaged in an effort to develop and establish a National Institution of Nutrition in Holland. I would meet him on his return home and be his house guest.

Before the war our inter-visitations had been a regular part of the Carnegie program. We felt they were valuable for criticism and suggestions and our friends abroad seemed also to favor the scheme. My tour in 1920 lasted four months, April to August. In all I visited nineteen cities: London, Edinburgh, Glasgow, Cambridge, Oxford, Paris, Brussels, Louvain, Amsterdam, Utrecht, Leyden, Groningen, Copenhagen, Lund, Stockholm, Hamburg, Berlin, Leipzig, and Vienna. This was my first trip abroad and how attractive it all seemed to me. The mission was to visit laboratories and scientists and every day was full of interest. Representing the Nutrition Laboratory and my colleagues I carried greetings to and visited many physiologists from J. Alquier in Paris to Prof. H. Zwardemaker in Utrecht. These scientists were cordial and wonderful hosts. Friendships began which have lasted through the years; such were the meetings and discussions with E. D. Adrian, Joseph Barcroft, Henry Dale, William Einthoven, August Krogh, Edward Mellanby, and Augustus D. Waller. My large book of photographs and notes has been reviewed and reviewed many times in the years that followed.

At the time of my European trip there were several psychologists who had established laboratories and were willing to welcome visitors. At Cambridge University there was an excellent laboratory. It was a new wing added to the physiology building and at the time Professor Frederick Bartlett was in charge. It was stimulating to meet him and to see the excellent provisions for experimental work in psychology. Charles Meyers had recently moved to London and was in the throes of establishing the National Institution for Applied Psychology and Physiology to investigate the problems of industry and commerce. This project had the support of Professor Charles Sherrington.

At a meeting of the British Psychological Association at Bedford College I listened with close interest to an address by Dr. E. W. Scripture on the subject of graphic records of normal and abnormal speech. Scripture had been the first to introduce Wundtian psychology at Yale. Carl E. Seashore was then his pupil so I was pleased to introduce myself as one of Professor Seashore's pupils. At University College London, the psychology laboratory was open at stated times and Professor C. S. Spearman had invited me to tea. We had a pleasant conversation in which Professor Fr. Aveling, J. C. Flugel, and Ll. Wynn Jones from North Wales took part. Jones was lecturing here and spoke about his plans to open a laboratory at Leeds University in October 1920.

At the University of Glasgow there had been a Department of Psychology housed in rooms loaned by the Department of Physiology. Now increases in student enrollment following war's end had made it necessary to give this space back to physiology, and so psychology was housed in an old private mansion outside but near the University. Here I had long conversations with Professor H. J. Watt. He had been a devoted student of Kulpe and just before the war had made a visit to Germany. War began and he was interned for two years. He was still obviously in a weakened condition.

At Oxford I found Professor William McDougall lately returned from Zurich where he had worked with Dr. Carl Jung on methods of psychoanalysis, a subject which McDougall had pursued during the war. With McDougall in charge, psychology had flourished at Oxford for a few years. Now with regret Professor Sherrington had, for lack of space, to turn out Professor McDougall and his students from these rooms. However, it was just at this time that Harvard invited McDougall to Cambridge. Professor Münsterberg had died quite early in the war and Harvard had delayed making a new appointment. At the time of my visit McDougall and his wife were pondering acceptance. They asked me many questions about life in Boston and Cambridge which I did my best to answer reassuringly.

At the Sorbonne I was honored to meet Professor and Madam Pieron, in their psychology laboratory. When I called they were determining the sensitivity of areas of the retina to different wave lengths of light. An American post graduate student, David Wechsler, showed me about. Pieron was now, he said, the successor of A. Binet. An Institute of Psychology seemed a possibility. It would include Pieron, Janet, and Dumas. Pieron might then do some lecturing in addition to his continuing research.

In Holland at the State University of Groningen an excellent laboratory of psychology had been included in the main University building which was at this time about ten years old. There I talked with Professor G. Heymans and Dr. Brugmans. They were working on problems of visual perception, some involving the hypothesis of thought transference. Our discussions were of great interest to me. I looked about in the psychological laboratory at the University of Copenhagen but Professor A. Lehman was on vacation. A suite of several rooms seemed well equipped and serviced also by a good department library.

At the University of Leipzig I was naturally most eager to visit the Institute of Experimental Psychology, the traditional birthplace of our modern science of psychology. My host here was Dr. A. Kirschmann, a German by birth, who had been for several years professor at the University of Toronto. To recuperate from an illness he returned to Germany in 1913 and was caught by the war. It was impossible for him to return to Canada. As a German in Germany he was dismissed from the Toronto faculty. Professor Wundt, still director of the Institute at the time, was greatly in need of an assistant in the absence of all the younger men. Kirschmann was therefore asked to join the Institute as an Ober Assistant, in the same position he had accepted in 1893. At the time of my visit Professor Wundt, now eighty-eight years old, had retired and was living in the country. The new director was Professor Kruger with whom I had a brief conversation. I was glad to have been in the founding laboratory although the atmosphere was gloomy at this time. In contrast I had a cheerful visit in the Physiological Institute conversing with Professor S. Garten. We had both worked on similar aviation pilot problems during the war. Now we could shake hands, compare results, and have a beer together. These brief visits made me want to see and know more. I was impressed with some of the strange effects of the war; many of them were in fact psychological phenomena.

At the time I visited these laboratories this type of experience was so new that I thrived on it. During my tour I observed the child feeding program of the American Friends Service Committee in Central Europe. Because of my interest in nutrition I had been asked to make a report of this work which I was glad to find carried on effectively and with a favorable degree of benefit to the seriously undernourished children.

Back in the United States I had much to tell and to show in photographs and collected reprints. My laboratory was still there, no one had taken back the space, and I was contented to be in it again and working. Now I turned back to the alcohol program beginning a long series of experiments using two and three-fourths percent alcohol beverages. Both psychological and some physiological data would be gathered and the results published in a Carnegie monograph. I was happy in our Boston life and associations. There was however one lack: the inquiring and driving impulse from younger minds. After Wesleyan I missed the contact with students.

Yet it was through no solicitation on my part that Dr. Ray Lyman Wilbur, President of Stanford University, requested me to meet him in Boston for a discussion of their new psychology situation needs, following the retirement of Professor Frank Angell, their early Wundtian disciple. Professor L. M. Terman, no laboratory man, had been lifted from the education department to head psychology. He wanted to round out his staff with laboratory and experimental workers. Dr. Wilbur's presentation of the situation intrigued and attracted me. I saw that he was evidently enthusiastic for this development. He emphasized for my consideration that the University was growing rapidly. New strength had been added in several departments. Funds for research were increasingly available. The psychology department was especially favored by the Thomas Welton Stanford Fund. Living conditions were favorable for faculty families. The University at that time granted scholarships to accredited faculty children.

Professor Terman was known to me especially for his work during World War I on the Army classification tests. He had impressed me most favorably at psychology meetings where we had met. The Stanford opportunity pleased me. Soon I was able to write my acceptance to President Wilbur. It was difficult for me to inform Dr. Benedict of my decision which I knew he would not wish to accept. It was difficult to leave the dear Carnegie Laboratory and Boston. Why was I doing this? I believe it was essentially because of the teaching opportunity which I had enjoyed at Penn College and at Wesleyan, and which appeared to me to be the chief asset at Stanford. The number of graduate students was said to be increasing. During recent years in Boston I had often wished that I could have young ambitious psychologists working with me in exploratory development of problems, in thinking about methods, in designing instruments, and in meditating about results and conclusions. I had played a junior role with Coffin at Earlham, with Seashore at Iowa, and in a sense with Dodge in Boston. I felt this had been of definite importance in my own progress. Dr. Benedict was generous to me personally in donating and selling to Stanford much of the laboratory equipment Dodge and I had constructed, collected, and utilized in the Carnegie Laboratory.

In December 1922 the Miles family left Boston for California. On our Western way we were guests of an old friend of the Carnegie, Dr. John Harvey Kellogg, at Battle Creek, Michigan. After family visits in Oregon we arrived in due time in Palo Alto. Already housing had been arranged for us in one of the two Hoover residences on the Stanford campus with the Termans as near neighbors. We received a warm reception from the psychology group and their associates.

In our first year at Stanford I had besides preparing my lectures the task of building up a working laboratory equipped with modern apparatus and supplies. The material from Boston was a great help in giving an almost immediate opportunity to start some graduate students in research. Thus available to us was photographic equipment for recording magnified eye movements during visual perceptual tasks, the ataxiameter (1922a) which gave integrated readings of voluntary control in steadiness of standing, and an advanced form of electrical apparatus for developing and measuring skill in tracking—the electrical-pursuit meter (1921). We also had the Einthoven string-galvanometer to record heart action and other bodily phenomena and other minor pieces of new or novel equipment.

A piece of apparatus designed to provide a task for a human subject and to give a score or measurable record of his performance seems to me to offer a standing invitation to research curiosity. In our apparatus stockroom I could now introduce some of our senior majors to available equipment.

I enjoyed teaching and came to it full of enthusiasm. No doubt my methods were unskillful based as they were on meager experiences. I attempted to select materials suitable to attract student interest. My procedure in the introductory course was to present first a rather brief historical introduction and then turn to illustrative problems that could be described in detail and in some cases worked out in the classroom. A requirement in the introductory class was that each student serve as a subject for two hours in some investigation in progress in our department.

In the early 1920's Stanford was in a state of flux. For three decades the general plan for the admission of students had brought in those recommended by many preparatory schools of unequal status. Every student on admission had to select a major subject of study; all else was elective. Now the old order was under attack. Two committees especially were charged with two major curriculum considerations. These were the Committees on Admissions and on the Lower Division (freshmen and sophomores). Terman and I were equally concerned about these problems and he was kind enough to delegate membership on these two committees to me. I had thus an opportunity to learn the history of the problems involved and to search my psychological training, experience, and possibly insight as to ways and means for arriving at some new conclusions.

The problem of admissions was paramount. The number of applications was much larger than Stanford could accept. The majority of these applicants seemed to have adequate backgrounds and training. But early dropouts occurred too frequently. Special tests had quite recently become available and their use had now to be carefully evaluated. For two years scholastic aptitude tests were given, and their results evaluated. These were found to be indicative of information not previously available. At the end of these two years the faculty accepted the Admission Committee's recommendation that test scores be added to the other available pre-admission criteria of student competence. Now our committee had a more complicated task but the student results proved more rewarding.

The second urgent problem in the early 1920's resulted from the rapid growth in available curricula. Whereas President David Starr Jordan had from his wise and wide experience emphasized the human right of freedom of choice, a system suited to the earlier limited possibilities had become unwieldy. Now in its fourth decade the Stanford pendulum was swinging away from complete freedom toward the recognition of certain basic essentials. A required set of content courses now seemed to offer these essentials whatever the student's major academic choice. These required courses were assigned to the curriculum of the first two years. Some experimental courses were developed. One called "Civilization" failed to catch on, whereas another, "The History of Western Civilization" proved brilliant and popular. As a member of the Committee on the Lower Division I learned much, while most of all learning to know and value my fellow committeemen.

My third assignment gave me an opportunity to come in close contact with faculty members in the biological sciences. This committee had the responsibility of structuring a School of Biology. The usefulness of an introductory course in science was debated, accepted, and instituted with good results. Our university colleagues at this time seemed to expect psychologists to have special knowledge on all these subjects, an attitude of course challenging but also humbling. I enjoyed committee work, but important as it was, my primary interest was in teaching students.

Early in the first years we began a study of the effect of loss of sleep on mental work. Laslett carried this out to a Ph.D. thesis. With George Branner a problem was developed in the static equilibrium of pilots. Thomas McQuarrie was working out his ingenious motor and mechanical ability test series. Franklin Fearing worked on the factors influencing static equilibrium. Ellen Sullivan did research on attitude in relation to learning, and there were others.

From January 1922 to mid-1925 I was busily occupied with experimental work with students, with my classes and lectures, and also with formal committees and family interests. My wife and children had adjusted happily to the change in our environment and associations. The children liked the California schools. We all enjoyed our new work and new friends. We were in the midst of planning a pleasant house of our own on the Stanford campus facing the foothills and near the Hoovers, the Termans, the Strongs, and others of our congenial acquaintance.

In 1924 I had accepted an invitation to carry Professor George Stratton's class work for the autumn semester at Berkeley. Our family expected to move into the new house at the end of the summer, but our happy life was suddenly ended by the death of my dear wife Elizabeth following necessary surgery from which no such tragic result was anticipated. The children and I passed through the sad summer and in the autumn we all went to Berkeley where our friends generously helped us to re-establish our thinking and go on with life.

Berkeley has much charm to share with newcomers. The psychology group at the University gave me excellent support. Seven mature graduate students (Katherine Adams, V. M. Bathgate, M. H. Elliott, Lloyd Jeffress, D. A. Macfarlane, Otto L. Tinklepaugh, Robert C. Tryon) served as my teaching assistants in the introductory psychology course that enrolled more than 700 students. I lectured to the entire group two or three times each week in Wheeler Hall. The class on other days was divided into sub-groups of thirty each for demonstrations, discussions, and quizzes. As a teaching team we tried hard to put psychology over to this assemblage. Stratton's other classes I could manage by myself. The graduate students were conducting studies on the learning behavior of animals. Here I had my first opportunity to observe monkeys as experimental subjects. I recorded some of this with my motion picture camera. I gained much from my contacts with the Berkeley faculty and graduate student group and I was renewed and enriched by their friendship.

Returning to begin the year at Stanford old friends stood by giving aid and encouragement. Classes were resumed, faculty meetings were attended, and I had to catch up with my University committees. Four graduate students got going on a study of handedness with some newly designed motor tests. Miles A. Tinker began his fruitful research on eye movements and fixations in reading mathematical and chemical formulae. K. W. Thompson studied eye dominance in workers skilled in use of a single eyepiece microscope. Frank Fearing continued his work on equilibrium with the ataxiameter, adding a study on the human knee-jerk with excellent equipment Dodge had designed. Eugene Shen working with several Chinese student subjects was recording their eye movements and comparing their reading speed for Chinese characters arranged in horizontal lines as compared with the usual vertical display.

A young German, Heinrich Klüver, came to Stanford in 1924 and was associated with me as a graduate student with Ph.D. intent. He was familiar with German philosophical typology and in our laboratory undertook experimentation with subjects found to be of eidetic type. This research was quite successful and instructive to all of us. Here began another valued friendship that has continued through the years.

Contact with some experimental work at Berkeley aroused my interest in the maze as a useful instrument for the investigation of patterned space learning. This suggested a psychological sector in which animal and human learning might be compared. Enclosed mazes were of course traditional. In fact a maze was defined as a complicated enclosure; however, open elevated and high-relief forms could be easily designed and readily constructed. I described several such arrangements in articles (1927b, 1927c) and showed these mazes to my good friend Walter S. Hunter when he visited us at Stanford. He took up the idea and went on to develop three-dimensional mazes.

At Berkeley I had made an elevated narrow path maze for rat learning. This was composed of interchangeable wooden frames. I wished now to compare this type with an alley form of the same linear path scale. I could set up this experiment in my garage at home, so as to spend more time with my children. I needed a student assistant and advertised for one without explaining the type of work. The student who came was an English major. At first I was doubtful. But I have never found a more careful and keen associate. His name was Harry F. Harlow. Later in 1930 he completed his work for the Ph.D. at Stanford guided by Professor Calvin P. Stone, my able colleague in comparative psychology.

The Western Psychological Association was helping to stimulate research at Stanford in these years. At the annual meetings, reports by our students on experimental problems gave an opportunity for the presentation of early research efforts allowing also critical discussions of the work. As secretary of this Association I prepared and published in the *Psychological Bulletin* reports of the third, fourth, and fifth meetings, 1924, 1925, and 1926.

In the summer of 1927 Professor Terman prevailed on Dr. Catharine M. Cox, a former graduate student and associate, to leave Cincinnati where she was working in the Central Mental Hygiene Clinic. His offer was participation as Research Associate in an area of the gifted research. Our family had known her for some years. This friendship developed and she and I were married in September. My children warmly approved the marriage and we remained as before a closely integrated family.

That autumn I had a number of studies in progress with graduate students. A problem in eye movement research started with Laslett should have been followed up. He and I photographed a reflected light beam from the human cornea when the eye executed forty-degree horizontal movements and then forty-degree vertical movements. The latter gave consistently shorter tracings as if the center of rotation had changed. With Fearing studies of periodic changes in mental and physical efficiency continued until he left Stanford for Ohio Wesleyan. R. W. Husband was working on human learning with our four-section high-relief finger maze. Clarence Young's problem involved the function of inner speech in reading and thought. B. Graves worked with me on research still mentioned in athletic circles. In this study we used a multiple chronograph on the football field for measuring the charging time of each of the seven men in the line of players (1928a, 1928b, 1931a). Maze learning in blind as compared with blindfolded seeing children by J. R. Knotts was an interesting study (1929c). Further investigations by Chinese students, notably S. K. Chow, enlarged our understanding of the reading of Chinese. Dr. Robert Seashore, eldest son of Dean Seashore, as an N.R.C. Fellow, worked with us at Stanford for a year and developed the Seashore Motor Skills Battery of tests. Hugh Bell made with me a preliminary investigation of the eye movements of university students engaged in study. The results gave a practical indication of the effectiveness of the students when at work. For Homer Weaver's research, the large eye-movement camera was located on top of a grand piano to record the eye-movement patterns in reading the music while playing it on the instrument. It was a valuable study and the first of its kind.

Studies of color-blindness were popular at this time. Sybil Walcutt made a carefully arranged attempt to grade and classify types of defect. E. Lowell Kelly was attracted to the problem of producing chromaesthesia artificially by a conditioned response technique. About this time L. P. Herrington, later for many years with Professor Winslow in the Pierce Laboratory at Yale, produced a careful research on the physiological psychology of college student introverts and extraverts.

Time, fatigue, and work studies had become popular in industry. Questions as to the older workers' competence and the problem of retirement were being debated. Scattered studies of the abilities and interests of middle-aged workers were appearing. We had done some studies involving capacities and abilities of adults under certain conditions. Industrialists as well as psychologists were asking about these and related questions: Could we at Stanford plan a research program for the study of the adult that might balance to some extent the great Terman research on the early growth period? Into a study of the later years it seemed we might fit many various researches of psychophysiological skills, intelligence, interests, even personalities.

Looking back now one sees the rapid development in problems of this area going on throughout our country and in Europe. But in the 1920's the research field was relatively new. Terman, Strong, Stone, and I were all involved in working out a plan. Strong would set up his vocational studies; Stone would work on aging in rats with excellent controls; I was delegated to carry out the details of laboratory housing, securing the needed age range of human subjects, and the general supervision of the work of the graduate students who enlisted in the project. We presented our detailed program to the Carnegie Corporation of New York and were rewarded by a grant of $10,000, and so the Stanford Later Maturity Study began. Graduate students were attracted to this research opportunity and the detailed planning of the first group of studies was undertaken with enthusiasm.

Problems of where and with whom were now before us and as our thinking and searching continued we came to see how the success of the project would depend on the rightness of some of our initial efforts. At once a research center must be established easily accessible to the people of the community. Also it seemed desirable to disassociate the project from the University psychology department.

This research program served as I had hoped as a framework for major graduate studies. The principal programs of experimental work were carried out in March to August 1930 and, supported by a second Carnegie grant, in April to June 1932. My wife assisted in working with our subjects in both studies.

A new problem developed as we tried advertising and other ways of soliciting individuals as subjects. Employment agencies were not successful as helpers in this respect. At length a scheme was devised of inviting social clubs and philanthropic organizations of all kinds to send us their members and friends, the club or organization, not the individual, receiving payment for the time and effort given. Since it was essential for our research to secure as many subjects as possible in the older age decades, payment was calculated on the age of each individual subject. This scheme proved successful in bringing out relatively large numbers in the decades from forty onward and even past sixty and seventy. The clubs were delighted with this novel means of raising funds. Individuals who had previously declined our invitation to participate now gladly came and brought others. The result was high motivation and I believe near maximum effort.

Our first Ph.D. thesis result of the Later Maturity Program was an excellent study completed by Floyd L. Ruch in which he compared the performance of three age groups (forty subjects in each group), including one of teen-agers, a second of middle age (thirty-five to fifty-eight) and one of older people (sixty to eighty-one). Ruch used tasks of motor and verbal learning requiring different levels of reorganization of partial patterns previously learned. In the young group individual competence increased with age, in the middle and older groups decrement occurred. The more complex the learning requirement, the more noteworthy was the contrast between the learning of young and older subjects.

Other doctoral theses followed: Roger G. Barker, on muscular work abilities of the hands; Bronson Price, on immediate verbal memory; and Charles Marsh, Jr., who used a series of seven tests including a Dearborn form board, the Healey picture completion test No. II, and Porteus mazes. Albert Walton studied motor abilities in athletes using Stanford students for his younger group and older men from the Athletic Club of San Francisco. Paul Butterworth made a comprehensive study of the relation of age to skill in expert chess players. Keith Sward did a postdoctoral study of various abilities in younger and older college professors matched for professional fields.

Three tests of practical or occupational competence and two tests of intelligence completed the Later Maturity test battery. A sex difference appeared where the experience of men and women is radically diverse. On the McFarlane Coat assembly test, where in terms of norms the women excelled the men in speed in every decade, a group of male tailors indicated their special occupational skill by exceeding the mean score for the women (1931b, 1931c, 1931d, with C. C. Miles, 1932b).

Over 2000 individuals worked diligently on a time-limited Otis Group test. The results showed the typical age decrement, the downward curves from decade to decade. Men and women of equal education scored equally with similar test material. When a similar Otis test was administered with unlimited time allowance, the age decline was lessened.

In summary, the Stanford Maturity Studies gave a broad working basis for later investigators. Our large and representative samples of subjects in each decade from the twenties to the nineties, while they brought out no decisively new or startling results, did show with emphasis the persisting trend of age decline in whatever aspects of activity whether mental, sensory, or motor. Sex similarity of achievement and decline in intelligence was demonstrated as was sex difference in tasks of every kind where the experience and training of men and women characteristically differ. Age decline was the persisting conclusion.

Now thirty years later we know how age and aging studies have continued to be of wide scientific interest. But when Cowdry brought together the material for his first volume of studies of aging, he included my report as representative in the psychological area. This was in 1939. Since then the field has enlarged and the researches have proliferated. In the 1930's Wechsler credited our results with suggesting to him the desirability of a sliding scale of intelligence quotients for older people. Lorge, Shock, and many others with present day compendia by Birren have shown what can be done and is still to be done in the psychology of aging.

We left Stanford after completing the second Later Maturity Study series in 1932. The data had been gathered and some of the reports were in. We were sorry to leave California and our many good friends at Stanford. There was much to remember in the stimulating comradeship of those years and we were grateful. Our three older children attended and graduated from Stanford. A brief halt was made after our drive to New Haven in the company of our daughter Marjorie and our new daughter, Anna Mary, who was not quite three years old. Then we were off for an ocean voyage and rest with relatives in England. I attended and took part in the Centenary Celebration of the British Medical Society. The International Congress of Psychology then drew us to Copenhagen where Professor and Mrs. August Krogh were our kind hosts. That Congress brought together good friends and scientists: Pavlov, Niels Bohr, Cattell, Margaret Washburn, and many others. The return voyage to New York and a quick journey by car found us in Ithaca for the fortieth Annual Meeting of the APA. As president for that occasion I read my paper on "Age and Human Ability," which was duly published in the *Psychological Review* (1933).

How had our transfer to Yale come about? The plan for the later maturity research had been in the making when in 1929 I attended the International Congress of Psychology in New Haven. For me that Congress represented a high point of scientific and personal experience. Pavlov was present and we were able to communicate with him through his interpreter. Dodge had arranged symposia on vision including some of our eye-movement recordings and he had included me as one of the speakers. In addition, I appeared on two other programs.

The talk in New Haven, especially among the Yale group, was of President Angell's achievements for the University and especially his newest plan for the Institute of Human Relations. Months later, after my return to Stanford, with considerable correspondence intervening, Professor Dodge came out West to use his persuasive powers to bring us into the Institute. I will not attempt to trace or outline the discussions. A memorandum, a brief statement of the President's plan brings together what had already been accomplished by the Psychology Institute and Dr. Ruggles' work in the University. It seemed to reach a climax in Dean Winternitz's ambition for medicine in the future. The ideas formulated in these statements were discussed again and again from every angle. In the end I agreed to go to New Haven during my Sabbatical leave the following year. This I did. Then we returned for one last year at Stanford and in 1932 transferred finally and definitely to Yale. The points of view and aspirations expressed in the "Memorandum on the Institute" had largely influenced me in my decision.

The Institute of Human Relations at Yale was an early enterprise of President Angell who as psychologist had seen and entered into the expansion of that science at Chicago and later at Yale. He believed that psychologists working closely with men in related fields could advance knowledge through an integrated attack. He envisaged a definite but flexible organization that would bring together scholars from sociology, anthropology, pedagogy, psychology, and medical science, especially psychiatry. His thinking developed in the atmosphere and with the enthusiasm engendered by the possibilities of combining three excellent existing sources and building further upon them.

The previous Institute of Psychology at Yale, which had engaged the efforts of Dodge, Yerkes, and Wissler, had demonstrated its success. Dr. Arthur Ruggles, Professor of Psychiatry, had developed since 1925 an unusual and effective mental hygiene program in the University student health department. Dean Milton Winternitz had brought the zeal and vigor of Johns Hopkins to an expanding medical school at Yale, in Simon Flexner's opinion "the most promising institution of its kind in the country." Dean Winternitz was directing effort and planning beyond the already achieved level of standard efficiency in the hospital and in the medical school. He believed that existing medical skills and knowledge were ready to achieve a leap forward, specifically in the prevention of illness and in the promotion of good health. He championed the view that psychiatry was important in all clinical teaching. The purpose of the Institute of Human Relations was to provide teams of medical and other related scientific specialists who could coordinate researches designed to gain the broadest possible understanding of human beings as socially functioning individuals. The importance of studying normal persons was specifically urged.

There were also those outside Yale who approved the announced objective of the Institute. Dr. Adolph Meyer, a warm supporter of "common-sense" in psychiatry, believed the Institute plan could be realized in fact. He organized a symposium on the material of human nature and conduct. I was included along with Malamud, Rado, Cobb, Whitehorn, Bender, and Meyer who linked the presentations and emphasized the common ground. A reviewer concluded, "The result is a kinship of material and methods characteristic of trained pluralistic but consistently objective common sense of today free of the residuals of animistic tradition and without the dogmatism of the traditional types of the superscientific materialism of the 18th and 19th centuries. The material of human nature and conduct is equally open to the contributions from the basic sciences and from the cultural sciences dealing with man and is a domain calling for its own specific status and cultivation. The Symposium . . . presents a panorama that is both factually and in perspective a practical attainment of the goal and an encouragement for a growing shaping of a plastic and fertile consensus." Here was the goal, and I believe that the striving toward it was not all in vain.

Dr. Eugene Kahn, a student of Kraepelin, had been brought from Munich as head of the Department of Psychiatry and Sterling Professor of Psychiatry and Mental Hygiene at Yale. Dr. Kahn was now in charge of the clinic and the clinic patients who made up the two groups of individuals for possible study in the Institute. Dr. Kahn proved to be a skillful diagnostician and we thought him a good teacher. He and Professor Dodge were closely associated and enjoyed philosophical discussions of personality problems.

In my laboratory I set up equipment for conducting research in metabolism, relaxation, respiration, and sensory perception combined with interview type studies. Dr. Kahn approved my program and invited my participation in the psychiatric staff meetings and also in the daily staff rounds which served as an essential part of his teaching plan. Our laboratory studies were offered to all available and more or less cooperative patients. My wife made clinical tests and observations of personality types and behavior reactions. We reported our findings to staff conferences.

Conferences with Dodge were always a pleasure and we carried on continuing studies and discussions in which our assistant Neal Miller often took part. Miller, previously my assistant at Stanford, had accompanied me in the transfer to Yale. Dodge and I were interested in his plan to go to Vienna for a didactic psychoanalysis, as a basis for later more exact study of certain concepts. After Vienna, Miller returned to Yale where he has continued his work. His friendship has meant much to me through the years. Until 1935–36 the Institute of Human Relations program proceeded about as originally planned. Interest in the Institute was general and for a time many visitors claimed attention. The routine of psychiatric conferences and interviews became increasingly demanding. There were always interested students. The psychiatric interns referred many of their patients to our service, wanted full written reports on them, and would come to discuss the cases. Outpatient clinic patients were referred more and more often as local agencies became aware of the available service.

I found special interest in referrals of unusual types—a Korsakof, a case of Pick's disease, and several cases of psychic or so-called hysterical damage. Amnesias and aphasics turned up. The neuro-surgeons were interested in frontal lobe problems at this time.

Dr. Clements Fry, psychiatrist in the University health department, set up a regular psychological program for selected clinical studies of university students under his care. And the School of Nursing made referrals and requested a testing program of entering students.

In the middle 1930's a State Commission on Jails with some Federal funds available for employing out-of-work personnel made a survey of the jail population of Connecticut. The Institute of Human Relations cooperated in this project by furnishing space for offices and also by making available psychiatric and psychological specialists to test and evaluate the jail population. My wife and I, using our car, took part in this project and had the assistance of four clinical psychologists. We spent a day or more at each jail gathering data. Group tests were made of some 800 men and individual studies were made of 503 persons. Appraisals of such traits as cooperation, adaptability, persistence, intelligence, and emotionality were made on the basis of our tests and observations. In addition social and personal data were gathered by welfare workers. The results of this survey were used by the Connecticut Legislative Commission on Jails in their planning and recommendations especially with respect to rehabilitation.

In 1935 Dr. Winternitz ended his fifteen years as Dean of the Yale Medical School and with this change in administration the originally planned program for the Institute was given up as practically impossible of realization. Professor Mark May now became director of the Institute of which he had previously been secretary and his keen insight and practicality were seen in the ensuing developments. As these were ultimately realized, they salvaged what at that time could be utilized from the original plan. According to the new plan a staff of senior professors was selected from the several disciplines already represented in the Institute and conducting research in the field of behavioral studies. I was included in this group. Our responsibility was the general planning for the work of young men in pre- or postdoctoral interneship. Dr. John B. Wolfe was one of these postdoctoral students, the first assigned to me. He came with an N.R.C. fellowship. I continued my relationship with the psychiatry department although with a difference, and other activities developed. In the psychology department I now took a somewhat more active part. I was already a member of the graduate school faculty and now served on its committees. Graduate students consulted me more frequently. In the medical school I came to have charge of the Neurological Study Unit, an important teaching clinic which met weekly and required continuous planning.

From 1939 to 1944 World War II called for total support from science and our activities. Yale men were deeply involved. The undergraduates in eight of the ten colleges were in uniform. Committee work and voluntary aid as called for by government agencies were the order of the day. National Research Council committees now had special goals for wartime research and planning. Under the Office of Scientific Research and Development my heaviest and most prolonged duty was with the Committee on Aviation Medicine of which Dr. Eugene F. DuBois, a Naval Reserve Captain, was chairman. We were meeting, supervising government contracts, organizing conferences, or traveling on inspections much of the time, and served from

November 12, 1940 to June 30, 1946. In 1940 and throughout the war period I worked on problems of vision involved in current needs and was at the New London Submarine Base from time to time (with Carson and Stevens, 1943c; 1943d; 1943e; 1945b; with D. W. Bronk, 1948). Dark adaptation was an important problem for research. I had excellent equipment in my laboratory at Yale and alert young men to serve as observers. I became aware that the presence of a red light in the dark room did not much influence the rate and resulting level of dark adaptation. I made up some dozens of pairs of red goggles and sent them to different U.S. military stations for trial. The military found them effective aids in preparation for night seeing. They were introduced in Great Britain and elsewhere and were not patented.

In 1942 I was sent to England to serve as consultant on flying stress in the Royal Air Force. Here I served with or under the director general of medical services, Dr. Whittingham. I shared an office in the U.S. Embassy in London and had for several months a wide opportunity to consult with British scientists and to relay to Washington such information as seemed desirable at that time. On returning home I had much to do in reporting and in catching up with the work of committees from whose membership I had been absent. One or two new ones were started. During the war I was in and out of Yale but when it was over, I came back, with gladness in my heart. It was wonderful to talk with graduate students again about science for science's sake. My capable laboratory assistant Alphonse Chapanis had finished his doctoral requirements in 1943. His ability and training later made him valuable at Wright Field, in the laboratory concerned with visibility and optics in connection with aviation. Again after the war I established contact with most of the graduate students in psychology and they all knew they could come to talk to me if they so desired. With some of them I talked about the possibility of doing research at Orange Park at the chimpanzee colony established there by Professor Robert M. Yerkes. For some time I was secretary of a Yale committee that had to do with the continuation of this research opportunity.

At Yale I was not responsible for as many Ph.D. theses as at Stanford but I had some contact with a large number of graduate scholars and had with many of them stimulating discussions. Among these I think of Merideth Crawford, James and Eleanor Gibson, Robert Malmo, Austin Rieson, Robert Ross and his friend Lloyd Embry who painted Professor Raymond Dodge's portrait, Richard Rouse, Robert and Pauline Sears, Lillian Wolfe, Jane B. Birge, Marion Rowe, Shirley Spragg, and Wallace Wulfeck. Dr. Lloyd Beck and I started some research on olfaction which resulted in my making a field study on honeybees (with L. H. Beck, 1949a). This problem still interests me.

With the founding of the residential colleges a new phase of academic life came into being at Yale. Under President Angell and made possible by gifts of Edward S. Harkness, ten colleges were established in order to recover the social and educational values of small groups in what had become a large university. Each college had its resident Master and a group of Fellows at first selected from teachers of the undergraduates. Before the end of the 1930's a few professors from the Graduate School were added to college groups. I had the honor of being chosen as a Fellow of Jonathan Edwards College. The Master, Robert Dudley French, and his wife Margaret became our valued friends. The Fellowship of the College built on the Oxford pattern has contributed a very special and precious aspect to the life at Yale. For several years I had the honor of being president of Jonathan Edwards Senior Common Room. The Fellowship continues now long after my retirement and means much to me.

In 1953, I reached the Yale automatic retirement age. Visits to relatives and a sojourn at our small farm in Otsego County, New York, followed. Then quite unexpectedly early in 1954 came an invitation from Professor Mümtaz Turhan, head of the Department of Psychology at the Turkish University in Istanbul, to join their faculty group. We knew little of the conditions for living and working in Turkey but decided to accept.

Moving to Turkey for an uncertain period made it necessary to resign from positions I had enjoyed for several years. As chairman of the Board of Examiners for Connecticut Certified Psychologists I had with others enjoyed working with Dr. Marion A. Bills who knew the law and most of the candidates who wished to qualify. I had been chairman of the Board of Directors of The Psychological Corporation of New York for ten years. They gave me a gold watch which I wear. It had been a pleasure to work with President Dr. George K. Bennett in this forward looking organization founded by my good friend Cattell. I had been chairman, Board of Directors, for the American Institute for Research, Pittsburg, since it was founded by its very capable Dr. John C. Flanagan. I continue to be interested in these and similar organizations that apply tested psychological facts and principles in the accomplishment of human needs.

We encountered in Turkey three years of fascinating and rewarding oriental life and the experience of contact with Turkish teachers, scholars, and students modern in their thinking while holding fast to the historical culture from which their young nation had emerged. At the University all professors were under the Turkish civil service. Permission to leave the city for a month or more must be obtained. It was readily granted us for the purpose of visiting universities of Southern Europe in the summer of 1955. The following summer we remained in Turkey visiting many historical and interesting sites. In 1957 we again went abroad, finally attending the International Congress of Psychology in Brussels.

At the University there were a few professors from Germany, France, and England, as well as the great majority who were Turkish. Each non-Turkish professor lectured in his own language which was then translated one paragraph at a time by a Turkish assistant. The result, an opportunity for the students to learn or increase their learning of the foreign language while imbibing what they can of the subject matter of the lecture. I used material presented on charts prepared at home and also slides and motion picture reels as illustrative devices.

My assistant, Beglan Birand, was an able Istanbul Ph.D. who had spent a profitable year at Stanford University as a Fulbright scholar. I had not met her before we went to Turkey. As a result of outstanding achievements in her examinations she was awarded at Istanbul the rank of Docent in 1957. Another able student was Halide Yavuz who after my first year in Istanbul came to the United States and graduated Ph.D. at Connecticut University; her fields were experimental and clinical. A group of students too numerous to name individually became and remain our friends.

In the three years we learned to know and admire Turkish art and architecture and also came in contact with Byzantine, Greek, and even Hittite remains of enormous interest.

Shortly before we left Istanbul a suggestion reached me that I should become scientific director at the U.S. Naval Submarine Base Medical Research Laboratory of New London, Connecticut. Commander Dean Farnsworth and Captain Joseph Vogel encouraged me to accept. The former was a long-time friend and fellow worker on Navy problems of vision; the latter was the officer-in-charge at the Laboratory.

My earlier experiences with the scientific staff at the sub base and knowledge of the work done there inclined me to the suggestion. And so we came to our beloved Connecticut again and located in Gales Ferry about three miles from the north gate of the submarine base. The focus of the research work in this laboratory is directed toward achieving results of benefit to the health, motivation, and effective service of the submariners. The atomic submarines capable of long periods of submergence have posed many new questions that demand research. And now there is a new and long-range problem before us. It is that of man living, exploring, and working in and from undersea dwellings on the continental shelf. Under the stimulating and far-sighted leadership of Captain George F. Bond, M.C., U.S.N., recently our officer-in-charge, this Laboratory, belonging to the Bureau of Medicine and Surgery, has through a long series of researches with animals and men developed and tested scientific information pertinent to this objective. A trial run with four men, all experienced divers, living in a "sea-house" on the sea bottom 192 feet down near the Argus Tower, was successfully carried out for nearly two weeks in late summer 1964. This complicated experiment came to have the name Sealab I. And now as I write these lines elaborate plans are far advanced for Sealab II to be located on the Pacific Coast in deeper colder water and involving more men and a wider spectrum of scientific data and planned undersea accomplishments.

In the psychophysiological research of the Navy there are many challenging possibilities and new problems especially in the opening areas involved in oceanography. I am happy to have shared in the developing insights and to have served with the able scientific groups engaged in the several programs of the research.

The joy of being a living creature is multiplied by there being others somewhat like one's self and by having or sharing children who develop into useful adults and who likewise have children. And there is enjoyment in associating with other life forms with which nature surrounds us. We may touch them and in memory recall their charms. I like to recall bringing the dozen little redwood trees down the mountain and planting them in a circle behind our home on Gerona Road at Stanford. When last we saw them some were more than sixty feet tall; they could cast a shadow ten times as long as a man's shadow. Perhaps if they escape man's tree cutting desires one of them may be living there a thousand years hence. To plant ideas or to plant trees? I have enjoyed trying to do a bit of both.

# REFERENCES

*Selected Publications by Walter R. Miles*

A comparison of elementary and high school grades. *Pedag. Sem.,* 1910, *17,* 429–450.

Accuracy of the voice in simple pitch singing. *Psychol. Rev. Monogr.,* 1914, *16,* No. 69.

Some psycho-physiological processes as affected by alcohol. *Proc. nat. Acad. Sci.,* 1916, *2,* 703–709.

*Effect of alcohol on psycho-physiological functions.* Washington, D.C.: Carnegie Institution, 1918, No. 286. (a)

The effect of a prolonged reduced diet on twenty-five college men. *Proc. nat. Acad. Sci.,* 1918, *4,* 152–156. (b)

The sex expression of men living on a lowered nutritional level. *J. nerv. Ment. Dis.,* 1919, *49,* 208–224. (a)

(with F. G. Benedict, P. Roth, & H. W. Smith) *Human vitality and efficiency under prolonged restricted diet.* Washington, D.C.: Carnegie Institution, 1919. (b)

A pursuit pendulum. *Psychol. Rev.,* 1920, *27,* 361–376.

A pursuit-meter. *J. exp. Psychol.,* 1921, *4,* 77–105.

Static equilibrium as a useful test of motor control. *J. Industr. Hyg.,* 1922, *3,* 316–331. (a)

The comparative concentrations of alcohol in human blood and urine at intervals after ingestion. *J. pharm. exp. Therapeut.,* 1922, *20,* 265–285. (b)

(with H. F. Root) Physical measurements of diabetic patients. *J. Metabol. Res.,* 1922, *2,* 173–197.

*Alcohol and human efficiency.* Washington, D.C.: Carnegie Institution, 1924, No. 333.

(with H. F. Root) Physical measurements on operated hyperthyroids. *Proc. Soc. exp. Biol. Med.*, 1926, 23, 727–728.

Rapid weight changes reflected in physical measurements on adults. *Arch. int. Med.*, 1927, 39, 605–617. (a)

The two-story duplicate maze. *J. exp. Psychol.*, 1927, 10, 365–377. (b)

The narrow-path elevated maze for studying rats. *Proc. Soc. exp. Biol. Med.*, 1927, 24, 454–456. (c)

Studies of physical exertion: I. A multiple chronograph for measuring groups of men. *Amer. J. physical Educ.*, 1928, 33, 379–387. (a)

The measurement of speed in football-charging. *Scientific American*, March 1928, 226–229. (b)

British scientific instruments. *Psychol. Bull.*, 1928, 25, 480–486. (c)

Human body-weight: I. Correlation between body widths and other physical measurements on young men. *Science*, N.S., 1928, 68, 382–386. (d)

Visual illusions of motion. *Sci. Mon.*, 1928, 27, 481–491. (e)

Horizontal eye movements at the onset of sleep. *Psychol. Rev.*, 1929, 36, 122–141. (a)

Duration of sleep and the insensible perspiration. *Proc. Soc. exp. Biol. Med.*, 1929, 26, 577–580. (b)

(with Knotts) The maze learning ability of blind compared with sighted children. *J. genet. Psychol.*, 1929, 36, 21–50. (c)

One hundred cases of color blindness detected with the Ishihara test. *J. genet. Psychol.*, 1929, 2, 535–543. (d)

Individuality in heart-rate response to work and rest. *Psychol. Bull.*, 1929, 26, 594–595. (e)

Ocular dominance in adults. *J. genet. Psychol.*, 1930, 3, 412–430.

Studies in physical exertion: II. Individual and group reaction time in football-charging. *Res. quart.*, 1931, 2, 5–13. (a)

Change of dexterity with age. *Proc. Soc. exp. Biol. Med.*, 1931, 29, 136–138. (b)

Measures of certain human abilities throughout the life span. *Proc. nat. Acad. Sci.*, 1931, 17, 627–633. (c)

Correlation of reaction and coordination speed with age in adults. *Amer. J. Psychol.*, 1931, 43, 377–391. (d)

The normal sensitivity of the cardio-inhibitory center. *J. Industr. Hyg.*, 1932, 14, 3–17. (a)

(with C. C. Miles) The correlation of intelligence scores and chronological age from early to late maturity. *Amer. J. Psychol.*, 1932, 44, 44–78. (b)

Age and human ability. *Psychol. Rev.*, 1933, 40, 99–123.

A metabolic study of three unusual learned breathing patterns practiced in the cult of Yoga. *Amer. J. Physiol.*, 1934, 109, 75.

Training, practice and mental longevity. *Science*, 1935, 81, 79–87. (a)

Age and human society. In C. Murchison (Ed.), *A handbook of social psychology*. Worcester, Mass.: Clark Univer. Press, 1935, 596–682. (b)

(Ed. and contrib.) Psychological studies of human variability. *Psychol. Monogr.*, 1936 (Whole No. 212). (a)

The reaction time of the eye. *Psychol. Monogr.*, 1936, 47, No. 212, 268–293. (b)

Changes in respiratory pattern associated with different types of vocalization. *Science*, 1937, 85, 444. (a)

Psychological factors in alcoholism. *Ment. Hyg.*, 1937, *21*, 529–548. (b)

Mental performance with bilateral frontal area defect. *Proc. Int. Congr. Psychol.*, 1938, 413.

Psychological aspects of ageing. In E. V. Cowdry (Ed.), *Problems of ageing.* Baltimore, 1939, 535–571. (a)

Performance of the Einthoven galvanometer with input through a vacuum tube microvoltmeter. *J. Exp. Psychol.*, 1939, *25*, 76–90. (b)

Reliability of measurements of the steady polarity potential of the eye. *Proc. nat. Acad. Sci.*, 1939, *25*, 128–136. (c)

The ocular polarity potential in cases with unilateral enucleation. *Proc. nat. Acad. Sci.*, 1939, *25*, 349–358. (d)

The steady polarity potential of the human eye. *Proc. nat. Acad. Sci.*, 1939, *25*, 25–36. (e)

Modification of the human eye potential by dark and light adaptation. *Science*, 1940, *91*, 456.

The development of psychology. In L. L. Woodruff (Ed.), *Development of the sciences.* New Haven, Conn.: Yale, 1941, 247–290. (a)

Coördination of psychological services in the national emergency. *J. consult. Psychol.*, 1941, *5*, 216–220. (b)

(with C. C. Miles) Psychological changes in normal ageing. In E. G. Stieglitz (Ed.), *Geriatric medicine.* Philadelphia: Saunders, 1943, 99–117. (a)

Contributions to "Psychology for the fighting man," E. G. Boring and M. Van de Water (Ed.), *The infantry J.*, Washington, D.C., 1943. (b)

(with Carson and Stevens) Vision, hearing and aeronautical design. *Sci. Mo.*, 1943, *56*, 446–451. (c)

Night vision: light sensitivity vs. form acuity. *Yale Sci. Mag.*, 1943, *18*, 10–11, 28, 30. (d)

Red goggles for producing dark adaptation. *Proc. Fed. Amer. Sci. exp. Biol.*, 1943, *2*, 109–115. (e)

Psychological aspects of military aviation. *American Scientist*, 1945, *33*, 146–158. (a)

Entoptic plotting of the macular area. *Army-Navy OSRD, vision Com. Proc.*, 14th meeting, 1945, 15–28. (b)

(with D. W. Bronk) Visual problems. In *Advances in military medicine.* Boston: Little, Brown, 1948, 261–277.

(with L. H. Beck) Infra-red absorption in field studies of olfaction in honeybees. *Proc. nat. Acad. Sci.*, 1949, *35*, 292–310. (a)

On the central zone of the human fovea. *Science*, 1949, *109*, 441–442. (b)

Selected psychomotor measurement methods, Sec. III. In R. W. Gerard (Ed.), *Methods in medical research, vol. III.* Chicago: The Year Book Medical Publishers, 1950, 142–218.

Methods of using binoculars. *Army-Navy NRC vision Com. Proc.*, 29th meeting, 1951, 63–89.

Effectiveness of red light on dark adaptation. *J. opt. Soc. Amer.*, 1953, *43*, 435–441. (a)

Light sensitivity and form perception in dark adaptation. *J. opt. Soc. Amer.*, 1953, *43*, 560–566. (b)

(with B. M. Shriver) Ageing in Air Force pilots. *J. Geront.*, 1953, *8*, 185–190. (c)

Comparison of functional and structural areas in the human fovea, I. Method of entoptic plotting. *J. Neurophysiol.*, 1954, *17*, 22–38.

(Ed. and contributor) *Istanbul studies in experimental psychology*, Vol. I, Istanbul, Turkey: Istanbul Univer., 1956. (a)

Comparison of simultaneous tests of right and left hand grip with separate successive tests. *Istanbul Stud. exp. Psychol.*, 1956, *1*, XX, 22–32. (b)

(with Beglan Birand) Lightness of some surface colors compared for stereo-kinetik depth effects. *Istanbul Stud. exp. Psychol.*, 1956, *1*, 86–103. (c)

Improvement of judgments for small horizontal distances. *Istanbul Stud. exp. Psychol.*, 1956, *1*, 122–143. (d)

### Other Publications Cited

James, William. *Psychology, briefer course.* New York: Holt, 1892.
Pillsbury, W. B. *Essentials of psychology.* New York: Macmillan, 1911.

Gardner Murphy

# Gardner Murphy

Over the years my classes have heard about the predicament of a small boy who lived in a New England town, and encountered some problems in getting himself sorted out in terms of "identity." The town was Concord, Massachusetts, and the years were at the beginning of this century. In the sketch, drawn on many blackboards, the Boston and Maine railroad tracks are indicated. On one side lived people who were of Anglo-Saxon derivation, business class membership, Protestant faith; in general, they were commuters to Boston. On the other side of the tracks, known in the vernacular as "Texas," lived people who were of Irish extraction, worked with their hands, were of Roman Catholic faith, and did not commute. The problem of the small boy in question arose from the fact that he belonged to the majority group on the "good" side of the tracks, but his name placed him spang in the middle of "Texas." This problem of divided loyalties, and uncertain identity, has been with me for a lifetime. It goes with the fact that when we moved from the North for a short time, to Montgomery, Alabama, the boys across the street asked what language we spoke. It appeared again when it became evident, as we moved North again, that my father was not only of remote Irish extraction, but was a Southerner and a Democrat.

Mavericks and minorities were "my kind" of people. I vividly remember an episode in Kerrville, Texas, where my uncle had taken us to share his hunting trip. It involved a huge, floppy-eared, otherwise nondescript brown dog who was very hungry. Nobody would feed him. Everybody knew that stray dogs would attach themselves to you if you fed them. I asked my mother if I could have my weekly allowance, consisting of a dime, and when the dog had followed us all the way back to San Antonio, I paid my cousin the dime to buy a big plate full of rations for the brown dog. This business of being "for the underdog" was deeply ingrained very early, and burrowed deeply in. I am sure it had a little to do with my being minority-groupish myself. It had something to do also with being admired for being generous, and enjoyed various other "operant" attributes. For whatever reasons one may assign, it has not extinguished. It has in fact been reinforced by a good many fairly obvious social factors, not necessarily or always very lovable.

After two and a half years in Montgomery, Alabama, where my father,

Edgar Gardner Murphy, was rector of an Episcopal church, and a year in San Antonio, Texas, the family came North. There was Concord, where my mother, Maud King, second of three sisters who were daughters of old New England stock, had herself grown up before she went off to Vassar and thence on to the South, teaching, and meeting my father. Concord was always the home base and rallying point, with my extraordinarily loving and companionable Gran'pa and Gran'ma King, and with aunts, uncles, cousins, who gave me a very intense feeling of really belonging. Indeed, belonging just as much as if my father had not come from San Antonio, and the University of the South. It was as if my life were a pure culture of the Emerson, Thoreau, Alcott world in which we were steeped. We soaked in Gran'pa King's continuous and exquisite quotations from Shakespeare, the Bible, and miscellaneous English literature, often slyly and adroitly adapted to capricious purposes. (When lunch was late, he asked if there was a "Distant Prospect of Eton," and when the melon was green, he suggested letting it wait over, "making the green one red.") With Gran'ma King, in her gentle, steady Stoicism, I identified to the same full degree.

After two and a half years in Concord we moved to Branford, Connecticut, so that my father, founder of the National Child Labor Committee, who was traveling in the interests of education in the South, could more easily run up from New York and see us. His health was deteriorating with a heart condition, and after several terrible sieges in Branford, and in New Haven, where we moved in 1905, he became a semi-invalid, struggling on through much writing on issues—Southern and national—to make a considerable dent in American public opinion on education, race relations, and other themes.

Those years in New Haven, 1905 to 1910, were years of intense curiosity and intellectual development, with a passion for religious clarification, as I became what my elder brother, DuBose, later called an "evangelical Catholic"; that is, within the Anglican fold, but both evangelical and historically oriented. I went off to Hotchkiss School, 1910 to 1912. Here I was somewhat isolated and intensely concerned about intellectual and religious matters, and was absorbed in my studies, particularly Greek, Latin, and English. In 1912 I entered Yale and went on with a narrow and intense scholarly preoccupation. My father, devotedly struggling to understand me, and to help me, and pouring out an affection which I reciprocated, died in 1913. My mother, always close to me, drew even closer, and remained a profound and sustaining force through all my later years—at college, in professional training, and during the years of my marriage and parenthood—living to the age of 92 and to the end vigorously sharing our intellectual efforts and our joy in our children.

With the aid of family savings and scholarships, I was able to continue at college and to graduate in 1916. My closest friends during that period were those destined for the ministry. My interest in psychology was intense, and as told in another narrative (1957), it was in considerable measure what I had known about psychical research, as conveyed to me by Gran'pa King and my father, that made me feel that there was a vital challenge here. The psychology at Yale was not then very strong, but I responded strongly to it, and much more to the very extraordinary anthropology taught me by Albert G. Keller. He presented a vivid, dramatic, Darwinian evolutionary viewpoint, which I telescoped into a broad social science point of view, with a good deal of economic, linguistic, and political material which I found enormously gratifying. My general world outlook took shape rapidly during this junior year at Yale, and there came about an erosion of my religious beliefs, which were to be assaulted more rapidly in the following two years. My primary extracurricular activity was the debating team—in itself very gratifying, and certainly the most important single factor in training me for public speaking, and for the delights of the teaching craft. John Chester Adams, who coached the debating team, and who taught me sophomore English, was the greatest influence in my college years, and to him ran second Chauncy Brewster Tinker, with whom I had both freshman English and in my senior year the "Age of Johnson." One other vital course for me was zoology, magnificently taught.

With the major in psychology and the minor in anthropology it became clear to me where I was going. I was admitted to the Harvard graduate school in September of 1916, working with Yerkes, Münsterberg, Langfeld, Holt, and Troland—all good courses, but none brilliant. Troland, however, offered a good workout in the literature of psychical research, as he was at that time Richard Hodgson Fellow in Psychical Research, and I latched on and worked under his direction. There I became acquainted with large masses of interesting research material which were, and still are, largely unknown—indeed, taboo—wherever orthodox psychology is organized. It began to be plain that I *could* train myself for an academic career in psychology, and handle psychical research on the side.

The United States declared war on Germany in April, 1917, and June saw me in the Yale Mobile Hospital Unit, a small medical-surgical outfit sent overseas in September, 1917. We did not see much active service. I learned a good deal from the other men, and from the French families with whom we chatted. I came back in the summer of 1919, and on the basis of friendly and effective guidance from R. S. Woodworth, settled down for what was destined to be a period of twenty-one years at Columbia. My response to Woodworth is contained in an obituary notice (1963). Not only was the experience with him a fine one, but I enjoyed membership in the group, especially the brilliant teaching of H. L. Hollingworth, the friendly support of A. T. Poffenberger, and many staff friendships, of which by far the strongest was that with Otto Klineberg. At Columbia also in those years were Ruth Benedict, Margaret Mead, and a little later, Robert and Helen Lynd, of *Middletown* (1929) fame, whom I had met in Florence in 1923; all of these became life-long and intimate friends.

While doing graduate work at Columbia (1919 to 1922), I was also taking courses at the New School for Social Research, a brilliantly organized new educational effort, and at Union Theological Seminary, where the work included some of the greatest teaching of my life, notably Fosdick's "The Use of the Bible," and Scott's "Life of Christ."

Thanks largely to Woodworth, I began in 1920 to teach in "The Extension," later known as General Studies, and went on with this while commuting back and forth to Boston as holder of the Richard Hodgson Fellowship in Psychical Research, for which McDougall had suggested I might apply. My collaborators there were Harry Helson and George Estabrooks. The strain involved in the double responsibility and the travel probably had something to do with my succumbing to a bad case of the grippe in March, 1925, from the consequences of which I did not recover for nine years. As a semi-invalid, I carried on with my teaching, but I could not do much research.

One of the courses I greatly enjoyed teaching all during this time at Columbia was entitled the History of Modern Psychology, organized while on a wandering summer trip in Europe in 1923. My life-time friend, Frank Lorimer, together with Theodore Newcomb, and a particularly thoughtful and challenging student back from France, Ruth Munroe, enlivened that course for me in 1924–25.

H. L. Hollingworth asked one day at the Faculty Club, "Now you've done the work of pulling all this material together, why don't you write a book?" I was surprised, and delighted. In those years there was, of course, no "history of psychology" that was used much by psychologists. Brett's three-volume *History of Psychology* (1921) was a useful survey of a philosopher's psychology, with a little bit in Volume III about modern experimentalism, but not a very clear indication of how modern psychology came into being; and the preface showed that Brett intended anyway to stop at the year 1900. In addition to Brett, I had a fair reading knowledge of the history of philosophy, absorbed during a wonderful five weeks in the summer of 1916, cycling in from Concord to the new Widener Library at Harvard, reading philosophy all day every day. This was profoundly satisfying to me. An indelible impression was made on me then and later by Heraclitus, Socrates, Epicurus, and the Pythagoreans, and my enthusiasm was kept alive by applying them, year by year, to new situations. But it was the growth of modern psychology that I wanted to emphasize. Ladd and Woodworth's *Elements of Physiological Psychology* (1911), William James' *Principles* (1890), which I had read in 1920, and a few other mainstays got me organized. When the course began in the fall of 1923, the lectures went well.

In 1926 the stenotyped lectures were read back to me by three devoted Columbia students, my eyes being at that time unequal to the task of reading; through dictating corrections to them the typescript was put through several revisions; however, in 1927 in response to the very unorthodox methods of Dr. Frank Marlow, my eyes recovered so that I could read the proofs. I had made a contract with C. K. Ogden of the International Library of

Psychology, using Harcourt Brace and Company as American outlet. The book appeared in January, 1929. It was really in the nick of time, for E. G. Boring's *History of Experimental Psychology* (1929) had not come out. When it did, I found a generous appreciation of my *Historical Introduction* (1929) in Boring's words, and as things worked out, his book and mine never really "competed" in any serious sense. All psychologists were grateful for his book, and a number could see the utility of my own effort, which dealt with some things which he had not touched upon; the same applied, actually, to the revisions of these books, for as it happened, he and I were both revising in 1948, and the 1949 revision of my book could not have been a competitor to his, nor was it so designed. It still represents, quite well, my general perspective regarding the evolution of psychology. Of course, it does not do justice to social psychology or personality study or parapsychology, but these were dealt with in separate works. An *Outline of Abnormal Psychology,* edited in the spring of 1928, appeared a few weeks after the *Historical Introduction* in 1929; Arthur H. Bachrach and I brought out a revised edition in 1954.

I gave up the Richard Hodgson Fellowship (June, 1925) and settled down to an instructorship at Columbia.

## MARRIAGE

The following spring, when Ruth Munroe invited me over, I met her roommate, Lois Barclay, a student at Union Seminary, with whom a new kind of world began. Despite my poor health, we explored many things in heaven and earth, especially during the year following, when she was teaching in Baltimore; on my weekends there we talked and walked, and rode in Baltimore's "dainty car" taxis, getting to know each other well. We were married in 1926. Her interest in education, in clinical psychology, and in comparative religion, deeply reinforced my own, and we began a sharing of intellectual, esthetic, philosophical, and other concerns like music, mountains, and travel, which has never diminished. The summer of 1929, spent in Europe, strengthened all these interests and gave us a common fund of rich experience. Her interest in psychical research, as a challenging pioneer field, was a primary factor in maintaining my own morale.

Our son, Al, born in 1930, and our daughter Midge, coming to us in 1932, gave another rich dimension to life—Al through his incredible clarity of perception and expression, his unlimited devotion to high standards in literature and music, and his Olympian sense of humor, and Midge for her robust directness, her earthy healthiness, her creativity, and her enthusiasm, gaiety, and warmth.

We lived in New York from the time of our marriage until 1935. Lois' major professional activity was teaching at Sarah Lawrence College in Bronxville. After two years in Tuckahoe, we moved to Bronxville in 1937, the year in which she completed the Ph.D. degree at Teachers College. I was teaching, in addition to the history, a course in social psychology for graduate students, and at times, a course in abnormal psychology, and I supervised a very large number of master's essays. My preoccuption with Ph.D. dissertations, mainly in social psychology, began with Rensis Likert in 1929, and continued through a period of eleven years in which Eugene Hartley, Muzafer Sherif, Sol Diamond, Joan Criswell, Ruth J. Levy, and others enriched my experience.

In 1934, having tried everything on the face of the earth recommended by orthodox medicine—and that includes literally dozens of ingenious devices —to try to get over the severe sequelae of the grippe which I had in 1925, I ran across Dr. William H. Hay's combination of diet and general physical revamping, regarded by most medical men as sheer quackery. Within a month I found myself restored to excellent health. As Lois said at the time, when she saw me after coming from Hay's sanitarium, "Why, Gardner, you're all pink now, instead of sallow." This, and the experience with Doctor Marlow, were among the things that convinced me that the unorthodox could be the thing that really worked.

## EARLY PSYCHOLOGICAL PERSPECTIVES

The kind of psychology that I found myself believing in during the early Columbia years was simply the broadest, deepest, most comprehensive psychology that I knew how to comprise. I did not believe that being systematic necessitated giving up varied interests in rich material wherever it can be found. In the summer of 1920, while working with F. L. Wells at McLean Hospital, I had read through the two-volume William James' *Principles of Psychology* (1890), and loved it utterly. Working with Woodworth was a delight, and I held the "middle of the road" position so firmly that I could never see how anybody could want to give up the large vista which you could see if you are willing to turn your head. This did not mean at all being orthodox in beliefs. It meant getting a stance from which you can see everything as you travel along. It made sense at Columbia, and although there was no very strong positive "ism," doctrine, dogma, or even method to be obtained there, I was happy in the catholicity of the spirit which radiated from Woodworth, and to some degree from all of his associates.

Such efforts as I made along systematic lines appear in my *Historical Introduction to Modern Psychology* (1929), especially in the 1949 revision; the introductory chapter to the *Experimental Social Psychology* (1931); and in the introduction to an elementary text, *A Briefer General Psychology* (1935). I had begun as general editor for the Harper Psychology Series in 1931, and continued until just now (1965), turning it over to Wayne H. Holtzman; this undoubtedly played a part in keeping me oriented to a rather wide range of interests. I became, to some degree, a specialist in social psychology; that is, I handled the dissertations in that field from 1929 onwards, often working together with Otto Klineberg in this area of responsibility.

The most important components in my broad or eclectic or tolerant or flexible, or whatever I like to call my beliefs (of course, they would be called chaotic, confused, fragmented, and a lot of other things by those not congenial to them), were first a passionate conviction that things are best understood through the study of their origins and evolution; second, a belief that psychology is *only* separable from the biological sciences on the one hand, and the social sciences on the other, through some sort of arbitrary compartmentalization which is likely to do much more harm than good; third, that if psychology is seriously the study of the whole organism, the whole individual, it is necessarily a study of experience, attitude, immediacy, as well as a study of what is observed from outside; fourth, that behavioral studies are good, and behavioristic beliefs are bad for science; fifth, that inclusiveness, and an accent on the positive, necessitates encouraging many primitive, groping efforts which might sometime *become* science, though it will be a long way to get there. Tinker taught me in freshman English the slogan "plus ultra." He explained that this phrase symbolized the open world after the Pillars of Hercules had been bravely passed; before, it was *ne plus extra,* but thereafter, the words ran simply *"plus ultra"*: "There is more beyond." If I have a focused philosophy, this is the center of it.

As far as the tasks of psychology are concerned, I would always say that they are bigger than anyone dreams; the methods are more numerous; the dimensions are greater; and the ultimate contributions greater than can be guessed. When Lois and I discovered Walt Whitman, he became for us the poet of this belief in limitlessness. One other poetic message has been lifeblood to me: John Masefield's series of sonnets on the self, beginning, "Here in the self is all that man can know/ Of beauty, all the wonder, all the power," and including the one that begins "If I could get within this changing I." This vision of man's resonance to the world is what I think psychology is all about.

## SOCIAL PSYCHOLOGY

Now for some more specific words about my interest in social psychology. As an undergraduate at Yale, I had responded to J. M. Baldwin's *Mental Development in the Child and the Race* (1895), including *Social and Ethical Interpretations,* and as I have noted above, the anthropology with Keller was deeply impressive. Though the social psychology of the period was largely centered in McDougall (Woodworth, for example, built his course largely on McDougall) there were striking new beginnings.

Floyd H. Allport, whom I had known when we were both graduate students at Harvard in 1916 and 1917, was of course, pointing towards a new scientific systematization of social psychology. I met him on a road in France, back of the lines, in 1918, and bumped into him again in New York in the mid-1920's. He had plainly shown the importance of the experimental method, elaborating and transcending the experiments of Moede and others in pre-World War I Germany. When I began, in 1924, to think of social psychology as my professional specialization, I gratefully went along with Floyd Allport. In fact, he was good enough to recommend me to pinch-hit for him, teaching social psychology at Syracuse University in the summer session in 1927; and I organized my teaching, to some degree, in his terms. I was, however, much dissatisfied with what I thought was over-emphasis upon the "behavior viewpoint" which I thought left out the personal world of the social initiator and the social responder—the very issues which Muzafer Sherif later brought into the picture, in 1934 and 1935.

When, in 1924, Woodworth decided not to offer his evening graduate class in social psychology, he asked if I was interested in taking it, and of course, I was. From 1924 to 1929, during each fall term I dealt with a more or less systematic picture of hereditary and acquired components in social behavior, including the usual thing on suggestion, imitation, and sympathy, the self, the group, etc., and during the spring dealt with individual differences in social attributes. When, however, the Lynds' *Middletown* came out in 1929, I began to use that as the basis for the spring semester and built up in each spring term a social psychology with a more or less sociological orientation, emphasizing the *mores* as I had come to know them through Keller, and of course, using the institutional system of the Lynds as a way of introducing psychological concepts.

I had, however, other aims in the field. The time was coming for an organized presentation of the experimental possibilities extending in every direction which human ingenuity would allow. Owing largely to the interest of Robert S. Lynd, I attended the "personality and culture" discussion organized by Edward Sapir for the Social Science Research Council at Hanover in 1930. These problems brought us into contact with Lawrence K. Frank, then of the General Education Board, who became an intimate friend. In many summers in Holderness, New Hampshire, Larry and Mary Frank have afforded us warm and deep sharing of professional and personal interests.

That fall found Lois and me hard at work organizing the research materials which we had been able to find in the field—Lois doing the child material, and I the adult. Simultaneously with my becoming Psychology Editor for Harpers, we brought out, in June of 1931, the first edition of *Experimental Social Psychology;* the Butler Medal at Columbia was awarded me the following year for this book. Of course, the most important thing was that Lois and I found ourselves with a specialization which we could share, and have shared ever since. This book helped to introduce me as a serious social psychologist, and doubtless helped me attract some of the stimulating students who came to the social psychology course. In 1937 we were joined by our dear friend, T. M. Newcomb, in revising this book.

Lois' background in child and clinical psychology made a huge impact on me too; she was constantly seeing personality issues of which I was astonishingly unaware. Her work, together with Eugene Lerner, Benjamin Spock, L. Joseph Stone, and their colleagues at Sarah Lawrence, leading to the studies on *Personality in Young Children* (1941), embodying her kind of sensitive study of the whole individual child, became primary in the development of my empirically grounded field theory of personality. While the term "field theory" was used generally to describe Kurt Lewin's approach, the actual meaning of the concepts as developed in my *Personality* (1947) book and in *Human Potentialities* (1958), were derived in large measure from the rich empirical material on child development which she was constantly working through.

The 1930's were exciting years in the New York intellectual world, with the gifted emigrés from Europe contributing to ongoing research as well as to therapy and the social sciences at the New School for Social Research inspired by their presence. Lois met Erik Erikson, Peter Blos, and Fritz Redl through her collaboration with Carolyn Zachry's psychoanalytically oriented adolescent study. Her collaboration with Anna Hartoch Schachtel led to our joint reading of Rorschach's *Psychodiagnostics* (1921).

This concern with personality development continued, and has played a big part in our years at The Menninger Foundation, where she has carried out intensive longitudinal studies of normal children who had been studied as infants, combining psychological, pediatric, psychiatric, and educational materials in a rich study of individuality. Her psychoanalytic training in Topeka deepened her approach and led to new concepts, building on the foundations she had built from her contact especially with Erikson.

But during the remaining years at Columbia (to 1940), social psychology was my major concern. I had made up a small project in 1928–29 for the study of social attitudes, organized around concepts of liberalism and conservatism, and Rensis Likert (who was then C. J. Warden's assistant in the animal laboratory) decided to work with me on this new project. It was then that he developed the Likert method of scaling attitudes. Actually he worked with me in the entire planning of the project, with support from the Columbia University Council for Research in the Social Sciences, during the years 1929 to 1932, when he got his Ph.D. It took a good deal of my time from 1932 to 1938 to write up the material which finally appeared under the title, *Public Opinion and the Individual* (with R. Likert, 1938). But this had started me on research in social psychology, and the next few dissertations were attitude and propaganda studies. Then they became more diversified. Several of them became studies which we would today call straight personality, rather than social research. I responded vigorously to David

Krech's organization of the Society for the Psychological Study of Social Issues, having taken part in the organizational meetings in Hanover in 1936, and becoming chairman in 1938. That was the same meeting of the APA in which I took part in J. L. Kennedy's symposium on ESP research. My professional life in those years was about two-thirds social psychology and most of the rest was parapsychology.

But this matter of the growth of personality study within the field of social psychology was penetrating more deeply into my whole outlook, and the kind of social psychology that meant most to me was personality research on a social basis, such as that of Ruth Benedict's *Patterns of Culture* (1934), Margaret Mead's *Cooperation and Competition Among Primitive Peoples* (1937), and Abraham Kardiner's *The Individual and his Society* (1939). The efforts at field theory, already mentioned, became the core of a personality theory on which I worked with intense delight, responding very keenly indeed to Harry Murray, to Kurt Lewin, and to J. L. Moreno. The key concept was the notion that the biological and the social are *literally the same events*. Defining a specific process in biological terms makes sense if we are looking at the organism at that moment; when we are looking at the social context, the same event is a part of social reality. Dozens of problems in the definition and measurement of personality suddenly change when viewed in this way.

The 1947 book on *Personality* evolved largely from the effort to integrate, in full-fledged literary form, all the major conceptions with which I had been working, just as the book on *Human Potentialities* in 1958 was an attempt to spell out the implications of field theory for the personality-and-culture problem, as it emerges with the question where man and his society are going, and what elements of planning and education are available for the fuller realization of the latent resources within, and the latent cultural structures which may emerge, to permit new man-world interactions.

The use of psychology in international relations had taken shape dimly in my thinking in the college years dominated by World War I. (In 1915 I gave an address in an oratorical competition entitled "A Larger Neutrality.") During the 1920's this came with increasing clarity to be seen as an important part of social psychology; Rensis Likert and I included "internationalism" among the issues dealt with in his 1932 dissertation. A good many "peace activities" occupied me at varying levels of effectiveness: Fellowship of Reconciliation, American Friends Service Committee, etc., and I edited a volume for The Society for the Psychological Study of Social Issues (SPSSI) entitled *Human Nature and Enduring Peace* (1945) which took up a good deal of time between 1941 and 1945. Some of the rudiments of a psychology relative to the prevention of war gradually became clear.

The whole groping effort found much more practical form when Robert Angell and Otto Klineberg asked me, in the fall of 1949, whether I was available to go to India for UNESCO to study the Hindu-Muslim conflict. This was to be financed by UNESCO, but involved reporting to the Government of India. In fact, Lois and I had always been interested in India, as we had both been students of comparative religion who felt somewhat at home in studies of Hinduism, Buddhism, Islam, and the other religions of South Asia. We had, of course, deep respect and enthusiasm for what Gandhi had been doing. Accordingly, with the enormously generous and wise guidance of Pars Ram of Forman Christian College, who was at the moment in New York, and the very helpful practical counsel of Professor C. N. Vakil of the Bombay School of Economics and Sociology who stopped in New York in March, 1950, we made a six months' visit in India from August of 1950 to January of 1951. Lois had simultaneously been invited to be a consultant on a plan for the B. M. Institute for Child Development initiated by Gautam Sarabhai of Ahmedabad, a leader in Indian educational and cultural activities. The trip gave her an opportunity for many village contacts and observation of child life and education, while for me it offered an opportunity to travel about from one Indian university to another, getting the help of Indian educational leaders at conferences, and in several cases in establishing research teams at these universities. The report on this exciting venture would probably have gathered dust for a long time, perhaps forever, had not Arthur Rosenthal of Basic Books asked for my report in book form, which appeared in 1953 under the title *In the Minds of Men*. This did *not* have a marked effect on Indian foreign policy, but it *did* have an effect on attitudes within the Indian universities towards the possibilities of doing social research which might make a difference in the national life.

I continued actively interested and worked with APA and SPSSI groups, giving many lectures on "psychology in international relations," and have learned much from the important new steps taken, as for example by Dan Katz through the Center for Conflict Resolution at the University of Michigan, Charles Osgood's worldwide studies by the semantic differential, Donald Michael's work at the Institute for Policy Studies, and Robert North's large-scale studies of war origins. My belief that a tiny dent on the war problem is being made by psychology is deeply gratifying.

## PERCEPTION AND COGNITION

A specific research focus began to take shape about 1935 when I offered a course in personality in the Columbia summer session, worked the personality material into my social psychology more and more, and formulated problems for a psychology of the person in the social situation; these appeared in master's theses and doctor's dissertations.

Almost simultaneously, in 1935 and 1936, my own version of field theory emerged (of which more below), and I began to formulate hypotheses for experimental testing in this field. Sherif was teaching me a great deal about the control of perception by factors in the person and in the environment which had been grossly neglected both by psychology and by the social sciences. Kurt Lewin, though I then knew him but slightly, soon began to push me too. Lois and I were both discovering more about Freud and Bleuler. All of this contributed to a conception which synthesized these, plus some Sherrington, to the effect that personality study has to be defined with an emphasis on the "input," the perceptual-cognitive side; that the personality is largely a way in which the world is viewed; that the problems of social psychology are determined by the confluence of outer and inner determiners, as in the following diagram later published in the book on *Personality* (1947, p. 8).

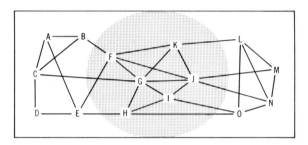

*All the functional relations within the shaded area, and between the shaded and unshaded areas, constitute personality. The shaded area is the organism.*

A personality is a structured organism-environment field, each aspect of which stands in dynamic relation to each other aspect. There is organization within the organism and organization within the environment, but it is the cross organization of the two that is investigated in personality research. (1947, p. 8)

To get at these problems of perception and cognition it was necessary, with Sherrington, to regard the exteroceptive, interoceptive, and proprioceptive systems as merging or pooling their energies in the centers, and to regard a psychology of personality as focused largely on the issue of how the interaction of these three input factors is actually effected. This meant, for experimental purposes, that there must be a systematic study of the role of drive in perception and thought. Looking back over the years, it began to be clear that many heroic figures in the history of psychology had grasped this, among them Nietzsche and Freud, and that the first great insight into a method for experimentally examining such phenomena was expressed in the work of Rorschach.

A large factor in my going to City College in 1940 was the opportunity to pursue this research theme. For it was here, in the years between 1940 and 1943, that the honors studies of Robert Levine, Harold Proshansky, Roy Schafer, Jerome Levine, and Leo Postman were carried out under my general guidance.

Robert Levine's study, taking much of the inspiration from H. A. Murray and from the published studies of R. Nevitt Sanford, showed, in response to pictures, the relation of frequency of food-naming responses to the time since eating. Harold Proshansky found that objects seen with difficulty in a dark room took on characteristic associations with monetary rewards. Roy Schafer reported that in an ambiguous figure-ground situation, a *rewarded* component tends to stand out as figure. Jerome Levine found that political attitudes influenced the learning and forgetting of controversial material. Leo Postman's study showed that attitude influenced associative memory.

Historically, the primary credit for laboratory studies of these influences of drive, feeling, affect, motive, etc., upon perception belongs to Harry Murray and his associates at Harvard, with R. N. Sanford the first to publish a report on such effects. Our City College studies followed for several years thereafter, and were of course, followed, and in many ways extended, elaborated, and improved by Bruner and Postman at Harvard immediately after World War II. These interests remained keen with me during the City College period, and in 1951 Julian Hochberg and I reformulated them. But the City College situation became less and less favorable for the prosecution of such studies, as practically all able psychology students were heading for clinical psychology and saw relatively little significance in these laboratory approaches. It was also obvious that a larger canvas was necessary on which to work. The opportunity to pursue this kind of investigation at The Menninger Foundation, beginning in 1952, was again my primary reason for a professional shift. During the years here at The Menninger Foundation as Director of Research, my own primary research interest has been in the continuation of these studies, which were integrated into a book mainly written by my collaborator, Charles M. Solley, in 1960, and in a series of papers.

## PERSONALITY THEORY

This conception of the relation of perception and cognition to the affective life, and to the learning process, was really the core of a complete personality system, as I saw it. It appears in brief form in Chapter 39 of *Personality* (1947), and is spelled out a bit more in the *Human Potentialities* (1958), and various short papers. But perhaps the growth of my general outlook on personality is best indicated by first describing the components in such a system as I used in the 1930's, and the mode of their articulation. This will, in a sense, "place" and likewise "date" me, but it may have the advantage of showing what I accept from the major systems of the modern era.

Some inkling of the direction in which I was going emerged in 1931, when Lois and I were in the Grand Canyon. It became clear to me that it was the inner world of the person that was most real to me, and that personality study would be my primary concern. Within a few months of that time I found myself writing and editing *Approaches to Personality* (with F. Jensen, 1932), which presented six systematic positions. First came the "Psychology and Mental Elements" which was classical sensationistic or associationistic psychology, the representation of which by Titchener had delighted me. I could readily follow his conception of sensations, images, and feelings, and the various ways in which higher-order realities were represented by association and attention. This kind of elementarism was compared with the elementarism of Janet in which the mind is reducible, at any one time, to components which may be put together in various ways under the influence of "psychic tension." Then I went on to the behaviorist approach which, in those years, meant mainly Watson, from which I expected to borrow a good deal, especially with reference to the use made of classical conditioning in normal and psychopathological events. Here close friendship with Harold and Mary Jones, who later established the Institute of Child Welfare Research at Berkeley, did much to bring the system close. Working on the Russian and American backgrounds for the *Historical Introduction to Modern Psychology* (1929) had given me a positive feeling towards the Watsonian system, although I felt that it was grossly defective in its handling of the learning processes and arbitrary and arrogant in its neglect of problems for which it did not have any tools. Then came the Gestalt approach, to which I had been awakened when R. M. Ogden described it at the APA in 1922. I was delighted with Köhler and Koffka as they came to our shores in this era, and poured into this little treatment of my own an enthusiastic account of the conception of personality as Gestalt which Wertheimer, Wolff, and Arnheim had been sketching out in Germany. Participation in a conversation with Wertheimer and Stern at the King's Crown Hotel in New York in 1933 was one of the great events of my professional life: Wertheimer pleading for universal Gestalt, Stern insisting that there was also *Ungestalt*. In the latter half of that 1932 book, my collaborator, Friedrich Jensen, handled psychoanalysis, analytical psychology, and individual psychology—his bias being towards the last of these. My good friend, John Levy, an analyst, added an appendix on the child guidance approach to personality.

This six-fold conception of *Approaches to Personality* (with F. Jensen, 1932) stayed with me until 1935 and 1936, when I found myself inclining to make less and less of the Titchenerian approach, and more and more of the evolutionary background, and to emphasize both phylogenetic and ontogenetic approaches to personality. I decided to call this the "organic" approach, meaning the approach in terms of *organism* (believing then, as I do still, that the distinction in psychiatry between "functional" and "organic" is slippery and often unmanageable, and that all psychological functions can be viewed as functions of an organic system, whether intact, or slightly disturbed, or patently damaged). I began at the same time to be more and more impressed with the anthropological contributions to personality study.

By the end of the 1930's the seven major approaches which I used in my own thinking and teaching were: (1) the organic approach (with a good deal of genetics and physiology); (2) the behavioristic, with emphasis upon classical conditioning (a little on operant conditioning too, but without a very sharp and clear theoretical separation of the two); (3) the Gestalt approach, emphasizing mainly perceptual learning and finding ways in which both the organic system as a whole, and the classical conditioning concepts helped to explain emotionally loaded forms of perceiving and thinking—what I came to call, after Bleuler, "autism." (4) Then the discussion of perception led to a fairly ambitious self-psychology, which led on into the presentation of (5) Freudian psychoanalysis, followed by brief concern with Jung and Adler, leading then (6) into a social science definition of personality utilizing all the foregoing concepts, and culminating in (7) field theory.

I have sufficiently indicated my biases, but will say just a few words more. I still think the sensationist and other atomistic approaches are entirely legitimate but have a very limited scope; the same for all systems which claim to be "objective"; for as Hollingworth shrewdly pointed out, systems called objective are systems preferring exteroceptive over other sources of information, but there are also good enteroceptive, proprioceptive, and memoric sources; no magical results are achieved for science by being so "objective" as to exclude them.

Regarding Freud's psychoanalysis, on which I have expressed myself a number of times, I believe we are dealing with the greatest genius which has appeared in psychological history, and that the question of finding the ultimate realities underneath this magnificent system will keep us busy for at least a century. The ideas essential for the general psychologist and the personality psychologist can probably be stated in a few hundred pages; and the primary problem today is probably not *testing psychoanalytic hypotheses*, but rather, in the manner of an astronomer or a geologist, *systematizing observations,* using now an experimental, now a developmental, now a comparative, now a mathematical approach.

To write, however, that psychoanalysis is the most challenging and the most comprehensive system we now have is not to say that it is correct, or what part of it is correct. I believe that anyone who tosses it aside as "unscientific" might profit by reading Jonathan Swift's gay little essay embedded within *Gulliver's Travels,* tossing off Newton and his new universe. Newton was wrong on many points, and paranoid on some, but that does not settle any procedural issues for his followers. On the other hand I think the devotion of Freudians to Freud—and sometimes to ideas which he himself revised or even rejected—puts them into continuous binds. A hundred years after Darwin's *Origin of Species* one does not spend a large part of one's time in biological research deciding exactly what Darwin meant and why he was right here and wrong there, or justify one's own conceptions as against those of others. One spends one's time not defending Darwin, but using him as a guide to fresh observations. Psychoanalysis could be the most important part of modern psychology if it were treated in the way evolutionary theory is treated, as a way of schematizing observations in a process involving endless vital redefinition of concepts in the light of fresh experience, and fresh method.

Perhaps I am color blind to Jung. I like to float along with his prose, but do not feel that his brilliant descriptions help me to understand the *why* of what he helps me to observe. Regarding Adler, the shoe is on the other foot: I think he was painfully correct, as Thomas Hobbes was painfully correct, in his ultra-simple formulations of inferiority, compensation, life style, and the social definition of health and illness. He kept saying the same thing on and on, and there is not very much more that one can say except to repeat what he said. We do not seem to be able to use ultra-simple, clear ideas in psychology. They have to be complicated to hold our interest.

## RECURRING EMPHASES

Among the more specific ideas which I have invested with strong self-quality, which I think of as "really me," are the ideas of autism, canalization, Spencerian three-phase evolutionary theory, feedback (especially proprioceptive feedback theory), and the type of field theory which I have described above. It would be tedious to spell them out in detail here; I will just tag them for anyone who cares to pursue them.

By autism (cf. 1947, p. 365) I mean the movement of the cognitive processes in the direction of need satisfaction. (This is similar to, but a bit simpler than either Bleuler's "autistic thinking" or Freud's "primary process.") By canalization I mean approximately what Pierre Janet meant by this term (and by his concept of "draining"): *diffuse and scattered energies (tensions) tend to flow into dominant channels;* that is, needs tend to become more specific in consequence of being satisfied in specific ways. This simple idea I have compared and contrasted with McDougall's "sentiment-formation," Woodworth's "mechanisms which become drives," Gordon Allport's "functional autonomy," Tinbergen and Lorenz's "imprinting"—though had I known of the work on imprinting in 1947, I would have done a better job. I still think the concept of canalization has value.

By Spencerian three-phase evolutionary theory I mean the doctrine that all reality (physical, biological, psychological, sociological) tends to move from homogeneous (undifferentiated) through heterogeneous (differentiated) to structured (integrated) reality. But J. Hughlings Jackson and Heinz Werner have done such magnificent things with these conceptions that I am content to let my elaboration shine entirely through their light.

With feedback theory, which derives, as I use it, from Helmholtz and

Sherrington (and owes little to modern cybernetics), I have attempted in recent years to construct a *theory of reality-testing,* and of the mode of escape from autistic self-deception. This is partially incorporated in a book now seeking its way into published form, with Herbert Spohn as co-author, and I will not jeopardize its chances by prematurely trying to blurt out what it must say slowly and sensibly.

These are all *developmental* concepts. Since my approach is always couched in developmental terms, I was early drawn to a concern with genetics; one of the big events of my professional life was a conference on behavior genetics at Bar Harbor, 1946, and I am constantly trying to view personality problems simultaneously in genetic and in socio-cultural terms.

## PSYCHICAL RESEARCH

But all through these years I was leading a double life, for psychical research was just as real and important to me as it had ever been. It had become obvious that the problems were much more complicated than I had seen, and that I was by no means as good an experimenter—either in this or in other fields—as I thought I was. I found excellent collaborators in J. G. Pratt and Ernest Taves, who worked with me at Columbia on ESP problems a little later after J. B. Rhine's first book on that subject came out, and with J. L. Woodruff at City College. With the stipend from the Richard Hodgson Fund of Harvard, I guided some studies by these men. Later I was able to use the stipend from this fellowship, 1942 to 1951, for the studies by Dr. Gertrude R. Schmeidler (with McConnell, 1958), looking for attitudinal and deeper personality factors in the successes in ESP which continued to come our way under controlled conditions in which materials were randomized and concealed. When they were treated by standard statistics, they consistently showed positive results to depend upon intra-organismic factors of sorts which we crudely described under the term "attitude," and later, under personality dimensions that enter into the more complex Rorschach, TAT, Rosenzweig, and other such personality evaluation techniques.

Thus while writing the *Personality* book, I was at the same time guiding the parapsychological studies just mentioned, and a series of other studies led by Laura Dale and others at the American Society for Psychical Research, of which I became a vice-president. A large quiet room was available, and I did far more experimentation and writing, both in the personality field and in psychical research, than I ever could have done under ordinary academic conditions. Incidentally, when Hall and Lindzey prepared their book on *Theories of Personality* (1957), they had the graciousness and the patience to get the whole story of my interest in parapsychology compressed in clear, orderly terms, quite faithfully representing the kind of belief and the kind of research activity which is characteristic of my life in this field.

The removal to The Menninger Foundation in no way impaired these opportunities, and as good chance would have it, two grants came to The Menninger Foundation for me to administer, dealing with "Creativity and Its Relation to Extrasensory Perception." Investigators were chosen, wherever they were, who had shown interest and competence in these problems, and given support to expand their work in their own institutions. Believing that it is not only legitimate, but imperative, for psychologists to work in areas far beyond the beaten path of existing methods or full-fledged conceptualized systems, I believe, as Donald Hebb (1951) well puts it, that if one were to judge as one ordinarily judges evidence, one would accept ESP. Hebb, at this point, says that the reason why he does not accept it is that it "does not make sense." If this statement recognizes that events which do not make sense from the point of view of science at any given time, can make sense as science advances, I would fully agree. How far can any new science get by laying down rules as to what can and what cannot happen? My interest was not in odds and ends; it was in the extension and maturing of a psychology which I thought now big enough to struggle with what it could not easily fit into its systems.

But any system will disintegrate sooner or later if it is brought into confrontation with fundamental facts which it cannot assimilate. Although a dozen powerful minds have made the attempt, I do not know anyone who has effectively assimilated the literature of psychical research into a general psychological system, nor, on the other hand, anyone who has found a way of building a separate system for parapsychological findings in which they have their own nontroublesome, independent existence. The scientific challenge to create a kind of field theory sufficiently open to provide a place for the main parapsychological findings still stands. I have published extensively along these lines, but the best I can do today is still a pretty poor thing. It would make use of a monism, rather of Spinoza's type as taught me by Troland at Harvard in 1916, according to which all reality is both physical and mental, seen on the one side through the exteroceptors (especially when aided with microscopes looking at brains) and seen on the inside as we describe our own experiences. Yet this kind of double aspect theory is not, as of now, able to handle very well what seem to be the realities of telepathic and clairvoyant contact with events occurring outside the living organic system. I rather suspect that we are dealing here with difficulties in the definition of time and space, and we confront a "rubber sheet" type of phenomenon in which the events with which we make contact are not really "at a distance," or "in the future." The little figure and comment which I am enclosing here may perhaps convey something of the time-space and cognition theory (1964, p. 243).

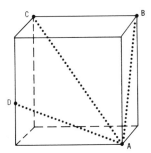

*Time-space schema in the form of a transparent cube.*

I am going to attempt here a graphic image of the ordinary time-space schema which I have set up in the form of a transparent hollow cube. Imagine that ordinarily we move along the surface, but not within, and not outside of this cube. Imagine the time-space relations as binding us to travel or make communication only along the six surfaces of this cube. I suggest that all the space within this hollow cube allows straight lines to be drawn from one point to another, which is possible, hypothetically, just because the cube is hollow, and the lines visible just because it is transparent. From this viewpoint, I suggest that getting from A to B, or from B to C, or to any other determined point on the surface of the cube, is similar to the ordinary sensory contacts that we make with other events at other points in space or time; but I also suggest that there are, as we envisage the possibility, other ways of getting from one point to another, other ways of transcending the time-space problem. I suggest that the paranormal may force us to consider communication within and outside of the cube, types of communication not limited to the six surfaces already indicated.

One must probably accommodate to what appear to be facts, but without giving up the essentially monistic or double-aspect theory of mind; mind is seen as an aspect of the living system. If you ask what it would mean to say that this theory is "true," the reply would be that it is not "true" or "false," but has a fifty-fifty chance of being in the right direction, and in the meantime is open-ended, ready to be stretched by facts into new forms.

## TEACHING PSYCHOLOGY

As a college teacher beginning in 1920, and a teacher of graduate students beginning the following year, I developed at Columbia some rather strong convictions about effective teaching of psychology. There was plainly a need for a strongly factual empirical presentation. We reorganized the elementary course in 1930, using selections and mimeographed portions of the work of Watson, Piaget, Margaret Mead, and whoever proved to be interesting and challenging. There was patently a need for a chance for students to learn by discussion, either through question-answer argumentive discussion in the lecture period or in a special discussion hour. Going to City College in 1940, I pushed a little further in this direction, teaching a course on personality from the systematic viewpoint as described, with emphasis upon facts and ideas considered useful in a large lecture class, and then meeting small sections for discussion thereafter.

I loved my teaching, partly because it was satisfying to offer a balanced conception of the field and to exchange ideas with eager students. At Columbia I was in charge of the undergraduate psychology and taught the large lecture classes in the introductory course, and the history and social to graduate students. During the years at City College I went back three years to teach Otto Klineberg's Monday afternoon social psychology classes at Columbia when he was away. These years also included teaching at the New School one evening a week, alternating between the history course and a course on the psychology of personality. It was what I taught that I really began to understand and to organize; and the publications followed, in large measure, from such efforts.

I have done a great deal of public extramural lecturing too, and have felt just as strongly in those situations that feedback, argument, discussion, learning by confrontation of more or less incompatible ideas, were esssential in all real education. Believing strongly in an active, rather than a passive, kind of learning, I also believe that the teacher as a person is a very vital part of the teaching process. It was gratifying when the John Dewey Society asked me to give in 1961 a lecture on my conception of this role of the teacher. I was likewise grateful to Eugene Hartley and John Peatman for saying a bit about my convictions and habits in the teaching stiuation, which they generously put into the preface of the *Festschrift* given me in 1960.

But, of course, teaching at the person-to-person level was also possible in a very rewarding way in the handling of master's essays and Ph.D. dissertations at Columbia, Honors Research Studies at City College, and contact with post- and pre-doctoral research people at The Menninger Foundation. With the years I find myself being taught more and more in such encounters, because a modern generation of students has gone through a lot of psychology that I was never taught, and a great deal of it rubs off on me in one way or another. The teaching process then becomes mainly a dyadic way of trying to solve a problem, and the conversation never really ends. It is self-evident to anyone who knows me that I have learned a great deal more psychology from Lois than from any other living person.

This conception of the multidisciplinary study of man which has taken shape with such vigor and such rich promise in the last few decades has meant for me a really radical change in the conception of psychological *method.* As a psychology major at Yale, I had believed intensely in the transcendent importance of experimentation as against all other methods. R. P. Angier and Horace English assigned us reaction time, warm-cold-touch-pain

spots, association tests, perimetry, and the rest, following Titchener's guide-
lines, as devotedly as anyone could. Horace said one day in the laboratory,
"There are your facts, Gardner; go after them." There was no possible alternative, either in external behavior or in internal commitment. At that time
I was sure that this devotion to the facts (mainly at the level of sensory and
associative processes) would ultimately lead to a sound and systematic experimental psychology dealing with every issue to which the term "psychological" can be applied.

Gradually, the teaching of developmental psychology and the interest
in heredity, which began to mean more and more to me in the early 1920's,
led to a changed perspective. Exposure everywhere to comparative psychology enriched the evolutionary approach which I had been assimilating at
a deeper level ever since the course with Keller at Yale. Charlotte Bühler's
studies of children were really, as she said, *social science* contributions. I
began to see how all these ideas, in connection with Freud, made psychopathology a part of a general psychological system and not a special recess
or eddy at the fringe.

Various approaches or methods began to be seen in relation to one another. The concept of ecology, as it slowly made its way into social psychology, seemed to require that all events be seen as transactions (as Dewey and
Bentley were to say) and that quantitative studies of environments—both its
components and its structural organization—were absolutely essential if even
the simplest psychological reality were to be grasped. What Egon Brunswik
was so magnificently developing conceptually and experimentally, filtered
through to me in a somewhat more turbid form as I struggled with anthropological and historical materials, preparing materials, for example, for the
Committee on Historiography of the American Historical Association as it
worked for the Social Science Research Council. All of this, of course, began
to come together under high pressure, enriching the rather abstract schema
of field theory that I had begun to sketch in 1936.

For many problems, such as those problems we are working on here
at The Menninger Foundation, the *experimental* method has to be *salient*.
At the same time, the experimental method does very different things with
a problem when it is seen in terms of the methodological system I have been
trying to sketch.

Of course, one must remember the tragedy of today's psychology in
which experimentalists and clinicians, from their earliest days, take a sort
of Hannibalian oath against one another. The clinicians swear that they will
never take the piddling, petty, rigid, narrow, atomistic approach of the experimentalists, and the experimentalists take an equally turgid vow that they
will never be concerned with the vague, amorphous, intuitive, sloppy, confused, unsystematic, and irresponsible position of the clinician. Naturally,
many of those who represent the great tradition in other sciences look at us
with "a plague on both your houses" or with a feeling of utter helplessness,

wondering why the study of man has to split him as in the judgment of Solomon. Perhaps if he were torn apart like a Chinese laundry ticket, and the parts could still be put together, he would be viable. But with the way we teach the Ph.D. candidates today, how is this going to happen?

## RESONANCE TO WILLIAM JAMES

My devotion to William James began very early, waxed strong in encountering his *Varieties of Religious Experience* in 1916, and became a steady passion as I read through the whole *Principles* in the summer of 1920 when working with Fred Wells at McLean Hospital. I encountered him in new contexts when working on the *Historical Introduction to Modern Psychology;* put him to use in connection with the theory of the self during the 1930's; read aloud, with Lois, his 1920 collection of letters published by his son, and, again with Lois, read through the two-volume *Thought and Character of William James* by Ralph Barton Perry in the 1940's. I used James constantly in connection with psychical research over all these and later years; gladly accepted Robert Ballou's suggestion that we edit together a volume on *William James on Psychical Research* (1960); and found him standing nearby, always ready to be consulted, and often profoundly helpful in connection with studies at The Menninger Foundation on perception, attention, thought processes, the will, and the whole evolutionary approach to the growth of the mind. I have several times attempted brief characterizations of him, as in the *Historical Introduction to Modern Psychology,* especially in the revised edition (1949, pp. 207–209), and in *Personality* (1947, pp. 22–27), as well as in the introduction and summary to *William James on Psychical Research* (1960). Several times I have taught courses on the psychology of William James.

Regarding "systems" in psychology, it nearly always happens that facts discovered by people with radically different viewpoints ultimately have to be comprised and integrated within a conceptual scheme. Every science does this, and psychology, the data of which are so extraordinarily complex and of so many different orders, has to do it on almost every page of its systematic effort. With a strange lack of perspective regarding the history of such matters, this integration is often called "eclectic," and is said to involve the wrenching of shreds and patches from different systems in which they have meaning into a new crazy quilt in which they have no meaning. This misses, I think, the entire substance of the issue. The facts which have arisen in many different systems or moods of observation or with tools of precision must be carefully scrutinized and their status thought through with reference to one's own coherent position. This issue was briefly discussed in *Approaches to Personality* (1932, ch. 8), and I have lived with such a faith ever since. My book *Personality* (1947) gratefully accepts observations from many systems, but attempts its own system. *I believe firmly in system;* in much more system than is ordinarily found. But in addition, I very firmly reject the idea that in order to build a system you must look only at certain corners or only through certain tubes.

My objection to the behaviorist system, for example, is that there are vast regions of human experience at which it cannot, dare not, or will not (choose your own term) look. I think, for example, that dreams, images, joys, griefs, and experiences of frustration are, in their own right, of enormous importance. It does not help me to say that behaviorists want to study "verbal reports" of these experiences. That would be like saying that an astronomer would like to study "verbal reports" of nebulae or comets. An astronomer experiences a comet, but he integrates the observation with much other evidence. The behaviorist is right in using exteroceptive channels, but so are other people right when they use enteroceptive channels or observe states that are not exteroceptively observable. In studying affects, we need verbal reports, but we likewise need much other evidence—some of it physiological, some of it clinical, some of it phenomenological. If psychology makes up its mind that it will only use a certain kind of sensory input, or certain modes of perceptual or conceptual analysis, it dooms itself to a warped picture. From an evolutionary point of view, it was the whole species that survived, and in terms of genetic and embryological realities, it is the whole individual that has survived in the growth process. To say that certain aspects of this total individual are irrelevant to science seems to me to impoverish science. Events may differ in the order of their objectivity and specificity. But it has been the rule in the history of science that the fuzzy and nonspecific out at the fringe get pulled into the focus of the real and become, in time, data of central significance.

Again, just as one might say that everything is good about behaviorism except its unwillingness to look in certain quarters, the only thing that is wrong with Gestalt psychology is that there are kinds of realities at which it does not look. The enormous importance of the role of feeling or drive in the perceptual and cognitive life was oddly enough overlooked as long as possible by the Gestalt psychology, which had been looking for principles of closure, membership-character, and so forth, in the cognitive life, but reluctant to find the same principles appearing in the perceptual-affective-impulsive integrations. Fortunately, this narrowness is disappearing, but Gestalt psychology laid itself open to the same criticism to which behaviorism is subject, namely, unwillingness to look.

Regarding psychoanalysis and the other psychotherapeutic or psychopathological systems, the same principle holds. Freud had an exceptionally brilliant moment in 1895 when he wrote the "Project for a Scientific Psychology," for there was a way in which physiological and psychological realities could all be seen in terms of one broad mountain-top outlook. He put it away in the belief that it was premature. Maybe it was. It is fascinating today to see the skill with which investigators like Hernández-Peón are writing a sort of double-language system in which psychophysiological realities are one, not two; or rather, in which a double language-system refers to the same central biological realities. Just as Spinoza in the seventeenth century saw, there are two (or more) aspects of all psychological realities; indeed, today it is entirely possible to write an experiential, a preconscious, an unconscious, a neurophysiological, a biochemical, or a broadly functional description of the same system of events. All of these are aspects of something which in nature is not divided up according to disciplines or techniques.

The only thing uncongenial to me in any school or system of psychology is its tendency to put up exclusive barriers or throw things into "wastebaskets." Wastebaskets, like those of the Middle Kingdom in Egypt, have turned out to yield most interesting things to people of another era. The one great danger to the jet-like scientific development in psychology is that it will throw out the things that cannot be picked up while going at its present speed, and using the present instruments of observation. It will pay terribly. In fact, it is already paying in the sense of losing contact with the thoughtful people in other sciences (many of whom cannot understand why psychology is so narrow and pedantic), and of course, likewise historians, creative artists, and the professional men who very much want a psychology that aspires at least to completeness and to closeness to the human nature which makes up their primary interest in life.

## PHILOSOPHY

I have mentioned my excitement and delight from reading history of philosophy in the Widener Library in the summer of 1916. I went on reading philosophy off and on in connection with teaching the history of psychology, in connection with the elements of social philosophy that came nearest to social psychology, and in connection with the whole attempt to see where psychology stands among the divisions of knowledge and research. Naturally I wanted to think through some problems and state them clearly enough to have some impact, and it was partly along these lines that the book *Human Potentialities* (1958) was conceived and written. I have always, however, been more ambitious regarding a possible contribution to philosophy and a contribution which such a publication might make to contemporary thinking. Apparently here, as in some other branches of thought, I exaggerated what I could do. But the considerable amount of traveling that we have done, and the delight which Lois and I have had in reading philosophy aloud to one another—Bergson, for example, and Nietzsche—have served to make this a considerably more important part of my professional life as a psychologist than has been evident to my friends.

This belief that I have something to offer, in a philosophical vein, expresses itself also in an ambitious effort that Lois and I have made for a multivolume presentation of the world's psychological classics—ancient and modern, Eastern and Western—which is rather far along at this writing, under the general title, *The World of the Mind*. We are not making a frantic struggle to complete this at the moment, but if we live to complete it, it will give a somewhat more rounded picture of the interrelations of philosophy and psychology than is generally available, and it will work out more fully the position which I hold on many fundamental psychological concepts and the ways in which they can be resolved by combinations of experimental, genetic, comparative, physiological, sociocultural methods of investigation.

This much can be said here about the philosophical position which I have held for some forty-odd years: while I cannot agree with James' suggestion for a "pluralistic universe," a universe lacking essential unity of form or process, I do believe that from the tiny little gob of time-space which we occupy, we cannot see the universe as a whole. We can only sample it by short-range terrestrial observations and by spotty snatches into time and space by the methods of astronomy. We must pay a great deal of attention to the range of experiences that come to us as a result of exceptional sampling from rare, unusual stimulation. Our joys and griefs in the normal course of life have to be eked out by studies of stress, fatigue, psychosis, the effects of special training techniques like some of those from India, and of special biochemical states induced by psychedelic drugs, as well as by studies of more extraordinary experiences of prophetic and inspirational leaders and indeed of those poets, painters, sculptors, architects, and composers who translate us into a world so very different from the ordinary world of our eyes, ears, and skin. Not that I really believe that we can "see life steadily and see it whole"; but I do believe that by combining and extrapolating beyond all these ways of experience, we can make educated guesses that are slightly better than those which we can make without them. I believe also that the methods of science, piercing as they do into mathematical and logical structure and into the physical world which is only represented here and there by a ripple of visible reality, lead to a conception that the unknowable, to put it mildly, is probably "pretty big," and the knowable but not yet realizable, though not as big as the unknowable, is still pretty big also. From this point of view, any statement such as "science has conclusively proven" or "the world certainly is . . . ." strikes me as immature. I think our main task in psychology is to increase the fringe around the present fragmentary little facts and to extend our methods not only towards the development of richer sampling of the immediate reality but towards greater comprehensiveness, bolder probing of the infinite unknown.

This viewpoint would make me regard man as probably a very small portion of life, and life as a very small portion of the world. Yet insofar as man's makeup may be isomorphic with the broader nature of life or even of the cosmos, we might steal a march on nature frequently by looking more closely within ourselves. The importance of majestic creativeness like that of Rembrandt or Beethoven or Shakespeare lies not in its being a "special case," but rather in its being a general case, that is, a finger pointing towards realities we have not well sampled; and in this same way, unusual states, states of ecstasy, revelation, or "cosmic consciousness" may have implications not just for psychology, but for the meaning of the whole show.

It is quite likely also that the oddments, the little fragmented particles which come our way in the realm of parapsychology are important. Perhaps they are important in the same way as the odd behavior Galvani noted in a frog's nerve, or the odd behavior of the dark "companion of Sirius" confirming Einstein's general theory of relativity—as telltale indications of something which will be explored and ultimately assimilated in a kind of knowledge of which our present little slice of increasing knowledge from Galileo through Einstein and Planck and Heisenberg may be only a tiny droplet.

Certainly Dewey was right that one's personality shapes one's philosophy. An enduring and growing trait of mine has been a passionate need for *inclusiveness*. My attempt to have in the picture everything that could be gotten into it, my need for an absolutely inclusive structure barring nothing, may be related perhaps to the "underdog" pattern, or to the "don't leave me out" pattern. But it probably had other components, particularly some that became prominent in the college years. I became restless with one-sided approaches or oversimplified solutions.

This certainly has some relation to my strong feeling that psychology is sound and vital only when it accepts and welcomes all the evidence, all the viewpoints, all the facts, all the systematic potentialities that can be offered. You have to conduct test tube isolation and mathematical abstraction in all science, but you do not do this by throwing away the things that do not get into the test tube or the abstraction. Other test tubes and other abstractions are always available. Other pockets and other ways of generalizing can be found; it is all of reality that we want and the context is important for the understanding of any specific datum. He proceeds at his peril who takes a cavalier attitude towards anything in heaven or earth. The conception that we know what makes sense, the conception that the world, after three centuries of science, is at last clear and known to us by the methods of today, strikes me as one of the most extraordinary blind spots of the ages; and that it occurs among psychologists, not only among men of the marketplace, strikes me as one more confirmation of the terrific need, if reality is to be seen, that all kinds of people, all kinds of methods, all kinds of ideas be winnowed, screened, and studied; none arbitrarily rejected and none arbitrarily accepted, but all brought humbly yet systematically before the reviewing stand of determined reality seeking.

# REFERENCES

*Selected Publications by Gardner Murphy*

*Historical introduction to modern psychology.* New York: Harcourt, Brace & World, 1929.

(Ed.) *An outline of abnormal psychology.* New York: Modern Library, 1929.

*Experimental social psychology.* New York: Harper & Row, 1931.

(with F. Jensen) *Approaches to personality.* New York: Coward-McCann, 1932.

*A briefer general psychology.* New York: Harper & Row, 1935.

(with L. B. Murphy & T. M. Newcomb) *Experimental social psychology.* (rev. ed.) New York: Harper & Row, 1937. (original edition, 1931)

(with R. Likert) *Public opinion and the individual.* New York: Harper & Row, 1938.

(with H. Proshansky) The effects of reward and punishment on perception. *J. Psychol.,* 1942, *13,* 295–305.

(with R. Levine & I. Chein) The relation of the intensity of a need to the amount of perceptual distortion: a preliminary report. *J. Psychol.,* 1942, *13,* 282–293.

(with R. Schafer) The role of autism in figure-ground relationships. *J. exp. Psychol.,* 1943, *32,* 335–343.

(with L. Postman) The factor of attitude in associative memory. *J. exp. Psychol.,* 1943, *33,* 228–238.

(Ed.) *Human nature and enduring peace.* Boston: Houghton Mifflin, 1945.

*Personality: a biosocial approach to origins and structure.* New York: Harper & Row, 1947.

*Historical introduction to modern psychology.* (rev. ed.) New York: Harcourt, Brace & World, 1949. (original edition, 1929)

(with J. E. Hochberg) Perceptual development: some tentative hypotheses. *Psychol. Rev.,* 1951, *58,* 332–347.

*An introduction to psychology.* New York: Harper & Row, 1951.

*In the minds of men: a UNESCO study of social tensions in India.* New York: Basic Books, 1953.

(with A. J. Bachrach, Eds.) *An outline of abnormal psychology.* (rev. ed.) New York: Modern Library, 1954. (original edition, 1929)

Affect and perceptual learning. *Psychol. Rev.,* 1956, *63,* 1–15.

Notes for a parapsychological autobiography. *J. Parapsychol.,* 1957, *21,* 165–178.

*Human potentialities.* New York: Basic Books, 1958.

Organism and quantity: a study of organic structure as a quantitative problem. In B. Kaplan & S. Wapner (Eds.), *Perspectives in psychological theory: essays in honor of Heinz Werner.* New York: International Universities Press, 1960, 179–208.

(with R. Ballou, Eds.) *William James on psychical research.* New York: Viking, 1960.

(with C. M. Solley) *Development of the perceptual world.* New York: Basic Books, 1960.

(with the collaboration of Laura A. Dale) *Challenge of psychical research: a primer of parapsychology.* New York: Harper & Row, 1961.

*Freeing intelligence through teaching: a dialectic of the rational and the personal.* New York: Harper & Row, 1961.

Robert Sessions Woodworth, 1869–1962. *Amer. Psychologist,* 1963, *18,* 131–133.

Lawfulness versus caprice: is there a "law of psychic phenomena"? *J. Amer. Soc. psych. Res.,* 1964, *58,* 238–249.

## Other Publications Cited

Baldwin, J. M. *Mental development in the child and the race.* New York: Macmillan, 1895.

Benedict, R. *Patterns of culture.* Boston: Houghton Mifflin, 1934.

Boring, E. G. *A history of experimental psychology.* New York: Appleton-Century-Crofts, 1929.

Brett, G. S. *History of psychology.* London: G. Allen, 1921. 3 vols.

Freud, S. Project for a scientific psychology. In *Origins of psychoanalysis.* New York: Basic Books, 1954. (Originally circulated in 1895).

Hall, C. S. & Lindzey, G. *Theories of personality.* New York: Wiley, 1957.

Hebb, D. The role of neurological ideas in psychology. *J. Pers.,* 1951, *20,* 39–55.

James, W. *Principles of psychology.* New York: Holt, 1890. 2 vols.

Kardiner, A. *The individual and his society.* New York: Columbia, 1939.

Ladd, G. T. & Woodworth, R. S. *Elements of physiological psychology.* (rev. ed.) New York: Scribner, 1911.

Locke, J. *Essay concerning human understanding.*

Lynd, R. & Lynd, Helen M. *Middletown: a study in contemporary American culture.* New York: Harcourt, Brace & World, 1929.

Masefield, J. *Poems.* New York: Macmillan, 1955.

Mead, M. *Cooperation and competition among primitive peoples.* New York: McGraw-Hill, 1937.

Murphy, Lois B. *Personality in young children.* 2 vols. New York: Basic Books, 1956. (Originally published in 1941).

Peatman, J. G. & Hartley, E. L. (Eds.) *Festschrift for Gardner Murphy.* New York: Harper & Row, 1960.

Rorschach, H. *Psychodiagnostics.* Berne: Hans Auber, 1942. (Originally published in 1921).

Schmeidler, G. R. & McConnell, R. A. *ESP and personality patterns.* New Haven: Yale, 1958.

Spencer, H. *First principles.* New York: Appleton, 1900.

Swift, J. *Gulliver's travels.* (part III, chs. 2–3).

Henry A. Murray

# Henry A. Murray

## PROLOGUE

It occurred to me that the easiest way for a veteran examiner of men to cope with this present assignment would be to hold the mirror up to the manifestations of his own nature pretty much as he would do in the case of any individual who volunteered as subject for exposure to the threatening and dubious procedures of assessment. This notion was particularly inviting at this moment since it offered me a chance to illustrate the applicability of some unfamiliar ideas to which I am nowadays attached, and since, by so doing, I might alleviate to some extent the tedium of a long parade of unexciting and unilluminated facts. Full of enthusiasm I embarked on the execution of this plan with the special purpose of representing and explaining the professional mentational history of my subject, whose pseudonym is Murr, in terms of the theoretical system to which I currently subscribe; but in due course I found myself involved in the conceptualization of the *concrete* system of mental operations by which Murr had arrived at the *theoretical* system, the very terms of which I was then using to conceptualize the concrete system which produced them. It was not till I arrived at these complications that I concluded that this mode of coping with the task would be impossible within the space that was fittingly allotted us. I had been yielding, once again, to an expansive, omnivorous, sanguine disposition (the "sanguine surplus," let us say for short) which leads me to start by envisaging every new, appealing undertaking in the most voluminous dimensions, huge and teeming with every possibility of adventure and achievement. I have illustrated this impediment to sound science at the outset because it is one of those temperamental forces which, however exhilarating and fructifying, has rocked or wrecked a whole procession of enterprises, despite the continued existence in my head of the corrective maxim: limitation of aim is the secret of success.

The functionally autonomous governor of my conscious ego system (the little self) is now definitely resolved to ostracize theory and the sanguine surplus (from the larger Self) and cleave to the corrective maxim. And so, in order to improve its chances of carrying out this resolution I have decided:

285

(1), to omit those experiences and activities and those components of personality which Murr has shared with the majority of his colleagues and, at the risk of portraying him as a repellent freak, focus on his peculiarities and eccentricities; and (2) from these peculiarities select those that are pertinent to one or more of these four topics: (i) Murr's discovery of psychology as his vocation, (ii) his conception of his role in this domain, (iii) his accomplishments, and (iv) his retrospective critical evaluation of his professional endeavors. [To facilitate the victory of the corrective maxim, there is the presence in the bibliography of two papers written by Murr which taken together constitute a sizable chunk of what could be termed his intellectual autobiography. When necessary in the ensuing text the first of these papers will be referred to as Auto. 1, the second as Auto. 2.] Finally there is the task of steering a fitting course for Murr between the Scylla of concealment and mendacity and the Charybdis of the "meanest mortal's scorn."

## THE CASE OF MURR

### Murr's Vocational Choice

*The Improbability of Murr's Vocational Choice.* The first question relevant to the purposes of this volume is: what were the determinants of Murr's exultant selection of academic psychology in 1926 as the domain for his vocational life from then on? Could his decision have been anticipated by the experts? In 1926, when Murr was admitted to the Harvard Department of Philosophy and Psychology, his past history differed from all but a small fraction of one per cent (as a crude estimate) of the membership of the American Psychological Association (as it was then and as it has been over the years, so far as I can tell) in *most* of ten respects. In view of the compounding of these peculiarities, what could an actuarial psychologist have said except that the probability of Murr's making this decision was virtually nil. In an actuarial sense, there were no empirical, positive determinants: his record consisted of nothing but items which correlated negatively, to a highly significant degree, with the records of the vast majority of professional psychologists. For instance: (1) Murr's experience was restricted by his never having studied at a public school. For his first six years of education he went to two small private schools in New York City and for the next five years attended boarding school at Groton, Massachusetts. (2) Throughout those eleven years at school and throughout the four subsequent years at Harvard College, where he received below average grades, none of his scholastic records were indicative of intellectual interests or aptitudes; even less promising was the decline of his marks from year to year in each of the institutions he attended. (3) One of the several determinants of Murr's continuously low academic standing at school and at college was his unremitting youthful passion for athletic achievement, an ambition which was thwarted in most areas of endeavor partly by a basic sensori-motor defect, but not in rowing, a sport in which endurance, not speed, is at a premium; and, by sweat and luck, he managed to "make" the crew at Harvard. (4) After medical school, Murr enjoyed a two-year surgical internship at the Presbyterian Hospital in New York. (5) This surgical experience was preceded and followed by what amounted to five years of experimentation and research relating to the biochemical aspects of various phenomena, for example: blood as a physicochemical system; changes in the chemistry of the blood as found in various diseases and as experimentally produced by parathyroidectomy and pyloric occlusion; biochemical, metabolic, and tissue changes as a function of age in chicken embryos—researches which were conducted in this country at Harvard, at Columbia, and at the Rockefeller Institute for Medical Research, and in England at Cambridge, from which university he received a Ph.D. in biochemistry. (6) Instead of mathematics or physics, Murr's earliest avenue of approach to psychology was history (his field of concentration) and biography, with an emphasis on alienated rebels, I suspect, since he won the history prize at Groton with a short life of John Brown of Osawatomie; and much later, a year before he reached psychology—after discursive readings in the world's literature which found their peak in the works of Herman Melville—Murr, regardless of the unpropitious fact that at school he had received his consistently worst marks in English composition, zestfully embarked on a biography of that alienated genius. (7) In the Easter vacation of his year at Cambridge University—working next to Joseph Needham and J. B. S. Haldone in the laboratory of the Nobel prizewinner F. Gowland Hopkins—Murr spent three weeks of daily sessions and long weekends with Dr. Jung in Zurich, from which explosive experience (already described in Auto. 1) he emerged a reborn man. (8) Having been for twenty-four years an incurable stutterer with a very-seldom-overcome repugnance to public speaking, and (9) having never taken a single course in psychology, Murr was clearly an extremely reckless applicant and an extremely risky choice for a life-long job as lecturer in this complex domain of knowledge, when, at the late age of thirty-three, he was squeezed into the Harvard faculty by some sort of high-hushed finaglings engineered by Professor L. J. Henderson. (10) Murr was advantaged by having an independent income which allowed him to accept the offer of a meagre $1800 to serve as the assistant of the famous psychopathologist Dr. Morton Prince in inaugurating and carrying on research and teaching at the Harvard Psychological Clinic.

*The Determinants of Murr's Vocational Choice.* A few of the items which I have listed as actuarial negative determinants of Murr's vocational choice were, in fact, positive determinants. This discrepancy is readily explained by the fact that Murr's initial intention was to combine experimentation and psychotherapy in an institutional setting, such as might presumably be found in the clinic of a mental hospital. As it happened, Dr. Prince had had the wisdom to foresee that if in 1926 the clinic (for the running of which he had raised barely enough funds) were attached to a hospital, research would inevitably give way to the more urgent demands of therapy. The establishment of a clinic for the treatment of psychoneurotics under the auspices of a college department of philosophy and psychology was, so far as I know, an innovation, not only in America but in the world. And so it is to the occurrence of this highly improbable arrangement that one may attribute Murr's enrollment as a member of an understandably reluctant academic department. This being the case, my part, at this point, is to list the more probable determinants of Murr's analytic interest in people, his curiosity regarding the "causes" of normal and abnormal human states, thoughts, and actions, and of his hopeful resolution to reveal them by suitable scientific means. The determinants that stand out are as follows: (1) Murr's first shadowy memory is that of experiencing what he calls the "marrow of his being," the nature of which will be described in a later section. Suffice it to say here that it seems to have sensitized the boy to the sufferings of other people and to have played a part in his decision, first to become a surgeon and subsequently a psychotherapist. (2) Murr was exposed to and may have been somewhat moved by the presence in his environment of two neuropsychiatric sufferers, younger sisters of his mother: one, the victim of seasonal psychotic depressions, and the other, a sweet hysterectomized hysteric, whose daily state of quavering health was, for forty years, the focus of her four healthy sisters' dutiful and compassionate regard, each of them vying with the rest for the crown of exemplary charity. (3) Murr was intrigued by what he saw of the patients in mental hospitals whose expressions of emotion struck him as more naturally human and appealing than the perfunctory, official behavior of the tired doctors whose role it was to label them. (4) At medical school and later, there were many occasions to be astonished, stimulated, and instructed by Dr. George Draper's pinpoint observations and brilliant intuitive diagnoses of patients with what was later to be called psychosomatic illness. For some years he was Murr's most uniquely influential teacher, both by exhibiting these talents and by expounding his very original conceptions respecting varieties of human constitution, many of which would eventually be more systematically set forth by W. H. Sheldon. (5) While working at the Rockefeller Institute, Murr was repeatedly confounded by a radical theoretical (if not metaphysical) opposition between the Institute's then-most-famous members, Jacques Loeb, who stood for an extreme version of mechanism, and Alexis Carrel, the defender of some type of vitalism. How, Murr asked himself, can one account for such irreconcilable interpretations of identical phenomena? The notion that science is the creative product of an engagement between the scientist's psyche and the events to which he is attentive prepared Murr for an enthusiastic embracement of Jung's *Psychological Types* on the very day of its timely publication in New York (1923). Except for Herbert Spencer and the admirable William James, no theorists in the realm of subjective events were known to Murr; and this book by Jung came to him as a gratuitous answer to an unspoken prayer. Among other things, it planted in his soil two permanent centers of preoccupation: the question of varieties of human beings and in what terms they can be most significantly represented and discriminated, and the question of what variables of personality are chiefly involved in the production of dissonant theoretical systems. These questions were at the root of Murr's first spurt of veritable intellectual interest in the direction of psychology. The transaction with Jung led to an omnivorous and nourishing procession of readings through the revolutionary and astonishing works of Freud and his disciples, heady liquor for the young chemist.

(6) I am venturing the hypothesis that from 1915 to 1923, the chronological order of the classes of phenomena and of applicable concepts to which Murr was successively attracted corresponded to the emergent phases of an epigenetically-determined program of mental maturations. It is chiefly to the slow pace of this program from birth on that one must attribute the protracted sleeping span of his intellectual potentials (he was a slow developer physically and sexually as well); and now I am proposing that, once awakened, the temporal order of his mental preoccupations was determined in part by the sequence of objects and events to which he was exposed at medical school and in part by the recurrence, on a theoretical level, of a sequence of cortical developments, such as those (as Piaget has shown) that are manifested in early years by the chronological order in which certain abstract concepts (of increasing difficulty) become comprehensible to the child. In Murr's case, the sequence of his devotions was as follows: a staunch affectionate affair with anatomy and surgery was succeeded by a brief flirtation with physiology, which led to a fairly stable, amorous dyad with biochemistry, a relationship that deepened when the two of them became involved with the wonders of embryological metabolism; but, as Fate (the epigenetical program plus other factors) would have it, this amicable union ended in a separation when Murr contracted a responsible marriage with psychology until death them do part. What calls for an explanation is the fact that although at the start of medical school Murr was simultaneously exposed to three distinguished sister disciplines, two of them, biochemistry and physiology, were wallflowers so far as he was concerned, and anatomy, a subject that is nonseductive to the majority of students, immediately became the target of his libido. And then in need of explanation is the fact that it was not until Murr arrived at surgery and visualized his role as that of an emergency carpenter manipulating visible macro-structures that he began wondering with serious intent about the invisible micro-events that were pumping along in the tissues he was grossly handling and turned for answers to physiology, then to biochemistry (the only subject in which he got a B in medical school), then to physical chemistry (including a course in

calculus!) and finally to chemical ontogeny. In shifting his focus of attention in this manner Murr was both descending into the hidden and obscure depths and genesis of living creatures (in compliance with a disposition described in Auto. 2) and ascending the Jacob's pecking ladder of the angelic sciences, although not to a point that was within earshot of the trumpet of the seraphic physicists. And besides all this, what struck me as indicative of epigenetical cortical developments was Murr's apparent repetition of certain trends of conceptual emphasis that have characterized the history of the sciences, such as from macro to micro, from matter to energy, from structure to process, from single entities and processes to systems of entities and processes, from permanence to change, and so forth; and, generally speaking, in the case of each of these pairs of complementary aspects of natural phenomena, it is easier to comprehend and deal conceptually with the earlier than with the later emphasis.

Finally, there remains to be explained, by reference to another part of the epigenetical program of interior developments, the fact that up to 1923 Murr had been immune to the enticements of all encountered versions of the science of psychology: a single lecture at Harvard by Professor Münsterberg, the course in psychiatry at the Columbia College of Physicians and Surgeons, and a single hour at the hospital with Freud's *Interpretation of Dreams* had been enough to cancel whatever potential gust for that sort of thing was in the offing. But then suddenly Murr was in a blaze, a blaze which would go on for three years and eventually pressure him to embrace psychiatry and psychology, and so to take the last step in his slow and devoted recapitulation of the order in which the disciplines pertinent to modern medicine were founded: anatomy (Vesalius), physiology (Harvey), biochemistry (Claude Bernard), and psychiatry (Kraepelin), with the significant omission of biophysics, and with evolutions to be subsequently experienced in the realms of sociology and culturology. All that I have said so far is in behalf of my thesis that the publication of Jung's book at just that moment in the course of Murr's mental and emotional metamorphoses is an example of what Pasteur called chance and the prepared mind.

(7) The actualizations of the genetical program may be mentational in nature, as I believe they were in Murr's psyche from 1915 to 1923, or they may be emotional, or both mentational and emotional. From 1923 to 1926, during which span Murr's bonds of affinity with the creative processes in chicken embryos were step-wise disengaged and attached to the germinal affects of human beings, the actualizations he experienced were in part mentational but predominantly emotional. Throughout his hospital activities, his emotions had been engaged in empathizing with the somatic discomforts and anxieties of each patient, especially on the female ward; but these involvements were necessarily brief and superficial, and when it came to chicken embryos, lovely as they were, the opportunities for empathy were critically curtailed. In short, in view of the profound affectional upheaval

that swept Murr into the unruly domain of psychology—and thereby down the pecking order of the sciences—I am assuming, first of all, that up to that time an assemblage of emotional potentialities had been denied adequate participation in his work, and, secondly, that the evolving genetical program had arrived at a new stage, comparable in a way to that of puberty, because what surged up was not merely what had been previously excluded, as in the "return of the repressed," but something wholly novel and astonishing, never dreamt of in his philosophy, with a dimension of depth and elevation which landed him in a vast brew outside the husk of his contemporary world. Instrumental in effecting and reinforcing this transition were influences emanating from the up-to-then-neglected realm of art, from artists and art-sensitive associates: a galaxy of seminal books, especially the works of Nietzsche, Dostoevski, Tolstoy, Proust, and Hardy; the music of Beethoven, Wagner, and Puccini; the poetry of E. A. Robinson and the plays of Eugene O'Neill, meeting both of them as well as a number of other poets and dramatists, actors and actresses, and attending rehearsals of their plays; endeavoring to sculpture in clay a head of his beautifully-featured wife in their backyard; communing with a circle of kindred spirits, including Dr. Alfred E. Cohn, his boss at the Institute, Robert Edmond Jones, Dr. Carl Binger, who was about ready to shift from experimental physiology to psychiatry, and Christiana D. Morgan, who was destined to experience visions which would occupy the attention of Dr. Jung for twelve memorable seminars and then to join Murr at the Harvard Psychological Clinic; attending thought-kindling lectures at the New School for Social Research; and more besides, in this country and in Europe, not to speak of a *femme inspiratrice* here and there along the way. (8) As I have said already, Melville was a very potent factor, not only, like Beethoven, as a deep prime-mover from the sphere of art and a model of powerful metaphorical speech, but as an illustrator of nearly everything that Murr was finding and about to find in Freud and Jung. (9) The revolutionary sessions with Dr. Jung in Zurich in 1925 (described in Auto. 1) have been mentioned earlier. This first encounter with an analytical psychiatrist of the new order provided Murr with an exemplar of genius that settled the question of his identity to come. (10) Murr's unswerving addiction to scientific research cancelled the possibility of his devoting the bulk of his time and energy to private practice, and so (11) when Dr. Morton Prince made the unprecedented offer of a position as his research assistant in founding a clinic at Harvard College, this struck Murr as another glorious instance of chance and the prepared mind.

## Murr's Conception of His Role and Some Determinants Thereof

I have pointed out that Murr was an eccentric in about ten respects when he became an academic psychologist at Harvard in 1926, and now is the moment for me to add that within the next few years it became all-too-obvious that he was a deviant in other respects besides those already mentioned, such as his being woefully ignorant of the content of academic psychology, which at that time consisted mostly of psychophysics and animal conditioning. In the first place, as I have said, Murr was vitally interested in persons, intent on understanding each of them as a unit operating in his or her environment. And then, coming from medicine, he was at first especially attentive to abnormalities of functioning, the psychoneuroses, no sufficient explanations of which are possible (as he learnt from Dr. Prince and from all breeds of psychoanalysts) without the concept of unconscious psychic processes. Believing in addition (against the sturdy opposition of Dr. Prince) that Freud's theoretical system was more applicable than any other to an understanding of dysfunctionings, Murr became one of the founders of the Boston Psychoanalytical Society, went through the then-existing course of formal Freudian training, including an analysis by Dr. Franz Alexander (described in Auto. 1) and several control analyses supervised by Dr. Sachs, and for a number of years practised orthodox psychoanalysis, modified by ideas derived from Jung, Adler, and Rank. These were the activities which incurred the disapproval of Karl Lashley and through him of President Conant, whose inclination to fire Murr was eventually overruled by various considerations advanced by Gordon Allport, Whitehead, and several other brave supporters.

As time went on, Murr became more interested in normal than in abnormal personalities, partly because there was no existing theoretical system which was anywhere near as applicable to the representation and understanding of the activities and achievements of healthy and supernormal human beings as the Freudian system was in dealing with the fears, fixations, and regressions of neurotics. As a starting point, Murr turned to what seemed most self-evident to him, in the light of common human experience, namely, that the most critical of all the variables involved in the determination of situational reactions and proactions was the nature of the goal-directed motive force (the subject's needful aim). As it happened at that juncture, this concept was not acceptable to the leading lights of Murr's department. McDougall, who had called the motive force "instinct," had been knocked out of the ring by Watson, and the triumphant champion had managed to persuade the brethren that they could get along without this imperceptible energizing and orienting factor. Watson's proposal to limit the science of psychology to concepts that pointed only to perceptibles struck the former biochemist—all of whose critical concepts had referred to imperceptibles—as a naive, juvenile perversity, even though it succeeded in rescuing psychology from the meanderings of the traditional form of introspectionism. A budding psychologist who was devoting fruitful hours listening to reports of the ongoing stream of consciousness—dreams, fantasies, memories, feelings, and thoughts—of other people (experiential psychology, as Murr would call it) could scarcely have been disposed to adopt with zest the dogmas of those whose avowed conscious purpose was to convince us that consciousness and purpose were nonexistent, or—considering that life is short and the art long— to pay close attention to the latest advances in psychophysics. William James (who was said by a later member of the Harvard department to have done unparalleled harm to psychology) had become one of Murr's major exemplars by that time, and the young man found himself agreeing with almost everything his hero had to say—completely, for example, with the heretical statement that "Individuality is founded in feeling; and the recesses of feeling, the darker, blinder strata of character, are the only places in the world in which we catch real fact in the making, and directly perceive how events happen and how work is actually done." (James, 1903, p. 501)

This idea that the "real facts" are to be found not on the surface of the body nor in the full light of consciousness, but in the darker, blinder recesses of the psyche was of course anathema to the majority of academic psychologists who were militantly engaged in a competitive endeavor to mould psychology in the image of physics, a competition in which positive reinforcements would be reserved for those who could bring forth experimental findings with the highest degree of face-validity, statistical significance, and verifiability in all cases, obtained by the most reliable and precise methods. To be among the leaders in this race it was necessary to legislate against the "blinder strata," to keep away from those events which intellectuals at large assumed to be the subject matter of psychology, to disregard individual and typological differences, and to approximate universality and certainty by measuring the lawful relationships of narrowly restricted forms of animal behavior, of physiological processes in general, and of the simplest sensory and sensorimotor processes of human beings in particular. In short, methodological excellence was dictating (more than it did in any other science) the phenomena to be investigated, with the result that in those days psychologists were not the experts to be consulted about problems involving varieties of human nature, as biochemists, botanists, and ornithologists, for example, are consulted about problems involving varieties of chemicals, plants, and birds. On this general issue Murr, at variance with his contemporaries, was facing in the opposite direction with the hope of devising the best possible methods for the investigation of obscure phenomena, realizing that it is the part of an educated man, as Aristotle said, to know what degree of precision is appropriate at each stage in the development of each discipline. Although, for various reasons, Murr did not attempt any direct exposures of the blinder strata of feelings, he would in due course find ways of eliciting feelingful imagery and fantasies from which one could infer the nature of some of the components of the blinder strata.

The chief determinants of all these eccentricities of Murr have been listed in the previous section. What remains to be presented here are the reasons why it took no courage on his part to stick to views which were diametrically opposed to those that were winning all the prizes: (1) Having been trained in a more exact science, he did not feel compelled for the sake of self-esteem to put exemplary technical competence in a less exact science at the top of his hierarchy of aims. (2) He had come to psychology with the hope of advancing current knowledge about human beings, not to raise his status on the totem pole of scientists. (3) There was nothing original about his ideas: they were derived from a score of world-famous medical psychologists whose practical aims had kept them far closer to the raw facts than occupants of the groves of academe had ever got. (4) Murr's varied, intimate relations with hospital patients, ranging from a notorious gangster and dope-addict to a champion world politician with infantile paralysis, together with privately-experienced emotional revolutions, upsurges from below consciousness, had given him a sense of functional fitness, the feeling that all parts of his self were in unison with his professional identity as he defined it, and that he was more advantaged in these ways than were many of the book-made academics who talked as if they had lost contact with the springs of their own natures. (5) Despite his obnoxious behavior now and then (after Dr. Prince retired and Murr took over the running of the Clinic), the permanent members of the department, Professor Boring and Professor Pratt, were invariably friendly, helpful, and indulgent: they included him in all official and unofficial gatherings, yet let him go his independent way uncriticized, except for a rare paternal hint, such as the warning after he had written one of his first papers, "Psychology and the University," that if he published it he would be *persona non grata* in the APA. (6) He was not much of a teacher, but because of the drawing power of psychoanalysis he was reinforced from the beginning of his career by having a number of promising graduate students—such as Donald MacKinnon, Saul Rosenzweig, Nevitt Sanford, Isabelle Kendig, Kenneth Diven, and Robert White—come his way to get their Ph.D.'s. (7) He was not tempted to toe the line of rewarded theories and experiments, as some others were, by economic need or even by any continuing, unrealistic want for recognition from the élite of his profession. (The reward of tenure, for example, was not granted until he had arrived at the seldom-equaled, late age of fifty-five.) The scientific reference group whose standards had shaped his aspirations in the past— composed of men who were both specialists and generalists, such as his teachers and good friends L. J. Henderson, Hans Zinnser, Raymond Pearl, and others I have mentioned—was now marginal to the line of his vision, and at the focus there were no equivalent replacements, except perhaps the next generation or a shadowy posterity, because I am sure that Murr was confident that the ideas and values he supported were slanted toward an allied future.

In due course the practice of introspection and the concept of motive force, in altered forms and disguised by fresh labels, surreptitiously regained their lost respectability; and after World War II, Freudian theory *in toto* overran large areas of American psychology as Napoleon overran Europe. In short, much that was pretty generally tabooed in academic circles between 1926 and 1936—the ideas and practices that gave Murr the brand of a dispensable eccentric on the Harvard faculty—became popular commonplaces within a single generation, things to be taught in general education courses, and, as a consequence of this cultural expansion, Murr found himself occupying a position of discomforting respectability. He was not the real McCoy, however, because of his conception of his role as that of an unstatistical naturalist and differentiating generalist who believed that all members of the human species were not birds of the same feather.

## Flash-Back

*Apologia.* The corrective maxim dictated that no space be devoted to an account of the parents and the childhood of my subject because there is nothing back there that qualifies as an aid to our understanding of his mind when it came to wrestling with the problems of psychology. In his twenties, so far as I can see, Murr's headpiece was like the island of Nantucket, standing off shore, "all beach, without a background." But, sad to say, the protests of the caucus of friends who frequent my boardinghouse drowned out the feeble voice of conscience and pressured me to cancel the corrective maxim for the nonce. And so, with suppressed scruples, I shall offer some passages extracted from the autobiography that Murr wrote in performing the first task in the usual order of assessment procedures. Here is his potpourri of sheer facts dished out for those who have a taste for them.

*Parents.* "My father was a Scot, born near Melbourne, Australia, where his father, a British Army officer, was sent and stationed until he died a few years after his fourth son's birth. This son, my father, was about nine when he and his mother rounded the tempestuous Cape in a schooner, with cascades of ocean pouring into their cabin, and eventually arrived in England as destitute relatives of some studbook uncles and cousins who were not inclined to be disturbed beyond using their influence to get my father entered at the famous "bluecoat" charity school in London, Christ's Hospital, where Coleridge, Leigh Hunt, and Lamb had studied. And so, to keep the home pot boiling, my grandmother—who was equipped with French and Irish genes as well as British—called on whatever talents for artistic compositions she could muster. In view of the attractive portrait by her brush that I now have in my possession, I shall gladly ascribe to her the honor of the A's in drawing I received in primary school. As for the uninspired novels of the then-current feminine brand which she managed to get published (one entitled *Ella Norman, or a Lady's Perils*), the genetical potential for creative writing they exhibit could not have been enough to count for anything in later generations.

"After his mother's premature death my father, a penniless orphan without a college education, came by way of Toronto to New York City. His anonymous arrival must have been as different as it could have been from that of his great-grandfather, the flamboyant and irascible Earl of Dunmore, who a hundred years earlier, being sent there to serve as Governor of the State, seems to have done more than he should have done to antagonize the citizens of Manhattan and was soon removed to become the last Royal Governor of Virginia, where he lived in that grand mansion at Williamsburg which we can see today in a restored state. In no obvious way resembling this ancestor, my father came to New York as an unknown and unassuming young man, presumably to seek his fortune, an outcome which looked dubious when he was given his first job cleaning ink-pots in the offices of a stock company. Inevitably he went up as time went on, though he proved less fortunate in making money than in making friends, and not so fortunate in making friends as he was in courting the liveliest of the six daughters of a highly respected merchant, president-to-be of the Mutual Life Insurance Company, whose fortune was both ample and secure for succeeding generations. My father and his bride actually lived happily ever after.

"All my mother's near ancestors were made out of English seeds transported to this country in the seventeenth century, the original American population of them being distributed in Connecticut, Rhode Island, and Pennsylvania; but eventually a number of their carriers converged and united in the City of New York. On the way down from the first immigrants, these seeds produced a doctor and jurist, his son, an Eli and Revolutionary colonel whose mind became unhinged, a minister, a sea captain, and a score of merchants of one sort or another, and a wife for each of them whose merits and demerits are matters of conjecture. Of all these progenitors I was acquainted only with my daughter-venerated grandfather, aloof toward me, but a kindly gent whose white-bearded visage resembled God's as painted, say, by Tintoretto. Remembering him I have been led to surmise that the image and concept of Jahveh must have come not from the all-too-familiar father figure, but from the more remote and lordly grandfather, the overruling patriarch of the clan.

"If, as countless philosophers have held, happiness, resulting from this or that variety of conduct, is the only state that a rational man will endeavor to secure, then my father was as successful as anybody I could name, provided one correlates happiness with a continuing state of unperturbed serenity, cheerfulness, enjoyment of sheer being, trust, and mutual affection, or, in other words, a life of moderate, solid, predictable satisfactions, free from choler, anxiety, guilt, and shame. In Aristotelian terms, the key to it all was his adherence to the *res media*; and in William James' somewhat comparable terms, the secret lay in the willingness of this man (who was no great shakes as a businessman and banker) to renounce in good faith unrealizable ambitions: 'With no attempt there can be no failure; with no failure no humiliation.' (James, 1950, p. 310)

"As for Freud, he seems to have had no concepts at all to represent such an unself-centered, even-tempered, unpretentious, undemanding, acquiescent, firm yet nonauthoritarian, jolly father who is scarcely capable of a veritable splurge of anger, even when he breaks the door down to put a stop to a voyeuristic-exhibitionistic party of mixed doubles initiated by his little daughter and her younger brother. Anyhow, in the analysis of my life's course conducted by Dr. Alexander, no indications of any hidden resentment against my father nor any memories of a persisting rage-reaction—following, say, one of the two just spankings I received from him—were ever brought to light. In short, so far as I recall, my father, though not installed as a charismatic hero, was always a positive univalent figure in my mind, a dependable guide and teacher in the Hellenic mode, rather than a threatening, awesome, high and mighty judge. Consequently, in later life when I came upon Freud's conception of the father-son side of the oedipus complex, it did not strike home with any vibrant shock of recognition. Furthermore, in my case there was no confirmation of the tenet that antagonisms to authority figures in later life (several in my history) can invariably be traced to the person's original hostility to his father.

"It was my mother who was the ambivalent parent: more often the focus of attention, affection, and concern than my father was, year in and year out, but also more resented now and then, mostly for correcting my abominable manners, for nagging about minutiae, or for enforcing duties or requesting services which interrupted my activities. Of the two, she was the more energetic, restless, enthusiastic, enterprising, and talkative—giving us daily reports of her personal preoccupations, her doings, encounters, worries, and frustrations—also the more changeable, moody, and susceptible to melancholy. I resemble my mother in all but one of these respects: like my fortunate father, I have never been plagued by endogenous anxieties and worries, and, like him again, I adopted at a very early age the role of physician to these perturbations in my mother and later to comparable but slighter perturbations in my more rational and steady wife.

"My mother was an effective, though over-exacting, administrator of the household, and I'm afraid there was good ground for her imbedded feeling that her unusual industry, thrift, and competence in carrying out these functions—keeping the seven domestics busy as could be—were not duly appreciated by her children, but taken for granted as the given order of nature. My mother was even more sedulous in the performance of her role as supervisor of the health and of the social development of her three children more than three years apart in age: a fascinating, mischievous daughter with flashes of ungovernable temper, followed by two more-easily manageable sons, me in the middle and my brother, the cute kid, with a repertoire of precocious tricks indicative of real brilliance in the future."

*Past History, Memories.* Here again I will have Murr speak for himself. But since he cannot recall his birth, nor anything of his sojourn in the

maternal claustrum, nor earlier when the particles that made him were located in two places, neither one of these in heaven, it is up to me to announce that on May 13, 1893, in a brownstone residence, where nowadays
the Rockefeller Center's sky-assaulting piles of concrete blocks irreverently
stand, the little cherub, trailing humors of the original sin of selfishness,
came from darkness into light in a shorter time, I wager, than it has taken
me to reach this beginning of his life. In addition let me say that this was
the location in New York City of his first and second winter homes up to
the time of his marriage at the age of twenty-three. His summers were spent
on Long Island near the seashore, with visits to boyhood friends in other
places, except for four longish trips to Europe (his father loved England,
his mother was a fervent Francophile and had her children learn French),
during the course of which Murr compliantly dragged his feet through most
of the great museums, cathedrals, and historic buildings between Naples
and the Highlands of Scotland. At home on Long Island he built sand-
fortresses and claustra of barrel-stays (his mother fantasied that he was cut out
to be an architect) until his father taught him how to swim, fish, and sail,
and later to play tennis, golf, and baseball with limited proficiency. More
enticing than those games, however, were his animals—goat, dog, and hens—
and the woods back of the house where he could climb trees, put up a
teepee, and pretend he was an Indian. He read every accessible French and
English fairy tale, all about the Knights of the Round Table, and boys'
books about animals, Indians, frontiersmen, and the American Civil War.
His father, who was steeped in the British classics, encouraged him to extend
his range to a few of the works of Scott and Dickens. But almost invariably
the greater lure was outdoor physical activity, and, on the whole, he seems
to have grown up as an average, privileged American boy of that era (before the days of automobiles, motorboats, movies, and all that), with an
identity in the eyes of his miniature social surround which could not be
captured in terms of either docile or rebellious, timid or reckless, awkward
or agile, dull or bright, hopeless or promising, in or out. He got on famously
with his younger brother but infamously with his older sister until he was
nine and had gathered up enough muscle to subdue her. Despite the experience gained in coping with this tempestuous sibling, come puberty he
was shy in his approach to girls and did not know the pangs of calf-love
until he was sixteen. In college there was a three-year period of devoted
courtship of Josephine L. Rantoul of Boston before he got around to the
long-since-predetermined question and answer the day after the Harvard-
Yale boat race. Since I have already called attention to Murr's mediocre
scholarship record up to the age of twenty-two, I have only two items to add:
one, that no bona fide intellectual ever crossed the threshold of his home,
and two, that his parents were Episcopalians and Republicans, his father
being a great admirer of Disraeli, his character, his policies, and his novels.
So much as a prelude to the memories that follow. Here is Murr speaking.

*"The Marrow of My Being. Memory* (about four years of age): Absorbed
in looking at a fairy-book picture of a sad-faced queen sitting with her sad-
faced son, I learn from my mother that it is the prospect of death that has
made them sad. Translated briefly into today's words, my melancholy feelings
and thoughts were of this nature: 'death . . . . sad for the queen if her son
is going to die, sad for the son if his mother is going to die . . . pitiful that
this must be and nothing can be done about it.' My present free associations,
starting from this first recalled encounter with the idea of death and its sever-
ance of affectional bonds between mother and son, have carried me back in
time to a few items which suggest that one crucial affectional bond between
mother and child had already been severed: (i) the fact that I was abruptly
weaned at two months because my mother, for some reason, was too upset to
continue nursing me (the possibility that sucking interfered with breathing
and that I 'fought' the stifling breast as some infants do to the great discom-
fort of their mothers), (ii) the fact that I was a feeding problem for a year
or more and in my earliest photograph look decidedly undernourished and
forlorn, and (iii) the fact that my mother was at most times far more occupied
with my older sister, her favorite child however troublesome, and at this time
was especially occupied with my cunning baby brother. These facts and a
score of other consonant filaments from the remembered past have led me
to the following hypothetical *Chronology of Events:* Quite a while before the
traditional oedipus hunting season, that infant had come to the grievous (and
valid) realization that he could count on only a limited, third-best portion of
his mother's love; and since his spectacles of hypersensitive grief and his
petitions for an ample supply of reassuring consolation—such as his tearfully
saying, 'you make my feelings hurt me'—since these led only to frustration
and shame, he proudly withdrew, with some of the murderous resentment
of an abandoned child ('you'll be sorry if I die'), into a private, maternal-like
claustrum of his own making, where, bathed in narcissistic self-pity for a
while, he could lick his own wounds until nature healed them. In this way,
that special bond of mutual affinity, which depends, in an extremity, on a
child's need to receive and his mother's capacity to bestow a sufficiency of
emotional nurturance, was forever severed; in this one respect they were now
dead to each other, an outcome which was, once in a while, tragically experienced by the child (as in the memory), despite his early gain in emotional
self-sufficiency ('I can get along without you') and in venturesome autonomy,
coupled with the repression of the residues of suffering, the abatement of his
resentment, and the displacement of pity from the self to some sufferer in
his environment. Needless to say the pitied sufferer was none other than his
mother who took to her couch periodically with a sick headache, and, being
given to understand that if he made a noise or misbehaved in any way, his
mother's headache would become unbearable ('you'll be sorry if I die'), pity
soon became one of the most influential ingredients of his conscience. This
reversal of roles was vividly illustrated in the one really astonishing (and un-

interpreted) dream I had in my analysis with Dr. Alexander: I was comforting my mother in my arms as if she were a baby, while she was vomiting over my left shoulder. All this is susceptible to a great deal more analysis; but let this much suffice because the determinants of this complex are of less interest than some of its *Consequences.* These included (i) a marrow of misery and melancholy repressed by pride and practically extinguished in everyday life by a counteracting disposition of sanguine and expansive buoyancy [described in the Prologue]; (ii) a profound attraction, coming from the marrow, for tragic themes in literature, which drew me to Herman Melville, Shakespeare, and other authors (the saddest of all circumstances being the loss of a beloved person), and incidentally disposed me to select many gloomy pictures for the TAT; (iii) also coming from the marrow, an affinity for the darker, blinder strata of feeling (as mentioned in connection with William James), this being a representative of the feminine component of my nature which, evoked by art, was influential in converting me to psychology; (iv) for some thirty years of my life, also coming from the marrow, a hypersensitivity to the sufferings of other individuals, especially women, which inclined me towards medicine and psychotherapy with the sanguine confidence that I could restore their health and joy; (v) coming out of pride, denial, and repression, the conviction that I could get along well enough with a minimum amount of aid, support, appreciation, recognition, or consolation from others; anyhow, I could never depend on it and should never seek it; in solitude and privacy I could be happily independent of all that; (vi) the (unnoticed) concept of inviolacy in Explorations; (vii) the concept of nurturance, of receiving and transmitting it; and finally (viii) later when new ideas began bubbling autonomously in my head, these became the foci of my nurturant disposition and there was not much energy left over for the miseries of others.

"*Nansen and the Exploration of Remote, Unknown, and Unspoiled Regions of Nature, Solitude and Pantheism. Memory* (3.8 years of age): Pacing back and forth one evening in the presence of my parents and saying that I would not go to bed until they promised to give my (one-month-old) brother the name of Nansen. *Explanation:* A few days earlier my parents told me about a lecture at the Metropolitan Opera House by Nansen, the arctic explorer, and this, together with a fine picture of him in the newspaper, was enough to get his figure immediately established as my first grand hero, having been prepared by *Robinson Crusoe* to be captivated by this chance encounter with a venturer into unstaked territory. *Consequences:* (i) choosing Nansen's *Farthest North,* in two volumes, as the first book to read alone from cover to cover; (ii) incorporating later generations of similar exemplars —American Indians, pioneers, woodsmen, explorers, mountain climbers— whose wilderness achievements depended on know-how, endurance, and fortitude; (iii) positive cathection, with pantheistic fervor, of the more remote, less frequented and unspoiled regions of nature, resulting in the development of a major territorial system of my personality exemplified by camping, fishing, and hunting trips in the Adirondacks, New Mexico, California, Oregon, British Columbia, Manitoba, Ontario, Quebec, New Brunswick, Newfoundland, the traverse of Mt. Blanc from the Italian side, and the building of solitary hide-outs, here and there, at some distance from 'the madding crowd'; and (iv) a psyche prepared by empathic communions with nature—receiving impressions 'fresh from her own virgin voluntary and confiding breast'—to appreciate nature poetry, the writings of Herman Melville, and the earth, animal, and sky mythologies of our earliest ancestors (closed books to city-dwelling theorists); and on the other hand, prepared to detest all the landscape horrors of commercial advertising. *Later consequences:* (i) the replacement of alluring geographical territories by the more enticing, primitive, mysterious, and unsurveyed regions of the psyche (explorations of personality); (ii) a miniature of nature in the form of a garden next to each of the four Clinic buildings we inhabited; and (iii) the concepts of egression, ingression, ascension, descension, and so forth to represent movements in social and cultural space as well as in territorial space.

"*A Sensori-motor Defect. Memory* (nine years old): Returning from school innocent as could be one day to find the dining room transformed into an operating room, with two white-gowned surgeons and an anaesthetist awaiting my arrival, and my mother confronting me with the option of a pain-eliminating general anaesthetic or an aquarium as prize for getting on without it. *Explanation:* Four years earlier, my mother, ever on the lookout for deviations from the norm, detected a slight crossing of my eyes (internal strabismus) which became steadily more accentuated despite the therapeutic efforts of New York's most eminent ophthalmologist, and so now the time had come for this worthy to cut some of the hyperactive orbital muscles. *Consequences:* Although I was pleasured by an aquarium of enchanting fish, it turned out that I had been somewhat disadvantaged by the expert surgeon's having cut a few more muscle fibers than was necessary to correct the crossing of my vision, and I came forth with the opposite defect, an external strabismus, which, though far less obvious than the previous condition, left me nonetheless as incapable as ever of focusing on a single point with more than one eye at a time, and hence incapable of stereoscopic vision. But I was entirely unconscious of the significance of this defect until as a medical student I went to the office of Dr. Smith Ely Jeliffe, a spectacular New York psychiatrist, to consult him about my stuttering which had set in shortly after the operation. To my amazement, Dr. Jeliffe's first question was: 'Have you found any difficulty in playing games, such as baseball, tennis, or squash, which necessitate catching or hitting a fast moving ball?' 'Yes, I certainly have,' I said, 'but how did you know?' 'Well,' Dr. Jeliffe replied, 'I noticed that one eye was not looking at me directly but turned out a bit, and that would be enough to unfit you for games of that sort and also for swift, precise manual movements.' The doctor's astonishing powers of observation and of inference succeeded in casting a penetrating ray of illumination into uprushing memories of humiliating incidents, particularly in baseball games, when I had struck out or let an easy one slip through my fingers, and so forth and so forth. Dr. Jeliffe went on to relate this elementary sensori-motor defect to my stuttering, but whatever wisdom he had to offer on that issue has long-since passed beyond recall. Today I am partial to the notion that a primary suffocation experience which, as mentioned earlier, involves a panicky inco-ordination of sucking, breathing, an inturned eye, and hands lunging at the breast could have established a predisposition to all three of the disabilities I have mentioned. But to return to Dr. Jeliffe's office, what surprises me now is that it never occurred to me that the revelation I had been vouchsafed had any bearing on my intention to become a surgeon; and it was not until three years later that the realization that my manual dexterity was definitely limited became clear enough to fortify my decision to devote myself exclusively to research."

Murr is so convinced that personality is revealed only vaguely in the empty abstractions derived from questionnaires and factor analyses, but substantially in the minute, concrete details of critical and typical episodes in the life history of an individual, that even after deleting most of the detail in the three memories I have offered you, I find that these have already usurped more than the allotted space. Consequently, instead of allowing him to go on in this fashion, I shall give the bare gist of three of the last dozen clusters of memories that he submitted. (1) *A non-Freudian child*. Murr tells of Dr. Alexander's boredom when his analysand, despite continuous scratching at his unconscious, failed to bring forth the expected array of polymorphic episodes. With the advent of passionate love in post-adolescence, Murr exultantly experienced and reciprocally expressed, as related in one of his papers, pretty nearly every Freudian component of the sex instinct, showing that none of these dispositions were absent in his constitution, and, incidentally, that Freud erred in affirming that men of our civilization are necessarily doomed to renunciation and incurable discontent. But, except for a few banal universals, there were no veritable exhibitions of these tendencies in his early dreams and memories, either, perhaps, because of the rarity in his protected environment of suitable stimulations and opportunities, or perhaps because of a too-firmly established barrier of repression. (2) *Possibly an Adlerian boy*. Freud's theories are consistent with a concept of the child as an armless and legless torso and head, with three cathected orifices in constant need of stimulation, a concept which offered Murr another possible reason for his failure to qualify as a typical Freudian child. Perhaps the locomotive and manipulative activity of his appendages were functionally more important to him than the superficial sensitivity of the orifices per se. Anyhow, from nine to eighteen, football heroes (which excluded his father) and playing football were at the top of his system of values, which suggests that an Adlerian factor was at work, because he, a confirmed stutterer, always played quarterback—not too well, but he persisted and, for some reason, never stuttered when he gave the signals. Another Adlerian story that Murr related with some pride was of being licked in a fight during recess at primary school and then taking up boxing until he won the featherweight championship. (3) *Egression from the husk of his youth.* Murr had been brought up on the conservative Republican Episcopalian side of the traditions of a relatively stable society, with a moral code, cluster of tastes, and privileged status that were taken for granted by his parents and unobtrusively exemplified. Molded by these values, which had been reinforced by the Rev. Endicott Peabody of Groton, Murr arrived at medical school, not suspecting that in due course his analytical mind would identify their ethnocentric determinants, and that before he graduated he would refute a basic Marxian theorem by saying good-bye to his implanted prejudices in favor of Christianity, the Republican Party, and the class of people with whom he had been reared. Foremost among his redeemers was a brilliant classmate, Alvan Barach, his first intimate (and life-long) Jewish friend, who was headed for a distinguished career as a practitioner and scientific innovator. Murr had chosen to go to the P & S in New York with the express purpose of detaching himself from his playboy and athletic friends in the Harvard-Boston area; but the separation that was intended to be temporary turned out to be a permanent divorce of interests and viewpoints with no remaining valid bridges of communication. But not so in his own family, since they had found a way of getting along happily together, all talking at the same time, without more than an occasional reference to basic issues.

## Murr's Accomplishments

Murr is known here and there in professional circles as an imprecision instrument maker because of his part in the fashioning of the Thematic Apperception Test (1935), and as a theorist because of his part in the building of the edifice of principles, concepts, methods, case material, and experiments entitled *Explorations in Personality* (1938). And here let me immediately record that in Murr's opinion the major determinant of the volume, quality, and pre-timeliness of that cooperative book was the exceptional spirit, character, competence, and imaginative scope of the students and colleagues who worked in companionship with him at the Harvard Psychological Clinic from 1934 through 1936. In Auto. 2 Murr gratefully named each member of that body and of later bodies of congenial and talented collaborators (some forty in all), so many of whom went on to surpass him, each in his own way as a productive contributor to the science of psychology, that, in some quarters, Murr is thought of not as an author so much as an author of authors, a diversity of them, none bound to his ideas.

Murr, with modesty in abeyance, is disposed to claim more than half the credit for the following endeavors to advance the science of human nature in 1938: *Methodological:* the *multiform system of assessment,* the more practical part of which consists of multifarious procedures administered by multifarious specialists to each of a number of subjects, followed by staff meetings in which the data obtained from one assessee is presented, discussed, interpreted, and organized (by an appointed personographer) into an explanatory formulation of the history of that assessee's personality. The general design of this system of operations was determined by a mere transfer of learning from medicine to psychology, with the crucial difference that the terminal process is not simply the assignment of each subject to a known diagnostic category, as it commonly is in medicine, but a novel, creative composition (consisting of universal, typological, and unique features) the validity of which is susceptible to judgments in terms of various criteria. These lengthy personographies based on data obtained from some forty procedures and revised to take account of the diverse judgments of other generalist-assessors canceled for Murr all further confidence in the rating of any variable by a single test or in the representation of a personality by a list of traits or, indeed, in any representation (except a truly creative one) that has escaped exposure to a variety of insights. But the point, overlooked by most readers, is that the superordinate purpose of these assessment procedures, repeated in modified versions with other assemblages of subjects, is to permit the periodic exemplification, testing, correction, expansion, and reconstruction (and hence the continuous evolution) of a personological system of concepts and theories. (2) *Technical: special methods* several of which, like the TAT (better named "eductors" than "projection tests"), were designed to educe (draw forth) words, sentences, or stories as ground for verifiable or plausible inferences in regard to influential components of the personality which the subject is either unable or unwilling to report. (3) *Synthetical:* the incorporation into the sphere of academic concern of a large portion of Freud's theoretical system integrated with contributions from Jung, Adler, McDougall, Lewin, and others. (4) *Conceptual:* (i) the first version of a reasonably comprehensive classification of aimed motive forces (needs, wants, drives) as a necessary revision and extension of Freud's irrational, sentimental, and inadequately differentiated division of instincts into Eros and Thanatos, and so forth; (ii) the first version of a classification of the salient properties of the "behavioral environment" (Koffka, Lewin) into varieties of *press,* and (iii) a number of concepts which define different dynamic relationships between needs and between needs and press. The chief determinant of these taxonomic endeavors was merely a transfer of learning from chemistry, medicine, and the biological sciences, all of which were launched on their careers as differentiated systems of knowledge by extensive classifications of the entities and phenomena that lay within the circumference of their responsibility.

The absence in *Explorations* of any clearly stated, testable propositions contributed by Murr is definitely to his discredit, as Hall and Lindzey have properly pointed out. Of little weight in his defense would be the observation that here and there are passages expressive of tacit propositions which could easily be made explicit, and many of these could be ordered in relation to one theme: the various components of personality (such as interests, emotions, needs, sentiments, defenses, and past experiences) that operate as determinants or modifiers of a person's apprehensions (perceptions, estimations, interpretations, predictions, recollections, conceptualizations, and theoretical explanations) of observed phenomena. Another factor to be considered in this connection is Murr's perverse antipathy to any odor of scientific pretentiousness, any greater methodological refinements than the nature of the data warrants, having too often been a witness of a mountain of ritual bringing forth a mouse of fact more dead than alive. To me this perversity in Murr looks like a wilful addiction to foreseeable negative reinforcements.

After editing the manuscript of *Explorations* for delivery to the Oxford University Press (whose consultant argued strongly for rejection), Murr left for an official absence from Harvard that would extend over nine of the subsequent eleven years. The first among other things he did was to sojourn and travel in Europe with his wife and daughter Josephine (who was destined to become a pediatrician). They travelled in Germany, where in 1937 they saw the frenzied Hitler and noted with horrible forebodings the unmistakable premonitory signs of a collective Faustian explosion, then in Switzerland, where they visited Dr. Jung at his Bollingen retreat and listened to his analysis of Hitler's syndrome of symptoms, and finally in Hungary and Austria, where he spent a memorable evening with Dr. and Anna Freud in the room where that astounding corpus of cultural history had been shaped. Four years later, in the fall of 1941, when Murr returned to his cherished workshop in Cambridge—succinctly described in his day as "wisteria outside, hysteria inside," but now progressing on a saner course under the steadier and more competent directorship of the beloved Robert White—he was greeted by the largest and liveliest group of knowledgeable and diversified investigators that had ever gathered there or ever would. Some of these men—Leo Bellak, Elliott Jaques, Silvan Tomkins, Frederick Wyatt and others—were prepared to engage in the multiform assessment of another aggregate of subjects, but this time with an expanded and improved conceptual system and an elegant statistical design composed by Daniel Horn. There was promise of a considerable advance in both methodology and theory; but Pearl Harbor and its consequences for the staff brought the whole program to a halt after the thorough study of only eleven subjects. Only some of the gathered data were salvaged for publication, some by White, Robert Holt, and others, and some by Murr and Christiana Morgan in a monograph entitled "A Clinical Study of Sentiments" (values), which, finished under pressure amid wartime duties, failed, by an inexcusable oversight, to mention the names of the numerous collaborators to whom they were unequivocally indebted. Between 1943 and 1948 Murr was primarily engaged in the operations of the OSS Assessment Staff, in company with several of his former colleagues, James G. Miller, Morris Stein, and a few previously mentioned, especially Donald MacKinnon, able director of the main assessment station near Washington (not to speak of almost fifty other "behavioral scientists"). After the war was over Murr was busy with some of the chapters of *Assessment of Men* (1948), which contains a full account of the exciting history and ambiguous results of that wholly absorbing world-wide enterprise. Finally, before returning to Harvard Murr wrote a 100-page introduction to Melville's bizarre yet profound *Pierre* (1949) and several other pieces.

From 1950 to 1962 Murr was in charge of grants from foundations and from the government (NIH) which covered the expenses of four successive assessment programs, each consisting of a three-year examination and analysis of the performances in testing situations and in experiments of twenty or more Harvard undergraduates. One result of all of these endeavors was a collection of eighty-eight copious case histories (including in all about 4,000 story compositions), teeming with grist for whoever has the time, bent, and capability to make scientific sense of it. Of the many collaborators in these projects, some (to whom Murr is especially grateful and indebted)—starting with the dynamo of 1950, the disciplined and effective Gardner Lindzey, and ending with the dynamo of 1962, the contagiously zestful and productive Ed Shneidman (not to speak of many other wonders, such as Gerhard Nielsen of Copenhagen, in between)—are already notable for their accomplishments along the way; but, except for a sketch of the icarian personality and an article on the heart rate in stressful dyadic disputations, Murr's bibliography is mute as regards all the grain-full information garnered in those years, and unless he has something creditable to exhibit in his sections of the cooperative volume with which he is currently involved (to be entitled *Aspects of Personality*), there will be no substantial accomplishments to record for those twelve years of industrious activity.

One determinant of the barrenness of Murr's record in the sphere of personological research after World War II was the spontaneous propulsion of his thoughts by the sanguine surplus into other, continuously expanding regions of concern. For ten years or more he and his wife would rise at 4:30 A.M., and by 5 Murr was at his desk ready to set down the bubblings of images and ideas which would invariably invade his stream of consciousness, sometimes in league with a set task but more often not. One of the main regions of concern was one which might be called the world's dilemma. The OSS assessment job had taken Murr around the world to check up on the errors they had made, and he happened to be in Kunming, testing officer candidates for the Chinese Nationalist army, when the news of Hiroshima, announced over the radio of his jeep, set off a hectic procession of horrendous images of the world's fate, which ever since have magnetically directed the path of countless currents of imagination toward some far-off ultimate solution, in the constant view of which, year by year and month by month, short-range international strategies and tactics could be more creatively designed. While others were thinking of ways of reducing momentary tensions and quieting the anxieties of their fellow citizens, Murr was oriented toward the total abolition of war. Peace must be insured by a world government of an unprecedented type, which would never be established or never last without a radical transformation of ethnocentric sentiments and values on both sides of our divided world; and a transformation of this nature would never occur without some degree of synthesis of the best features of the two opposing cultural systems; and this would not take place creatively except in sight of an unprecedented vision and conception of world relationship and fellowship, a kind of superordinate natural religion, or mythologized philosophy. This line of thinking, which brought Murr to a consideration of the determinants of the genesis and history of Judaeo-Christianity, issued in a number of papers listed in the bibliography.

Murr's other absorbing region of concern contained potential constituents for a basic revision and expansion of his theoretical system. It is impossible to summarize 2000 pages of diagrams, notes, and scribblings; but to deprive those voyages of thought of a little of their strangeness, let me just mention a few of the incorporated components that can be readily identified: (1) Keith's group theory of evolution; (2) role theory which Murr, as a member of the newly formed Department of Social Relations, learnt from Talcott Parsons in conjunction with much that he received from Clyde Kluckhohn regarding the pervasive influence of culture; (3) general systems theory, the abstract essence of which Murr derived from Whitehead; (4) adoption of the on-going processes of metabolism (the anabolic composition, $Co$, and the catabolic decomposition, $De$, of energy-binding substances) as the *sine qua non* of the givenness of life, the source of psychic energy (psychometabolism), and the *core* (with additional variables) of his basic paradigm for a host of analogous phenomena at different levels; (5) the application of this paradigm to the problem of the genesis of life from non-life, to the theory of the creative (emergent) evolution of genetical systems, to the life cycle of a single individual, and to the compositional activities of the mind, and so forth, and so forth. A little of all this was included in Auto. 2, which Murr wrote for Sigmund Koch, but not enough to give any of the more recent expositors of contemporary theories of personality the impression that Murr had inched his thoughts a measurable distance beyond their original positions some thirty years ago.

Anyhow, the impression he has given others of a stationary mental apparatus is not very likely to be corrected. After being vouchsafed an extremely happy and full-freighted life, with a few trough and many peak experiences, he was confounded in 1962, on the one hand, by the sudden death of his superlatively good and loyal wife, and, on the other, by the fading of the mental energies on which he had been counting to deal with one or two at least of the ten half-finished books that are calling for completion, residual products of his sanguine surplus.

## EPILOGUE

I told you at the start of this case portrait that my functionally autono-mous will, the conscious governor of my ego system (the little self) had re-solved to check the incontinence of the sanguine surplus from the larger Self and adhere to the corrective maxim. But it must have been apparent to you almost from the start that although I was managing to focus pretty well on the eccentricities of Murr, there was more functional autonomy in the Self than in the self: the legs of the portrait came out too long and lanky, the belly of childhood memories was too bloated, and I had hardly stretched above the eyebrows when I found myself simultaneously at both the ordained space limit and the time limit. Down came the blade of the editor's guillotine, and my last section, the forehead and crown of the portrait, which contained what-ever retrospective bits of wit and wisdom Murr could muster, rolled into the basket with a thud. In short, I need not have taken a paragraph of the pro-logue to describe the sanguine surplus, because it was fated to make a dis-astrous spectacle of itself in the ensuing pages, and to leave Murr and myself, the viewed and the viewer, with one residual query: Would I not have been capable of contributing more substantially to my profession if that eminent ophthalmologist had left my right eye focusing on something just beyond my nose which I could seize and scientifically contain in the hollow of one hand, instead of allowing his own sanguine surplus to take hold of his scalpel and send me off with a right eye that was bound to wander, joyfully but waste-fully, beyond the standard circumference of healthy vision?

## REFERENCES

*Selected Publications by Henry A. Murray*

*Autobiographical and Theoretical*
What should psychologists do about psychoanalysis? *J. abnorm. soc. Psychol.,* 1950, 35, 150–175. (Auto. 1)
Preparations for the scaffold of a comprehensive system. In S. Koch (Ed.), *Psy-chology: a study of a science,* vol. 3. New York: McGraw-Hill, 1959. (Auto. 2)

*Theoretical*
(with staff) *Explorations in personality.* New York: Oxford, 1938.
(with C. D. Morgan) A clinical study of sentiments. (ch. II) *Genet. Psychol. Monogr.,* 1945, 32, 3–311.
Toward a classification of interactions. In T. Parsons, E. A. Shils, E. C. Tolman, *et al.* (Eds.) *Toward a general theory of action.* Cambridge, Mass.: Harvard, 1951.
(with C. Kluckhohn) Outline of a conception of personality, and Personality formation: the determinants. In C. Kluckhohn, H. A. Murray, and D. M.

Schneider (Eds.), *Personality in nature, society, and culture*. New York: Knopf, 1953.

Drive, time, strategy, measurement, and our way of life. In G. Lindzey (Ed.), *Assessment of human motives*. New York: Holt, Rinehart and Winston, 1958.

### Methodology and Methods

(in addition to *Explorations in personality* and A clinical study of sentiments, ch. III)

(with C. D. Morgan) A method of investigating fantasies. *Arch. neurol. Psychiat.*, 1935, *34*, 289–306. Reprinted in R. C. Birney and R. C. Teevan (Eds.), *Measuring human motivation*. Princeton: Van Nostrand, 1962.

Principles of assessment. In H. A. Murray, D. W. MacKinnon, J. G. Miller, D. W. Fiske, & E. Hanfmann, *Assessment of men*. New York: Holt, Rinehart and Winston, 1948.

(with A. Davids) "Preliminary appraisal of an auditory projective technique for studying personality and cognition. *Amer. J. Orthopsychiat.*, 1955, *25*, 543–554.

Introduction. In G. G. Stern, M. I. Stein, & B. S. Bloom, *Methods in personality assessment*. Glencoe, Ill.: Free Press, 1956.

Historical trends in personality research. In H. P. David & J. C. Brengelmann (Eds.), *Perspectives in personality research*. New York: Springer, 1960.

### Research and Case Studies

The effect of fear upon estimates of the maliciousness of other personalities. *J. Psychol.*, 1933, *4*, 310–329.

(with H. A. Wolff & C. E. Smith) The psychology of humor. *J. abnorm. soc. Psychol.*, 1934, *28*, 341–365.

The psychology of humor. II. Mirth responses to disparagement jokes as a manifestation of an aggressive disposition. *J. abnorm. soc. Psychol.*, 1934, *29*, 66–81.

(with D. R. Wheeler) A note on the possible clairvoyance of dreams. *J. Psychol.*, 1936, *3*, 309–313. (concerned with the kidnapping of the Lindbergh baby)

(with C. D. Morgan) Eleven case studies (chs. IV–VII) in A clinical study of sentiments. *Gen. Psychol. Mono.*, 1945, *32*, 3–149.

Introduction. In A. Burton & R. E. Harris (Eds.), *Clinical studies in personality*, Vol. I. New York: Harper & Row, 1947.

American Icarus. In A. Burton & R. E. Harris (Eds.), *Clinical studies of personality*, vol. 2. New York: Harper & Row, 1955.

Notes on the Icarus syndrome. *Folia psychiatrica, neurologica, et neurochirugica Neelandica*, 1958, *61*, 204–208.

Studies of stressful interpersonal disputations. *Amer. Psychologist*, 1963, *18*, 28–36.

### Miscellaneous: State of Man, Evolution, Creativity, and Mythology

Individuality: the meaning and content of individuality in contemporary America. *Daedalus*, 1958, *87*, 25–47. Reprinted in *The American style*, New York, 1958; and in H. M. Ruitenbeek (Ed.), *Varieties of modern social theory*, New York: Dutton, 1963.

Vicissitudes of creativity. In H. H. Anderson (Ed.), *Creativity and its cultivation*. New York: Harper & Row, 1959.

Beyond yesterday's idealisms. Phi Beta Kappa Oration, Harvard Chapter, 1959; printed in C. Brinton (Ed.), *The fate of man*. New York: George Braziller, 1961; also in *Man thinking*, United Chapters of Phi Beta Kappa, Ithaca, N.Y.: Cornell.

Two versions of man. In H. Shapley (Ed.), *Science ponders religion*. New York: Appleton-Century-Crofts, 1960.

The possible nature of a "mythology" to come. In H. A. Murray (Ed.), *Myth and mythmaking*. New York: George Braziller, 1960.

Unprecedented evolutions. *Daedalus*, 1961, *90*, 547–570. Reprinted in H. Hoagland and R. W. Burhoe (Eds.), *Evolution and man's progress*. New York: Columbia, 1962.

Prospect for psychology. *International Congress of Applied Psychology*, Copenhagen, 1961. Reprinted in *Science*, 1962, *136*, 483–488.

The personality and career of Satan. *J. soc. Issues*, XVIII, 1962, 28, 36–54.

### Herman Melville

Introduction with footnotes. In H. A. Murray (Ed.), *Pierre or the ambiguities*. (H. Melville) New York: Farrar, Straus, Hendricks House, 1949.

In nomine diaboli. *The New England Quart.*, 1951, XXIV, 435–452. Reprinted in *Moby-Dick Centennial Essays*, Melville Society (Ed.), 1953; also in *Discussions of Moby-Dick*, M. R. Stern (Ed.), Boston, 1960; and in *Melville, a collection of critical essays*, R. Chase (Ed.), New York: Prentice-Hall, 1962.

### Other Publications Cited

James, William. *The varieties of religious experience*. New York: Longmans, 1903.

———. *The principles of psychology*, vol. I. New York: Dover, 1950.

Jung, C. G. *Psychological types*. New York: Harcourt, Brace & World, 1923.

311

# Sidney Leavitt Pressey

In previous volumes of *Psychology in Autobiography* some contributors have made little or even no mention of their personal lives. I must be more frank; my professional interests had origins in my youth and have continued to relate to my own life—thus my research in gerontology was stimulated by concern over my father's problems of aging and my own. Throughout, I have worked with the conviction that psychology has major contributions to make to human welfare. Now seventy-six, I can comment more freely than a younger man about certain issues and see them in a long perspective.

## NEW ENGLAND HERITAGE

Both my parents came from a little southern New Hampshire village where their families had long lived; part of Grandfather Little's farm had been in his family since before the Revolutionary War. My mother taught country school, attended the New England Conservatory of Music, and played the pipe organ in the Congregational church where Grandfather Pressey was long a deacon. My father graduated from Williams College and Union Theological Seminary after a struggle as regards both finances and health, a year being spent in Colorado because of a diagnosis of incipient tuberculosis. He thereafter served Congregational churches mostly in the Midwest, but always returning whenever he could to visit his aging parents. The most recurring recollections of my childhood are of this then-lovely New England countryside and the kindly people there.

I was born December 28, 1888, in Brooklyn, New York, where my father had his first pastorate; but since I was troubled greatly by asthma, the family moved to Vermont and then to a little Illinois town from which (my father suffering a sunstroke) we went to the cooler climate of St. Paul, Minnesota; in a suburb of that city my childhood and youth were spent. There was much illness in the little family (which included a younger sister) and anxiety about health, also about income and tenure, though my father was among the most successful and respected of the pastors in each community he served. As usual in ministers' families, that service included all of us. My mother kept various women's groups going. I delivered the church newsletter over the parish, played in the Sunday school orchestra, and was handy-boy. We might attend four church meetings a week and had always to be exemplary in this turn-of-the-century, middle-class Puritan suburb where there was no card playing, dancing, nor even bicycle riding on Sunday. My father was always thinking about his work, shy, humorless, often impractical, and moody; my mother was devoted to him and her children, liked by everyone, the wise counselor in times of difficulty though overworked and often ailing herself.

Like most ministers' sons, I was irked by the demands of my father's profession on all our lives, and I came to question the beliefs he preached. But my adolescent idealism was impressed by the selfless commitment to his work of both my parents. For his denomination and his time my father was a liberal and much interested in what would now be called pastoral psychology; he read everything he could find which might help him better understand his own religious convictions and his parishioners' problems. In that middle-class suburb sixty or more years ago, his church was the one institution serving the whole community, and very broadly; there were lectures, entertainments, organizations of various types, opportunities for all to participate in a variety of worthwhile undertakings. In all this, my parents tried to give unobtrusive wise leadership. The concept of one's profession as dedicated to service, but the conviction also that there should be more adequate beliefs and service, more understanding of people's needs and problems, became basic elements in my own educational and vocational plans.

## EDUCATIONAL WASTE, FRUSTRATION, FINDING

Helped by my mother I began reading before entering school. The family subscribed to excellent magazines, my father's library was sizable and included such compendia as the *Encyclopedia Brittanica*; I became an omnivorous reader. I also had a workbench; thus I early developed an interest in handicraft and gadgets which has remained with me. With such a background, elementary school was, for me, often a sitting it out while the teacher taught what I already knew or could more quickly get by myself. For many of my classmates also, the eighth grade was mostly a repetitious waste of time.

In high school four years of Latin was not only drudgery but blocked off other desired courses such as the sciences. Most broadly educative was a summer job in a department store; I made special deliveries all over town including the red-light district, wrapped bundles, and chummed with fellow workers very different from people I had known before. The most valuable course was in typing and shorthand, which resulted in a secretarial job the next summer and has aided me ever since right up to and including the writing of this paper. Also valuable was a "literary society," giving experience in debate. But mostly high school was dreary, and the last year seemed largely surplus.

My first college year was at the University of Minnesota, where in a physical education program I learned to swim, play handball, and tennis; these continued to be my physical recreations so far as I had time for them, till middle life when I turned to fishing and golf. The last three years (the family having moved to Massachusetts) were at Williams, an old New England college in a lovely setting, where student life was then dominated by fraternities and athletic interests. Required were a fifth year of Latin, also mathematics, composition, and English literature, largely repetitive of work had before. Courses in philosophy gave none of the orientation to life I sought. But a course in social psychology, using McDougall's book so titled as chief reference, did give something regarding the dynamics of personality for which I had been groping. It was taught by a student of Royce and James, J. B. Pratt. Through him I obtained a Harvard scholarship, and there I went with high hopes in 1912.

Certain difficulties began at once. Psychology was then in the Department of Philosophy, and my first adviser, the philosopher R. B. Perry. He protested my desire to take Walter B. Cannon's medical school course in physiology as a foundation for psychology and Dean Holmes' basic course in the new Graduate School of Education, where I sought ways schools might be made less bumbling than I had found them. Perry said I needed instead more epistemology and metaphysics. I insisted but so did he; the result was a very busy year, not only because of the course load (and time taken in the old streetcars across town to the medical school), but also because of the diversity of associates and, indeed, basic points of view in graduate school, medical school, and the school of education. But it was all very educative . . . ! As a result, in all my student advising, I have tried to give greater freedom, and for forty years have been active in efforts to improve graduate programs.

For further study I needed money, and if, as I now thought, I desired to teach in college, I should try it. Here my father had not only a suggestion —why not broaden my experience by teaching in a missionary college—but a place found, a little home-missionary college in Alabama. So there I went, never having known a Negro except for one college classmate, nor been in the South. Not only did the race prejudices there shock me, but even more the gross irrelevance of the educational program to student needs. For those students attending at great sacrifice and presumably going back to live in the South, there was a conventional arts program; in the little theological seminary Hebrew was taught, but nothing about the problems to be faced in a struggling Negro southern crossroads church. The students sensed these inadequacies; a protest meeting turned into a mild riot so blunderingly dealt with by the president that the faculty chose a committee (of which I was a leader) to ask the home office in New York to review the whole situation.

That review was made with such arrogant disregard of basic problems that all the younger faculty left at the end of the year. I again had a Harvard scholarship, and returned there almost exhausted.

The next year was a dreary struggle with ill health, language requirements, and a Titchnerian psychology barren of significance for me. When I saw him about a thesis topic, Münsterberg explained (with his famous accent) that each student should select his own, but went on to remark that psychological effects of color much needed investigation; he had been told that walls tinted a soft blue soothed hospital patients, that French women working in the red light of photographic darkrooms seemed thereby made more erotic, that clerks in offices with pastel green walls worked more efficiently. Then he paused. My cue was evidently to choose this topic. I did so.

After much preliminary experimenting, the following setup and procedure were arrived at. The subject sat in a darkroom at a small table covered with unglazed white paper over which was a light fixture giving either red, green, or blue light of the same brightness, or bright medium or dim ordinary light. In a given hour, each of the three hues or brightnesses was on for about twelve minutes with about four minutes' intermission between. In each period various records were obtained including pulse and respiration, judgments of the pleasantness of substances touched, rate of free association, recall of nonsense syllables, tapping at most comfortable speed, rate of multiplying one-by two-place numbers, and rate of continuous choice reaction. The last three tests seemed to show a somewhat faster rate with bright lights than dim; no data evidenced any effect of hue (1921). Such dynamogenic effect of brightness seemed plausible—and of possible interest to electric light companies! But it seemed obvious that twelve minutes with a given brightness in a laboratory darkroom at odd inconsequential tasks (and a total for three years of only twenty-six subjects) told little about possible effects of similar brightness continued throughout the day while working at tasks more substantial, in shop or office or schoolroom. I became impatient of the artificialities and limitations of the laboratory. And meantime I had begun work with the man most influential on my career—R. M. Yerkes.

Here was a man dedicated to his work and of notable competence in it. And he also was impatient of the philosophers; one afternoon he took me into his office and pointed to a place over his desk where had hung a reproduction of a group portrait of James, Royce, and Palmer—in their place he had pictures of three apes. "These," he said dryly, "are my new friends!" The range of his research was exhilarating: from worms and frogs and mice not only to the apes but also to humans, from idiots to "that most superior of all persons, the physician!" He was then directing psychological work at the Boston Psychopathic Hospital and chronically in friction with the staff there. Venturing into this last work, I found it fascinating, and Yerkes appointed me as a psychological intern there.

The hospital was a relatively new institution then, handling about 2,000 cases a year, keeping each long enough for first diagnosis and reference to state hospitals, social agencies, or other provision for treatment. To it the police brought chronic alcoholics, criminals possibly psychotic, girls off the streets; physicians, employers, social agencies referred individuals exhibiting symptoms of mental illness or disability; into the outpatient department came problem children from schools and juvenile courts and agencies for child care, and immigrants the Port Authority had doubts about admitting. The excellent staff was headed by E. E. Southard, outstanding among psychiatrists of his time; there were also psychologists and social caseworkers. As intern I made acquaintance with all these various groups, had access to the wards and case records and excellent staff library, and attended morning staff rounds and staff meetings. Here were abundant opportunities for study of personality problems. The prevailing psychiatry saw causation as organic rather than psychogenic, but with some interest in Freud, I saw cultural conflicts and socioeconomic stresses as often major but neglected causative factors.

Research was encouraged. I had projects under Southard and also chief-of-staff Herman Adler, but of course primarily with Yerkes. At his suggestion I gave his Point Scale of General Ability (having essentially Binet-type material but with like items together rather than scattered through age levels) to dementia praecox and chronic alcoholic patients whose histories indicated that they had attained adult intelligence. These results were compared in detail with results from feebleminded and normal children of the same total or mental age and a distinctive profile found, the psychotic doing especially poorly on tests of immediate memory and learning but well on vocabulary. The sum of the differences of the psychotics from the merely feebleminded was used as a measure of irregularity; and by counting only those five tests on which differences were greatest, a "differential unit" was formed which distinguished with greater clarity the psychotic from the feebleminded. These results could be put in terms of a differential table showing the percentage probability that a given case was (for example) a feebleminded case with some psychotic symptoms rather than a deteriorated alcoholic (1917). Also, adult feebleminded gave a somewhat different profile from feebleminded children of the same mental age. It is believed that these were the first differentiating mental measurements of psychotics and, using irregularity to distinguish deterioration from adult defect, also adult from child mental profiles.

So at long last in 1917 at the age of twenty-eight I obtained my Ph.D., having essentially completed two doctorate projects and other research besides. In the process I had taken four graduate school years instead of the then-usual three, and, in spite of my initial advisors, I got what I wanted but spent about half my time on what I did not want and became physically almost exhausted from overwork (plagued with insomnia, episodes of dizziness, and indigestion). Yerkes obtained for me an outstanding appointment for the next year as a special research assistant at Indiana University to investigate problems of mental deficiency and disease in that state. Postponement of that appointment seemed likely when, shortly after the United States entered the First World War, I was drafted, and then when Yerkes offered me a commission for participation in the Army Psychological work; but on both occasions I was rejected as physically in such condition as to be unfit for any military service. So in September at Indiana I began what was then a largely new type of service by a state university for the schools and also state welfare institutions.

One of the social caseworkers at the Boston Psychopathic Hospital was a Vassar graduate with some work in psychology there, who showed interest in my research. Though a childhood victim of polio, corrective operations and remedial exercises had carried her through to unusual physical vigor, but with certain psychological residuals such as morbid fear of operations, cancer (from which her mother had died), childbirth, storms, and closed places—on a European trip she had slept on a deck chair, finding a cabin intolerable. We talked over our problems, became very well acquainted, and planned marriage. This was delayed until after my rejection for military service, but early in 1918 she joined me in Indiana and, desiring a career, began graduate work and obtained the doctorate with my guidance, using part of the total project for her research.

## TOWARD A PSYCHO-EDUCATIONAL TECHNOLOGY

The initial task at Indiana University was to determine the number of subnormal children in the schools of the county, but a secondary interest was also to locate those of superior ability. It soon became evident that, even for a very first rough sorting out, the teachers could not be depended upon; one was found who had herself never progressed beyond the fourth grade! So a multitest group examination for grades three through twelve was devised, and all the schools in the county were visited by me and my wife travelling in a buggy, or by a graduate student. In the little one-room schools the group test was first given and quickly scored, then the Stanford-Binet given to doubtful cases. By such relating to the Binet, also by giving the group examination (a) to all who could take it in the state school for the feebleminded and comparing results with Binet and case records there, and (b) to classes for the gifted in the Louisville schools, evidence was obtained validating that the examination did indeed differentiate the very dull and very bright.

Clearly the schools of this largely rural southern Indiana county were burdened with many subnormal children; also bright children were being held to a slow-average lockstep pace, though a few who had accelerated illustrated how successful such expediting might be. All this was reported in local and state conferences. Further surveys evidenced that schools in the same small city might differ markedly in their "pupil material," also different rural areas, in congruence with the socioeconomic status of the areas served; and different promotion policies showed unexpected, significant results (1919). We had many requests for more such work.

I therefore began construction of very inexpensive and easy-to-give-take-and-score tests markedly different from the elaborate batteries then appearing and prevalent since—hoping to make tests a convenient, welcomed aid rather than a resented burden in the schools. For grades three through twelve the first "crossout" test, on the front page of a little six-by-nine-inch four-page folder, consisted of twenty-five items such as "see a I man on," the task being to draw a line through the word not belonging in the sentence. The second test consisted of twenty-five lines such as "dog cow horse oak cat," in which the item that did not belong with the others was to be crossed off. A number series and an abstract meanings test were similarly simple and of some intrinsic interest. The blanks cost only $1.25 per hundred, a class could be tested in twenty-five minutes, blanks scored one per minute. Another inexpensive easy-to-use folder made up what is believed to have been the first group objective examination for grades one through three. The first test consisted of twenty-five patterns of dots with one extra to be marked off; the second test had groups of pictures, for example two dogs and a cat, and the incongruent object was to be checked; a paper form board and picture-absurdities test followed, having surplus or wrong elements to be crossed out (with L. C. Pressey, 1919). Very practical validating research showed that this little four-test folder, given in the first month of the first grade, sectioned pupils better than a teacher could then do, in terms of the sectioning she had arrived at by the end of the year. The two cross-out folders thus roughly surveyed general ability for grades one through twelve. Similarly simple little folders sampled attainment in the basic school subjects, and a double-entry table then facilitated location of "under-achievers."

Most original was a personality inventory which in its most-used form had on three six-by-nine-inch pages a total of 450 items all covered by the average student in about twenty-five minutes—a record as regards compactness and yield of score in a given time which apparently still stands after forty years. On the first page, the directions were to cross out everything considered wrong in twenty-five lines listing a variety of borderland social and moral taboos such as "begging smoking flirting spitting giggling," then go back and circle the one item in each line thought worst—in effect, each word was a question and each line one more. The second and third pages similarly sampled worries and interests. The total number of words crossed was considered the total affect, and the number of lines in which the circled word was other than the one which had been found modal was total idiosyncrasy. These were called "X-O" tests because of the crossing and circling. "Differential units" for various purposes were to be empirically determined; thus certain words were found distinctively more or less often marked by good as compared with poor students; these were scored as a subscale and found in combination with a test of general ability to give better prognosis of academic success than that test alone (1927, pp. 71–80).

In 1923 I used the inventory in a survey from the middle grades through college, finding a progressive liberalization of attitudes especially through the college years; and I repeated the survey in 1933, 1943, and 1953, finding a continuing liberalization over the thirty-year period. Analysis showed especially a consistent and striking change in sex-social attitudes—less marking of immodesty as wrong, more frank checking of kissing and flirting as liked, and more worry about marriage. Data from adults in 1953 showed progressive increase with age in items marked wrong, which cross-comparison indicated was not due to increasing conservatism with age, but rather to a persistence of attitudes established in the young adulthood of the earlier time (with A. W. Jones, 1955). These in total appear to be the most systematic measures yet of cultural change over a substantial period of time and in relation to developmental change.

The four years at Indiana University resulted in fifty-three papers by myself, my wife, local teachers, and the departmental secretary—I at once began bringing others into the program and giving them such recognition. I had some clerical and secretarial help, usually taught one class sometimes in extension, presented papers at local, state, and national meetings, and worked in schools and state institutions. It was an almost ideal way to begin a professional career and resulted in an invitation to Ohio State University as assistant professor in 1921, where I insisted on an appointment for my wife also.

There the feverish pace continued. In the next dozen years were produced three books, two laboratory manuals and a monograph, some seventy-five professional papers, and four teaching machines. I also had a full teaching load, increasing numbers of graduate students, and committee assignments. I also attended regional and national meetings in both psychology and education, usually participating in some way. It was a marvelously stimulating, challenging life. In 1926 I was given the rank of full professor.

The first book (with L. C. Pressey, 1922) brought together in very practical fashion then-current work in testing of both ability and attainment in the school subjects. The book was widely used and reissued in England and in a French translation. The second text (with L. C. Pressey, 1926), based on my experience at the Boston Psychopathic Hospital and in the Indiana surveys, attempted an overview of the full range of mental abnormalities and deficiencies with avoidance of both psychiatric and psychoanalytic technicalities. It featured a reassuring consideration of the average person as typically having some mental quirks and so not to be unduly alarmed thereby. It emphasized cultural and socioeconomic stresses as causative of, or at least involved in, psychopathologies, and the importance of a more widespread understanding of problems of mental health.

Most original was a volume (with others, 1927) reporting eighteen investigations regarding problems of higher education—with which two-thirds of all doctoral projects under my direction have been concerned, on the double ground of need therefor and appropriateness for students looking toward college positions. The first chapter differentiated most effective methods of study by contrasting those used by superior and failing students; a laboratory course based on the findings was shown to be a great help to probationers; case reports made vivid their problems. Some students in a required course in educational psychology were able to pass the final examination at the beginning of the course; some topics were so generally known as to need no teaching, the understanding of a few students was actually confused thereby, and some very important topics were left out—pretests and both curricular and instructional research seemed clearly needed. A simple test of sensitivity to blank verse showed many freshmen to have none, even after all that high school Shakespeare. Why, then, should it be taught in high school? Unsuspected gross deficiencies in preparation (for example, inability to handle common or decimal fractions) were found to hamper some students but were readily remediable. Incisive experiments regarding teaching methods led to substantial improvements, evidenced for example by more students electing further courses in the subject. Inclusion in doctorate programs of consideration of the problems of higher education was urged. I introduced such a course and gave it for many years.

Such research was continued. Thus I persuaded a courageous graduate student to take four oral examinations under four different faculty committees with concealed stenographers taking down all questions asked. Most of the questions in one examination were irrelevant; two committees failed the candidate and two passed her (with L. C. Pressey and Elinor J. Barnes, 1932). As a result the department made certain changes in its examining procedure. But I was most interested in what might be called psycho-educational technology in the public schools. Thus having noted a remark by Leonard Ayres that certain features of handwriting might hamper legibility though not affect appearance, I collected samples of handwriting from elementary school through college and from adults, had these read by a laboratory class, illegibilities being checked. Relatively few malformings ("a" written to look like "u" or "d" like "cl", or "g" like "y", "r" or "e" like undotted "i") accounted for the most difficulties in reading. A simple chart facilitated identifying and tabulating such errors. Remedial work concentrating on each pupil's specific difficulties was very effective: thus a fourth grade class so aided showed not only gains over a control class in speed of writing and quality, but also a fifty percent increase in the rate at which its writing could be read.

Problems in English composition were analogously investigated. Thus uses of capital letters in magazines, newspapers, and business letters were tabulated, also, capitalization errors in samples of writing from elementary school through college and from adults, and both usage and errors data brought together in one table in terms of frequencies per 10,000 words. The few needed usages not mastered were then evident (1924). Individual conferences with pupils about their capitalization errors gave insight as to causes (with Pera Campbell, 1933). Rules for capitalization were then formulated, taking account of actual usage, errors, and pupils' misunderstandings, and a little six by nine inch test sheet was made up, systematically covering these rules. Essentials in punctuation, grammar, and sentence structure were similarly determined (most conventional material on these last two topics being found irrelevant to practical needs) and simple diagnostic tests covering them prepared, also a little pamphlet, *Guide to Correctness in Written Work*, giving rules which if followed would eliminate nine-tenths of all errors in composition. These materials were very widely used.

Special attention was given to that most important tool subject—reading. A 1000-word sampling method of measuring the vocabulary burden of books (with Bertha Lively, 1923) showed even some primers having sizeable loads; a junior high school science text had a technical vocabulary of over 2000 terms. But a series of master's degree studies taking account of frequency of use, judgments as to importance by experienced teachers, and adult needs, usually showed essential terms to be perhaps a quarter of those used—most texts were barnacled with excess terminology. The goal was to prepare for each public school subject a classified list of important technical terms and simple tests systematically covering them, which would serve as both appraising and instructional devices. All this was part of the great general interest around 1925 in the "psychology of the school subjects." But the "teaching machine" I exhibited at the APA meeting that year proved ahead of the times.

In a window of the little apparatus showed a four-choice question to which the student responded by pressing the key corresponding to the answer he thought right. If it was, the next question turned up, but if not, he had to try again until he did find the right answer—meanwhile a counter kept a cumulative record of his tries. Moreover (two features no device since has had) if a lever were raised, the device was changed into a self-scoring *and* rewarding testing machine: whatever key was pressed, the next question turned up, but the counter counted only rights; also when the set on a reward dial was reached, a candy lozenge was automatically presented (1926). A paper the next year reported a device which, on successive times through an objective lesson sheet, presented again only those questions on which a mistake had been made before the right answer was found the previous time through, that is, there was selective review. And a third device automatically marked each error on a student's test-answer strip, printed on it the total of his errors, and kept a cumulative count of number of errors on each question so that the instructor could at once see which questions had been most missed and center his discussion about them (1932). Carefully controlled experiments evidenced that class use of this last little machine as an instructional

aid significantly increased learning as measured by midterm and final examinations, and the first type of device even more. My former student Hans
Peterson and his brother devised and similarly attested the value of a very
simple paper feedback "teaching machine"; if a wrong answer on a test answer
slip was moistened, it at once turned red, but the right answer green. If such
feedback devices were used with materials derived from curricular and instructional research such as described above, an "industrial revolution" in
education seemed possible (Lumsdaine-Glaser Sourcebook, pp. 32–93, 497–
505).

However, by this time the Great Depression was making it ironic to
facilitate the progress of young people into careers when there were no
careers to be found or to save labor in teaching when there were many more
teachers than jobs. The manufacturer of the one crude teaching machine I
had been able to get on the market withdrew it from sale. The publisher of
my tests went out of business. And—my wife asked for a divorce, having plans
for a second marriage. The fault may chiefly have been mine: we were too
much together, I too often insisted on correcting what I considered hasty in
her work while she thought me overly careful, my compulsive absorption in
my work was undoubtedly at times hard to live with. So not only my marriage,
but a professional partnership, broke up. After thirty-four years the hurt is
still with me. But in the crisis, friendships were found stronger than I had
realized. Two colleagues, who had been more aware than I of my wife's dis-
affection, willingly served as witnesses for me to obtain the divorce on
grounds of desertion; the departmental chairman and dean and university vice
president, all of whom knew us well, assured me that my university status
would not be affected. And when I talked with my wife's best friend (also a
woman on the university faculty) about the situation, her sensible kindly
understanding was in healing contrast to the tense irritability to which I had
been accustomed. The association ripened into a marriage which over the
past thirty years has been vital for my well-being and the most precious experience of my life. Thus at the age of forty-five, both my personal and my
professional life were largely reconstituted. So far as possible I dropped work,
especially at the public school level with which my first wife had been associated and which she wished somewhat to continue, to build something of a
second career. And for that, a major undertaking was ready at hand.


## TEACHER-TRAINING, LIFESPAN VIEW, ACCELERATION

Around 1930 the College of Education began an attempt to remake its
entire program; I was a member of the central committee and some dozen
subsidiary groups. I agreed to criticisms that then-current textbooks in educational psychology were loaded with charts showing the anatomy of the spinal

chord, progress of rats in a maze, and nonsense-syllable learning in the laboratory, but had too little about children in school and their work there. And I agreed that the complex meaningful learning going on there was little explained by theory derived largely from research with animals. I countered that the required courses in education were also not close to educational realities, notorious on campus as poorly taught and inconsistent—200 students given an uninterrupted lecture on the importance of small classes with full pupil participation and free discussion! And I accepted the challenge to build a course in educational psychology which would in content *and* method be accepted as basic to a sound program of teacher education. In this effort I brought out a text (1933) radically different from those in the field at that time, with a congruent sourcebook and laboratory manual. I developed instructional methods yet more venturesome and a supportive graduate program.

The first half of the text, "Development During the School Years," included chapters on physical growth and health, stressing interrelationships with personality; on interests manifested in play and reading, radio, and movie likes; on the social psychology of these years, stressing the often conflicting social worlds of home, school, peers, and adults; on emotional stress, seeing causes therefor especially in these conflicts; on the individual child with brief case studies illustrating the need for a teacher to understand each pupil as a person. Material came from pediatrics, psychiatry, and sociology as well as education and psychology. The volume's second half, "Learning in School," featured curves of progress in arithmetic, reading, and composition with evidence that curricular and instructional research could make learning more effective. Curves for forgetting showed how little might be retained months or years after of what had been learned in a school or college class. Transfer data showed how little Latin benefited English, or Algebra "trained the mind," but stressed "applicational transfer"—how a school safety campaign might be made to reduce accidents. Omitted was all the research with animals and in the artificialities of the laboratory and also theory based essentially thereon, in favor of cognitive concepts of meaningful learning. Again sources were various, including *Science Education, English Journal, Journal of Home Economics,* as well as the more commonly cited psychological periodicals. The book was very widely used, issued in a Swedish edition, and translated into Japanese and Turkish—but comparatively little noted by psychologists, perhaps because too apostate in theory and sources.

Also distinctive was the *Casebook of Research in Educational Psychology* (with J. E. Janney, 1937): seventy-six very readable and interesting reports showing that, for instance, training therein can increase leadership in children, that first-grade tots using self-instructional matter can teach themselves to read, that history may best be taught backward, that a motion picture may have long-lasting effects on adolescent attitudes, that educational effectiveness can literally be weighted—that youngsters in a course in vocational agriculture increased the yield of pork per sow on their farms by over 200 pounds! A *Laboratory Workbook in Applied Educational Psychology* (with N. E. Troyer, 1936) began with a data sheet to be filled out and turned in by each student regarding his background and interests, thus acquainting his instructor with him and illustrating knowledge a teacher should have about her pupils. Simple exercises in tabulating, finding percentiles, making and interpreting graphs were based on data as to needs therefor to read texts in educational psychology and use tests. Since most public school teachers had been found unfamiliar with professional journals, another task called for selection and appraisal of three (from samples in the laboratory) most relevant to teaching plans. Yet another project involved selection, from samples available in the classroom, and evaluation of three standard tests each student might wish to use in his teaching. All the twenty-five projects were similarly practical—for example, a diagnosis of illegibilities in each other's handwriting, as described earlier.

The course, taken usually in the freshman year, met in five fifty-minute sessions for a quarter in sections of about thirty students each (five to eight sections each quarter), the instructors being doctoral candidates mostly in educational psychology and having as their research projects some issue of college teaching, often with this course serving as laboratory. I usually taught one section each quarter. It was understood that any instructor could visit any other class (including mine) any time. There were weekly staff meetings. I declared that under all these circumstances teaching by graduate students was *better* than by the average faculty member and invited my colleagues in education to come see. All sections met in a large room re-served exclusively for this course and having round tables seating five—cast-offs from a dormitory dining room and repaired as a class project by students in the course majoring in industrial arts, who also made cabinets holding sample tests and other materials used and exhibit cases displaying instructional material and other relevant matter, much of it brought in by the students and explained in class by them. On the wall were relevant pictures and charts and above them a frieze depicting children at play or in school, drawn on wrapping paper with crayons by fine arts students in the course.

Perhaps half the class hours went into very informal class discussion—never formal lectures. More often the students worked at the tables, going to the cases for laboratory materials and supplementary reading as needed, talking freely with each other and the instructor. Some laboratory work might be service to a school; thus when the school superintendent in a small city asked help in a survey, a young instructor and his wife and a student from each section spent three days there giving tests and forms, which were graded in the laboratory and first reports drawn up there (with others, 1940).

Beginning with the information on the student data sheet, each instructor was expected to get acquainted with his students and foster their getting acquainted with each other. At each table, such acquaintance proceeded rapidly and might be broadened by moving some students from one table to another. Sociometric appraisals evidenced that students became much more widely and closer acquainted than in the average class (with David C. Hanna, 1943). Indeed, alumni have told me of several marriages which so began. Since the quarter of educational psychology normally followed the required quarter course in general psychology, it was often possible to continue the same instructor with largely the same group through two quarters, thus increasing acquaintance yet more. An instructor might occasionally have lunch with groups of students or arrange class parties or picnics, all the time watching each youngster in a variety of situations and using them for the benefit of each. I have long felt that counselors and therapists grossly limited their understanding of cases and yet more their helpfulness by depending almost entirely on that highly special and often artificial methodology, the interview, when such informal classes as described above give opportunities for interviews when needed but permit observation of each student in various situations *and* use of them therapeutically. Both case studies and a variety of other evidence made clear such values.

As a result of the curriculum revision mentioned a few paragraphs above, all other departments in the College of Education were done away with and all other required courses merged in a series labelled Education number so and so. But the course in educational psychology had gotten itself a new and distinctive text, sourcebook, laboratory manual, and the most colorful, unique, and lively classroom in the college, often shown to visiting educators. It was handling some 800 students a year in classes of around thirty by methods advocated (but not practiced) by the "progressive educators" on the faculty, with tight supervision obtaining excellent instruction from graduate students while both training them in such teaching and fostering relevant research. Appraisals by seniors and recent graduates rated the course outstanding. The college agreed that educational psychology should remain independent, and the required course continue under my direction—as it did for some twenty-five years. But outcomes were not only local. The wide use of the text and other materials, the reports I gave at meetings and published in journals (for instance, 1940, 1942), and the influence of former instructors in the course, many of whom soon moved into positions of some importance, all presumably helped keep psychology explicitly in teacher-training and put educational psychology explicitly in the AAAP and then in the reorganized APA—as will be mentioned shortly.

Meanwhile from 1934 through 1939, I was working on what I appraise as my best book, *Life: A Psychological Survey* (with J. E. Janney and R. G. Kuhlen, 1939). Having experienced certain stresses in midlife, I wanted to study what life then looked like. The volume considered the full sweep of human development and change throughout the life span, with emphasis (surely appropriate in this time of depression and international turmoil) on socioeconomic and cultural factors affecting that development. In both respects the book was a radical departure from those then current. Most seemed to assume that development stopped at eighteen; one venturesome author gave fifteen pages to all the years from puberty till death, but forty-five pages to development from conception till birth; I left out the last topic completely and gave most space to the years after twenty. Another text gave thirty percent of its space to such topics as inheritance of wing color in the fruit fly, microscopic structure of various tissues, and behavior of chicks reared in darkness, but to socioeconomic and cultural phenomena only three pages; again I left out all the first type of material and gave a third of the book to the last (1940, also 1949).

For the wide-ranging library work involved, I assembled a little staff of students, paying them myself—during the Depression no funds therefor were available and many students were in great need. The two who were with the undertaking the full five years I made co-authors. And I used "quarters off" for relevant "field work": visits to settlement houses and housing developments and courts in New York and Washington, to congressional hearings and government bureaus, to CCC camps and WPA projects, to Mexico for a glimpse of a more primitive economy and culture. A summer's teaching at the University of Hawaii in 1937 was followed by four months work there using especially my friend Gregg Sinclair's Institute of Oriental Studies, and contacts with the many racial groups in the Hawaiian islands.

Part one of the volume dealt with "Conditions and Circumstances of Life," noting the population explosion (not much noted then) and the lengthening life span, with data on marriage and divorce and the family, on employment, and differences in different parts of the world in these respects. Again with many simple tables and graphs the next chapter considered living conditions in different world areas and from earlier times to now, also wealth, income, and education. A chapter on "the invisible environment—culture" dramatically illustrated changes as in the status of women, codes of conduct and humanitarianism, and in science and technology (and what changes since this 1939 book!). Then central issues were turned to: first physical growth—not only through adolescence but especially after and into age—in physique, strength, skill, and morbidity. The book considered many problems: Not only how does "intelligence" grow through the growth years but does it cease growing or even decline soon thereafter; when is there most creativity; and when warrant for retirement? What is and what should be the course of the work life? How do interests change not only from five to fifteen but to thirty, sixty, eighty? What changes occur in social life through all these years; in attitudes, character traits, personality? How do brief life stories of morons, criminals, psychotics, average citizens, and famous men and women illustrate these issues? And finally in the light of all this, how might a reader best try to increase his efficiency, better his adjustments, and plan his life?

The book was well received as a pioneering venture, tried in a few colleges as a beginning text, and found increasing use in courses in developmental psychology extended to cover the life span and in adult education for courses on "the psychology of adult life." I increasingly turned my efforts in these directions, had large evening classes in a course on "Psychology in Biography" (as I later found Elliott was doing), initiated the APA Division on "Adulthood and Age" (1948), and in 1957 published, with Kuhlen, *Psychological Development Through the Life Span.* All this in total has, I believe, contributed appreciably to increased recognition of the need that psychological phenomena be considered in the perspective of the total span of life--and with a broad scholarship reaching discriminatingly into the social as well as the biological sciences.

The outbreak of the Second World War brought great interest in ways to expedite various types of training and in educational acceleration. I suggested to Dean Klein of the College of Education that this last topic greatly needed intensive investigation (for which in sundry respects I was well prepared). He arranged (with the support in this as in many other matters of my good friend Harold Burtt, chairman of the Department of Psychology) that for several years my time was largely freed for such research, with a small staff and excellent campus-wide cooperation. The total project was reported in some twenty-four papers and a monograph (1949), with further papers since.

An historical survey emphasized the incoordinations in the total American educational system and possibilities of time-saving in both school and college. There, the freshman year often largely repeated secondary school work. Many, including President Eliot of Harvard, had advocated three instead of four college undergraduate years, and Clark College had for twenty years so operated (as did the English universities). Ph.D. programs, imported from Germany where they followed the *Gymnasium,* were here put on top of the American four-year college; we compiled data showing that, as a result, Americans obtained the doctorate about four years older than German students. The long summer vacation seemed a relic of an agricultural economy.

Many excellent investigations had also agreed that students entering college young did best, and those graduating young had the best records. We piled up the most extensive data so far emphasizing these findings and showing that young students were not maladjusted but rather participated more in student activities. We also showed that students who during the war years completed a four-year undergraduate program in three calendar years or less (a few in two years) did *better* academically than cases paired with them in ability and age at entrance, and were about as active in student affairs. Most common means of acceleration was by attending school four quarters, and we gathered evidence indicating no harmful effects therefrom or from the heavier-than-average course loads sometimes taken; and students taking credit by examination thereafter did well in courses thus advanced to. It seemed clear that many students could progress more rapidly than the usual lockstep pace (begin school at six, then take twelve years in school and four in college); and there were intimations that functioning ability might be increased thereby (Pressey, 1962). Indeed, studies of precocious geniuses suggest that they may be in no small part the product of opportunity to progress rapidly (1955).

But might the accelerated student begin a career too young? We found that young women graduating from our College of Education at the age of twenty had a somewhat better professional record thereafter than cases paired with them as to ability but graduating at twenty-two. A ten-year followup of the above-mentioned students who during the war finished a four-year program in three years or less showed they were doing better than the controls who took four (Pressey and Flesher, 1955). Men graduating from an eastern college young more often had superior careers. And continuing investigation brought evidence that those obtaining the doctorate young tend more often to become outstanding. Thus, recently, median age of attaining the Ph.D. degree in psychology has been thirty-one, but for APA presidents it was twenty-five (1962; 1965). All this is congruent with Lehman's evidence of greatest creativity in the young adult years and more generally, of greatest vitality and liveliness of interests during those years (with R. G. Kuhlen, 1957).

Now over a quarter of the population of this country is in school, five million in higher education and this number likely to double soon, with increasing numbers of these continuing into some form of professional training. As things are now, half of such a man's life may pass before he can begin his life-work. As Dael Wolfle has recently declared in a striking editorial in *Science,* "It almost seems as if a conspiracy existed to delay the age at which the formal educational system lets go of a young scientist and allows him to be on his own" (1964, p. 104). And he goes on to specify how from the first grade (half as many children enter at five now as twenty years ago) to the doctorate (now taken a year later than formerly) there is delay—and now more often a post-doctorate to delay further. For many years (really since the beginning of my career) I have been fighting that conspiracy. There is abundant evidence that more bright children should begin school at five, go on to obtain the undergraduate degree by twenty, and complete professional training by twenty-five. Years would thus be added to a career in the most creative time of life—also more students would thus be able to complete such training and university facilities freed therefor.

## APA, AUTOMATION, AGEING

Like most applied psychologists, I was sympathetic with and did all I could to foster the organization of the American Association of Applied

Psychology before the Second World War. And I urged friends to join and set up a section in educational psychology; many were moving toward the American Educational Research Association. Of that section I was chairman during the war. However, psychology then again became greatly interested in applications, and I was sympathetic with Yerkes' efforts to bring the two associations back together but with such reorganization as would meet the needs which had caused the fission. In 1944–45 I was a member of both the governing board of the AAAP and the council of the APA and appointed to a joint committee to consider proposals for again having one association but composed of divisions giving recognition to the many various types of work then evident in the total field of psychology. After many meetings, essentially the present organization of the APA was arrived at. I then did my best, as the one person on both Board and Council, to obtain approval by these groups and then a vote-through at the business meetings of both associations. After some uncertainties, all this was done. For several years thereafter, efforts (which I opposed) were made to reduce drastically the number of divisions, but all failed. And, as already mentioned, I initiated the first division (on maturity and age) thereafter added—thus also trying out the procedure for such addition. Perhaps it will now be generally agreed that, with the great growth in numbers of psychologists and diversification of their interests, some such structure was necessary to give these various interests an opportunity to develop and for those concerned to associate.

Early in the War I wrote the Navy Office of Research and Invention, telling of my teaching machines. A reply asked what they cost. I answered that they were not in manufacture but that I had working models which I would be glad to bring to Washington and demonstrate at my own expense. To this there was no reply. However, after the war Victor Raimy from Ohio State became a member of the staff of that office and suggested that I make application for a grant. This was obtained and renewed, supporting some eight doctoral projects and making possible the most systematic research in the field thus far—largely in the numerous sections in educational psychology. The device used most was a little three by five punchboard: a face-plate of thin press-board had thirty rows each of four one-eighth inch holes in two columns; under it could be inserted a slip of paper and under that a keyplate with holes only for the right answers, face-plate and guide strips for the inserts were riveted to a pressboard base. The "teach-test" questions were on a mimeographed sheet. The student answered each question by pushing his pencil-point into the hole in the face-plate of the punchboard corresponding to the answer he thought right. If it was, his pencil pushed through the paper on into the keyplate hole. But if he was wrong, the pencil-point barely broke through the slip of paper, and he had to try again until he did find the right answer, until the pencil-point did go deep (1950).

Using chiefly this very simple device, a variety of issues were investigated with a great variety of materials from nonsense syllables to college textbooks and in various ways. Such feedback with objective items was found to aid meaningful learning much more than rote learning and to show on write-in as well as objective end-tests. Analysis showed the feedback to aid in two ways: initial right answers about which the learner was somewhat uncertain were confirmed as right and so more likely to be made again, and (by far the most important effect) initial wrong answers were at once identified as such in immediate juxtaposition to the right answer, and wrongs were thereafter avoided. Items varied greatly in their instructional efficacy; difficult, challenging questions exposing common misconceptions were the best. With meaningful matter, the elucidative learning came mostly the first time through a teach-test, but repeating it added a little. If in a college course a teach-test was given only occasionally and incidentally, and a check test a day or so later repeated or paraphrased some questions and added some new ones on the same topic, gains over a control group were found to be relatively specific and did not extend to the new items. But an instructional aid should rather be used systematically as part of a total teaching plan.

To appraise one way of doing so, experienced instructors in some sections of the course in educational psychology began the hour when a reading assignment was due, by giving a teach-test thereon with a punchboard. As each student finished (usually in about fifteen minutes), he was free to look up any point in the reading (usually available in the classroom) or discuss it with another student or the instructor—for whom all this furnished points of departure for his further discussion of the assignment, to which two class hours were usually allotted. Toward the end of the second hour another punchboard test was given, with time for brief discussion afterwards. Though the teach-tests did not count on grades, they were an additional reason for preparing. Of the total sixty feedback questions, some were factual, others applicational, or judgemental; headings might group them with page references after each, indicating where consideration of it could be found. Half of the assignments were so handled, the others taught in the usual fashion of informal discussion. And half of the first and second half-quarter objective examinations were on these last assignments; of those questions on auto-instructed readings, a third were repeated from the teach-tests, a third paraphrased therefrom, and a third new.

Meanwhile, other sections went through the teach-test blanks but without the punchboard; answers were marked on an answer slip, then discussed with other students or the instructor, who thereupon collected the slips, later graded them, and returned them for possible further discussion. And meanwhile, control sections went through the entire course in the conventional fashion of informal class-meeting. Instructors were rotated and the special procedures soon became routine; the total research design seemed sound. On midterm and final examinations the punchboard-aided sections (even though so aided on less than half the assignments) scored strikingly higher than the controls and above those going through all the teach-tests but without that immediate feedback. Item-analysis showed the punchboard sections doing best not only on questions repeated or paraphrased from the teach-tests but also on new questions on both the assignments auto-instructed *and* those not. In short, when teach-tests with feedback were made part of the total instructional procedure, the gain was not simply on items thus dealt with but was spread so as somewhat to raise performance in the entire course—as had been found in the earlier research already mentioned and similar in design.

The above work all involved classes meeting the usual class periods and time so used in those periods. Other experiments, believed potentially more important, showed that students could with the help of teach-tests cover a five-hour course in one two-hour evening meeting a week, in an independent study laboratory finish the course in the first half of the quarter, and in even less time so prepare to pass the course by examination. A wide range of usefulness for objective instructional tests with feedback, such as aid in study of books or other material, seemed attested; and various possible values to the Navy were indicated. Thus, the use of new equipment sent to a distant port might be expedited if explanations included feedback teach-tests. A three-by-five-inch "chemo-card" was put in limited manufacture which seemed almost the ultimate in inexpensive convenience; on its face were the thirty rows each of four one-eighth-inch squares which the student checked with an inexpensive fountain pen filled with a special red ink; when he checked the right square, his mark instantly changed to black. He thus was guided to the right choice for each question; the marks remaining red were his errors (easily counted to give his error score); and the card could be kept as a detailed record. I had high hope of general use not only in the Services but also the schools.

However, personnel in the Navy office had changed again, and the cards were rejected offhand on the ground that the trainees would always be stealing the pens; a clumsy form of punchboard was made up and tried in ways regarding which I was not consulted, then dropped. Again my whole effort had apparently failed. But Leslie Briggs, who had taken his doctorate with me and in one phase of the project, continued an interest; Lumsdaine became interested; and Skinner wrote me and we had several delightful conferences. Being now near retirement I planned no more such work.

Then I was startled, at an Air Force conference on the subject in December of 1958, by the learning theorists' ignorance of the great amount and variety of research regarding learning in school and assurance in applying there concepts derived primarily from rat maze-running or paired-associate memorizing. And I was shocked at what followed: the most extraordinary commercialization of a new idea in American educational history—hundreds of teaching machines were put on the market, some sold door-to-door with extravagant claims, others costing thousands of dollars, hundreds of "programs" published with as many as 16,000 frames, all involving many millions of dollars investment. Then millions of research dollars went into, first, the confident elaboration of these ideas and only slowly into any questioning of them. The last chapter of the conference report (Galanter, 1959) gives my critique thereof. Reluctantly, I further attacked both programming methods and basic theory (1963, 1964), as exemplified in most of this work.

My recent critical articles focused on the Holland-Skinner programmed college text *The Analysis of Behavior* (1961) as the authoritative pioneer of its type, involving, as had my research, an undergraduate course in psychology—and also involving processes of reading and study which I had much investigated. Such investigations had stressed the importance of reading for larger meanings and of noting paragraphs, headings, and summaries to find and structure those meanings, also to guide preview and review of main points. But the programming eliminated such cues to structure and aids to overviewing; instead there was interminable bit-learning of specific responses to interminable "frames," with interminable writing in of "constructed" completions for each and interminable page turning. I illustrated how simple little class experiments could prove that (a) such time-taking busy-work brought no more learning than simply silent reading; (b) objective questions with feedback did not, with meaningful matter, mislead the learner with their wrong alternatives (as Skinner had assumed on a priori grounds) but did clarify meanings; and (c) such questions used to check on and clarify the understanding of organized subject matter could get better understanding than Skinner-type programs at a fraction of the cost in time and paper.

I also made more explicit than before research procedures for the best development of such questions in aid of study-reading: the reading should first be assigned and very broad essay-type questions asked to find what aid is needed; where there is need, questions should be formulated using mistakes most often occurring (usually only one or two and thus warranting no more than three-choice questions) as wrong alternatives and the most colloquially clear as the right one. The first trial should eliminate not only all questions but also all alternatives not evidenced as aiding learning (with J. R. Kinzer, 1964). Methodology thus seemed clarified, and the value of objective questions with feedback as aid in use of, but *not* replacement of books and like matter, was repeatedly evidenced for over thirty years. However, at seventy-six I could hardly continue such research. Programming has become a magic word, and the "write-in" response generally accepted. Though my criticisms thereof might be listened to, my concept of feedback material as elucidating rather than replacing organized matter was apparently not understood. To no other undertaking have I devoted so much time and effort. I remain of the conviction that a distinctive cognitive theory rather than an animal-derived stimulus-response theory is still to be found to explain meaningful human learning adequately, and that simple objective feedback devices could so greatly facilitate such learning as largely to remake our educational procedures.

At the Boston Psychopathic Hospital I had seen many senile cases often complicated by alcoholism or physical illness and usually of poor socio-economic status. But as I came to know well certain older faculty members, I realized that deterioration might not be a major feature of age. Then in 1944 my eighty-eight-year-old father came to live with us. He was still active and alert, read avidly, and had wide interests; there even seemed to be certain gains with age—a relaxed mellowing of mood, more humor and good humor, more tolerant judgement. Though slowing down physically, in intellect and personality he remained intact until his death at the age of ninety-three. Here was an issue relatively neglected and surely appropriate for study by an aging psychologist—what are the potentials in contrast to the liabilities of age, and how might those potentials be increased?

To make practical contact with such issues, I became active in the committee concerned with the old of the local welfare organization and later became chairman of such a committee of the state welfare council. I was a member of the first Ohio governor's commission on age, the first national conference on aging in Washington, and also joined state and national adult education organizations. As already mentioned, I initiated and became first president of the division on maturity and age of the APA, and I also became a fellow of the national Gerontological Society. My wife and I regularly attended meetings of these various groups, expanding the trips involved (and summer school appointments in California and British Columbia) to visit institutions, housing, recreation centers, other programs for the aged across the country.

What I saw in these visits and heard discussed in these meetings disappointed me in that the always younger investigators or Senior Center directors seemed to presume decline, and thus set investigatory tasks or provided recreational opportunities of a relatively trivial nature. And the usually well-educated, well-adjusted, and often still-active superior old people were not seen. About them I especially wanted information.

As a first exploratory effort to find out about them, I asked advanced students in summer sessions at Ohio State University, the University of Southern California, and the University of British Columbia to prepare case studies about the finest old person they had known well and the oldster most a problem. The able old were a fascinating group, many were employed either gainfully or in community service activities, had wide interests and many social contacts; the problem old were lacking especially in these respects (with Elizabeth Simcoe, 1950). Since hiring and retirement policies seemed of special practical importance, through the University Development Fund I obtained several fellowship grants from an interested wealthy alumnus to investigate these problems.

These studies, in the Columbus area, were intended as a service to the

cooperating companies as well as research. For instance, a company was retiring its salesmen at sixty-five. But we found that those sixty and over were
outselling those in their thirties by over fifty percent and that turnover was
much more rapid in the younger group; we urged that retirement age might
better be seventy or made flexible. A big establishment shorthanded during
the Korean crisis was venturing to hold workers past seventy; we found evidence that even those retained until seventy-five were doing well, as were
new workers taken on at sixty. A big department store had trouble maintaining a pool of occasional workers for sales and such rush times as before
Christmas; we showed that older people in this pool remained available about
four times longer and were more often given wage increases than the young
people usually turned to for such work. Several stores permitted older sales-
women to come during the middle of the morning and leave the middle of
the afternoon, thus avoiding rush traffic and filling in over the noon hour;
we found that (for example) the greatest sales in one store were made by
a perky little eighty-year-old with a long-established clientele. Reports were
made to the cooperating companies and ten papers were published about
such work. A later paper brought together many examples of people, from
Churchill to a local barber, still working at eighty and even ninety.

At my suggestion an APA committee was set up (of which I was made
chairman) which circularized psychologists sixty years or older regarding
retirement plans or present activities if already retired. Almost all emeriti
were professionally active in some way, and those not retired hoped then to
be. It was recommended that the APA appointments office (and department
heads also) give special consideration to emeriti desiring a retirement opportunity, that possibilities of tapering or flexible retirement be considered, and
that there be a social hour for older psychologists at the annual meetings.
This last was tried for at least two years and seemed much enjoyed by those
attending. A similar paper was published in the American Association of
University Professors' (AAUP) Bulletin, and shortly afterwards a special
office for placement of emeriti in all fields was set up in AAUP headquarters
under subvention of the Ford Foundation; I was on the initial advisory committee.

In all my research with older workers and also earlier clinical and personal contacts with the old, I had been much dissatisfied with tests available
for their appraisal. Almost all these tests were devised for use with young
people or derived therefrom or made very artificial so as not to be influenced
by differences in adult experiences. Rather, it seemed to me that tests for
adults should appraise ability practically to interpret such experience. Various adults were therefore asked about daily activities and problems met; from
a variety of such matter, some twenty group tests of practical information,
judgement, and social perception were made up and given first trial. And
three were appraised further. Given to various groups including those admitted to the Ohio penitentiary, steady *rises* in score were found from the

twenty through twenty-four to the over-fifty age brackets, but the usual marked drops were observed on Army Beta, Otis intermediate, and Minnesota paper form board tests (with J. A. Demming, 1957). Unfortunately, the project could not be continued. Such work should be. A young investigator cannot fairly infer, because oldsters do poorly on such child-play tasks as an alphabet maze and a puzzle board, that they suffer general loss in problem-solving ability; perhaps if he were faced with sample problems in the idiom of oldsters' lives, he would do worse than they!

To search out yet more adequately any possible gains with age (as perhaps in wisdom, courage, and kindliness, if not more specific abilities) a grant was obtained from the National Institutes of Health to find and study especially outstanding oldsters in the Columbus metropolitan area. The staff included two married veterans and the pastor of a local church, all graduate students specializing in gerontology, and also three very capable older people widely acquainted and respected in the city—a retired YWCA worker, a retired high school principal, and the wife of a labor leader. The staff met every Saturday morning. It had initial suggestions concerning oldsters worth studying and used its acquaintance to get more. I got suggestions from Faculty Club and community contacts, also in my classes; I was now giving a seminar on age, had a large evening course on adulthood and age serving mostly adults, many of these caseworkers dealing with the aged, and another large evening class on psychology in biography.

There were no medical check-ups, no physical or mental tests: these could hardly be asked of people like the former dean of the medical school and president of the American Medical Association, or the former mayor seen in the home of his son who was a judge. But I had known the dean, knew the judge and talked with him about his father. Our charming elderly caseworker became a welcomed guest in each home. Many people knew such cases; we got much information. The result was a series of nonquantified but very broad-based personality studies including the following: three centenarians still largely mentally and characterologically intact but three other fine old people disintegrated by personal problems; some oldsters heroically mastering great physical handicap but others mastered thereby; some continuing usefulness into the nineties but others not useful who could have been; some more happily social than ever before and others withdrawing into psychosis. Though the search was always for the superior, such contrasting cases were also noted, and constructive suggestions were attempted. Potentials of age seemed often great and means for their realization available. In a recent brief paper I have suggested that somewhat as very carefully selected and trained astronauts explore the outer reaches of space, so analogously selected "agenauts" (or "agenots") might have the benefit of every medical and psychological resource to find out what their greatest potentials may be for length of life, with continuance of well-being and perhaps usefulness (1963).

In 1959 I retired at the mandatory age of seventy—with an invitation to teach the coming year at the University of California in Los Angeles. While in that area I decided to do some psychological exploring: after spending so much of my youth in church (and the disillusionment with church bureaucracy mentioned earlier), for fifty years I had been to no church; I wondered now what church would seem like? So every Sunday we sampled around (what better city in which to find variety); and we finally decided that Unitarianism offered us a liberalism, a companionship with like minds, and an opportunity to support undertakings of worth, and so we joined. The next two years (made especially pleasant by my being given an honorary LL.D. by Ohio State University) were spent back in Columbus doing research and writing, and then for two years I was a visiting professor at the University of Arizona. At the 1964 meeting of the APA, the Division of Educational Psychology gave me the first E. L. Thorndike award. In 1965 I was chosen to be a charter member of the new National Academy of Education. For the past year we tried living in a retirement community to see whether an elderly gerontologist might find special opportunities there for both study of and usefulness in age, as we both did. Now we are living in an apartment near the University where I have a desk and continue Faculty Club membership and other associations, and here I am writing this paper—my eighteenth since retirement.

So at seventy-six I look back at my life, trying to decide whether my psychology helps me understand it. It doesn't, much! It should be evident to any reader who has stayed with me thus far, that I am a product of the Puritan ethic of work and hope for a larger usefulness: I hoped that integrating the study of psychology and psychiatry might yield significant gains in understanding personality; that teaming together new techniques of curriculum-building, measurement, and educational automation might remake our schools; that bold action research might reconstitute psychology's contribution to the preparation of teachers; that viewing life in full length and higher education in relation thereto might substantially improve both education and life-planning; that studying the aged both before and after I was old, and then living with them, might yield more adequate understanding of age. To each of these undertakings I have devoted myself to the point of exhaustion, and each one brought disappointment—but perhaps there have been residual contributions of some value. And I have plans for further work.

# REFERENCES

*Selected Publications by Sidney Leavitt Pressey*

Distinctive features in psychological test measurements made upon dementia praecox and chronic alcoholic patients. *J. abnorm. Psychol.*, 1917, *12*, 130–139.

A comparison of two cities and their school systems by means of a group scale of intelligence. *Educ. Admin. Supervis.*, 1919, 5, 53–62.

(with L. C. Pressey) Cross-out tests—with suggestions as to a group scale of the emotions. *J. appl. Psychol.*, 1919, 3, 138–150.

The influence of color upon mental and motor efficiency. *Amer. J. Psychol.*, 1921, 32, 326–356.

(with L. C. Pressey) *Introduction to the use of standard tests.* New York: World, 1922.

(with Bertha Lively) A method for measuring the "vocabulary burden" of textbooks. *Educ. Admin. Supervis.*, 1923, 9, 389–398.

A statistical study of usage and of children's errors in capitalization. *English J.*, 1924, 13, 727–732.

A simple apparatus which gives tests and scores—and teaches. *Sch. & Soc.*, 1926, 23, 373–376.

(with L. C. Pressey) *Mental abnormality and deficiency: an introduction to the study of problems of mental health.* New York: Macmillan, 1926.

(with others) *Research adventures in university teaching.* Bloomington, Ill.: Public School, 1927.

(with L. C. Pressey) Analysis of 3,000 illegibilities in the handwriting of children and adults. *Educ. Res. Bull.*, 1927, 6, 85, 270–275.

A third and fourth contribution toward the coming "industrial revolution" in education. *Sch. & Soc.*, 1932, 36, 668–672.

(with L. C. Pressey and Elinor J. Barnes) The final ordeal. *J. higher Educ.*, 1932, 3, 261–264.

(with Pera Campbell) The causes of children's errors in capitalization. *English J.* (college edition), 1933, 22, 197–201.

*Psychology and the new education.* New York: Harper & Row, 1933; rev. ed. with F. P. Robinson, 1944.

(with N. E. Troyer) *Laboratory workbook in applied educational psychology.* New York: Harper & Row, 1936; rev. ed., 1945.

(with J. E. Janney) *Casebook of research in educational psychology.* New York: Harper & Row, 1937.

(with J. E. Janney and R. G. Kuhlen) *Life: a psychological survey.* New York: Harper & Row, 1939.

(with others) The laboratory concept and its functioning. *Educ. Res. Bull.*, 1940, 19, 187–216.

Fundamentalism, isolationism, and biological pedantry versus sociocultural orientation in psychology. *J. gen. Psychol.*, 1940, 23, 393–399.

Report of the committee on contributions of psychology to problems of preparation for teaching. *J. consult. Psychol.*, 1942, 6, 165–167.

(with David C. Hanna) The class as a psycho-sociological unit. *J. Psychol.*, 1943, 16, 13–19.

The new division on maturity and old age: its history and potential service. *Amer. Psychologist*, 1948, 3, 107–109.

*Educational acceleration: appraisals and basic problems.* Columbus: Ohio State University Press, 1949.

Place and functions of psychology in undergraduate programs. *Amer. Psychologist*, 1949, 4, 148–150.

(with Elizabeth Simcoe) Case study comparisons of successful and problem old people. *J. Geront.,* 1950, *5,* 168–175.

Development and appraisal of devices providing immediate automatic scoring of objective tests and concomitant self-instruction. *J. Psychol.,* 1950, *29,* 417–447.

War-time accelerates ten years after. *J. educ. Psychol.,* 1955, *46,* 228–238.

Concerning the nature and nurture of genius. *Scient. Mon.,* 1955, *81,* 123–129.

(with A. W. Jones) 1923–1953 and 20–60 age changes in moral codes, anxieties, and interests as shown by the "X-O Tests." *J. Psychol.,* 1955, *39,* 485–502.

The older psychologist: his potentials and problems. *Amer. Psychologist,* 1955, *10,* 163–165.

(with R. G. Kuhlen) *Psychological development through the life span.* New York: Harper & Row, 1957.

Potentials of age: an exploratory field study. *Genet. Psychol. Monogr.,* 1957, *56,* 159–205.

(with J. A. Demming) Test "indigenous" to the adult and older years. *J. counsel. Psychol.,* 1957, *4,* 144–148.

(with F. P. Robinson and J. E. Horrocks) *Psychology in education.* New York: Harper & Row, 1959.

Age and the doctorate, then and now. *J. higher Educ.,* 1962, *33,* 153–160.

Teaching machine (and learning theory) crisis. *J. appl. Psychol.,* 1963, *47,* 1–6.

Most important and most neglected topic: potentials. *The Gerontologist,* 1963, *3,* 69–70.

Psycho-technology in higher education versus psychologizing. *J. Psychol.,* 1963, *55,* 101–108.

(with J. R. Kinzer) Auto-elucidation without programming. *Psychol. in Sch.,* 1964, *1,* 359–365.

Autoinstruction: perspectives, problems, potentials. *63rd Yearbook of the Nat. Soc. for the Study of Educ.,* Chicago: The Univ. of Chicago Press, 1964.

Two basic neglected psychoeducational problems. *Amer. Psychologist,* 1965, *20,* 391–395.

(with Alice D. Pressey) Two insiders' searchings for best life in old age. *The Gerontologist,* 1966, *6,* 14–17.

## Other Publications Cited

Galanter, E. (Ed.) *Automatic teaching: the state of the art.* New York: Wiley, 1959.

Holland, J. G. & Skinner, B. F. *The analysis of behavior.* New York: McGraw-Hill, 1961.

Lumsdaine, A. A. & Glaser, R. (Eds.) *Teaching machines and programmed learning.* Washington: National Education Association, 1960.

Wolfle, D. Editorial. *Science.* 1964, *143,* 104.

Carl R. Rogers

Charles Schneider

# Carl R. Rogers

I assume the purpose of an autobiography is to reveal the person as he is to himself and, either directly or indirectly, to reveal some of the factors and forces which entered into the making of his personality and his professional interests. So perhaps the first question to answer is Who am I? Who is this person whose life history is to be explored?

I am a psychologist; a clinical psychologist I believe, a humanistically oriented psychologist certainly; a psychotherapist, deeply interested in the dynamics of personality change; a scientist, to the limit of my ability investigating such change; an educator, challenged by the possibility of facilitating learning; a philosopher in a limited way, especially in relation to the philosophy of science and the philosophy and psychology of human values. As a person I see myself as fundamentally positive in my approach to life; somewhat of a lone wolf in my professional activities; socially rather shy but enjoying close relationships; capable of a deep sensitivity in human interaction though not always achieving this; often a poor judge of people, tending to overestimate them; possessed of a capacity for setting other people free, in a psychological sense; capable of a dogged determination in getting work done or in winning a fight; eager to have an influence on others but with very little desire to exercise power or authority over them.

These are some of the ways I would describe myself. Others, I am sure, often see me quite differently. How I became the person I am is something of which I am not at all sure. I believe the individual's memory of his own dynamics is often decidedly inadequate. So I shall try to give enough of the factual data for the reader to draw his own conclusions. Part of this data consists of the feelings and attitudes which I remember in various events and periods throughout my life to date. I will not hesitate to draw some of my own inferences from the data, with which the reader can compare his own.

## EARLY DAYS

Though as a clinician I feel that the individual reveals himself in the present and that a true history of his psychogenesis is impossible, I will yield

343

to the traditional mode and give my own memory and perception of my past, pegged to such objective facts as are available to me.

I was born January 8, 1902, in Oak Park, a Chicago suburb, the fourth of six children, five of whom were boys. My parents had both been reared on farms and were highly practical, "down to earth" individuals. In a day when college education was not widespread, my father had completed his engineering degree and even some graduate work at the University of Wisconsin, and my mother had also attended for two years. In spite of this they both tended to be rather anti-intellectual, with some of the contempt of the practical person toward the long-haired egghead. They both worked very hard and, more important than this, had a strong belief in the virtue of work. There was almost nothing that a little hard work would not cure. My mother was a person with strong religious convictions, whose views became increasingly fundamentalist as she matured. Two of her biblical phrases, often used in family prayers, stick in my mind and give the feeling of her religion: "Come out from among them and be ye separate"; "All our righteousness is as filthy rags in thy sight, oh Lord." (The first expressed her conviction of superiority, that we were of the "elect" and should not mingle with those who were not so favored; the second her conviction of inferiority, that at our best we were unspeakably sinful.) My father was involved too in the family prayers, church attendance and the like, but in a less emotional way. They were both devoted and loving parents, giving a great deal of time and energy to creating a family life which would "hold" the children in the way in which they should go. They were masters of the art of subtle and loving control. I do not remember ever being given a direct command on an important subject, yet such was the unity of our family that it was understood by all that we did not dance, play cards, attend movies, smoke, drink, or show any sexual interest. For some reason swearing was not quite so strictly tabooed—perhaps because father would, on occasion, vent his anger in that way.

My father formed his own business—contractor and civil engineer—in partnership with an older man. Due to hard work (and doubtless good fortune) the business prospered, and by the date of my birth the early "hard times" were past and we were a middle-class or upper-middle-class family. Our home was one of good family times, occasional pleasant gatherings of young people (the friends of my oldest brother), and much family humor which very often had a cutting and biting edge on it. We teased each other *unmercifully*, and I did not realize until I was adult that this was not a necesary part of human relationships.

I learned to read long before I went to school—from my older siblings, I presume—and was reading heavy Bible story books before I went to first grade at age seven. The principal, being informed of this, took me to the second, third, and fourth grade rooms for a brief trial at their reading material. I could read all of it. Nothing was made, at school or at home, of this (as I now realize) rather unusual performance. I was placed in second grade, which pleased me because I was very fearful of the stern-looking first grade teacher. I soon had a crush on Miss Littler, my teacher. This was repeated in fifth grade when I was so devoted to Miss Kuntz that I stayed after school to help her with tasks around the school room. This was flying in the face of the family expectation that children came *directly home* when school was out. It was perhaps my first minor personal independence.

I was a dreamy youngster all through these grammar school years, so lost in fantasy most of the time that my absent-mindedness was legendary. I was teased a great deal about this and called "Professor Moony," an absent-minded comic strip character of the period. I was buried in books—stories of Indian and frontier life to the extent that I could lay hands on them, but *anything* was grist to my mill. If there was nothing else, I read the encyclopedia or even the dictionary. I can still recall some of the attempts to gain sex information through these channels, only to come to a dead end at a crucial point.

I felt guilty about my reading since it so often meant that I was not doing my "chores," or had blissfully forgotten all the things I had been told to do. To "have your nose in a book," except perhaps in the evening, was not a good or practical or hardworking thing. (Years later, as a college professor, vaguely guilty feelings would still arise when I sat down to read a book in the *morning!*)

I felt that my parents cared more for my next older brother than they did for me. This feeling must have been quite strong, for I recall that I developed the theory that I had been adopted. (It was many years later that I learned how common this fantasy is.) As might be expected, there was much rivalry and hard feeling between me and this brother, Ross, who was three years older. There was also, however, much companionship since we went to school together and shared in many activities. My closest family link was with my next younger brother, Walter. He and John, my youngest brother, were less than two years apart in age and were respectively five and seven years younger than I. In spite of this age difference we were a very close trio. I had an attitude of real hero-worship toward my oldest brother, Lester, though the age difference was too great for us to have much companionship. I remember the pride I felt when it was reported in the newspapers that he had made the highest score of any recruit (on the old Army Alpha Intelligence Test) at Camp Grant in World War I.

I had almost no social life outside the family, but I have no recollection of being disturbed by this. Our family life seemed sufficient. I recall just one fist fight while in elementary school. I was frightened to death but did my best in what ended as pretty much of a draw.

I recall one experience which seems to indicate that my parents were concerned about my withdrawn, dreamy, and impractical nature. At about the time of my twelfth birthday, while in seventh grade, plans were made for me to take a long trip of two or three weeks with my father, while he visited various construction jobs in the South and East. Permission was obtained for me to leave school on the basis that I would present a written report of my experience when I returned. Father and I visited New Orleans, Norfolk, Virginia, and New York City, spending much time visiting construction projects. I enjoyed myself, though I did not become enamored of engineering as a result. It is only as I look back at this trip that I realize its unusual nature. I do not recall that my brothers were taken on similar trips. My best guess is that it was an attempt to help me become more interested in real life than fantasy and to help me become aware of the fact that the world was one of work and that I should be thinking about my future occupation. I am not sure that the trip accomplished these aims, but it was an exciting and broadening experience. I came back thrilled by the chanting Negro workers on the New Orleans docks and with a passionate taste (acquired in Norfolk) for raw oysters!

When I was twelve my parents bought a large farm some thirty miles west of Chicago, and after spending weekends and a summer there, a home was built and we moved to the country. There were several reasons for this step. My father liked farming and made a hobby of having the farm handled in the best scientific fashion. Mother too liked gardening and cared little for the social life of the suburb. The major reason, however, was that with six growing children, ranging at that time from six to twenty, they were concerned about the temptations and evils of suburban and city life and wished to get the family away from these threats.

When we moved to the farm, I loved it. To play in the woods (the "forest" to me) and to learn the birds and animals was bringing my frontier stories to life. Many are the Indians I have crept up on, all unsuspecting, in those wooded glades. What if they were only imaginary? My brothers and I thoroughly enjoyed the new setting.

I recall two events—the first very vividly—occurring before I was fifteen, which turned me toward the world of science. To provide background for the first I should say that Gene Stratton-Porter was at that time writing her "Girl of the Limberlost" books, in which nature, but particularly the large night-flying moths, played an important part. I had of course read all these books. So I was in a responsive mood when I discovered in the woods close to home, against the dark fissured bark of a black oak tree, two lovely luna moths, just emerged from their cocoons. These beautiful pale green creatures, large as a small bird, with long "swallowtail" wings spotted with purple, would have intrigued anyone. They fascinated me. I began my first "independent study project," as it would be termed today. I obtained books on moths. I found and raised their caterpillars. I hatched the eggs and raised caterpillars through their whole series of moults, into the cocoons, until the twelve-month cycle was complete and they emerged again as moths—Polyphemus, Cecropia, Prometheus, or one of the dozens of other varieties I

came to know. I even "tied out" a female moth on the roof to attract males—
a very successful experiment—and was continually busy getting leaves of
the special sorts which the caterpillars demanded as food. In my own very
small and specialized field I became something of a biologist.

A less sharply focused experience has to do with scientific agriculture.
My father wanted his farm conducted in the most modern way and brought
in agricultural scientists from the universities to instruct the farm foreman,
herdsman, and others. He also acquired many books on the latest approaches
to agriculture. I can remember reading these books—particularly the heavy
scientific tome by Morison on *Feeds and Feeding*. The descriptions of all
the scientific experiments on feeding, on milk and egg production, on the
use of different fertilizers, different varieties of seed, of soil, and so forth,
gave me a thoroughgoing feeling for the essential elements of science. The
design of a suitable experiment, the rationale of control groups, the control
of all variables but one, the statistical analysis of the results—all of these
concepts were unknowingly absorbed through my reading at the age of
thirteen to sixteen.

My experience in high school was very fragmented. I attended three
different high schools and in each case had to travel from our farm home to
attend high school—by horse and buggy, by train, by automobile, and combinations of these. It was expected that I would return home at once, after
school was over, in order to do chores and work at home. Consequently, I
made no lasting associations or friendships in any of these schools. I was a
good student and never had any difficulty with the work. Neither did I have
any problems in getting along with the other students so far as I can recall.
It is simply that I knew them only in a very surface fashion and felt decidedly
different and alone, but this was compensated for by the fact that my
brother and I went together much of this time and there was always the
family at home.

When I speak of working at home, both morning and night, while
going to high school, I do not mean light work. I was up at five o'clock or
earlier and milked a dozen cows morning and night while attending high
school. I remember this particularly because the milking was evidently more
than my muscles could stand and my hands and arms were continually
"asleep" during the day. I could never get them quite free of the prickles.
I recall that at one time also I took care of all of the pigs on the farm. During
the summer months I rode a cultivator all day long, usually being assigned
to the cornfield at the far end of the farm which was full of quack grass. It
was a lesson in independence to be on my own, far away from anyone else.
When the cultivator needed repair or adjustment, when the team was
troublesome, or the soil or weather conditions not right, I had to make the
necessary decisions and take appropriate action on my own. It was a type of
responsibility experienced by few young people today.

At school my best work was in English and science. I received straight

A grades in almost all my courses. I remember best Miss Graham, a spinster-ish teacher of English at Naperville High School. Though she was a strict disciplinarian and rarely if ever smiled, she had a true scholarly interest in her work. I somehow felt that she would understand what I wrote, so for themes in English I wrote personal accounts as well as rebellious papers on "Shakespeare as an overrated author."

I never had a real "date" in high school. In my junior year I was elected president of the class (presumably because I had good grades and did not belong to any of the cliques.) The one social event of the year was a class dinner to which it was necessary to take a girl. I remember the agony I went through in inviting an auburn-haired lass whom I had admired from a distance. Fortunately for me, she accepted. If she had not, I do not know what I would have done.

There is one summer during this period which tells a great deal about me and about my upbringing. It was the summer between high school gradu-ation and the beginning of college. I was seventeen. It was part of the family tradiiton that of course I would work during the summer. On this particular occasion my father arranged for me to work in one of a string of lumberyards throughout the Northwest, owned by three of my uncles. I was excited by the opportunity of going all by myself to a small town in North Dakota for the summer. I had been given a graduation present of fifty dollars and spent it on the beautifully printed, small leather-bound books which were all the rage at that time. I took my books with me and was given a room in the lumberyard itself, where I lived and slept, being the only person on the premises. I worked hard from about eight o'clock in the morning until five o'clock, loading and unloading lumber, filling customers' orders, shoveling coal, unloading bricks, and the like. I ate at a boarding-house and remember no contact beyond superficial conversation with any of the individuals at the boardinghouse. My relationship with the kindly boss of the lumberyard was similar. We worked together and I felt he was fair and friendly. He invited me twice to his house during the summer. Aside from that I remember no social life at all. I was not too lonely, however, because I spent the long evenings with my new books. During that period I read Carlyle, Victor Hugo, Dickens, Ruskin, Robert Louis Stevenson, Emerson, Scott, Poe, and many others. I found this most stimulating. I realize that I lived in a world of my own, created by these books.

## COLLEGE

At some point in my high school years I had chosen scientific agri-culture as my field. I went to the University of Wisconsin in 1919. It was an appropriate place to go because it had a very good college of agriculture. This, however, was not my real reason for going to Wisconsin. It was simply assumed that every member of the family would go to Wisconsin since my parents and my two older brothers and sister had all studied there. I roomed with my next older brother, Ross, at the YMCA dormitory.

Following my own religious inclinations—built on the religious traditions at home—I became a member of a Sunday morning YMCA group composed of students of agriculture. Professor George Humphrey was the leader. I saw him then as a well-intentioned individual but somewhat weak. To this day I do not know whether he really understood what he was doing in leaving everything up to the group, but it was (I realize now) an excellent example of facilitative leadership. Left to our own decisions and choices, the group set up its own curriculum, organized all kinds of social and educational activities, conducted its business in first class parliamentary fashion, discussed topics deeply, and became very close-knit. For the first time in my life outside of my family I found real closeness and intimacy. The friendship and companionship which developed in this group of about twenty-five young men was an exceedingly important element in my life. We came to know each other well and to trust each other deeply. We were completely free to engage in any kind of activity and we became involved in many different types of projects. One of the results was that I acquired a good grasp of parliamentary law and have never been fearful of chairing any type of parliamentary assembly, an ability which has from time to time stood me in good stead. Another experience of that period was that as part of the activity of this "Ag-Triangle" group, I took on the leadership of a Boys' Club and tried myself out as leader of a group of younger individuals.

It was during the first summer vacation that I began writing personal letters to Helen Elliott, a tall, graceful girl interested in art, whom I had known since grammar school days in Oak Park, where we had ridden our bicycles together. I had dated her a few times during my freshman year at Wisconsin since she had come there to study art, and I found her very attractive.

It was during the Christmas vacation of my sophomore year, I believe, that I went to a conference of Student Volunteers at Des Moines. The Student Volunteer movement had at that time as its slogan, "Evangelize the world in our generation," and this was a meaningful purpose to me with my religious interests. The speakers were inspiring and there was a great deal of mass emotion engendered. I find it embarrassing to read the highly emotional and idealistic diary I kept during that period. I decided at this conference that I should change my life goal and go into Christian work. Though the Student Volunteer movement was specifically oriented toward the foreign field, I do not recall that I had any particular intention of going into foreign work. I did, however, feel that religious leadership was now my goal. In many ways the Student Volunteer movement was the Peace Corps of that day and appealed to some of the same sentiments.

Having made this decision, agriculture no longer seemed to be a very suitable field. I felt that I should shift to some subject which would prepare me for the ministry and decided that history, which had always been one of my interests, was a good background for that type of work. Consequently, I shifted from agriculture to history.

In the midst of my junior year there occurred a sequence of events which had a great deal of impact on me. I was selected as one of ten students from this country to go to a World Student Christian Federation Conference in Peking, China. When I was informed of this I wept with joy and surprise. I couldn't understand how or why they would have chosen *me*. Realistically, I have realized since that my very active work in the YMCA, my good grades, and the fact that my parents would be able to pay most of the expenses of the trip, probably accounted for the choice. At the time, however, it seemed like an utterly incredible and exciting thing to be selected from all of the students in the United States for a most unusual experience of this sort.

A delegation of students and professional workers, mostly from the YMCA, went over together on board ship. John R. Mott, who at that time was a world leader, Professor Kenneth Latourette from Yale, David Porter of the YMCA, and a number of others constituted the professional group. The students too were naturally a selected group. Here was a very congenial intellectual group and our shipboard discussions and reading constituted a most enriching experience.

I was most privileged to have this whole trip. We met highly cultured and well-informed individuals throughout all our sojourn. The foreign representatives of the YMCA were a statesmanlike group in their approach to intercultural relations. A number of them, such as Jack Childs, became very well known as philosophers, diplomats, and the like. They were not at all the evangelical missionary type and I learned a great deal from them.

I was gone more than six months, since in addition to the slow voyage and the conference in Peking, I was part of one of the delegations which made speaking tours to student centers—in my case to West China. Following this I accompanied Professor Latourette, who was gathering data for a book, on a tour of South China and the Philippines.

This voyage bears curious testimony to the fact that speed of communication is not always desirable. During the trip I kept a long typed journal of the various events I was living through and my reactions to them. I was rapidly becoming much more liberal in religion and politics due to my exposure to a wide spectrum of opinion, a wide range of cultures, and to such specifically challenging experiences as trying to understand the interchange between French and German students and faculty members who were still filled with hatred and suspicion from the days of World War I. My intellectual horizon was being incredibly stretched all through this period, and this growth was recorded in my journal. I sent a copy of this journal to Helen, who was now definitely my sweetheart, and another copy to my family. Since we did not have the benefit of airmail it took two months for a reply to arrive. Thus I kept pouring out on paper all my new feelings and ideas and thoughts with no notion of the consternation that this was causing in my family. By the time their reactions caught up with me, the rift in outlook was fully established. Thus, with a minimum of pain I broke the intellectual and religious ties with my home.

This independence was furthered on the return trip, when shipboard conversations with Dr. Henry Sharman, a student of the sayings of Jesus, were very thought-provoking. It struck me one night in my cabin that perhaps Jesus was a man like other men—not divine! As this idea formed and took root, it became obvious to me that I could never in any emotional sense return home. This proved to be true.

Due to this six months' trip I had been able freely, and with no sense of defiance or guilt, to think my own thoughts, come to my own conclusions, and to take the stands I believed in. This process had achieved a real direction and assurance—which never after wavered—before I had any inkling that it constituted rebellion from home. From the date of this trip, my goals, values, aims, and philosophy have been my own and very divergent from the views which my parents held and which I had held up to this point. Psychologically, it was a most important period of declaring my independence from my family.

A few more comments might be made in regard to my junior and senior years at Wisconsin. I joined a fraternity, Alpha Kappa Lambda, noted for its scholastic excellence, in my junior year, in spite of the opposition of my parents to "frats." I became much involved in my scholastic work and fortunately had a number of gifted teachers. Historians Carl Russell Fish, George Sellery, and Eugene Byrne all had an impact on me. I came to have a real respect for scholarship and scholarly activities. I did a paper for Professor Sellery on "The Source of Authority in Martin Luther." I realize that the idea I formed at that time—that man's ultimate reliance is upon his own experience—has been a theme which has stayed with me. I also did a paper on Benjamin Franklin and an undergraduate thesis on "The Pacifism of John Wyclif." All of these were highly independent papers in which the idea was my own and the manner of working was my own. I feel that they were reasonably scholarly and I learned to use historical research as a way of exploring my interests and ideas.

Another important experience of those years was my work on the university debating team. I found it both surprising and thrilling to realize that I could tackle a subject on which I knew nothing—in this case the compulsory arbitration of labor disputes—put in eight solid hours a day working at it over a period of weeks, and come out reasonably "well informed." It somehow gave me a feeling of confidence in my own ability to tackle a new intellectual problem and to master it.

Shortly after I returned from the Orient, I was increasingly troubled by abdominal pains which I had had intermittently since the age of fifteen. They were now properly diagnosed as being due to a duodenal ulcer, and I was in the hospital for some weeks and on an intensive treatment regime for six months. Something of the gently suppressive family atmosphere is perhaps indicated by the fact that three of six children developed ulcers at some period in their lives. I had the dubious distinction of acquiring mine at the earliest age.

During this period of medical treatment it was of course expected, by me as much as my parents, that I would work. It seems so typical, both of my own attitudes and those of my family, that the only considered alternative to college, even though I was not too well, was hard physical work. I think that to a considerable extent I shared my parents' views that work would cure anything, including my ulcer. So I obtained a job in a local lumberyard, while living at home. I remember that one time my model-T Ford—my first car—was hemmed into a tight parking spot at the lumberyard. I simply lifted the rear end of the car and moved it a few inches. I strained my back in doing so. It seemed never to have occurred to me that I could have asked someone to help me. This attitude, too, has been a typical one for me.

While working in the lumberyard I made no effort to keep up my college work, except that I took a correspondence course from the University of Wisconsin in introductory psychology. This was my first acquaintance with psychology. I was not particularly impressed. I used William James as a text but thought our assignments were a bit dull. The only portion of the course I remember is that I got into an argument by mail with my instructor as to whether dogs could reason. It was his claim that only human beings could reason. I was quite able to prove to my own satisfaction that my dog, Shep, was definitely able to solve difficult problems by reasoning!

One advantage of being out of school was that it kept me close to Helen, who had given up university work to take professional art training in Chicago. Consequently, there was much courting during this period although each visit involved a thirty-mile drive in my Model-T, over roads quite different from modern highways, after a hard day's work at the lumberyard. I returned to the university in the autumn, but during a visit home Helen and I became engaged on October 29, 1922, an event which made me ecstatically happy. I had felt very uncertain that I could win her and floated on clouds for some time after this day.

I graduated in June of 1924 with a bachelor's degree in history, having had my one correspondence course in psychology. I had been delayed one year in my graduation by my six-month trip to China and by the half year of illness and work. Because I had shifted from the class of '23 to the class of '24 and because I had shifted from agriculture to history, the close contacts I had built up in my freshman year were greatly weakened. But I had friends in the fraternity and good times there. It was still true, however, that I had few friends with whom I was close all during the four years of college.


## THE NEW YORK YEARS

Helen and I were married on August 28, 1924, and set out in a second-hand Model-T coupe of which I was inordinately proud and for which I had paid $450. We headed for New York and Union Theological Seminary. My parents had opposed the marriage, not because they were opposed to Helen, but because it was at that time considered absurd for a man to marry while he was still going to school. Her parents shared this same feeling. Helen was at first reluctant to give up her good job as a commercial artist, but I convinced her that we should be together in facing all the new learnings and challenges of graduate work. We both realized later that we had been wiser than we knew in making this decision.

I had chosen Union Theological Seminary because it was the most liberal in the country and an intellectual leader in religious work. Knowing my plan for going to Union, my father had made one offer which was very close to a bribe. I suspect he was not proud of himself afterward for this. Certainly I rejected it indignantly. He told me that he would pay all the expenses for both of us if I would go to Princeton Seminary, which was at that point a center of fundamentalist thinking. Instead, I took some competitive examinations and won a good scholarship at Union Seminary and we made our plans for going there. My parents were then generous in gifts to help us get underway, though it was still necessary for me to earn a considerable amount of money for our expenses.

Helen and I were both very naive at the time we married (though I had loaned her a book on sex-life and marriage, a mark of how avant garde I was in my thinking!). Whether in spite of or because of our lack of sophistication, we had a delightful honeymoon and it was a great and independent venture to drive all the way to New York City in our own car.

We started our life together in a tiny new apartment. At that time there were no dormitories for married students, and hence we were somewhat separated from my classmates as I began to attend Union Seminary. I found it to be a stimulating and exciting place. I made friends, found new ideas, and fell thoroughly in love with the whole experience. Harry Emerson Fosdick was in his heyday and his course was one which Helen and I took together, gaining a feeling for a modern and liberal religion.

Goodwin Watson and Joseph Chassell, both young fellows at that time, were in charge of a course on "Working with Individuals." In addition to their own teaching they brought in psychologists and psychiatrists from the New York area. It was this course which introduced me to the whole field of clinical work and I found it most exciting. Harrison Elliott and his wife (on the faculty of the seminary) were also much involved in both individual work and the group discussion approach. For the first time I realized that working with individual persons in a helping relationship could be a professional enterprise.

I had great respect for Arthur Cushman McGiffert, who at that time was head of the Seminary. He was a remarkable teacher and a profound scholar. He created an exciting philosophical climate at Union Seminary. His course on "Protestant Thought before Kant" and other similar courses introduced me to a new level of teaching excellence. As we heard him present the thinking of one philosopher or theologian we in the class would become convinced that, "Aha! This is the person with whom he really agrees." The next week he would present someone else with equal conviction and persuasiveness. In the long run we found that we had to do our own thinking. (It is of interest to me that Miss Graham in high school and Professor McGiffert at Union were both grave, scholarly, almost scholastic teachers; not at all the sort I would tend to select as faculty members today. Yet they were both highly independent in their thinking and had a deep respect for the independence of their students.)

While at Union Seminary, either during the first or second year, I was involved in an amusing but highly significant venture. Knowing universities and graduate schools as I do now—knowing their rules and their rigidities—I am truly astonished at the freedom which was granted to us at Union. A group of students, of which I was one, felt that ideas were being fed to us and that we were not having an opportunity to discuss the religious and philosophical issues which most deeply concerned us. We wanted to explore our own questions and doubts and find out where they led. We petitioned the administration that we be allowed to set up a seminar (for credit!) in which there would be no instructor and in which the curriculum would be composed of our own questions. The Seminary was understandably perplexed by this request but they granted our petition. The only restriction was that in the interests of the Seminary a young instructor was to sit in on the course but to take no part in it unless we wished him to be active. This seminar was deeply satisfying and clarifying. It moved me a long way toward a philosophy of life which was my own. The majority of the members of that group, in thinking their way through the questions that they had raised, thought their way right out of religious work. I was one, Theodore Newcomb was another. Various other members of the group have gone on in sociology and psychology. The whole seminar was very freewheeling. It took up profound philosophical, religious, and social problems. My own reason for deciding at that time to leave the field of religious work was that although questions as to the meaning of life and the possibility of the constructive improvement of life for individuals were of deep interest to me, I could not work in a field where I would be required to believe in some specified religious doctrine. I realized that my own views had changed tremendously already and would very likely continue to change. It seemed to me that it would be a horrible thing to have to profess a set of beliefs in order to remain in one's profession. I wanted to find a field in which I could be sure my freedom of thought would not be limited.

During my second year at Union Seminary I was taking courses both in the Seminary and in Teachers College, Columbia University, which was located just across Broadway. At "T. C." I found my course in philosophy of education with William H. Kilpatrick very stimulating indeed—not only the lectures and question and answer periods, but also the small group discussions which were a part of the course. It was my first acquaintance with the thinking of John Dewey (who has since that time been so generally misunderstood) and introduced me to a philosophy of education which has been influential in my thought ever since. A course with Leta Hollingworth, in clinical psychology, also stands out. She was a warm human being, concerned about individuals, as well as a competent research worker. It was under her supervision that I first came in actual *clinical* contact with children—testing them, talking with them, dealing with them as fascinating objects of study, and helping to make plans for their welfare.

By the end of my second graduate year I decided to shift entirely out of Union Seminary and over to Teachers College, working in clinical and educational psychology. Again this was a relatively painless transition since, as I have indicated, I had already been taking courses there.

Something of my own attitudes during my graduate work may be indicated in my reactions to examinations. I look back on these with some surprise myself. Preparation for examinations was a well-organized affair for me. It never gave me any trouble because it never entered my head that I would not be successful. When it came to the matriculation exam for the doctoral degree, I remember my surprise at discovering that some people were frightened of this. I took the examination and passed as I had expected to do. Months later I was amazed to find, quite by chance, that I had the highest score of that particular group on a Thorndike test of intellectual power, and also that I had received the highest grades on the content examinations.

Perhaps it would be appropriate to try to describe at this point my very limited experience with educational failure. I remember once in the fifth grade I failed an examination when I had simply loafed and paid no attention to a history class. As a consequence, I had to take a second examination on the same material and I well remember the panic I felt. I even cheated a little by checking one answer with a girl who was taking the same examination. The next failure I can recall was a statistics course at Teachers College. I had never had a first course in statistics, but I was perfectly confident that I could pass the second course which came at a more convenient hour. The instructor was very abstruse in his explanations and I simply could not catch on. It was a new experience for me to be in a situation where I could not *grasp* the material. When it came to the final examination I answered it as best I could but I was sure that I had failed the course. Consequently, I took the opportunity of telling him, in the examination blue book, what I thought of the course and his methods of teaching, which were far from the best. Whether because of this personal outburst or in spite of it, I have never known which, he passed me.

Our first child, David, was born in 1926, and we experienced all the excitements, apprehensions, and satisfactions of caring for our first born. We endeavored to raise him "by the book" of Watsonian behaviorism, strict scheduling, and the like. Fortunately, Helen had enough common sense to make a good mother in spite of all this damaging psychological "knowledge."

During these two years in New York, I was working as director of religious education at a Mt. Vernon church, spending all my weekends there in order to support myself, my wife, and child. As my own interests changed away from religion, I became increasingly uncomfortable in this work. I was pleased to give it up when Goodwin Watson, my brilliant young sponsor, offered me a job. He always had many irons in the fire, and he turned over to me almost complete responsibility for an extensive survey he had initiated. I employed a sizable group of research assistants, conducted the analysis of some very complex material, and organized and wrote the presentation, all under pressure of an unyielding and imminent deadline.

I presume it was in the latter part of 1926 that I applied for a fellowship or internship at the new Institute of Child Guidance which was about to be formed. Child guidance work was just coming into its own and an elaborate Institute of Child Guidance was established by the Commonwealth Fund in New York City in order to provide training for such clinical workers. The $2500 fellowship would keep us afloat financially and I would be working in a field to which I had become increasingly attached. I was awarded the fellowship. Then shortly before the year was to begin I received an embarrassed letter from Dr. Frankwood Williams, the psychiatrist who headed the selection committee. He had just discovered that psychiatrists were to get $2500. The fellowships for psychologists were to be only $1200. It was the financial rather than the professional insult which roused my dander. I wrote him a very strong letter, saying essentially that the fellowship had been awarded, I had been informed of it, I had made all my personal plans on this basis, and I needed the money to support my family. On the strength of my letter he made an exception and I received a $2500 fellowship. It is interesting and symbolic that I started my professional training —through a fluke—on the same level with psychiatric residents.

The year 1927–28 at the Institute for Child Guidance was an extremely stimulating year. I was still working toward the completion of my doctor's degree at Teachers College where such things as emotions and personality dynamics were completely scorned by Percival Symonds and other members of the Teachers College faculty, and Freud was a dirty word. The whole approach was through measurement and statistics. At the new Institute for Child Guidance the emphasis was primarily an eclectic Freudianism and contrasted so sharply with the Teachers College approach that there seemed to be no common meeting ground. I experienced very sharply the tension between the two views.

I did well at the Institute for Child Guidance. For my doctoral research I developed a test for measuring the personality adjustment of children (see 1931), building on the attitudes present at the Institute, but also utilizing some of the technical procedures more congenial to Teachers College. It amazes me that this test is still used some thirty-five years later. I also began to realize that I had real clinical skill, both in dealing with individuals and with colleagues. I remember one case conference with an uncooperative caseworker from outside, discussing a boy with whom I had been working. I was late because of a sleet storm that morning. When I arrived the conference was obviously stalemated because the outside worker was totally unsympathetic and uncooperative. I won her over by my explanation of the situation, though I was the youngest and least experienced member of the conference group. It was this boy who was the first individual with whom I carried on regular therapy (though when psychologists did it, it was called remedial work or some such name). I made real progress in helping him, though I was full of the psychoanalytic theories which I was trying out at that time.

The eclecticism of the Institute was very helpful to me in the long run. There were different shades of psychoanalytic thinking and other psychiatric and psychological views. Alfred Adler lectured to us, for example, and shocked the whole staff by thinking that an elaborate case history was not necessary. I remember how misinformed I thought he must be, since we routinely took case histories fifty to seventy pages in length. David Levy was chief of staff and a stimulating leader who introduced us to the then new Rorschach. E. K. Wickman, the chief psychologist, was thoughtful, balanced, a good research worker, and genuinely interested in discovering the truth.

As this year drew toward an end, the question of what I would do next was a very important one. For the first time in my life I was really seeking a job. By the spring of 1928, David was two years old and our second child was on the way. Jobs for psychologists were not plentiful. I remember I was interviewed for a position at Culver Military Academy and felt I might have to take this. Then I was interviewed for a position at the Rochester Society for the Prevention of Cruelty to Children which had a Child Study Department composed of psychologists. I would be studying children and making recommendations in regard to them. It might even be possible to see some of them for treatment interviews. This sounded like what I wanted to do. There were three psychologists in this department and the salary offered was $2900 per year.

I look back at the acceptance of that position with amusement and some amazement. The reason I was so pleased was that it was a chance to do the work I wanted to do. That it was, by any reasonable criterion, a dead-end street professionally, that I would be isolated from professional contacts and universities, that the salary was not good even by the standards of that day, seems not to have occurred to me, as nearly as I can recall. I think I have always had a feeling that if I were given some opportunity to do the thing I was most interested in doing, everything else would somehow take care of itself.

## THE ROCHESTER YEARS

The next twelve years in Rochester were exceedingly valuable ones. For at least the first eight of these years, I was completely immersed in carrying on practical psychological service, diagnosing and planning for the delinquent and underprivileged children who were sent to us by the courts and agencies, and in many instances carrying on "treatment interviews." It was a period of relative professional isolation, where my only concern was in trying to be more effective with our clients. We had to live with our failures as well as our successes, so that we were forced to learn. There was only one criterion in regard to any method of dealing with these children and their parents, and that was "Does it work? Is it effective?" I found I began increasingly to formulate my own views out of my everyday working experience.

Three significant illustrations come to mind, all small, but important to me at the time. It strikes me that they are all instances of disillusionment—with an authority, with materials, with myself.

In my training I had been fascinated by Dr. William Healy's writings, indicating that delinquency was often based upon sexual conflict, and that if this conflict were uncovered, the delinquency ceased. (This at least was my understanding.) In my first or second year at Rochester I worked very hard with a youthful pyromaniac who had an unaccountable impulse to set fires. Interviewing him day after day in the detention home, I gradually traced back his desire to his sexual impulses regarding masturbation. Eureka! The case was solved. However, when placed on probation, he again got into the same difficulty.

I remember the jolt I felt. Healy might be wrong. Perhaps I was learning something Healy did not know. Somehow this incident impressed me with the possibility that there were mistakes in authoritative teachings and that there was still new knowledge to discover.

The second naive discovery was of a different sort. Soon after coming to Rochester, I led a discussion group on interviewing. I discovered a published account of an interview with a parent, approximately verbatim, in which the caseworker was shrewd, insightful, clever, and led the interviewee quite quickly to the heart of the difficulty. I was happy to use it as an illustration of good interviewing technique.

Several years later, I had a similar assignment and remembered this excellent material. I hunted it up again and reread it. I was appalled. Now it seemed to me to be a clever legalistic type of questioning by the interviewer which convicted this parent of her unconscious motives and wrung from her an admission of her guilt. I now knew from my more extensive experience that such an interview would not be of any lasting help to the parent or the child. It made me realize that I was moving away from any approach which was coercive or strongly interpretive in clinical relationships, not for philosophical reasons, but because such approaches were never more than superficially effective.

The third incident occurred several years later. I had learned to be more subtle and patient in interpreting a client's behavior to him, attempting to time my interpretations in a gentle fashion which would gain acceptance. I had been working with a highly intelligent mother whose boy was something of a hellion. The problem was clearly her early rejection of the boy, but over many interviews I could not help her to this insight. I drew her out, I gently pulled together the evidence she had given, trying to help her see the pattern. But we got nowhere. Finally I gave up. I told her that it seemed we had both tried, but we had failed, and that we might as well give up our contacts. She agreed. So we concluded the interview, shook hands, and she walked to the door of the office. Then she turned and asked, "Do you ever take adults for counseling here?" When I replied in the affirmative, she said, "Well then, I would like some help." She came back to the chair she had just left and began to pour out her despair about her marriage, her troubled relationship with her husband, her sense of failure and confusion, all very different from the sterile "case history" she had given before. Real therapy began then and ultimately it was highly successful—for her and for her son.

This incident was one of a number which helped me to experience the fact—only fully realized later—that it is the *client* who knows what hurts, what directions to go, what problems are crucial, what experiences have been deeply buried. It began to occur to me that unless I had a need to demonstrate my own cleverness and learning, I would do better to rely upon the client for the direction of movement in the process.

While I was in Rochester I had a reasonably comfortable relationship with the psychiatric profession. We had a consultant psychiatrist in the Child Study Department. He was a rather weak person and for the most part we told him what we thought he should say and he said it, thus giving our recommendations more force and authority. Later when I became director of the Child Study Department, I employed Samuel Hartwell as consultant psychiatrist and I had real respect for him. He was actually able to accomplish things with children which I could not. Later on I employed a full-time psychiatrist on the staff. I also had many colleague relations with psychiatrists at the University of Rochester, and these were friendly relationships until the dispute arose which I will mention later.

It was while I was in Rochester that, due to the interest of another psychologist in the work of Otto Rank, we decided to bring him there for a weekend. This was very profitable. I was not too impressed with Rank's theories but I was very much impressed with his description of his therapy. By this time some of my own staff workers were also interested in Rank's work and some of them had taken courses at the Pennsylvania School of Social Work which was decidedly Rankian in its orientation. All of this had an important impact on my thinking.

During the summer of 1935 I was invited to teach at Teachers College, Columbia. I found this highly rewarding and ego strengthening. I was much surprised that the classes, even though enormous (150 to 300) seemed to respond to me very favorably and had good learning experiences. My approach at that time was to give a lecture but with ample opportunity for questions and discussion from the group. I particularly remember one course which was broken into thirds. I taught the first part, a much more experienced psychologist taught the second portion, and I was to teach the third portion of the course. When I returned for this last portion the class applauded loud and long when I came in. I was bowled over by the message that this contained, namely, that they were glad to see me back and really liked me better than the more experienced faculty member who had been teaching them. I began to realize not only that I loved to get people excited about new ideas and new approaches, but that they loved this too.

During 1937 and 1938, the social agencies of Rochester, in which I took a very active part, decided that a community guidance center was a needed organization and that the Child Study Department, of which I was the director, should be its core. The decision was to form a new Rochester Guidance Center. At this point my psychiatric friends made a strong case to the Community Chest, to my board of directors, and to all who would listen, that such a clinic should be headed by a psychiatrist. So far as I know there was little criticism of the job I had done. The argument was simply that a psychiatrist was in charge of almost all similar clinics in other cities, and must be in charge here. This led to a prolonged and sometimes bitter battle, with many facets, which I finally won, becoming the first director of the Rochester Guidance Center.

During this period I began to doubt that I was a psychologist. The University of Rochester made it clear that the work I was doing was not psychology, and they had no interest in my teaching in the psychology department. I went to APA meetings and found them full of papers on the learning processes of rats and laboratory experiments which seemed to me to have no relation to what I was doing. The psychiatric social workers, however, seemed to be talking my language, so I became active in the social work profession, moving up to local and even national offices.

I began to teach courses at the University under the Department of Sociology on how to understand and deal with problem children. Soon the Department of Education wanted to classify these as education courses, also. Before I left Rochester, the psychology department, too, finally requested permission to list these courses, thus at last accepting me as a psychologist. Simply writing these paragraphs makes me realize how stubbornly I have followed my own course, being relatively unconcerned with the question of whether I was going with my group or not.

In 1940 I accepted a position at Ohio State University as a full professor. I deeply regretted leaving my newly won position as Director of the Rochester Guidance Center and might have turned down the offer had it not been for Helen's gentle insistence in pointing out that I had for a long time wished to have a university position, and that these did not grow on trees. So I showed an interest in the offer and finally accepted it. I am sure the only reason I was considered was my book on the *Clinical Treatment of the Problem Child* (1939), which I had squeezed out of vacations and brief leaves of absence. I heartily recommend starting in the academic world at the top level. I have often been grateful that I have never had to live through the frequently degrading competitive process of step-by-step promotion in university faculties, where individuals so frequently learn only one lesson—not to stick their necks out.

It was in trying to teach what I had learned about treatment and counseling to graduate students at Ohio State University that I first began to realize that I had perhaps developed a distinctive point of view of my own, out of my experience. When I tried to crystallize some of these ideas, and presented them in a paper at the University of Minnesota in December 1940, I found the reactions were very strong. It was my first experience of the fact that a new idea of mine, which to me can seem all shiny and glowing with potentiality, can to another person be a great threat. To find myself the center of criticism, of arguments pro and con, was disconcerting and made me doubt and question. Nevertheless I felt I had something to contribute, and wrote the manuscript of *Counseling and Psychotherapy* (1942), setting forth what I felt to be a somewhat more effective orientation to therapy. I also included the first complete verbatim case, electronically recorded and laboriously transcribed.

Here again I realize with some amusement how little I have cared about being "realistic." When I submitted the manuscript, the publisher thought it was interesting and new, but wondered what classes would use it. I replied that I knew of only two—a course I was teaching and one in another university. The publisher felt I had made a grave mistake in not writing a text which would fit courses already being given. He was very dubious that he could sell 2000 copies, which would be necessary to break even. It was only when I said I would take it to another publisher that he decided to make the gamble. I don't know which of us has been more surprised at its sales—nearly 80,000 and still continuing.

I had arrived at Ohio State at an opportune time. Many graduate students had been thoroughly trained in a largely laboratory approach which they found unexciting. When I came upon the scene—a psychologist interested in working with real human beings—they flocked to my seminars and courses and many asked me to sponsor their doctoral researches. I was too naive to realize that by accepting them for sponsorship I was stirring up jealousies in the other faculty members. On the other hand, many of my lifelong friendships were formed in my dealings with this choice group of doctoral students.

I have been told that the practicum in counseling and psychotherapy which I established in 1940 was the first instance in which supervised therapy was carried on in a university setting—that neither Freud nor any other therapist had ever managed to make supervised experience in the therapeutic relationship a part of academic training. I am not certain that this statement is true. I do know, however, that I had no such brash thought in mind when I inaugurated this practicum. It simply seemed essential that if students were to study therapy they must also carry it on and should have the opportunity to analyze and discuss what they were doing. Nearly all of the discussion was based on recorded interviews, and this was an exciting venture for the whole group. I realize now that too much of our discussion dealt with individual responses and with techniques, but nonetheless it was a growing experience for all of us.

I was much involved in professional activities during my Ohio State years. I plunged into the newly formed American Association for Applied Psychology, became chairman of its clinical division, and president in 1944–45. Meanwhile Robert Yerkes was arguing that if the parent organization, the APA, could be reorganized so as to be democratic in its structure, all of psychology might again be brought together. I was responsive to this and there were many meetings involving Yerkes, Hilgard, Boring, and various others which laid the basis for a constitutional convention and the eventual reunification of psychology. It was a privilege to be involved in this statesmanlike enterprise.

Though Columbus was our home for only five years, it seems longer because it was a period of intense growth for the whole family. We built and enjoyed our own home, and it was a period rich in friendships. David and Natalie, our children, went through their adolescence here. David pointed toward medicine and has gone on to an outstanding career as chairman of the Department of Medicine at Vanderbilt University. Natalie became sensitively involved in art, the teaching of art, and psychology, with a special interest in interpersonal relationships. She has continued all these interests, adding to them the responsibilities of a wife and mother. Among other things, she helped her active professor husband, Lawrence Fuchs, to establish the Peace Corps in the Philippines. She is now working in the child guidance field as well as being involved in her husband's wide-ranging activities. We have had enormous satisfaction in the integrity and sensitivity of our children. But this gets somewhat ahead of my story.

## THE MOVE TO CHICAGO

I was flattered to be invited to teach at the University of Chicago during the summer of 1944. Toward the end of the summer, Ralph Tyler, who held several important posts at the University, surprised me by extending an invitation to come to Chicago permanently and establish a counseling center there. This was a very appealing offer. I could not accept it for the coming year because I was already committed to aid the war effort by teaching simple counseling methods to the staff members of the USO, whose staff was being besieged by servicemen with personal problems. I did, however, accept a professorship in psychology and the responsibility of establishing a counseling center, my duties to begin in the autumn of 1945.

In August of 1944, before I left Chicago, Dr. Tyler and Lawrence Kimpton, then Dean of Students, asked me to draw up a memorandum as to my views regarding a possible university organization for the counseling of students. This memo was written for university administrators—non-psychologists all—but I am quoting from it here because it served as the basis for the development of the Center a year later.

The primary purpose of the student counseling organization is to assist the student to help himself, to aid him in becoming more intelligently self-directing.

In order to achieve this goal, the purpose of the counselor is to create a situation of deep understanding and acceptance which will enable the student to think through his problems and perplexities more clearly, and to direct himself more intelligently and rationally, as a result of this counseling experience.

It is the purpose of the student counseling organization to deal with the student as a total individual. There is no attempt to treat the individual as a bundle of separate parts—educational problems, vocational problems, social problems, etc. There is a clear recognition that difficulties in adjustment are difficulties in adjustment of the whole individual.

It is not the purpose of the counselor to assume responsibility for the life of the student, nor to control him in the ways in which the counselor or others regard as satisfactory. Neither is it the purpose of the counselor to control the student's environment by manipulating the curriculum, rules, or other factors so as to make it possible for the student to adjust.

In short, the counselor controls neither the student nor the college environment. Rather the counselor provides a situation in which the student may work out clearly and independently the adjustment to his college experiences and to later life which is realistic for him and which satisfies his own desire for increasing maturity.

It is the purpose of the student counseling organization to be freely available to the student. The counselor should be physically and psychologically accessible. How many counselors there should be in order to be satisfactorily accessible remains to be seen.

The criterion of success of the counseling organization will not lie in elaborateness or completeness of the records, nor in the complexity of organizational machinery, but in the feeling of the student that he has achieved a satisfying plan of action for himself.

## THE ESTABLISHMENT OF THE
## COUNSELING CENTER

The development of the Counseling Center—its staff, its therapeutic principles, its research, its administrative procedures—was a most exciting process. I believe I learned more and contributed more during the twelve years at the Center (1945–1957) than at any other period. I learned to set the staff free, to make all of us jointly responsible for the work of, the welfare of, and the future of the Counseling Center. It was a period in which our basic views about the helping relationship came to fruition. These views developed out of a heavy service function. The Center had 2800 counseling interviews with 605 individuals during its first ten months of work and the number steadily increased after that. It was a time of innovation in our educational methods and in our freewheeling administrative process. It was a germinal period for research hypotheses and theoretical formulations. Although our efforts were essentially task oriented, we were also experimenting with much freedom of expression of interpersonal feelings (negative and positive) in our staff meetings and staff relationships. Hence, without consciously planning it, the staff became a very close and personally nourishing group. Graduate students, clerical staff, and faculty members worked as equals in our undertakings. There was enormous freedom for creativity. I think it is safe to say that anyone who worked for as much as a year in that climate, regards his time there as one of the most significant experiences of his life.

Some of the closeness of the group grew out of the fact that though Deans Tyler and Strozier gave us complete freedom and solid backing, we lived in a general University context of skepticism, criticism, and strong antagonism. The antagonism was mostly from the Department of Psychiatry, in which successive chairmen strongly rejected each of our bids for better relationships and cooperation. Our relationship with the Department of Psychology was friendly and gradually became close under the chairmanship of James Miller.

For myself, this was the period when I wrote *Client-centered Therapy*

(1951), many papers, and formulated a precise statement of my whole theoretical position, which was first widely distributed in duplicated form for criticism and was finally published as a long chapter in Sigmund Koch's mammoth series, *Psychology: A Study of a Science* (1959).

It was also a period in which my dreams of research in psychotherapy came true. Up to this point I had been unable to get more than piddling amounts for research, but with Dr. Miller's assistance we obtained a large grant from the Rockefeller Foundation, and this was followed by other grants. These funds enabled us to carry out the dozen or more coordinated investigations which we reported in the volume *Psychotherapy and Personality Change* (1954). Other studies followed.

During these years I sponsored many fine graduate students who have gone on to make significant records for themselves. The staff and students contributed greatly to my personal growth, to the greater depth I was achieving in therapeutic relationships, to my development as a facilitative administrator, and to the enrichment of my theories about therapy and interpersonal relationships.

I would like to mention a few of those who have contributed most significantly to my own thinking and development, listing them roughly in the order in which I came to know them: Victor Raimy, Thomas Gordon, E. H. Porter, Jr., William Snyder, Donald Grummon, Nicholas Hobbs, Arthur Combs, George Muench, John Butler, Julius Seeman, Oliver Bown, Nathaniel Raskin, Douglas Blocksma, Stanley Lipkin, Bill Kell, Louis Cholden, John Shlien, Elaine Dorfman, Eugene Gendlin, Gerard Haigh, Richard Hogan, Madge Lewis, Desmond and Rosalind Cartwright, Richard Farson, Godfrey Barrett-Lennard, Jerome Berlin, Leif Braaten.

## PROFESSIONAL ACTIVITIES AT CHICAGO

My manner of conducting courses had never been orthodox, but at Chicago I became more and more radical. The hypothesis which came to be central to me is the first one presented in the chapter on "Student-centered Teaching" in *Client-centered Therapy*. It is that "We cannot teach another person directly; we can only facilitate his learning." This hypothesis had grown largely out of my therapeutic experience, and I endeavored increasingly to find new methods of implementing it. Even in large courses where some presentation of issues at least seemed essential, I found ways of setting students free to pursue their own goals and providing the resources from which they could learn. My classes became exciting clusters of small groups, informing themselves in depth on topics of real interest. To find themselves set free was often a shocking experience. One outstanding student, who later became a leader in the Counseling Center, withdrew from his initial course with me, saying in disgust to his companion, "That son-of-a-bitch calls himself a teacher!" Yet the ferment he had felt continued to work in him until he returned more than a year later. This same phenomenon occurred in a Harvard conference on teaching in 1952. I presented a ten-minute paper ("Some Personal Thoughts on Teaching and Learning") in order to initiate a discussion. It is hardly correct to say that it initiated a discussion—it set off an explosion! Yet, constructive reverberations from that paper (included in *On Becoming a Person*, 1961) continue to this day.

Though I shall not further discuss this aspect of my interests, my concern with what I believe is a much needed revolution in education at all levels has continued. I have tried increasingly to point out and to demonstrate that we do not need *teaching,* as that term is ordinarily used or defined in the dictionary. What is needed, from nursery school to the Ph.D., is an intelligent and resourceful facilitation of *learning.*

Especially during the early portion of my Chicago years, I was extremely active in professional affairs. I was president-elect of the APA in 1945–46, and president in 1946–47. These were years of great change and expansion in psychology following the war, and I was deeply involved in formulations regarding clinical training, the formation of the American Board of Examiners in Professional Psychology, and the continuing attempt to resolve the tensions between psychiatry and psychology.

For my presidential address in 1947, I determined to try to work out and present my emerging views regarding the importance of the phenomenological world of the individual as a source of data, and the centrality of the self-concept as the determiner of behavior. Because I was in the midst of struggling with these new ideas, the paper ("Some Observations on the Organization of Personality") is not a masterpiece of clarity. It did, however, push forward into areas which have since received much more recognition. I felt it was neither understood nor well received by psychologists. In fact, I have one vivid memory of this. Following the address in a beautiful auditorium in Detroit, Chairman John Anderson and I went to the men's room which was crowded with psychologists, buzzing loudly with talk. When I entered, all conversation stopped. The silence was deafening. I felt I had interrupted many highly critical comments. I received very few congratulations, and it is only the increasing number of times that this paper has been selected for books of readings in psychology which has given me the feeling that though it was perhaps a somewhat groping first attempt, it has come to be recognized as at least a significant groping.

## A PERIOD OF PERSONAL DISTRESS

There were two years while I was at Chicago which were years of intense personal distress, which I can now look back upon coolly but which were very difficult to live through.

There was a deeply disturbed client (she would be regarded as schizo-phrenic) with whom I had worked at Ohio State, who later moved to the Chicago area and renewed her therapeutic contacts with me. I see now that I handled her badly, vacillating between being warm and real with her, and then being more "professional" and aloof when the depth of her psychotic disturbance threatened me. This brought about the most intense hostility on her part (along with a dependence and love) which completely pierced my defenses. I stubbornly felt that I *should* be able to help her and per-mitted the contacts to continue long after they had ceased to be therapeutic, and involved only suffering for me. I recognized that many of her insights were sounder than mine, and this destroyed my confidence in myself, and I somehow gave up *my* self in the relationship. The situation is best summa-rized by one of her dreams in which a cat was clawing my guts out, but really did not wish to do so. Yet, I continued this relationship, destructive to me, because I recognized her desperately precarious situation, on the brink of a psychosis, and felt I *had* to be of help.

Gradually I realized I was on the edge of a complete breakdown myself and then suddenly this feeling became very urgent. I *had* to escape. I am everlastingly grateful to Dr. Louis Cholden, the promising young psychiatrist, who was working in the Counseling Center at that time, for his willingness to take over the client on an hour's notice. She, within moments, burst into a full blown psychosis, with many delusions and hallucinations. As for me, I went home and told Helen that I must get away, at *once*. We were on the road within an hour and stayed away two or three months, on what we can now calmly refer to as our "runaway trip." Helen's quiet assurance that I would come out of this distress in time and her willingness to listen when I was able to talk of it, were of great help. However, when we returned I was still rather deeply certain of my complete inadequacy as a therapist, my worthlessness as a person, and my lack of any future in the field of psychol-ogy or psychotherapy.

For a time before I left, I was in therapy with one member of my staff. When I returned I felt my problems were so serious it would only be threat-ening to ask a staff member to help me with them. I am deeply grateful that one member of our group simply told me that it was obvious I was in deep distress, that he was not afraid of me or my problems, and that he was offering me a therapeutic relationship. I accepted in desperation and gradu-ally worked through to a point where I could value myself, even like my-self, and was much less fearful of receiving or giving love. My own therapy with my clients has become consistently and increasingly free and spon-taneous ever since that time.

I have often been grateful that by the time I was in dire need of per-sonal help, I had trained therapists who were persons in their own right, not dependent upon me, yet able to offer me the kind of help I needed. I have since become rather keenly aware that the point of view I developed in therapy is the sort of help I myself would like, and this help was available when I most needed it.

## A BROADENING VISTA

During these Chicago years, I had many choice opportunities for gaining a broader perspective, both personally and professionally. During various summers I taught at UCLA, Harvard, Occidental College, Brandeis University, and spent a visiting semester at the University of California at Berkeley. While there I counseled a client in front of my large seminar group for about ten sessions, an experience which I think none of us have forgotten.

It was in these years also that Helen and I began to take the winter quarters off, getting away from the cold and slush of Chicago to various isolated hideaways in Mexico and the Caribbean where no one knew I was a psychologist. Here, snorkeling, painting, and color photography appeared to be my major activities. Yet in these spots, where I almost never put in more than four hours a day in professional work, I have produced, I believe, some of my most creative and solid writing. It is when I am alone, when there is neither physically nor psychologically anyone "looking over my shoulder" that I have done some of my best work.

## WISCONSIN

I was invited to spend one semester in the Department of Education at the University of Wisconsin in the spring of 1957 as the honorary Knapp Professor for that period. The individual who sponsored this idea, and worked hard to bring it about, was Virgil Herrick, a dynamic professor of education whom I had known previously, but who was to become one of my very closest personal friends during the ensuing years.

The five-month appointment was a fruitful one. I held a seminar for faculty members in which I was, I fear, rather rigidly "student-centered." I had not yet learned how to place full responsibility with the group and yet give freely of myself. Nevertheless it was an exciting and unusual experience for most of the participants. I also held a large seminar for graduate students in counseling, psychology, and education. This was highly successful and, judging from letters over the years, had a significant impact on the lives of the members. During this time, Helen and I had many warm personal and social contacts with faculty members in education, psychiatry, and with several of the psychologists.

These months gave me a great deal of time for my own work. I listened to dozens of recorded therapeutic interviews, seeking for the elements of the process of therapy. I determined to make this the subject of my paper before the APA, the paper demanded of each recipient of the APA Distinguished

Scientific Contribution Award, which I had received in 1956. As with my APA presidential address, I was still struggling with emerging ideas as I tried to meet the deadline, but the paper, "A Process Conception of Psychotherapy" (1958), has since stimulated many research investigations and a number of instruments for measuring process movement in psychotherapy.

Meanwhile, Virgil Herrick was working devotedly and selflessly behind the scenes to bring me to Wisconsin. I had assured him that nothing could lure me from Chicago, and he had challenged me to write out the description of a position which would entice me. I wrote a description of an impossible position—appointments in both psychiatry and psychology, opportunity to train psychologists and psychiatrists, time for therapy and research with psychotic and normal individuals (the two extreme groups where I felt my experience was deficient), and other improbable requirements. To my amazement, he was able to bring this about, though the approval of ten separate committees, besides his persuasive talks with many individuals, was necessary to achieve this.

This faced me with a difficult decision. I felt I could continue at Chicago along the same lines I had been following, but I could go little further. I could continue to have the encouraging environment of the Counseling Center which had permitted my ideas to grow. Or I could launch out into a skeptical psychology department and a somewhat skeptical department of psychiatry, and try to establish myself and my ideas in a more pervasive setting. I could also have the opportunity to pursue research with psychotic individuals, which I felt was my next challenge. In addition, we would have a more pleasant and friendly environment for living. We decided to accept.

The staff members of the Counseling Center were incredulous and greatly upset. They found it hard to understand my view that I had contributed what I could at Chicago, that the Counseling Center was a vigorous and viable organization (which it has proven to be), and that for my own personal growth and development it was challenging to move on. Despite their protests, I held to my decision.

So in the late summer of 1957 we moved to Madison, where for seven years we enjoyed gracious living in a beautiful home of contemporary architecture, situated on the shore of Lake Monona, and where we made many very close and dear friends and thoroughly enjoyed our personal experiences.

Professionally there were ups and downs. It was the first time in my professional life that I tried to be a *member* only, rather than a leader. I did not do too well in several respects. In psychiatry I tried to play down any leadership role on my part. This submerging of myself was probably not quite genuine and made some members suspicious of me. I was also frankly appalled at the poor caliber of the psychiatric residents, in comparison with graduate students in psychology. However, by the end of the seven years, many changes had come to pass, due in large measure to Dr. Robert Roessler, chairman during most of that period. The caliber of residents greatly improved, I was doing a much better job of stimulating their learning in my time with them, and much research, which had been almost nonexistent at the time of my arrival, was being carried on.

In psychology I had an ample number of students in my seminars and under my sponsorship, and I enjoyed them. I had had few illusions about the attitudes of the department in general, which was highly laboratory oriented and very distrustful of clinical psychology. But I had felt that it would be healthy for students working with me to have laboratory as well as clinical training and believed that I could carve out an area of interest in which my students and I could work together, engaging both in clinical practice and in research.

What I did not foresee or recognize was that the department had come to place such stress on "rigorous" examinations, on failing large proportions of students, that no one in any field could turn out a significant number of Ph.D.'s. In the department as a whole—though it took me a number of years to recognize this—about one out of seven of our carefully selected graduate students ever received the Ph.D. Some were failed, some of the most creative minds and the best clinicians left in disgust, and I was in the peculiar position of training graduate students who had only a minute chance (a chance which did not have too much to do with merit) of obtaining a degree. I made every effort in my power to change what appeared to me as both an incredibly wasteful and foolishly punitive system, but without avail. A majority of the department would put through some liberalizing change, only to have it negated by some new policy (all of course in the interest of "high standards"). In April of 1963 I finally resigned from the department, retaining only my appointment in psychiatry. I felt I would be lacking in integrity to do otherwise. As persons, the members of the department constituted an interesting and often likable lot. Collectively, they were destroying everything I valued in the development of scientists and practitioners.

Meanwhile, I was deeply involved in research. After a considerable period of planning and fund raising, I began assembling a small and devoted staff for the most complicated and difficult research of my life—a study of the impact of the therapeutic relationship upon relatively chronic hospitalized schizophrenic patients. The difficulties of implementing such a study were fantastic but it was at last launched. I am tempted to mention the names of those who contributed the most, but since more than 200 individuals were eventually involved it is impossible to know where to stop.

But there were flaws in the way I organized the research staff; flaws which were to be nearly fatal. Because I was spread too thinly over many activities, I did not take the time to develop a staff which was unified in philosophy and outlook, as at the Counseling Center. The task was so large, it seemed there was hardly time for this. Although I wished the group to be responsible for itself, I did not devote time enough or energy enough to implement this, so that the staff never felt completely responsible for itself and its activities.

Consequently, when an important member of the group engaged in behavior which I (and others) regarded as unethical, there was not a solid basis for handling this. The fact that most of the turmoil which then occurred happened while I was away for a year at Palo Alto, multiplied the problems. My difficulty in believing that a person I had known and trusted as an effective colleague might also be unethical made me vacillate in my own attitudes. Because of the emergency I tried to pull back some of the authority, which I had freely given to the group, into my own hands. This was a grave mistake also. The ensuing uproar, recriminations, disappearance of data, misunderstandings, and involvement of many outsiders constitutes without doubt the most painful and anguished period in my whole professional life. The major portion of the research analysis had to be completely redone, at the insistence of the staff. I agreed to its necessity, but was skeptical that we had the time and strength to do it. It was, however, achieved, and a fearfully complex investigation, developed and reported by many members of the staff, is at long last ready for publication. I hope it will prove to be worth the suffering it has caused so many people.

There were, fortunately for my personal balance, many positive events occurring during this period. Two occurred during the summer of 1960. I was a leader in a ten-day workshop at the University of Denver for influential young men in the field of college counseling and personnel work. This was successful beyond our hopes, and was a most satisfying experience.

Following this, Helen and I retreated to a lovely log home near Estes Park, built sixty years earlier, and in a three-week period I drew together the material for my book, *On Becoming a Person* (1961). This book had been germinating in my mind and my notes for several years but the final selection of the papers, the editing out of overlap, the writing of material which would introduce and link the papers, was all accomplished in these three intense weeks. Even so I found time to hike in the rocky peaks behind the cabin, enjoying the deer and other wildlife which were plentiful.

During the summer of 1961 we embarked on a trip to Japan, a goal for which a group of Japanese had been toiling long and hard. On the way over, on a Japanese freighter, I prepared for the lectures and workshops which I was to hold. In Yokohama I was met by Logan Fox, an American born and brought up in Japan but very familiar with my work, who was to serve as my exceedingly able interpreter and friend, and Mr. Endo, a Japanese counselor who had gradually developed his own type of helping relationship, only to be greatly strengthened in his approach when he learned of my work. During a seven-week period I conducted five one-week workshops for college counselors, industrial executives, and individuals in the correctional and probation fields, as well as giving many lectures. I was flattered at being one of the few Americans brought to Japan on Japanese funds. I came to know some very dedicated counselors and therapists. I came to understand why, to a Japan seeking new directions and a new philosophical base, my work was extremely important. (Though I am still overawed by the fact that there will soon be sixteen volumes of my books and articles in Japanese translation!) It was an exciting, hard-working summer, in which we came into close contact with a culture so vastly different from our own that we could not truly understand it. But in the therapeutic relationship, I was most interested to see that individuals, Oriental or Occidental, appeared to go through the same process of personal exploration and reorganization.

The year 1962–63 I spent as a Fellow at the Center for Advanced Study in the Behavioral Sciences at Stanford. It was in many ways a meaningful and stimulating year, but the greatest single impact on me was my close contact with two Britons, Michael Polanyi, the physicist turned philosopher of science, and Lancelot Whyte, the historian of ideas. I was excited to find that many of my own developing ideas regarding the unfortunate and out-of-date philosophy of science to which American psychology seems committed were not only shared but strongly reinforced by these men who were much more competent scholars in the field than I. Another important influence was my contact with Erik Erikson, a splendid person whose very appearance is therapeutic, and several other psychoanalysts, foreign as well as American. From them I learned what I had strongly suspected—that psychoanalysis as a school of thought is dead—but that out of loyalty and other motives, none but the very brave analysts mention this fact as they go on to develop theories and ways of working very remote from, or entirely opposed to, the Freudian views.

Before returning to Wisconsin, I had obtained from the president of the University permission to conduct a continuing, interdepartmental, non-credit seminar, open to both faculty and graduate students. After resigning from Psychology, I felt that I would like an opportunity to facilitate real learning in a way which would cut across all boundaries and which would be free of the horribly constricting influence of evaluation, grades, and degrees. I decided upon the topic "the philosophy of the behavioral sciences," for the first semester. There were so many who applied that the seminar could accommodate less than half, and still was too large. It was, partly because of its size, not entirely successful, but it was a stimulating experience for almost all and a beginning experiment in breaking the lock-step of American graduate education.

## THE WESTERN BEHAVIORAL SCIENCES INSTITUTE

Quite unwittingly I had had a part in the formation of an adventurous new organization on the cutting edge of the behavioral sciences. Richard

Farson, Thomas Gordon, and I had conducted a workshop in human relations in California in the summer of 1958. Dr. Paul Lloyd, a California Institute of Technology physicist who had become increasingly interested in the field of interpersonal relationships, was one of the participants. As a result of many discussions following that workshop, Farson and Lloyd founded the Western Behavioral Sciences Institute, a nonprofit organization devoted to humanistically oriented research in interpersonal relationships, with a particular focus on the manner in which constructive change in interpersonal relationships comes about. At the time of its establishment in 1959, I accepted their invitation to serve on its board of directors. My motive was to encourage what seemed to me to be a pioneering venture in an area in which pioneering is often unwelcomed by established institutions.

From the first, Farson, whom I had known for many years, urged me to come out as a Visiting Fellow, to join the staff, or in any other way I chose to affiliate more closely than as a remote board member. I had never accepted any of these invitations, partly because of other obligations, partly because I felt that my contribution could certainly best be made through a university. While I was at the Center in Stanford in 1963, he repeated over the phone this invitation to join their staff. I gave my stock response but later began to mull over the question. What was a university, at this stage of my career, offering me? I realized that in my research it offered no particular help; in anything educational, I was forced to fit my beliefs into a totally alien mold; in stimulation, there was little from my colleagues because we were so far apart in thinking and in goals. On the other hand, WBSI offered complete freedom from bureaucratic entanglements; the stimulation of a thoroughly congenial interdisciplinary group; the opportunity to facilitate learning without becoming entrapped in the anti-educational jungle of credits, requirements, examinations, more examinations, and grudgingly-granted degrees. As Helen and I talked it over, we were very reluctant to leave our Madison friends and our lovely home, but I recognized that professionally I could now leave university life without too much regret, and that from a realistic point of view I would have a much deeper membership in a "community of scholars" at WBSI than at any university I knew. So we decided to make the move, beginning our new life in January, 1964.

Our wildest hopes have been exceeded. I could not have believed, in advance, how much relief I would feel on being freed from the constrictions of university life. I have always done pretty much what I wanted to do, but I have had to discover that doing what you want to do, against skepticism and opposition, is a very different thing from doing what you want to do in an atmosphere of encouragement and congenial interdisciplinary stimulation. I have been more creative and productive than I have been for years. Curiously enough, I have had deeper and much more significant contact with faculty members and more significant contact with eager learners than I have ever experienced before. This demands a word of explanation.

Having completed our work with schizophrenics, I have been eager to turn to working with "normal" individuals—the other end of the spectrum. A potent way of doing this, as I learned as early as 1950, is through the intensive group experience (often called a workshop, or a T-group, or a basic encounter group). So I have held intensive workshops of from two-and-one-half to ten days in length, with graduate students, faculty members, business executives, therapists (psychologists and psychiatrists), government officials, executive leaders with their spouses, and others, in this country as well as in Australia, Japan, and France. The impact has been striking for them and rewarding to me. In a very real sense it has been an adaptation of my therapeutic approach to the facilitation of learning and the self-enhancement of the well-functioning person. It involves feelings as well as cognition, experiencing as well as ideas, learning by the whole person as contrasted to learning "from the neck up." It involves intensive experience in a group rather than the spaced contacts of individual therapy. I am embarked on a study of the process in such basic encounter groups that I hope may eventuate in theoretical propositions which can be tested empirically.

As to my contacts with faculty members, I have had a continuing consultant relationship to the California Institute of Technology, in which I have spent many, many hours in intensive discussion with a group of twenty faculty members around profound issues in education—the preservation and enhancement of creativity, the development of persons rather than technicians, the many ways of facilitating learning, the crippling effect of over-stress on grades, and so forth. To a lesser degree I have had this type of contact with the faculty of Lewis and Clark College in Portland and with a faculty group at Sonoma State College. So I feel definitely fulfilled in my opportunities to explore deeply, with other faculty members, the basic issues in education today.

I have also had the opportunity to freely pursue my second major current interest in the assumptions and philosophy of the behavioral sciences. A seminar with behavioral scientists, psychological practitioners, physicists, philosophers, and others was a beginning. We have held a small deliberative conference composed of outstanding individuals in the field, including Michael Polanyi. But since the fruition of much of this lies in the future, I will not discuss it here.

If I have conveyed the impression that my life at WBSI is full of new directions, challenging new opportunities, and professional excitement, then I have correctly described my present situation. As Helen and I turn from looking at our flower-filled patio to the view of surf and coastline and mountains to the north, we feel very pleased that we had the courage to embark on this venture which has given us both a new zest for living.

## WHAT ARE THE MEANINGS IN MY CAREER?

What meanings, what significant threads, do I see in the events of my professional life and thought? The drafting of this autobiography has made me think seriously about this question for almost the first time, since I have not ordinarily been one to look backward. Let me describe a number of the meanings which I can distil out of my experience.

I have never really *belonged* to *any* professional group. I have been educated by, or had close working relationships with, psychologists, psychoanalysts, psychiatrists, psychiatric social workers, social caseworkers, educators, and religious workers, yet I have never felt that I really belonged, in any total or committed sense, to any one of these groups. When psychology was taking directions I did not like, I joined the social work profession. When psychology became more interested in the human being, I returned to psychology. When the APA showed a rejecting attitude toward clinical psychologists, I left it to become a very active member of a rebel group, the American Association for Applied Psychology, splitting off from the main stream of the profession. When more democratically-minded individuals became concerned about the rigidities of the APA, I worked hard to help bring applied psychology back into the main stream. At the present time, most of psychology seems to me so sterile that I have no feeling of attachment to it. If some new profession were formed which more closely fitted my interests, I would join it without so much as a backward glance at psychology.

Because of this attitude, I was deeply touched, to the point of tears, when I was awarded one of the first three Scientific Contribution Awards by the APA. I was astonished that psychologists deeply and significantly regarded me as "one of them." In spite of all the work I had done in professional organizations of psychologists, in spite of working in departments of psychology, I had never regarded myself in quite that way.

It should be obvious that whatever its disadvantages, this lack of belonging has left me free to deviate, to think independently, without any sense of disloyalty to my group.

Lest one think I have been a complete nomad professionally, I should add that the only groups to which I have ever *really* belonged have been close-knit, congenial task forces which I have organized or helped organize, or which have used my ideas as a part of their central core. Thus, for example, I fully belonged to the Counseling Center of the University of Chicago, and I belong deeply now to the Western Behavioral Sciences Institute. One may look upon this as evidence of egotism or whatever. I simply mention it as a fact.

I was fortunate in never having a mentor, and thus never had any professional father-figure on whom I was dependent or against whom I had to rebel. Many individuals, organizations, and writings were important to me in my education, but no one source was paramount. There was no great intellectual or emotional indebtedness to one person or one institution. This too made it easy to think for myself, without any sense of guilt or betrayal.

I was similarly fortunate in having broken from my family and my early religious beliefs, clearly and cleanly, with very little bitterness and only a moderate amount of rebellion. Because the break came at the right time, the differences could be open and above-board, not furtive and festering. This too helped me to feel comfortably self-reliant.

The types of isolation or "unrootedness" which I have been describing have made for what I think of as a very positive kind of aloneness. A proverb which has for many years meant a great deal to me is, "He travels fastest who travels alone." I feel this has been a central theme for me. I have no great desire to bring colleagues along with me. I am too impatient. I tend to "go it alone," confident that if I am in error my efforts will be disregarded, and equally confident that if I am doing something worthwhile, others will at some point discover this.

I have never felt particularly insecure in regard to exams, degrees, positions, titles, promotions, tenure, and the like. I cannot account for this, for I have often felt *very* insecure as to my abilities, my knowledge, the value of my work or my writings. But I have never worried to any significant degree as to whether I could pass an exam, fill a position, or win a promotion. This is in spite of the fact that my first positions, held during the great depression, *were* insecure. I have cared so little for permanent tenure that I have on three separate occasions forfeited tenure in order to take a position I wanted.

I have always been inwardly quite certain that I could pass examinations and that I could do whatever was required to hold a job. I have also felt that in any position, I could build the job into exactly what I thought it ought to be—and have been naively astonished on the few occasions when superiors have thought otherwise. I have never felt that pleasing my superiors was a major goal. Sometimes they have understood what I was doing, sometimes not. It has never been a matter of great importance to me.

If all of this sounds extraordinarily secure and self-sufficient, it is not. I regard myself rather as having been exceedingly fortunate. I feel very strongly that if I had been continually evaluated as our graduate students are today, frequently failed in such examinations, scrutinized and supervised closely during my early professional years, put through the academic ladder, I would probably have been destroyed as an original worker. I am sensitive to any judgment which I think is a competent judgment, can readily be made to feel that I and my thoughts are worthless and inadequate, and could very easily have been crushed by even the ordinary experiences of academic and professional life in my earlier years. By the time I was forty, I was beginning to have a confidence in myself which would not have been easily beaten down but, before that, negative judgments from competent people would almost certainly have destroyed me.

As a corollary of not belonging firmly to any group, I have never felt myself a part of the mainstream of psychology. Probably the major concern of psychology during my lifetime has been in learning theory. I used to be embarrassed by the fact that I found this field totally uninteresting. I felt it was additional proof that I was not really a psychologist, when such highly regarded work seemed to me to be mostly a pompous investigation of the trivial. Now that some others also share this view, I dare to voice it.

I have had some sort of a penchant or gift for being in the forefront of developments which were on the verge of occurring. I certainly take no credit for this. It is nothing I have tried to do. It seems purely intuitive. Let me explain what I mean with a number of examples.

I became interested in clinical psychology when it was a piddling and insignificant appendage on the fringe of the respectable portions of psychology. I could never have dreamed that in twenty-five years it would constitute much the largest portion of the psychological profession.

I became interested in psychotherapy (the "treatment interview") when it scarcely was a field of endeavor for anyone and when the one certain thing about it was that it was solely the province of the physician. If someone had told me that in thirty-five years psychotherapy would be a major interest of more than one-third of American psychologists, I would have regarded the statement as utterly absurd.

I thought that valuable raw data could be obtained by the electronic recording of therapeutic interviews and made such recordings beginning in 1938 or 1939. At the time, every reputable therapist in the country was certain that it was impossible to carry on any real therapy if either the therapist or the client knew it was being recorded. I sometimes chuckle at the fact that even the psychoanalysts—who were the most adamant—are now involved in and advocating recording, and opening the sacrosanct analytic hour to professional scrutiny and study.

I became interested in research in psychotherapy a couple of decades before it became fashionable and respectable for psychologists and psychiatrists to invest themselves in this field.

When I first began to realize that a theory of the self and the self-concept might fit the emerging facts of my experience, I felt both lonely and apologetic for emphasizing a line of thought which had died out with introspectionism. I certainly did not foresee today's burgeoning of self-theory.

I was surprised to find, about 1951, that the directions of my thinking and the central aspects of my therapeutic work could justifiably be labeled existential and phenomenological. It seemed odd for an American psychologist to be in such strange company. Today these are significant influences on our profession.

Perhaps these examples will make clear that in many instances the directions in which I have felt impelled to move are directions which many psychologists and psychiatrists have later followed. This has, to me, seemed a strange thing.

On the basis of experiences such as these it is not surprising that I believe that my current concern with the basic assumptions and philosophy of the behavioral sicences, with the implications of the prediction and control of human behavior, with the potency of the intensive group experience (the "T-group" or "basic encounter group"), with the development of a humanistically oriented psychology, will also, within the next decade or two, become central concerns of the whole field of psychology.

I enjoy discovering the order in large bodies of complex experience. This has been a very persistent theme. It seems inevitable that I seek for the meaning, the underlying order, and the lawfulness in every major area of my interest. I tried to discover the underlying framework in the conglomeration of things clinicians did for children, and out of this came my book on *The Clinical Treatment of the Problem Child* (1939). I have tried to discover the orderly principles in the work of the therapist and in the process of change in his client. I found it very satisfying to write a paper on "The Process Equation of Psychotherapy" in which I tried to describe the interaction in hard, parsimonious, and general terms. "A Tentative Formulation of a General Law of Interpersonal Relationships" (ch. 18 in *On Becoming a Person,* 1961) is a still bolder attempt to sense the lawful pattern which exists in a fantastically complex area of life. I am currently at work trying to discern whatever order exists in the richly varied process of the intensive group experience.

I have come to realize that both empirical research and the process of theory construction are aimed, essentially, at the inward ordering of significant experience. These activities are justified because it is subjectively satisfying to perceive the world as having order and because rewarding results often ensue when one understands the lawful relationships which appear in nature.

Another theme which stands out is the tension and division within me between the sensitively subjective therapist and the hard-headed scientist. I suspect I am not as sensitively attuned to human experience as some therapists. I am sure that I am not as purely motivated by curiosity as the best of the scientists. Yet, both this sensitively subjective understanding and this detached objective curiosity are very real aspects of my life. It is the working out in me of the tensions between them which has been the basis for whatever contributions I have made to psychology. I have expressed this tension most clearly perhaps in my paper "Persons or Science?" (1955). I thoroughly enjoy the complete immersion in a highly subjective relationship which is the heart of psychotherapy. I thoroughly enjoy the hard-headed precision of the scientist and the elegance of any truly great research. If I try to give up either one of these aspects of me, I am not complete. So some people, knowing me only as a "soft" therapist, are surprised to learn that I am also "tough." A few, knowing me primarily from my research, are surprised that I can be at times a delicate artist in the therapeutic relationship. I feel myself fortunate in having these two sharply different selves. I like both of them, and they are both a real part of me.

I have often been a so-called "controversial person." This has meant that I have been involved in a variety of professional struggles and battles. I realize that my strategy has almost invariably been one of "island hopping." In World War II, MacArthur—a great strategist but not otherwise one of my heroes—never attacked the next island in the South Pacific, which was always heavily fortified and defended. Instead he slipped a task force through to some island far beyond, and captured and held that. Then the island heavily defended by the Japanese simply died on the vine, without ever having been attacked, simply because it could no longer be supplied or supported. This very well describes my own intuitive strategy in professional struggles. When psychiatrists have argued that psychotherapy is a medical function and psychologists should not be allowed to practice it, I have spent very little time arguing this directly but have simply gone far beyond it trying to improve psychotherapy and to strengthen research in psychotherapy. It has been my conviction that the argument would lose all its force if psychologists were *doing* good therapy and expanding the area of knowledge in that field through research. I feel this view has been borne out. When the psychology department at Chicago had what I felt were unreasonably constrictive rules for obtaining the Ph.D., I simply encouraged my students to take their degrees through the Committee on Human Development. As psychology lost students, it modified its rules in a more liberal direction. (In the psychology department at the University of Wisconsin, I was unsuccessful in finding the island to which I might "hop," hence had to engage in a more and more frontal attack on their—to me—antiquated and punitive structure of graduate education, and hence was thoroughly defeated.) In instance after instance in my professional life, I have felt it wasteful and foolish to battle directly to achieve my goals. I much prefer to establish a beach-head in the future, a beach-head which will make the current controversy meaningless. Thus, for example, it has never been of any importance to me to convince my professional colleagues that what I am doing is significant. This seems to me a most futile endeavor. But to interest *students*, who will be the next generation of faculty members and practitioners, in what I am doing—this has been of the greatest importance to me. I prefer, in other words, to hop the present generation and concentrate on the coming one.

This relates very directly to the next theme of my life. I want to have *impact*. I am not a person who is ambitious in the ordinary sense. It has never made much difference to me whether I have prestige, position, or power. In fact when power has been bestowed on me, I have usually given it away to the group. But it *is* important to me to have influence. I want what I do to *count*, to make a difference somewhere. I am not one of those persons who can do his thinking and research in an isolated corner, with never a care as to whether someone else finds it meaningful. I definitely want my work to have an influence. This can be regarded as good or bad— I suspect it is both—but it is most certainly a fact in me.

Very closely related is what I think of as my enjoyment of facilitation. I get great pleasure out of facilitating the development of a person in therapy, the development of growth-promoting interaction in a group, or serving as a facilitative "change agent" in an institution. I realize that my sense of "power" comes from the confidence I have that I can serve as a catalyst and produce the unpredictable! This is truly exciting.

I think this is a rather rare trait. Most individuals who have attained some status tend to dominate a situation—they are brilliant in conversation, tend to be the center of attention in any group, simply cannot be ignored. I, on the contrary, am absolutely at my worst if I am expected to be a "leading figure," or an "exciting person." As my wife can testify, I simply "clam up," and seem to be the dullest person around. If, however, I am received as a person (by a group or an individual) and can sense an opportunity to facilitate change and growth (in myself as well as the other), I can be a sparkling person whose expressiveness focuses attention not particularly on myself but on each person's sensing of change within himself. I feel most deeply rewarded when the group or the individual leaves me, not with the feeling, "what a brilliant leader (or speaker, or thinker)" but with the feeling, "I feel myself changing—within myself and in my relationship to my wife (or my children or my boss, or my thinking and professional interests.)" This ability to facilitate change, to free people for change, is something I greatly prize in myself.

Another important aspect of my development is my liking for writing. As a shy boy, I found I could express myself much more freely in writing than face to face. My love letters to Helen, as my wife-to-be, are far more eloquent than anything I could express to her verbally. I enjoyed writing stories and essays and poetry and even my attempts at scholarly papers in college. My work on the college debating team was helpful. The course in homiletics I took at Union Seminary helped me to develop clarity. But the experience which perhaps contributed most to my psychological writing was the twelve years of preparing comprehensive reports on each child we studied or dealt with at the Child Study Department and later the Guidance Center in Rochester, New York. Frequently these reports had to meet a deadline of a court hearing or an agency decision. If they were to have any influence they had to be accurate, penetrating, comprehensive, persuasive in presenting the reasons for our recommendations, clear and interesting enough to be read, and able to stand the test of time, since we would continue to be in contact with both the agency and the child, often for long periods. This was excellent training in writing and strengthened both my desire and ability to write with clarity. I have realized, as the years have gone by, that some writers desire to mystify. They want (consciously or unconsciously) for the reader's reaction to be, "What is this complex thing you're trying to say? I'll have to read it again." My desire, on the other hand, has been, even from childhood, to be understood. I would like to communicate so clearly that you cannot mistake my meaning. This long-standing attitude has made a difference, and a frequent comment on my writing, even from critics, is that it is lucid.

In more recent years I have assimilated another learning which has, I believe, improved my writing, my speaking, and hence my impact. I have expressed it as the knowledge that "what is most personal is most general." I have come to realize that if I can drop some of my defenses, can let myself come forth as a vulnerable person, can express some of the attitudes which feel most personal, most private, most tentative and uncertain in me, then the response from others is deep and receptive and warming. If I can be deeply myself in my expression this sets up a resonance in the other—whether an individual or an audience of 2000—which is very rewarding both for the other and for me. I have gradually become much more bold in revealing myself.

An important theme of my life is that I have had a personal existence and security quite apart from my professional life. If by some strange circumstance I were completely barred from all psychological practice, research, speaking, and writing, I would still have a full and rich life. I have a security in my relationship with my wife which has been a rich resource to me, and at times an even desperately needed one. Because of early difficulties in sexual adjustment we were fortunate in learning that open communication in problem areas, though difficult, is the only avenue to a better relationship. So we have enjoyed each other and supplement each other in many, many ways. She is naturally social where I tend to be a loner; she dreams up trips and enterprises which I reluctantly accept and then

thoroughly enjoy; she has kept our life from being narrow. She has been
a true helpmate (a term which is unfortunately growing old-fashioned), in
every sense of the word.

In addition I have many fields of interest. I enjoy color photography,
especially close-ups; we both have enjoyed (through snorkeling) the undersea life of the Caribbean; I like to garden and nurse each plant and bud;
I like to make mobiles; I have an interest in art and have tried my hand
at painting; I enjoy carpentry; I have an interest in foreign cultures, especially primitive ones. All this has meant that my professional work is not
the be-all and end-all of my existence. Somehow I have an inwardly light
touch in regard to my work. It is not all there is to life. Sometimes I am
struck with the absurdity of my earnest effort to help a person, complete
a research, write a paper. Placed in the perspective of billions of years of
time, of millions of light-years of interstellar space, of the trillions of one-
celled organisms in the sea, of the life struggle by billions of people to
achieve their goals, I cannot help but wonder what possible significance
can be attached to the efforts of one person at one moment of time. I can
only do my part as one infinitely small living unit in this vast ongoing
universe. But such a perspective helps to keep me from feeling too self-
important.

There is one final thread in my career which has surely been woven
in and out through the years. It is that I have had a great deal of plain
luck, that chance and good fortune are elements which should be clearly
recognized in the shaping of my career. I do not wish to be unduly modest
or to say that the recognition I have received is all luck. But chance *has*
entered in, as two illustrations may indicate.

By chance, my book on *The Clinical Treatment of the Problem Child*
came out at the very time (1939) that Ohio State University was making
every effort to establish a major position in clinical psychology. As a consequence, I entered university life as a full professor, I became visible na-
tionally, instead of being involved in a local service agency, and a part
of that was pure luck.

When I wrote *Counseling and Psychotherapy,* in 1942, neither my
publisher nor I could have foreseen that the minuscule field of counseling
would suddenly expand at the end of the war into an enormous field of
great public interest. To have written one of the very few books on the
subject was to boost me again into national visibility, and again the timing
was simply lucky.

As I have been writing this section in which I have attempted to
discover the major themes of my professional life, I have been surprised
at a certain smugness or assurance which has crept in. At first I thought
this was quite unlike me and should be edited out. As I have thought it

over further, I believe this is a real part of me and should be permitted to remain in the manuscript. It was most certainly not present in my earlier years, when I often felt a great lack of assurance, but it does describe a part of me now. I *do* believe in what I am doing; I *do* trust my own experience more deeply than any authority; I *am* inwardly sure that the directions in which I am moving are, and will prove to be, significant directions. I do, in some very basic sense, believe in myself. Intellectually, I know with equal assurance that I and my thinking may be shown to be completely erroneous; that the directions in which I am moving may prove to be blind alleys; but in spite of this openness of *mind*, I believe, at the *feeling* level, in myself and in what I am doing. This degree of assurance I *do* have.

# REFERENCES

### Selected Publications by Carl R. Rogers

This selection is intended to include what I regard as important expressions of what were for me at the time, new directions in my thinking and work.

*Measuring personality adjustment in children nine to thirteen.* New York: Teachers College, 1931. 107 pp.

*The clinical treatment of the problem child.* Boston: Houghton Mifflin, 1939. 393 pp.

*Counseling and psychotherapy.* Boston: Houghton Mifflin, 1942, 450 pp.

Significant aspects of client-centered therapy. *Amer. Psychologist,* 1946, *1,* 415–422.

Some observations on the organization of personality. *Amer. Psychologist,* 1947, *2,* 358–368.

*Client-centered therapy: its current practice, implications, and theory.* Boston: Houghton Mifflin, 1951. 560 pp.

(with Rosalind F. Dymond, Ed.) *Psychotherapy and personality change.* Univ. of Chicago Press, 1954. 447 pp.

Persons or science? A philosophical question. *Amer. Psychologist,* 1955, *10,* 267–278.

The necessary and sufficient conditions of therapeutic personality change. *J. consult. Psychol.,* 1957, *21,* 95–103.

A process conception of psychotherapy. *Amer. Psychologist,* 1958, *13,* 142–149.

A theory of therapy, personality and interpersonal relationships as developed in the client-centered framework. In S. Koch (Ed.), *Psychology: a study of a science, Vol. III. Formulations of the person and the social context.* New York: McGraw-Hill, 1959, 184–256.

The process equation of psychotherapy. *Amer. J. Psychother.,* 1961, *15,* No. 1, 27–45.

*On becoming a person.* Boston: Houghton Mifflin, 1961. 420 pp.

Learning to be free. In S. M. Farber and R. H. Wilson (Eds.), *Conflict and creativity: control of the mind, Part 2.* New York: McGraw-Hill, 1963, 268–288.

Toward a science of the person. In T. W. Wann (Ed.), *Behaviorism and phe-nomenology: contrasting bases for modern psychology.* Univ. of Chicago Press, 1964, 109–140.

Graduate education in psychology: a passionate statement. *WBSI Reports.* Western Behavioral Sciences Institute, La Jolla, California, 1964.

The process of the basic encounter group. In J. Bugental (Ed.), *The challenge of humanistic psychology.* New York: McGraw-Hill, in press.

Fabian Bachrach

# B. F. Skinner

## EARLY ENVIRONMENT

My Grandmother Skinner was an uneducated farmer's daughter who put on airs. She was naturally attracted to a young Englishman who came to America in the early 1870's looking for work, and she married him. (He had not found just the work he wanted when he died at the age of ninety.) My grandmother's aspirations were passed on to her son, William, who "read law" while apprenticed as a draftsman in the Erie Railroad shops in Susquehanna, a small town in northeastern Pennsylvania. He went on to a law school in New York City and passed his bar examination in Susquehanna County before getting a degree. He suffered from his mother's ambitions all his life. He was desperately hungry for praise, and many people thought him conceited; but he secretly—and bitterly—considered himself a failure, even though he eventually wrote a standard text on Workmen's Compensation Law which was in its fourth edition when he died.

My mother, Grace Burrhus, was bright and beautiful. She had rigid standards of what was "right," and they never changed. Her loyalties were legendary. At eleven she began to correspond with a friend who had moved away, and they wrote to each other in alternate weeks, without missing a week, for seventy years. Her father was born in New York State. He lied about his age to enlist as a drummer boy in the last year of the Civil War. After the war he came to Susquehanna looking for work as a carpenter, and eventually he became foreman of the Erie Carpenter Shops there. My Grandmother Burrhus had the only claim to quality in the family: an ancestor, a Captain Potter, had fought under Washington.

My home environment was warm and stable. I lived in the house I was born in until I went to college. My father, mother, and I all graduated from the same high school. I saw a great deal of my grandparents. I had a brother two and a half years younger than I. As a child I was fond of

[1] Preparation of this manuscript has been supported by grant K6-MH-21, 775–01 of the National Institute of Mental Health of the U. S. Public Health Service and by the Human Ecology Fund.

him. I remember being ridiculed for calling him "honey," a term my mother used for both of us at home. As he grew older he proved to be much better at sports and more popular than I, and he teased me for my literary and artistic interests. When he died suddenly of a cerebral aneurism at the age of sixteen, I was not much moved. I probably felt guilty because I was not. I had once made an arrowhead from the top of a tin can, and when I made a test shot straight up into the air, the arrow fell back and struck my brother in the shoulder, drawing blood. I recalled the event with a shock many years later when I heard Lawrence Olivier speaking Hamlet's lines:

> . . . . Let my disclaiming from a purpos'd evil
> Free me so far in your most generous thought,
> That I have shot mine arrow o'er the house,
> And hurt my brother.

Susquehanna is now half deserted, and it was even then a rather dirty railroad town, but it is situated in a beautiful river valley. I roamed the hills for miles around. I picked arbutus and dogwood in early Spring, chewed sassafras root and wintergreen berries and the underbark of slippery elm, killed rattlesnakes, and found flint arrowheads. With another boy I built a shack in the hills alongside a creek, and I learned to swim in the pool we made by blocking the creek with a sod-and-stone dam, sharing the pool with a poisonous watersnake. Four other boys and I once went three hundred miles down the Susquehanna River in a fleet of three canoes. I was fifteen at the time and the oldest in the party.

I was always building things. I built roller-skate scooters, steerable wagons, sleds, and rafts to be poled about on shallow ponds. I made seesaws, merry-go-rounds, and slides. I made slingshots, bows and arrows, blow guns and water pistols from lengths of bamboo, and from a discarded water boiler a steam cannon with which I could shoot plugs of potato and carrot over the houses of our neighbors. I made tops, diabolos, model airplanes driven by twisted rubber bands, box kites, and tin propellers which could be sent high into the air with a spool-and-string spinner. I tried again and again to make a glider in which I myself might fly.

I invented things, some of them in the spirit of the outrageous contraptions in the cartoons which Rube Goldberg was publishing in the *Philadelphia Inquirer* (to which, as a good Republican, my father subscribed). For example, a friend and I used to gather elderberries and sell them from door to door, and I built a flotation system which separated ripe from green berries. I worked for years on the design of a perpetual motion machine. (It did not work.)

I went through all twelve grades of school in a single building, and there were only eight students in my class when I graduated. I *liked* school. It was the custom for students to congregate outside the building until a

bell rang and the doors were opened. I was a constant problem for the
janitor, because I would arrive early and ask to be let in. He had been
told to keep me out, but he would shrug, open the door just enough to
let me through, and lock it after me. As I see it now, the school was good.
I had four strong years of high school mathematics using no-nonsense texts
by Wentworth. In my senior year I could read a bit of Virgil well enough
to feel that I was getting the meaning in Latin. Science was weak, but I
was always doing physical and chemical experiments at home.

My father was a sucker for book salesmen ("We are contacting a few
of the town's more substantial citizens"), and as a result we had a fairly
large library consisting mostly of sets—*The World's Great Literature, Mas-
terpieces of World History, Gems of Humor,* and so on. Half a dozen small
volumes on applied psychology, published by an "institute," were beautifully bound, with white spines and embossed seals on blue covers. I remember only one sample: it was said that an advertisement for chocolates
showing a man shovelling cocoa beans into a large roasting oven was bad
psychology.

An old-maid school teacher named Mary Graves was an important figure in my life. Her father was the village atheist and an amateur botanist
who believed in evolution. Miss Graves once showed me a letter he had
received from the Prince of Monaco offering to exchange specimens of
pressed plants. Miss Graves was a dedicated person with cultural interests
far beyond the level of the town. She organized the Monday Club, a literary society to which my mother belonged. The club would spend a winter
reading Ibsen's *Doll's House.* Miss Graves did her best to bring the little
town library up to date. When I was in high school, she once whispered
to me in a conspiratorial tone, "I have just been reading the strangest book.
It is called *Lord Jim.*"

Miss Graves was my teacher in many fields for many years. She taught
a Presbyterian Sunday school class, taking six or eight of us boys through
most of the Old Testament. She taught me drawing in the lower grades,
and she was later promoted to teaching English, both reading and composition. I think it was in the eighth grade that we were reading *As You
Like It.* One evening my father happened to say that some people believed
that the plays were not written by Shakespeare but by a man named Bacon.
The next day I announced to the class that Shakespeare had not actually
written the play we were reading. "You don't know what you are talking
about," said Miss Graves. That afternoon I went down to the public library
and drew out Edwin Durning-Lawrence's *Bacon is Shakespeare* (1910). The
next day I *did* know what I was talking about, and I must have made life
miserable for Miss Graves for the next month or two. Durning-Lawrence
had analyzed act five, scene one of *Love's Labours Lost,* proving that the word
*honorificabilitudinitatibus* was a cipher which, when properly interpreted,
read, "These works, the offspring of Francis Bacon, are preserved for the

world." To my amazement I discovered that the same act and scene in *As You Like It* was also cryptic. The philosopher Touchstone (who else but Bacon?) is disputing with the simple William (who else but Shakespeare?) for the possession of the fair Audrey (what else but the authorship of the plays?). The clincher was that William says that he was born in the Forest of Arden, and Shakespeare's mother's name was Arden. (O, the lovely adolescent obscenity of that "forest"!) I have long since lost interest in the Bacon-Shakespeare controversy, but in my defensive zeal I read biographies of Bacon, summaries of his philosophical position, and a good deal of *The Advancement of Learning* and *Novum Organum*. How much it meant to me at the age of fourteen or fifteen I cannot say, but Francis Bacon will turn up again in this story.

Miss Graves was probably responsible for the fact that in college I majored in English literature and afterwards embarked upon a career as a writer, and probably also for the fact that I have dabbled in art. I have never painted or sculpted really well, but I have enjoyed trying to do so.

My father had played the trumpet (then called the cornet) in a small orchestra, but he gave it up when he married. I never heard him play more than a few notes; he had "lost his lip." My mother played the piano well and had an excellent contralto voice. She sang at weddings and funerals— and the same songs at both. I still have her copy of J. C. Bartlett's "A Dream." It begins, "Last night I was dreaming of thee, love, was dreaming . . ." A sacred text for use at funerals is added in her own hand: "Come, Jesus, Redeemer, abide thou with me-e . . ." At the age of eight or nine I studied the piano for a year with an old man who sucked Sens-sens and jabbed me in the ribs with a sharp pencil whenever I made a mistake. For a while I gave up the piano in favor of the saxophone. My father was then local attorney for the Erie Railroad, and he arranged for me to play with an employee's band. We never got beyond "Poet and Peasant," "Morning Noon and Night in Vienna," and other overtures by von Suppe, but I learned to love ensemble playing. I played in a jazz band during my high school years. When I returned to the piano again, a friend of the family who taught piano noticed that I was limited to my mother's sentimental music and a few volumes of *Piano Pieces the Whole World Loves,* and she sent me a copy of Mozart's Fourth Sonata. Shortly afterward I bought all the Mozart sonatas, playing at first only short passages here and there. Later I came to play them all through once a year in a kind of ritual.

I was never physically punished by my father and only once by my mother. She washed my mouth out with soap and water because I had used a bad word. My father never missed an opportunity, however, to inform me of the punishments which were waiting if I turned out to have a criminal mind. He once took me through the county jail, and on a summer vacation I was taken to a lecture with colored slides describing life in Sing Sing. As a result I am afraid of the police and buy too many to their annual dances.

My mother was quick to take alarm if I showed any deviation from what was "right." Her technique of control was to say "tut-tut" and to ask, "What will people think?" I can easily recall the consternation in my family when in second grade I brought home a report card on which, under "Deportment," the phrase "Annoys others" had been checked. Many things which were not "right" still haunt me. I was allowed to play in the cemetery next door, but it was not "right" to step on a grave. Recently in a cathedral I found myself executing a series of smart right-angle detours to avoid the engraved stones on the floor. I was taught to "respect books," and it is only with a twinge that I can today crack the spine of a book to make it stay open on the piano.

My Grandmother Skinner made sure that I understood the concept of hell by showing me the glowing bed of coals in the parlor stove. In a travelling magician's show I saw a devil complete with horns and barbed tail, and I lay awake all that night in an agony of fear. Miss Graves, though a devout Christian, was liberal. She explained, for example, that one might interpret the miracles in the Bible as figures of speech. Shortly after I reached puberty, I had a mystical experience. I lost a watch which I had just been given by my family, and I was afraid to go home ("You would lose your head if it were not screwed on"). I took my bicycle and rode up along the river and followed the creek up to our shack. I was miserably unhappy. Suddenly it occurred to me that happiness and unhappiness must cancel out and that if I were unhappy now I would necessarily be happy later. I was tremendously relieved. The principle came with the force of a revelation. In a mood of intense exaltation I started down along the creek. Halfway to the road, in a nest of dried grass beside the path, lay my watch. I have no explanation; I had certainly "lost" it in town. I took this as a Sign. I hurried home and wrote an account in biblical language and purple ink. (The ink I had made by dissolving the lead from an indelible pencil, and it had an appropriate golden sheen.) No other signs followed, however, and my new testament remained only one chapter in length. Within a year I had gone to Miss Graves to tell her that I no longer believed in God. "I know," she said, "I have been through that myself." But her strategy misfired: I never went *through* it.

## COLLEGE

A friend of the family recommended Hamilton College, and I did not think of going anywhere else. It was then at the nadir of its long career. I took an absurd program of courses, but in some curious way I have made good use of every one of them. I majored in English and had good courses in Anglo-Saxon, Chaucer (for which I wrote a modern translation of "The Pardoner's Tale"), Shakespeare, Restoration drama, and Romantic poetry. I minored in Romance languages. Hamilton was proud of its reputation for public speaking, and I had four thin compulsory years of that. I elected biology as my freshman science and went on to advanced courses in embryology and cat anatomy.

The most important thing that happened to me at Hamilton was getting to know the Saunders family. They were abroad during my freshman year, recovering from the tragic death of their elder son, a brilliant student who had been killed in a hazing accident the year before. All the Saunders children were prepared for college at home; and when the family returned, they asked my mathematics professor to suggest a tutor for their younger son. I agreed to serve.

Percy Saunders was then dean. Hamilton College students called him "Stink" because he taught chemistry, but his great love was hybrid peonies. He and his family lived in a large frame house alongside the campus. It was full of books, pictures, sculpture, musical instruments, and huge bouquets of peonies in season. Dean Saunders played the violin, and there were string quartets at least one night a week. Louise Saunders took in a few students each year to prepare them for college, among them usually a pretty girl with whom I would fall in love. We would walk through the Root Woods, returning for tea before a fire in the music room in the late afternoon. Once in a while on a clear night a telescope would be set up among the peonies, and we would look for the moons of Mars or Saturn's rings. Interesting people came to stay—writers, musicians, and artists. Beside my chair as I listened to Schubert or Beethoven I might find a copy of the avant-garde *Broom* or a letter from Ezra Pound. I remember a page from the score of George Antheil's *Ballet Mécanique* with the words COMPLETELY PERCUSSIVE printed diagonally across it. Percy and Louise Saunders made an art of living, something I had not known was possible.

I never fitted into student life at Hamilton. I joined a fraternity without knowing what it was all about. I was not good at sports and suffered acutely as my shins were cracked in ice hockey or better players bounced basketballs off my cranium—all in the name of what was ironically called "physical education." In a paper I wrote at the end of my freshman year, I complained that the college was pushing me around with unnecessary requirements (one of them daily chapel) and that almost no intellectual interest was shown by most of the students. By my senior year I was in open revolt.

John K. Hutchens and I began that year with a hoax. Our professor of English composition, Paul Fancher, was a great name-dropper in the field of the theater. Hutchens and I had posters printed reading, in part:

"Charles Chaplin, the famous cinema comedian, will deliver his lecture 'Moving Pictures as a Career' in the Hamilton College Chapel on Friday, October 9." The lecture was said to be under Fancher's auspices. In the early hours of October 9 we went down to the village, plastered the posters on store windows and telephone poles, threw a few into lobbies of apartment houses, and went back to bed. That morning Hutchens called the afternoon paper in Utica, the nearest city, and told them that the president had announced the lecture at morning chapel. By noon the thing was completely out of hand. The paper ran Chaplin's picture on the front page and even guessed at the time he would arrive at Union Station, which, I am ashamed to say, was swarming with children at the appointed hour. In spite of police road-blocks it was estimated that 400 cars got through to the campus. A football pep meeting was mistaken for a Chaplin rally, and a great throng began to mill around the gymnasium. The editorial which appeared next day in the college paper ("No man with the slightest regard for his alma mater would have done it") was one of the best things Hutchens ever wrote.

As a nihilistic gesture, the hoax was only the beginning. Through the student publications we began to attack the faculty and various local sacred cows. I published a parody of the bumbling manner in which the professor of public speaking would review student performances at the end of a class. I wrote an editorial attacking Phi Beta Kappa. At commencement time I was in charge of Class Day exercises, which were held in the gymnasium, and with the help of another student (Alf Evers, later a well known illustrator) I covered the walls with bitter caricatures of the faculty.

One of the most sacred of Hamilton institutions was the Clark Prize Oration. Students submitted written orations, six of which were selected to be spoken in an evening contest, from which a winner was chosen by a committee of judges. Four of us decided to wreck the institution. We submitted orations which we thought would be selected but which were potentially so bombastic that we could convert the evening into an uproarious farce. We misjudged the judges, however. Only mine was selected. I found myself on the program with five serious speakers. I decided there was nothing for it but to go through with the joke alone, hoping that my friends would understand. Very few did. We also made a shambles of the commencement ceremonies, and at intermission the President warned us sternly that we would not get our degrees if we did not settle down.

## LITERARY INTERLUDE

My Hamilton College activities seemed to be pointing toward a career as a writer. As a child I had had an old typewriter and a small printing press, and during my grade school years I wrote poems and stories and typed or printed them "artistically." I started a novel or two—sentimental stuff on the model of James Oliver Curwood: Pierre, an old trapper, lived in the woods of colonial Pennsylvania with his lovely daughter, Marie (how they got down from Quebec I never thought it necessary to explain). In high school I worked for the local *Transcript*. In the morning before school I would crib national and international news from the Binghamton papers which had come in on the morning train. Occasionally I did a feature story or published a poem in the manner of Edgar Guest. When I got to college I contributed serious poems to the *Hamilton Literary Magazine*. Free verse was coming in, and I tried my hand at it. Here is a sample:

### CONCUPISCENCE

An old man, sowing in a field,
Walks with a slow, uneasy rhythm.
He tears handfuls of seed from his vitals,
Caressing the wind with the sweep of this hand.
At night he stops, breathless,
Murmuring to his earthy consort,
"Love exhausts me!"

And I had not yet heard of Freud. Once, when in love, I wrote five or six rather derivative Shakespearean sonnets and enjoyed the strange excitement of emitting whole lines ready-made, properly scanned and rhymed.

The summer before my senior year I attended the Middlebury School of English at Breadloaf, Vermont. I took a course with Sidney Cox, who one day invited me to have lunch with Robert Frost. Frost asked me to send him some of my work, and I sent him three short stories. His comments came the following April. The letter is printed in the *Selected Letters of Robert Frost,* edited by Lawrance Thompson (1964). It was encouraging, and on the strength of it I definitely decided that I would be a writer. My father had always hoped that I would study law and come into his office. My birth had been announced in the local paper in that vein: "The town has a new law firm: Wm. A. Skinner & Son." I had taken a course in political science my senior year just in case I might indeed go into law. My father was naturally unhappy that I had decided against it. He thought I should prepare myself to earn a living—say, as a lawyer—and *then* try my hand at writing. He eventually agreed, however, that I should live at home (in Scranton, Pennsylvania, to which my family had moved) and write for a year or two. I built a small study in the attic and set to work. The results were disastrous. I frittered away my time. I read aimlessly, built model ships, played the piano, listened to the newly-invented radio, contributed to the humorous column of a local paper but wrote almost nothing else, and thought about seeing a psychiatrist.

Before the year was out, I rescued myself and my self-respect by taking on a hack job. The FBI has occasionally expressed interest in that two-year gap in my educational history, but I was not writing for the *Daily Worker*. On the contrary, I was way out on the right wing. In 1904, after a bitter coal strike, President Theodore Roosevelt had set up a Board of Conciliation to settle grievances brought by unions and companies. The decisions which had since been handed down were increasingly cited as precedents, and the coal companies wanted them digested so that their lawyers could prepare cases more effectively. I read and abstracted thousands of decisions and classified them for ready reference. My book was privately printed under the title *A Digest of Decisions of the Anthracite Board of Conciliation*. (My father was listed as coauthor, but for prestige only.) The book was intended to give the coal companies an advantage, but the lawyer who prepared all the union cases had a copy within the year.

After I had finished the book, I went to New York for six months of bohemian living in Greenwich Village, then to Europe for the summer, and on to Harvard in the fall to begin the study of psychology. In New York I worked in a book shop, dined at Chumleys', and drank hot rum Punchino's at Jimmy's, a speakeasy on Barrow Street. My friends were liberal and even intellectual. On Saturday nights eight or ten of us would somehow manage to have an all-night party on one quart of prohibition gin. That summer Paris was full of literary ex-patriots and I met some of them, but a violent reaction against all things literary was setting in.

I had failed as a writer because I had had nothing important to say, but I could not accept that explanation. It was literature which must be at fault. A girl I had played tennis with in high school—a devout Catholic who later became a nun—had once quoted Chesterton's remark about a character of Thackeray's: "Thackeray didn't know it but she drank." I generalized the principle to all literature. A writer might portray human behavior accurately, but he did not therefore understand it. I was to remain interested in human behavior, but the literary method had failed me; I would turn to the scientific. Alf Evers, the artist, had eased the transition. "Science," he once told me, "is the art of the twentieth century." The relevant science appeared to be psychology, though I had only the vaguest idea of what that meant.

## TOWARD PSYCHOLOGY

Many odds and ends contributed to my decision. I had long been interested in animal behavior. We had no household pets, but I caught and kept turtles, snakes, toads, lizards, and chipmunks. I read Thornton Burgess and Ernest Thompson Seton and was interested in folk wisdom about animals. The man who kept the livery stable once explained that the cowboys in the rodeo let themselves be thrown just before "breaking the spirit" of the bucking broncos to avoid spoiling them for future performances. At a county fair I saw a troupe of performing pigeons. The scene was the facade of a building. Smoke appeared from the roof, and a presumably female pigeon poked her head out of an upper window. A team of pigeons came on stage pulling a fire engine, smoke pouring from its boiler. Other pigeons with red fire hats rode on the engine, one of them pulling a string which rang a bell. Somehow a ladder was put up against the building, and one of the firepigeons climbed it and came back down followed by the pigeon from the upper window.

Human behavior also interested me. A man in Binghamton who gave me advanced lessons on the saxophone had entertained soldiers during the war with a vaudeville act. He wrote the alphabet forward with his right hand and backward with his left while adding a column of figures and answering questions—all at the same time. It gave him a headache. I remember being puzzled by an episode at some kind of church fair where there was a booth in which you could throw baseballs at dolls mounted on a rack. The dolls were restored to their place by pulling a rope from the front of the booth. When the woman who ran the concession was gathering balls near the dolls, some wag pulled the rope. Everyone laughed as the woman dropped to the ground in alarm. Why had she confused the sound of the rack with the sound of a ball?

Some of the things I built had a bearing on human behavior. I was not allowed to smoke, so I made a gadget incorporating an atomizer bulb with which I could "smoke" cigarettes and blow smoke rings hygienically. (There might be a demand for it today.) At one time my mother started a campaign to teach me to hang up my pajamas. Every morning while I was eating breakfast, she would go up to my room, discover that my pajamas were not hung up, and call to me to come up immediately. She continued this for weeks. When the aversive stimulation grew unbearable, I constructed a mechanical device that solved my problem. A special hook in the closet of my room was connected by a string-and-pulley system to a sign hanging above the door to the room. When my pajamas were in place on the hook, the sign was held high above the door out of the way. When the pajamas were off the hook, the sign hung squarely in the middle of the door frame. It read: "Hang up your pajamas!"

My earliest interest in psychology was philosophical. In high school I began a treatise entitled "Nova Principia Orbis Terrarum." (That sounds pretentious, but at least I got it out of my system early. Clark Hull published his Principia at the age of fifty-nine.) Two pages of this great work survive. It begins: "Our soul consists of our mind, our power of reasoning, thinking, imagining, weighing, our power to receive impressions, and stimulate action of our body; and our conscience, our inner knowledge of write (sic)." I engaged in a good deal of self-observation, and I kept notes. Once in a rather noisy street I was trying to talk to a friend in a store window. Though I strained to hear him, I could not make out what he was saying. Then I discovered that there was no glass in the window and that his voice was reaching me loud and clear. I had dismissed it as part of the ambient noise and was listening for a fainter signal.

College did little to further my interest in psychology. The only formal instruction I received lasted ten minutes. Our professor of philosophy (who had actually studied under Wundt) once drew a pair of dividers from his desk drawer (the first Brass Instrument I had ever seen) and demonstrated the two-point limen. My term paper for a course in Shakespeare was a study of Hamlet's madness. I read rather extensively on schizophrenia, but I should not care to have the paper published today. At Breadloaf I wrote a one-act play about a quack who changed people's personalities with endocrines, a subject which was then beginning to attract attention in the newspapers.

After college my literary interests carried me steadily toward psychology. Proust's *A La Recherche du temps perdu* was just being translated. I read all that was available in English and then carried on in French. (I bought Part VIII, *Le Temps retrouvé*, in Algiers in 1928. The uncut pages indicate that I abandoned literature on page ninety-six.) Proust intensified my habit of self-observation and of noting and recording many tricks of perception and memory. Before going to Harvard I bought Parson's book on perception, and I suppose it was only my extraordinary luck which kept me from becoming a Gestalt or (so help me) a cognitive psychologist.

The competing theme which saved me was suggested by "Bugsy" Morrell, my biology teacher at Hamilton. He had called my attention to Jacques Loeb's *Physiology of the Brain and Comparative Psychology* (1900), and later he showed me Pavlov's *Conditioned Reflexes* (1927). I bought Pavlov's book and read it while living in Greenwich Village. The literary magazine called *The Dial,* to which I subscribed, was publishing articles by Bertrand Russell, and they led me to Russell's book, *Philosophy,* published in 1925, in which he devoted a good deal of time to John B. Watson's *Behaviorism,* emphasizing its epistemological implications. I got hold of Watson's *Behaviorism* (1924–25) (but not his *Psychology from the Standpoint of a Behaviorist,* 1919), and in the bookstore in New York I read the store's copy of his *Psychological Care of Infant and Child* (1928) between customers.

The Department of Psychology at Harvard did not strengthen any particular part of this hodgepodge of interests, but two graduate students did. Fred S. Keller, who was teaching part time at Tufts, was a sophisticated behaviorist in every sense of the word. I had seen the regal name of Charles K. Trueblood spread across the pages of *The Dial,* for which he wrote many reviews. Now I found Trueblood himself, in white coat and gumshoes, moving silently through the corridors of Emerson Hall carrying cages of rats, the performances of which he was studying in a rotated maze. I welcomed the support of another renegade from literature.

At Harvard I entered upon the first strict regimen of my life. I had done what was expected of me in high school and college but had seldom worked hard. Aware that I was far behind in a new field, I now set up a rigorous schedule and maintained it for almost two years. I would rise at six, study until breakfast, go to classes, laboratories, and libraries with no more than fifteen minutes unscheduled during the day, study until exactly nine o'clock at night and go to bed. I saw no movies or plays, seldom went to concerts, had scarcely any dates, and read nothing but psychology and physiology.

My program in the department was not heavy. Boring was on leave, writing his history. Troland gave a course, but I found it unbearably dull and withdrew after the first day. Carroll Pratt taught psychophysical methods and was always available for discussions. I took Harry Murray's course in Abnormal Psychology the first year he gave it. I could reach French but needed German as well, so I took an intensive course which met five days a week. To pass statistics I simply read G. Udney Yule's *An Introduction to the Theory of Statistics* (1911). His use of Greek letters to refer to the absence of attributes explains my symbols $S^p$ and $S\Delta$, the awkwardness of which has plagued many psychologists since.

The intellectual life around the department was of a high order. A weekly colloquium, loosely structured, was always exciting and challenging. We argued with Pratt, Beebe-Center, and Murray on even terms. The informality is shown by a letter which I wrote to Harry Murray, of which he recently reminded me. He had given a colloquium on his theory of "regnancy." I wrote to tell him that there were some things about himself I felt he ought to know. When he was a child, he had obviously been led to believe that it was urine which entered the female in sexual intercourse. This had wreaked havoc in his scientific thinking, and he was still trying to separate *p* from *pregnancy*.

A joint reception for new students in philosophy and psychology was held each year at Professor Hocking's. My first year I turned up at the appointed hour, which was, of course, too early. A little old man with a shiny bald head and deep-set eyes soon arrived and came straight toward me in the friendliest way. He wore a wing collar and ascot tie. He stammered slightly and spoke with an English accent. I sized him up as a clergyman—perhaps an imported preacher in one of the better Boston churches. He asked me where I had gone to college and what philosophy I had studied. He had never heard the name of my professor and was only puzzled when I tried to help by explaining that he was an Edwardian (meaning a disciple of Jonathan Edwards). He told me that a young psychologist should keep an eye on philosophy, and I told *him*, fresh from my contact with Bertrand Russell, that it was quite the other way around: we needed a psychological epistemology. This went on for fifteen or twenty minutes, as the room filled up. Others began to speak to my new friend. Finally a student edged in beside me, explaining that he wanted to get as close to the professor as possible. "Professor who?" I asked. "Professor Whitehead," he said.

My thesis had only the vaguest of Harvard connections. Through a friend who had come to Harvard to study under Percy Bridgman I got to know the *Logic of Modern Physics* (1927). I read Poincaré and Mach. I began to spend a good deal of time in the Boston Medical Library and in the summer of 1930 wrote a paper on the concept of the reflex, adopting the semihistorical method from Mach's *Science of Mechanics*. Early that fall I was discussing my future with Beebe-Center. I outlined the work I intended to cover in my thesis. His comment was typical: "Who do you think you are? Helmholtz?" He encouraged me to get a thesis in at once. I was already well along in my work on changes in rate of eating and had written two short papers on drive and reflex strength. I combined these with my paper on the reflex and submitted them as a thesis to Professor Boring, who was now back in residence. I still have his long reply. He was bothered by my selective use of history. A thesis on the history of the reflex should be quite different. He suggested an alternative outline. I felt that he had missed my point, and I resubmitted the thesis without change. Suspecting that he was bothered by my behavioristic leanings, I attached a quotation from Thomas Hood:

> Owning her weakness,
> Her evil behavior,
> And leaving, with meekness,
> Her sins to her Savior.

Boring accepted the role of Savior. He appointed a thesis committee of which he himself was not a member; the thesis was approved, and I passed my orals at the end of the fall term of 1930–31. I stayed in my laboratory, supported by the balance of a Harvard Fellowship, until June.

Meanwhile I had come into close contact with W. J. Crozier and Hudson Hoagland. Hoagland had taken his Ph.D. in psychology but was teaching in Crozier's department of General Physiology. It was felt, I think, that Crozier was stealing students from psychology. He certainly offered enthusiastic encouragement, and after I got my degree he put me up for National Research Council Fellowships for two years, but I was never under any pressure to adopt his principles or move into his field. During my first postdoctoral year I spent every other day working on the central nervous system at the medical school under Alexander Forbes and Hallowell Davis. For the rest of my time Crozier offered me a subterranean laboratory in the new biology building. I moved my animal equipment into it and worked there for five years, the last three as a Junior Fellow in the Harvard Society of Fellows.

I have traced the development of my research in detail elsewhere (see 1956). Russell and Watson had given me no glimpse of experimental method, but Pavlov had: control the environment and you will see order in behavior. In a course with Hoagland I discovered Sherrington and

Magnus. I read *Körperstellung* and proposed to do a translation (fortunately I failed to find a publisher). I felt that my thesis had exorcised the physiological ghosts from Sherrington's synapse, and I could therefore maintain contact with these earlier workers. In writing *The Behavior of Organisms* (1938) I held doggedly to the term "reflex." Certain characteristics of operant behavior were, however, becoming clear. My first papers were challenged by two Polish physiologists, Konorski and Miller. It was in my answer to them that I first used the word "operant." Its function, then as now, was to identify behavior traceable to reinforcing contingencies rather than to eliciting stimuli.

## MINNESOTA

In the spring of 1936, the low point of the depression, the end of my Junior Fellowship was approaching and I had no job. The best offer the Department of Psychology could pass along to me was from a YMCA college; but Walter Hunter was teaching that summer at Minnesota, and he mentioned me to R. M. Elliott, who was looking for someone to teach small sections of a big introductory course. The beginning salary was $1900.

At Minnesota I not only taught for the first time, I began to learn college psychology, keeping a jump or two ahead of my students in Woodworth's text. I chose two sections of twenty students each from about eight hundred in the beginning course. Many of them were already committed to particular careers, such as medicine, law, journalism, and engineering, but five percent of the students I had during five years went on to get Ph.D.'s in psychology and many more to get M.A.'s. I stole W. K. Estes from engineering and Norman Guttman from philosophy. I have never again been so richly reinforced as a teacher.

## VERBAL BEHAVIOR

I did not quite give up literature. At Harvard I met I. A. Richards, who managed somehow to blend psychology and literary criticism, and I discussed books and techniques with other literary friends. I wrote an article for the *Atlantic Monthly* under the editor's title of "Has Gertrude Stein a Secret?" In it I showed that a paper which Gertrude Stein had published when at Radcliffe contained samples of her own automatic writing which resembled material she later published as literature. Gertrude Stein wrote to the editor in reply: "No, it is not so automatic as he thinks. If there is anything secret it is the other way too. I think I achieve by xtra consciousness, xcess, but then what is the use of telling him that, he being a psychologist and I having been one."

I began to look at literature, not as a medium for portraying human behavior, but as a field of behavior to be analyzed. A discussion with Whitehead after dinner at the Society of Fellows set me to work on my book *Verbal Behavior* (1957). The chairman of the Society, L. J. Henderson, cautioned me that such a book might take five years. The following summer he sent a postcard from France: "A motto for your book—'Car le mot, ç'est le verbe, et le verbe, ç'est Dieu'—Victor Hugo."

As a boy I knew two interesting cases of verbal behavior. My Grandmother Skinner was an almost pathological talker. My grandfather had stopped listening to her while still a young man, and when any visitor came to her house she would begin talking and would repeat, without pausing, a string of anecdotes and stereotyped comments which we all knew by heart. More predictable verbal behavior I have never seen. The other case was Professor Bowles, the principal of my high school, who taught mathematics. He had a long list of favorite topics, and almost any stimulus would set him off an a digression. He would eventually return to mathematics with a perfunctory bow to the comment which had first set him off. One day I made running notes of the topics he was touching upon. There were two long harangues that day, and to my surprise he concluded the second by returning to the topic with which he had begun and concluded the first!

When I was in the Society of Fellows, another verbal phenomenon came to my attention. On a beautiful Sunday morning I was in my subterranean, soundproofed laboratory writing notes against a background of rhythmic noise from my apparatus. Suddenly I found myself joining in the rhythm, saying silently, "You'll never get out, you'll never get out, you'll never get out." The relevance of the remark seemed worth investigating. I built a phonographic system in which patterns of vowels (separated by glottal stops) could be repeated as often as desired. Playing each sample softly to a subject, I could maintain the illusion that it was actual speech and could collect a large sample of "projective" verbal responses. Harry Murray supplied me with subjects from his research on thematic apperception.

My renewed interest in literature was encouraged by my marriage in 1936 to Yvonne Blue. She had majored in English at the University of Chicago, where she had taken a course in English composition with Thornton Wilder. She is an active reader (and a rapid one—she reads exactly twice as fast as I), and there were always new books around the house. When I had a chance to give a summer school course in the psychology of literature, she attended my lectures and reinforced me appropriately. I gave the course again and broadcast it over an educational radio station. To fill out the term I roamed rather widely, from *The Meaning of Meaning* (1945) through psychoanalysis, and thus explored the field of verbal behavior rather more widely than I should otherwise have done. As a rule the material in which I had least confidence proved to be most popular, but I did not wholly abandon my scientific principles. After several persuasive demonstrations of alliteration as a verbal process, for example, I became suspicious and made a statistical analysis of a hundred of Shakespeare's sonnets. I found that, although an occasional line might have as many as four stressed initial s's, such lines occurred almost exactly as often as one would predict from chance. (A similar study of Swinburne, I was glad to find, not only demonstrated alliteration, but showed an alliterative tendency extending over several syllables.)

In the fall of 1941 on a Guggenheim Fellowship I began to write a final draft of *Verbal Behavior*. The war intervened, but I picked up the Fellowship again in 1944–45 and finished the greater part of the manuscript. I gave a course from it in the summer of 1947 at Columbia, and my William James Lectures at Harvard that fall were based on it. I put off a final version in order to write *Science and Human Behavior* (1953). *Verbal Behavior* was published, not five, as Henderson had predicted, but twenty-three years after it was begun, in 1957. It was completed under heavy competition from research and from another book, *Schedules of Reinforcement* (1957), which Charles Ferster and I published at about the same time.

## PROJECT PIGEON

By the end of the 1930's the Nazis had demonstrated the power of the airplane as an offensive weapon. On a train from Minneapolis to Chicago in the spring of 1939, I was speculating rather idly about surface-to-air missiles as a possible means of defense. How could they be controlled? I knew nothing about radar, of course, but infrared radiation from the exhaust of the engines seemed a possibility. Was visible radiation out of the question? I noticed a flock of birds flying alongside the train, and it suddenly occurred to me that I might have the answer in my own research. Why not teach animals to guide missiles? I went back to Minneapolis and bought some pigeons. The rest of the story of Project Pigeon has already been told (1960).

## THE "BABY BOX"

Toward the end of the Second World War, we decided to have another child. My wife remarked that she did not mind bearing children but that the first two years were hard to take. I suggested that we mechanize the care of a baby. There is nothing natural about a crib. Wrapping a baby in several layers of cloth—undershirt, nightie, sheets, and blankets, with a mattress underneath—is an inefficient way of maintaining a proper temperature, and it greatly restricts the child's movements. I built, instead, an enclosed space in which the baby, wearing only a diaper, could lie on a tightly stretched woven plastic sheet, the surface of which feels rather like linen and through which warm air rises, moved by convection or a fan, depending on the outside temperature.

When our second daughter, Deborah, came home from the hospital, she went directly into the device and used it as sleeping space for two and a half years. I reported our happy experience in an article in the *Ladies Home Journal,* and many hundreds of babies have been raised in what is now called an Aircrib. Child care is conservative, and the method has been adopted fairly slowly, but medical and behavioral advantages should be studied. Predictions and tales of dire consequences have not been supported. Deborah broke her leg in a skiing accident but presumably not because of "the box." Otherwise she has had remarkably good health. She is now in college, interested in art and music, from Bach to Beatle, and she usually beats me at chess. To complete the story of the shoemaker's children, our older daughter, Julie, is married to a sociologist, Ernest Vargas, and is finishing her work for a Ph.D. in educational research. Their first child, Lisa, is of course, being raised in an Aircrib.

## WALDEN TWO

In the spring of 1945 at a dinner party in Minneapolis, I sat next to a friend who had a son and a son-in-law in the South Pacific. I expressed regret that when the war was over they would come back and take up their old way of life, abandoning their present crusading spirit. She asked me what I would have them do instead, and I began to discuss an experimental attitude toward life. I said that some of the communities of the nineteenth century represented a healthy attitude. She pressed me for details and later insisted that I publish them. I was unaware that I was taking her seriously. A paper on "The Operational Analysis of Psychological Terms" (1945) was due on June 1, and I met that deadline. Then, to my surprise, I began to write *Walden Two* (1948). It began simply as a description of a feasible design for community living. I chose the unoriginal utopian strategy of having a few people visit a community. The characters soon took over.

In general I write very slowly and in longhand. It took me two minutes to write each word of my thesis and that is still about my rate. From three or four hours of writing each day I eventually salvage about one hundred publishable words. *Walden Two* was an entirely different experience. I wrote it on the typewriter in seven weeks. It is pretty obviously a venture in self-therapy, in which I was struggling to reconcile two aspects of my own behavior represented by Burris and Frazier. Some of it was written with great emotion. The scene in Frazier's room, in which Frazier defends *Walden Two* while admitting that he himself is not a likeable person or fit for communal life, I worked out while walking the streets near our house in St. Paul. I came back and typed it out in white heat.

I receive a steady trickle of letters from people who have read *Walden Two,* want to know whether such a community has ever been established, and, if so, how they can join. At one time I seriously considered an actual experiment. It could be one of the most dramatic adventures in the twentieth century. It needs a younger man, however, and I am unwilling to give up the opportunity to do other things which in the long run may well advance the principles of *Walden Two* more rapidly. A conference organized to consider an actual experiment was recently attended by nearly one hundred people.

## INDIANA

In the fall of 1945 I became chairman of the Department of Psychology at Indiana. I took with me from Minnesota the unfinished manuscript of *Verbal Behavior,* the manuscript of *Walden Two,* the Aircrib with its lovely occupant, and a miscellaneous lot of apparatus. I was inexperienced as an administrator, but the department survived my brief chairmanship. I did no undergraduate teaching, but the chapter in *Science and Human Behavior* on self-control is to a large extent the joint product of a seminar in which, for almost the only time in my life, I successfully managed group thinking. In spite of my administrative responsibilities I ran a number of experiments —all with pigeons—on reaction time, differential reinforcement of slow responding, two operanda, and matching-to-sample. These studies are mostly reported in "Are Theories of Learning Necessary?" (1950)

## THE EXPERIMENTAL ANALYSIS OF BEHAVIOR

Other people were now beginning to do research along the same lines. W. K. Estes, who went on to get a Ph.D. at Minnesota, wrote a thesis on the effects of punishment which became a classic. At Columbia Fred Keller was teaching graduate students from *The Behavior of Organisms* and, with W. N. Schoenfeld, was planning a revolutionary introductory course in the college. A problem in communication arose, and Keller and I started what became a series of annual conferences on the Experimental Analysis of Behavior. Those who attended the first of these at Indiana in the spring of 1946 are pictured in volume five (1962) of the *Journal of the Experimental Analysis of Behavior.* Eventually we began to meet at the same time as the American Psychological Association and later as part of its program. When Division 3 could no longer provide space or arrange time for our expanding activities, we took the probably inevitable step of forming a separate division—Division 25.

Meanwhile, the need for a special journal had become clear. I proposed an inexpensive newsletter, but more constructive opinions prevailed. A small holding society was formed and the *Journal of the Experimental Analysis of Behavior* founded. The history of the discipline can also be traced in the increasing availability of excellent apparatus, reflecting the growing complexity and subtlety of the contingencies of reinforcement under analysis.

## HARVARD AGAIN

While giving the William James Lectures at Harvard in 1947, I was asked to become a permanent member of the department, and we moved to Cambridge in 1948. Remembering my introductory teaching at Minnesota I proposed to add a course in human behavior to the Harvard list. The first year was nearly a disaster. More than four hundred students, anticipating a "gut" course, signed up. I had no appropriate text and could only supply hastily prepared mimeographed sheets. My section men were loyal but puzzled. Later the course was incorporated into the General Education program and gradually improved. By 1953 *Science and Human Behavior* was available as a text.

Meanwhile I had set up a pigeon laboratory in which Charles Ferster and I worked very happily together for more than five years. It was the high point in my research history. Scarcely a week went by without some exciting discovery. Perhaps the behavior we dealt with most effectively was our own. Near the end of our collaboration we found ourselves with a vast quantity of unanalyzed and unpublished data, and we proceeded to design an environment in which we could scarcely help writing a book. In it we both worked as we had never worked before. In one spring term and one long hot summer we wrote a text and a glossary and prepared over a thousand figures, more than 900 of which were published.

The success of my laboratory in the 1950's and early 1960's was due in large part to many excellent graduate students, not all of them under my direction, of whom I may mention Douglas G. Anger, James A. Anliker, Donald S. Blough, Richard J. Herrnstein (now my colleague on the Harvard faculty), Alfredo V. Lagmay, William H. Morse, Nathan H. Azrin, Ogden R. Lindsley, Lewis R. Gollub, Matthew L. Israel, Harlan L. Lane, George S. Reynolds, A. Charles Catania, Herbert S. Terrace, and Neil J. Peterson. With very little direct help from me they all made and are continuing to make important contributions.

## TECHNOLOGICAL APPLICATIONS

At Minnesota W. T. Heron and I had studied the effects of certain drugs on operant behavior. In the 1950's a strong interest in psychopharmacology suddenly developed. Almost all the large drug companies set up operant laboratories, some only for the screening of new compounds but many providing an opportunity for basic research. Much of this interest was generated by Joseph V. Brady of the Walter Reed Army Medical Center. Peter Dews of the Department of Pharmacology in the Harvard Medical School began to work in close cooperation with my laboratory and soon organized an active program in his own department.

In the early 1950's Dr. Harry Solomon, then chairman of the Department of Psychiatry at the Harvard Medical School, helped me set up a laboratory for the study of the operant behavior of psychotics at the Metropolitan State Hospital in Waltham, Massachusetts. Ogden R. Lindsley took over, and the work he initiated there has now been carried forward in many other laboratories. Azrin and others have extended operant principles to the management of psychotic patients in hospital wards, and there is increasing interest in applications to personal therapy.

Sporadic research on operant behavior in children goes back to the 1930's. Sidney Bijou, among others, has been particularly active in applying the principles of an experimental analysis to the behavior of children in nursery schools, clinics, and the home. Ferster turned from our work on schedules to the study of autistic children, and there are now many operant laboratories for the study of retardates. Almost all these practical applications have contributed to our understanding of behavior. Fortunately, they have not overshadowed the basic science; many laboratories continue to study operant behavior apart from technological significances.

In the late 1930's, looking ahead to the education of our first child, I began to write a book called *Something to Think About*. It was never completed, though I got as far as having an artist work on the illustrations. It contained examples of what later came to be called programmed intruction. When our daughters went to school, I showed the usual interest as a parent but carefully refrained from speaking as a specialist in the field of learning. In 1953 our younger daughter was in fourth grade in a private school in Cambridge. On November 11, as a Visiting Father, I was sitting in the back of the room in an arithmetic class. Suddenly the situation seemed perfectly absurd. Here were twenty extremely valuable organisms. Through no fault of her own the teacher was violating almost everything we knew about the learning process.

I began to analyze the contingencies of reinforcement which might be useful in teaching school subjects and designed a series of teaching machines which would permit the teacher to provide such contingencies for individual students. At a conference on Current Trends in Psychology at the University of Pittsburgh in the spring of 1954 I demonstrated a machine to teach spelling and arithmetic. Within a year I found myself caught up in the teaching machine movement. A series of projects at Harvard led eventually to a Committee on Programmed Instruction, in which I had the invaluable collaboration of James G. Holland.

Economics, government, and religion are farther from psychology than linguistics, psychotherapy, or education, and few people have the kind of joint interest needed for an examination of common principles. I have seen myself moving slowly in this direction, however, and I am now working under a Career Award from the National Institutes of Health which will permit me to explore the social sciences from the point of view of an experimental analysis of behavior.

## MY BEHAVIOR AS A SCIENTIST

It is often said that behaviorists do not view themselves as they view their subjects—for example, that they regard what they say as true in some sense which does not apply to the statements of the people they study. On the contrary, I believe that my behavior in writing *Verbal Behavior,* for example, was precisely the sort of behavior the book discusses. Whether from narcissism or scientific curiosity, I have been as much interested in myself as in rats and pigeons. I have applied the same formulations, I have looked for the same kinds of causal relations, and I have manipulated behavior in the same way and sometimes with comparable success. I would not publish personal facts of this sort if I did not believe that they throw some light on my life as a scientist.

I was taught to fear God, the police, and what people will think. As a result I usually do what I have to do with no great struggle. I try not to let any day "slip useless away." I have studied when I did not feel like studying, taught when I did not want to teach. I have taken care of animals and run experiments as the animals dictated. (Some of my first cumulative records are stamped December twenty-fifth and January first.) I have met deadlines for papers and reports. In both my writing and my research I have fought hard against deceiving myself. I avoid metaphors which are effective at the cost of obscuring issues. I avoid rhetorical devices which give unwarranted plausibility to an argument (and I sometimes reassure myself by making lists of the devices so used by others). I avoid the unwarranted prestige conferred by mathematics, even, I am afraid, when mathematics would be helpful. I do not spin impressive physiological theories from my data, as I could easily do. I never convert an exploratory experiment into an *experimentum crucis* by inventing a hypothesis after the fact. I write and rewrite a paper until, so far as possible, it says exactly what I have to say. (A constant search for causes seems to be another product of that early environment. When my wife or one of my daughters tells me that she has a headache, I am likely to say, "Perhaps you have not been eating wisely" or "You may have been out in the sun too much." It is an almost intolerable trait in a husband, father, or friend, but it is an invaluable scientific practice.)

I must admit that all these characteristics have been helpful. Max Weber could be right about the Protestant Ethic. But its effect is only cautionary or restrictive. Much more important in explaining my scientific behavior are certain positive reinforcements which support Feuer's answer to Weber in which he shows that almost all noted scientists followed a "hedonistic ethic." I have been powerfully reinforced by many things: food, sex, music, art, and literature—and my scientific results. I have built apparatuses as I have painted pictures or modelled figures in clay. I have conducted experiments as I have played the piano. I have written scientific papers and books as I have written stories and poems. I have *never* designed and conducted an experiment because I felt I ought to do so, or to meet a deadline, or to pass a course, or to "publish rather than perish." I dislike experimental designs which call for the compulsive collection of data and, particularly, data which will not be reinforcing until they have been exhaustively analyzed. I freely change my plans when richer reinforcements beckon. My thesis was written before I knew it was a thesis. *Walden Two* was not planned at all. I may practice self-management for Protestant reasons, but I do so in such a way as to maximize non-Protestant reinforcements. I emphasize positive contingencies. For example, I induce myself to write by making production as conspicuous as possible (actually, in a cumulative record). In short, I arrange an environment in which what would otherwise be hard work is actually effortless.

I could not have predicted that among the reinforcers which explain my scientific behavior the opinions of others would not rank high, but that seems to be the case. Exceptions are easily traced to my history. I take a silly pride in the fact that "Freedom and the Control of Men" (1955–1956) appears as an example of good contemporary prose in textbooks written for college freshmen; Miss Graves would have been pleased. But in general my effects on other people have been far less important than my effects on rats and pigeons—or on people as experimental subjects. That is why I was able to work for almost twenty years with practically no professional recognition. People supported me, but not my line of work; only my rats and pigeons supported *that*. I was never in any doubt as to its importance, however, and when it began to attract attention, I was wary of the effect rather than pleased. Many notes in my files comment on the fact that I have been depressed or frightened by so-called honors. I forego honors which would take time away from my work or unduly reinforce specific aspects of it.

That I have never been interested in critical reactions, either positive or negative, is probably part of the same pattern. I have never actually read more than half a dozen pages of Chomsky's famous review of *Verbal Behavior*. (A quotation from it which I have used I got from I. A. Richards.) When Rochelle Johnson sent me a reprint of her reply to Scriven's criticism of my position, it only reminded me that I had never read Scrivin. Clark Hull used to say that I did not make hypotheses because I was afraid of being wrong. Verbal statements are, indeed, right or wrong, and in some sense I want my statements to be right. But I am much more interested in measures for the control of a subject matter. Some relevant measures are verbal, but even so they are not so much right or wrong as effective or ineffective, and arguments are of no avail. For the same reason I am not interested in psychological theories, in rational equations, in factor analyses, in mathematical models, in hypothetico-deductive systems, or in other verbal systems which must be *proved* right.

Much of this attitude is Baconian. Whether my early and quite accidental contact with Bacon is responsible or not, I have followed his principles closely. I reject verbal authority. I have "studied nature not books," asking questions of the organism rather than of those who have studied the organism. I think it can be said, as it was said of Bacon, that I get my books out of life, not out of other books. I have followed Bacon in organizing my data. I do not collect facts in random "botanizing," for there are principles which dictate what Poincaré called *le choix des faits,* and they are not, as Poincaré argued, hypotheses. I classify not for the sake of classification but to reveal properties.

I also follow Bacon in distinguishing between observation and experimentation. Bacon no doubt underestimated the importance of extending the range of human sense organs with instruments, but he did so in emphasizing that knowledge is more than sensory contact. I would put it this way: *Observation* overemphasizes stimuli; *experimentation* includes the rest of the contingencies which generate effective repertoires. I have also satisfied myself that Bacon's four Idols can be translated into an acceptable behavioral analysis of faulty thinking.

My position as a behaviorist came from other sources. Perhaps, like Jeremy Bentham and his theory of fictions, I have tried to resolve my early fear of theological ghosts. Perhaps I have answered my mother's question, "What will people think?" by proving that they do not think at all (but the question might as well have been "What will people *say?*"). I used to toy with the notion that a behavioristic epistemology was a form of intellectual suicide, but there is no suicide because there is no corpse. What perishes is the homunculus—the spontaneous, creative inner man to whom, ironically, we once attributed the very scientific activities which led to his demise.

To me behaviorism is a special case of a philosophy of science which first took shape in the writings of Ernst Mach, Henri Poincaré, and Percy Bridgman. Bridgman himself could never make the extension to behavior. He is one man I *did* argue with. When he published *The Way Things Are* (Bridgman, 1959), he sent me a copy with a note: "Here it is. Now do your damnedest!" I was busy with other things and did nothing. But I could never have convinced him, for it is not a matter of conviction. Behaviorism is a formulation which makes possible an effective experimental approach to human behavior. It is a working hypothesis about the nature of a subject matter. It may need to be clarified, but it does not need to be argued. I have no doubt of the eventual triumph of the position—not that it will eventually be proved right, but that it will provide the most direct route to a successful science of man.

I have acknowledged my indebtedness to Bertrand Russell, Watson, and Pavlov. I never met or even saw Watson, but his influence was, of course, important. Thorndike (not a behaviorist but still an important figure in a science of behavior) I met briefly. He knew of my interest in verbal behavior and sent me his *Studies in the Psychology of Language* (Thorndike, 1938). When I wrote to thank him, I told him about my analysis of alliteration and added, "Hilgard's review of my book [*The Behavior of Organisms*] in the *Bulletin* has reminded me of how much of your work in the same vein I failed to acknowledge . . . I seem to have identified your point of view with the modern psychological view taken as a whole. It has always been obvious that I was merely carrying on your puzzle box experiments but it never occurred to me to remind my readers of the fact." Thorndike replied, "I am better satisfied to have been of service to workers like yourself than if I had founded a 'school.'"

Walter Hunter I knew well. He gave me professional advice. I recall his wry smile as he told me, "It only takes one little idea to be a success in American psychology." (He measured the idea with thumb and forefinger.) Clark Hull visited my laboratory in Cambridge and made suggestions, which I never followed. I talked to his seminar at Yale and was invited to the unveiling of his portrait shortly before he died. I have a bound volume of my papers which was once on his shelves under the title *Experimental Studies in Learning*.

Tolman taught summer school at Harvard in 1931, and we had many long discussions. I had been analyzing the concept of hunger as a drive. In my thesis I had called it a "third" variable—that is, a variable in addition to stimulus and response occupying the intervening position of Sherrington's synaptic states. I have always felt that Tolman's later formulation was very similar. When *The Behavior of Organisms* appeared, he wrote:

I think the two words *operant* and *respondent* are swell . . . I do think, as I have said so many times before, that what you ought to do next is to put in two levers and see what relationships the functions obtained from such a discrimination set up will bear to your purified functions where you have only one lever. No doubt you were right that the "behavior-ratio" is a clumsy thing for getting the fundamental laws, but it is a thing that has finally to be predicted and someone must show the relation between it and your fundamental analysis. I congratulate you on coming through Harvard so beautifully unscathed! . . .

P.S. And, of course, I was pleased as Hell to be mentioned in the Preface.

Another behaviorist whose friendship I have valued is J. R. Kantor. In many discussions with him at Indiana I profited from his extraordinary scholarship. He convinced me that I had not wholly exorcised all the "spooks" in my thinking.

## THE CONTROL OF BEHAVIOR

I learned another Baconian principle very slowly: "Nature to be commanded must be obeyed." Frazier in *Walden Two* speaks for me here:

I remember the rage I used to feel when a prediction went awry. I could have shouted at the subjects of my experiments, "Behave, damn you! Behave as you ought!" Eventually I realized that the subjects were always right. They always behaved as they should have behaved. It was I who was wrong. I had made a bad prediction.

But that coin has another face: once obeyed, nature can be commanded. The point of Solomon's House in the *New Atlantis,* as of The Royal Society founded on Bacon's model, was that knowledge should be useful. A hundred years later—in an epoch in which I feel especially at home—Diderot developed the theme in his *Encyclopédie.* A hundred years after that, the notion of progress took on new significance in the theory of evolution. *Walden Two* is my *New Atlantis;* I suppose it could also be said that in applying an experimental analysis to education I returned to a motto which Bacon as a child saw in his father's house: *Moniti Meliora* (instruction brings progress). I believe in progress, and I have always been alert to practical significances in my research.

I began to talk explicitly about the control of human behavior after I had written *Walden Two.* Control was definitely in the air during my brief stay at Indiana. In *Science and Human Behavior* and the course for which it was written, I elaborated on the theme. In the summer of 1955, on the island of Monhegan, Maine, where we had a cottage, I wrote "Freedom and the Control of Men" for a special issue of the *American Scholar* (1955–1956). In it I took a much stronger stand on freedom and determinism. My position has been rather bitterly attacked, especially by people in the humanities, who feel that it is in conflict with Western democratic ideas and that it plays down the role of the individual. I have been called Machiavellian, a Communist, a Fascist, and many other names. The fact is, I accept the ends of a democratic philosophy, but I disagree with the means which are at the moment most commonly employed. I see no virtue in accident or in the chaos from which somehow we have reached our present position. I believe that man must now plan his own future and that he must take every advantage of a science of behavior in solving the problems which will necessarily arise. The great danger is not that science will be misused by despots for selfish purposes but that so-called democratic principles will prevent men of goodwill from using it in their advance toward humane goals. I continue to be an optimist, but there are moments of sadness. I find the following in my notebook, dated August 5, 1963.

### End of an Era

Last night Deborah and I went to the Gardner Cox's for some music in their garden. A group of young people, mostly current or former Harvard and Radcliffe students, sang a Mass by William Byrd. It was *a cappella* and, for most of the singers, sight reading. Very well done. The night was pleasant. Ragged clouds moved across the sky, one of them dropping briefly a fine mist. The garden has a circular lawn surrounded by shrubs and a few old trees. Half a dozen lights burned among green branches. Several kittens played on the grass. We sat in small groups, in folding chairs. Except for a few jet planes the night was quiet and the music delightful. *Kyrie eleison* . . . I thought of *Walden Two* and the B-minor Mass scene. And of the fact that this kind of harmless, beautiful, sensitive pleasure was probably nearing the end of its run. This was Watermusic, floating down the Thames and out to sea. And why?

Phyllis Cox may have answered the question. As I said good night, she motioned toward the young man who had conducted the music and said, "You know, he thinks you are a terrible person. Teaching machines . . . a fascist . . ."

Possibly our only hope of maintaining any given way of life now lies with science, particularly a science of human behavior and the technology to be derived from it. We need not worry about the scientific way of life; it will take care of itself. It would be tragic, however, if other ways of life, not concerned with the practice of science as such, were to forego the same kind of support through a misunderstanding of the role of science in human affairs.

The garden we sat in that evening once belonged to Asa Gray. In high school I studied Botany from a text by Gray, called, as I remember it, *How Plants Grow*. One passage impressed me so much that I made a copy which I have kept among my notes for nearly fifty years. It is the story of a radish. I would reject its purposivism today but not its poetry, for it suggests to me a reasonable place for the individual in a natural scheme of things.

So the biennial root becomes large and heavy, being a storehouse of nourishing matter, which man and animals are glad to use for food. In it, in the form of starch, sugar, mucilage, and in other nourishing and savory products, the plant (expending nothing in flowers or in show) has laid up the avails of its whole summer's work. For what purpose? This plainly appears when the next season's growth begins. Then, fed by this great stock of nourishment, a stem shoots forth rapidly and strongly, divides into branches, bears flowers abundantly, and ripens seeds, almost wholly at the expense of the nourishment accumulated in the root, which is now light, empty, and dead; and so is the whole plant by the time the seeds are ripe.

# REFERENCES

*Selected Publications by B. F. Skinner*

*Behavior of organisms.* New York: Appleton-Century-Crofts, 1938.

The operational analysis of psychological terms. *Psychol. Rev.,* 1945.

*Walden two.* New York: Macmillan, 1948.

*Science and human behavior.* New York: Macmillan, 1953.

Freedom and the control of man. *American Scholar,* special Winter 1955–56, Vol. 25, No. 1.

*Verbal behavior.* New York: Appleton-Century-Crofts, 1957.

(with C. Ferster). *Schedules of reinforcement.* New York: Appleton-Century-Crofts, 1957.

*Cumulative record.* (enlarged ed.) New York: Appleton-Century-Crofts, 1961. (Includes a selection of the author's more important articles.)

*Other Publications Cited*

Bridgman, P. *Logic of modern physics.* New York: Macmillan, 1927.

———. *The way things are.* Cambridge: Harvard, 1959.

Durning-Lawrence, E. *Bacon is Shakespeare.* London: Gay and Hancock, 1910.

Feuer, L. *The scientific intellectual.* New York: Basic Books, 1963.

Loeb, J. *Physiology of the brain and comparative psychology.* New York: Putnam, 1900.

Mach, E. *The science of mechanics, a critical and historical account of its development.* LaSalle: Ind. Open Court Publ. Co., 1942.

Magnus, R. *Körperstellung.* Berlin: Springer, 1924.

Pavlov, I. *Conditioned reflexes.* London: Oxford, 1927.

Richards, I. A. & Ogden, C. K. *The meaning of meaning.* New York: Harcourt, Brace & World, 1923.

Russell, B. *Philosophy.* New York: Norton, 1925.

Sherrington, C. S. *The integrative action of the nervous system.* New Haven: Yale, 1906.

Thompson, L. (Ed.) *Selected letters of Robert Frost.* New York: Holt, Rinehart and Winston, 1964.

Thorndike, E. L. Studies in the psychology of language. *Arch. Psychol.,* 1938, No. 231.

Watson, J. B. *Behaviorism.* New York: People's Institute Publ. Co., 1924–25.

———. *Psychological care of infant and child.* New York: Norton, 1928.

———. *Psychology from the standpoint of a behaviorist.* Philadelphia: Lippincott, 1919.

Yule, G. *An introduction to the theory of statistics.* London: Griffin, 1911.

Morris S Viteles

# Morris S. Viteles

## EARLY EDUCATION AND FAMILY BACKGROUND

I was born in a small village in the Bessarabian region of Russia, bordering upon Roumania, on March 21, 1898. My parents migrated to Leeds,
England, when I was approximately six months of age, so that my earliest
recollections are associated with life and education in this Yorkshire city.

My schooling began at age five, and by the time the family left England
to emigrate to the United States, in January 1904, I had already had the
equivalent of the first grade of elementary school education in the United
States. I was enrolled in the first grade of a Philadelphia school immediately
upon arrival and completed my elementary and secondary schooling in
Philadelphia public schools. I was allowed to skip two grades in the eight-
year elementary program. This acceleration, which made possible graduation
from high school at age sixteen, and the completion of the Ph.D. requirements in 1921, at age twenty-three, contributed enormously to an early start
in the making of my professional career.

Along with an older sister and an older brother, I was raised in the
milieu of a middle-class Jewish family. My father had been employed as a
manager of forest holdings in Russia. In the United States, he started as a
factory worker but soon entered the restaurant and summer hotel business,
in which he was engaged until retirement in 1931, because of illness.

The economic status of the family was never bad, in the sense that
there were never any lacks in the way of food and basic comforts of life.
The economic status of the family was never good, in the sense that there
was frequently question as to whether outstanding bills would be met or
whether something more than basic comforts could be provided. By the time
I graduated from high school, I was already working to contribute to my
support and continued doing so throughout my college career, as a teacher
in the schools of the Jewish community, made possible by a knowledge of
Hebrew and of history of the people obtained during my early years of religious training and later through a program of evening studies at Gratz College, a Philadelphia center of sectarian learning.

My father had had little in the way of secular education, but he had a

417

thirst for knowledge and a great respect for scholarship. In the midst of a very busy life, he found time for reading—even modern works—and time to discuss with his children what they were learning and reading. His particular fondness was for music, and I have known him in leaner times to forego buying a new hat in order to attend the opera. My mother was occupied in maintaining a clean, orderly house and in catering to the needs of her children and, later, also in doing the cooking in the family restaurant and hotel business. She had little time to pursue intellectual activities. However, there was intellectual alertness, and when time became available in the later years of her life she read avidly and was able to keep up with her children in discussing current events and other matters of intellectual interest.

The fact that all their children—including my sister and brother as well as myself—would go on to a higher education was simply taken for granted by my parents, even during periods of economic stress. The fact that both my brother and I went on beyond college, to graduate studies, unquestionably reflects interests and aspirations to which we became accustomed in early life and the strong support provided by our parents—even to the point of sacrificing personal welfare—to help us achieve educational goals and career aspirations.

## SECONDARY EDUCATION AND CAREER CHOICE (1910–1915)

It was within this framework that, in 1910, I enrolled as a freshman in the Central High School of Philadelphia. My choice among available programs was the classical course, which included four years of Greek, three years of Latin, two years of French, extensive content in history, English language and literature, and also rigorous courses in mathematics and the basic sciences. Curiously enough, my introduction to psychology came in high school, in the form of a course entitled Fundamentals of Psychology taken as an elective during the senior year. There would be a certain elegant consistency in career choice if I were able to say that a course given by a great teacher of psychology at the high school level led at once into my professional career. However, I can recall no evidence of this. In fact, what later attracted me to psychology was entirely absent in the course—given by a teacher of physics—which brings to mind, in retrospect, what Baldwin, in volume one of this series, describes as "a sort of propaedutic to metaphysics and theology, taught in most American colleges," in his student days.

By the end of my senior year in high school, in 1914, I had nevertheless made a career decision, that of preparing for teaching history in the secondary school. However, before another year had elapsed, this choice was replaced by a firm decision to seek a career in psychology. The impact toward this decision came primarily from a teacher, named Melville, on the staff of the Philadelphia School of Pedagogy which I attended, for a year, while awaiting enrolment in the University of Pennsylvania on a scholarship which had been granted for entrance in the academic year 1915–1916. Melville never became a great figure in psychology, but he was a dedicated psychologist, with great vision concerning the promise of the new science of psychology for enhancing our knowledge of mental processes through research. He had an intense interest in individual differences and a broad view of the possibilities of the objective measurement of such differences in adapting the educational process to the abilities, interests, and motivation of the individual. Such views, and others presented with conviction, produced an interest in psychology and a firm decision to prepare myself for a career in this field, rather than for that of teaching history.

## COLLEGE YEARS (1915–1918)

The decision to become a psychologist was a firm one, but it quickly became apparent that I must plan my education in such a way as to have available, upon graduation from college, the funds needed for postgraduate work. The plan called for preparation at the undergraduate level for teaching history in a secondary school, with the anticipation that employment as a teacher would provide both the time and the funds for postgraduate study in psychology.

My undergraduate major in the College of Arts and Sciences was, in fact, history. I feel sure that my strong and continuing concern with the historical perspective for graduate study in psychology and my interest in the history of institutions (such as business) and of social movements (such as labor organization) comes, in large part, from work done during formative years with great historians at the University of Pennsylvania. Their influence is to be seen, I think, in the historical chapter, "Work Through the Ages," which opens my more or less popular text on industrial psychology, entitled *The Science of Work,* published in 1934. However, my strong involvement in history did not preclude progress in other ways toward the accomplishment of the objective of the educational plan. I managed to fit in —or really "bootleg"—a few courses in education which helped to meet the requirements for a secondary school teaching certificate in Pennsylvania. More important still, in spite of a major in history, my undergraduate courses in psychology were numerous and varied.

As I think about my undergraduate work in psychology, I detect two strong trends in the program which, I am sure, greatly influenced the direction of my interests in the field and the values which I apply in assessing both my own research and that of others. In the first place, *the orientation of the program was strongly experimental.* For example, the introductory course included four hours of laboratory work and one hour of lecture per week during each of two terms—a pattern which was virtually unique for the era. A second strong feature of the undergraduate instruction which influenced my development and work in industrial psychology was a *strong concern with individual differences.*

These two features of my undergraduate education in psychology were not chance occurrences. The oldest American laboratory of psychology with a continuous existence is that organized at the University of Pennsylvania by James McK. Cattell in 1889. It is highly probable that Cattell, among the first to hold the title of Professor in Psychology in this country, initiated the experimental orientation in the program of undergraduate instruction. There is no question that Lightner Witmer, whose interest in psychology was aroused by Cattell and who also obtained his Ph.D. under Wundt, was responsible for maintaining and strengthening this approach when, in 1892, following Cattell's departure for Columbia, he became director of the laboratory of psychology.

The emphasis on differential psychology in the curriculum of the Department of Psychology also reflected the interests and influence of both Cattell and Witmer. As is well known, Cattell, even as a student of Wundt, expressed strong objection to the latter's preoccupation with only the central measures in experimental findings, and Cattell was largely responsible for the initiation of systematic research on individual differences in the United States. Witmer, like Cattell, insisted upon the central importance of a knowledge of individual differences for the understanding of human behavior.

The orientations in the teaching of psychology referred to above were also present in advanced undergraduate courses in psychology. By the time my senior year was completed, I was already involved in semi-independent research of the type that frequently was available only in postgraduate work in other universities. Problems in the area of individual differences were extensively explored in advanced courses. In addition, several such courses brought clearly into focus a third feature of instruction in psychology at the University of Pennsylvania that strongly influenced my later work in the field of industrial psychology. This was the concern with *the study of the total individual,* from the viewpoint of adaptation and maladjustment to diverse life situations, which is the province of *clinical psychology.*

Almost forgotten today is the fact that Witmer brought into use the term "clinical psychology," and organized, in 1897 at the University of Pennsylvania, a *psychological clinic* for implementing his views with respect to the utilization of psychology, along with such associated disciplines as education and sociology, for the study and promotion of individual adjustment. Clinical psychology did not represent to Witmer a departure from the scientific and experimental orientation in psychology. In fact, Witmer protested against the direct application to the schoolroom and elsewhere of the results of laboratory experimentation, in the absence of experimentation bearing upon and conducted in the life situation (Witmer, 1925). At the same time, he took a strong stand in the way of directing clinical psychology toward useful applications, in concordance with his conviction that "in the final analysis, the progress of psychology, as of every other science, will be determined by the amount of its contribution to the advancement of the human race" (Witmer, 1907).

## GRADUATE STUDY IN PSYCHOLOGY AND BEGINNINGS OF MY CAREER AS AN INDUSTRIAL PSYCHOLOGIST (1918–1922)

The impact of such orientations in undergraduate work in psychology became stronger when I started graduate work at the University of Pennsylvania. Progress toward a career in psychology came faster than had been anticipated in my "master plan." Upon graduation from college, in the spring of 1918, I was awarded a graduate scholarship in history. The prospect for making use of this was, however, slight, since I needed to consider seriously the question of war service. During the summer of 1918, I made an effort to enlist in the division for psychological service in the Army directed by R. M. Yerkes, and, when rejected on the grounds of insufficient preparation for work in the area, I sought enlistment in the Chemical War Service of the Army, also without success. Very shortly thereafter I learned of the Student Army Training Corps (SATC) and, in September of 1918, was sworn in for officer training in the branch located at the University of Pennsylvania.

The SATC program provided for the continuation of studies and the major portion of time available for graduate studies was devoted to psychology. Within a few days after being discharged from the SATC in December 1918, I was offered a position as an assistant in the Department of Psychology. On the following day I was offered an instructorship in history. The firmness of my decision to make a career in psychology is illustrated by my rejection of that offer, in spite of the doubling of salary which this involved.

In a sense, my professional career as a psychologist started on December 18, 1918, when I started my work as an assistant—more commonly known as a "dog"—in the Department of Psychology. Although I quite quickly started to carry a heavy load of work in the department, I was able to move along with my graduate studies, and to obtain the A.M. degree in June 1919. Both my graduate studies and also my work as an assistant brought closer associations with Witmer, but even during the first year of graduate work, and also later, I can see the influence of other staff members.

Outstanding was that exercised by Edwin B. Twitmyer. Although hardly known to other psychologists either in the past or now, he was probably the first psychologist in the United States to observe the conditioned reflex. At least, his was the first report (Twitmyer, 1902, 1905) on this phenomenon in the United States—antedating that of Pavlov—but the skepticism and even ridicule with which his findings, as reported at a meeting of the American Psychological Association in 1904, were received by the pundits of the day was apparently a potent factor in turning a sensitive and promising young man away from further research pertaining to either this or other psychological phenomena. Nevertheless, Twitmyer remained a great teacher, and to conduct research under his direction proved to be a memorable learning experience.

Although Twitmyer and a few other members of the Department of Psychology had an impact upon my development, it is chiefly the influence of Witmer that is to be seen in much of my work, especially in the 1920's and early 1930's. E. G. Boring, with his usual perceptiveness, recognized this and shows me as an offshoot of Witmer on the chart which he has used to depict the growth and diversification of branches in the family of psychologists. It is no accident, for example, that my first article described a study of performance on mental tests and of the school achievement of children in an orphanage, in comparison with performance of a normative population. This and another article, describing a case examined in the psychological clinic, were the earliest in a series published during succeeding years which reflect strong involvement in mental testing, in clinical psychology and, in more general terms, a leaning toward applied rather than experimental psychology. This preference moved in the direction of industrial application of psychology in about 1920.

As I consider the question of how and why I became committed to industrial psychology, it becomes apparent that there was an underlying receptivity to a career in this field, since I was already interested not only in psychology and in the individual, but in the social sciences, in social institutions, and in social movements. I read the novels of such authors as Butler, Wells, Balzac, Tolstoy, Dostoievski, Maeterlinck, and Rolland, not only because of their literary implications, but also because they were concerned with problems of social significance. My political and social views as a young man were what might be called "liberal." My friends came from among those who were concerned with social welfare and through some of these —especially the members of two families which produced two justices of the Supreme Court—I came to know many American and also British liberals who exercised a great influence on the making of social change in later years.

It seems possible that such views and such experiences helped to produce a predisposition toward a career that has involved dealing to some extent with social change. However, it seems quite certain that a number of books, already available at the time, helped to stir my interest in industrial psychology. Among these was the volume by H. C. Link (1919) entitled *Employment Psychology*. I was familiar with the informative text on *Vocational Psychology* by H. L. Hollingworth (1916) and know that this provided background materials for my work in developing procedures for the description, analysis, and classification of job requirements. I feel quite sure, too, that the classic text *Psychology and Industrial Efficiency* by Münsterberg (1913) was known to me, but it was not until somewhat after the events described above that I came to consider his program in detail. On the other hand, I feel quite sure that in the years under consideration I had not read the book *Influencing Men in Business* by W. D. Scott (1911), and had little, if any familiarity with his activities and those of others at the Carnegie Institute of Technology.

While I cannot now properly assess the influence of the factors discussed above, I am certain that *three* events, occurring during the period 1918 to 1920, definitely foreshadowed a commitment to industrial psychology. The *first* was an opportunity, early in 1919, to observe the work of counselors and to assess the possibility for psychological research in the Philadelphia office of the Federal Bureau of Vocational Rehabilitation. There was little interest on the part of the chief administrator of the Philadelphia office in this project, which had been suggested by a junior staff member. However, the situation quickly changed when I undertook to construct and put into use a short test of reading proficiency after a counselor had brought embarrassment to the agency by recommending training in bookkeeping for a veteran who could not read. I made a sufficiently good impression in this and other ways to be given a paid job in the agency during the summer of 1919. By the fall, when I returned to continue graduate work and to my job as an assistant—in spite of the opportunity to triple my salary by continuing to work for the federal government—I was already much aware of the potential of work in the area of vocational assessment both as a promising career and as a source of personal satisfaction.

The *second* significant event was participation in a study group on vocational guidance, conducted by Arthur J. Jones, Professor of Education at the University of Pennsylvania, during the academic year 1919–20. This strengthened my awareness of the promise of psychology and of psychological techniques for the study of job requirements and for the measurement of vocational aptitudes, and furthermore, of the need for research in this area.

The two experiences described above had an initial impact in directing my attention to vocational guidance and in leading me to undertake, in 1921, the organization, within the framework of the psychological clinic, of a *vocational guidance clinic* which, so far as I know, was the first center for teaching, research, and service associated with a university, specifically devoted to the application of tests and clinical methods for purposes of vocational guidance. However, I see this also as a step in progress toward a career in industrial psychology, because of the close connection between the two areas, at least insofar as the assessment of vocational competence is concerned. Nevertheless, as will appear later, industrial psychology gradually became my predominant interest.

This shift of interest is already to be observed in the events noted above, since, for example, my work with the study group in vocational guidance resulted in a paper "Tests in Industry" (1921), which not only deals with the implications of job analysis and tests for the selection of workers, but takes issue with what was then the prevailing common practice of placing almost exclusive reliance upon the measurement of general intelligence for assessing vocational aptitudes. This view was further expanded in an article I published soon after (1922a) which raises questions concerning the generality of "intelligence" itself, as measured by available tests. I still find gratification in the fact that this was later noted by Spearman (1927) as a "damaging criticism," of assumptions pertaining to the dimensions of human ability and of work in intelligence testing.

Perhaps even more pertinent, among initial impacts toward commitment to a career in industrial psychology, was a *third* event, in the form of a research project, involving an analysis of job requirements and the development of selection tests conducted, in 1920, in the Naval Aircraft Factory at the United States Navy Shipyard in Philadelphia. The opportunity to conduct the study was made available through the good offices of Joseph H. Willits, at that time Assistant Professor of Geography and Industry at the University of Pennsylvania, who later became Dean of the Wharton School of Finance and Commerce and, still later, Director for the Social Sciences, Rockefeller Foundation. The research experience was interesting and valuable, but I value it more as the beginning of a long and rewarding association with Willits to whom I owe much for introducing me to the broader areas of industrial relations; for helping me gain insight into the problems involved in working with people in industry; for helping enrich my understanding of the broader social problems of industry and of the social obligations of professional consultants in the industrial situation.

It is within the framework of the events and experiences noted above that, in the summer of 1920, there came my first opportunity to conduct research as a paid consultant in an industrial organization. The invitation to do so came from Arthur J. Rowland, who, in 1919, as the administrator of the Philadelphia office of the Federal Bureau of Vocational Rehabilitation, had looked so skeptically at the possibility of applying tests and other psychological techniques and psychological principles in vocational counseling. Rowland had left Philadelphia to become Director of Education in The Milwaukee Electric Railway & Light Company and, in 1920, he approached me with the suggestion that I come to Milwaukee for the summer in order to investigate the possibility of developing a test for the selection of street car motormen.

My association with this company, which was carried on through long visits during holidays and recesses at the University and through correspondence involving the direction of research on the motormen selection test and other problems, continued until the middle of 1922. One of the chief outcomes of my work with T.M.E.R.&L. Company was the validation of an instrument *(Viteles Motorman Selection Test)*, later cross-validated by Shellow, which is still being used in the selection of motor vehicle operators (1925; Shellow, 1925). I also quickly became aware of the wider potentials of psychology in areas of training, accident prevention, employee-supervisory relations, and so forth, and had an opportunity to initiate work in these areas. Perhaps most important is the fact that my experience with the Milwaukee Railway & Light Company led me to think about standard methods for the study, description, and classification of job requirements and resulted in the formulation of the concepts and methodology for constructing *job psychographs* and what are now called "job families." This work, as originally reported in my doctoral dissertation (1922b), led, among other developments, to the now widely known method of analyzing worker trait requirements used by the U.S. Employment Service (Stead, *et al.*, 1940) and has otherwise come to be known as an important contribution to the methodology of industrial psychology.

The last and most far-reaching consequence of my work with The Milwaukee Electric Railway & Light Company was the conviction that continued association with the academic atmosphere was necessary for me both to achieve personal satisfaction and to provide the basis for worthwhile contributions to the field of industrial psychology. During discussions held in the summer of 1921, after I had been awarded the Ph.D. degree, I accepted an offer to join the company on a full-time basis at the close of the academic year 1921–1922. I remember the discussions with my father after this decision had been made. While he was very much pleased that I was invited to join a large industrial organization, he nevertheless was much upset by my decision to leave the University, on the grounds that he felt that my life could best be lived as a "scholar." The same opinion was emphatically expressed by Arthur J. Jones, who predicted with no equivocation that I would be returning to university life.

In spite of the views expressed by my father and Jones, I continued to plan for separation from the University of Pennsylvania. However, with each passing month I found myself questioning my decision more and more. This was the situation when, in December 1921, I saw a notice concerning the availability of American Field Service Fellowships for study in France. Study in France seemed particularly appropriate both because of my competency in reading and speaking French, and by reason of the opportunities which were available for study in areas, particularly motivation and psychopathology, in which I felt the need for an enrichment of knowledge. And, as a sort of gilding of the lily, was the prospect of work with Pierre Janet, with whose contributions in psychopathology I had become quite familiar through readings and to whom I was strongly attracted.

The result was a hastily prepared application for study at the University of Paris and the College de France. Notice of the award of the fellowship in the spring of 1922 placed me in a serious quandary, since I had made a commitment to join The Milwaukee Electric Railway & Light Company. This was ended, however, by acceptance of the fellowship with the very reluctant "blessing" of the company.

## A YEAR OF STUDY AND TRAVEL IN EUROPE (1922–1923)

The year in Europe actually started in July 1922, since needs for personnel by the American Joint Distribution Committee in Europe, and the knowledge of my interests by my brother, who was associated with this organization, led to my employment to conduct a trade education survey in the eastern portion of Czechoslovakia, including the Slovakian and sub-Carpathian areas of this country. While the summer yielded good results in terms of valuable work experience and also in the opportunity to travel and to become acquainted with the cultures of central Europe, it was my studies in Paris and the opportunity to learn about work in industrial psychology in Western European countries that made my year abroad a rewarding one.

With the few exceptions noted below, I did not attend courses regularly during the year in Paris, but devoted myself to sampling various courses, observing the work done in laboratories and clinics, and taking advantage of every opportunity to meet and talk with psychologists and scholars in other fields (1923a). Among the courses which I did attend regularly was that given by Janet at the College de France. I still have vivid recollections of the sixty minutes (never more nor less) of the always lucid and scintillating lectures upon theory and practices in dealing with mental aberrations. The skill with which he could dissect theories—always with good taste—is something never to be forgotten. Janet not only contributed much to my knowledge of psychopathology, but he also raised the level of my aspirations with respect to performance as a teacher. Only one other individual exercised an influence in this respect approaching that of Janet, namely Stokowski, whose virtuosity in drawing-out and coordinating the tones of diverse orchestral instruments I saw as a pattern of what the teacher should be doing with the diverse students in the classroom.

In the field of psychopathology, my program included also regular attendance at the lectures on abnormal psychology given by G. Dumas and at his clinics, conducted on Sunday mornings at either the Cliniqe Asile or Cliniqe St. Anne, I forget which. The way in which he handled cases in his clinic and his clear and insightful discussion of the problem under consideration presented impressive examples to the clinician and the teacher in the field.

The chief representative of classical experimental psychology at the University of Paris at the time was Henri Piéron. While I neither took courses nor conducted research under his direction, I came to know him well and to appreciate intensely his happy faculty for combining a strong concern for theory and experimental psychology with a strong and fruitful interest in applied psychology, and he did much to make me aware of the importance of the theoretical framework for research in applied psychology. In this and in many other ways, I benefitted from and cherish the associations which I had with him in 1922–1923 and throughout the years which followed.

There was little activity in the field of industrial psychology in France during the early 1920's. However, I became acquainted with the work of J. M. Lahy who as early as 1905 had conducted a study of psychophysiological factors in learning by typists and later conducted research in many other areas, including the selection of motor vehicle operators. I was not attracted to Lahy's work, although we became great friends in the years which followed and found much in common through our mutual interest in the International Psychotechnical Association (known since 1955 as the International Association of Applied Psychology), of which he was Secretary-General for many years. Knowledge of the way in which he was hounded by the Nazis during the occupation, because of his associations with USSR, and of his unhappy end are among my sadder recollections.

In terms of professional development, the fellowship year produced another major impact in the way of an opportunity to learn about what was going on in industrial psychology through fairly extended visits to England and Germany. In both of these countries, work in industrial psychology, stimulated by World War I, was expanding at a rapid rate (1923b). As of 1922, approximately twenty large concerns in Germany had their own psychological laboratories, and institutes for the industrial application of psychology were to be found in all of the larger cities in Germany. In England the Industrial Fatigue Research Board (later the Industrial Health Research Board), organized in 1915, already had completed or had under way a large number of investigations. The National Institute of Industrial Psychology, established by C. S. Myers in 1921, was functioning actively. Psychologists attached to universities, such as T. H. Pear at Manchester and J. Drever at Edinburgh, were engaged in investigations bearing upon the applications of psychology in business.

What impressed me most in both Germany and England was the scope of the program in industrial psychology as contrasted with the predominant commitment to personnel selection and classification on the part of industrial psychologists in the United States. The Europeans were also working in this area, but, to a much greater extent than in the United States, industrial psychologists were doing research in the area of training and methods and conditions of work, including wage payment systems—as related particularly to fatigue and boredom—and, to some extent, with the study of industrial organization. Also more evident, particularly in England, was a greater interest than was to be found in the United States in the *adjustment of the individual* and the *welfare of society* as distinct goals in the application of psychology in industry.

In general, I was impressed by the amount of work being done in Germany and much less impressed by the quality of much of the work. There were exceptions, as in the case of the activities of F. Giese, O. Lipmann, and W. Stern, and of investigators in the area of the physiology of work. Nevertheless, largely under the influence of W. Moede and G. Piorkowski, industrial psychology in Germany had moved in the direction of "psychotechnology." In contrast was the persistent effort on the part of industrial psychologists in England to relate what they were doing to basic laboratory research in experimental psychology and to theory.

This effort was particularly apparent in the work of Myers, whose earlier broad interests in cultural anthropology and applied psychology had led him, in 1921, to leave his post as director of the Psychological Laboratory at Cambridge to organize the National Institute of Industrial Psychology —to move, in his own words, from "the fairly peaceful academic life at Cambridge in *pure* psychology to a wider, less tranquil life in *applied* psychology in London." Myers consistently underlined the research aspect of the institute's work and insisted that psychologists engaged in research in industry must continually look to the pure sciences of psychology and physiology for guidance, and that such research could bring important returns to these sciences in the way of revealing wide gaps in knowledge and suggesting important problems for laboratory research. I am sure that his views strongly influenced the position on the role of an experimental and theoretical framework in industrial psychology taken in my book *Industrial Psychology* and also in later years—in fact, until the present time.

Myers may have influenced both my career and my outlook in other ways. I was excited by his cultural interests and breadth of knowledge outside of the field of psychology. His quiet sense of humor, his well-balanced tolerance, the quality of Myers' relations with his associates in the National Institute of Industrial Psychology and with other colleagues, and the sympathy with which he dealt with ideas which were not congruent with his own made more than a casual impression upon me.

## PROGRESS IN THE MAKING OF A CAREER
## IN INDUSTRIAL PSYCHOLOGY (1923–1934)

I enjoyed and profited from the fellowship year, but I was also happy to return, in June 1923, to my teaching at the University of Pennsylvania and to my work in industrial psychology and vocational guidance. One important event which occurred shortly thereafter was my promotion, in 1925, from instructor to the rank of assistant professor.

Almost immediately after my return, I again became active in industrial work. On April 1, 1924, I became associated with the Yellow Cab Company of Philadelphia and continued to act as consultant to this company until 1965, except for the period between 1927 and 1936. Most of my work here was in the area of personnel selection and research and consultation on accident prevention. However, I also became involved with labor relations and conducted a number of studies bearing upon both labor negotiations and the arbitration of grievances. A gratifying aspect of my work came from my associations with E. S. Higgins, president of the company, who vividly stated what I think should be one of the functions of a consulting industrial psychologist in describing me as his "intellectual irritant"—a function which was carried out almost as frequently in the course of long rides on horseback over trails in the parks of Philadelphia as in the offices of the company.

My major commitment in industry through the years, from the viewpoint of both time and scope of responsibility, has been with the Philadelphia Electric Company, which I joined in 1927. Being invited to join the company was, in a sense, a "stroke of luck" since just a few days before I was asked to consider doing so I had resigned from the Yellow Cab Company of Philadelphia, because of dissatisfaction with the atmosphere created by the management of the organization, Philadelphia Rapid Transit Company, which had purchased the company.

My original engagement with the electric company was as a consultant for a period of one year, to be spent in the development of tests for the selection of electric substation operators. By the end of that time I had made considerable progress in the validation of a test battery which has, in fact, consistently yielded satisfactory outcomes, both at the Philadelphia Electric Company and elsewhere, in helping to reduce the number of operating errors (1930a). I also quickly became involved in other matters—and in 1930 I was given the status of a "regular" employee, with the title of Director of Personnel Research and Training.

My associations with the Philadelphia Electric Company continued until the end of September 1964, when I requested retirement in order to assume new duties at the University. It is not possible to deal in any detail with the great variety of activities in which I was involved during my years with this company. The preparation and validation of tests for selection purposes was extended through the years to the point where these are used in employment for all entry jobs, with the exception of sales jobs. An interesting and possibly unique activity was that of developing a series of trade knowledge and trade skill tests to the point where virtually all promotions in manual and office jobs in the company now include the requirement of passing such qualifying examinations. My program with the company involved the development of an extensive series of training programs, including those devoted to training of management personnel (1933a, 1946). In fact, I think that a training program given to practically all members of the supervisory personnel in 1933 and 1934 represents one of the earliest management development programs in the country. Attitude measurement and even a little work on the design of electric substation instrument and control boards are among the other activities in which I was engaged.

I feel much disturbed because space limitations make it possible to devote only these few lines to nearly forty years of work which, as a matter of fact, has been cited as representing a contribution to the well-being of the Philadelphia Electric Company in its official history (Wainwright, 1961). Furthermore, I feel that I am doing many of my former associates an injustice by failing to list the names of all who contributed to my own accomplishments. There is, nevertheless, need for special mention of the many ways in which George W. Fewkes, as Manager of the Personnel Department, facilitated my work and, also, to acknowledge the encouragement and support given by members of the executive staff—most particularly N. E. Funk, H. P. Liversidge, W. H. Taylor, and R. G. Rincliffe.

As I write this, I begin to suspect that the reader may be wondering whether I did any work at the University. The fact is that, except for the years in which I was involved in the World War II effort, I carried a full teaching load. I developed new courses at the undergraduate level, including an introductory course for students in the school of business, courses in differential psychology, vocational psychology, and so forth, and also a program of graduate instruction in industrial psychology. I participated fully in other responsibilities generally assigned to department personnel. This was made possible chiefly by an adjustment of my work schedule, which consisted largely of rostering some of my courses on Saturdays so that I could have an extra free day during the week, in addition to the usual free day granted as a matter of policy to every staff member. This concession involved, of course, recognition of the fact that I could not hope to contribute to the development of the new field of industrial psychology unless I became thoroughly conversant with industry and was in a position to utilize the industrial organization as my research laboratory.

I continued also to act as director of the Vocational Guidance Clinic at the University and to be involved with the vocational guidance movement. Most particularly, during the early 1930's, I participated in the work of the National Occupational Conference. Meetings held in various parts of the countries at which local workers had an opportunity "to meet the experts" proved to be exciting experiences which contributed to my understanding of the practical problems of guidance in the school situation. However, the experience also increased an already growing dissatisfaction with work in the area that led to withdrawal from active involvement in the field of vocational guidance. I have a few publications in the area subsequent to 1934, including a volume entitled *Vocational Guidance Throughout the World,* written in collaboration with F. J. Keller (1938) and also a critical assessment of psychological research in vocational guidance, written as late as 1961 (with A. H. Brayfield & L. E. Tyler, 1961). However, my active interest in the area has progressively decreased since about 1935.

By contrast, both my own recollections and my publications reveal a growing commitment to industrial psychology during approximately the decade in question. There were occasional forays into other areas (see 1928, 1929), but the majority of my publications at the time are in the field of industrial psychology. Of particular significance among these, in terms of career development, was a series of comprehensive reviews of the literature, written at the request of the editor, for the *Psychological Bulletin* (1926, 1928, 1930b). I recall that, upon receiving the first of these reviews, the editor expressed great surprise with respect to the scope of industrial psychology since, in common with the other academic psychologists of the time, he had thought of industrial psychology as generally synonymous with personnel testing and classification. The three reviews, which covered approximately 1000 titles culled from at least double that number of books and articles published in the United States and abroad, led directly to the preparation of my book *Industrial Psychology* (1932) which was followed shortly by a condensed, semipopular version entitled *The Science of Work* (1934).

Publication of *Industrial Psychology* represents, I think, the most important of my activities during the period 1923–1934, at least in terms of the recognition which it brought and of my impact upon industrial psychology both in the United States and abroad. The book received very favorable reviews both in the psychological literature and elsewhere, as illustrated by the reference to it as the "Bible" of industrial psychology at a meeting of the British Psychological Association which I addressed in 1935. I was reminded of this only recently when the book was again referred to in the same terms by the chairman of the meeting which I addressed in Washington. The book, in my opinion, is still a basic source, in the sense of providing necessary background for research today and even in foreshadowing current events, but I begin to suspect that, like the Bible, it is to be more frequently found on the book shelves than on the reading tables of the new generation of industrial psychologists.

The story of the years under consideration would be incomplete if I failed to mention at least some of the many people with whom I associated during the period and who had an influence on my career. I recall, with gratitude, S. W. Fernberger's practice of making a point of introducing me to his many friends at meetings of the American Psychological Association. It was through him, in the main, that I came to know J. F. Dashiell, R. S. Woodworth, E. G. Boring, Knight Dunlap, H. S. Langfeld, S. I. Franz, and other well-known American psychologists who, at least in an indirect way, may have helped to direct my thinking and to formulate my goals.

Among those who contributed more directly to the development of my career was W. V. Bingham. He made it possible for me to participate in meetings organized by the Personnel Research Foundation. He encouraged me to write and publish my speeches and articles in the *Journal of Personnel Research* (later the *Personnel Journal*), which he edited for many years, and showed his interest in me in many other ways. In a curious kind of way, Bingham did all of this in spite of very significant differences in our backgrounds and outlooks that became apparent from time to time. We became and remained good friends in our work in this country in spite of such differences, and we saw much of each other as United States members of the Executive Committee of the International Psychotechnical Association.

During the years in question, I came to know Elton Mayo. He had been brought to the University of Pennsylvania by Willits. While I never felt quite comfortable with the looseness of his research and with the extent to which his observations and conclusions were determined by his own particular perspectives, I was impressed and influenced by the broad view he took with respect to the social role of business and by his efforts to deal with emotional aspects of behavior in industry. It was also through Mayo that I became interested in considering the role of the psychiatrist and of the psychiatric orientation in dealing with personnel problems, although I also soon came to question both the validity and practical value of the psychiatric approach (see 1929). Nevertheless, I see Mayo as an intellectual catalyst in dealing with human problems in industry and, also, as being largely responsible for such important concepts as came out of the Hawthorne experiments which, however, for various reasons I have come to call the *Legend of the Hawthorne Works* (1959).

Among members of my own generation with whom I established particularly close friendships were Donald G. Paterson and Arthur W. Kornhauser. Paterson and I had similar views on many issues, and I always felt close to him—as reflected in an address given by me at a testimonial meeting in his honor held in September 1960 (with A. H. Brayfield & L. E. Tyler, 1961), I established an even closer friendship with Kornhauser. We had much in common in the way of a highly critical attitude and of little hesitation in expressing our opinions. At meetings of the American Psychological Association, we came to be known as "the raspberry twins" because of the frequency with which—although quite independently of one another—we chose to express disagreements and criticisms of the speakers. This does not mean that we always agreed with each other, but this did not mar our respect for one another or our friendship. I could mention many other psychologists working in industry and in other applied fields—such as H. E. Burt, D. Fryer, H. D. Kitson, H. C. Link, B. V. Moore, L. J. O'Rourke, E. K. Strong, and M. Trabue—but any effort to assess their impact would be onerous for me and boring for readers of this chapter.

There remains, however, the need to mention influences that grew out of associations with psychologists abroad. In 1926 I attended the meeting of the International Congress of Psychology in Groningen, Holland, and in 1928 the meeting of the International Congress of Psychotechnology in Utrecht. During both years I also visited universities and other research centers in many Western European countries and thereby had opportunities to meet many of the European psychologists—to establish the personal contacts and to initiate the exchange of publications which through the years have helped me to keep in close touch with what was going on in industrial psychology abroad.

## A YEAR IN THE USSR (1934–1935)

In general, the years 1923 through 1934 represent the most productive period of its length within the span of my career. Be this as it may, toward the end of the ten-year period I was beginning to feel "fed-up" and started to think about the possibility of going abroad for another year of study and intellectual refreshment, and late in 1933 I applied for a Social Science Research Council Fellowship, for study and observation in the USSR. When the fellowship was awarded, I found myself in the same quandary that had faced me in 1922 when I received the fellowship for study in Paris. However, this was happily resolved by favorable action on the request for a year's leave from my work at the Philadelphia Electric Company which was, in fact, accompanied by word that the company would pay half of my salary while I was on leave. I had already been granted leave by the University of Pennsylvania, and my wife Rebecca—to whom I have been most happily married since 1931—and I prepared for departure early in August of 1934.

The selection of the USSR for the fellowship year was made not only because I felt that it would be of interest and importance to know what was going on in the way of psychological research and practice, but also because of an interest in learning about what was then known as the "great experiment" in social change. I had met a few of the Russian psychologists at the international congress in Utrecht in 1928, and again at Yale in 1929, and also had an opportunity to talk to I. N. Spielrein and others in the course of the International Congress of Applied Psychology held in Prague in September 1934, which I attended en route to Moscow. Nevertheless, I arrived in the USSR with little specific foreknowledge of what I might find of interest in my field.

In spite of rather rigid restrictions placed upon work and travel by foreigners, I managed to visit most of the important centers in the European section of the USSR. Actually, I acquired unusual freedom of movement because of the replacement of my "tourist" visa by a "foreign specialist" visa which was obtained largely because of the intervention of Spielrein. I sometimes wonder whether the loss of his job and his banishment to what was for him the unhealthy climate of Tashkent were associated with the fact that he had been so close to a foreigner, as well as with the fact that he was one of the "old Bolsheviks" who were so freely liquidated in 1935.

In the course of my stay in the USSR, I came to know some of the experimental and also educational psychologists such as K. N. Kornilov, A. R. Luria, A. N. Leontiev, N. D. Levitov, M. B. Sokolov, A. A. Smirnov, and others. However, my attention was focused on industrial psychology, and I found that there had indeed been considerable progress in the development of a program in this area in the USSR. In general, the distribution of research activities was much more like that of Western Europe than that in the United States in terms of the relative emphasis upon areas other than employee selection, although there was considerable activity in this direction, at least until testing was officially denounced as an evil practice in 1935. Much attention was being given to the application of principles of learning to the training of workers and also to research on training problems. There was much research on rest pauses, methods of work, machine design, and so forth, from the viewpoint of fatigue elimination. This, to a much greater extent than in other countries, involved a team approach which coordinated the efforts of psychologists, physiologists, time and motion study men, and others concerned with the fatigue phenomenon. Several of the industrial psychologists were concerned with problems of motivation. Paradoxically, however, piece-rate systems and other wage incentive plans, embodying extremely large wage differentials, were being used on a scale unknown in "bourgeois capitalistic countries." Significantly, this was defended on the ground that it was employee enthusiasm for "voluntary socialistic competition" which produced the increased production that, in Western countries, would have been largely attributed to the wage incentive itself.

In one respect I found the practice of industrial psychology to be very much like that in the United States, in the form of a predominant emphasis on increasing production. On the whole, I concluded that in industry in the USSR there were much the same problems that were to be found in plants in "capitalistic" countries, and also that these—as is still apparent in the USSR today—could not be solved by dependence on unsubstantiated social dogma.

I had many opportunities to observe the pernicious effects of political and social ideology upon science and scientists. For example, I brought back to the United States data from an experiment on transfer effects, conducted by a leading psychologist, which could not be published in the USSR because the conclusions were not in accord with the official party line bearing upon methods to be used in training the masses to overcome technical illiteracy. Pavlov, with whom I spent a little time in Leningrad in 1935, had been leading his life as though there had been no change in the political regime in his country, even to the point of closing his laboratories on Sundays in spite of the official six-day work week with staggered days of rest observed in industry and schools throughout the country. However, even Pavlov had reached the point of being unable to obtain an exit visa for one of his students who had been granted a fellowship by the Rockefeller Foundation for study in the United States.

I discovered that my book *Industrial Psychology* had been translated into Russian and was available in the university libraries in mimeographed form. However, two chapters—dealing with the nature and origins of individual differences—had not been reproduced. Not long after my arrival, I was asked to cooperate in the preparation of an official translation for which, upon publication, royalties would be paid to me. I found it necessary to refuse to do so upon learning that it would be necessary for me to revise these chapters in order to bring them into accord with official Communist ideology concerning the nature and origin of individual differences. The request that this be done strikingly reflects the enforced marriage between political ideology and science which led, for example, to the elimination of the work of the "pedologists" and the use of tests in schools and in industry in 1935, shortly after Lysenko won his battle with the traditional geneticists and his views became the official doctrine for dealing with problems in the field of genetics. I could describe many other incidents which led me to close an article on industrial psychology in Russia with a word that their progress is a "tribute to the sincerity and integrity of Russian scientists who must struggle not only against the inadequate financial support which hampers scientific workers throughout the world, but also against the intolerance of a political creed and system which denies to them the freedom of thought and opinion that is basic to real accomplishment in every field of science" (1938a, pp. 18–19).

## A PERIOD OF "SETTLEMENT" (1935–1940)

Upon returning to the United States in the summer of 1935, I resumed my activities at the University—now at the rank of associate professor—and also my work with the Yellow Cab Company of Philadelphia and the Philadelphia Electric Company. The period from 1935 to approximately 1940 was, with few exceptions, devoted to continuing what I had already been doing and represented a relatively calm period of "settlement" into my career.

This does not mean that I settled into a rut, from either the viewpoint of writing or of undertaking new projects. When Frederick J. Keller, who was then directing the work of the National Occupational Conference, visited me in the USSR, we talked about the idea which he had conceived of jointly writing a book describing and comparing vocational guidance programs throughout the world. I started work on this soon after my return and, as noted earlier, the book was published in 1938 (with F. J. Keller, 1938). Although many years have elapsed since the writing of *Vocational Guidance Throughout the World,* it still represents, I think, a unique contribution to the literature of vocational guidance.

During the same five-year period I also prepared two chapters on vocational psychology for a text, *Fields of Psychology,* edited by J. P. Guilford (1940) and also approximately twenty articles in various technical and other journals. As I review these, I detect a continuing interest in the criterion problem (1936a) and concern with the academic program for training industrial psychologists (1941a) and with their responsibility to industry and to society at large. Moreover, I find indications of a growing interest in the problem of employee motivation (1938b, 1941b) which, as will be seen later, grew in the succeeding years and resulted in a major publication in this area.

As the decade of the 1940's approached, the publisher of *Industrial Psychology* suggested that there would be merit in bringing out a revised edition in 1942, ten years after the original publication of this book. My work at the University (where I was promoted to full professor in 1940) and in industry was going well, and I responded favorably to this suggestion and started to assemble materials and to plan the revision. However, I did not get far with this, because even before World War II started I was drawn into a series of projects sponsored by civilian and military agencies of the federal government which grew in magnitude with our entry into World War II in December 1941.

## WORK ON MILITARY PROJECTS (1940–1951)

My first association with such a project was as a representative of the National Research Council on the Technical Board for the Occupational Research Program of the U.S. Employment Service. This involved participation, with M. R. Trabue, W. Dietz, W. H. Stead, C. L. Shartle and others, in laying the groundwork for what became an extensive program in research and for the widespread application of psychology in job analysis and in occupational placement, both for civilian and military purposes.

My first association with a project pointing directly toward the military applications of psychology came in the form of research on behalf of the U.S. Navy, in 1940, on the effects of atmospheric conditions and noise upon the performance, physiological states, and attitudes of personnel in plotting and charting rooms of naval vessels. This was conducted in collaboration with Kingsley R. Smith, a former student whom, along with J. L. Otis and Albert S. Thompson, I consider to be among the best of those who took their degrees under my direction (with K. R. Smith, 1946). The experiment provided evidence that an *effective temperature* (ET) of 94°F was highly detrimental to performance and also to individual well-being. Most important were clear indications—noted for the first time in any experiment —of a "danger zone," at the level of approximately 87°ET, which suggested the need for experiments with effective temperatures of 80°F and 90°F to determine more exactly the point at which atmospheric conditions became critical for performance. I find considerable satisfaction in the confirmation, provided in later experiments by Mackworth (1948, 1950) and Pepler (1953), of the existence of a critical area within the range of effective temperature of 83°F and 87.5°F on a variety of tasks.

My longest association with the military and its problems was in the field of aviation psychology. This started in 1940 when, with the collaboration of A. S. Thompson, I undertook research on the development of objective measures of flight performance for use as criteria in evaluating the outcomes of studies on the selection and training of civilian aircraft pilots. This project was part of a program sponsored by the National Research Council Committee on Selection and Training of Civilian Aircraft Pilots which had been organized in 1940, largely through the foresight and influence of D. R. Brimhall, to develop and supervise research supported by the Civil Aeronautics Administration.

The program was soon extended to include research on the selection and training of pilots for the U.S. Navy. With the onset of World War II, this was expanded to include research on many aspects of human performance during flight, supported by and conducted in cooperation with the military services. The broadened scope of the program was acknowledged, later in the 1940's, by changing the name of the committee to NRC Committee on Aviation Psychology.

On February 1, 1942, when J. G. Jenkins, who was its chairman from the start, joined the Medical Aviation Section of the U.S. Navy, I became chairman of the committee and directed its program until the committee was disbanded in 1951. As chairman of the committee I became involved in the design of many experiments and in the administration of research on perception, learning, and emotional disturbance, as well as on selection, training, fatigue, air-sickness, accident prevention, and so forth, conducted by investigators working at university and military centers throughout the country. I also assumed the responsibility for editing and seeing to the publication of reports which numbered approximately 125 before the work of the committee was completed. Much of the early work is described in the five-year report published in 1945 (see 1945), but, unfortunately, most of the research reports have not found their way into the open literature.

Of course, much of the burden of such responsibilities was carried by staff members, including J. W. Dunlap who acted as research director for a period of time, and by a number of highly competent staff assistants, particularly H. S. Odbert, A. S. Thompson, E. S. Ewart, and R. Y. Walker. In addition—and of utmost importance—was the constant help of an Executive Subcommittee which included not only psychologists, but representatives from many disciplines, e.g., physiology, medicine, and engineering, and also members of the military forces. D. R. Brimhall, L. Carmichael, and W. R. Miles are only a few among the many of the highly competent and devoted psychologists who gave freely of their time and of their skills, as members of this subcommittee, in planning and evaluating research projects. I also enjoyed and profited from associations with many others, such as J. P. Guilford, H. M. Johnson, E. L. Kelly, C. Landis, F. A. Geldard, N. L. Munn, K. W. Spence, and G. R. Wendt, who served as investigators on such projects. In addition, I have derived great satisfaction from my work and continuing associations with the quite large number of younger men, including many who have since made important contributions and achieved reputations as psychologists, who started their research careers as staff members on such projects.

During the entire decade of the 1940's, a considerable portion of both my time and energy was devoted to the Committee on Aviation Psychology. Much of the remaining portion was also devoted to the war effort, through work with the National Defense Research Committee (NDRC) of the Office of Scientific Research and Development (OSRD) and as a consultant to various branches of the military services.

Entry into the NDRC program came almost casually, in the fall of 1941, when Gaylord P. Harnwell—then chairman of the Department of Physics and now president of the University of Pennsylvania—asked me to become a member of a committee on the Selection and Training of Underwater Sound Operators, Division 6.1, NDRC, of which he was chairman. My major work in this connection, which continued until shortly after V-J day, involved the development and original validation of a battery of tests and the preparation of test manuals which were used during most of the war in the selection of underwater (sonar) operators.

My other activities with NDRC included membership—along with W. S. Hunter, C. H. Graham, L. Carmichael, C. W. Bray, G. K. Bennett, and others—on the Applied Psychology Panel, which had the responsibility for supervising nation-wide research and action programs on many aspects of military performance. I also served as a consultant to a number of NDRC divisions. Most particularly, I was directly responsible for the administration of a series of projects, conducted for NDRC under contract between the University of Pennsylvania and OSRD. These, carried on in naval installations between Norfolk and Newport, Rhode Island, on the East Coast, between San Diego and Seattle on the West Coast, and at army centers in between, included work on the selection, classification, and training of antiaircraft gun crews; the formulation of doctrine and training of personnel operating main batteries aboard naval vessels; training of engineering division personnel; the development of improved procedures for the assignment of personnel to billets on naval vessels ranging from destroyer escorts through small aircraft carriers to battleships, and so forth.

The mission of the NDRC University of Pennsylvania projects was largely programmatic, in the sense of finding ways of applying to the military situation such psychological principles and procedures as could be immediately useful in dealing with personnel problems faced by the military services, and resulted in the preparation of a large number of procedural manuals. However, there were provisions for research on pertinent problems, and outcomes from research conducted by the staff were far from negligible. Of particular interest among these are the findings of a study, conducted in collaboration with D. D. Wickens, A. B. Bayroff, M. H. Rogers, H. A. Voss, and others, designed to examine the transfer effects to performance in range estimation from instruction on a synthetic range estimation trainer which, in accordance with current practice at the time, had been widely distributed for use without prior evaluation. This experiment, which showed negligible transfer from the synthetic device to performance on the firing line, and that short periods of systematic training on the firing line produced both significant improvements in range estimation and a reduction in the variability of performance, proved to be of value not alone in connection with the training of antiaircraft gunners, but also in leading toward later large-scale evaluation of proposed synthetic training devices as a necessary condition to their adoption.

As I think about the multiplicity of the activities involved in work with the NDRC, I sometimes wonder how I was able to do what was required along with the work involved with the NRC Committee on Aviation Psychology. Familiarization with the problems involved called for firing line practice; trial runs on simulated bombing and fighter flights in naval aircraft; participation in precommissioning and shakedown cruises in American waters; observing and participating in antisubmarine warfare exercises in Bermuda waters, as well as many other varied contracts and activities. Frequent trips were required to these various stations in planning and coordinating the activities of the project. However, relief in the way of partial leave from the University and an adjustment of my work schedule in industry helped sufficiently to ease the situation for me to come through the hectic period without any signs of having suffered physically or otherwise from the demands of the situation.

Most of the NDRC projects in which I was engaged came to an end in 1946. Research administered by the Committee on Aviation Psychology continued for a few more years, and it was not until 1951 that all of the research reports were completed and the committee was dissolved. However, in that year, at the urgent request of the Air Force, I made a nation-wide survey with the objective of determining what could be done to implement research that had already been completed and to outline what was needed in the way of new research to deal with severe personnel problems in the early warning centers and other installations maintained by the Air Defense Command. With this mission accomplished, I closed out my work with the military and since 1951 have been involved to only a slight extent with military projects.

As I look back upon my work in the military situation, I experience a feeling of deep satisfaction in having had an opportunity to participate in and, hopefully, make a contribution to the war effort. I found pleasure and profit, too, in working closely with the military people who were almost uniformly unstinting in their efforts to facilitate the work under way, and established friendships with many of them—such as Captain W. E. Kellum, Group Captain Percy A. Lee—which continue until today. From the viewpoint of this autobiographical chapter, there is need however to consider the question of what I learned and how my career as a teacher and as an industrial psychologist was influenced by more than a decade of intensive work on military projects. I see the following as major effects.

There was much profit to me in the way of intellectual stimulation and enrichment. By 1940, the Department of Psychology at the University of Pennsylvania had lost its strength and its glamor, at least at the level of the senior staff. There were a few exciting young people around—especially Francis W. Irwin and Malcolm G. Preston—and an exchange of ideas with them was and continues to be a stimulating experience. However, a most rewarding outcome of my work was what I gained in the way of a broader background in psychology and of greater experimental sophistication through my associations with psychologists representing diverse areas of psychological research and practice.

I also learned much about the problems encountered in administrative work and how to deal with them. Nevertheless, I had never been interested in administrative work as a career, and my experience in administering military research intensified my desire to devote myself to teaching, research, and professional practice, rather than become a professional administrator. This conviction was intensified by what I observed in the way of changes that occurred in a number of promising young psychologists who turned into administrators—who turned from the manipulation of ideas to the manipulation of money, men, and organizations.

As shown in my publications, I have always taken a strong stand on the importance of a close identification between experimental and applied psychology. I am convinced that the fact that experimental and other psychologists worked closely together during the war contributed to mutual understanding and tolerance. Many applied psychologists learned something about the need for sound experimental designs and a theoretical background for research; many experimental psychologists learned that they could do research which had practical objectives without losing their identity as experimentalists.

This does not mean that the schism has completely disappeared, although I am not particularly disturbed about it. I am highly pleased, for example, at the amount of miltary funds that is going into basic research. Nevertheless, at times I sense a neglect of the implications of such research for dealing with problems which need to be solved in the public interest and tend to recall a suggestion, included in my report at the completion of my work with the Air Force in 1951, which made me very unpopular with many psychologists engaged in research for the Air Force, to the effect that those engaged in research be placed in military installations for a period of six months to do what could properly be done in implementing already available research findings. Of course, I did not seriously expect that this suggestion would be followed *in toto,* but I was glad to find that something was accomplished in providing for the greater utilization of research findings in dealing with the many and serious problems encountered in Air Defense Command installations.

Reference to the influence of the war upon psychology and psychologists would not be complete without mentioning another significant development that became prominent in the 1940's. I refer here to the expansion of what is now commonly called "human engineering" which is concerned, primarily, with the psychological aspects of the design and operation of man-machine systems. I neither found myself attracted to nor became active in this field. Nevertheless, it seems necessary to call attention, in passing, to the stream of developments in an area of research and practice that has considerable significance to industrial as well as to military psychology and also in terms of rapprochement between "experimental" and "applied" psychology.

## THE RETURN TO "NORMALCY" (1951–1963)

As noted earlier, my work on military projects virtually came to an end in 1951. However, even before that time, I had started the return to "normalcy." For example, in 1946 I spent approximately two months in Germany on behalf of the Technical Industrial Intelligence Division, Department of Commerce. This was the only time throughout the war period that I was clothed in military garb and reported through military channels (Field Information Agency Technical, Office of Military Government of Germany U.S. Army), although, paradoxically, I was mostly engaged in examining wartime developments in industrial psychology and in industrial relations. In fact, the chief outcome of this trip was a report on significant developments in the selection and training of supervisory personnel in German industry. There were, however, opportunities for many other interesting observations in my field, and I also learned, in passing, that caste had not disappeared in the American army, when a colonel was forced out of his room at the Hotel Schloss in Heidelberg in spite of my protestations, because as a civilian carrying a simulated higher military rank, I was entitled to the room which had been assigned to him.

During the late 1940's, I also traveled to Europe to attend two interesting meetings of psychologists, the International Congress of Psychology in Edinburgh in 1948, and that of the International Psychotechnical Association (International Association of Applied Psychology) in Berne in 1949. Although there were military involvements in both trips, attendance at the meetings provided an opportunity to learn what was going on in the field of industrial psychology during these postwar years and also to renew associations with professional colleagues and friends in the field.

During the late 1940's, I also found time to turn to the revision of my book *Industrial Psychology*. I succeeded in updating a goodly portion of the book to about 1945, and began to bring such sections up to about 1950, and also to work on chapters untouched since about 1940. Among the first of the latter to which I turned my attention, because of a growing interest in problems of employee motivation (see 1947), was the chapter entitled "Motives in Industry." Under this caption I had been able, in 1932, to cover essentially all of the significant research which had been done on employee motivation both in the United States and abroad up to that time. It soon became evident that a book was needed to cover adequately what had been done in this field. I therefore dropped the revision of *Industrial Psychology* and turned to the preparation of a volume that was published in 1953 under the title of *Motivation and Morale in Industry*.

The theme and content of this book reflect, in part, the concern of industry with the problem of motivating employees which grew in magnitude after World War II. The theme and content of *Motivation and Morale in Industry* reflect also a highly significant change in the orientation of industrial psychology—in the form of increasing interest in motives, interpersonal behavior, small group influences, and the general social context of behavior—which came clearly into focus in approximately the mid-1940's. Supporting this change was the growth of an experimental social psychology which, along with other social sciences, provided the theories, the research techniques, and a set of values that have grossly affected psychological research and practice in industry, as well as in other fields, in the past quarter of a century.

Although already evident in the general field of psychology as early as the mid-1920's, this did not become a strong force in industrial psychology until the 1940's. It is not possible to deal with the people and the forces within and outside of psychology that produced the strong emphasis in industrial psychology upon the operation of social groups, but I think of Whiting Williams, A. W. Kornhauser, E. Mayo, F. Linton, T. M. Whitehead, K. Lewin, G. Friedmann, and, in the specific area of motivational theory, A. H. Maslow, as having had a particularly strong influence on my thinking.

It may be true, as has been suggested by a number of my associates and also more distant colleagues, that the publication of *Motivation and Morale in Industry* in 1953 reflects a transformation in my own role from that of a personnel psychologist to that of a social psychologist. If such a transition did take place, it occurred painlessly and without overt recognition on my part. Actually, I see the preparation of *Motivation and Morale in Industry* as an expression of a preoccupation with the problems of motivation and with the role of supervisory personnel and of the group in industry that is already strongly apparent in *Industrial Psychology* (1932). In fact, others have noted the degree to which recent concern with problems of motivation, management, and organization is anticipated early in this text (Katz, 1949). In this connection, too, I am intrigued by the extent to which the concept of a "systems approach" in management and organizational psychology, stressed by Stagner in a recent review of books in these areas (Stagner, 1966), coincides with what I (under the influence of Witmer) call the "clinical approach" in industry, and with my views on the influence of gestalt psychology, as expressed in an article (see 1930c) published in 1930.

Be this as it may, during approximately the past twenty years, I have become increasingly preoccupied with employee attitudes and employee motivation (1947, 1955a); with the study of organization (1955b, 1962a); with the problems of management behavior (1954) and management selection and development (1958); and with similar issues in which the influence of social psychology is most apparent. In addition, my attention has turned more and more to a number of other social issues, to some extent peripheral to the field of industrial psychology. Among these is a quite deep interest in the interaction between science and the humanities and in the role of humanistic education in a developing industrial civilization.

Opportunities for giving expression to such interests referred to above have been enlarged through my associations since 1951 with the Bell Telephone Company of Pennsylvania. To some extent accidental factors played a part in the initiation of my relationship with this company. Late in 1950, I gave an address on the "Problem of Boredom" (1952) which came to the attention of W. D. Gillen, president of the company, who was concerned with what appeared to be a high incidence of severe boredom among employees working on routine clerical tasks. In 1951, in the midst of one of the busiest years of my life, I agreed to devote a total of ten days during the year to an exploration of this problem.

Examination of the situation indeed suggested that something could be done about this through job enlargement and a number of other relatively simple steps. However, it also quickly became apparent that much more was involved, especially in terms of the constitution of the small groups and of the relationships, on the one hand, between the workers and their supervisors and, on the other, between supervisors and their superiors. I found it of interest to extend my study of these aspects of the situations and to other problems which were brought to my attention. As a result, I continued as a consultant with the Bell Telephone Company of Pennsylvania, and have enjoyed fifteen years of stimulating associations, especially with John Markle II, Vice President, Personnel, who himself has contributed much to the development and implementation of the programs with which I have been concerned.

One of the outcomes of my work with this company which gave me particular satisfaction is an extensive project, known as the Management Coordination Program, which was designed to bring fuller and more effective participation, particularly at lower levels of management, in arriving at decisions affecting both supervisory personnel and employees (see 1954). I have been involved in consultation and research on other problems, chiefly in the area of management development. Among all of these activities, I have been most interested in my involvement in the development and evaluation of a unique program of humanistic education for executives which was carried on at the University of Pennsylvania, for managerial personnel from the entire Bell System, during the years 1953–1960 inclusive. Especially gratifying was the demonstration, in an evaluation study, that a program of this kind—involving a full year of exposure to philosophy, literature, art, history, and social studies—did indeed bring the flight from "over-conformity," the liberalization of opinions, the changes in interest, and the modifications of value systems which were sought in the initiation of the program (see 1959).

My satisfaction with the outcomes of the program of humanistic education for executives reflects an interest in the humanities and in the full realization of the potentials of "humanistic" teaching with which I have been concerned throughout my years. In my teaching, where I frequently draw upon literature and the arts, especially in lecturing to undergraduates, I still find no better way, for example, of introducing a discussion of the nurture-nature controversy than by reference to Aldous Huxley's *Brave New World*, George Orwell's *1984*, or even by merely quoting, from W. S. Gilbert, the wondrous soliloquy which notes that "Every little boy or girl, that's born into this world alive, is either a little liberal or else a conservative." (Perhaps I overdo Gilbert and Sullivan. At least, my good friend Malcolm Preston found it necessary to place on the bulletin board a notice stating where the music to Viteles' *Industrial Psychology* could be purchased, when this book was published in 1932.) I find it difficult to discuss the psychological effects of a mechanized industrial civilization without reference to Samuel Butler's *Erewhon*, to Romain Rolland's *Revolt of the Machines,* and so on. There may be exaggeration in the statement, in a discussion of advertising strategy and of theories of motivation, that "possibly we are saved from the solemnities of Freud by the sanity of Rabelais" (Anon., 1956, p. 4). Nevertheless, especially in the present state of psychoanalytical theory, it would seem that understanding might be enhanced by asking students to read Mereschowski's *Leonardo da Vinci,* and also the biography by Antonina Vallentin, along with Freud's own treatment of Leonardo.

In emphasizing teaching that helps to establish the bonds between the science of psychology and the humanities, I am concerned not alone with arriving at a fuller view of the nature of human behavior, but also with problems in the areas of value judgments. I find myself increasingly questioning the assumption, so frequently made by scientists, that they are better capable of assessing the value of a variety of life events than are the playwright, the artist, the historian, and other creative people or scholars in the area of the humanities. More and more I find myself recalling the forceful appeal made by A. V. Hill that "scientists should be implored to remember that, however accurate their scientific facts, their moral judgments may be wrong" (Hill, 1951, p. 371).

This exhortation takes on particular importance to me because of a current tendency on the part of psychologists—especially the social psychologists—to report research findings in a manner which makes it increasingly difficult, especially for the layman, to determine when they are dealing with conclusions or principles derived from experiments, or when they are merely presenting their own value judgments. To say this is not to deny the right of the psychologist to his opinions—to his own value judgments. It is not his privilege, however, to clothe the frequently questionable sources and personal nature of such opinions in the language or form of scholarly speech or writing to the point where it would appear that they are the outcomes of scientific inquiries.

## THE PAST FEW YEARS (1963–1965)

My increasing concern with such matters has been dealt with in a paper entitled "The New Utopia" (1955c) and in an unpublished paper entitled "Humanistic Teaching: Opportunity and Dilemma." The latter reflects also my continuing interest in teaching, which has become an increasingly absorbing activity during the last decade, in large part because of a vibrant intellectual climate that exists since the reorganization of the Department of Psychology and of its goals, with the appointment of R. R. Bush as chairman, in 1957, and the addition of a group of highly stimulating younger psychologists, such as R. D. Luce, R. L. Solomon, P. Teitelbaum, and H. Gleitman, the current chairman, to the staff. In my "declining years" I still find time for research, but, more and more, whatever spare time I can find from teaching and administrative duties at the University is devoted to writing.

The revision of *Industrial Psychology* is proceeding more rapidly than in past years. I have long been interested in the effects of technological change upon employment and career adjustment (1933b, 1934, 1935, 1936b) and now find myself increasingly concerned with the immediate and long-range effects of accelerated mechanization and automation (1962b) and have undertaken to present its problems—for people and for society—in a book to be entitled *Man, Mind, and Machines,* which is approximately half-way to completion. Nevertheless, I still find I have difficulty in devoting as much time as I should like to spend on writing because of involvements in administrative work, undertaken in the later years of my life in spite of the fact that I always have found much more pleasure and satisfaction in teaching, research, and writing than in administration.

There has been, nevertheless, considerable satisfaction for me in one of these administrative activities—that of serving as president of the International Association of Applied Psychology since 1958. In general, through the years I have had no ambitions with respect to holding office in professional organizations, although at various times I have done so. However, I have thoroughly enjoyed my work with the I.A.A.P. and have found great pleasure in the opportunities which the office has provided for closer association with R. Bonnardel, C. B. Frisby, J. Germain, L. Canestrelli, G. Westerlund, and other colleagues and friends from many countries. I find additional and great satisfaction in what I believe has been a successful effort to enhance the value of the association, not alone as an agency for the exchange of scientific information, but as a medium for the promotion of the closer understanding and the mutual respect among scientists throughout the world that can have a significant impact in the area of improved international relations.

A much more extended and greater responsibility in the way of administrative responsibility came when I agreed to serve as acting-Dean of the Graduate School of Education at the University of Pennsylvania for the academic year 1963–64 and then to continue as dean when it became apparent that more time was needed to find a younger scholar, free from the taint of professional "educationalism" to serve as dean. It is not possible to deal with the circumstances that led me to do so, in spite of my adverse attitude toward administration, except to say that there was great need to make a start on the rehabilitation of this school, and I felt I owed this service to the University. Perhaps I am deluding myself in the belief that I was also moved by the challenge of making sure that the changes which were undertaken in the way of adding scholars to the staff, in the way of raising admission standards, and in the way of developing a program oriented toward excellence in scholarship would be continued after my departure.

Be this as it may, I am now a dean—a member of the always vulnerable administrative cadre of a university. However, I continue to teach and to do research and look forward, hopefully, to a period of extended writing, along with a modicum of consulting work, following my retirement from the University in 1968 at age seventy, and after fifty years of service.

## REFERENCES

*Selected Publications by Morris S. Viteles*

Tests in industry. *J. appl. Psychol.*, 1921, 5, 57–63.

A comparison of three tests of general intelligence. *J. appl. Psychol.*, 1922, 6, 392–401. (a)

Job specifications and diagnostic tests of job competency designed for the Auditing Division of a street railway company. *Psychol. Clin.*, 1922, 14, 83–105. (b)

Instruction in psychology in Paris. *Psychol. Bull.*, 1923, 20, 545–552. (a)

Psychology in business—in England, France, and Germany. *Ann. Amer. Acad. pol. soc. Sci.*, 1923, 110, 209–220. (b)

Research in the selection of motormen, Part I. *J. pers. Res.*, 1925, 3, 110–115; Part II, *J. pers. Res.*, 1925, 4, 173–197.

Psychology in industry. *Psychol. Bull.*, 1926, 23, 631–680.

Psychology in industry. *Psychol. Bull.*, 1928, 25, 6, 309–340.

Psychology and psychiatry in industry: the viewpoint of a psychologist. *Ment. Hyg.*, 1929, 13, 361–377.

The human factor in substation operation: specifications and tests for substation operators. *Personnel J.*, 1930, 11, 21–27. (a)

Psychology in industry. *Psychol. Bull.*, 1930, 27, 567–635. (b)

Die gestalt-betrachsungsweise in der angewandte psychologie, *Z. F. Ang. Psych.*, 1930, 35, 525–531. (c)

*Industrial psychology.* New York: Norton, 1932.

Adjustment in industry through training. *Personnel J.*, 1933, 11, 295–306. (a)

Training and unemployment. *The Human Factor*, 1933, 7, 307–311. (b)

*The science of work.* New York: Norton, 1934.

Psychology and reemployment. *Scientific Monthly*, 1934, 39, 271–273.

Le point de vue psychologique du chomage aux Etats-Unis. *Le Travail humain*, 1935, 3, 129–138.

A dynamic criterion. *Occupations*, 1936 (Section 1), 14, 1–5. (a)

How technological changes affect employees. *Mech. Engng.*, 1936, 58, 302–303. (b)

Industrial psychology in Russia. *Occup. Psychol.*, 1938, Spring issue, 1–19. (a)

The application of psychology in industrial relations. *A.M.A. Personnel Ser.*, 1938, 35, 23–26. (b)

(with F. J. Keller) *Vocational guidance throughout the world.* New York: Norton, 1938.

Caveat emptor. *J. consult. Psychol.*, 1941, 5, 118–122. (a)

The role of industrial psychology in defending the future of America. *Ann. Amer. Acad. pol. soc. Sci.*, 1941 (July), 156–162. (b)

The aircraft pilot: five years of research: a summary of outcomes. *Psychol. Bull.*, 1945, 42, 489–526.

*The role of leadership in supervisory management: human problems in business and industry.* New Wilmington, Penn.: The Economic and Business Foundation, 1945.

(with K. R. Smith) An experimental investigation of the effect of changes in atmospheric conditions and noise upon performance. *Trans. Amer. Soc. Heating and Ventilating Engr.*, 1946, 52, 167–180.

The measurement of employee attitudes. In C. W. Churchman, R. L. Ackoff, & M. Wax (Eds.), *Measurement of consumer interest*. Philadelphia: Univ. of Pennsylvania Press, 1947, 177–197.

L'homme et la machine: le problème de l'ennui. *Le Travail humain*, 1952, 15, 85–100.

*Motivation and morale in industry.* New York: Norton, 1953.

What raises a man's morale? *Personnel*, 1954, 30, 302–313.

Motivation and morale—whose responsibility? *Personnel Practice Bull.* (Australia), 1955, 11, 27–42. (a)

The human factor in organization. *University of Minnesota Industrial Relations Research and Technical Report 17*, 1955, 19–26. (b)

The new Utopia. *Science*, 1955, 122, 1167–1171. (c)

L'Identification du potentiel du personnel d'encadrement. *Bull. de l'association internationale de psychologie appliquée*, 1958, 7, 44–79.

"Human relations" and the "humanities" in the education of business leaders: evaluation of a program of humanistic studies for executives. *Personnel Psychol.*, 1959, 12, 1–28.

Fundamentalism in industrial psychology. *Occup. Psychol.*, 1959, 33, 98–110.

(with A. H. Brayfield & L. E. Tyler) Vocational counseling: a reappraisal in honor of Donald G. Paterson, *Minnesota Studies in Student Personnel Work No. 11*, Univ. of Minnesota Press, 1961.

Personality and organization: the indivdual and the system: an introduction. In G. Nielsen (Ed.), *Industrial and business psychology*. Munksgaard, 1962, 97–100. (a)

Man, mind, and machines. In G. Nielsen (Ed.), *Industrial and business psychology*. Munksgaard, 1962, 9–25. (b)

## Other Publications Cited

Anonymous. Advertising strategy and theories of motivation. *Cost and Profit Outlook*, 1956, 9, (12), 4.

Guilford, J. P. (Ed.) *Fields of psychology*. New York: Van Nostrand, 1940. (rev. ed., 1950)

Hill, A. V. The social responsibility of scientists. *Bull. Atomic Scientists*, 1951, 7, 371.

Hollingworth, H. L. *Vocational psychology: its problems and methods*. Appleton-Century-Crofts, 1916.

Katz, D. Morale and motivation in industry. In W. Dennis (Ed.), *Current trends in industrial psychology*. Pittsburgh: Univ. of Pittsburgh Press, 1949.

Link, H. C. *Employment psychology*. New York: Macmillan, 1919.

Mackworth, N. H. Definition of the upper limit of environmental warmth by psychological tests of human performance. *The Royal Society, Empire Scientific Conference Report*, 1948, *1*, 423–441.

———. Researches on the measurement of human performance. *Medical Research Council Special Report Series No. 268, H. M. Stationery Office*, 1950, 119–133.

Münsterberg, H. *Psychology and industrial efficiency*. Boston: Houghton Mifflin, 1913.

Pepler, R. D. *The effect of climatic factors on the performance of skilled tasks by young European men living in the tropics*. London: Medical Research Council, Royal Naval Personnel Research Committee, 1953 (February).

Scott, W. D. *Influencing men in business*. New York: Ronald, 1911.

Shellow, S. M. Research on selection of motormen in Milwaukee. *J. personnel Res.*, 1925, *4*, 222–237.

Spearman, C. *The abilities of man*. New York: Macmillan, 1927.

Stagner, R. New design for industrial psychology. *Contemp. Psychol.*, 1966, *11*, 145–149.

Stead, W. H., Shartle, C. S., *et al.*, *Occupational counseling techniques*. New York: American Book, 1940.

Twitmyer, E. B. *A Study of the knee jerk*. 1902.

———. Knee jerks without stimulation of the patellar tendon. *Psychol. Bull.*, 1905, *2*, 43ff.

Wainwright, H. B. *History of the Philadelphia Electric Co., 1881–1961*. Philadelphia Electric Co., 1961.

Witmer, L.. Clinical psychology. *The psychol. Clinic*, 1907.

———. Psychological diagnosis and the psychonomic orientation of analytic science: an epitome. *The psychol. Clinic*, 1925.